Denise Tyler

SAMS
Teach Yourself

Microsoft®
FrontPage® 2000

in 21 Days

SAMS

201 West 103rd St., Indianapolis, Indiana, 46290 USA

Sams Teach Yourself Microsoft FrontPage 2000 in 21 Days

Copyright © 1999 by Sams Publishing

International Standard Book Number: 0-672-31499-1

Library of Congress Catalog Card Number: 98-87800

Printed in the United States of America

First Printing: August 1999

01   00   99   4   3   2   1

Trademarks

Warning and Disclaimer

ACQUISITIONS EDITOR
Randi Roger

DEVELOPMENT EDITOR
Scott D. Meyers

MANAGING EDITOR
Charlotte Clapp

PROJECT EDITOR
George E. Nedeff

COPY EDITOR
Kim Cofer

INDEXER
Greg Pearson

PROOFREADERS
Maryann Steinhart
Mary Ellen Stephenson

TECHNICAL EDITOR
Bill Bruns
Lon Coley

SOFTWARE DEVELOPMENT SPECIALIST
Aaron Price

INTERIOR DESIGN
Gary Adair

COVER DESIGN
Aren Howell

COPY WRITER
Eric Borgert

LAYOUT TECHNICIANS
Brian Borders
Susan Geiselman
Mark Walchle

Contents at a Glance

Contents

About the Authors

Denise Tyler (dtyler@midplains.net) is a freelance author, graphics artist, animator, and Web designer, and has been an author for Sams/Macmillan Computer Publishing for five years. She has authored several FrontPage books in the Laura Lemay's Web Workshop series, including the best-selling *Laura Lemay's Web Workshop: Microsoft FrontPage 98*. She was also a contributing author for *Tricks of the Game Programming Gurus* in 1994, and author of *Fractal Design Painter 3.1 Unleashed* in 1995. Most recently, she contributed to the updated revision of the international best-selling book, *Sams Teach Yourself Web Publishing with HTML 4 in 21 Days*, by Laura Lemay.

David Beauchemin is a Microsoft Most Valuable Professional (MVP), a title awarded for his continued support and dedication in the Microsoft newsgroups. At only 19, he completed his training in computer programming, graduating at the top of his class, with honors. He works in the advanced technologies department at Future Electronics (http://www.future.ca) as a Web application developer while at the same time he is working to obtain his Microsoft certification as a systems engineer (MCSE). He maintains his personal Web site at http://www.web-dave.com. Even with this hectic pace, he still takes time to practice the piano, as he has for the past 13 years, and to zealously support his church, which takes priority in his life.

Lon Coley (LonColey@ariadne-webdesign.co.uk) is an IT professional, specializing in FrontPage and the whole Microsoft Office family of products. She has been working professionally within the Internet for 3 years (a long time in the UK!) designing and developing Web sites and Internet solutions for business and education. Her company site at http://www.ariadne-webdesign.co.uk holds far more information than we could put here and is updated as often as time allows.

Mark Fitzpatrick (markfitz@fitzme.com) is a Microsoft Most Valuable Professional (MVP) who specializes in Microsoft Internet technologies and products such as FrontPage, Visual Interdev, and Internet Information Server. He has been designing Web sites for businesses and organizations for five years. When he isn't writing, Mark can be found in the role of Director of Technology for the Inner Reach Corporation (http://www.innerreach.com), Webmaster for the Fibre Channel Community (http://www.fccommunity.org), or working on his own site at http://www.fitzme.com.

Dedication

To Ed, who continues to give me inspiration and support as I travel down the yellow brick road.

Acknowledgments

For starters, I'd like to thank Sams (and Macmillan) Publishing for allowing me to fulfill many dreams, and for giving me the opportunity to share my passion for learning with so many.

Each book is the product of a talented team of dozens of folks who dedicate themselves to getting the job done right, and I'd like to thank each and every one of them.

As always, I thank Mark Taber for his continued support and trust.

Also thanks to Randi Roger for the many inspirational phone calls and messages, as well as the humor and understanding that helped keep me plugging away.

To Scott Meyers for his expert care in ensuring that the book kept its focus.

To co-authors Dave Beauchemin, Lon Coley, and Mark Fitzpatrick, for adding fresh new perspectives and expertise to some of the more advanced topics in the book.

And last but not least, to the many technical editors, proofreaders, formatters, and graphics people, who put it all together in its final form.

—Denise Tyler

Tell Us What You Think!

As the reader of this book, *you* are our most important critic and commentator. We value your opinion and want to know what we're doing right, what we could do better, what areas you'd like to see us publish in, and any other words of wisdom you're willing to pass our way.

You can fax, email, or write me directly to let me know what you did or didn't like about this book—as well as what we can do to make our books stronger.

Please note that I cannot help you with technical problems related to the topic of this book, and that due to the high volume of mail I receive, I might not be able to reply to every message.

When you write, please be sure to include this book's title and authors as well as your name and phone or fax number. I will carefully review your comments and share them with the authors and editors who worked on the book.

Fax: 317-581-4770

Email: office_sams@mcp.com

Mail: Mark Taber
            Associate Publisher
            Sams Publishing
            201 West 103rd Street
            Indianapolis, IN 46290 USA

Introduction

FrontPage 2000 is Microsoft's strong entry into the foray of Web development tools that now flood the market. Its ease of use and complexity of design options are two of its strongest components, but it also provides other tools to help maintain and tweak your site with ease.

How to Use This Book

Week 1, "Starting with the Basics," does a little more than its title implies. After completing the lessons in this section, you will have a fully functional Web page, complete with images, links, tables, and other useful features. This first week's worth of exercises lays the groundwork for you to begin to enhance and develop your whole site. If you are unfamiliar with FrontPage or Web site development in general, this will get you up and running:

- Day 1, "FrontPage 2000 Basics," gives you a quick tour of FrontPage 2000, including its new features.

- Day 2, "Fast-Track to Webs and Pages," introduces the Web and page templates and wizards to help you get a page up and running quickly.

- Day 3, "Building Basic Web Pages," teaches you how to build a Web page from the ground up. You'll create an empty Web in which to store all the exercises throughout the book.

- Day 4, "Using Lists to Organize Information," describes how to use lists to arrange textual information on your page.

- Day 5, "Creating and Formatting Tables," explains how to insert, draw, and modify your tables for organization and layout.

- Day 6, "Adding Images, Sound, and Video," teaches you how to insert and manipulate multimedia objects on your Web site, including extensive information about images and image effects.

- Day 7, "Adding Links and Bookmarks," shows you how to start making your page interactive with other pages—whether they are on the Internet, your company's intranet, or on your own computer.

Now that the nuts and bolts of Web page basics have been covered, it's time to learn how to develop your pages more fully. Week 2, "Enhancing Your Presentation," gets your fingernails dirty with information about planning and maintaining your pages, as well as more advanced Web-related topics.

- Day 8, "Planning Your Own Web Site," describes structure and development of your pages, files, and folders.
- Day 9, "Changing the Appearance of Your Pages," gives you information about how to change what people see on your page—colors, borders, shading, and even themes are covered in this lesson.
- Day 10, "Using Style Sheets," explains how high-powered layout can be applied to your pages.
- Day 11, "Designing Navigation Systems," teaches you the ins and outs of letting people move around easily and efficiently in your site.
- Day 12, "Creating and Using Framesets," shows how frames work and how you can incorporate them into your pages.
- Day 13, "Working with DHTML and Positioning," describes how to make your page come alive with animations, layered images, and positioning through the use of Dynamic HTML.
- Day 14, "FrontPage Components," lets you on the inside of what can be done to really make your site look professional with FrontPage.

Week 3, "Advanced Features and Publishing," shows you the real power of FrontPage—how it is integrated in the Office 2000 family, how to add HTML and advanced Web technologies, how to build and edit forms, and taking care of the quotidian needs of a Webmaster.

- Day 15, "Integrating with Office 2000," describes how to make your Office files Web-ready.
- Day 16, "Adding Your Own HTML Code," shows how to make raw HTML code work for you in your FrontPage documents.
- Day 17, "Adding Advanced Web Technologies," explains how to incorporate sophisticated tools, codes, and applets into your Web site.
- Day 18, "Building and Editing Forms," gives you all the tools you need to build forms for users to fill out and give you information you need from them.
- Day 19, "Handling Forms with FrontPage Components," describes how different types of FrontPage form handlers (such as the Discussion, Registration, and All-Purpose form handlers) work.
- Day 20, "Testing and Publishing Your Web," shows you how FrontPage's powerful tools can test for bad links, as well as content and other errors. This lesson also describes how to make your Web pages known across the Internet.

- Day 21, "Tracking and Maintaining Your Webs," explains how to make reports, add security, and keep your pages in good condition.

Sams Teach Yourself FrontPage 2000 in 21 Days ends with several appendixes that can be referenced at any time.

- Appendix A, "HTML 4 Quick Reference," gives you tags and important information about the Web's most widespread coding language.
- Appendix B, "CSS Quick Reference," is a guide to making Cascading Style Sheets do your layout work for you.
- Appendix C, "Installing FrontPage 2000," shows the "How-Tos" of installing FrontPage 2000 on your computer.

WEEK 1

Starting with the Basics

1

2

3

4

5

6

7

DAY **1**

FrontPage 2000 Basics

FrontPage 2000 provides many features that enable you create and manage Web pages and Web sites with ease. If you are new to FrontPage, you will delight in the way it helps you create Web pages that incorporate many of the latest Web technologies. It also helps you maintain the integrity of the links in your site— imagine verifying dozens or hundreds of internal and external hyperlinks in a matter of minutes! These are some of the tried and true features that have made FrontPage a leading program for Web page developers.

Today you will get a quick overview of the new FrontPage interface and learn what each of the different views and toolbars are used for.

In today's lesson, you will

- Become familiar with the FrontPage interface
- Learn what the different views in FrontPage are used for and which chapters in this book provide additional information on them
- Learn how to display and customize the toolbars in FrontPage

What's New in FrontPage 2000?

With FrontPage 2000, you can design a complete navigation system that generates navigation bars for you. As you make changes to your Web site, the navigation bars automatically update to reflect the changes. Tired of your background and colors? Change the look of your entire site with the click of a button, choosing from dozens of professionally designed Web themes.

New to FrontPage 2000 is a combined interface. Whereas previous versions of FrontPage separated the FrontPage Explorer (Web management) from the FrontPage Editor (Web page design), the new interface combines both into one. The integrated interface makes it far easier to create and maintain your Web sites. In addition, the interface is designed to fully integrate with other Office 2000 applications such as Word, Excel, Access, and PowerPoint.

Also new to FrontPage 2000 are menus and toolbars that you can customize yourself. Menus can display all commands, or only those you use most often.

With the HTML specification in a transitional phase, many Web developers find it difficult to keep track of which HTML tags are on the way out, which are in, and which will work in both older and newer browsers. For those who are familiar with the current HTML 4 specifications, FrontPage designs pages that are HTML 4 transitional compatible, and then some. You can use FrontPage to design pages that are compatible with the HTML 4 specification while being aware of tags that are compatible with older browsers. You can configure FrontPage to disable commands that are browser-specific, or to display commands that work in both HTML 3 and HTML 4 browsers.

The FrontPage Interface

The FrontPage interface is customizable to fit the needs of the individual. There are different panes that serve different needs, and you can hide them until you're ready to use them. In addition, you can configure toolbars and menus to display all the commands, or only those that you use most.

To begin our tour, start FrontPage from the Windows 95/98 Start menu. When FrontPage opens, the interface displays Page View, which displays the page editor shown in Figure 1.1. Here is where you'll do most of your work.

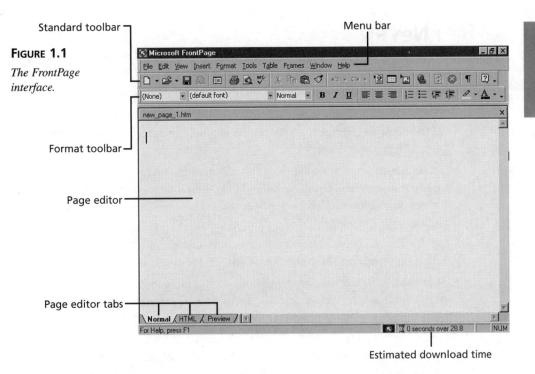

FIGURE 1.1

The FrontPage interface.

Standard toolbar

Menu bar

Format toolbar

Page editor

Page editor tabs

Estimated download time

Immediately obvious are the following areas, which will be discussed further in the sections that follow:

- The menu bar, located along the top of the page, contains nine categories of commands to help you build your pages.

- Beneath the menu bar are two of the many toolbars that FrontPage provides. The Standard toolbar and the Format toolbar contain buttons that allow you to quickly access the commands you most frequently use as you design your pages. Other toolbars are accessible only when you are using commands that are associated with them. You'll learn how to customize toolbars later in this chapter.

- The page editor allows you to design your Web pages in WYSIWYG (what you see is what you get) fashion. Figure 1.1 displays the Normal page editor screen.

- Tabs at the bottom of the page editor allow you to view and edit the HTML source code or preview your Web pages as they appear in a browser.

- The estimated download time of the current page displays in the right portion of the status bar. It helps you keep track of how long it will take for readers to download your Web page.

The Menu Bar

As with nearly all Windows programs, the Menu bar is located along the top of the inter-face screen. Nine categories of menu commands appear here. Briefly, the function of the commands in each menu is as follows:

- The File menu contains commands that deal with creation and maintenance of Webs and pages. Here are the commands that help you create, delete, publish, and print Web pages or entire Webs.
- The Edit menu contains commands that allow you to make changes to your pages and Web folders. You can undo and redo multiple actions, cut and paste items from the Windows clipboard, check pages in and out of a Web, and add tasks to your To Do list.
- The View menu contains commands that show or hide various elements in the FrontPage interface. These commands will be discussed later in this chapter.
- The Insert menu contains commands that allow you to insert several different types of content into your Web pages. Horizontal lines, line breaks, FrontPage compo-nents, pictures, video clips, sounds, hyperlinks, and other advanced features can be added to your pages with ease through commands found in this menu.
- The Format menu, in general, contains commands that control overall appearance and positioning of text, backgrounds, and other page content. These commands can be applied to one, several, or all pages in a Web.
- The Tools menu provides commands that allow you to customize features of the FrontPage interface and of FrontPage Webs.
- The Table menu provides commands that help you create, format, modify, and delete tables and cells.
- The Window menu provides commands that let you display and work on one or more pages at a time.
- The Help menu provides commands that display further information on the FrontPage commands and procedures, and current version information.

The FrontPage interface is divided into several panes, which can be displayed or hidden through commands in the View menu. In the following sections, you'll learn what each of the views is used for.

Page View (the Page Editor)

Page View is displayed when you first open FrontPage. You can also display Page View at any time by choosing the View, Page command, or by clicking the Page icon in the

Views Pane (described later in this chapter). This displays the current Web page in the main section of the FrontPage interface so that you can view or edit the page. You'll learn throughout this book how to add different kinds of content to Web pages.

Exercise 1.1: Viewing Your Pages in Page View

Try this simple exercise, which allows you to view a Web page in different page views. You will open a file from the CD-ROM that accompanies this book, and use the tabs in the bottom of the Page View to see what they do. Follow these steps:

1. Choose File, Open (Ctrl+O), or click the Open button on the Standard toolbar. The Open File dialog box appears.

2. Use the Look In drop-down box to locate the *D:\tyfp2k\chap12* folder on your CD-ROM (where *D:* is the drive letter of your CD-ROM drive).

3. Highlight frameset.htm and click Open to open the page in the page editor. FrontPage opens the Web page, and displays a folder list beside the Page View, as shown in Figure 1.2. The Folder List displays a list of all folders and pages in the Web. When the page opens, you view your page in Normal View. This view allows you to create and edit the content of your Web page.

> **Note**
>
> If the Folder List does not appear when you open the frameset page, choose View, Folder List to display it.

FIGURE 1.2

A frameset page is opened in Page View, and the Folder List displays a list of all folders and files in the Web.

4. Click the HTML tab (the third tab at the bottom of the page editor) to view your page in HTML View, shown in Figure 1.3. This view allows you to view and edit the HTML source code on your Web page. Don't let this view scare you, because FrontPage generates HTML code for you automatically. Advanced users who are more familiar with source code can quickly access and modify source code from this view.

FIGURE 1.3

The HTML tab allows you to view and edit the HTML code of your Web pages.

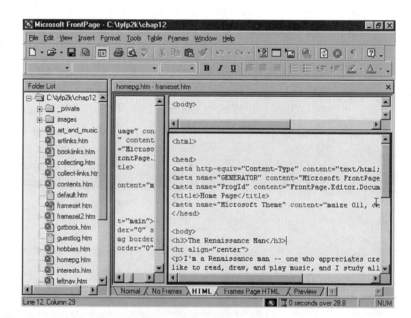

5. Next, click the Preview tab (the last tab) at the bottom of the page editor. The Preview mode, shown in Figure 1.4, allows you to navigate and test your Web pages as if you were viewing them through a Web browser.

The page that you currently have opened in the page editor is a frameset, which is a special type of page that divides the browser window into multiple panes, each of which displays a different Web page. Framesets are discussed on Day 12, "Creating and Using Framesets," and you'll learn more about each of these views there.

When you design or edit framesets, two additional tabs are displayed. Continue the exercise as follows to view them:

6. Click the No Frames tab (the second tab) at the bottom of the page editor. The No Frames editor, shown in Figure 1.5, allows you to design and edit the page that appears in place of the frameset when a browser does not support frames.

FIGURE 1.4

Preview mode of the page editor allows you to preview and test your Web pages as if you were viewing them in a Web browser.

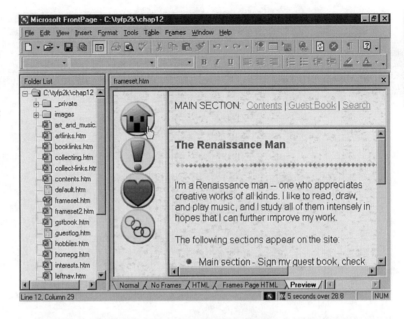

FIGURE 1.5

The No Frames tab allows you to create and edit the page that displays in place of a frameset when a browser does not support frames.

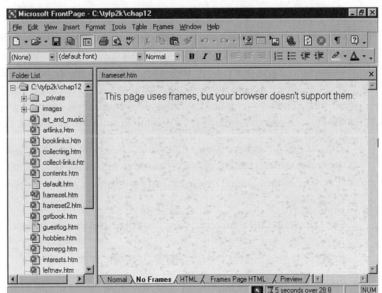

7. Finally, click the Frames Page HTML tab (the fourth tab) at the bottom of the page editor. This tab, shown in Figure 1.6, allows you to view and edit the HTML source code for the frameset.

FIGURE 1.6

The Frames Page HTML tab allows you to view and edit the HTML source code for a frameset.

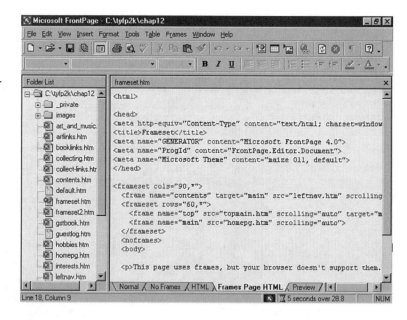

The Views Bar

FrontPage is much more than a Web page editor. Hiding behind the scenes are many other views that allow you to track and maintain all of the links on your Web pages. There are several other views that allow you to examine and repair links, create Web reports, design navigation systems, and more. You can display and hide each of these views by choosing commands in the View menu. You can also display the Views bar, which is shown in Figure 1.7. To display or hide the Views bar, choose View, Views Bar.

The Views bar, which appears along the left side of the FrontPage interface, enables you to choose one of many ways to view and maintain the folders and content in your Web sites. The main screen in the FrontPage workspace changes, depending on the view you select.

The views, and their functions, are described and shown in the following sections.

Folder List and Folders View

Figure 1.7 displays the Folder List in the middle pane, and Folder View in the right pane. As previously mentioned, you choose View, Folder List to display or hide the Folder List, which displays a graphic tree of all of the folders and files in a Web. You can collapse or expand the Folder List to display a list of the pages that are contained within each folder.

FIGURE 1.7

Use the Views bar to select one of several views that help you manage pages and links in your Web site.

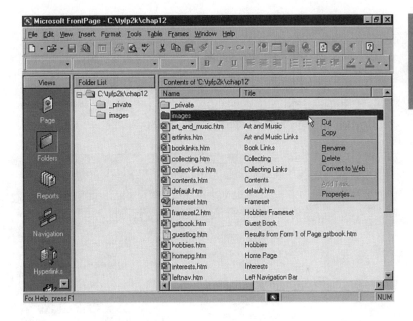

To display or hide Folders View, select the Folders icon in the Views bar, or choose the View, Folders command. Folders View displays a more detailed list of all the pages that are contained within a specific folder in a Web site. Folders View displays the size and type of file, the date the page was last modified, who modified the file (if multiple users are working on the same Web site), and additional comments about the file.

When you right-click on a folder name in Folder View, the pop-up menu shown in Figure 1.7 appears. You can easily relocate, copy, delete, or rename a folder from this menu. The Convert to Web command in the pop-up menu allows you to convert any subfolder in your Web into a sub Web that can use a different set of themes and Web settings than the original Web.

Tip

Use Folders View to change the title of a page without opening it in the page editor. The first time you click on a title in Folders View, it selects it as the active page. The second time you click, a bounding box surrounds the page title and allows you to change it. Edit the title as necessary, and then press Enter to complete the task. You can also edit the filename in the same manner.

When you right-click on a file in Folders View, the pop-up menu shown in Figure 1.8 appears. You can cut or copy pages into your clipboard and paste them into another folder in your Web. You can also rename or delete pages. When you choose Open from the pop-up menu, the page opens in the page editor. Choose the Open With command to open the selected file in any editor that you have configured to use in conjunction with FrontPage. The Add Task command allows you to create a to-do task for the currently selected page, as discussed further on Day 21, "Tracking and Maintaining Your Webs."

FIGURE 1.8

Folders View allows you to cut, copy, rename, and delete pages in your Web.

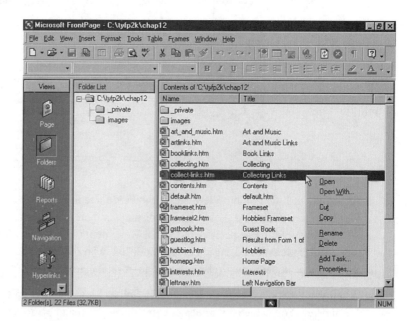

<table>
<tr><td>Note</td><td>To configure additional editors, choose Tools, Options to open the Options dialog box. Select the Configure Editors tab. Enter the file extension in the File Type field, and then use the Browse button to locate the executable file that you want to use to open any file with that extension. For example, when you enter xls in the File Type field, you can configure FrontPage to open Microsoft Excel anytime you select a file with an xls extension.</td></tr>
</table>

When you display Folders View and the Folder List concurrently, you can select one or more files and move them to a different folder in your Web. When you move files, FrontPage automatically edits all pages that link to the files you move so that your links do not break.

Reports View

Reports View, shown in Figure 1.9, allows you to track and maintain the status of links and pages in your Web sites and generate reports on the status of your Web site. You can display or hide Reports View by choosing the Reports icon in the Views bar, or by choosing the View, Reports command. You'll learn more about these commands on Day 21.

FIGURE 1.9

Reports View allows you to track and maintain the pages in your Web, while viewing your Web content in several reporting categories.

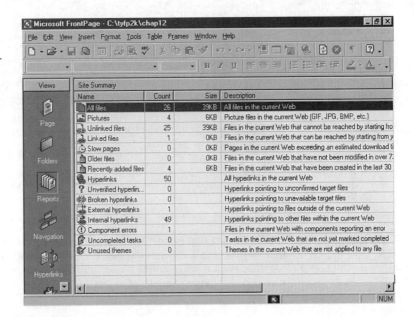

Navigation View

Navigation View, shown in Figure 1.10, allows you to create and maintain a navigation system for a Web site. In the figure, the Folder List has been toggled off by choosing View, Folder List. When you right-click in Navigation View, you can choose a different zoom level for Navigation View, view a specific subtree, create a new top page, or configure Web settings for the view.

You use Navigation View to quickly plan and design the navigation system in your Web site. Similar to an organizational chart, pages can be added, deleted, and moved around in a tree. Navigation bars and buttons are generated for you automatically when you add pages to your navigation tree. To switch to Navigation View, select the Navigation icon in the Views bar, or choose the View, Navigation command. You'll learn more about this view and its associated commands on Day 11, "Designing Navigation Systems."

Navigation View helps you build a complete navigation system by placing your Web pages in a tree. Navigation bars and buttons are generated automatically for you.

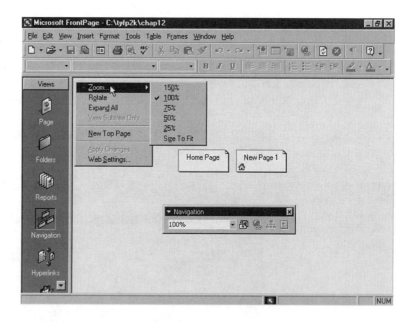

> **Note**
>
> The Web pages that you are viewing use framesets to help the reader navigate through the Web. Typically, framesets and navigation bars are not used together. For a more complete picture of what a Web looks like when displayed in Navigation View, refer to Day 11.

Hyperlinks View

Hyperlinks View, shown in Figure 1.11, displays hyperlinks to and from the pages in your Web in a graphical format. The currently selected page is shown as a large icon in the center of hyperlinks View. Pages that link to the current page are displayed at the left of the current page, while pages that the current page links to are displayed to the right of the current page.

Select the Hyperlinks icon in the Views bar, or choose the View, Hyperlinks command to display your Web in Hyperlinks View. To view the pages that link to a page or file in your Web, select a page from the Folder List. When you highlight the page, it appears in the Hyperlinks pane at the right.

The pop-up menu shown in Figure 1.11 appears when you right-click anywhere in Hyperlinks View. This allows you to select additional information to display in Hyperlinks View:

- Show Page Titles displays titles of your Web pages in place of the filename.

- Hyperlinks to Pictures displays hyperlinks to any pages that appear on the current page.

- Repeated Hyperlinks displays a link to items that appear on your page more than once.

- Hyperlinks Inside Page displays a link to bookmarks that are included on the page.

- Web Settings opens the Web Settings dialog box, where you can rename the Web and display or hide hidden folders in your Web, among other tasks.

FIGURE 1.11

Hyperlinks View provides a graphic representation of pages that link to or from a page in your Web site.

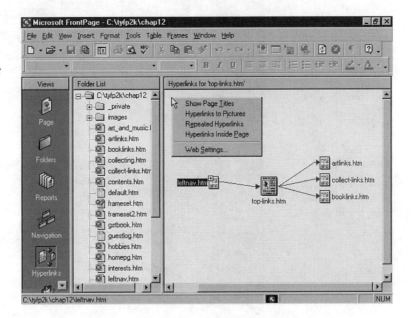

When a plus sign (+) appears beside a page, you can expand the tree to continue your way forward or backward through your Web, as shown in Figure 1.12. Conversely, click the minus sign (-) to contract the tree.

Tasks View

Tasks View, shown in Figure 1.13 and discussed in more detail in Day 21, allows you to add, complete, or delete to-do tasks as you build your Web sites. The pop-up menu allows you to quickly add a task to a selected page or file. Select the Tasks icon in the Views bar, or choose the View, Tasks command to display Tasks View.

FIGURE **1.12**

*Click the plus sign (+)
to expand the tree and
continue your way for-
ward or backward
through your Web.*

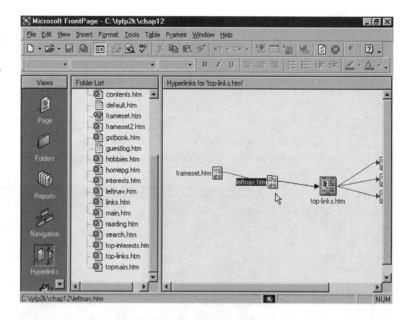

FIGURE **1.13**

*Tasks View allows you
to create, edit, and
complete to-do tasks.*

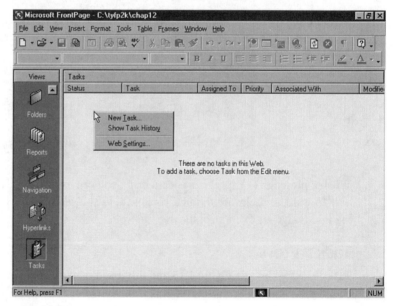

The FrontPage Toolbars

FrontPage 2000 has several toolbars, each of which provides access to frequently used commands and features. The toolbars, which are located either just below the Menu bar or just above the status bar at the bottom of the screen by default, can be displayed or hidden through commands in the View, Toolbars menu.

Each of the toolbars is described briefly in the following list, and discussed further in the chapters noted.

- Choose View, Toolbars, Standard to view the Standard toolbar, which displays commands you most commonly use to create new pages and Webs. Refer to Day 3, "Building Basic Web Pages," for additional information about this toolbar.

- Choose View, Toolbars, Formatting to view the Format toolbar, which displays commands you most commonly use to format text and paragraphs on your pages. This toolbar is also discussed on Day 3.

- Choose View, Toolbars, DHTML Effects to display the DHTML Effects toolbar. This toolbar is discussed on Day 13, "Working with DHTML and Positioning."

- Choose View, Toolbars, Navigation to display the Navigation toolbar while in Navigation View. This toolbar is discussed on Day 11.

- Choose View, Toolbars, Pictures to display or hide the Pictures toolbar while an image is selected. This toolbar is discussed on Day 6, "Adding Images, Sounds, and Video."

- Choose View, Toolbars, Positioning to display or hide the Positioning toolbar. This toolbar is discussed on Day 13.

- Choose View, Toolbars, Reporting to display or hide the Reporting toolbar while in Reports View. This toolbar is discussed on Day 21.

- Choose View, Toolbars, Style to display the Style toolbar. This toolbar is discussed on Day 10, "Using Style Sheets."

- Choose View, Toolbars, Tables to display or hide the Tables toolbar when working on a table in your Web page. This toolbar is discussed on Day 5, "Creating and Formatting Tables."

Customizing and Creating Toolbars

You can customize any of the toolbars, as well as create your own toolbars. Normally, the toolbars that are provided with FrontPage display all the buttons. However, you can choose to hide some of them so that the toolbars take up less space.

At the right end of each toolbar, you'll see a small arrow that points downward. Click on this arrow to choose the Add or Remove Buttons command. Then modify the toolbar as follows:

- To remove a button from a toolbar, click the check mark that appears to the left of the associated command name. The check mark disappears, indicating that the button will no longer appear on the toolbar.

- To add a button to a toolbar, click the blank area that appears to the left of the associated command name. A check mark appears, indicating that the button will appear on the toolbar.

- Choose the Reset Toolbar command to reset the toolbar to its default configuration.

- Choose the Customize button to create and configure your own toolbars. Alternatively, you can choose the View, Toolbars, Customize command. The Customize dialog box shown in Figure 1.14 appears. The following exercise shows you how to use this dialog box.

FIGURE 1.14

You can add or remove buttons from any toolbar.

Exercise 1.2: Creating a New Toolbar

You use the Customize dialog box to create your own toolbars. Let's say, for example, that you want to create a toolbar that displays commands associated with the Frames menu. Follow these steps:

1. The Customize dialog box initially opens to the Commands tab. To create a new toolbar, select the Toolbars tab shown in Figure 1.15.

FIGURE 1.15

Use the Toolbars tab in the Customize dialog box to create your own toolbars.

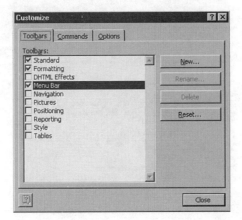

2. Click the New button. The New Toolbar dialog box appears. Enter Framesets and click OK. The Framesets toolbar appears in the list of available toolbars, and a check mark displays beside its name.

Note

The Rename command in the Toolbars tab allows you to rename your custom toolbar. This option is disabled for the default toolbars provided with FrontPage.

The Delete command in the Toolbars tab allows you to delete a custom toolbar. This option is also disabled for the default toolbars.

The Reset command in the Toolbars tab allows you to reset the default toolbars back to their original configuration. This allows you to add commands back in if you have removed them.

3. Select the Commands tab to display it. This tab, shown in Figure 1.16, allows you to choose the commands that appear in your custom toolbar.

4. From the Categories section, highlight Frames. The commands associated with frames display in the Commands section.

5. Select a command from the Commands section, and drag it into your new toolbar. Drag all six commands into the toolbar (Figure 1.16 shows three of the six commands, with the fourth in process of being dragged toward the toolbar).

FIGURE **1.16**

*Use the Commands tab
in the Customize dia-
log box to add com-
mands to a custom
toolbar.*

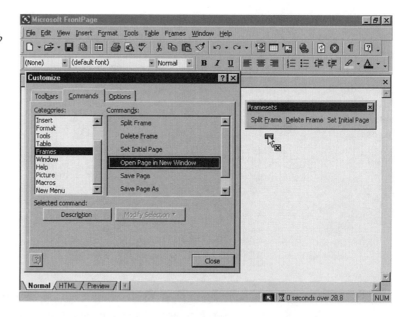

After you have added commands to the toolbar, you can use the Modify Selection command in the Commands menu to select how to display the commands in the toolbar.
Figure 1.17 shows the commands that are available in this menu. Briefly, the commands
serve the following functions:

- *Reset*—Resets a toolbar command to its original (default) state.

- *Delete*—Deletes a command from the toolbar.

- *Name*—Allows you to change the name of a toolbar command, or to assign a
  hotkey to it. To assign a hotkey, precede the letter you want to use with an amper-
  sand (&).

- *Copy Button Image*—Copies an icon that you have assigned to a toolbar command,
  and places it into the clipboard.

- *Paste Button Image*—Pastes the icon from the clipboard into another command on
  the toolbar.

- *Reset Button Image*—Removes the icon from the toolbar command.

- *Edit Button Image*—Choose this command to open the Button Editor shown in
  Figure 1.18. This editor allows you to create a custom icon, or to modify one of the
  icons that you select from the Change Button Image command (described next).
  After you create or edit your icon, choose OK to assign it to the toolbar command.

- *Change Button Image*—Select the command and drag to the right to select a
  generic image for your toolbar command.

1

- *Default Style*—Displays all toolbar commands with icons only. The command name displays in a pop-up when you hover the mouse button over the icon.

- *Text Only (Always)*—Displays all toolbar commands as text.

- *Text Only (in Menus)*—A variation of Text Only (Always). Displays the toolbar icon in the toolbar.

- *Image and Text*—Displays an icon and a text command for the toolbar option.

- *Begin a Group*—Adds a dividing line between two toolbar commands, allowing you to display related icons in groups.

- *Assign Macro*—Assigns a macro to a button or menu command.

FIGURE 1.17

Commands in the Modify Selection menu allow you to choose options for displaying the commands in your custom toolbar.

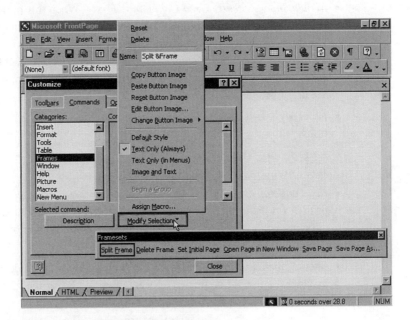

FIGURE 1.18

The Button Editor, accessible through the Edit Button Image command, allows you to create your own button images.

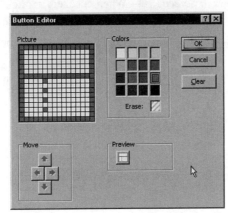

Other Toolbar Options

The Options tab in the Customize dialog box allows you to select other options for your toolbars, as well as options to display the FrontPage menus. This tab is shown in Figure 1.19. The options are as follows:

- *Standard and Formatting Toolbars Share One Row*—Choose this option to display the Standard and Formatting toolbars on the same line, instead of on two separate lines as default. Note that you might want to select this option if you design your pages at lower resolutions, because it will reduce the number of icons that are visible at one time.

- *Menus Show Recently Used Commands First*—When this option is checked, FrontPage displays the commands you most recently used in each menu. Commands you use less frequently are not displayed, but will be displayed after a delay if the Show Full Menus After a Short Delay option is checked. When you deselect the Menus Show Recently Used Commands First option, all commands are displayed in their respective drop-down menus.

- *Reset My Usage Data*—This option resets all menus to their original configurations.

- *Large Icons*—This option displays large icons in toolbars in lieu of the default small icons.

- *List Font Names in Their Font*—When this option is checked, the Change Font drop-down list in the Formatting toolbar displays each font exactly as it appears, allowing you to preview what each font looks like. When not checked, all font names are displayed in Arial text.

- *Show ScreenTips on Toolbars*—When this option is checked, a pop-up window that displays the toolbar command appears after you hover the mouse over the toolbar icon. When not checked, the pop-ups will not appear.

- *Show Shortcut Keys in ScreenTips*—When checked, shortcut keys are displayed with the command names. When unchecked, only the command name appears.

- *Menu Animations*—This option allows you to choose the method in which menus expand. The choices are None (displays entire menu at one time), Random (varies between all options), Unfold (menu reveals itself from top-left to bottom-right corner), or Slide (slides open from the top of the screen).

FIGURE 1.19

The Options tab in the Customize dialog box presents several additional options for displaying your menu commands.

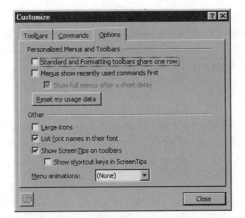

Previewing Your Pages in Browsers

If you're relatively new to browsing the Internet, you might only be familiar with what the Internet looks like in one Web browser. The screen shots throughout this book will display pages as they look in Internet Explorer 5.0. Be aware, however, that pages will not necessarily look the same in all browsers.

You may ask, "Why is this the case? Isn't FrontPage supposed to create Web pages and display them exactly as they appear on the Internet?" The answer to this question is, "Well, yes... and no."

There are many different computers out there in the real world, and several different operating systems are used to run the software on them. Each of these operating systems has to speak to the Internet, which presents a problem. DOS doesn't speak Windows, Windows doesn't speak OS/2, OS/2 doesn't speak Macintosh. How did they get it all to work?

Enter the HTML language, which was written to be cross-platform. Web browsers developed for each operating system are the key. The browser looks at the cross-platform HTML code and interprets it so that your computer and operating system know how to display it correctly.

As the Internet grows up, the HTML specifications grow and change with it. Browser manufacturers have to keep up with the latest trends, and sometimes they incorporate features that add enhancements that are not found in other browsers. Over time, this has resulted in a situation where there is a conglomeration of many different browsers in the real world. Not everyone keeps up to date with the latest and greatest developments on the Web, and you have to consider those who view the Internet differently than you do.

When you design your Web pages, it is *always* a good idea to preview them in as many different Web browsers as you can, including older versions of browsers. The reason for this is because browsers display Web pages differently, and you want to make sure that your pages look good in as many browsers as possible. You want your site to be viewed by as many people as possible.

FrontPage allows you to select different browsers in which to preview your Web pages. The "big two" (Internet Explorer and Netscape Navigator) should always be included in your choices. Quite often, online services such as CompuServe, AOL, and MSN use slightly customized versions of these Web browsers, and are also good choices for page previews.

After you install other browsers on your system, you can configure them in the Preview in Browser dialog box, shown in Figure 1.20. Choose File, Preview in Browser to open this dialog box.

FIGURE 1.20

Use the Preview in Browser dialog box to choose and configure the browsers in which you want to preview your Web pages.

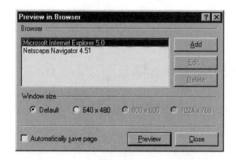

To add a browser, click the Add button. Enter the name of a browser that you have installed on your computer, then click the Browse button in the Add Browser dialog box to locate the executable file that starts the browser. After you locate the browser, choose the Open command to return to the Add Browser dialog box, and choose OK to return to the Preview in Browser dialog box.

To preview a Web page in one of the browsers that you have configured, open the Web page that you want to preview in the page editor. Then, choose the File, Preview in Browser command again to open the Preview in Browser dialog box.

By default, the browser previews your Web page in the resolution that your computer is set at. If your video display is set to a higher resolution than 640×480 (additional options are 800×600 and 1024×768), you can select additional window sizes in which to preview your page. The display options will not exceed your current display resolution.

FrontPage will not preview pages unless you save changes to the pages you are editing. Check the Automatically Save Page check box to automatically save any changes that you make to your pages before you preview them.

Configuring Browser Compatibility

Related to the browser issue is keeping track of which commands are compatible with which browsers. This can sometimes be a daunting task, but fortunately FrontPage 2000 makes it a lot easier for you. Choose Tools, Page Options to display the Page Options dialog box, then select the Compatibility tab shown in Figure 1.21. This tab configures FrontPage to help you design pages that will be compatible with specific browsers and features. Any commands that do not work with the features you select will be disabled.

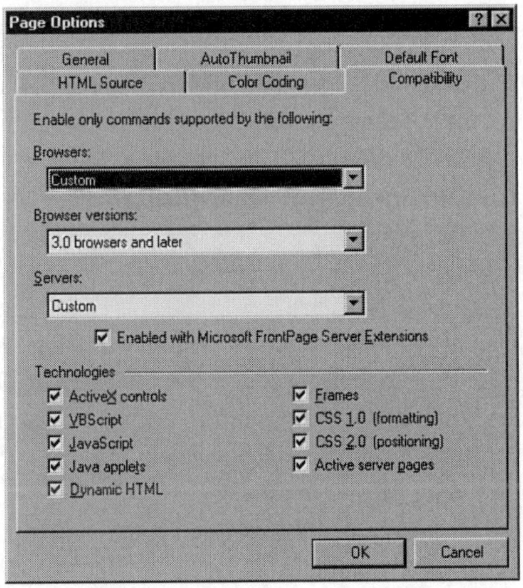

FIGURE 1.21

The Compatibility tab in the Page Options dialog box lets you specify the types of browsers and features that you want your pages to be compatible with.

The following options are available on the Compatibility tab of the Page Options dialog box:

- The Browsers drop-down menu allows you to develop pages for Microsoft Internet Explorer only, Netscape Navigator only, both Internet Explorer and Netscape Navigator, MS Web TV, or Custom.
- The Browser Versions menu allows you to choose between HTML 4.0 browsers or later, HTML 3.0 browsers or later, or Custom.

- The Servers drop-down menu allows you to choose between Microsoft Internet Information Server 3.0 or later, Apache servers, or Custom.
- If your Web server does not have the FrontPage Server Extensions installed, uncheck the Enabled with Microsoft FrontPage Server Extensions check box.
- If you want design pages that include additional Web technologies, check or uncheck any additional options in the Technologies section.

You might find it too soon in the game to decide which of these technologies you should include in your pages. For this reason, you might want to leave the settings at their default values until you learn more about the technologies and which browsers support them. And that is exactly what this book will help you learn!

Summary

Now you have a general idea of how to find your way around the FrontPage interface, and you are ready to journey down the road of Web page design. You've learned what each of the views in FrontPage are used for. You also got a quick review of the toolbars, and learned how to customize the FrontPage interface. You also learned how to preview your pages in Web browsers, and why it is important to do so.

Workshop

Each chapter in this book will be summarized with a workshop that lists common questions and answers about the topic discussed in the day's lesson. You'll also get a couple of exercises in each lesson that will help reinforce what you learned. In addition, a quiz will test you on some of the most important points in the lesson. Today's wrap-up will focus on the basics of the FrontPage interface.

Q&A

Q Can I open other types of documents in FrontPage besides Web pages?

A You can open a variety of word processing formats, including Rich Text Format and text documents. The FrontPage Editor also enables you to open and edit processed .html pages that use extensions such as .asp (Active Server Pages), .htx (for Internet Information Server Internet database connection), and others.

Q Can I use FrontPage to edit Web pages that reside on my hard drive instead of those that exist in a FrontPage Web?

A Yes, you can. FrontPage 2000 makes it easy for you to generate Web sites on a hard disk as well as on a Web server. Web sites that you generate on a local or network hard disk are called disk-based Webs. The projects that you create in this chapter are created on disk-based Webs.

However, many of the features discussed in Week 3 require you to test and run your pages on a Web server that has the FrontPage server extensions installed. When this is indicated, you will need to install a personal Web server on your own computer, or publish and test your pages on an Internet server that has the server extensions.

Q Can I create toolbars that combine commands from the standard toolbars that are furnished with FrontPage? For example, if I want to create a toolbar that contains only commands to make image maps, can I do that?

A As long as there is an equivalent menu command, you can add it to a toolbar. However, if you want to create a toolbar that includes icons that do not have a menu equivalent (such as many that are found in the Picture toolbar), you won't be able to add them to a custom toolbar.

Quiz

1. True or false: The pages I design in FrontPage will really be WYSIWYG. FrontPage displays them exactly the way that I will see them on the Internet.

2. Which of the FrontPage views allows you to edit your Web pages?

3. When you customize a toolbar, can you create custom icons to appear on the toolbar?

4. Can you preview your pages in any Web browser?

5. How does FrontPage help you design pages that are compatible with the browsers that you select?

Exercises

1. Experiment with adding icons to the commands that you added to your custom Frames toolbar. Select pre-made icons from the Change Button Image selections, or design your own using the Edit Button Image command.

2. Try to decide which additional browsers you want to preview your pages in. Remember that not all browsers are created equal, and you might want to add a couple of browsers besides the "big two"—Internet Explorer and Netscape Navigator. Install the browsers on your computer, and use the File, Preview in Browsers command to add the new browsers to your preview list.

Answers to Quiz

1. A trick question, because it depends on what browser you view your pages in. Though there are minor differences between Internet Explorer and Netscape Navigator, FrontPage displays your Web pages reasonably similar in both of these

browsers. Older browsers may display your pages considerably different, so be sure to preview in as many browsers as you can.

2. You can edit your pages in Page View. Choose View, Page or click the Page icon in the Views pane to enter the page editor.

3. Yes you can. The Button Editor helps you generate icons for your toolbars.

4. Yes, the Preview in Browser dialog box lets you select any browser that you have installed on your computer.

5. You use the Compatibility tab in the Page Options dialog box to select the browsers, servers, and Web technologies to include in your pages. FrontPage allows you to select the commands and features that are compatible with those browsers.

DAY 2

Fast-Track to Webs and Pages

Now that you know a little bit about how to find your way around FrontPage, you'll begin to learn more about the power beneath the FrontPage hood. Today you will build a couple of Web sites using some of the templates and wizards provided with FrontPage. You'll also learn how to add template-built pages to these Webs.

If you are pressed for time or short on ideas for pages, FrontPage has a bountiful supply of Web and page templates and wizards that will quickly help you set the groundwork for your Web site. There are templates and wizards designed to accommodate both personal and corporate needs. You can modify the content in any way you choose.

In this chapter, you get a quick overview of the many Web and page templates and wizards provided with FrontPage.

Some of the things you'll accomplish today:

- Introduce yourself to the Web and page templates and wizards furnished with FrontPage 2000
- Create personal and corporate Web sites containing several pages that are automatically linked for you
- Create a page from a template and add the page to a Web site
- Save pages to your current Web or to a folder on your local or network hard drive

Web Building Basics

If you're new to Web site construction, you might find it helpful to begin your site by using one of the FrontPage Web templates or wizards to generate some pages. The Web templates generate one or more pages that are automatically linked together. They set the groundwork for your Web site, after which you can customize the content to suit your needs. The Web wizards differ slightly from the Web templates in that the wizards allow you to customize which pages you want to include in your Web site and offer other choices such as how you want your Web pages to look.

There are five simple steps involved in creating a Web site in FrontPage. You begin with the File, New, Web command, which opens the New Web dialog box shown in Figure 2.1. The following sections describe the remaining steps in more detail.

FIGURE 2.1

The first step to creating a FrontPage Web.

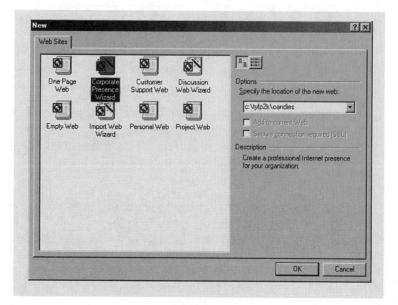

Selecting a Template or Wizard

After you open the Web Sites tab in the New dialog box, the next step is to choose a template or wizard with which to create your pages. In the example shown in Figure 2.1, the Corporate Presence Wizard is selected to create a Web site for a small business.

FrontPage provides five Web templates and three Web wizards that help you get a Web site up and running very quickly. Two of the Web templates set up a Web site in which you want to design your own pages. The remaining templates and wizards generate several pages that are automatically linked together for you or help you import existing content into a FrontPage Web.

- The two Web templates that get you started creating your own original pages are the Empty Web and One Page Web. You'll work with one of these two Web templates tomorrow, when you generate your first Web page.

- The three remaining Web templates that generate several pages automatically with little intervention are the Customer Support Web, the Project Web, and the Personal Web.

- The three Web wizards, which allow you to make choices about which pages are included in your Web site, are the Import Web Wizard, Discussion Web Wizard, and Corporate Presence Wizard.

Specifying a Location for Your Web

FrontPage allows you to create Web sites on your local or network hard drive or on a Web server. To specify the location of the Web, you enter either a file path or a URL in the Specify the Location of the New Web field in the New dialog box. Again, referring back to Figure 2.1, you will see a Web named `Candies` that is about to be created beneath the `C:\tyfp2k` directory on a local hard drive.

 Note

By default, the New dialog box displays information from the Web that you most recently created. If, for example, the last Web that you created was located at `C:\tyfp2k\candies`, the Specify a Location for the New Web field will default to `C:\tyfp2k\candies2` the next time you open the New dialog box to create a new Web.

You specify the location of a new Web as follows:

- In FrontPage terminology, a Web that resides on a local or network hard drive is called a *disk-based Web*. Disk-based Webs allow you to create Web sites when you don't have access to a Web server.

After you design your disk-based Web pages, you can publish them on the Internet. To create a disk-based Web, you specify a file path on a local or network hard drive, as shown in Figure 2.2. For example, if you want to store your Web pages in the My Documents folder on your C drive, you enter the following path in the Specify the Location of the New Web field:

C:\My Documents\My Webs*webname*

FIGURE 2.2

To create a disk-based Web, specify a file path in the New dialog box.

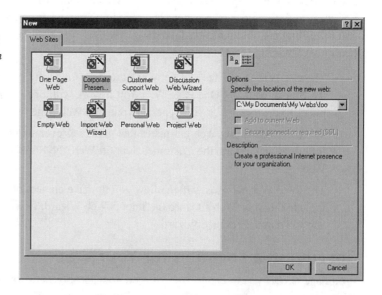

Some FrontPage features will not work unless they reside on a Web server that has the FrontPage Server Extensions installed.

Throughout this book, I will note occasions where the Extensions are required. It is important to note that disk-based Webs *will* allow you to design full-featured Web sites that include these advanced FrontPage features. However, you won't be able to fully test them until your pages are published on a server that has the FrontPage Server Extensions installed. If you are using FrontPage on Windows 98 and need the ability to design and test your pages offline, you can install the Microsoft Personal Web Server. This personal Web server is furnished on your Windows 98 CD-ROM at D:\add-ons\pws\setup.exe (where D: is the drive letter for your CD-ROM drive).

When you have a server installed on your computer, you create your Web site by specifying a URL instead of a file path.

- To create a Web site on a Web server (whether it be the Microsoft Personal Web Server on your local computer, an Internet server on the World Wide Web, or your corporate intranet server), you specify a URL as shown in Figure 2.3. Begin the URL with **http://**, followed by the name of the server in which you want to create the Web, and follow that by the name of the Web you want to create. For example, if your server is located at `http://www.foo.com`, and you want to create a Web called `mysite`, you enter a URL as follows:

`http://www.foo.com/mysite`

When you specify a URL location for your new Web but do not have a Web server installed on your local computer, FrontPage assumes you want to connect to a remote location to create the Web. The Connect To dialog box appears and allows you to connect to the Internet.

2

FIGURE 2.3

To create a FrontPage Web on a Web server, enter a URL in the New dialog box.

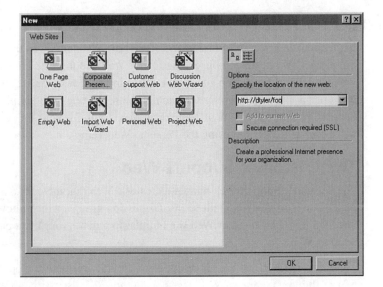

Adding a Web to a Current Web

FrontPage allows you to combine templates and wizards to create a larger Web site. For example, let's say you have already designed a business Web site with pages that describe the products you sell.

Now you want to add a discussion group to your existing Web site, enabling you to interact with your customers in a threaded newsgroup style format.

First, open the existing Web that contains your products pages. To add the discussion group, choose File, New, Web. Because you already have the first Web opened in FrontPage, you will now notice that the Add to Current Web option is enabled in the New dialog box. To add the discussion group to your currently opened Web, click the Add to Current Web check box. This will add the pages from the Discussion Group Wizard into the site that contains your product pages.

Connecting to SSL

Some Web sites (for example, those that allow customers to purchase products and services on the Internet) use what is called a Secure Sockets Layer to communicate sensitive data between the Web server and the customer. If your Web site resides on such a server, check the Secure Connection Required (SSL) option in the New dialog box before you create your Web site.

The FrontPage Web Templates

In the preceding section, I briefly mentioned the Web templates that are available in FrontPage. Two of the templates, the Empty Web and the One Page Web, get you started with a totally original Web site. In the following sections, you'll learn more about what types of pages are generated with each of the remaining Web templates: the Customer Support Web, Project Web, and Personal Web. Then, for your first exercise today, you will generate a Web site using the Personal Web Template.

The Customer Support Web

The Customer Support Web template creates a Web that includes a number of different pages, some of which contain forms. Discussion groups, which allow you to place threaded messages on your Web site (similar to a newsgroup), are part of the Customer Support Web.

The Customer Support Web is designed to provide interactive support with your customers through the use of Web pages and a threaded discussion group. Though it is primarily designed to provide support for software products, it can easily be modified to suit any purpose. Included in the collection of pages in the Customer Support Web are the following sections:

- *A Customer Support section*—Complete with Bug Report Form, Discussion Group, Download page, Customer Feedback page, Frequently Asked Questions page, Search Page, Suggestions from Customers page, Technical Notes, and What's New Page

- *A Customer Support discussion group*—Complete with its own Search page, article submission form, Welcome page, and page headers and footers

Note Discussion groups will not function properly unless they are tested and located on a Web server that has the FrontPage Server Extensions installed. Discussion groups and the FrontPage Server Extensions are discussed further on Day 19, "Handling Forms with FrontPage Components."

The list of pages that are generated by the Customer Support Web is shown in Figure 2.4, displayed in Folder View.

FIGURE 2.4

The Customer Support Web creates a collection of fully editable pages for your customer support Web site.

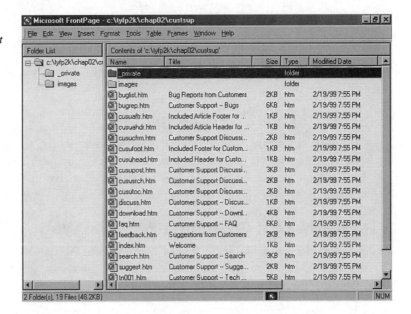

The Project Web

The Project Web includes two discussion groups and is roughly divided into two main sections. The first section of the Project Web is designed to store files and pages and to provide a discussion group that relates to project design and development. The second section of the Project Web stores knowledge base articles and a related discussion group. Figure 2.5 shows a partial list of the pages generated by the Project Web, displayed in Folder View.

FIGURE 2.5

The Project Web template creates two discussion groups and additional pages that help you coordinate projects on an intranet or the Internet.

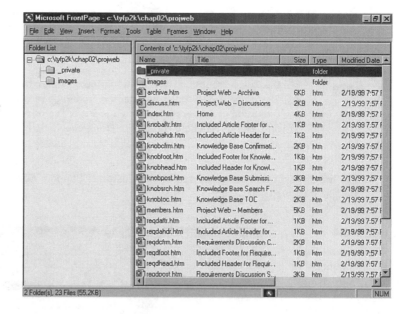

The Personal Web Template

For those of you who want to create a personal site very quickly, FrontPage includes a template that will get you well on your way. The Personal Web Template creates a home page along with four additional pages that display your favorite links and interests. In the following exercise, you'll create a personal Web using this template.

Exercise 2.1: Creating a Personal Web

In today's first exercise, you'll build a small personal Web site using one of the FrontPage templates. Also, the steps outlined here are those you would use to generate a Web site with any of the Web templates that have already been mentioned in this chapter.

The Personal Web template creates a personal Web site with five Web pages. Besides a home page, the site includes a Favorite Sites page, an Interests page, a Favorites page, and a Photo Album page. Figure 2.6 shows how the pages link to each other in Navigation View. The only page that does not appear automatically in Navigation View is the page titled myfav3.htm. You'll learn more about how to add additional pages to Navigation View on Day 11, "Designing Navigation Systems."

Note

When you generate Webs with any of the FrontPage templates and wizards, navigation systems are generated automatically for you. To include the navigation buttons on your Web pages, you need to place shared borders on your Web pages. You'll learn more about this procedure on Day 11.

FIGURE 2.6

The Personal Web Template creates a home page and some additional pages that list personal favorites and interests.

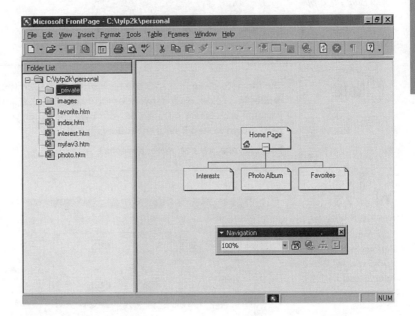

To create a personal Web using the Personal Web Template, follow these steps:

1. Choose File, New, Web; or click the arrow just to the right of the New Page icon on the Standard toolbar, and then select Web from the drop-down menu (see Figure 2.7).

2. The New dialog box shown in Figure 2.8 appears. From the icons displayed in the Web Sites tab, select Personal Web.

3. In the Specify the Location of the New Web field, enter the following file path to create a Web named `personal` in the `tyfp2k` directory on your C drive:

   `c:\tyfp2k\personal`

FIGURE 2.7

To create a new Web from the Standard toolbar, click the arrow to the right of the New Page icon and select Web from the drop-down menu.

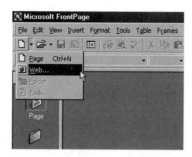

Note

The file path given in step 3 creates a *disk-based Web* (that is, a Web that resides in a folder on a network or local hard drive). If you have the Personal Web Server installed on your own computer, you can replace the path shown in step 3 with the following URL:

`http://your server name/personal`

FIGURE 2.8

The Web Sites tab in the New dialog box allows you to select from several Web templates and wizards.

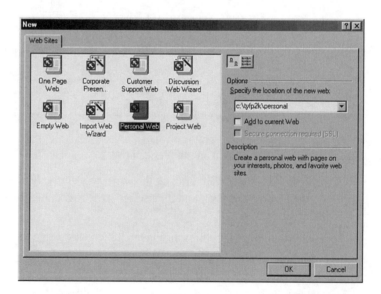

4. Choose OK. FrontPage generates five pages for you. If you have previously used FrontPage to create a Web, your new personal Web will be created using the theme that was applied to the previous Web.

In four easy steps, you've created five pages. The purpose of each of these pages is as follows:

- Favorites (favorite.htm) is a page where you can create and display links to your favorite Web sites. Three links are automatically included on the pages, but you can modify them as discussed on Day 7, "Adding Links and Bookmarks."

- Home Page (index.htm) is the first page people see when they navigate to the site. This page provides a place for you to introduce yourself or the purpose of the Web site. Links to the remaining pages in the Web also appear on the page. The filename of your home page may vary, depending on the type of Web server you develop your Web pages on. When you create a disk-based Web, the home page is named index.htm. When you use the Microsoft Personal Web Server or Internet Information Server, the home page is named Default.htm. Many UNIX-based Web servers default to index.html. Most Web servers today can be configured to search through an array of popular index pages, including all of the above-mentioned filenames.

- Interests (interest.htm) is a page that displays your hobbies or interests and can include pictures, text, or hyperlinks.

- My Favorite Site 3 (myfav3.htm) is a page that has been created as a destination page for the links on the Favorites page. You can either delete this page and replace the associated links on the Favorites page with links to other sites on the World Wide Web, or use it as a starting point for another page in your own Web.

- Photo Album (photos.htm) is a page where you can display your favorite photos. You'll learn how to insert images on pages on Day 6, "Adding Images, Sounds, and Video."

The FrontPage Web Wizards

The FrontPage Web wizards are somewhat similar to the Web templates in that they generate sites with several pages that are automatically linked together for you. However, unlike the Web templates that give you no choices as to the pages you include in the site, the wizards put you in control of the choices. You decide which pages to include (or omit), make selections for content to appear on pages, and even choose how you want the pages to look. The wizards guide you to customizing your site by prompting you to make the selections in a series of screens. If you need help, there is easy access to the built-in Help from each screen in the wizard.

Note | FrontPage creates the folder for your Web site before the wizard starts. If you choose the Cancel button during the process of using a wizard, the folder for the Web you were creating still resides in the directory location in which you were creating the new Web. The steps to delete Webs are discussed on Day 21, "Tracking and Maintaining Your Webs."

The Import Web Wizard

The Import Web Wizard differs slightly from the other wizards. Instead of creating *new* pages, it helps you create a FrontPage Web site from pages that already exist somewhere else. The main purpose for this Web wizard is to help you import Web content from another Web site or hard drive location.

Say, for example, you've already created some Web pages and have them stored on your hard drive or "somewhere out there" on the Internet. You've now decided that you want to use FrontPage to enhance the pages and maintain your site. It's very easy, and this is exactly what the Import Web Wizard was designed to do. The Import Web Wizard imports your existing Web pages without changes.

Because this wizard is rather unique in its purpose, I'll discuss it more on Day 8, "Planning Your Own Web Site," where you'll learn how to import existing content into a FrontPage Web.

The Discussion Web Wizard

The first screen of the Discussion Web Wizard is shown in Figure 2.9. This wizard creates a customized discussion group in a new or existing Web site. As mentioned previously, FrontPage discussion groups require that the FrontPage Server Extensions reside on the server to function correctly. If you cannot use the FrontPage Server Extensions, you will be unable to create FrontPage discussion groups in your Webs.

Note | If your Web server does not have the FrontPage Server Extensions installed, you can use custom scripts or Java applets to create discussion groups in your Web site. There are many nice scripts and applets freely available on the Internet that allow you to accomplish this. You'll learn more about advanced scripting languages and Web technologies in Week 3.

FIGURE 2.9

The Discussion Web Wizard helps you design discussion groups for public and private Web sites.

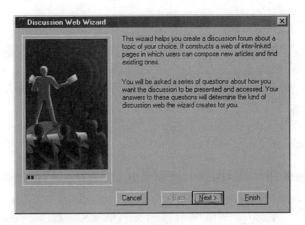

2

Discussion groups can be private or public, and can be placed within framesets or on regular pages. An article submission form is automatically created for you. You can also add a Table of Contents, search form, threaded replies, and a confirmation page. You'll learn how to create and configure a discussion group on Day 19.

The Corporate Presence Wizard

The Corporate Presence Wizard creates several pages that get a corporate Web site up and running quickly. The following is an overview of the pages that are generated. The pages that require FrontPage Server Extensions are noted. If your Web is destined to reside on a server that does not have the extensions, deselect those options in the Wizard.

- The home page provides a general introduction to your company. It can include an introduction, a mission statement, a company profile, and contact information.

- The What's New page announces recent changes to your site and links to pages that tell recent news about your company.

- Products and Services pages describe the products and services that your company has to offer. Each product sheet can contain a product image, pricing information, and an information request form. Each service page can include a list of capabilities, reference accounts, and an information request form. The Information Request Forms on the Products pages and the Services pages require the FrontPage Server Extensions or a custom form handler. Deselect the option to include the Information Request Form on these pages if you cannot use them.

- The Table of Contents page contains a list of all the pages on your site. It is generated automatically through the use of a Table of Contents component.

- The Feedback Form enables users to tell you what they think about your company, your Web site, or your products and services. You can store users' results in an HTML or text file on your Web site. The Feedback Form requires the FrontPage Server Extensions or a custom form handler. Deselect this option if you cannot use them.

- The Search Form enables users to search through all the pages in your site for words or a combination of words. The Search Form requires the FrontPage Server Extensions. Deselect this option if you cannot use them.

Exercise 2.2: Creating a Corporate Presence Web

In the following exercise, you'll create a site for a fictitious small business called Andy's Candies. You'll also get a sneak peak at Web themes, which are discussed in more detail on Day 9, "Changing the Appearance of Your Pages."

Andy's Candies doesn't provide services (although he did consider hiring an onboard dentist). However, the owner has spent a considerable amount of time and effort choosing many tasty products to offer. The site is a perfect example to show you how FrontPage wizards allow you to make choices for the types of pages to include in your Web site. We'll start out very simply with five basic pages.

To begin your corporate presence Web, follow these steps:

1. Choose File, New, Web. The New dialog box appears.
2. From the Web Sites list, select the Corporate Presence Wizard icon.
3. In the Specify the Location of the New Web field, enter `c:\tyfp2k\candies` to create a disk-based Web, or `http://yourservername/candies` to create a server-based Web. Replace *yourservername* with the name of your Web server.
4. Choose OK. FrontPage creates the Web folders, and the first screen of the Corporate Presence Wizard appears (see Figure 2.10). Click Next to proceed with the Wizard.

Selecting Your Pages

The second screen in the Wizard, shown in Figure 2.11, asks what types of pages you want to include in your Web site. The home page is required, and you do not have the option of unchecking that page. For the time being, we will avoid pages that contain forms and other features that require the FrontPage Server Extensions or custom scripts. In this screen, complete the following steps:

1. Select the following additional pages for your Web site:

   What's New

   Products/Services

   Table of Contents

2. Click Next to continue.

FIGURE 2.10

The introductory screen of the Corporate Presence Web Wizard.

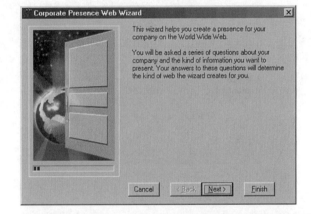

FIGURE 2.11

Select the pages you want to include in your Web from this screen.

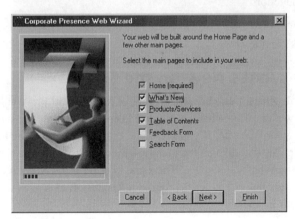

Choosing Your Home Page Content

The third screen of the Corporate Presence Web Wizard prompts you to choose the sections you want to appear on your home page. Andy is a pretty direct person and wants to get right down to business. An introduction of what his shop provides and contact information on how to reach the shop are all he wants on the page. To complete the screen shown in Figure 2.12, follow these steps:

FIGURE 2.12

Select the sections you want to appear on your home page from this screen.

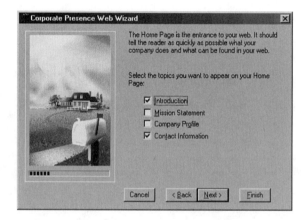

1. Select the following options:

   Introduction

   Contact Information

2. Click Next to continue.

Telling What's New on the Site

In the fourth screen, you choose the types of information you want to report on your What's New page. The What's New page keeps visitors to your site informed of recent changes to your Web site. If you select the Press Releases option here, FrontPage creates additional pages that display the press releases. Links to the press release pages will appear on the What's New page. The same is true for the Articles and Reviews option, which provides links to pages that quote magazine articles or newspaper reviews that mention your business.

Andy wants to keep this simple by only announcing the new products that he features on his Web pages. Here, you select only one option. To complete the screen shown in Figure 2.13, do the following:

1. Select Web Changes.

2. Click Next to continue.

FIGURE 2.13

Select the content for your What's New page in this screen.

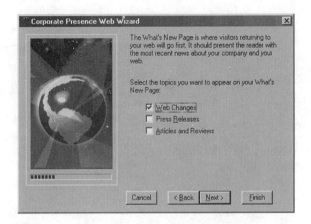

Selecting Your Products and Services

In the fifth screen, you select how many products and services pages you want to add to your Web site. Andy's Candies doesn't provide services. For the time being, you will create one Products page to give you a feel for what is included on the page. To complete the screen shown in Figure 2.14, follow these steps:

1. In the Products field, enter 1.

2. In the Services field, enter 0.

3. Click Next to continue.

Selecting Your Products Page Options

In the sixth screen, shown in Figure 2.15, you choose the options for your products pages. The services pages options are disabled because you elected not to include them in the previous screen. You won't select the Information Request Form option in this example, because the form requires the FrontPage Server Extensions or a custom form handler. To complete this screen, follow these steps:

1. Select the following options:

   Product Image

   Pricing Information

2. Click Next to continue.

FIGURE 2.14

From this screen, select how many products and services pages you want to create.

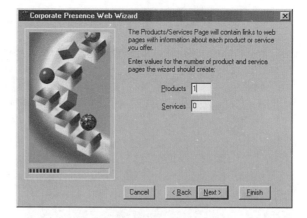

FIGURE 2.15

Select the options for your products pages in this screen. The service page options are disabled because you elected not to create them.

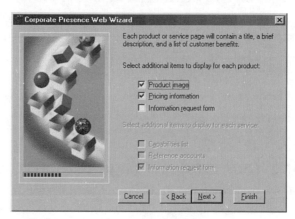

Choosing Your Table of Contents Page Options

In the seventh screen, you select the options for your table of contents page. The options are as follows:

- *Keep Page List Up-to-Date Automatically*—This option, when checked, updates the list of pages in the table of contents every time you add, move, or delete pages from your Web site. If you expect that your Web site will be large, you should to consider unchecking this option to reduce the amount of time that FrontPage needs to calculate the pages and links in your Web site. You can regenerate the table of contents list manually at any time by opening the table of contents and resaving it to your Web.

- *Show Pages Not Linked into Web*—This option, when checked, will list every page that is stored on your Web site, including those you might not want people to see (for example, partial pages that contain headers, footers, or navigation bars that are repeatedly included within other pages). It is recommended that you leave this option unchecked. By doing so, the table of contents lists only those pages that can be hierarchically reached by following links from the home page.

- *Use Bullets for Top-Level Pages*—This option, when checked, will precede the top-level pages in your Web site with bullets.

To complete the screen shown in Figure 2.16, follow these steps:

1. Select Use bullets for top-level pages.
2. Click Next to continue.

FIGURE 2.16

Select your Table of Contents Page options in this screen.

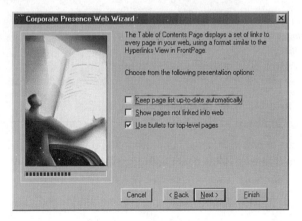

Selecting Options for Your Header and Footer

In the eighth screen of the Corporate Presence Web Wizard, shown in Figure 2.17, you are asked what you want to appear at the top (or page header) and bottom (or page footer) of each page. The choices are pretty self-explanatory, but one of them should be mentioned.

Notice that you have the option to include links to your main Web pages at either the top or bottom of the page or both. The decision, of course, is up to you.

However, here's a point to consider. Think about how you typically navigate Web sites, and what happens when you come across a Web page that is very long. In cases like this, there are generally two things you can do: either put a link near the bottom of the page that says "Back to Top", or include navigation links that let the user choose where he or she wants to go from there. By including links to your main Web pages at both the top and the bottom of each Web page, you have both bases covered.

FIGURE 2.17

Select what you want to appear at the top and bottom of each page in this screen.

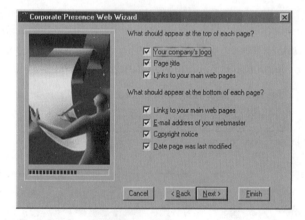

For Andy's Candies site, follow these steps to complete the screen:

1. You are asked what should appear at the top of each page. Select all three options (Your Company's Logo, Page Title, and Links to Your Main Web Pages).

2. You are asked what should appear at the bottom of each page. Select all four options (Links to Your Main Web Pages, E-mail Address of Your Webmaster, Copyright Notice, and Date Page Was Last Modified).

3. Click Next to continue.

Adding an Under-Construction Icon

In the ninth screen (see Figure 2.18), you are asked whether you want to include an under-construction icon on your pages. Some folks like to put them on their pages as a reminder that there is something left to do on the pages.

I elected not to include them in my Andy's Candies site by choosing No. Many Web developers consider them to be somewhat unprofessional, and most people who browse the World Wide Web realize that sites are always under construction. If you would rather include the under-construction icons, choose Yes (but remember to remove the icons when your pages are done!). Click Next to continue after you make your choice.

FIGURE 2.18

If you want to include an under-construction icon on unfinished pages, choose Yes in this screen.

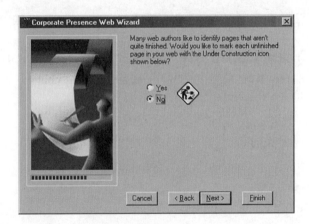

Entering Your Company Location

In the 10th screen (see Figure 2.19), you enter your company name and location. The one-word version of the name is an acronym that will appear in all of the page titles. You can edit them later. To complete this screen, respond as follows:

1. What Is the Full Name of Your Company?

   Andy's Candies

2. What Is the One-Word Version of This Name?

   ANDYCAN

3. What is Your Company's Street Address?

   123 Sweet Street, Hershey, PA 55555

4. Click Next to continue.

FIGURE 2.19

Enter your company name and location in this screen.

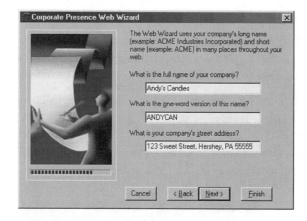

Enter Your Company Contact Information

In the 11th screen (see Figure 2.20), you enter company contact information. To complete this screen, respond to the questions as follows:

1. What Is Your Company's Telephone Number?

   555-555-3452

2. What Is Your Company's FAX Number?

   555-555-3453

3. What Is the E-mail Address of Your Webmaster?

   webmaster@andycan.com

4. What Is the E-mail Address for General Info?

   sales@andycan.com

5. Click Next to continue.

Choosing Your Web Theme

On the 12th screen (see Figure 2.21), you decide to choose or not choose a graphical theme for your Web. To bypass selection of a theme, continue to the next screen of the Corporate Presence Wizard by choosing the Next button.

Note

See Day 9 for more information about how to choose and create Web themes.

FIGURE 2.20

Enter your company contact information in this screen.

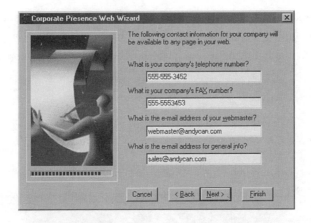

FIGURE 2.21

The 12th screen gives you the option to select a graphical theme for your corporate presence Web.

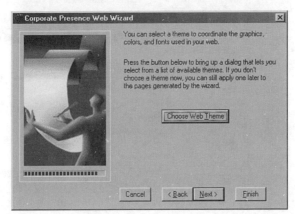

There is a perfect theme for Andy's Candies site furnished with FrontPage, although if you didn't install the extra themes during FrontPage installation you might not see this theme.

If it turns out that you did not install the extra themes, simply substitute the Sweets theme with a theme of your choice in step 3 of the following list.

To select a theme for your sample site, follow these steps:

1. Click the Choose Web Theme button. The Choose Theme dialog box appears (see Figure 2.22).

2. From the left portion of the screen, choose to apply the theme to All Pages.

3. If you elected to install additional themes during installation of FrontPage, you

should have in the list a theme called Sweets. If you don't have this theme avail-able, highlight another theme that you feel is appropriate for a candy shop.

4. Select the following options (which will be described in more detail in Day 9):

   Vivid Colors

   Active Graphics

   Background picture

5. Choose OK to return to the Corporate Presence Web Wizard.

6. Click Next to continue to the next screen.

FIGURE 2.22

Choose a graphical theme for your Web site in this screen.

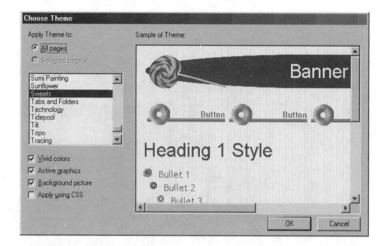

Creating the Web

The final screen in the Wizard (see Figure 2.23) asks whether you want to display your Web in Tasks View after FrontPage generates your custom pages. Task View, which allows you to organize and keep track of the tasks that you need to complete in your Web site, is described in more detail in Day 21.

For purposes of this example, uncheck the option that says Show Tasks View after Web is uploaded, and then click the Finish button.

After FrontPage generates your Web pages, the Andy's Candies Web appears in FrontPage, displaying five Web pages. These are the pages that you selected and cus-tomized during your progress through the Wizard. If this was your own corporate or business Web site, the next step would be to customize the content on the pages, and that's basically what the remaining chapters of this book are all about.

FIGURE 2.23

Check or uncheck the option to display your Web in Tasks View.

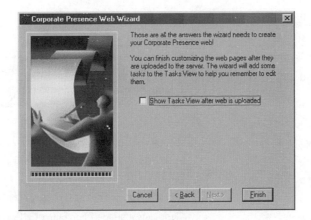

Building Pages the Fast Way

Now that you've learned how to generate Web sites the fast way, you'll learn how to add pages to your Web site the fast way. Here, FrontPage provides even more goodies. There are many Web page templates from which to choose. While some serve specific purposes, others give you an advanced start at a more professional page layout.

Several of the page templates that have been designed for specific purposes contain FrontPage components, forms, and additional features that you'll learn about throughout this book. These pages are listed in Table 2.1. Where the FrontPage Server Extensions or other custom form handlers are necessary, they are noted as such.

TABLE 2.1 Page Templates Designed for Specific Purposes

Page Template or Wizard	Comments
Normal Page	Blank page—used to start your pages from scratch. You can create a normal page quickly by using the New button on the Standard toolbar.
Bibliography	Presents a list of reference material, including author and publication name and publisher information.
Confirmation Form	A form that is returned to a user after he or she submits data into a form on your page. Requires the FrontPage Server Extensions.
Feedback Form	A general-purpose feedback form that can be modified for any purpose. Requires the FrontPage Server Extensions or custom form handler.

continues

TABLE 2.1   CONTINUED

Page Template or Wizard	Comments
Form Page Wizard	A wizard that helps you create forms by entering the questions you want to ask. Discussed in Day 18, "Building and Editing Forms." Pages generated by the wizard require the FrontPage Server Extensions or custom form handler.
Frequently Asked Questions	Presents a list of questions and links to their answers.
Guest Book	Enables users to place comments on your site. Requires the FrontPage Server Extensions or custom form handler.
Search Page	Enables users to search through your site for a word or phrase. Requires the FrontPage Server Extensions.
Table of Contents	Generates a table of contents of all pages on your site, beginning with a specified page.
User Registration	A form to enter a username and password to gain entry into a protected Web. Requires the FrontPage Server Extensions.

Other page templates furnished with FrontPage create pages that are more general in nature. Some of these templates use tables to arrange Web page content into two or three columns. Some pages feature sidebars where you can place your navigation items. The general pages are identified by names such as Centered Body, One-Column Body, Two-Column Staggered Body, and so on. As you select the page templates, you see a thumbnail preview of each page in the New dialog box.

To show you how easy it is to add a page to an existing Web site, you'll add a new page to the Web you created for Andy's Candies.

Exercise 2.3: Creating a Page from a Template

Pages generated with templates can be added to any Web that you have opened in FrontPage. To add a template-generated page to the Andy's Candies Web, follow these steps:

1. With the Web opened, choose View, Page. FrontPage displays Page View in the main screen.

2. Choose File, New, Page (Ctrl+N). The New dialog box shown in Figure 2.24 appears. It displays three tabs that list the various pages you can generate with FrontPage templates and wizards:

- The General tab allows you to choose from many different page templates that display in a full browser window or within a frame in a frameset. You'll add one of these pages to your Web in this exercise.

- The Frames Pages tab allows you to select one of several different frameset templates. These will be discussed further on Day 12, "Creating and Using Framesets."

- The Style Sheets tab allows you to choose or create style sheets that you can use to control the appearance of one or more pages in your Web. These will be discussed further on Day 10, "Using Style Sheets."

FIGURE 2.24

When you work in Page View with an open Web, the New dialog box allows you to select a template or wizard from which to create a Web page.

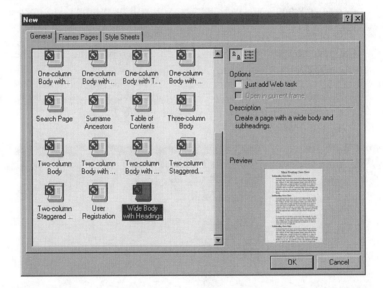

3. For this example, highlight the Wide Body with Headings page template. When you highlight a page template, a thumbnail preview of the page appears in the lower-right portion of the New dialog box.

4. Choose OK or press Enter. The new page opens in the page editor, and FrontPage applies the default Web theme to the new page.

Note Navigation bars and banners will not appear on your pages until after you design your navigation system. Many theme elements will take the form of comments until you do so. The procedures to do this are discussed on Day 11, "Designing Navigation Systems."

Saving Pages to Your Current Web

After you create or edit your pages, you should save them to your FrontPage Web. The Web can be located on your server or on your local or network hard drive. If there is no Web open when you save the page, you will be prompted to open a Web and save the page again.

The page you just generated with the page template has not yet been saved to your FrontPage Web. To proceed, follow these steps:

1. Choose File, Save or Ctrl+S, or click the Save button on the Standard toolbar. The Save As dialog box appears (see Figure 2.25).

FIGURE 2.25

The Save As dialog box.

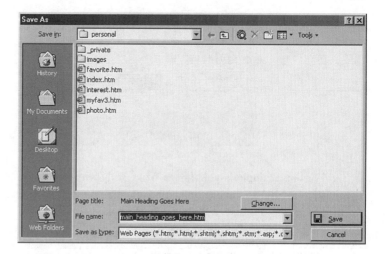

2. By default, FrontPage prompts you to save the new page in the root folder of your current Web. For purposes of this exercise, this is what you want to do.

You can also use the Save As dialog box to navigate to a different folder in which to save your new pages. You can choose a new path from the Save In drop-down menu or double-click the folder icons within the screen area of the Save As dialog box to select another folder in your current Web.

3. To change the title of your new page, click the Change button located to the right of the Page title display. The Set Page Title dialog box appears (see Figure 2.26). For purposes of this example (since you're not going to publish this site to the Internet), call the page something simple. Enter `Cinnamon Swizzle Sticks`.

The page title is the title that displays in the title bar in your visitors' browsers when they visit the site. The title of the page is also important when people look through search engines such as Yahoo! or Alta Vista. A better real-world example for a page title here is `Andy's Candies Products: Cinnamon Swizzle Sticks`. This identifies the company name and the product in World Wide Web search engines, and will probably generate more hits to the page.

4. In the File Name field, enter `cinnamon.htm`.

5. Click OK or press Enter to save the page to the current Web.

FIGURE 2.26

The Set Page Title dialog box allows you to specify the title of your Web page.

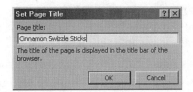

Summary

This chapter discussed many of the built-in templates and wizards provided with FrontPage. Much work and thought has gone into these pages. The Webs and pages generated with FrontPage can save you a great deal of time. And look at what you've accomplished today: You've generated two Web sites, assigned a theme to the pages to give them a special appearance, and added an additional page to one of the Web sites. Congratulations on a day well spent!

Workshop

Q&A

Q You mentioned some of the pages I create won't work unless I have the FrontPage Server Extensions or a custom form handler, but yet I can design pages that use those features. I'm confused—what exactly does this mean?

A You can *design* pages that use all of the features you find in FrontPage's page editor. However, when it comes time to *test* the pages in your browser, you may get error messages that certain files do not exist in your Web site. This is especially true regarding forms, which need to communicate through a Web server to work correctly. When you create a disk-based Web, the files necessary to communicate between your browser and the FrontPage form handlers do not exist in the Web (this is what the FrontPage Server Extensions do). Many of the questions that you will have in relation to this are discussed in Day 19.

Q So are you saying it's bad to create a disk-based Web?

A No, not at all, and especially when your Internet Service Provider does not have the FrontPage Server Extensions installed on its server. By creating your Web sites on a disk-based Web, FrontPage will notify you when pages you create contain features that need to be published before you can fully test them. In a roundabout way, FrontPage is telling you, "There are some features on this page that aren't going to work without the extensions." It serves as a checkpoint that lets you know that something on your page needs to be changed or omitted.

Q The `_private` and `images` folders are created in every FrontPage Web that I generate with a template. Do I always have to store my images in that folder? Also, what exactly is that `_private` folder for?

A You don't *have* to store all of your images in the `images` folder, but it is the default folder where FrontPage assumes your images will be stored. If you have several subfolders in your Web and it's better to store graphics in folders that make more sense, you can easily switch the path when you save your Web pages. This is discussed in more detail in Day 6.

The `_private` folder is there to store any pages that you don't want people to see. This not only hides pages from people that visit your site, it also hides them from robots that automatically catalog all of the pages in your sites on the World Wide Web. You can create additional folders beneath the _private folder if you need additional file organization.

If you are working on pages that you know you won't finish for a while (or have "partial pages" such as page headers, footers, navigation bars, and other similar pages), the _private folder is a good place to store them. You can optionally create additional "hidden" folders of your own—any folder name that begins with an underscore will not be found by Web robots.

It is also important to mention that you should never change the folder properties of your private folder to allow files to be browsed. Most Web sites have a private directory, and it is the first place that an unscrupulous visitor will look for hidden information.

Q **Can I delete the _private and images folders in the Webs if I don't use them?**

A Certainly. It won't hurt your Web site or break anything if they aren't there.

Quiz

1. How does FrontPage know whether you want to create a disk-based Web or a server-based Web?

2. True or false: You can combine more than one Web template to create a single Web site.

3. True or false: The Web templates allow you to choose which pages you want to include in your Web site.

4. Is it always a good idea to keep page lists in a table of contents page up to date automatically?

5. Why is it a good idea to include links to the main pages in your Web at the bottom of a page?

Exercises

1. Begin a personal or business site of your own, selecting one of the Web templates or wizards that you learned about today. Explore the features and structure of the pages. You'll be amazed at the tricks you'll discover on your own when you study the examples that are already provided for you.

2. Add some additional pages to your new site, using some of the other page templates and wizards. Again, studying the features in the page templates will help you learn more on your own.

Answers to Quiz

1. When you create a Web that points to a path on a local or network hard drive, FrontPage knows you are creating a disk-based Web. When you create a Web site that points to a URL, FrontPage knows you are creating a server-based Web.

2. True. You can add pages generated by any Web template or wizard to an already existing FrontPage Web by first opening the existing Web site, and then checking the Add to Current Web check box in the New dialog box before you create the new Web.

3. Trick question! The Web templates generate several pages that are added to a Web, but you don't get choices. It's the Web wizards that give you the opportunity to choose.

4. Not all the time. If your site contains many pages, you might want to consider disabling this option. The time it takes to regenerate page lists is better spent designing more pages.

5. If the page is long (requires a lot of scrolling to get from top to bottom), it saves the visitors to your site some time by placing links at the bottom of your page.

DAY 3

Building Basic Web Pages

Now that you have had an introduction to the templates and wizards, you probably want to start building your own pages. Hopefully, you have a fairly good idea of the types of pages you want to put in your Web. Roll up your sleeves—it's time to start building some simple pages. This chapter starts with the basics: working with headings, paragraphs, and text styles.

In today's lesson, you will

- Learn about the basic content elements that are contained in a page.
- Use headings to identify the contents on your page.
- Learn about the basic types of paragraph styles and what they are used for.
- Format text and paragraphs to add style without images.

Commonly Used Toolbars

As you design your Web pages, there are a couple of toolbars in FrontPage that you will use frequently. Most of the commands on them are those you'll encounter in this chapter. The Standard toolbar (discussed next) and the Format toolbar (discussed in "Formatting Your Text," later in this chapter) provide quick access to the commands you will use most frequently when you create and edit Webs and pages.

The Standard toolbar, shown in Figure 3.1 provides a quick way to access common page creation and editing commands. Table 3.1 shows the toolbar buttons as they appear—from left to right—and the menu commands associated with them.

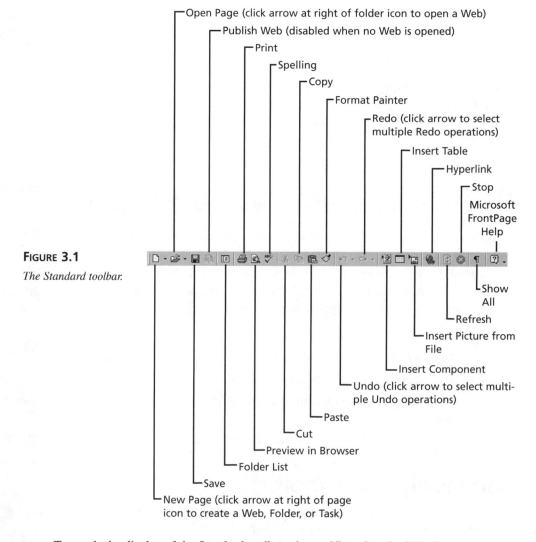

FIGURE 3.1

The Standard toolbar.

To toggle the display of the Standard toolbar, choose View, Standard Toolbar.

TABLE 3.1 Commands on the Standard Toolbar

Toolbar Button	Associated Menu Command
New Page	File, New, Page (select Normal Page)
New Web	File, New, Web
New Folder	File, New, Folder
New Task	File, New, Task
Open	File, Open
Open Web	File, Open Web
Save	File, Save
Publish Web	File, Publish Web
Folder List	View, Folder List
Print	File, Print
Preview in Browser	File, Preview in Browser
Spelling	Tools, Spelling
Cut	Edit, Cut
Copy	Edit, Copy
Paste	Edit, Paste
Format Painter	No menu equivalent
Undo	Edit, Undo
Redo	Edit, Redo
Insert Component	Insert, Component
Insert Table	Table, Insert, Table
Insert Picture	Insert, Picture
Hyperlink	Insert, Hyperlink
Refresh	View, Refresh
Stop	No menu equivalent
Show All	No menu equivalent
Help Tool	Help, Microsoft FrontPage Help

Exercise 3.1: Creating an Empty Web

In yesterday's lesson, you learned how to use some of the FrontPage templates and wizards to generate pages for you automatically. When you start building pages of your own, you typically add them to a FrontPage Web that you have already created.

When you want to build a complete Web site with original pages, you will typically start with one of two Web templates: the Empty Web or the One-Page Web. The only difference between the two is that the One Page Web creates a blank home page for you.

In this exercise, you'll create an Empty Web to store the pages that you'll build in this chapter. You might want to bookmark these steps so that you can easily find them when you create new Webs for other projects in this book. The exercise will create a disk-based Web that resides in the tyfp2k folder on your C drive. The Web, named chap03, will store your Web pages for this chapter.

To create your Empty Web, follow these steps:

1. From FrontPage, choose File, New, Web. The New dialog box appears, opened to the Web Sites tab.

2. Highlight the Empty Web icon in the template list.

3. In the Specify the Location of the New Web field, enter **c:\tyfp2k\chap03** to create a Web named chap03 in the tyfp2k folder on your C drive.

4. Choose OK. FrontPage creates a Web that contains only two folders: _private and images. Figure 3.2 shows the two folders displayed in the Folder List in the left panel of the interface screen.

FIGURE 3.2

The Empty Web contains only two folders: _private and images.

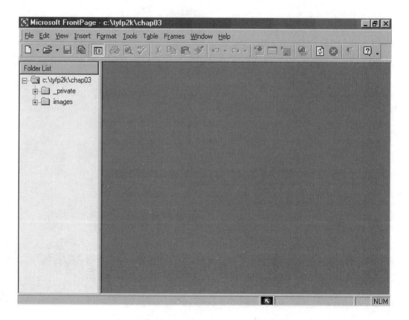

Starting a Web Page from Scratch

Now you'll learn how to build your *own* Web pages and begin to make use of the page template you will probably use most often: the *Normal page template*.

The Normal page template creates a blank Web page that includes all the correct header information that identifies your page as an HTML document. If you don't have a theme applied to your current Web site, the new page displays with a white background. The text and links you add to your page will be displayed with standard text and link colors. Normal text is black, unvisited links are blue, visited links are purple, and active links are red.

 Note   When your Web site uses a FrontPage theme, the background and text colors will differ from the default colors mentioned in the previous paragraph. The appearance of your pages will depend on the theme you select for your Web site.

3

Exercise 3.2: Creating a Normal Page

In the previous exercise, you created a new Web site on your hard drive. Right now, there are no pages in the Web, and you're about to complete the easiest task in this chapter.

It only takes one simple step to create a normal page. Simply click the New Page icon on the Standard toolbar. A new page appears in the Web and defaults to a filename of new_page_1.htm. The cursor stands waiting for you to begin your page design.

Adding Headings to Your Page

You use headings to identify sections or subsections in your Web pages. Web pages use six levels of headings. The HTML tags associated with them are <h1> through <h6>, with <h1> being the highest level in the hierarchy and <h6> being the lowest. You select the heading level from the Style drop-down list in the Format toolbar.

You can design a Web page in many different ways. One way to start is to plan a page by entering headings on the page first. This gives you an idea about how your content can be organized on the page.

Many times your Web pages will contain subheadings that divide your pages into subtopics. Each of the subheadings acts as a bookmark that marks the beginning of a subtopic. It is easier to create bookmarks before you add the text beneath the headings. This way you have less to scroll through when you create the links to the bookmarks.

Note

Bookmarks, or anchors, are placeholders that allow you to jump to a specific section on a page. You'll learn how to create them on Day 7, "Adding Links and Bookmarks."

Figure 3.3 shows a page that contains three levels of headings. The first line (Popular Software Applications) is a level 1 heading. It is followed by two level 2 headings (Word Processors and Software to Manage Data), which are followed by two level 3 headings (Spreadsheets and Databases), and ending with another level 2 heading (Presentation Software). The organizational structure of your page begins to take shape.

FIGURE 3.3

Different levels of headings can be used to define the sections and subsections on the page.

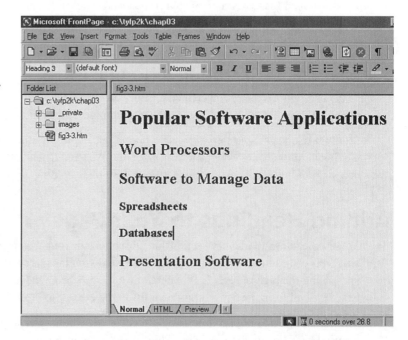

To create a page that contains only headings, begin by selecting the first heading style that you want to use (typically Heading 1) from the Style drop-down list (see figure 3.4). Enter the text for the first heading. When you press the Enter key, the insertion point moves to the next line. By default, FrontPage formats the new line as a Normal paragraph so you can enter content beneath it. To change this to another heading, select another heading style.

Tip

> When you position the insertion point at the *end* of a heading and press Enter, the next line is automatically formatted as a normal paragraph.
>
> When you position the insertion point at the *beginning* of a heading and press Enter, the current heading moves down one line. The space it formerly occupied retains the same heading style.

Another way to create a page that only contains headings is to enter all items as normal text. Then click and drag your mouse to select (highlight) one or more lines that you want to change into the same heading level. Choose the new heading style from the Style drop-down list in the Format toolbar to reformat the headings appropriately, as shown in Figure 3.4.

FIGURE 3.4

You can select multiple lines of text and format them as headings using the Style drop-down list.

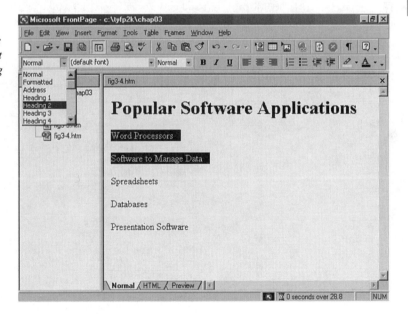

Basic Paragraph Types

With headings explained, now I'll talk about the three different types of paragraphs you can add to your Web pages: *normal*, *formatted*, and *address*. You can choose these paragraph styles from the Style drop-down list in the Format toolbar. In addition, you can easily change a paragraph from one style to another by selecting text and choosing a different paragraph style from this same menu. The following sections demonstrate typical uses for each of these paragraph styles.

Normal Paragraphs

Normal paragraphs are the meat-and-potatoes paragraphs of your Web pages and are typically used for the majority of your text content. When you look at the HTML code on your page, you'll see Normal paragraphs enclosed with <p>...</p> tags that mark the start and end of each paragraph. The text you see after the first heading in Figure 3.5 is a normal paragraph.

Tip

> Interested in seeing where HTML tags appear in relation to the content on your Web page while you're in the page editor? Choose View, Reveal Tags (or press Ctrl+/). The HTML tags appear within yellow icons, and show where HTML tags start and end. For example, a p within an icon marks the start of a paragraph, and a /p within another icon marks the end of a paragraph.

FIGURE 3.5

Normal paragraphs are the most frequently used type of paragraph.

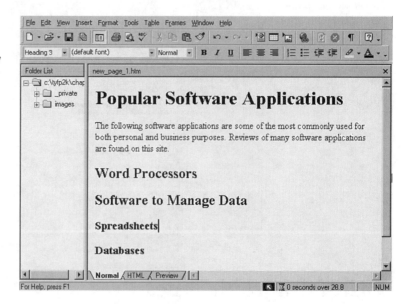

There are several ways that you can insert a normal paragraph on a page:

- Position the insertion point on the page and choose Normal from the Style drop-down list in the Format toolbar.
- Position the insertion point at the end of a heading or another normal paragraph and press Enter. The new line is automatically formatted as a normal paragraph.
- Position the cursor at the end of the last item in a list and press Enter twice or press Ctrl+Enter. The new line is formatted as a normal paragraph.

Formatted Paragraphs

In HTML code, formatted paragraphs are identified with <pre>...</pre> tags, which mark the beginning and end of the paragraph. These paragraphs use a fixed-width font, such as Courier or Courier New, to display information. Multiple spaces are allowed in formatted paragraphs, which makes them ideal for displaying tabulated data without using tables.

Formatted paragraphs are also used to display ASCII art, code, and programming or other types of instructions. Figure 3.6 shows an example of a formatted paragraph.

FIGURE 3.6

Use formatted paragraphs when you need to display information in a fixed-width font or tabular form.

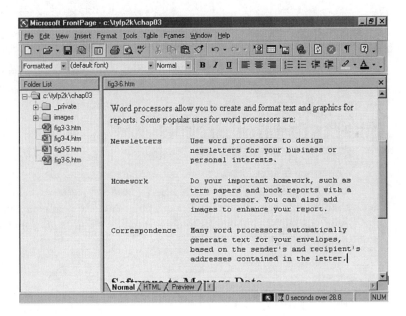

Address Paragraphs

Address paragraphs, identified by `<addr>...</addr>` at the start and end in HTML code, use an italic font to display information. Traditionally, address paragraphs are used to place company addresses, authorships, or copyright information on your pages. Most commonly, this information is placed at the end of a page, as shown in Figure 3.7.

FIGURE 3.7

Use address paragraphs to place author information or other italicized content on a page.

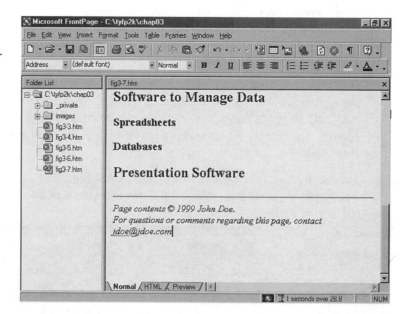

Inserting Line Breaks

When you press the Enter key to start a new line on a page, a new paragraph begins. Whitespace is added between the current paragraph and the one that precedes it. Sometimes, however, you need to begin a new line *without* creating whitespace between it and the line that precedes it. For example, the formatted paragraphs displayed in Figure 3.8 include line breaks to prevent the text in the right column from being presented with extra whitespace.

Tip

> To view placement of line breaks on your page, press the Show All button (second from the last in the Standard toolbar). This allows you to see all of the paragraph and line break marks on your Web pages.

FIGURE 3.8

The Show All button allows you to see where line breaks and other format marks appear on the page.

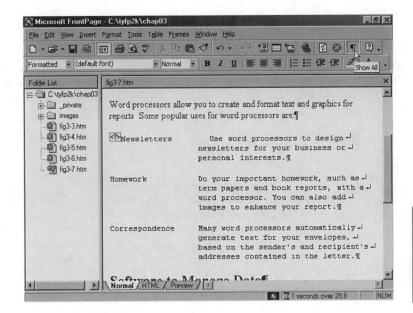

You can use line breaks to begin a new line of text without adding whitespace. Line breaks are created in HTML through the use of the <br> tag. In FrontPage, you add a line break with the Insert, Break command or by pressing Shift+Enter at the end of a line. By default, a line break starts a new line of text on the line directly beneath it—in FrontPage, this is called a *normal* line break.

There are also three additional attributes that control how text clears other inline content such as images. These additional types of line breaks are mentioned next, but will be discussed further on Day 6, "Adding Images, Sound, and Video."

Briefly, the four types of line breaks are

- *Normal line break*—This forces a line break without clearing images in the left or right margin. The new line of text appears on the line that directly follows the break. This is the type of line break created when you press Shift+Enter at the end of a line.

- *Clear left margin*—The text after the line break is positioned in the next clear line after an image that appears in the left margin.

- *Clear right margin*— The next line of text moves to the next clear line after an image that appears in the right margin.

- *Clear both margins*—If an image is in either or both margins, the next line of text moves until both margins are clear.

Exercise 3.3: Building Up Your Page

If you completed the preceding exercise, you should have a blank Web page ready and waiting for you to add content. The following exercise puts into practice what you've learned since you created that page. You'll build a basic Web page that includes several different headings, three different types of paragraphs (normal, formatted, and address), and line breaks to control the layout of text. This Web page provides information about an upcoming music festival.

 Tip

> Worried about making mistakes? FrontPage has a multiple-level Undo function. To undo one action, choose Edit, Undo, press Ctrl+Z, or click the Undo button in the Standard toolbar. To undo multiple steps, click the arrow located at the right of the Undo icon in the Standard toolbar and select the number of steps you want to undo. The steps to redo operations are similar: choose Edit, Redo, press Ctrl+Y, or click the Redo icon or arrow on the Standard toolbar.

To build your first Web page, do the following:

1. With the insertion point at the upper-left corner of the page, choose Heading 1 from the Style drop-down list in the Format toolbar. (If the Format toolbar is not displayed, choose View, Format toolbar.)

2. Enter the following:

   `The Springtown Music Festival`

3. Press Enter. By default, the next line is formatted as a normal paragraph. Choose Heading 2 from the Change Style drop-down list and enter the following:

   `About the Festival`

4. Press Enter and choose Heading 2 again. Enter the following text, after which your page will look similar to Figure 3.9:

   `Schedule of Events`

5. Position the insertion point after the first heading (The Springtown Music Festival), and press Enter. The new line is formatted as a normal paragraph. Enter the following text:

   `Welcome spring by attending the 15th Annual Springtown Music`
   `Festival. Scheduled to take place April 16th through April 18th at`
   `the Springtown Convention Center, the festival is enjoyed by people`
   `of all ages, and is one of our most widely anticipated events.`

FIGURE 3.9

Organize your thoughts by placing headings on your page first.

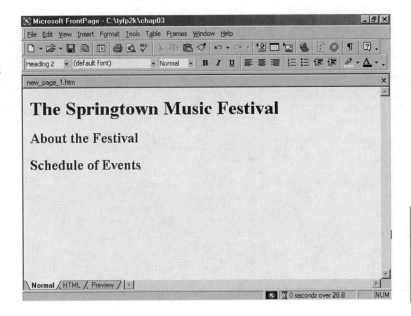

Tip

Are you prone to spelling errors, or do you have fingers that can't seem to find their way around a keyboard? Use the built-in spell checker to help you solve the problem. When FrontPage suspects a word is spelled wrong, you'll see a word underlined with a squiggly red line. This lets you know that something's wrong with the word. You can also choose Tools, Spelling or press F7 to spell check an entire page at once.

6. Position the insertion point after the second heading (About the Festival), and press Enter. The new line is formatted as a normal paragraph. Enter the following text, after which your page should look like Figure 3.10:

   ```
   The Springtown Music Festival is sure to provide something of inter-
   est to everyone. Along with good food, good company, and an amuse-
   ment park for the youngsters, the highlight is three days of live
   music performances. For a complete list of performers, see the
   Performance Schedule on this site.
   ```

7. Now enter some formatted paragraphs that use line breaks to begin new lines within each paragraph. Position the insertion point after the third heading (Schedule of Events) and press Enter. Choose Formatted from the Style drop-down list in the Format toolbar. Enter the following text:

   ```
   DATE (add 10 spaces) TIME (add 10 spaces) HIGHLIGHTS
   ```

FIGURE 3.10

Normal paragraphs are added after the first two headings.

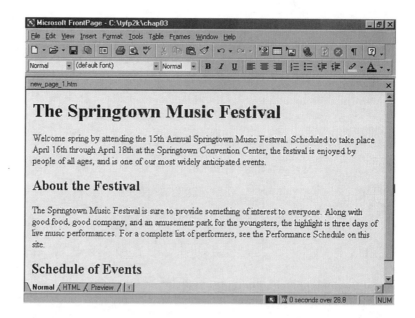

8. Press Enter to begin a new paragraph. FrontPage automatically formats the next line as a formatted paragraph. Enter the following text, adding spaces between the date, time, and event to align them with the headings you entered in the previous step:

    ```
    Fri Apr 18   11AM to 10PM   Amusement Park and Carnival
    ```

9. Press Shift+Enter to add a line break at the end of the line. Press the Space bar until your cursor appears in the time column and enter the following:

    ```
    11AM to 8PM   Pavilion open for sit-down meals
    ```

10. Press Shift+Enter to add a line break at the end of the line. Complete the first day's schedule by adding the final event. Use line breaks (Shift+Enter) to end the first two lines, and press Enter to end the last line:

    ```
    3PM to 10PM   Live music performances featuring
                  popular folk, Country/Western, and
                  bluegrass artists
    ```

11. Press Enter to begin a new paragraph. Using steps similar to those described in steps 8–10, complete the schedules for the remaining two days. When you are finished, your page will look similar to Figure 3.11:

    ```
    Sat Apr 19   11AM to 10PM   Amusement Park and Carnival
                 11AM to 8PM     Pavilion open for sit-down meals
    ```

```
              11AM to 10PM   Live music performances featuring
                             popular rock artists

              2PM to 8PM     1999 Regional Battle of the Bands
                             Competition

 Sun Apr 20   11AM to 6PM    Amusement Park and Carnival
              11AM to 2PM    Pavilion open for sit-down meals
              11AM to 6PM    Live music performances featuring
                             popular blues and jazz artists
```

FIGURE 3.11

Formatted paragraphs and line breaks are used to display a schedule of events.

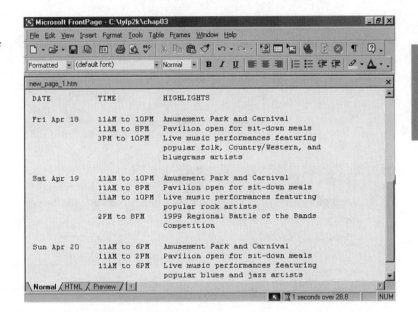

12. Press Enter to begin a new paragraph. Now you'll add some copyright information at the end of the page, using an address paragraph and line breaks. From the Style drop-down list in the Format toolbar, choose Address and enter the following two lines. Figure 3.12 shows the last portion of the page:

```
Copyright 1999, Springtown Music Festival Committee.
For questions or comments, contact springtownmus@smusfc.org
```

13. Choose File, Save, press Ctrl+S, or use the Save button on the Standard toolbar. The Save As dialog box appears.

14. The page title defaults to The Springtown Music Festival, which it obtains from the first heading on your page. In the File Name field, enter the filename `music.htm`.

15. Choose Save to save the page to the root folder in your FrontPage Web.

FIGURE 3.12

An address paragraph displays copyright and contact information at the bottom of the page.

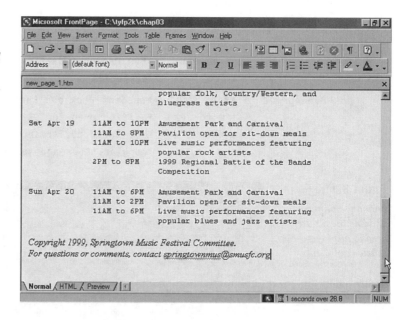

Formatting Your Text

Some of the information on your Web page could use additional emphasis to attract attention. There are several ways you can add emphasis to your Web pages: You can use character styles, different fonts, or Cascading Style Sheets.

Note You'll learn more about using different fonts and Cascading Style Sheets on Day 10, "Using Style Sheets."

Today you'll learn about using character styles, which provide the widest browser compatibility. This is because the character styles that I discuss here have been in use since the earliest versions of HTML. And, because even today's browsers are backward compatible to those early days, you have a reasonable assurance that just about any browser out there will view your Web pages pretty much as you see them in your own browser.

The Format toolbar, shown in Figure 3.13, includes several buttons that can help you format the text on your pages. The menu commands for the toolbar buttons are listed in Table 3.2.

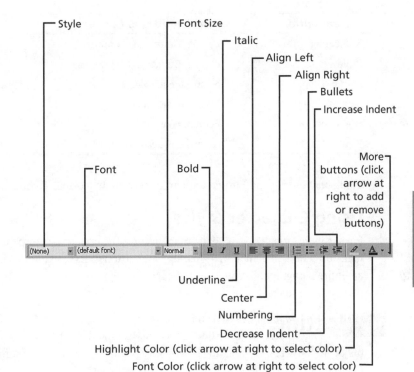

FIGURE 3.13

The Format toolbar.

TABLE 3.2 Commands in the Format Toolbar

Toolbar Button	Associated Menu Command
Style	Format, Paragraph
Font	Format, Font
Font Size	Format, Font
Bold	Format, Font
Italic	Format, Font
Underline	Format, Font
Align Left	Format, Paragraph
Center	Format, Paragraph
Align Right	Format, Paragraph

continues

TABLE 3.2   CONTINUED

Toolbar Button	Associated Menu Command
Numbering	Format, Bullets and Numbering
Bullets	Format, Bullets and Numbering
Decrease Indent	No menu equivalent
Increase Indent	No menu equivalent
Highlight Color	Format, Font
Font Color	No menu equivalent

To display or hide the Format toolbar, choose View, Format Toolbar.

Using Character Styles

Earlier in this chapter, you learned about three different types of paragraph styles—normal, formatted, and address —that use proportional, fixed-width, or italic text to format an entire paragraph. If you want to change the appearance of a *portion* of text within a paragraph, you can apply *character styles* to selected text.

NEW TERM   *Character styles* add emphasis to selected text (for example, changing text to bold, italic, or underlined text), but use the default fonts the user has specified in his or her browser. By default, Times New Roman is used for proportional font and Courier or Courier New is used for fixed-width font.

Other character styles are designed for specific uses. For example, to format a definition for a phrase, you can use the Definition character style; to cite a reference to a book or magazine article, you can use the Citation character style.

Table 3.3 shows the list of character styles that are still in common use. You can apply these styles to selected text by choosing the Format, Font command. Examples of these character styles are shown in Figure 3.14.

TABLE 10.2   Character Styles in the Special Styles Tab of the Font Dialog Box

Style	HTML Tag	Typical Use
Blink	`<blink>`	Causes selected text to blink on and off in Netscape browsers. This style is deprecated in HTML 4.0 and replaced with an equivalent command in Cascading Style Sheets. Use it sparingly, as it can be distracting and a *lot* of people find it very objectionable.

Style	HTML Tag	Typical Use
Citation	`<cite>`	Used to mark a citation from a book or other published source. Most often rendered in a proportional italic font.
Code	`<code>`	Marks computer source code. Most often rendered in a fixed-width font.
Definition	`<dfn>`	Used to mark a definition and is usually preceded by a term. Most often rendered in a proportional italic font.
Emphasis	`<em>`	Renders text as italic. Similarly, you can use the Italic button on the Format toolbar to apply the `<i>` tag.
Keyboard	`<kbd>`	Marks instructions that a user enters by keyboard. Rendered as fixed-width text in FrontPage Editor; rendered as mono-spaced text in some browsers.
Sample	`<samp>`	Renders sample text or special characters. Most often rendered in a fixed-width font.
Strikethrough	`<strike>`	Renders text with a line through it and is used to represent revisions in a Web document.
Strong	`<strong>`	Renders text as bold. Similarly, you can use the Bold button on the Format toolbar to apply the `<b>` tag.
Subscript	`<sub>`	Renders text below the normal text baseline by a specified amount.
Superscript	`<sup>`	Renders text above the normal text baseline by a specified amount.
Underline	`<u>`	Underlines text with a single line.
Variable	`<var>`	Marks a variable used in computer code, equations, or similar work. Usually rendered in a proportional italic font.

3

Note

There are five other styles listed in the Effects section of the Font dialog box: Overline, Small Caps, All Caps, Capitalize, and Hidden. These styles use Cascading Style Sheet techniques to display the font styles, and are viewable only in browsers that support HTML 4 and later.

FIGURE 3.14

FIGURE 3.14

Examples of character styles rendered in FrontPage.

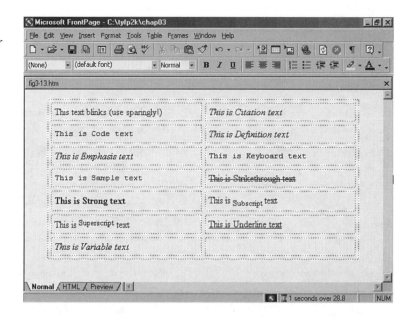

Exercise 3.4: Adding Emphasis with Character Styles

In the following task, you'll add some formatted text to your page.

To apply character styles to your Web page, do the following:

1. Select (highlight) the text in the first paragraph that reads "15th Annual Springtown Music Festival."

2. From the Format toolbar, click the Bold and Underline buttons. The text you selected is displayed as bold, underlined text.

3. Position the insertion point at the end of the heading that reads "Schedule of Events." Press Enter to begin a new normal paragraph.

4. Enter the following text:

   `Important: In the event of bad weather, check this web site or phone 555-3456 to confirm which events, if any, are cancelled.`

5. Highlight the text you entered in the previous step. Choose Format, Font. The Font dialog box appears, opened to the Font tab.

6. From the Effects section, shown in Figure 3.15, check Emphasis. Optionally, you can choose more than one style (for example, Emphasis and Underline will create text that is rendered in italics and underlined with a single line).

7. Click OK to exit the Font dialog box. Your selection or selections are applied to the text.

8. This step demonstrates a *reasonable* use for the blink tag. In the line of text on which you're currently working, highlight only the word "Important:". Again, choose the Format, Font command, and select Blink from the Effects menu. Choose OK to exit the Font dialog box.

Note

By making the word "Important" blink on the page, the reader's eye is drawn toward an area on the page where an important notice appears. By applying the tag to *only one word* in the sentence, the effect is not over-bearing and gets the job done. Note, however, that the blink tag is a Netscape browser-specific enhancement and may not work in some browsers. As a result, the blink tag will soon become obsolete, and is replaced in HTML 4.0 with an equivalent Cascading Style Sheet command.

9. Scroll to the events for Saturday, April 19. Select the text that reads "1999 Regional Battle of the Bands" and click the Bold and Underline buttons on the Format toolbar.

10. Select the line that reads "Competition" and again use the Bold and Underline buttons on the Format toolbar to format this line.

11. Choose File, Save to update the changes to your Web site.

FIGURE 3.15

Choose a character style from the Effects section in the Font tab of the Font dialog box.

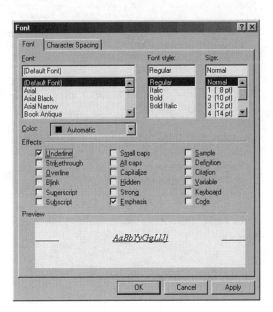

Now your page should look like the one in Figure 3.16. As you can see, you can use character formatting to achieve interesting effects without relying on graphics.

FIGURE 3.16

The Springtown Music Festival page, with some emphasis added to the text.

Tip

To remove all text formatting on a page, choose Edit, Select All to select all the text on the pages. Then choose Format, Remove Formatting or press Ctrl+Shift+Z. All custom formatting will be removed from the page.

Enhancing Your Page Footer

The page footer on your current page looks a little sparse and doesn't really stand out. We're going to dress it up a little with some features that are very handy to use: symbols, horizontal lines, and a time and date stamp.

Inserting Symbols

Symbols are items such as trademark, registration, and copyright symbols; accent marks on text; special currency symbols; and common fractions. In the "old days" of designing Web pages, you had to keep track of ASCII codes that told browsers which of these special characters to place in your Web pages. With FrontPage, you don't even have to know a single ASCII code. The basic steps to insert a symbol on your page are

1. Position the cursor on your page at the point where you want to insert the symbol.
2. Choose Insert, Symbol. The Symbol dialog box shown in Figure 3.17 appears.
3. Click the symbol that you want to insert on your page.
4. Choose Insert. The symbol appears on your Web page.
5. Repeat steps 3 and 4 if you want to insert additional symbols at the current location.
6. Choose Close to exit the Symbol dialog box and resume your Web page creation.

Inserting and Formatting Horizontal Lines

You use horizontal lines (traditionally known as horizontal rules) to distinguish the beginning or end of sections in your pages. For example, if you have a page that describes the main sections on your site, you can use horizontal lines at the end of each section's description. A horizontal rule can be added to your Web page with one simple step: choose Insert, Horizontal Line.

Once you have a horizontal line on your page, you can change its appearance in the Horizontal Line Properties dialog box, shown in Figure 3.18. The easiest way to open this dialog box is to double-click the horizontal line that you want to format.

3

FIGURE 3.17

The Symbol dialog box allows you to put special characters such as copyright and trademark symbols in your pages.

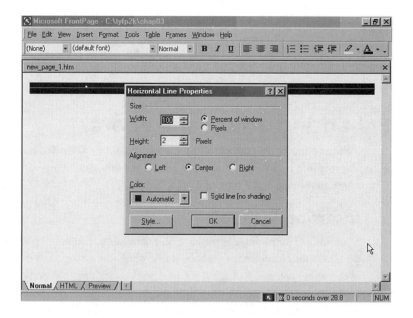

> **Note**
>
> When you edit the appearance of a horizontal line, FrontPage remembers the settings and continues to use them for new horizontal lines. This occurs until you close the program or choose new settings in the Horizontal Line Properties dialog box.
>
> Note that if your Web has a theme applied to it, the horizontal line properties will be defined by the theme. The only property that you will be able to adjust is the alignment option.

The following are options you can choose in the Horizontal Line Properties dialog box:

- *Width*—The figure you enter here creates a horizontal line that spans a portion or the entire width of the browser window. To specify a width by percentage, select the Percent of Window radio button, and enter a number in the Width field. To specify a width in pixels, choose the Pixels radio button and enter a number in the Width field.

- *Height*—Specify the height of the horizontal line in pixels. By default, the height of a horizontal rule is 2 pixels.

- *Alignment*—This setting specifies how the horizontal line is aligned on the page. Available choices are Left, which aligns the line with the left edge of your page;

Center, which centers it; and Right, which aligns it with the right side of your page.

- *Color*—By default, a horizontal rule is displayed as a shadowed line that appears to be indented in your page. When you choose Solid line (mentioned next), the horizontal line uses the same color as your text by default. You can change the color by choosing a value other than Automatic from the Color drop-down list.

- *Solid Line (No Shading)*—Choose this check box if you want to create a horizontal line that is the same color as your text.

- *Style*—The Style button allows you to format your horizontal lines using Cascading Style Sheet properties, which are discussed further on Day 10.

FIGURE 3.18

Specify settings for horizontal lines in the Horizontal Line Properties dialog box.

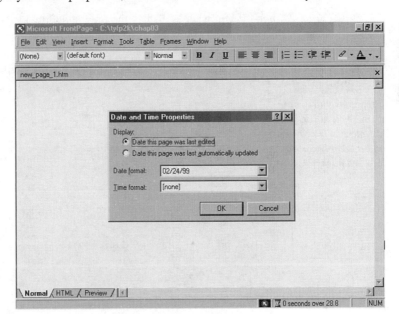

Inserting the Date and Time

Your Web site visitors might find it extremely handy to know whether or not a Web page has been updated since the last time they visited your site. One way that you automatically can let them know is to include an easy-to-configure FrontPage component on your page. By using this component, you don't even have to look at the calendar when you update a page. You simply insert the component, configure how you want FrontPage to display the date, and save the page. Each time you edit the page and resave it, FrontPage will display the date (and time, if you choose) that you last edited the page.

The Date and Time Properties dialog box, shown in Figure 3.19, appears after you choose Insert, Date and Time. The options you can choose from are as follows:

- *Date This Page Was Last Edited*—Choose this option if you are adding the Date and Time component to a Web page that you change manually.

- *Date This Page Was Last Automatically Updated*—Choose this option if you are adding the Date and Time component to Web pages that change automatically. Examples of these are pages that contain Table of Contents components or form results pages, such as guest books, that accept input from visitors to your site.

- *Date Format*—Choose a suitable format to display the date from the drop-down list.

- *Time format*—If you want to display the time in addition to the date, choose a value other than (none) from the Time format drop-down list.

FIGURE 3.19

The Date and Time Properties dialog box allows you to configure a Date and Time component that keeps track of when pages were last edited.

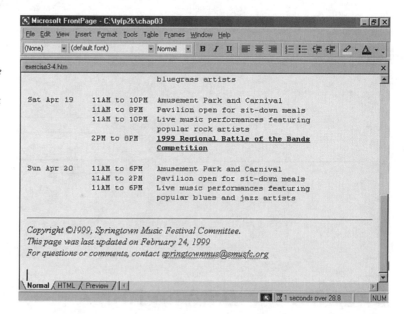

Exercise 3.4: Completing Your Page Footer

In the final exercise for today, you'll polish up your Web page by adding a horizontal line at the bottom of the page, before the page footer. You'll add a copyright symbol and a Date and Time component to the footer.

To complete your Web page, follow these steps:

1. Position the insertion point at the beginning of the line that reads "Copyright 1999, Springtown Music Festival Committee."

2. Choose Insert, Horizontal Line. A horizontal line appears on your page before the line you identified in the previous step.

3. Double-click the horizontal line to open the Horizontal Line Properties dialog box. Select the following settings to create a solid horizontal line that spans 90 percent of the browser window and is centered on the page:

Width	90, Percent of Window
Height	2 Pixels (default)
Alignment	Center
Color:	Automatic, Solid Line (No Shading)

4. Position the insertion point at the end of the word Copyright in the first line of the footer and add a space.

5. Choose Insert, Symbol. The Symbol dialog box appears.

6. Select the copyright symbol from the fourth row of symbols in the dialog box and click the Insert button. The copyright symbol appears on your page.

7. Choose Close to exit the Symbol dialog box.

8. Position the insertion point at the end of the first line in the page footer and press Enter to begin a new line.

9. Enter the following text, adding an extra space at the end of the line:

   `This page was last updated on`

10. Choose Insert, Date and Time. The Date and Time Properties dialog box appears.

11. From the Display section, select Date This Page Was Last Edited.

12. Select a date and time format of your preference. For my example, I selected the fourth date option, which displays a date such as March 21, 1999. I also decided not to display the time by selecting (none).

13. Choose OK. The date and time that you specified appear on your Web page. The bottom of your page should now look as shown in Figure 3.20.

14. Choose File, Save to save your changes to your Web page.

3

FIGURE 3.20

A horizontal line, copyright symbol, and date and time component are added to the page footer.

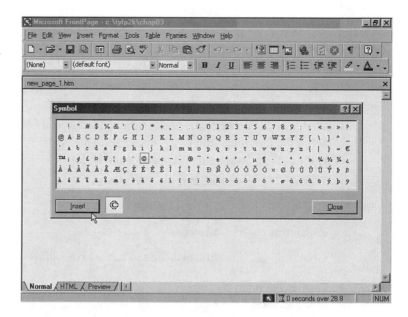

Other Web Page Editing Tips

You've read enough for today, but I'll point out some additional features for you to explore on your own. The following commands will help save you some time, or possibly additional work, as you design your pages:

- Choose Edit, Copy to copy and paste content that appears several times on one or more pages. For example, you might have several sections on your Web page after which a Back to Top link appears. You only need to create the first occurrence of this link. Then, copy it into the clipboard and paste it on your Web page in every other location where you want it to appear. A real time saver!

- To delete text, or any other Web page content, select the content you want to delete and choose Edit, Delete. This command removes the content from your page without placing it in the clipboard, so use it with care.

- Choose Edit, Find to find one or more occurrences of a certain word or phrase. This feature can be used on your current page, or can also find every page in the Web that contains that word or phrase.

- The clipboard can be a handy tool when you want to move content from one Web page to another. Select all the text you want to move, and choose Edit, Cut to place the content in your Windows clipboard. Open or create the page you want to move the content to, and choose Edit, Paste to place it at the current insertion point.

- When you have text formatting that you want to repeat in several locations on a Web page, you can use the Format Painter, which is available on the Standard toolbar. Highlight some text that uses a format you want to reuse. While the text is highlighted, click the Format Painter button on the Standard toolbar. Next, select the text that you want to apply the formatting to, and click the Format Painter again. The text remains selected, so you can repeat the procedure as many times as you want to apply the same formatting to other locations on your page.

Summary

As you have learned in today's lesson, FrontPage makes it very easy to create basic Web pages. When you use headings to initially plan your pages, you begin to organize your page content. Then you add text using three basic paragraph styles. Toolbar commands help you emphasize your page content with bold or italic text. Horizontal rules help to define where the main areas of your pages begin and end. Although you've only just begun your journey into Web page design, you'll learn that it's just as easy to add color, multimedia, and other Web page enhancements.

Workshop

Q&A

Q Can I change the text and link colors without using FrontPage themes?

A Yes, you can. With your Web page open in the editor, choose File, Properties, or right-click anywhere inside the page editor screen and choose File Properties from the pop-up menu. The Page Properties dialog box appears. The commands to change the background color and the text and link colors appear within the Background tab. This is discussed further on Day 9, "Changing the Appearance of Your Pages."

Q Can I change the default size of the font in the FrontPage Editor?

A Although you can change the default fonts you use, you cannot set the default font size. You must set the font size or use the Increase Font Size or Decrease Font Size buttons on the toolbar to change the size of your text.

Q I created a formatted paragraph while designing my page, but some people say that they can't see it all in their browser. They say they have to scroll toward the right to see some of the content. Did I do something wrong?

A I suspect that you created your Web pages while working in a higher resolution (perhaps 800×600 or 1024×768), and that the people viewing your pages are viewing them at a lower resolution (such as 640×480). Formatted paragraphs display exactly the way you create them and don't wrap around like normal paragraphs do. You'll want to keep in mind as you design your pages that some people navigate the Web at lower resolutions. Besides previewing your pages in different browsers, it's a good idea to preview your pages at different resolutions, too.

Q I created a Web page that shows my old company name on it several times. I've recently changed it—is there an easy way to make all changes at once?

A There sure is. You can use the Find and Replace features of FrontPage. Choose Edit, Replace or press Ctrl+H. The Replace dialog box appears. Enter the "old" company name in the Find What field, and the "new" company name in the Replace With field. To make the changes in your current page, choose the Current page radio button in the lower-left corner of the dialog box. To apply the changes in all pages in your Web, choose the All pages radio button.

Quiz

1. Which two Web templates are good to use when your Web site will contain all original content?

2. Which page template is most often used when designing pages in FrontPage?

3. What are the three types of paragraph styles, and for what are they used?

4. True or false: There are different character styles that you can use that will display pretty much the same in old and new browsers.

5. In what cases do you want to add a Date and Time component that updates itself automatically?

Exercises

1. You can use horizontal rules to create artistic borders before or after text. Try this: Use the Insert, Horizontal Line command to place three consecutive horizontal lines on a Web page. Select the first horizontal line, and set its properties to 500 pixel width, 5 pixels in height, center aligned, and change its color to a dark red solid line. Format the second horizontal line as a purple solid line, 400 pixels wide, 4 pixels high, and center aligned. For the third horizontal line, make it a red solid line, 300 pixels wide and 3 pixels high, center aligned.

2. You can use the Insert, Symbol command to create numbers that end with the fractions 1/4, 1/2, or 3/4. For example, to create the number 12-3/4, first enter the whole number (12) in normal text. Then choose the Insert, Symbol command and choose the 3/4 symbol (second to last symbol in the fourth row). If you prefer to display the fractional part of the number in superscript text, select the 3/4 symbol

and choose Format, Font. From the Font tab, select Superscript from the Effects section of the Font tab.

Answers to Quiz

1. The Empty Web template and the One Page Web template are good to start with when your entire Web will be original.

2. The Normal page template, which creates a blank Web page, is the most commonly used page template.

3. Normal paragraphs are the most commonly used paragraph type and are used for the majority of your page content. Formatted paragraphs are used to display information in a fixed width font and allow for multiple spaces so that you can align content in a tabular form. Address paragraphs are typically used to display copyright and authorship information at the foot of a Web page.

4. True. All but five of the character styles that you find in the Effects section in the Font tab of the Font dialog box will display fairly consistently in older and newer browsers.

5. Date and Time components should be updated automatically when they are placed on a page that accepts input from a site visitor, or on pages that FrontPage automatically updates for you. Examples of these pages are guest books, table of contents pages, and pages that display other results from survey forms or questionnaires that receive input from your visitors.

DAY 4

Using Lists to Organize Information

Do you have links to sites that you want to point people to? Have you written a great paper that shows people how to build, install, or complete something? Lists are among the best ways to organize information. They help information stand out clearly. You can use several types of lists in your pages, and this chapter shows you how to construct each of them.

In today's lesson, you'll learn how to:

- Use several different types of lists to organize your information
- Create nested lists that display information in a hierarchical manner
- Use different numbers, letters, and bullets in lists

Working with Numbered Lists

Numbered lists are used to place items in a definite order. They are good for describing steps, procedures, or sections in a book as the following examples will show. When you view the source code, you'll see your numbered lists enclosed within <ol>...</ol> tags (for *ordered lists*). Each item in the numbered list is enclosed within an <li>...</li> tag (for *list item*).

Numbered lists are usually rendered as paragraphs separated by white space and prefixed by numbers. By default, numbered lists begin with the number 1 (you'll learn how to change this later in this chapter). FrontPage numbers the items in the list for you automatically.

Exercise 4.1: Creating a Numbered List

To begin today's lesson, you'll create a simple list of sections in a book. The completed example is shown in Figure 4.1.

FIGURE 4.1

Use numbered lists when you need to arrange items in a specific order.

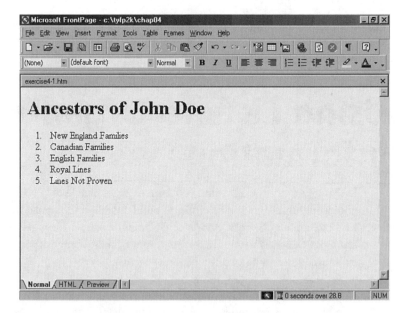

To create the numbered list shown in Figure 4.1, open a new Normal page (using the New Page button on the Standard toolbar) and do the following:

1. Position the insertion point on your page and choose Heading 1 from the Style drop-down list in the Format toolbar. Enter the following text:

   `Ancestors of John Doe`

2. Press Enter. The insertion point moves to the beginning of the next line and automatically changes to Normal paragraph style.

3. Choose Numbered List from the Style drop-down list in the Format toolbar, or click the Numbering button on the Format toolbar. FrontPage enters the first number for you automatically.

4. Enter the first item in the list:

`New England Families`

5. Press Enter to begin the next list item. Add the additional list items shown next, pressing Enter after each line except the last one:

`Canadian Families`

`English Families`

`Royal Lines`

`Lines Not Proven`

6. At the end of the last item, press Enter twice, or press Ctrl+Enter to complete the list.

Exercise 4.2: Creating a Nested Numbered List

So far, you have created a list of five sections of a book. Each of the sections in this book has several chapters that can be added to the list. In addition, each chapter in the book has several topics that are discussed within it.

To display the chapters and topics clearly, you can indent each section's sub-levels. Lists with multiple levels are more commonly known as *nested* lists. Basically, a nested numbered list is a list within a list. To create a nested numbered list in FrontPage, use the Increase Indent and Decrease Indent buttons, which are located on the Format toolbar.

In the following example, you'll add the chapters that are included in the first section of the book.

1. Position the insertion point at the end of the list item that reads "New England Families." Press Enter. The insertion point moves to the next line and starts a new list item. FrontPage renumbers the list as if you are adding a new list item in the middle.

2. Press the Increase Indent button on the Format toolbar twice. The insertion point indents, moves to the next line, and starts the indented level with number 1. The items in the previous level are automatically renumbered to their original sequence.

3. Enter the following five list items in the second level, pressing Enter at the end of each line but the last one. Your list will look like the one in Figure 4.2 when you are finished:

`The Doe Family of Weymouth, Mass.`

`The Jones Family of Saybrook, Conn.`

```
The Roberts family of Wethersfield, Conn.

The Smith Family of Dorchester, Mass.

The Williams Family of Salem, Mass.
```

FIGURE 4.2

You create a nested numbered list by using the Increase Indent and Decrease Indent buttons on the Format toolbar.

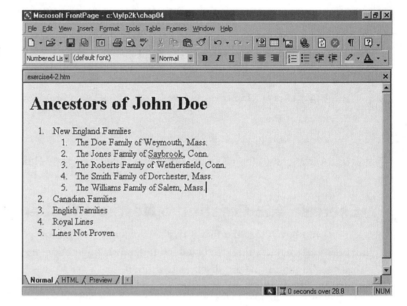

4. The third level in the list displays topics covered in each chapter. In this example, each topic is the name of an ancestor in a certain family. To add a third level to the Doe family, position the insertion point at the end of the line that reads "The Doe Family of Weymouth, Mass." Press Enter to begin a new list item.

5. Press the Increase Indent button on the Format toolbar twice. The list indents to a new level.

6. Enter the following three list items. When you reach the end of the last item, your list should look like the one shown in Figure 4.3.

```
John Doe, born 1609 in England

John Doe II, born 1646 in Weymouth, Mass.

Samuel Doe, born 1673 in Dorchester, Mass.
```

FIGURE 4.3

A third level is added to the numbered list.

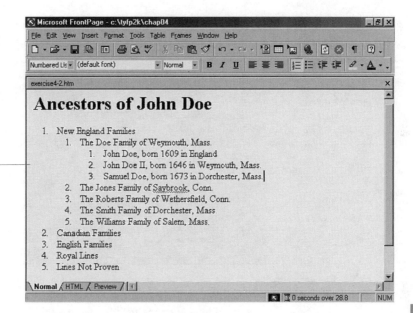

Exercise 4.3: Changing the Ordered List Type

Ordered lists don't always have to start with numbers. You can also begin numbered lists with large or small Roman numerals, large letters, or small letters. Be aware that browsers might handle these other attributes differently. Preview your pages in several browsers to view the differences.

In the case of our genealogy book example, we'll modify the list so that each section begins with a large Roman numeral, each chapter begins with a number, and each chapter topic begins with a large letter. To accomplish this, you choose Format, Bullets and Numbering.

To change the numbered list types in your book outline, use the following steps:

1. Position the insertion point anywhere within the "New England Families" list item.

2. Choose Format, Bullets and Numbering. The List Properties dialog box appears. The Numbers tab, shown in Figure 4.4, allows you to modify the numbering system for the list.

3. Select the Large Roman Numerals list type (third type in the first row, labeled I, II, III) and choose OK. All of the section list items in the first level change to large Roman numerals.

FIGURE **4.4**

Use the Numbers tab in the List Properties dialog box to select the type of numbered list you are creating.

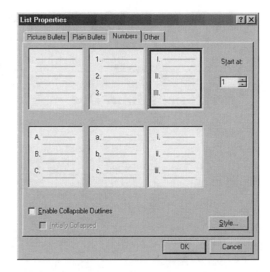

4. The second level of list items (the chapters in the book) will remain as numbered list items, but we need to change the list type for the third level. To do this, position the insertion point anywhere within the list item "John Doe, born 1609 in England."

5. Choose Format, Bullets and Numbering. The List Properties dialog box appears and defaults to the Numbers tab.

6. Select the Large Letters list type (first type in the second row, labeled A, B, C) and choose OK. All list items in the third level change to large letters. Your list should look like the one shown in Figure 4.5.

Note

You can also open the List Properties dialog box by positioning the insertion point within a list item. To change the list properties of all list items in a single-level list or of one level in a nested list, right-click and choose List Properties from the pop-up menu. To change the list properties of one item in a list, right-click and choose List Item Properties from the pop-up menu.

This completes the first page for the day. You'll be working with this file again later, so you'll want to save it to your hard drive or Web. Choose File, Save, press Ctrl+S, or click the Save button in the Standard toolbar. The page title defaults to Ancestors of John Doe. Assign a filename of **ancestors.htm**.

FIGURE 4.5

The numbered list now contains three different number types.

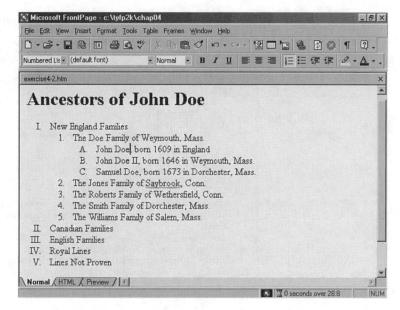

Exercise 4.4: Changing the Starting Number

There are also occasions when you will want to begin a numbered list with a different number. The page shown in Figure 4.6 is contained in a file named ezcheck.htm in the tyfp2k\chap04\samples folder on the CD-ROM that accompanies this book. Open this file in FrontPage to follow along with the next example.

In Figure 4.6, you see a portion of the ezcheck.htm page that shows installation instructions to set up a software program. A note follows the first six steps in the process, and then the instructions continue with three additional steps. You want the second list to begin where the preceding numbered list left off (with the number 7).

To change the starting number of the second numbered list, follow these steps:

1. Position the insertion point anywhere within the first list item in the list you want to change (in this case, in the "Enter your credit card…" item in the list that begins after the note).

2. Choose Format, Bullets and Numbering or right-click and choose List Properties from the pop-up menu. The List Properties dialog box appears, opened to the Numbers tab.

3. In the Start At field of the Numbers tab, enter the new starting number for the list. For this example, enter the number 7.

FIGURE **4.6**

FIGURE **4.6**

*The second list on this
page should begin with
the number 7.*

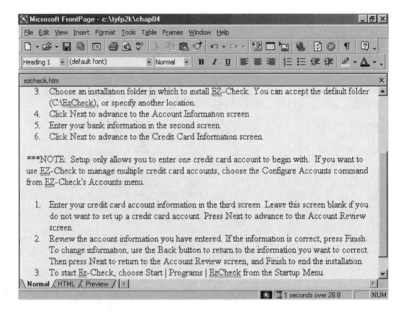

4. Choose OK. The second numbered list is renumbered from 7 through 9, as shown
   in Figure 4.7.

FIGURE **4.7**

*Using the Numbers tab
of the List Properties
dialog box, the second
list now starts with a
consecutive number.*

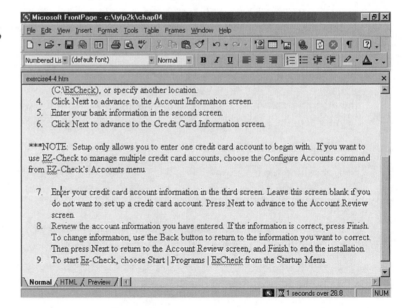

Working with Bulleted Lists

Bulleted lists are a close cousin to numbered lists. The HTML tag associated with bulleted lists is <ul>...</ul> (for *unordered lists*). Each list item is enclosed in an <li>...</li> tag as they are for numbered lists. Bulleted lists are typically used to display a list of items that don't have to appear in a specific order. Many people use bulleted lists to display links to their favorite Web sites, but there are many other applications for them as well.

Bulleted lists are usually rendered as paragraphs separated by white space. They are usually prefixed by filled or unfilled circles or squares, but some browsers display bulleted lists differently. For example, some browsers render bullets exactly the way you see them in FrontPage. Others render all bullets as solid circles, regardless of the bullet type you specify. Others render level 1 bullets as shaded circles, level 2 bullets as shaded diamonds, and level 3 bullets as shaded squares, regardless of the bullet you specify. WYSIWYG is WYSIWYG only to a point when it comes to bulleted lists, but the differences in the way that they are rendered are usually not objectionable.

Exercise 4.5: Creating a Bulleted List

4

Bulleted lists are created using procedures similar to those for numbered lists. In fact, the steps you'll follow here should feel quite familiar to you already. Create a new Normal page (using the New Page button on the Standard toolbar), and add a bulleted list to it using the following steps:

1. On the first line of the page, enter the following text:

   Some popular hobbies:

2. Press Enter. The insertion point moves to the beginning of the next line.

3. Choose Bulleted List from the Style drop-down list in the Format toolbar, or use the Bullets button on the Format toolbar. FrontPage enters the first bullet for you automatically.

4. Enter the first item in the list:

   Collecting

5. Add the following list items, pressing Enter at the end of each except the last:

   Creative Arts / Crafts

   Genealogy

   Sports

6. At the end of the last item, press Enter twice or press Ctrl+Enter to complete the list. Your list should look like the one shown in Figure 4.8.

FIGURE 4.8

Use bulleted lists to present a list of items that don't need to be arranged in a specific order.

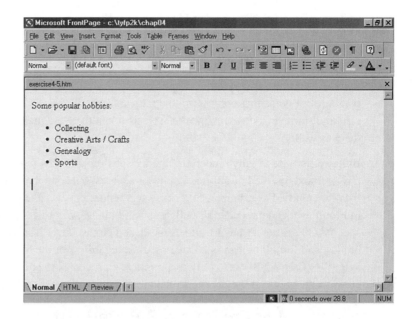

Exercise 4.6: Creating a Nested Bulleted List

The steps you use to create nested bulleted lists are basically the same as those you learned earlier in this chapter for nested numbered lists. When you create nested bulleted lists, a different bullet type represents each level in the list. The bullets can be solid or filled circles or squares. To add nested items to the hobby list, follow these steps:

1. Position the insertion point at the end of the list item that reads "Collecting." Press Enter. The insertion point moves to the next line and starts a new list item.

2. Double-click the Increase Indent button on the Format toolbar. The insertion point indents, moves to the next line, and changes the bullet to an unfilled circle.

3. Enter the following list items, pressing Enter at the end of each line except the last:

   `Antiques`

   `Art`

   `Books and Magazines`

   `Coins`

   `Figurines`

   `Ornaments`

   `Rocks and Crystals`

   `Stamps`

   `Toys`

4. Position the insertion point at the end of the line that reads "Antiques." Press Enter to begin a new list item.

5. Double-click the Increase Indent button on the Format toolbar. The list indents to a new level, and the bullet changes to a square.

6. Enter the following additional list items in the third level. When you reach the end of the last item, your list should look like the one shown in Figure 4.9:

```
Dishes

Dolls

Furniture

Radios

Quilts

Silverware
```

FIGURE 4.9

The bulleted list now contains three levels.

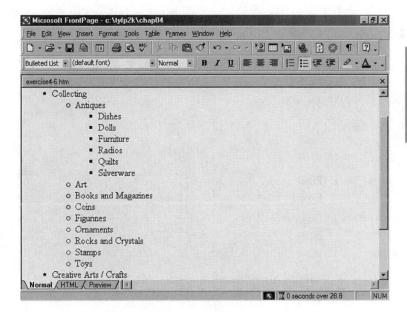

Exercise 4.7: Changing Plain Bullets

Though each level in a nested bulleted list automatically receives a different bullet type, you can change the bullets in the list. You can select one of two types of bullets: plain or image bullets. You'll learn how to modify the plain bullets in the following exercise.

Note

There are two ways to apply images to bullets in your lists. One way is to apply a theme to your Web pages, as discussed in Day 9, "Changing the Appearance of Your Pages." Your bulleted lists will automatically use the images associated with the theme. If you decide not to use themes in your Web site, you can still use images as bullets, as discussed in Chapter 6, "Adding Images, Sound, and Video."

Plain bullets (solid circles, unfilled circles, and squares) are used by default when you create a nested bulleted list. You can select a different type of plain bullet, but keep in mind that browsers render bullet types differently.

To change the bulleted list types in your Hobbies page, follow these steps:

1. Position the insertion point anywhere within the list item that reads "Antiques."

2. Choose Format, Bullets and Numbering. The List Properties dialog box appears, opened to the Plain Bullets tab shown in Figure 4.10.

FIGURE 4.10

Use the Plain Bullets tab to change the type of bullet in your bulleted list.

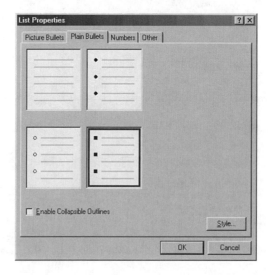

3. Select the square bullets list type (on the right in the second row) and click OK. All list items in the second level change to square bullets.

4. Position the insertion point anywhere within the list item that reads "Dishes."

5. Choose Format, Bullets and Numbering. The List Properties dialog box appears, opened to the Bulleted tab.

6. Select the unfilled circle bullet list type (first in the second row) and click OK. All list items in the third level change to unfilled circles. Your list should look like the one shown in Figure 4.11.

FIGURE **4.11**

The bulleted list uses bullet types that you specify.

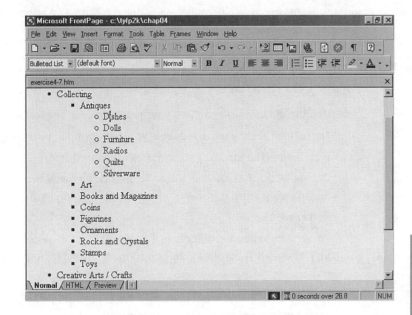

Now, you've completed your second page today. If you want to save the page, the page title defaults to Some popular hobbies. Assign a file name of **hobbies.htm**.

Working with Definition Lists

Definition lists, also sometimes referred to as glossary lists, are used for what the name implies. They typically display a list of terms, followed by definitions for each term. You can also use definition lists to provide a list of items and their descriptions. Three HTML tags are associated with definition lists. The <dl>...</dl> tag encloses the items in the list. The terms in the definition list are enclosed within <dt>...</dt> tags, and the definitions of each term are enclosed within <dd>...</dd> tags.

Generally, the defined term is aligned with the left margin of the page, and its definition is indented. Most browsers display definition lists in the same way, though the amount of indentation of the definition can vary slightly.

Exercise 4.8: Using a Definition List

It is very easy to create a definition list in FrontPage. You choose Defined Term from the Style drop-down menu to format the first list item. Pressing the Enter key automatically formats the next item as a definition. Pressing the Enter key again starts a new term, followed by a new definition, and so on.

The following exercise will help you remember the different types of lists that you're learning about in this chapter. Create a new page (using the New Page button on the Standard toolbar), and build a definition list as follows:

1. Position the insertion point on your page and enter the following text:

   `The different types of lists you can use in your pages are:`

2. Press Enter. The insertion point moves to the next line.

3. Choose Defined Term from the Style drop-down menu in the Format toolbar. Enter the following term:

   `Numbered Lists`

4. Press Enter to add the definition. The insertion point moves to the next line. The Style drop-down list shows the line formatted as a Definition. Enter the following text:

   `Used when the list must be arranged in a definite order.`

5. Press Enter to add the next defined term:

   `Bulleted Lists`

6. Press Enter again to add the next definition:

   `Used when the list does not have to be arranged in a definite order.`

7. Continue to add the remaining list items, pressing Enter at the end of each line:

Term:	`Definition Lists`
Definition:	`Used to display a list of terms and their definitions.`
Term:	`Directory Lists`
Definition:	`Used to list the contents of a directory. Primarily used by programmers, and not widely supported by browsers. Will soon become obsolete.`
Term:	`Menu Lists`
Definition:	`Used to list the contents of a menu or short items (20 characters or less). Not widely supported by browsers. Will soon become obsolete.`

8. At the end of the last list item, press Enter twice or press Ctrl+Enter to end the list. When you finish, your list should look like the one shown in Figure 4.12.

FIGURE 4.12

A definition list shows a list of terms and their definitions.

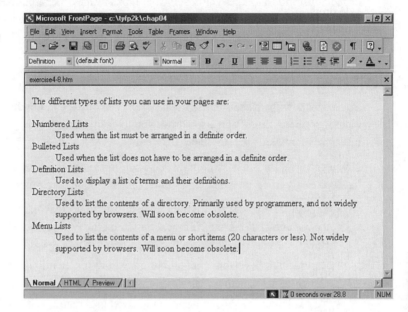

A third page done today! To save the page, use a page title of Different Types of Lists, and assign a filename of **definition.htm**.

Using Directory and Menu Lists

FrontPage supports two more types of lists: directory lists and menu lists. You'll find both of these list options in the Style drop-down list in the Format toolbar.

Both of these types of lists were originally intended for programmers and are not used very often any more. Directory lists were used to list the contents of a directory. Similarly, menu lists displayed the contents of a menu or short items of 20 characters or less.

Because these tags haven't really been used often, many browsers do not support them well. As a matter of fact, some browsers don't support directory and menu lists at all and don't quite know what to do with them. As a result, these two types of lists have been *deprecated* in the current version of HTML (HTML 4.0). What this means is that the HTML powers-that-be have kept these list types in to provide backward compatibility for older browsers (which is probably the very same reason why FrontPage still supports them). Eventually these lists will be obsolete.

If you want to go ahead and use a directory or menu list in your pages, the steps to create them are similar to those outlined for bulleted lists. In fact, if you create a directory list or menu list in FrontPage, you'll see what looks *exactly* like a bulleted list. Because there is no difference in appearance, and considering that these list types are on the way out, it stands to reason that it's easier just to use a bulleted list instead.

Editing Lists

You now know the basic steps to create each type of list and how to apply different formatting to them. FrontPage also allows you to easily change one type of list to another, insert new items in a list, or delete list items.

If you change your mind about how you want to present your lists, you can change the list type easily. Here are some notes and pointers about changing list types:

- You can easily convert a numbered list back to normal text by selecting all items in the list and clicking the Numbers button on the Format toolbar. Similarly, the Bullets button will convert all selected items in a bulleted list to Normal text.
- Basic (single-level) numbered lists convert to bulleted lists, and bulleted lists to numbered lists, with no problem.
- Nested bulleted lists and nested numbered lists retain their level structure, so you need to change one level at a time to change the list type.
- You can use a combination of bullets and numbers in a nested list (as the following task will show).
- When you change from any other type of list to a definition list, all the list items become formatted as definitions—not as terms. You can easily change the definitions to terms by selecting them all and choosing Defined Term from the Style drop-down list in the Format toolbar.

Exercise 4.9: Creating a Nested Numbered/Bulleted List

The following example demonstrates how to create a list that uses a combination of numbers and bullets. Though there are many ways to approach this, the quickest way is probably to create the entire nested list as a numbered list. Then you can change the appropriate sub-levels to bullets as necessary.

The genealogy book page that you worked on earlier in this chapter (ancestors.htm) is a good page with which to demonstrate this technique. We'll change the third list level from a numbered list with large letters to a bulleted list.

Reopen `ancestors.htm`, and modify it as follows:

1. Position the insertion point anywhere within the line that reads "John Doe, born 1609 in England" (the list item that begins with the letter A).

2. There are two ways that you can change the level to a bulleted list. The first way is to choose Bulleted List from the Style drop-down list in the Format toolbar. This changes the list to a bulleted list and formats the bullets as they would normally appear on whatever list level they appear (solid circles for the first level, unfilled circles for the second level, or filled squares for the third level).

   The second method allows you to choose the bullet type when you reformat the list. For example, to use solid circles in the third level, right-click in the list item and choose List Properties from the pop-up menu. From the List Properties dialog box, select the Plain Bullets tab. Select the bullet type you want to use (in this case, the solid circles in the top row). Click OK to apply the changes. Now, your list looks like the one shown in Figure 4.13.

FIGURE 4.13

A list with a combination of bullets and numbers is easily created using the List Properties dialog box.

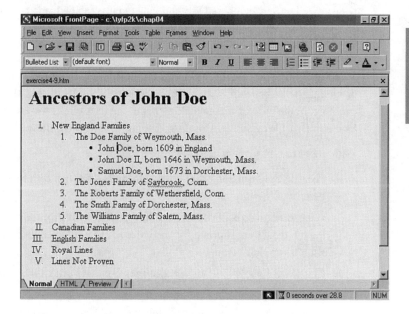

Exercise 4.10: Using Collapsible Outlines

Now that you've changed the third level of the nested list in the `ancestors.htm` page to bullets, we'll add another enhancement to the list. Here, you'll get a brief introduction to an advanced feature that you'll learn more about in Day 13, "Working with DHTML and Positioning."

Dynamic HTML, or DHTML for short, is a fairly recent Web page technology that extends HTML. It allows you to implement advanced positioning, display options, and much more in your Web pages. The effect you are about to learn won't work in older browsers that don't support DHTML. Although older browsers will display all of the items in the list, you won't be able to collapse them. To see how collapsible outlines work, you'll need to view the page in a browser that supports Dynamic HTML. Internet Explorer 4.0 or later or Netscape 4.0 or later will display these types of lists correctly.

A collapsible list does exactly what its name implies. When a user clicks on a list item, it shows or hides sub-levels beneath the list item that was clicked (if they exist). To get technical, this effect is accomplished through a Dynamic HTML list attribute named `dynamicoutline`. Fortunately, with FrontPage you don't have to worry about the list attribute that is used to create the effect—you can apply the effect from within the List Properties dialog box.

Note

Only numbered lists and bulleted lists can be made collapsible. This feature will be disabled with definition lists, directory lists, and menu lists.

Make note that you want to apply this effect to the list item that the user clicks to show or hide the level beneath it, and not on the part of the list that is shown or hidden. For example, in the case of the genealogy page, the user clicks the list item that reads "The Doe Family of Weymouth, Mass." to display or hide the bulleted list beneath it.

With `ancestor.htm` opened, follow these steps:

1. Position the insertion point anywhere within the list item that reads "The Doe Family of Weymouth, Mass."

2. Choose Format, Bullets and Numbering. The List Properties dialog box opens to the tab that is appropriate for the list you are editing (either Image Bullets, Plain Bullets, or Numbers tab).

3. Check the Enable Collapsible Outlines box, and click OK.

4. Save the page to your Web or hard disk (I saved my page under a new filename of **ancestors2.htm**). If you are using Internet Explorer 4.0 (or later), you can use the Preview tab in FrontPage to test how the collapsible list works. Click the list item to which you applied the property, and you should see the bulleted list appear and disappear as you click the list item. Figure 14.14 shows the list with the bullet items hidden.

FIGURE 4.14

A collapsible list hides items beneath a list item.

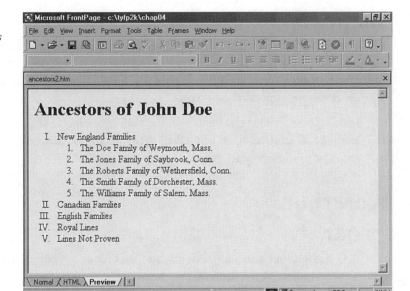

Inserting List Items

To insert list items, just place the insertion point where you want to insert the new item and press Enter. A new number, bullet, or term is started for you. Enter the new list item as you usually do.

Deleting Lists or List Items

Deleting lists or list items is easy to do. In the case of nested lists, you'll need to perform the following steps more than once to delete the entire list, because each nested level is treated as a separate list.

To delete a list or a list item from a page, you simply select the list item or list that you want to delete, and then choose the Edit, Clear or press the Delete key.

- To select a single list item, position the cursor in the selection bar at the left side of the page. (You know you're in the selection bar when the cursor changes to an arrow that points inward toward the list item). Single-click to select one list item.

- To select an entire list that is not nested, or to select one level in a nested list, position the cursor in the selection bar and double-click.

Summary

Organizing your information in lists is easy. The hardest part is thinking of the information that you want to include. Keep in mind that lists can appear differently in your visitors' browsers. While you develop your site, have a few different browsers on hand to check the appearance of your pages.

In this chapter, you learned how to format information into different types of lists. You learned how to create basic and nested lists and how to change their appearances by specifying different bullet and numbering types.

Workshop

Q&A

Q **How about a sneak preview...how do I make a bulleted list that uses graphics as bullets? I see them all the time.**

A Briefly, when you choose a FrontPage theme, bullet graphics are added automatically for you. If your page does not use a theme, you can customize the bullet graphic by using the Image Bullets tab in the List Properties dialog box. It's easiest to add the bullet images after you import the appropriate graphics into your Web first. Then you can use the Browse button in the Image Bullets tab to select your bullet image. Further details on all these procedures are discussed in Day 6.

Q **I want to create a definition list, but some of my terms have more than one definition. Is it possible to create more than one?**

A Yes, it's possible, but it's not automatic. FrontPage automatically formats the next line after a definition as a term, unless you end the list. You'll need to choose Definition from the Style drop-down list in the Format toolbar to create more than one definition in your list.

Q **I want to increase the indentation in my definition list. When I position the cursor in the selection bar at the left side of the list and click, only one list item gets selected. How do I select the entire list?**

A If you position the selection pointer at the lower-left corner of the entire list (to the left of the last line in the last definition), you should be able to double-click to select the entire list. Then you can use the Increase Indent button to indent the entire list at the same time.

Quiz

1. What three types of lists are most commonly used in Web pages?

2. What two types of lists are no longer commonly used, and what can be used place of them?

3. What FrontPage command or toolbar item is used to create a nested numbered or bulleted list?

4. By default, numbered lists begin with the numbers. What are the other ways that numbered lists can be displayed?

5. What types of bullets can be displayed in bulleted lists?

Exercises

1. Experiment with changing the definition list that you created in "Using a Definition List." Change this list into a nested bulleted list. (Hint: Select the entire list and use the Bullets button in the Format toolbar to convert it to a bulleted list. Then, select each definition and use the Increase Indent button to indent the definition).

2. Create a Web page that displays a list of Web sites that relate to a topic that interests you. You'll learn how to create the links in Day 7, "Adding Links and Bookmarks."

Answers to Quiz

1. The three types of lists that are most commonly used in Web pages are numbered lists, bulleted lists, and definition lists.

2. The two types of lists that are not used as frequently are menu lists and directory lists. Bulleted lists can be used in place of them.

3. The Increase Indent and Decrease Indent buttons on the Format toolbar are used to create nested numbered and bulleted lists.

4. Numbered lists can also begin with large Roman numerals, small Roman numerals, large letters, or small letters.

5. The bullets in bulleted lists can be filled circles, unfilled circles, filled squares, and unfilled squares. You can also assign images as bullets, as you will learn in Days 6 and 9.

DAY 5

Creating and Formatting Tables

FrontPage 2000 supports tables and table attributes to the fullest. Using tables, you can control the layout of a page in many ways, placing content and images where you want them. Well…sort of.

Browsers handle tables differently. Some older browsers don't recognize tables at all; they leave your hard layout work laying in the dust, displaying a jumble of text and images. You should keep several different browsers around to test your tables as you design them and make compromises when you can.

There is good news, though. The latest versions of Internet Explorer and Netscape handle tables quite well. Each of these browsers has its own nifty little tricks. When designing pages to view in Netscape 4.0 and Internet Explorer 4.0, you can specify different colors for individual cells. Internet Explorer adds even more flexibility in how you can view tables. You have the capability of specifying a separate background image for each cell, as well. Tables help you create a fancy layout that can be viewed by many popular browsers.

In today's lesson, you will

- Become acquainted with the elements that make up a table
- Learn how to insert tables onto your page
- Align tables, include borders, choose cell padding and spacing, and change the width of your tables
- Create advanced tables by splitting and merging cells and creating nested tables

What Makes Up a Table?

A table has several elements, and to understand them is to understand the terminology needed to create them. Figure 5.1 shows an example of a basic table.

FIGURE 5.1

The basic elements of a table are rows, columns, cells, and borders.

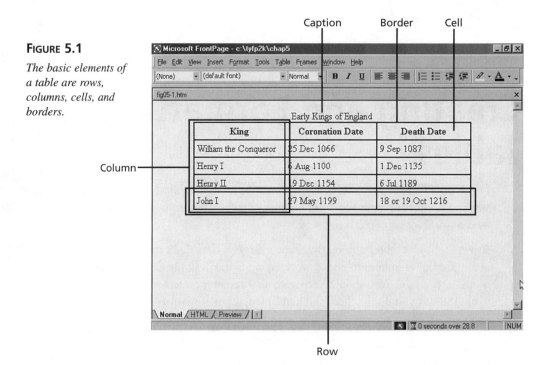

You see the following elements in Figure 5.1:

- *Rows and columns.* A table usually consists of multiple rows and columns. Rows run horizontally and columns run vertically.

- *Cells.* Each data field in a table is called a cell, sometimes referred to as a data cell. Cells used for table headings are called *header cells*.

- *Captions.* The table caption is a title or description of the contents of the table. Typically, it is located immediately above or below the table.

- *Borders.* A table can be created with or without a border. It can appear on all sides of the table or on selected sides through the use of extended attributes.

The Tables Toolbar

The Tables toolbar, shown in Figure 5.2, is used to create and edit tables and cells. Table 5.1 lists the buttons that are available in the Tables toolbar and the menu commands that are associated with them.

TABLE 5.1 Commands in the Tables Toolbar

Toolbar Button	Associated Menu Command
Draw Table	Table, Draw Table
Eraser	No menu equivalent
Insert Rows	Table, Insert, Rows or Columns
Insert Columns	Table, Insert, Rows or Columns
Delete Cells	Table, Delete Cells
Merge Cells	Table, Merge Cells
Split Cells	Table, Split Cells
Align Top	See Alignment option in Table Properties dialog box
Center Vertically	See Alignment option in Table Properties dialog box
Align Bottom	See Alignment option in Table Properties dialog box
Distribute Rows Evenly	Table, Distribute Rows Evenly
Distribute Columns Evenly	Table, Distribute Columns Evenly
Fill Color	See Background Color option in Table Properties or Cell Properties dialog box
Auto Fit	Table, AutoFit

5

To display or hide the Tables toolbar, choose View, Toolbars, Tables.

FIGURE 5.2

The Tables toolbar.

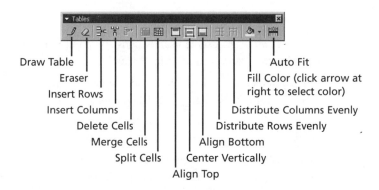

Draw Table
Eraser
Insert Rows
Insert Columns
Delete Cells
Merge Cells
Split Cells
Align Top
Center Vertically
Align Bottom
Distribute Rows Evenly
Distribute Columns Evenly
Fill Color (click arrow at right to select color)
Auto Fit

Exercise 5.1: Inserting a Basic Table

For your first exercise today, you'll create a very basic table using the Table, Insert, Table command. This command opens the Insert Table dialog box, from which you can specify several table attributes.

Tip

You can insert a table with up to five columns and four rows by using the Insert Table button on the Standard toolbar. Simply click the button and a grid appears. Click the cell that corresponds with the lower-right cell in the table you want to insert. The table appears on your page using the same settings that were last set in the Table Properties dialog box.

To create the table, follow these steps:

1. Using the steps you learned in Chapters 3, "Building Basic Web Pages" and 4, "Using Lists to Organize Information," create a new disk-based Web using the Empty Web template. Save the Web to your `c:\tyfp2k\chap05` directory. When you create the new Web, a blank page appears in the page editor.

2. The cursor appears on the first line in the page. Choose Table, Insert, Table. The Insert Table dialog box shown in Figure 5.3 appears.

3. Specify the following settings:

Rows:	3
Columns:	2
Alignment:	Center
Border Size:	5
Cell Padding:	3
Cell Spacing:	3
Specify Width:	Check this option, and enter **75**; then choose In Percent

4. Click OK to create the table. The table appears on your page.

FIGURE 5.3

The Insert Table dialog box allows you to specify settings for your new table.

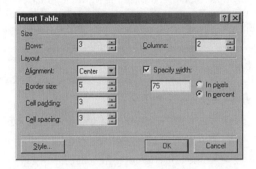

Tip

By default, when you create a table with the Insert Table command, each column in the table spans an equal percent of the table width. After you add your content, there is a quick way to adjust the column widths so that they fit better with the contents. Use the AutoFit command to adjust column width and give your table a more pleasing appearance.

To autofit a table, click anywhere inside the table and choose Table, AutoFit, or click the AutoFit button in the Tables toolbar. The columns adjust appropriately to fit the contents of each column.

Basic Table Parts and Properties

As you saw in the preceding section, the Insert Table command allows you to define some basic settings for your table. Now you'll learn a little bit about the options you can choose in the Insert Table dialog box.

Rows and Columns

The first two settings in the Insert Table dialog box define the number of rows and the number of columns that you want to create in your table. As the entries imply, you enter the number of rows you want in the Rows field (or use the up and down arrows to select a value from 1 to 100). Likewise, enter the number of columns in the Columns field (or use its up and down arrows to select a value from 1 to 100).

Table Alignment

The Alignment setting appears in the Layout section of the Insert Table dialog box. This setting controls how the entire table is aligned on your page.

5

> **Note**
>
> Some browsers don't recognize the right-alignment setting and align the table to the left side of the page instead. Test your table alignment in several different browsers to ensure you get the results you expect!

To choose a table alignment, select one of the following options from the Alignment drop-down list box in the Layout section of the dialog box:

- *Default* aligns the table to the position that was specified when the table was created.
- *Left* aligns the table to the left edge of your page.
- *Right* aligns the table to the right of your page. This choice is not recognized in some browsers.
- *Center* aligns the table to the center of your page.
- *Justify* spans the table across the full width of the page.

Figure 5.4 shows examples of left, center, and right alignment applied to a two-row, two-column table. The Alignment setting won't be noticeable unless the table width is set to a value of less than 100 percent.

FIGURE 5.4

Tables aligned to the left, center, and right of a page.

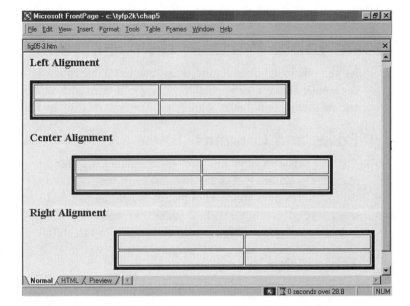

Border Size

The Border Size setting is found in the Layout section of the Insert Table dialog box. It controls the width of the border that appears around the outer edge of the table. If you want to create a borderless table, enter a value of **0**.

To set the border size, you can do one of two things:

- Enter a value in the Border Size field of the Layout section in the dialog box.
- Use the up and down arrows to select a value between 0 and 100 pixels.

Figure 5.5 shows some tables that have varying border widths. The top table has a border of **0** pixels, the middle table has a border of **5** pixels, and the bottom table has a border of **10** pixels.

Tip

> Borderless tables (those with a border width setting of **0**) are typically used to lay out several graphics side by side, giving the illusion that they are all one graphic. FrontPage displays the borders of borderless tables and cells in dotted lines. Not to worry—this is just a guide for you to place your content in the cells. When you view the table in other browsers, you won't see those border designations.

FIGURE 5.5

Borders of varying widths are added to the tables.

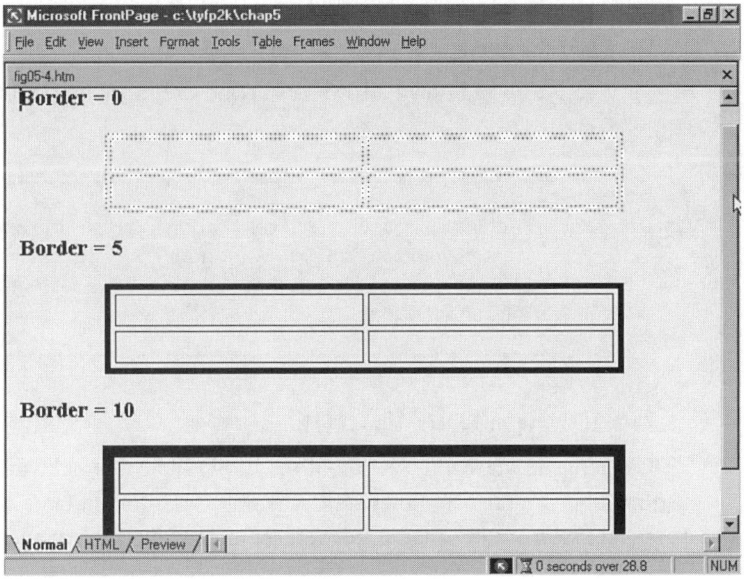

5

Cell Padding

The Cell Padding setting controls how far from the edge of the cell's border its contents appear. A value of 0 results in cell contents appearing immediately adjacent to its borders.

Compare the top and middle tables in Figure 5.6 to see what cell padding does in a table. The top table displays a table that does not use cell padding or cell spacing (which is described next). The middle table uses a cell padding setting of 10 pixels. As you can see, the contents in the table that uses cell padding stand out more readily.

You can specify cell padding settings in one of two ways:

- Enter the number of pixels in the Cell Padding field.
- Use the up and down arrows beside the Cell Padding field to select a value between 0 and 100.

Cell Spacing

The Cell Spacing setting controls the width of the borders between cells (the row and column dividers, so to speak). A value of 0 results in a table that does not contain extra spacing between the cells. Again refer to Figure 5.6, where the bottom table has *cell spacing* added. Compare it to the top table, which does not.

To set cell spacing, you can use one of the following two methods:

- Enter the number of pixels in the Cell Spacing field.
- Use the up and down arrows beside the Cell Spacing field to select a value between 0 and 100.

Tip

Adding cell padding and cell spacing improves the appearance of text content in your tables. If you want graphics to get as close to each other as possible to give the illusion that the table is one solid graphic, set cell padding and spacing to 0.

Changing Table Width

The settings in the Width section of the Insert Table dialog box control the width of the entire table. Figure 5.7 shows some examples of different table widths. Each table is aligned to the center of the page. You set table width in percentage of screen or in pixels.

FIGURE 5.6

Examples of cell padding and cell spacing.

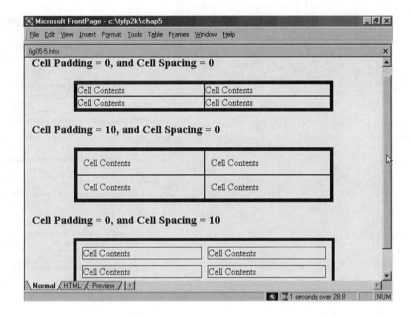

Tip

To create a table that automatically sizes itself to fit the contents of the table, uncheck the Specify Width option.

There are three choices when you specify table widths:

- *In Pixels*. If you're adding graphics to your tables, pixel settings help you plan your table layout before you insert the graphics. Note, however, that when users resize their browser windows or view your pages in a resolution that is less than what you designed your pages for, portions of your table might not be visible. A good rule of thumb is to size your table width for 640×480 resolution (or, generally, 600 pixels width as a maximum) and to size your graphics accordingly.

- *In Percent*. This is the most common setting. When users browse through your pages using different resolution settings, a table sized in percent will adjust itself to accommodate the width of the browser window.

- *No setting (Specify Width unchecked)*. When you uncheck the Specify Width option, the table sizes itself as necessary to accommodate the contents in the cells.

5

FIGURE 5.7

FIGURE 5.7

These tables use various width settings as configured in the Insert Table dialog box.

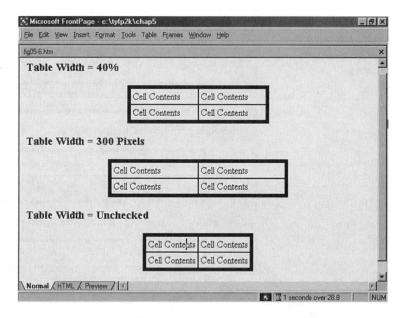

Adding and Formatting Table Captions

Tables don't always have captions, but in some cases, captions are necessary. They help you point out what the table is about. When you apply a caption to a table, it actually becomes part of the table instead of a separate line of text. Generally, a table caption uses one line.

To add a caption to a table, follow these steps:

1. Position the insertion point anywhere within the table.

2. Choose Table, Insert, Caption. The insertion point moves to a center location above the table, where you can type the table caption. If your table uses a background image, the caption uses the same image as the background.

To select a table caption, move the pointer to the left of the table caption and click to select it.

Drawing or Adding Tables

FrontPage 2000 also includes a feature that enables you to draw a table on your page. When you create a table in this manner, the table aligns to the center of the page. The border size, cell padding, and cell spacing settings that you last used in the Insert Table dialog box will be applied to the new table when you draw it.

Exercise 5.2: Draw a Basic Table

In this exercise, you'll use the Draw Table button on the Tables toolbar to draw a table on a new page. Follow these steps:

1. Click the New Page icon in the Standard toolbar to create a new page. The insertion point appears at the upper-left corner of the page.

2. Click the Draw Table button on the Tables toolbar (or choose Table, Draw Table). The cursor changes into a pencil.

3. Position the pencil cursor at the upper-left corner of where you want your table to appear. Click and drag to the lower-right corner of your new table. An outline of a table appears on your page, as shown in Figure 5.8. Note that if your display resolution is set differently than 640×480, your screen might appear different than the figure's.

FIGURE 5.8

Draw the outline of your table first.

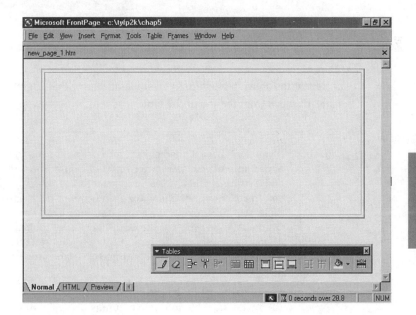

4. In this step, you'll add the first of two lines to the table to divide it into three rows. First, position the pencil cursor inside, but not touching, the left or right edge of the table, about a third of the way down from the top. Click and drag to the opposite side of the table. Release the mouse when you see a dotted line that attaches itself to the left and right borders of the table, as shown in Figure 5.9. A new row appears in your table.

FIGURE 5.9

*Drawing a row in
your table.*

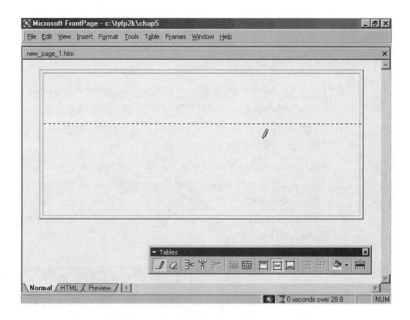

5. Repeat the above procedure to create another row that begins about two-thirds of the distance from the top of the table.

Tip

If you don't have a good eye for measurements, you can improve the appearance of your table after you've drawn it. The Distribute Rows Evenly and Distribute Columns Evenly commands and Tables toolbar buttons help you create rows and columns of even width or height. After you draw the table, select the rows you want to distribute evenly and choose Table, Distribute Rows Evenly or the equivalent Tables toolbar icon. Select the columns you want to distribute evenly and choose Table, Distribute Columns Evenly or use the equivalent button in the Tables toolbar.

6. Now, you'll divide the table into two columns using the draw tool. First, position the pencil cursor inside, but not touching, the top or bottom edge of the table, about a third of the distance into the table. Click and drag to the opposite side of the table. Release the mouse when you see a dotted line attach itself to the top and bottom borders of the table, as shown in Figure 5.10. A new column is added to the table.

FIGURE 5.10

Drawing a column in your table.

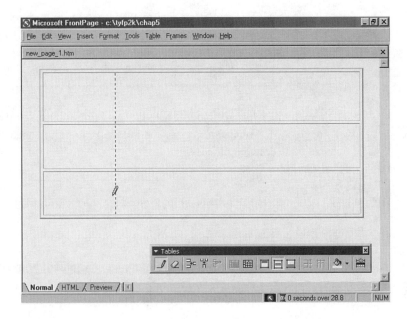

7. You can also use the Draw Table pencil to split one of the cells in a column into one or more cells. Try this: Position the pencil cursor near the top of the large cell in the second row, at about the halfway point. Click and drag to the bottom of the same cell. Now, the second row in your table has three cells, while the first and third rows still have two cells. (You can apply the same procedure to split a cell into more than one row as well.)

 Note

Another way to split cells is to select the cells that you want to split and choose the Table, Split Cells command, or right-click inside one of the selected cells and choose Split Cells from the pop-up menu. The Split Cells dialog box prompts you to split the cell into two or more rows or columns.

8. To merge cells while you're drawing, you use the Table Eraser, which is the second icon on the Tables toolbar. Click the icon to select the eraser. Position your mouse inside the first cell in the first row. Click and drag the eraser over the line that divides it from the cell in the second row. Release the mouse button when the line between the cells in the first and second rows in the first column turns red. The two cells will now be merged into one, as shown in Figure 5.11.

Note

> Another way to merge cells is to select the cells that you want to merge and choose the Table, Merge Cells command, or right-click inside one of the selected cells and choose Merge Cells from the pop-up menu.

9. To exit table drawing mode, click the Draw Table button on the Tables toolbar to toggle it off. You can also press the Escape key or click once outside the table to exit table drawing mode.

Note

> Keep this page open for Exercise 5.3, which follows the next section.

FIGURE 5.11

The finished table.

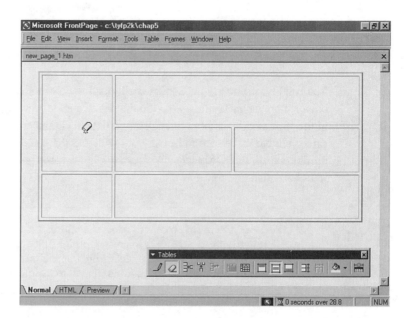

More Table Properties

Once you've added a table to your page, you can change or enhance its appearance using some additional settings in the Table Properties dialog box, shown in Figure 5.12. In addition to the settings that you have already learned about, the Table Properties dialog box contains the following settings:

- *Float*. If you want to create a table that allows text to flow to the right or left of the table, choose a setting other than Default in the Float section of the Table Properties dialog box. When you choose Left, the table appears on the left side of your page and text wraps around the right side. Conversely, when you choose Right, the table appears on the right side of your page and text wraps around the left side.

- *Specify Height*. Similar to the Specify Width setting, you can also define the height of a table by percent of screen height or in pixels.

- *Borders* (Color, Light Border, and Dark Border). By default, the color of your table border is the same as the text on your page. You can specify a different border color in one of two ways: Choose Color to specify a different solid border color for all four sides of the table. Choose Light Border to specify a color for the right and bottom borders, and Dark Border to specify a color for the top and left borders.

Note

Note that border colors are an Internet Explorer enhancement, and are not well supported in Netscape browsers.

Border colors will not display in tables that have a border width of 0.

- *Background*. By default, your table appears "transparent" over the page background, meaning that the cells of the table use the same background color or image as your page. To create a table that uses a different solid color in all of its cells, select a new color from the Color drop-down list in the Table Properties dialog box. If you want your table to use a different background image, select the Use Background Picture option, and select an image from your current Web or hard disk.

5

FIGURE 5.12

Additional settings for tables are available in the Table Properties dialog box.

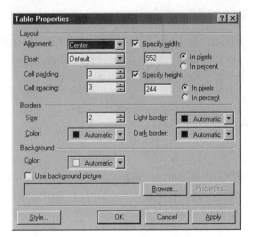

Exercise 5.3: Enhancing Table Properties

In the previous exercise, you drew a table using the Draw Table and Eraser tools in the Tables toolbar. Now you'll add some additional properties to that table by applying some of the settings from the Table Properties dialog box.

To enhance your table, follow these steps:

1. Position the insertion point anywhere within the table. Right-click and choose Table Properties from the pop-up menu. The Table Properties dialog box appears.

2. The following Layout settings create a table that uses default alignment. It allows text to flow along the right side of the table. Cell padding and cell spacing are set to 3 pixels each. The table will display a minimum of 50% width and 50% height of the browser window. Choose the following settings from the Layout section of the Table Properties dialog box:

Alignment:	Default
Float:	Left
Cell Padding:	3
Cell Spacing:	3
Specify Width:	50, In Percent
Specify Height:	50, In Percent

Tip

> You can click the Apply button in the Table Properties dialog box to apply new settings to the table at any time. This keeps the Table Properties dialog box open while you preview the new settings in your table.

3. The following Border settings create a 5-pixel-wide border that uses red for a light color and maroon for a dark color. Choose the following settings from the Borders section of the Table Properties dialog box:

Size:	5
Light Border:	Red (sixth color in second row of color squares)
Dark Border:	Maroon (fourth color in first row of color squares)

4. To choose a solid background color for all of the cells in your table, use the Color setting in the Background section of the Table Properties dialog box. Click the Color drop-down list and select More Colors from the bottom of the color selection

box. The More Colors dialog box appears. The center color in the color matrix is white. Choose the light yellow color that appears below and to the left of the white hexagon (the Value column should display Hex=(FF,FF,CC) when you have selected the right color).

5. Choose OK to return to the Table Properties dialog box.

6. Choose OK to exit the Table Properties dialog box and apply the settings to the table. Your table should look similar to Figure 5.13.

FIGURE 5.13

Background and border colors are added to your table.

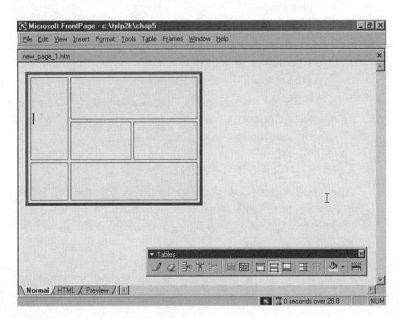

Changing Tables

It's time for a little more theory before your next exercise. The examples that you have worked with so far in this chapter have been applied to the table as a whole. You can also apply properties to one or more cells within the table, and this is where you can really improve the appearance of your tables.

Selecting Tables and Cells

To apply settings to one or more cells, rows, or columns, you first have to select the cells you want to change.

To select one or more cells, click inside the first cell you want to select and choose Table, Select, Cell. Press the Shift key and click inside each additional cell that you want to add to the selection.

To select one or more rows, use one of these methods:

- Place the insertion point in one of the cells in the row you want to select and choose Table, Select, Row. Press the Shift key and click in any other rows you want to add to the selection.
- Position the insertion point outside the left edge of the table, where it becomes a selection pointer. Click to select the table row. You can drag the arrow to select additional contiguous rows.

To select one or more columns, use one of these methods:

- Place the insertion point in one of the cells in the row you want to select and choose Table, Select, Column. Press the Shift key and click in any other columns you want to add to the selection.
- Position the insertion point above the top edge of the table, where it becomes a selection pointer. Click to select the table column. You can drag the arrow to select additional contiguous columns.

Changing Cell Layout

After you select the cells you want to change, use the Cell Properties dialog box shown in Figure 5.14 to apply new properties to them. Many of the settings that you learned about in the Table Properties dialog box are similar to those that you find in the Cell Properties dialog box.

FIGURE 5.14

Change properties of one or more cells using the Cell Properties dialog box.

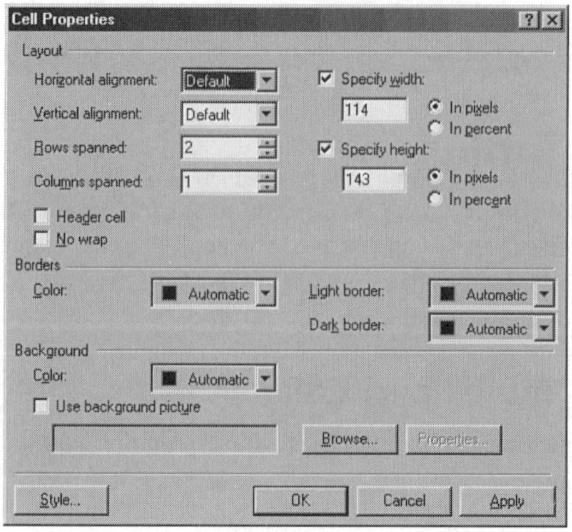

The Layout section of the Cell Properties dialog box contains the following settings:

- *Horizontal Alignment.* Whereas the Horizontal Alignment setting in the Table Properties dialog box controls how the table is aligned to your page, the Horizontal Alignment setting in the Cell Properties dialog box controls how the contents of the cell are aligned within the cell. If you are going to use style sheet properties to control table cell alignment, leave this setting at Default. To override style sheet properties, choose Left (to align cell contents to the left side of the cell), Right (to align cell contents to the right side of the cell), Center (to align cell contents to the center of the cell), or Justify (to create justified text in the cell). See Figure 5.15 for examples.

- *Vertical Alignment.* This setting controls how the contents of the cell are aligned from the top to bottom of the cell. By default, cell contents are aligned to the middle of cells unless overridden by style sheet properties. To override style sheet properties, choose Top (which aligns contents to the top of the cell), Middle (which aligns contents to the middle of the cell), Baseline (which aligns contents to the baseline of text in the cell), or Bottom (which aligns contents to the bottom of the cell). See Figure 5.15 for examples.

- *Header Cell.* Header cells are typically used in the top row or left column of a table to define the data that appears in each row or column. Header cells are typically rendered in bold, centered text, unless overridden with alignment settings as shown in Figure 5.15.

- *Specify Width.* Similar to the setting in the Table Properties dialog box, except that it specifies the width of the current cell or cells. Typically, width settings are applied to an entire column of cells. All of the cells in the table shown in Figure 5.15 have a width setting of 95 pixels.

- *Specify Height.* Similar to the setting in the Table Properties dialog box, except that it specifies the height of the current cell or cells. Typically, height settings are applied to an entire row of cells. All of the cells in the table shown in Figure 5.15 have a height setting of 60 pixels.

- *Rows Spanned.* The best way to merge cells is to select two or more cells and use the Table, Merge Cells command. This field will then display the number of rows that were merged to create the cell. See the examples in Figure 5.16 for some cells that span multiple rows.

- *Columns Spanned.* Again, use the Table, Merge Cells command to combine two or more cells from a column. This field displays the number of columns that were merged to create the cell. See the examples in Figure 5.16 for some cells that span multiple columns.

5

Figure 5.15

*Examples of horizontal
and vertical alignment
in cells.*

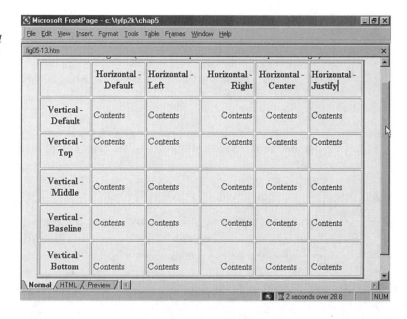

Figure 5.15

*Examples of horizontal
and vertical alignment
in cells.*

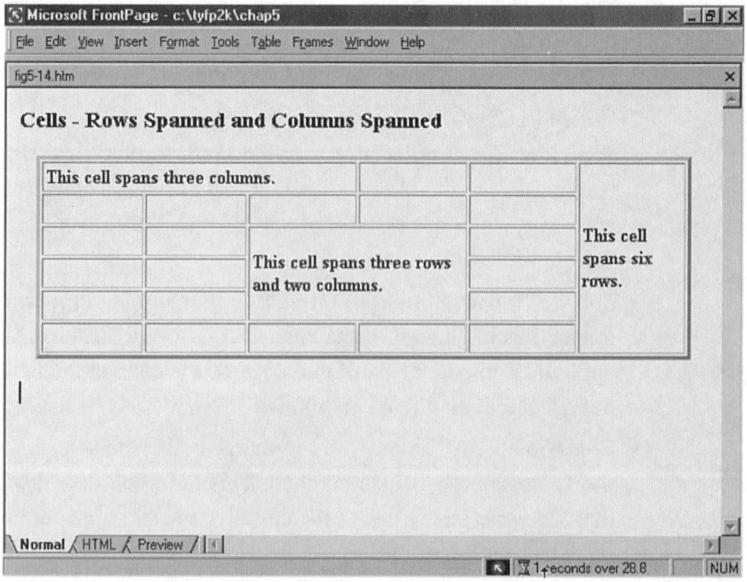

Figure 5.16

*Examples of cells that
span multiple rows and
multiple columns.*

- *No Wrap.* Select this option if you want to display the contents of a cell in a single
  line of text, instead of wrapping the text in multiple lines. A "before" and "after"
  example is shown in Figure 5.17.

FIGURE 5.17

A cell before and after No Wrap is applied.

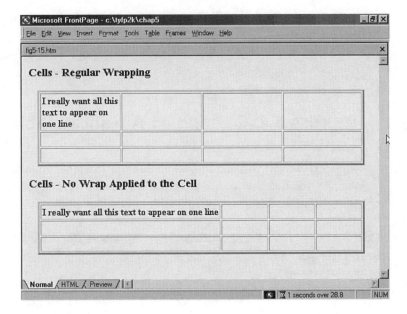

Changing Cell Borders

Earlier in this chapter you learned how to change the color of the table border. You can also change the colors of the borders of individual cells. The Borders section of the Cell Properties dialog box contains the following settings, which are very similar to those found in the Table Properties dialog box:

- *Color*—Changes the color of the top, bottom, left, and right borders of a cell or cells.
- *Light Border*—Changes the color of the bottom and right borders of a cell or cells.
- *Dark Border*—Changes the color of the top and left borders of a cell or cells.

Note

Cell border colors will not display in tables that have a border width of 0. You will need to adjust the border width setting in the Table Properties dialog box to see cell border colors.

Changing Cell Backgrounds

Just as you can change the background colors of an entire table, you can also change background colors of one or more cells in the table. The Background section of the Cell Properties dialog box contains the following settings for this purpose:

5

- *Color*—Applies a solid background color to the selected cell or cells.
- *Use Background Picture*—Applies a background picture to the selected cell or cells. Note that this feature will not display in older browsers. If you use background pictures in tables, test their appearance in a few different browsers to ensure that your entire table content is legible.

Exercise 5.4: Creating an Advanced Table and Adding Content

This next exercise will demonstrate all that you've learned so far in this chapter. Not only that, but you'll also get to add some content into the table as you go along. Figure 5.18 shows what the final result of your table should look like.

FIGURE 5.18

The table that you will create in this exercise.

1. Create a new blank page using the New Page icon in the Standard toolbar.
2. Choose Table, Insert, Table. The Table Properties dialog box appears. Enter the following settings to create a table with four rows and three columns, no border, and that spans 100 percent across the width of the browser window:

Rows:	4
Columns:	3
Alignment:	Default
Border Size:	0
Cell Padding:	10
Cell Spacing:	5
Specify Width:	100, In Percent

3. Choose OK. The table appears on your page.

4. Position your mouse along the left side of the table, where it turns into a selection pointer. Click to select all of the cells in the first row.

5. Choose Table, Merge Cells (or right-click and choose Merge Cells from the pop-up menu). All of the cells in the first row are merged into one large cell.

6. Click inside the cell in the first row and choose Heading 2. Enter `Bill's Travel Bureau: The Best in International Travel.`

7. Press Enter, and add the following normal text: `Book one of the following trips by September 1, 1999. Hurry, they are filling quickly.`

8. Click in the first cell in the second row. Choose Heading 2 and enter `London!.`

9. Click in the second cell in the third row. Choose Heading 2 and enter `France!.`

10. Click in the first cell in the last row. Choose Heading 2 and enter `Egypt!.`

11. Click inside the `London` cell, and choose Table, Select, Cell. Shift-click to add the `France` and `Egypt` cells to the selection.

12. Position the insertion point over one of the selected cells and right-click. Choose Cell Properties from the pop-up menu. Select the following properties for the cell:

Horizontal Alignment:	Center
Vertical Alignment:	Middle
Background:	Color: Yellow (first color in second row)

13. Choose OK to apply the settings to the selected cells.

14. Enter the following text in the cell located at the right of the `London` cell:

    `Visit the Big Ben, Winchester Cathedral, London Tower and more, including a trip to Stonehenge.`

15. Enter the following text in the cell located at the left of the `France` cell:

    `See Paris (the City of Lights) - the Louvre, the Moulin Rouge, and the Eiffel Tower. Includes a trip to Notre Dame Cathedral.`

5

16. Right-click in the cell you just completed and choose Cell Properties from the pop-up menu. Choose `Right` from the Horizontal Alignment options and then choose OK to exit the Cell Properties dialog box. The text aligns to the right of the cell.

17. Enter the following text in the cell located at the right of the `Egypt` cell:

    Who can resist the enigmatic Sphinx and the Pyramids of Giza? Will you encounter the curse of the mummy?

18. Click and drag to select the three remaining empty cells in the third column. Choose Table, Merge Cells (or right-click and choose Merge Cells from the pop-up menu) to merge them into one large cell.

19. Click inside the large cell you just created, and choose Bullets from the Format toolbar. Enter the following bulleted list items:

    Low Prices
    Fast Service
    Complete packages include round trip air fare and 2 meals per day
    Come see us today

20. Choose File, Save (Ctrl+S) or click the Save icon in the Standard toolbar. Save the page with a page title of `Bill's Travel Bureau` and a filename of `bills.htm`.

Note

> Without a doubt, Bill's Travel Bureau page would attract more attention with graphics and color added to the table. You'll work with this table more in tomorrow's exercises, so be sure to save it!

Inserting a Table Within a Table

There are times when a single table won't accomplish what you want to do with your layout. Say, for example, you want to display some information in three columns, and other information in four columns. After you do your splitting and merging of cells, you discover that the layout isn't quite what you expected.

In cases like this, it might be easier to insert a table within a table. These are called *nested tables* and they are often used to build very complex layouts in Web pages.

Here's a good example of using a table within a table. This isn't an "official" exercise, so if you want to try this on Bill's Travel Bureau page, don't save the changes to it.

Take a look at the table in Bill's Travel Bureau page. Right now, each column in the table spans 33 percent of the table width. If you split one of these cells in an attempt to make four cells in a row, what you'd end up with is two cells at 33 percent width, and two cells at 16.5 percent width. But you want your new row to contain four cells, each of which span 25 percent of the width of the table. An example is shown in Figure 5.19.

FIGURE 5.19

You can create more complex tables by inserting tables within tables.

Here's what you would do to accomplish your objective with Bill's Travel Bureau page:

1. Place the insertion point in the first row of the table.

2. Choose Table, Insert, Rows or Columns. The Insert Rows or Columns dialog box appears.

> **Note**
>
> When you insert rows or columns in your table, the new row uses the same number of cells as the row that you select to insert before or after. This is important to keep in mind when you insert new rows in tables that have split and merged cells.

3. Select the Rows radio button.

4. In the Number of Rows field, enter 1.

5. In the Location field, choose Below Selection.

6. Choose OK. A new cell appears in the second row.

7. Choose Table, Insert, Table. The Insert Table dialog box appears.

8. Enter the following settings in the Insert Table dialog box:

   Rows: 1

   Columns: 4

Alignment:	Default
Border Size:	0
Cell Padding:	5
Cell Spacing:	0
Specify Width:	100, In Percent

9. Choose OK to add the new table inside the original table. Now you have a row with four evenly spaced cells.

Other Table Tasks

I'll briefly mention a handful of other table commands that you might find useful. Two of these commands help you convert tables to text, or text to tables. You'll also learn how to delete cells, rows, columns, or entire tables.

Converting Tables to Text

FrontPage 2000 provides the capability to convert tables to text. When you convert a table to text, the data that was once contained in a cell is reformatted into a normal paragraph.

To convert a table to text, follow these steps:

1. Click anywhere inside the table that you want to convert.
2. Choose Table, Convert, Table to Text. The cells in your table appear on your page as normal paragraphs, with data from each cell appearing on a separate line. Figure 5.20 shows a portion of the Bill's Travel Bureau table after it has been converted to text.

Converting Text to Tables

Just as you can convert tables to text, you can also go the other way. FrontPage allows you to convert text into tables. This is ideal for text files that have been exported from database programs.

The key to good conversion is in choosing what delimiter defines each row and column in your table. You have one of four options to use as a delimiter:

- Choose Paragraphs if each line of text appears on a separate line.
- Choose Tabs if you have separated the data for each cell by tabs.
- Choose Commas if the data for each cell is separated by commas.
- Choose Other if the data for each cell is separated by another indicator, and enter the indicator that separates each item in the Other field.

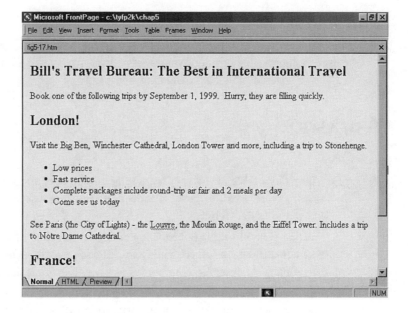

To convert text to a table, follow these steps:

1. Select the text that you want to convert into a table.

2. Choose Table, Convert, Text to Table. The Convert Text to Table dialog box appears.

3. Choose how you want to convert the table to text, based on how the items in your text are separated.

4. Choose OK. The text converts into a table.

Deleting Tables and Cells

To delete a table from your page, you need to select the entire table. To select the entire table, use one of these methods:

- Place the insertion point in one of the cells in the row you want to select and choose Table, Select, Table.

- Select all rows and columns in the table using any of the methods mentioned in the sections "Selecting Rows" or "Selecting Columns," earlier in this chapter.

It's pretty easy to delete cells from your table. All you have to do is select the cells, rows, or columns you want to delete and press the Delete key or use the Delete Cells button in the Tables toolbar. You can also use the Table, Delete Cells command.

Summary

This chapter covered the basics of table creation and gave you a glimpse of how they can be used to improve the layout of your pages. I hope I've started the wheels turning now that you've covered so much ground in this chapter.

Workshop

Q&A

Q **I inserted a table at the very beginning of my page, and now I want to add text up there. I can't figure out how to do that because my cursor won't go above the table. Help!!!**

A Position your cursor at the beginning of the top-left cell of the table (or click anywhere inside the top-left cell and choose Home to get to its beginning). Then press Ctrl+Enter. The insertion point moves to a new line immediately above your table.

Q **I'm using a background that puts a really neat design at the left side of my page. I used the Increase Indent button to position my text beyond that border, but some browsers put the text at the beginning of the page over the border. How can I fix that?**

A Put your page contents in a table. Create a table that contains one row and two columns and spans 100 percent of the page width. Create a spacer graphic that is as wide or slightly wider than the design on the left side of your background. This spacer graphic doesn't have to be that tall—even one pixel will do. After you insert the spacer graphic into the left table cell, use the Make Transparent button on the Image toolbar to add transparency so it doesn't show.

Q **I formatted my tables for 50 percent width and aligned them to the right side of my page. Now I want to put text on my page at the left side of the table, but I can't. What gives?**

A Did you remember to set the Float setting in the Table Properties dialog box? This will let you put text along the side of the table and allows it to wrap around the table as necessary.

You can also add an extra set of cells at the left side of the table, and place your text inside the new cell. This option will not wrap text around the table.

Q **I used background images in my tables and table cells, but I can't see them in some of my browsers. How come?**

A Background images in tables and cells are features that were introduced by Microsoft Internet Explorer 3.0. They are considered "browser-specific features" rather than being a part of the HTML specification. Because browser-specific features are not an official part of the HTML specification, other browser manufacturers support them at their own discretion. If you favor using a specific browser and its features when you design your pages, note on your site that your pages are best displayed using that browser. However, it's a good rule of thumb to also make sure that your pages still look good in other browsers!

Quiz

1. What are the basic elements that make up a table?
2. When is it good to use a borderless table?
3. What is the difference between cell padding and cell spacing?
4. When specifying the width of a table, which is most commonly used: percentage widths or pixel widths? Why?
5. What are nested tables, and what are they used for?

Exercises

1. Go to some of your favorite Web sites, and try to learn how tables enhance the appearance of their pages. Select one or two of them, and try to reproduce the tables yourself. No fair importing the page into FrontPage or peeking at the code!
2. Typically, newsletters and newspapers present information in multiple columns. Try your hand at creating a "front page" of a newspaper, putting titles, text, and images into two or three columns.

Answers to Quiz

1. The basic parts of a table are border, caption, cells, rows, and columns.
2. Borderless tables are good to use when you want to lay out several graphics side by side and give the illusion that they are one complete graphic.
3. Cell padding defines the amount of space between the cell border and the contents of the cell. Cell spacing defines the amount of space in between the cells.
4. Percentage widths are most commonly used because people browse the Internet at different resolutions. Percentage-width tables resize themselves to accommodate the varying resolutions.
5. Nested tables are tables inserted within tables. They are typically used for advanced page layouts, in situations where splitting and merging cells will not result in the desired outcome.

5

DAY 6

Adding Images, Sound, and Video

How many of you surfed the World Wide Web about three or four years ago? You might remember that most Web pages were displayed on gray backgrounds and contained little in the way of graphics. Today, things are much different. Due to advances in Web technologies and in the HTML specification, graphics and multimedia are running rampant on the Web. Everyone is taking notice. You're able to design past that old (and boring) WWW-gray background color. You can use tiled background images, specify custom colors, use images for links, and even place animation, video, and sound on Web pages.

Today you'll learn how to spice up your pages with images and multimedia, including how to

- Insert images and video files into your Web pages
- Import images and files into your FrontPage Web
- Convert images to graphic formats that most browsers can display

- Align text and images in several different ways
- Modify the rotation, position, size, and appearance of images
- Create transparent GIFs that make your images look like they're floating on your page background

Exercise 6.1: Inserting Images onto Your Page

Yesterday you designed Bill's Travel Bureau page, which includes a table that displays information about trips to exciting places. For your first exercise today, you'll dress up that page with images. If you didn't work through the example, there is a completed version of the page located on the CD-ROM that accompanies this book.

Importing Images into Your Web

When you add external content, such as an image or sound file, to your Web page, the external file doesn't actually become a part of the Web page. Instead, your Web page contains an internal link to the external file.

In most cases, you'll probably want to link to images and other media that are stored on your own Web site. When adding images to Web pages, you may find that it is much easier to import your images into a Web before you place them on your pages. This way, you are ensured that the links to the images are calculated correctly.

It's not that difficult to import files and images into a Web, and we'll start off with that process first. You'll create a new empty Web named chap06 in the tyfp2k directory on your hard drive. Then you'll import Bill's Travel Bureau page and the related images into your new Web.

To create the Web and import the files, follow these steps:

1. Choose File, New, Web. The New dialog box appears.
2. From the list of available templates in the Web Sites tab, select Empty Web.
3. In the Specify the Location of the New Web field, enter **c:\tyfp2k\chap06**.
4. Choose OK to create the Web.
5. Choose File, Import. The Import dialog box shown in Figure 6.1 appears.
6. Click the Add File button. The Add File to Import List dialog box appears.
7. From the Look In drop-down menu at the top of the dialog box, select your CD-ROM drive. Locate the tyfp2k\chap06\samples folder, and highlight bills.htm. Click the Open button to add the file to your import list.
8. From the Import dialog box, choose OK to import the Web page into your Web.

FIGURE 6.1

The Import dialog box allows you to import files into your current Web.

9. Now, from the Folder List, highlight the images folder in your new Web.

10. Again, choose File, Import. The Import dialog box appears.

11. Click the Add File button to open the Add File to Import List dialog box again. Locate the tyfp2k\chap06\samples folder on the CD-ROM and highlight four images: bills.jpg, egypt.jpg, england.jpg, and france.jpg. Click the Open button to add the files to your import list.

12. Choose OK to import the images into your Web's images folder.

Inserting Images from Your Current Web

Now that the images and the Web page are stored in your Web site, you'll find it very easy to place the images onto the Web page. In the process, we'll make a couple of minor changes to the previous Web page to make it look better with the new images that you'll add.

You use the Picture dialog box, shown in Figure 6.2, to insert an image onto your pages. The Picture dialog box enables you to insert images from several locations. In this example, you will insert the images from your current Web.

To insert the images into the table on Bill's Travel Bureau page, follow these steps:

1. Choose View, Folder List (if the Folder List is not already displayed). Double-click bills.htm to open the page in the editor.

2. The insertion point should default to the beginning of the first line, which is Bill's Travel Bureau: The Best in International Travel. (If it doesn't, click at the beginning of the line to position the insertion point there.)

3. Choose Insert, Picture, From File. The Picture dialog box appears. By default, the dialog box opens to the default folder in your current Web. Double-click the images folder to select it. You will see the four images you imported in the previous section, as shown in Figure 6.2.

6

FIGURE 6.2

Use the Picture dialog box to insert an image on your page.

4. Highlight `bills.jpg`. A preview of the image appears in the preview pane at the right side of the dialog box. The URL field displays `images/bills.jpg`.

5. Choose OK. The image appears on your page and the insertion point appears immediately after it. Press Enter to move the title to the next line (otherwise, when you view your Web page at higher resolutions, the title of the page will display immediately after the graphic you just inserted).

6. Click before the word `London!` in the first yellow cell. Using steps 2 through 4 as a guide, insert the `england.jpg` image into this cell. Press Enter after the image appears to move the text to the next line in the cell.

7. Click before the word `France!` in the second yellow cell. Insert the `france.jpg` image into this cell. Press Enter after the image appears to move the text to the next line in the cell.

8. Click before the word `Egypt!` in the third yellow cell. Insert the `egypt.jpg` image into this cell. Press Enter after the image appears to move the text to the next line in the cell.

9. The yellow background that surrounds the cells doesn't look too good with those images, so we'll change the background color of those cells back to the default white page background. Click in the first yellow cell and choose Table, Select, Cell. Use Ctrl-click to select the other two yellow cells.

10. Choose Table, Properties, Cell to open the Cell Properties dialog box. From the Background section of the Cell Properties dialog box, select Automatic from the Color drop-down menu. Choose OK to exit the Cell Properties dialog box.

11. Choose File, Save to save the changes to the Web page. Your page should look similar to the example in Figure 6.3 when viewed in Internet Explorer.

FIGURE 6.3

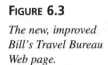

FIGURE 6.3

The new, improved Bill's Travel Bureau Web page.

Images: To Be or Not to Be?

6

As you can see, the addition of images on Bill's Travel Bureau Web page made a dramatic improvement to the appearance of the page. Not only does it look more professional, but also the images draw the eye toward the text that describes the trips he has to offer.

Now that you know how easy it is to insert images into your pages, I'll be bold and tell you about some of the design considerations you should think about when you use images. One of the keys to good Web page design is to keep your pages as lean and mean as you possibly can. Keep in mind that not everyone who browses the Web has a fast modem, a cable, or an ISDN connection.

Let me show you an extreme example of what *not* to do. On the CD-ROM that accompanies this book, you will find a page that our fictitious "Bill" designed himself. The page is located in the chap06 directory, and is named nono.htm.

Open this file in your Web browser by double-clicking the filename. Then you'll understand what was wrong with Bill's *very long* Web page, the beginning of which is shown in Figure 6.4.

FIGURE 6.4

Our fictitious Bill made a gallant attempt at a Web page, but he made some very common design errors.

As you can see, Bill liked the idea of putting images on his pages. He liked it *a lot*, but he couldn't understand why his Web page wasn't getting the responses he'd hoped for.

While there isn't anything really wrong with how the Web page looks in your browser, Bill broke some of the "unwritten codes" that many new Web page designers break. Notice how much you have to scroll to get from the top to the bottom of the page. Also, think about how long it will take for the browser to completely load all of the images on the page. Bill's customers noticed these things, too, and many of them lost patience and moved on to another travel bureau site. That wasn't good for Bill's site—and it won't be good for your site, either.

Note   FrontPage includes a report option that lists the "slow pages" in your Web. This is discussed in more detail in Day 21, "Tracking and Maintaining Your Webs."

As you work with images and multimedia, pay close attention to the "weight" of your page. FrontPage would definitely consider Bill's first attempt a "slow page." Fortunately, there are ways to keep track of them. The most immediate way is to look at the status bar in the Page Editor. As you insert content into a page, the estimated download time displays in the right corner of the status bar, as shown in Figure 6.5.

FIGURE 6.5

The FrontPage status bar informs you of how long it takes to download your Web pages at specific connection speeds.

Tip

FrontPage displays the estimated download time of your current page in the status bar. You can select one of several connection speeds: 14.4, 28.8, 56.6, ISDN, T1, or T3. Simply click the status bar over the text that reads *nn* seconds over *speed* (where *nn* is the number of seconds and *speed* is the connection speed). A pop-up menu appears, and you can select one of the other speed options. The number of seconds will adjust to reflect the new estimated download time.

For comparison's sake, I've also included an "improved" version of Bill's design in the chap06 Web on the CD-ROM. The better version involves three pages: better.htm, ustrips.htm, and int-trips.htm. While the total download time of these three pages isn't much less than the original design, each of the pages focuses on items that have something in common. One page introduces the new trips, a second page displays United States trips, and a third page displays international trips. Now the reader can choose the information that he or she is most interested in and ignore what he doesn't want to see.

Note

I've also included some additional "design tips" on the CD-ROM. Open the imagetips.htm file in the chap06 Web to view them.

6

Web Page Graphics Formats

FrontPage allows you to import several different graphics formats into your Web pages. However, most Web browsers commonly use one of two image formats—GIF or JPEG. A third image format, PNG, is becoming increasingly popular, but it is only supported in more recent browsers.

Note

FrontPage automatically converts images that contain 256 or fewer colors to GIF format. Images that use more than 256 colors are automatically converted to JPEG format.

GIF Images

When your images contain 256 or fewer colors, GIF graphics format is best to use. Some examples of images that are best suited for GIF format are

Cartoons

Line art and line drawings

Small icons

Buttons

Horizontal rules

Bullets

Small-to-medium-sized header graphics

In general, if your image contains only a few colors or has large areas of solid color, GIF format is probably your best choice. Black and white or monochromatic images are also suitable for GIF format, but may result in faster download times if you choose to save them in JPG format instead.

JPEG Images

Several graphics formats, such as TIF, TGA, BMP, and PCX, can contain as many as 16.8 *million* colors. These are most commonly referred to as *true-color* images. However, in their native formats, true-color images consume mass quantities of disk space. For example, a 600×400 true-color TGA image can soak up a whopping 700KB of disk space on your hard drive.

Tip

You can set the amount of JPG compression on an image by using settings in the Picture Properties dialog box.

The JPEG file format uses image compression to significantly reduce the size of true-color images. The size and quality of the file is controlled by the amount of compression you apply to the image. Higher amounts of compression make an image smaller in file size, but reduce the image quality. Too much compression will leave objectionable artifacts in your image. You'll need to experiment to find settings that strike a good balance between image size and appearance. If you use compression settings wisely, you won't see a lot of difference between the original true-color image and the compressed JPG version.

Tip

Once you compress a true-color image and save it as a JPG image, the data that was in your original file cannot be put back in. It's not a good idea to recompress an image that has already been saved in JPG format, because it further reduces image quality. Keep a copy of the original true-color image format (TGA, TIF, PCX, BMP, or other format) on hand as well, in case you have to make changes in the future.

PNG Images

The PNG graphics format is a relatively new graphics format that was developed in 1995 in response to a controversy that arose over the GIF file format. The earliest support for PNG images was supported in browsers through the use of plug-ins. More recent versions of Internet Explorer and Netscape Navigator provide built-in support to display PNG images.

The PNG format works equally well on true-color and 256-color images. File sizes are comparable to those that you can achieve with JPG compression.

Setting General Picture Properties

After you insert an image on your page, you can specify several properties for the image. You use the General tab in the Picture Properties dialog box (shown in Figure 6.6) to change the image type, specify alternative representations, or choose the URL to which that the image links. To open the Picture Properties dialog box, right-click your image and select Picture Properties from the pop-up menu.

6

Note

You'll learn more about using images as links in Day 7, "Adding Links and Bookmarks."

FIGURE 6.6

*Use the General tab in
the Image Properties
dialog box to alter the
image type, specify
alternative representa-
tions, and designate a
link or target frame.*

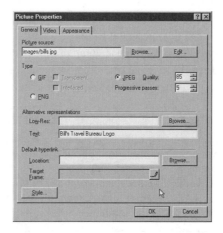

Choosing a File Type

The Type section of the General tab allows you to convert one image format to another
or to specify advanced settings for your images. There are several choices here:

- *Transparent* GIF files are images that contain transparent areas. They give the
  appearance that the image is floating over your page background. To create a transparent GIF, select GIF for file type, and check Transparent. You can select the
  transparent color by using the Transparent Color icon in the Pictures toolbar.

- *Interlaced* GIF files are progressively rendered as your browser downloads the
  image. Normally, an image doesn't appear until it is fully downloaded. However,
  an interlaced GIF file displays information in the image as it's downloaded to your
  browser. Interlaced GIF files appear blocky at first, but gradually give way to a
  clearer image as the image is downloaded. To create an interlaced GIF, select GIF
  for file type, and check the Interlaced check box in the General tab.

- Choose PNG to save or convert your image to PNG format. Note that older
  browsers may not support this format at all. Other browsers support them only if
  you include an appropriate plug-in.

- Choose JPEG to save or convert your image to JPEG format. The amount of compression applied to an image can be adjusted by varying the Quality setting. Higher
  values produce sharper images, but they increase the size of the file. Lower values
  reduce file size, but also affect the appearance of the images.

- *Progressive JPEG* images are similar to interlaced GIF files, in that a lower-quality
  representation of the image appears first. The browser loads a progressive JPEG in
  multiple steps, presenting a better quality image with each pass. To create a progressive JPEG image, enter a value higher than 0 in the Progressive passes field.

Using Alternative Representations

While a browser downloads an image, it's a good idea to display something on the page in its place. The Alternative Representation section of the General tab provides two options for image alternatives:

- *Low-Res*—You can display a low-resolution version of an image on your Web page while the higher-quality image is downloading. Black and white images or images that contain 16 or fewer colors are generally much smaller and download more quickly than images with many colors. To specify a low-resolution image, use the Browse button in the Alternative Representations section of the General tab to select another image from your Web or hard drive.

- *Text*—While the browser downloads an image, the text you specify in this field appears within the space that is allocated for the image. It's generally a good idea to include an alternative text description on all of your images. This is especially true when you use images as links to other pages in your Web. This way, if visitors have image display turned off in their browsers, they can still determine to which page the image was supposed to link.

Exercise 6.2: Converting Images with FrontPage

In the following exercise, you'll add a true-color image to a blank Web page, and you'll convert the image to a progressive JPG image.

To complete the exercise, follow these steps:

1. Click the New Page icon in the Standard toolbar to create a new Web page. A new page opens in the page editor.

2. Click the `images` folder in your Web. Use the File, Import command to import `true02.tif` into the images folder. This image is located in the `tyfp2k\chap06\samples` folder on the CD-ROM that accompanies this book.

3. Now here's a really easy way to place images on your pages. If you don't already have the folder list displayed, choose View, Folder List to display the folders at the left side of the page editor (see Figure 6.7). Expand the `images` folder in your Web to see all of the images that are saved in it.

5. Click and drag the `true02.tif` image from the folder list into the page editor. Release the mouse button after you position the image at the top of the Web page.

6. To convert `true02.tif` to a progressive JPG, click the image to select it, and press Alt+Enter on your keyboard (or, right-click on the image and choose Picture Properties from the pop-up menu). The Picture Properties dialog box appears, opened to the General tab.

6

FIGURE 6.7

When you display the Folder List alongside the page editor, you can drag and drop files from the folder list into your pages.

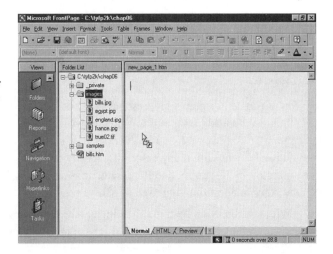

7. From the Type section of the General tab, select the following options:

    JPEG

    Quality: 90

    Progressive passes: 3

8. In the Alternative representations section, enter **Smiling Man** in the Text field. (Note that if you were going to use this image as a link, you'd want to add text that is more descriptive of the page to which the image links.)

9. Choose OK. The appearance of the image changes slightly due to the image compression.

Note

If your JPEG image contains too many objectionable artifacts, you may have set the Quality setting too low. At this point, before you save the page, it's very easy to fix the problem. First, choose Edit, Undo Properties (or press Ctrl+Z) to revert back to the original uncompressed image. Then repeat steps 7 through 9, but increase the Quality setting until you find results that are more pleasing.

Tip

Use the Restore button on the Pictures toolbar to restore your image to its original state if you don't like the results of your changes.

You can also undo one action at a time by choosing Edit, Undo Edit Image (Ctrl+Z) from FrontPage.

10. Choose File, Save, Ctrl+S, or click the Save button on the Standard toolbar. The Save As dialog box appears.

11. Save the page with a page title of **Converting Images**, and a filename of **convert.htm**.

12. After you press the Save button, the Save Embedded Files dialog box appears (see Figure 6.8). This dialog box also appears when you insert images that do not already exist in your Web, or when you make any changes to your image using the Pictures toolbar.

FIGURE 6.8

The Save Embedded Files dialog box appears when you add images from outside your Web or make changes to the images that you have placed on your page.

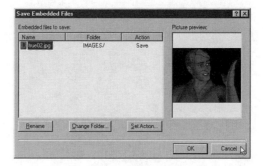

13. The filename defaults to **true02.jpg**. (You can change the filename, if you prefer, by clicking the Rename button. If you enter a new filename, be sure to add the **.jpg** extension at the end of the filename.)

14. Verify that the **images/** folder appears in the Folder column of the Embedded files to save list. If it doesn't, click the Change Folder button. Use the Look In box in the Change Folder dialog box (see Figure 6.9) to select the **images** folder in your current Web. Choose OK to return to the Save Embedded Files dialog box.

15. Choose OK to save the progressive JPG image to your Web. The page is now completely saved.

FIGURE 6.9

The Change Folder dialog box lets you specify the folder in which to save the embedded files on your Web page.

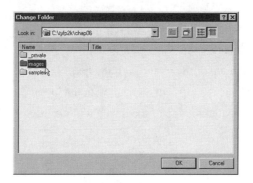

6

Setting Image Appearance Properties

The Appearance tab in the Picture Properties dialog box is shown in Figure 6.10. The settings in this portion of the Picture Properties dialog box allow you to control how text wraps around the image, the thickness of the border that surrounds the image, and how much spacing appears between the image and the text. You can also resize the image to display larger or smaller than it actually is.

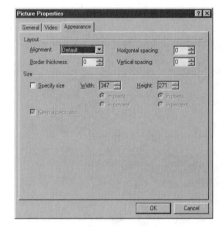

Picture Alignment

The Alignment settings in the Layout section control how the image appears in relation to the text. The options are as follows, and examples of the image settings are shown in Internet Explorer in Figure 6.11:

- *DEFAULT*—When no other style properties are applied, aligns the image to the left of the text.
- *LEFT*—Aligns the image to the left of the text. Good for wrapping text around an image.
- *RIGHT*—Aligns the image to the right of the text. Another choice for wrapping text around an image.
- *TOP*—Aligns the top of the image with the text.
- *TEXTTOP*—Aligns the top of the image with the top of the tallest text in the line.
- *MIDDLE*—Aligns the middle of the image with the text.

- *ABSMIDDLE*—Aligns the middle of the image to the middle point of the top and bottom text in the line.
- *BASELINE*—Aligns the bottom of the image with the baseline of the current text line.
- *BOTTOM*—Aligns the bottom of the image with the text.
- *ABSBOTTOM*—Aligns the bottom of the image with the bottom of the current line.
- *CENTER*—Aligns the bottom of the image to the center of the current line.

FIGURE 6.11

Examples of image alignment settings.

6

Border Thickness

You can use the Border thickness setting in the Alignment tab to add or remove a border around any image. Simply enter a value, in pixels, for how wide you want a border to be. This draws a solid border around the image. Don't make your border too wide. Most professional Web designers avoid them entirely. Anything wider than 2 or 3 pixels might be too distracting.

Horizontal and Vertical Spacing

The Horizontal spacing and Vertical spacing settings specify the number of pixels of whitespace between your image and the text on your page. For example, if you have an image that is aligned on the left side of the page, and you want text to wrap to the right and beneath the image, you can increase the Horizontal spacing and Vertical spacing to make the image stand out more. Figure 6.12 shows two examples of Horizontal spacing and Vertical spacing settings and border thickness.

FIGURE 6.12

Horizontal and vertical spacing settings control the amount of whitespace between an image and the text that surrounds it.

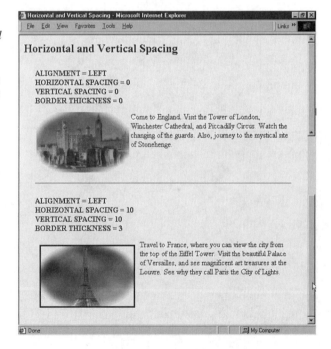

Modifying Your Image with FrontPage

The buttons on the Picture toolbar (shown in Figure 6.13) allow you to make several really interesting modifications to the images on your Web pages, all from within FrontPage. Many of the commands on the Pictures toolbar are not available in the FrontPage menus. However, don't overlook them—you'll learn in the following exercises that the buttons allow you to make some nice enhancements and changes to your images while you are working on your Web pages in FrontPage.

While FrontPage allows you to make several interesting modifications to the images you place on your pages, you should note that most Web developers prefer to use a graphics application to make modifications to images. FrontPage is primarily a Web page editing and management tool, and it succeeds well in that regard. However, you will achieve better results if you use a graphics software package to develop and revise your images. Adobe Photoshop, Fractal Design Painter, Paint Shop Pro, and Corel PhotoPaint are among the most popular graphics applications.

Note

There is one important thing to mention. If you have multiple copies of an image on your Web page (for example, if you use an image several times for buttons or icons), *all other instances* of the image with the same filename will update with the same changes you make to the first instance.

When you click an image to edit it, the Pictures toolbar should automatically appear at the bottom of your FrontPage workspace. If it does not appear, choose the View, Toolbars, Pictures command from FrontPage.

There's a bit of a dilemma when using the Pictures toolbar to modify JPG images, however. Let's say you place a JPG image on your page. Then you rotate it with the Rotate Left button in the Pictures toolbar. It's not the same image anymore because you changed the dimensions of the image by rotating it.

When you save your Web page, FrontPage prompts you to resave the image to your Web. As I mentioned earlier in this chapter, it's not a good idea to recompress a JPG image. Doing so removes even more data from an image that has already lost some of its data during the first conversion to JPG. The image will lose some of its clarity. If you try to circumvent additional compression by increasing the Quality setting to 100, the byte size of the file increases—sometimes considerably.

6

FIGURE 6.13

The Pictures toolbar provides commands that let you make changes to the images on your Web pages from within FrontPage 2000.

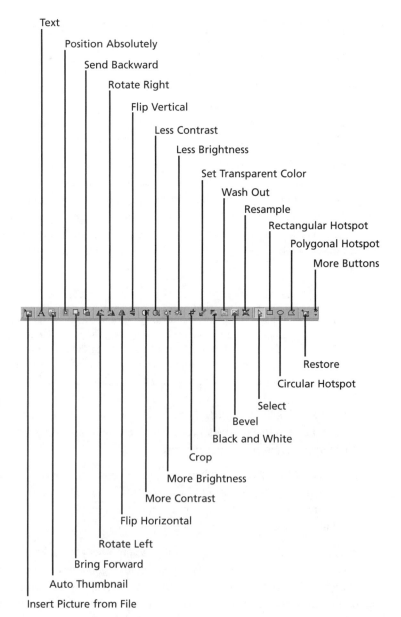

Text

Position Absolutely

Send Backward

Rotate Right

Flip Vertical

Less Contrast

Less Brightness

Set Transparent Color

Wash Out

Resample

Rectangular Hotspot

Polygonal Hotspot

More Buttons

Restore

Circular Hotspot

Select

Bevel

Black and White

Crop

More Brightness

More Contrast

Flip Horizontal

Rotate Left

Bring Forward

Auto Thumbnail

Insert Picture from File

...fications with the Pictures
...less, of course, you apply
...k of how the modifica-
...ntained fewer than 256
...mples use GIF images.

...ntation of your image.
...wise or flip your image
...6.14. These changes can

...k the Open button on the Standard toolbar. The

...s folder on your CD-ROM drive, and open the
...n the page in the page editor.

. Then choose the Rotate Left icon in the
...90 degrees to the left.

4. Click the top-right image to select it. Then choose the Rotate Right icon in the
Pictures toolbar to rotate the image 90 degrees to the right.

5. Click the bottom-left image to select it. Then choose the Flip Horizontal icon in the
Pictures toolbar to flip the image horizontally.

6. Click the bottom-right image to select it. Then choose the Flip Vertical icon in the Pictures toolbar to flip the image vertically.

7. If you choose File, Save, FrontPage will attempt to save the page back to its original location (which is your CD-ROM drive). Instead, choose File, Save As. The Save As dialog box appears.

8. Use the Save In box to locate the `tyfp2k\chap06` folder on your hard drive, and then click Save. The Save Embedded Files dialog box appears.

9. Click the Change Folder button, and select the images folder in your `tyfp2k\chap06` folder. Choose OK to return to the Save Embedded Files dialog box. Then choose OK to save the images with your page.

Changing Picture Size

The Appearance tab of the Picture Properties dialog box contains a setting that we haven't yet covered: the Specify size setting. This setting causes the browser to display an image in a size that is larger or smaller than the actual image is. It is important to note that these settings do not increase or decrease the download time of the image. Therefore, if you insert a 500×300 pixel image on your page, and change the Width and Height settings to 250×150 pixels, the browser will still download the original larger image, but will display it in a smaller space.

To change the dimensions of the image using the Appearance tab in the Picture Properties dialog box, check the Specify Size check box. If you check the Keep Aspect Ratio check box, you can enter a dimension in either the Width or Height field. The other dimension will automatically change appropriately to keep the image in its proper proportion.

There's also a way to resize an image visually while looking at the image in the page editor. First, click the image you want to resize. Resize handles (which appear as small squares of contrasting color at the ends and centers of each side of the image) appear, as shown in Figure 6.15.

- To resize the height and width of the image proportionally, position the mouse over the lower-right resize handle. Click and drag until the image is the size you want, and then release the mouse button.

- To resize the horizontal dimension of the image, drag the right-center or left-center resize handle.

- To resize the vertical dimension of the image, drag the top-center or bottom-center resize handle.

FIGURE 6.15

FIGURE 6.15

To resize an image, click and drag one of the resize handles and release the mouse button when the image is the size you want.

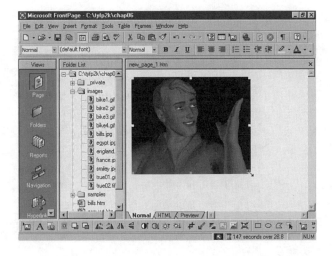

> **Tip**
>
> When you resize an image, it changes the dimensions of the file as it appears on your page, but it does not change the byte size of the file. If you reduce the dimensions in the Size field, use the Resample button on the Pictures toolbar to convert your image to that final size. That way, there is no excess download time.

Cropping Images

You can crop wasted space from the outer edges of your image by using the Crop button on the Pictures toolbar. You can also use the Crop button to crop an image so that it contains a smaller area in a picture. This helps reduce the file size of your image.

To crop your image, follow these steps:

1. Click the image that you want to crop.

2. Click the Crop button on the Pictures toolbar. A rectangular outline appears on your page with resize handles at the corners and centers.

3. Resize the crop rectangle to surround the area in the image that you want to retain, as shown in Figure 6.16.

4. Click the Crop button again. The portion of the image that appeared outside the outline is removed.

5. Click the Resample button to update the new dimensions of the image. This prevents the smaller cropped image from expanding to fit into the original dimensions of the file.

6

FIGURE **6.16**

*You can crop an image
to reduce its size and
download time.*

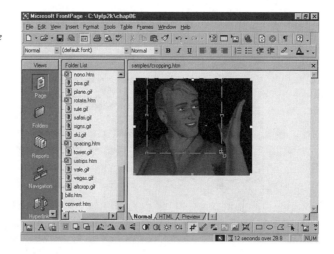

FIGURE **6.16**

*You can crop an image
to reduce its size and
download time.*

Improving Picture Appearance

Use the Contrast and Brightness buttons to increase or decrease the amount of contrast
between light and dark areas in your image or to lighten or darken it. You may need to
select the command more than once to achieve the effect you desire.

- The More Contrast button increases the contrast between the light and dark areas
  in your image.
- The Less Contrast button decreases the contrast between the light and dark areas in
  your image.
- The More Brightness button lightens your image.
- The Less Brightness button darkens your image.

Adding Picture Effects

The Pictures toolbar also allows you to create some interesting effects with your images.

For example, black and white images can sometimes be very effective on Web pages.
Figure 6.17 shows a simple example of this. You can also find the Web page on the
CD-ROM that accompanies this book. It is located in the `tyfp2k\chap06\samples`
folder, and is named `blkwht.htm`.

To create a black-and-white image, use the aptly named Black and White button on the
Pictures toolbar.

FIGURE 6.17

Black-and-white images can be very striking on a Web page.

Tip | You can also use black-and-white images as alternative low-resolution images that display in your Web pages until the color versions are able to load.

For Web pages with white backgrounds, washed out images can also be effective. Also, when you want to superimpose text over your images, it is sometimes difficult to read the text when an image appears beneath it. When the colors in your image are in the middle range, rather than being very light or very dark, it can be difficult to find a text color that is readable over the image.

For cases like this, you can use the Washout button in the Pictures toolbar to create a more pastel version of your image. An example is shown in Figure 6.18.

Adding a Text Label

The text labels in the preceding example were added with the Text button on the Pictures toolbar. Note that if you add text to a JPG image, FrontPage informs you that the image will be converted to GIF format when you save the page. As previously mentioned, this could reduce the number of colors in the image and also can increase its byte size.

If you want to add text to JPG images, it is probably best to add the text to the true-color version of the file. You can also add the text in an image-editing program, such as Microsoft Photo Editor or Adobe Photoshop, *before* you apply JPG compression.

6

FIGURE 6.18

*When you use the
Washout button on the
Pictures toolbar,
superimposed text is
much easier to read.*

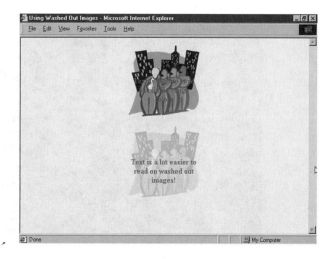

Tip

Use the Bevel button on the Pictures toolbar to create a beveled button or image very quickly. Use this in combination with the Text button (described in the following exercise) to create rectangular navigation buttons for your pages.

To add a text label to a GIF image, follow these steps:

1. Click the image to which you want to add the text label.

2. Click the Text button on the Pictures toolbar. A bounding box appears on the image, with the cursor centered within the box.

3. Enter the text label. The bounding box resizes to accommodate the text you enter. You can adjust the box as shown in Figure 6.19 to position the text exactly where you want it to appear.

4. From the Format toolbar, use the Change Font drop-down menu to change the font face and the Increase Text Size or Decrease Text Size buttons to change the size of the font. Use the Text Color button in the Format toolbar to change the color of the text.

5. To use the text for a hyperlink, choose the Create or Edit Hyperlink button in the Standard toolbar or press Enter when the text label is selected. The Create Hyperlink dialog box appears, and you can create your hyperlink. (This is more fully described in tomorrow's lesson).

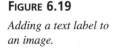

FIGURE 6.19

Adding a text label to an image.

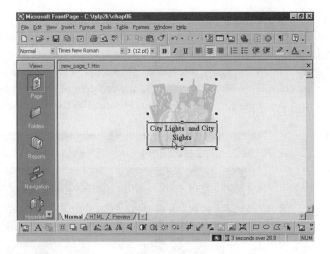

Positioning and Layering Images

The Pictures toolbar also includes a buttons that allow you to position an image *absolutely* and to layer images one atop another. The Position Absolutely button on the Pictures toolbar allows you to visually specify the exact top and left coordinates at which to display an image on your page. The Bring Forward and Send Backward buttons allow you to layer images one over another, much like you would stack cards in a deck.

These features jump ahead a little bit to things that you'll learn more about in Day 10, "Using Style Sheets." Absolute positioning and layering use properties found in cascading style sheets (or CSS for short). It is important to note that these features are only supported in browsers that fully support the HTML 4.0 specification. Among these browsers are Internet Explorer 4.0 (and later) and Netscape Navigator 4.0 (and later).

In the following exercise, you'll learn how to create a transparent GIF image. Then, using the Position Absolutely button, you'll place the image in a precise place on your page and view it in a browser that supports cascading style sheet properties.

Exercise 6.4: Creating a Transparent GIF

When you place a GIF image on your Web page, you can select one of the colors in the image to become a "transparent" color. This allows your page background to show through the image, giving the appearance that the image is floating on your page.

6

When you create transparent GIF images, keep the color or tone of your page background in mind. If your page uses a dark background, choose an image that has a dark background that you can select for your transparent color. Conversely, if your page uses a light background, choose an image that has a light background that you can select for your transparent color. This way you can avoid the problem of seeing "ghosting" or dark outlines around your transparent GIF images. Figure 6.20 shows you exactly what I mean.

FIGURE 6.20

Try to choose transparent colors that are similar to your page backgrounds.

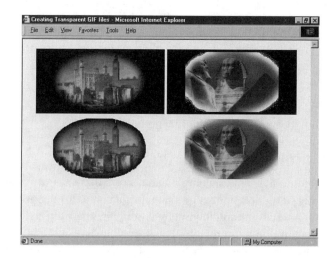

The page that you will work with in the following exercise is located on the CD-ROM that accompanies this book. The page uses a patterned image for a background. You'll import the Web page, the background image, and another GIF image into your chap06 Web, and then will add transparency to the GIF image.

This time, you'll import the Web page and associated images into your Web's main folder and move the images to your images folder. You'll see that FrontPage automatically updates the paths to the files when you move the images.

To complete the exercise, follow these steps:

1. With your chap06 Web opened, choose File, Import. The Import dialog box appears.

2. Click the Add File button. The Add File to Import List dialog box appears.

3. From the Look In drop-down menu at the top of the dialog box, select your CD-ROM drive. Locate the tyfp2k\chap06\samples folder, and highlight trans-gif.htm, back01.gif, and trans.gif. Click the Open button to add the file to your import list.

4. From the Import dialog box, choose OK to import the files into your Web.

5. Double-click the `trans-gif.htm` page to open it in the Page Editor. You should see a patterned background on the Web page.

6. Choose Insert, Picture, From File. From the Picture dialog box, locate the `trans.gif` image in your Web and choose OK to insert the image on your page.

7. Click the `trans.gif` image to select it. The Pictures toolbar appears at the bottom of the page editor.

8. Click the Set Transparent Color button on the Pictures toolbar. The cursor changes to the Set Transparent Color pointer.

9. Click the color in the image that you want to make transparent (in this case, click anywhere where the color white appears). All the pixels that use that color "disappear" from your image, enabling the background color to show through.

Note

If you want to change the transparent color, choose the Set Transparent Color button again and click your new choice.

To remove a transparent color, choose the Set Transparent Color button and click the transparent area in your GIF image; or, uncheck the Transparent check box in the General tab of the Picture Properties dialog box.

10. Now for the fun part. Click the Position Absolutely button in the Pictures toolbar. The cursor changes to a four-directional arrow. Move the image so that it looks like the image colors, the circles and squares in the background. Figure 6.21 shows an example of what your page looks like after you complete this step.

FIGURE 6.21

Use the Position Absolutely button on the Pictures toolbar to position an image in a precise location. Browsers that support HTML 4.0 and cascading style sheets display the image exactly where you specify.

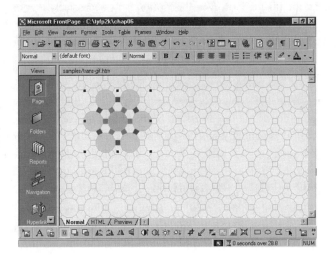

6

11. Choose File, Save. Save the page to your Web.

12. In the last step, I purposely had you save the images into the same directory that you saved the page. I want to demonstrate what happens when you move a page or image to another folder.

    With the page still opened, select the image and press Alt+Enter. Notice in the General tab that FrontPage reports the URL of the transparent GIF file as trans.gif. Choose OK to exit the Picture Properties dialog box.

13. Go to Folders view (View, Folders) and display the folder list (View, Folder List) if it is not already displayed. Select the back01.gif and trans.gif images and drag and drop them into the Web's images folder. FrontPage notifies you that it is renaming the paths to the images.

14. Return to Page view (View, Page), click the image on your Web page, and press Alt+Enter again. FrontPage now shows the image path as images/trans.gif. When you moved your image, FrontPage automatically kept track of the proper relative path to the image file and updated your page as necessary.

15. Choose File, Save to save the updated page to your Web.

Using Auto Thumbnails

Sometimes, you can't avoid placing large images in your Web, especially if you want to display some incredible full-screen images on which you worked very hard. You have two options to display them.

The first option is to create a text link on a separate Web page. The text link can also display the size of the file, so readers have an idea of how long it will take them to download the image. However, this option isn't necessarily a good solution, because the viewer has no idea what the image looks like. They might look at the size of the file and say, "I'm not sure I want to wait to see an image that might not be that good."

Here's where auto thumbnails come in as a great solution. The Auto Thumbnail command creates a small "preview" of what the larger image looks like. Basically, you place the large version on your Web page and then choose the Auto Thumbnail command. FrontPage replaces the large version of the image on your page with a tiny thumbnail version that automatically links to the larger file that is stored separately on your Web site. Users get a preview of your images and can choose those that interest them.

Setting Auto Thumbnail Options

The Auto Thumbnail tab in the Page Options dialog box allows you to set default options for your auto thumbnails. You can specify a default width or height for your thumbnails, set border thickness, or create a beveled edge.

To set default options for your auto thumbnails, follow these steps:

1. From FrontPage, choose Tools, Page Options. The Page Options dialog box appears. Select the Auto Thumbnail tab shown in Figure 6.22.

FIGURE 6.22

Use the Auto Thumbnail tab in the Options dialog box to configure default settings for your auto thumbnails.

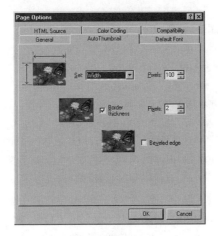

2. From the Set drop-down menu, choose one of the following options for sizing your auto thumbnail:

   - Width creates thumbnails that are always the same width. Enter the number of pixels of width in the Pixels field. When FrontPage creates the thumbnail, the width will always be the value you enter in the Pixels field. The height will be sized appropriately to create a proportionally correct miniature of your original.

   - *Height* creates thumbnails that are always the same height. Enter the number of pixels of height in the Pixels field. When FrontPage creates the thumbnail, the height will always be the value you enter in the Pixels field. The width will be sized appropriately to create a proportionally correct miniature of your original.

   - *Shortest Side* creates thumbnails where the shortest side (height *or* width) is always the value you enter in the Pixels field. The other dimension will be sized appropriately to create a proportionally correct miniature of your original.

   - *Longest Side* creates thumbnails where the longest side (height *or* width) is always the value you enter in the Pixels field. The other dimension will be sized appropriately to create a proportionally correct miniature of your original.

6

3. Because your thumbnail links to the larger image, a border displays around the thumbnail by default. The width of the border is 2 pixels. To change the width, verify that the Border Thickness check box is checked, and enter the desired width in the Pixels field at the right of the check box. To remove the border completely, uncheck the Border Thickness option.

4. If you want your thumbnails to be beveled so that they look more like buttons, check the Beveled Edge check box. Leave the option unchecked to create a flat thumbnail. You cannot adjust the width of the bevel.

5. Choose OK to configure your new settings. They take effect the next time you choose the Auto Thumbnail command.

Exercise 6.6: Creating an Auto Thumbnail

After you set your Auto Thumbnail options as described in the previous section, FrontPage will use these settings each time you generate an auto thumbnail.

In this exercise you'll create a new page. This time, instead of importing an image into your Web first, you'll insert an image directly from the CD-ROM drive. Then you'll create an auto thumbnail of the image. The original image and its thumbnail will be saved to your Web when you save your page.

 Note

> The following exercise demonstrates that you are able to select images from a local or network hard disk, floppy disk, or CD-ROM and place them onto your Web pages. As a general rule, however, FrontPage generates file references more reliably if you import images into your Web first, and then insert them into your pages.

To complete the exercise, follow these steps:

1. With your `tyfp2k/chap06` Web opened, use the New Page icon to create a new blank page.

2. Choose Insert, Picture, From File. The Picture dialog box appears.

3. Click the Select a File on Your Computer icon that appears to the right of the URL field. The Select File dialog box shown in Figure 6.23 appears.

4. Use the Look In box to locate your CD-ROM drive. Choose the `forest.jpg` image that is located in the `tyfp2k\chap06\samples` folder on this book's CD-ROM.

5. Click the image to select it, and then click the Auto Thumbnail button on the Pictures toolbar. The image is reduced to a thumbnail as shown in Figure 6.24.

FIGURE 6.23

Use the Select File dialog box to insert an image from a directory on a local or network hard drive, floppy drive, or CD-ROM.

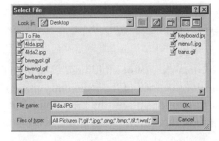

FIGURE 6.24

After you choose the Auto Thumbnail button, a smaller version of the image appears on your page.

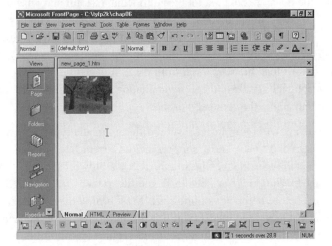

6. Choose File, Save (Ctrl+S). Enter a page title of **Creating Auto Thumbnails**, and a filename of **thumbnail.htm**. Click Save to save the page to your Web.

7. When the Save Embedded Files dialog box appears, you will see two images with similar names. One filename is for the original larger image that you inserted in your page (forest.jpg). The filename for the thumbnail has _small appended to it. Save both of these images to the images folder in your current Web.

8. Click the Preview tab at the bottom of the FrontPage Editor. Click the thumbnail. You should see the larger image open in a different page.

Adding Multimedia to Your Page

Many times you'll see animated graphics or videos on a Web page. Though they add a lot of "weight" to a page, they can be very eye-catching.

Animations add a lot of weight to your page because they are composed of several separate graphics that are saved in sequence into one larger file. The file size of one animation usually isn't as large as it would be to place each frame of the animation on your file individually, but they are considerably larger than a static (non-moving) image of the same size.

Typically, when a Web site contains a lot of multimedia, the Web designer places an announcement on the home page (or one of the main entry pages) that tells readers to expect long download times. He or she places the media on other pages that the visitor can choose to visit. Other times, the visitor clicks a link to download the file.

If your site doesn't contain a lot of multimedia, tasteful and wise use of animation or sound can attract attention and add interest to your pages. The key is not to *overuse* it. Animated logos and icons can enhance any type of Web site. If you place the same animation on several different pages (an animated logo, for example), the browser only needs to download the animation from the first page that includes the animation. Any subsequent pages that use the *same* animation file will load more quickly, providing that the file remains in the browser's cache.

FrontPage allows you to insert several different media types into your pages. However, all browsers don't necessarily support them. Current Internet trends are advancing toward several media types that can be *streamed* into a browser. Streamed media displays on your page as your browser downloads the file, rather than waiting for the entire file to download before it appears on the page. Most browsers require external viewers or plug-ins to display streamed media. You'll learn more about plug-ins and browser enhancements in Day 17, "Adding Advanced Web Technologies."

Currently, the most popular streamed media formats are Real Audio (.ra extension) and Real Movie (.ram) by Real Networks, and Shockwave Flash (.swf) by Macromedia. A more recent format, currently supported by Internet Explorer 5.0, is Advanced Streaming Format (.asf) developed in partnership by Microsoft, Adobe, Intel, Real Networks, and Vivo Software. This new streamed format may prove to be a standard that a larger number of browsers will support in the future.

Exercise 6.7: Adding Video Files

In this exercise, you'll learn about two of the easiest types of animation to add to your pages: animated GIF files and Video for Windows (.avi) animations.

Animated GIF files contain 256 colors or less, and are basically nothing more than a series of GIF images that are displayed in sequence in a single GIF file. The Video for Windows format offers some advantages over animated GIF files. In some cases, the size of an .avi file is much smaller than the equivalent animated GIF file because you can control the amount of compression that is applied to the file. The Video for Windows format also allows you to develop animations that are more realistic because they can use more than 256 colors. In fact, you can create a true-color Video for Windows animation. Another advantage is that Video for Windows animations can also include sound, making them more like a movie.

However, not all browsers can display Video for Windows animations. When you want to display a Video for Windows animation in browsers that support them, you'll probably want to display something in its place if a browser does not display Video for Windows files. The following exercise shows you a workaround that displays an AVI file in Internet Explorer, an animated GIF file in Netscape, and a still image in browsers that do not support Video for Windows files or animated GIFs. For the final exercise in this chapter, you'll open a page that is partially created for you. You'll add an animation to the page.

1. With your `tyfp2k/chap06` Web opened, choose File, Open. The Open File dialog box appears.

2. Use the Look In box to locate the `tyfp2k/chap06/samples` folder on your CD-ROM drive. Highlight the `swinfrno.htm` file and click Open. The page opens in the page editor.

3. Click inside the empty cell in the top row of the table. Choose Insert, Picture, Video. The Video dialog box appears.

4. Click the Select a File on Your Computer button located at the right of the URL field. Use the Select File dialog box to locate the `infrno.avi` animation in the `tyfp2k/chap06/samples` folder on your CD-ROM drive. Highlight the file and choose OK to insert the animation into the table, as shown in Figure 6.25.

FIGURE 6.25

Insert the animation into the top cell in the table.

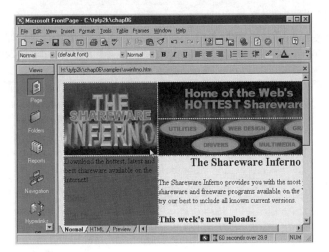

6

5. Choose File, Save As (Ctrl+A). The Save As dialog box appears.

6. Locate the `c:\tyfp2k\chap06` folder. Save the page to your Web with the default page title of **The Shareware Inferno** and filename of **swinfrno.htm**.

7. When the Save Embedded Files dialog box appears, save the three images (`infrno.avi`, `swinf1.jpg`, and `swinf2.jpg`) to the `images` folder in your Web.

   At this point, if you click the Preview tab to preview your page in FrontPage, you'll see the animation move for a brief time and then it will stop. This is because you have to add additional properties to the video. Return to the Page Editor and follow the next steps.

8. Click the animation and press Alt+Enter to open the Video Properties dialog box shown in Figure 6.26.

FIGURE 6.26

Use the Video tab in the Picture Properties dialog box to apply additional settings to the video file.

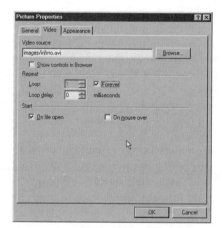

9. Check the Forever check box in the Repeat section of the dialog box. This repeats the animation for as long as the page is displayed in the browser.

Note

Additional options in the video properties dialog box are:

- *Show Controls in Browser*—This displays standard "VCR"-type controls that allow the viewer to start and stop the animation as desired.

- *Loop Delay*—Enter the number of milliseconds that you want to pause an animation before it starts again.

- *Start: On File Open*—The browser begins playing the animation as soon as it is completely downloaded.

- *Start: On Mouse Over*—The animation begins to play when the user places the mouse cursor over the animation.

10. Choose OK to exit the Picture Properties dialog box and apply the loop setting to the video.

11. Click the Save button in the Standard toolbar to update the page to your Web.

There is still one problem to tackle. Microsoft Internet Explorer supports the display of AVI files, but many browsers will not play them at all, or require a plug-in to do so. So I've thought ahead and devised a solution for you.

Also included on the CD-ROM that accompanies this book is an animated GIF file that looks exactly like the AVI file you now have on your page. The filename is `infrno.gif`, and you'll have to import this file into the `images` folder in your Web.

Then you have to edit the code manually, by hand, to add the animated GIF as an alternative for Netscape Navigator. I realize that this is jumping ahead to lessons you'll learn about in the third week, but because you're learning how to insert video on your page, I think it is important to show you how to make things work right in as many browsers as possible. Besides, this will give you a little sneak preview of what it's like to edit HTML code. It's a very simple code addition—I promise!

Continue the exercise as follows:

12. Choose View, Folders, or click the Folders icon in the Views pane.

13. Highlight the images folder and choose File, Import. Click the Add File button and locate `infrno.gif` in the `tyfp2k/chap06/samples` folder on your CD-ROM drive. Click Open to add the file to your import list, and OK to import the file into your `images` folder.

14. Return to Page View, and click the video file. Then, click the HTML tab in the editor. You'll see the code for the video file highlighted in the HTML editor. The code looks like the following:

```
<img border="0" dynsrc="images/infrno.avi" start="fileopen"
loop="infinite" width="200" height="150">
```

15. The `dynsrc` tag tells Internet Explorer that it should display the Video for Windows file as an animation. However, Netscape Navigator and other browsers don't recognize this tag. Instead, you can instruct other browsers to display the animated GIF in its place. To do this, you have to add the relative path to the animated GIF. It's a simple addition, and all you have to do is add `src="images/inferno.gif"` between the `border="0"` and `dynsrc` statements in the previous code. The result should look like the following:

```
<img border="0" src="images/inferno.gif" dynsrc="images/infrno.avi"
start="fileopen" loop="infinite" width="200" height="150">
```

6

16. Choose File, Save, or click the Save button in the Standard toolbar. Use the File, Preview in Browser command to preview the page in Internet Explorer, Netscape Navigator, and other browsers.

Summary

Graphics, when used effectively, can really make a page. On the other hand, when graphics aren't used properly, they can break a page. The best way to learn how to use graphics effectively is to carefully examine pages that catch your eye. In this chapter, you learned how to insert image files into your Web pages and how to modify them from within FrontPage. The workshop that follows will help you remember some of the most important points that you learned today.

Workshop

Q&A

Q I put an animated GIF on my page and then I made it transparent in FrontPage. It doesn't animate anymore. What's wrong?

A When you add transparency to the image, FrontPage recognizes that the image has been altered and saves it over the previous version. However, animated GIFs are special in that they contain more than one image in the file. You only added the transparency to the first frame.

After you save the altered image into your Web, the only frame that remains in the GIF animation is the one to which you added the transparency. It's not something that you did wrong. There are special programs that allow you to assemble animated GIF files, and you have to add transparency to each frame in the animation before it is assembled and placed on your page.

If you want to add transparency to an animated GIF file that doesn't already have it, you'll need to obtain a GIF animation program. If you go to CNET Download.com (`http://www.download.com`) and do a search for `animated GIF`, you'll find links to download several shareware and demo versions of popular GIF animation programs.

Q Can I use an animated GIF or video file for a link?

A You can assign an animated GIF or AVI file as a link as you do any other image. Click the image, click the Create or Edit Link button, and away you go.

Q **I notice that there is a button near the URL field in the Picture dialog box that lets you insert an image from the World Wide Web. Will that page get imported into my Web too?**

A No, it won't. When you use the Use your Web Browser to Select a Picture or File button, FrontPage uses the original URL on the other site as the source of the picture file. If you're linking to images on other sites that you have created on the Internet, you can be fairly safe in using links to other sites on the Web, because you have control of when the pages are moved. However, if you're linking to an image on someone else's site, ask his or her permission to link to it. Keep in mind that URLs change all the time as well.

Quiz

1. Which two alignment settings are good to use when you want to wrap text around an image?

2. What do the horizontal and vertical spacing settings control?

3. When using the buttons on the Pictures toolbar, which graphics format should you avoid making changes to? Why?

4. When you use FrontPage to change the size of an image, what additional step should you remember to perform?

5. True or false: When you position images in a precise location, all browsers can display the image correctly.

Exercises

1. You'll find lots of "top picks" on the Web—some good starting points for "best of the Web" picks are: Project Cool (http://www.projectcool.com), Best of the Web (http://www.botw.org), and Starting Point (http://www.stpt.com). Check out some of the award winners for various ideas. How were colors used on the page? What was it about the page that got your interest? Try to apply the same principles to your own pages.

2. Study other pages on the Internet to see how other people use images on their pages. In particular, notice how long it takes to download pages—how much time seems reasonable to you when you are interested in the topics on the pages? Conversely, how much time seems reasonable when the topic isn't one of keen interest? The answers you learn will help you decide when it's best to keep your pages trim.

6

Answers to Quiz

1. The Left and Right alignment settings allow you to position an image to the left or right side of the page. The text wraps along the other side and bottom of the image.

2. The horizontal and vertical spacing settings control the amount of whitespace between the image and the text that wraps around it.

3. It is generally not a good idea to make modifications to JPG images. Doing so might deteriorate the appearance of the image because it will be compressed again as you save the revised image to your Web.

4. After you resize an image, use the Resample button to set the new dimensions of the image.

5. False. Positioning and layering of images is only supported in browsers that support cascading style sheet properties. Among these are Internet Explorer 4.0 (and later) and Netscape Navigator 4.0 (and later).

DAY 7

Adding Links and Bookmarks

Most of the skills that you've learned this week have been practiced on stand-alone Web pages that don't go anywhere else. You've learned most of the basics for developing text content, but today you'll learn what really makes the World Wide Web work. *The Web is about reaching outward*, and hyperlinks are the fuel behind it all.

Without hyperlinks and bookmarks, you cannot easily enable people to see what is on your site or to find other sites with similar information. With hyperlinks and bookmarks, a user can simply click on text or a graphic to navigate to all types of pages, download files, find newsgroups, and send email.

In today's lesson you will

- Create bookmarks on your pages and navigate to specific places on them
- Create hyperlinks to Web pages, files, and other Web protocols

- Use images as hyperlinks and designate specific areas in an image for navigating to other pages
- Use FrontPage to follow hyperlinks

Hyperlinks and Bookmarks Explained

Hyperlinks and bookmarks help you define areas where you want people to visit, but they serve slightly different purposes. In basic terms, a hyperlink takes your readers to another Web page or file, whereas a bookmark serves as a "destination point" that marks a specific location on the Web page.

To explain further, a hyperlink is a text or graphic area on a Web page that, when clicked, takes you to another location. Hyperlinks can take users to other pages in your own Web site, to pages in other people's sites, to newsgroups, and to other types of files. You can also put a hyperlink on your page to get email delivered to your mailbox. FrontPage helps you easily create hyperlinks from text or images. Figure 7.1 shows a Web page that displays several links to pages on the World Wide Web.

FIGURE 7.1

Hyperlinks are used to take readers to other Web pages or files.

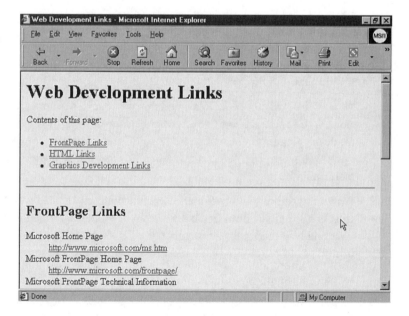

Occasionally, you will want to point your readers to a specific location on a Web page. A *bookmark*, most commonly referred to as an *anchor*, serves to identify a specific place on a Web page by a name. The name of the bookmark is appended to the hyperlink, so that the browser knows which point on the page to position at the top of the browser window. By following one of the hyperlinks shown in Figure 7.1, the reader is taken to the top or bottom of a Web page, or any point in between as shown in Figure 7.2.

FIGURE 7.2

A bookmark, or anchor, marks a specific point at the top or bottom of a Web page, or any point in between.

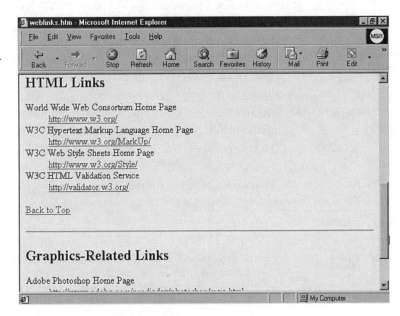

Where You Can Hyperlink

In the following tasks, you'll learn how to create hyperlinks to the most common types of destinations. Table 7.1 shows examples of the many different file and Web protocols that you can hyperlink to, and examples of what the URLs to those destinations might look like.

TABLE 7.1 Web Protocols

Protocol	Description and Sample URL
file	Specifies a file on your local or network computer. Sample URL is `file://localhost/directory/filename.ext`.
ftp	File transfer protocol. Used for a file that is accessible across the Internet. Sample URL is `ftp://www.anyserver.com/downloads/program.zip`.
gopher	Gopher protocol. Creates a link to a directory-based protocol. Sample URL is `gopher://anygopher.tc.university.edu/`.

7

continues

TABLE 7.1 CONTINUED

Protocol	Description and Sample URL
http	Hypertext transfer protocol. Enables Web clients to retrieve information from Web hosts. Sample URL is `http://www.anyserver.com/mylink.htm`.
https	Hypertext transfer protocol with Secure Systems Layer (SSL) support. Enables Web clients to retrieve information from Web hosts using secure connections. Sample URL is `https://www.secureweb.com/mylink.htm`.
mailto	Creates a link to an email address. Sample URL is `mailto:myemail@www.myprovider.com`.
news	Retrieves files from a Usenet newsgroup. Sample URL is `news://news.server.edu/news.alt.example.nosuchgroup`.
telnet	Used for a remote telnet login session. Sample URL is `telnet://yourname:password@yourhost:port`.
wais	Provides hyperlinks to database information on Wide Area Information Servers. Sample URL is `wais://yourhost:port/database`.

Note

Your files might end up on a system that is case sensitive. This is typical of servers that run on UNIX systems. As a general rule, most Web developers use all lowercase letters when they enter URLs to avoid conflicts with case sensitivity.

Exercise 7.1: Hyperlinking to a Page on the World Wide Web

When you create a hyperlink to a page, file, or protocol on the World Wide Web, you can enter its URL in the URL field of the Create Hyperlink or Edit Hyperlink dialog box. You can also select the Use Your Web Browser to Select a Page or File button, shown in Figure 7.3, to locate the page with your browser. The following steps describe both methods.

In the following exercise, you'll create a new Web to store the pages that you'll build in this chapter. Then you'll create a simple Web page that links to two pages on the World Wide Web. You'll enter a URL for the first hyperlink, and use your Web browser to locate a page to link to for the second hyperlink. Follow these steps:

1. Choose File, New, Web. Create a One Page Web and locate it in the `c:\tyfp2k\chap07` directory on your hard drive. A new blank page appears in the page editor.

2. Position the insertion point at the beginning of the page and choose Heading 1 from the Style drop-down list. Type `FrontPage Links`.

3. Press Enter to begin a new line. The line is formatted as a Normal paragraph. Click the Bullets button on the Format toolbar to change the line to a bulleted list item.

4. Type `Microsoft FrontPage Home Page`.

5. Select the text that you just entered, then click the Hyperlink button on the Standard toolbar. The Create Hyperlink dialog box shown in Figure 7.4 appears.

FIGURE 7.3

Select the Use Your Web Browser to Select a Page or File button to link to pages that you find with your Web browser.

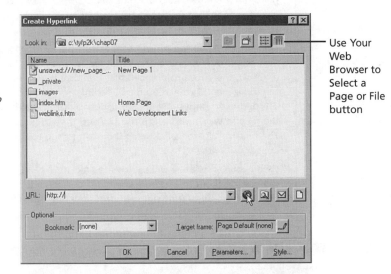

Use Your Web Browser to Select a Page or File button

FIGURE 7.4

The Create Hyperlink dialog box allows you to create hyperlinks to other pages or files in your site or on the World Wide Web.

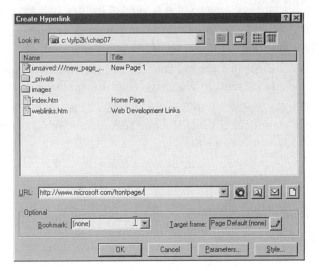

7

6. Enter (the *absolute URL*) to the page or file that you want to link to in the URL field. For the Microsoft FrontPage home page, you enter the URL as follows:

`http://www.microsoft.com/frontpage/`

Note

In the HTML world, there are two ways that you can enter the path to a page or file on the World Wide Web. An *absolute URL* lists the complete path—that is, it displays the protocol, server path, and filename. An example of an absolute URL of a home page is `http://www.foo.com/index.htm`. Another page that resides in an interests folder in the same Web might have an absolute URL of `http://www.foo.com/interests/hiking.htm`.

Relative URLs, on the other hand, are partial URLs, and are used to describe how pages or files relate to each other as far as their location goes. For example, the above-referenced files are located in two different folders in the same Web. If you created a hyperlink from the home page to the interests page, its relative URL would appear as `interests/hiking.htm`. Going the reverse way, an ellipsis is used to designate going back one directory. The relative URL for a link from the hiking page to the home page would appear as `../index.htm`.

When you use relative URLs to create links between pages in your Web, you can publish them to another server without damaging the integrity of the links. Fortunately, FrontPage generates relative URLs for you automatically.

7. Choose OK to exit the Create Hyperlink dialog box. You have created a link to the first Web page.

8. Position the insertion point at the end of the first link. Press Enter to create a new bullet list item.

9. Type **FrontPage Web Presence Providers**.

10. Select the text that you just entered, then click the Hyperlink button on the Standard toolbar. The Create Hyperlink dialog box opens again.

11. Click the Use Your Web Browser to Select a Page or File button located immediately to the right of the URL field. Your default Web browser opens and prompts you to navigate to a URL.

12. Using your browser, navigate to the following URL:

`http://microsoft.saltmine.com/frontpage/wpp/list/`

13. After you reach the URL you want to hyperlink to, return to FrontPage. The URL of the page that you navigated to appears in the URL field of the Create Hyperlink dialog box.

14. Click OK to create the hyperlink.

15. Choose File, Save (Ctrl+S), or click the Save button on the Standard toolbar. The Page title defaults to FrontPage Links, and the filename defaults to frontpage_links.htm. Click Save to save the page to your Web.

Hyperlinking to Files

If you are designing a Web site for a corporate intranet, you can easily create links to pages or files on any computer on the network. Note that these types of links will not be appropriate if your Web site resides on a server that is hosted by an Internet service provider. In this case, links to files on your local or network hard drive will result in a File Not Found message when a user tries to navigate to the page.

When you create a hyperlink to a page, file, or protocol on your local or network hard drive, you can enter its path in the URL field or select the Make a Hyperlink to a File on your Computer button shown in Figure 7.5.

FIGURE 7.5

Select the Make a Hyperlink to a File on Your Computer button to hyperlink to a page or file on your local or network hard drive.

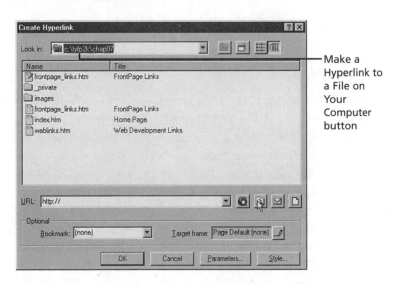

Make a Hyperlink to a File on Your Computer button

After you click the button, the Select File dialog box shown in Figure 7.6 appears. You can use the Look In drop-down list to locate the drive and directory that contains the file to which you want to link. Once you find the proper folder, select the file and choose OK to create your hyperlink.

7

FIGURE 7.6

Use the Select File dialog box to create a hyperlink to a file on your local or network hard drive.

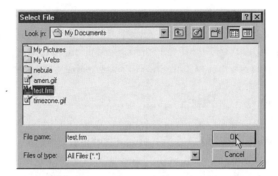

Exercise 7.2: Hyperlinking to New Pages

Right now, you don't have many pages in your Web to which to link. In FrontPage, it's very easy to create a new page and link to it at the same time. When you create a new page in this manner, you can base the new page on one of the many page templates provided with FrontPage 2000.

In this exercise, you'll add some very basic content to the home page in your Web. You'll add hyperlinks to several other pages that will be saved to your current Web site. Use the following steps:

1. Display the Folder List (View, Folder List) if it is not already displayed. Double-click index.htm to open it in the page editor.

2. From the Style drop-down list in the Format toolbar, choose Heading 1. Type
   `My Simple Home Page`.

3. Press Enter to begin a new line. Enter the following text:
   `Welcome to my first home page. I'm just beginning my site, but I have a few pages here that you can visit. Select any of the following pages to view them:`

4. Press Enter to begin a new line. Click the Bullets button in the Format toolbar, and type:
   `First, please visit my Guest Book. I'd appreciate it if you would share some comments about the site. But please be nice, I'm just learning!`

5. Select the words `Guest Book` from the text you just typed. Then click the Hyperlink button on the Standard toolbar. The Create Hyperlink dialog box appears.

6. The last icon that appears to the right of the URL field is the Create a Page and Link to the New Page button. Click this button to open the New dialog box.

7. From the New dialog box, highlight the Guest Book template, then choose OK to create the hyperlink to the Guest Book. The new Guest Book page appears in the page editor.

8. Choose File, Save (Ctrl+S) or click the Save button on the Standard toolbar. The Save As dialog box appears.

9. Click the Change button to open the Set Page Title dialog box. Change the page title to **Guest Book**, and choose OK to return to the Save As dialog box.

10. Enter the filename **guestbk.htm** in the File Name field, then click Save to save the page to your current Web.

11. Choose File, Close (Ctrl+F4) to close the Guest Book page. You return to the home page, and the link to the Guest Book page is complete, as shown in Figure 7.7.

FIGURE 7.7

A link to a new Guest Book page is created on your home page.

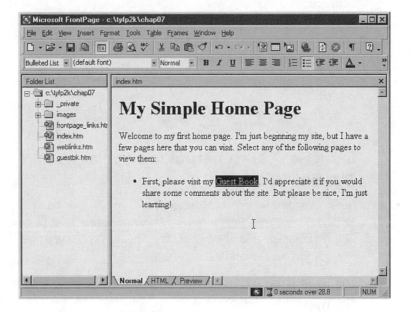

Dragging and Dropping Files to Create Text Links

Your Web grows quickly, and as you add pages to your site you'll want your readers to find them easily. FrontPage provides one very easy way to create links from one page in your current Web to another. To use this method, however, you should make sure that the page you want to link to has a page title that is descriptive of the content on the page.

When the Folder List is displayed beside the page editor, as shown in Figure 7.8, you can click and drag a page from the Folder List and drop it into your currently opened

7

page. After you release the mouse button, the title of the page that you dragged and dropped appears as a hyperlink on your current page.

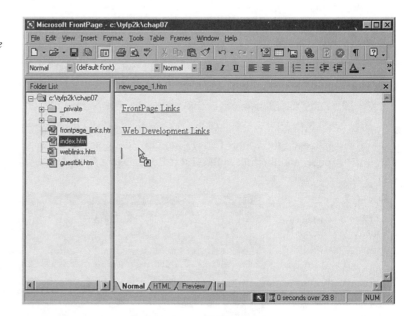

Exercise 7.3: Hyperlinking to Pages in Your Current Web

In the preceding section you learned a quick way to add a link to a page in your current Web. However, you might not always want to display your links in a bulleted list, or display the complete title of the page. You can use the Create Hyperlink dialog box to link to pages in your current Web.

The Create Hyperlink dialog box allows you to link to any page in your current Web, and keeps track of the locations of the files. You can link to a page whether you have it opened or closed. If you examine the list of files that are displayed in Figure 7.9, you'll notice that two pages appear above the list of folders in the Web. These are pages that you have opened in the page editor.

When you have one or more pages opened in the page editor, they appear at the top of the list in the Create Hyperlink dialog box, and a pencil appears over the little page icon to signify that you are currently working on the page.

Pages in your Web that you do not have opened in the page editor appear beneath the list of folders in your Web, and no pencil appears over the page icon.

FIGURE 7.9

The Create Hyperlink dialog box displays all pages in your Web. Pages that you have opened in the page editor are displayed at the top of the list.

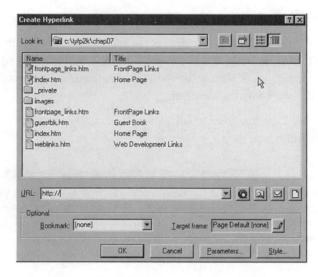

Now you'll create a hyperlink to the FrontPage Links page that you created in Exercise 7.1. Follow these steps:

1. Return to the `index.htm` page that you started in Exercise 7.2 if it is not your current Web page.

2. Position the insertion point at the end of the first bulleted list item on the page and press Enter to begin a new list item. Enter the following text:

   I created my web pages with Microsoft FrontPage. For more information about it, see my FrontPage Links page.

3. Click and drag to select the words `FrontPage Links` in the list item you just entered on your page. Then click the Hyperlink button on the Standard toolbar. The Create Hyperlink dialog box appears.

4. From the list of files in your current Web, click to highlight the FrontPage Links Web page (`frontpage_links.htm`). Choose OK to create the hyperlink. You return to the home page.

Note

If the page to which you want to link appears in a different folder in your Web, you can use the Look In drop-down list to locate the correct folder.

5. Choose File, Save (Ctrl+S) or click the Save button in the Standard toolbar to save the revised page to your current Web.

7

Exercise 7.4: Sending Mail Through a Hyperlink

Do you want to learn an easy way to get people to contact you right from your Web site? Use the Hyperlink dialog box to create a hyperlink to your email address. When the user follows this link, he or she can compose an email message and send it to the email address designated by the hyperlink.

You create a hyperlink to an email address by choosing the Make a Hyperlink That Sends E-mail button shown in Figure 7.10.

FIGURE 7.10

Select the Make a Hyperlink That Sends E-mail button to create a hyperlink to your email address.

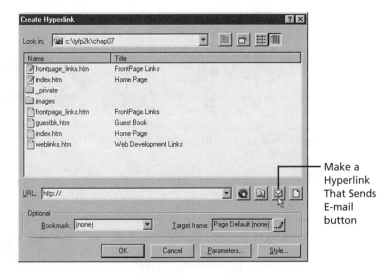

Make a Hyperlink That Sends E-mail button

Now you will modify your home page, and add a hyperlink to your email address. Follow these steps:

1. Position the insertion point at the end of the last bulleted list item and press Enter to begin a new list item. Enter the following text:

   If you have questions or comments about my pages, please send an e-mail message.

2. Click and drag to select the words send an e-mail message in the list item you just entered on your page. Click the Hyperlink button on the Standard toolbar to open the Create Hyperlink dialog box.

3. Click the Make a Hyperlink That Sends E-mail button (the third button that appears at the right of the URL field, as shown in Figure 7.10). The Create E-mail Hyperlink dialog box shown in Figure 7.11 appears.

4. Enter your email address in the dialog box (example: jdoe@msn.com). Then choose OK to return to the Create Hyperlink dialog box.

5. Choose OK to create the hyperlink. You return to the home page.

6. Choose File, Save (Ctrl+S) or click the Save button in the Standard toolbar to save the revised page to your current Web.

Bookmarks

Now that you've learned several ways to create text hyperlinks, you'll learn how to create and link to bookmarks. As you learned earlier in this chapter, a bookmark marks a specific spot on a Web page. You can then create a hyperlink that takes your readers to this exact spot when they choose the link.

You use the Bookmark dialog box, shown in Figure 7.12, to create a bookmark. If other bookmarks appear on your page, they are listed in the dialog box. Each bookmark on the page must have a unique name—generally, they are named in all lowercase letters.

When you first open the Bookmark dialog box, the text that you selected for the bookmark appears in the Bookmark Name field. It is important to note that bookmark names that contain spaces may not work in some browsers, so in many cases you'll have to modify the bookmark name. Try to keep the names of your bookmarks brief, and use names that you can easily relate to the topic of each bookmark.

FIGURE 7.12

The Bookmark dialog box helps you create bookmarks on a Web page. The names of all other bookmarks on the page appear in a list in the dialog box.

7

Exercise 7.5: Creating Bookmarks

The Frequently Asked Questions page template that is provided with FrontPage shows a good example of how to use bookmarks in Web pages. As you'll see in this exercise, the page displays a table of contents at the top of the page. Each of the bulleted list items in the table of contents will take the reader to a question on the page. After the user reads the answer to the question, he or she can jump back to the top of the page. This page already has six bookmarks created for you. We'll add a seventh one to the page.

To create the page and the bookmarks, follow these steps:

1. Choose File, New, Page (Ctrl+N). The New dialog box opens.

2. From the General tab, highlight the Frequently Asked Questions page template, and choose OK. The page opens in the page editor.

3. Scroll to the bottom of the page. Position the insertion point at the beginning of the line that reads Author information goes here. Press Enter to insert a new line.

4. Place the insertion point on the new line that you created, and choose Heading 3 from the Style drop-down list in the Format toolbar. Type `What happens when ... ?`.

5. Press Enter to begin a new line of normal text. Type `[This is the answer to the question.]`.

6. Press Enter again, and choose Heading 5 from the Style drop-down list in the Format toolbar. Type `Back to Top`.

7. Press Enter and choose Insert, Horizontal Line to add a horizontal line to end the section.

8. Highlight the entire `What happens when ...` question in the section that you just added to the page. You will create a bookmark from this heading.

9. Choose Insert, Bookmark. The Bookmark dialog box appears.

10. In the Bookmark Name field, enter `whathappens`. Choose OK to create the bookmark. When you return to the page, you see a dotted line beneath the text that you selected for the bookmark. This confirms that the bookmark is created. Your page should now look like in Figure 7.13.

FIGURE 7.13

A new bookmark is created for the new question you added to the page.

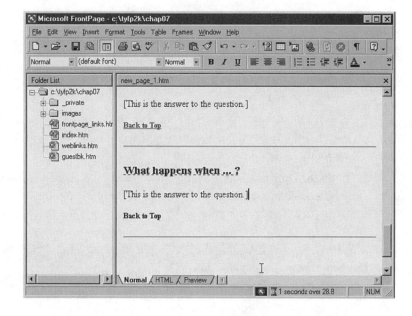

> **Tip**
>
> If you make a mistake when you create the bookmark, you can clear the bookmark without removing the text that you used to create it. Open the page on which the bookmark appears, and position the insertion point anywhere within the text of the bookmark. Choose Insert, Bookmark and verify that the correct bookmark name appears in the Bookmark Name field. Then choose Clear to remove the bookmark.
>
> To delete both the bookmark and the text that you used to create it, select the appropriate text on your Web page and use the Delete key.

Exercise 7.6: Creating and Testing Hyperlinks to Bookmarks

Now that you have created your first bookmark, you'll learn how to create hyperlinks to the bookmark. You'll create two hyperlinks: One hyperlink will appear on the Frequently Asked Questions page (the same page that the bookmark appears on), and another hyperlink will appear on the home page.

7

To create your hyperlinks, follow these steps:

1. With the Frequently Asked Questions page still open, scroll to the Table of Contents that appears at the top of the page.

2. Position the insertion point at the end of the last item in the contents list. Press Enter to add a new list item.

3. Type **What happens when...?**, and then select the text.

4. Click the Hyperlink button on the Standard toolbar. The Create Hyperlink dialog box appears.

5. In the Optional section near the bottom of the dialog box, you'll find the Bookmark drop-down list. Press the arrow to expand the list of bookmarks on the page, as shown in Figure 7.14.

FIGURE 7.14

Select the bookmark to which you want to link from the Bookmark drop-down list in the Create Hyperlink dialog box.

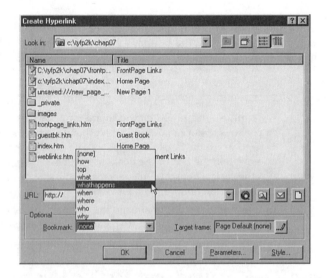

6. Locate the whathappens bookmark in the list, and select the option. When you release the mouse button, the bookmark name appears in the Bookmark field. You also see the same bookmark name appear in the URL field, where it is preceded by a pound sign.

7. Click OK to complete the bookmark and return to your Web page.

8. Choose File, Save (Ctrl+S) or click the Save button in the Standard toolbar. The Save As dialog box appears.

9. Change the page title to **Frequently Asked Questions**, and enter **faq.htm** in the File Name field. Then choose Save to save the page to your Web.

10. Open or return to the `index.htm` page in your Web. Position the insertion point at the end of the last bulleted list item, and press Enter to begin a new item. Enter the following text:

   A new question has been answered on my Frequently Asked Questions page. What happens when you link to a bookmark on another page?

11. Select the text that reads `link to a bookmark on another page`. Then click the Hyperlink button on the Standard toolbar. The Create Hyperlink dialog box appears.

12. From the list of current pages in your Web, highlight the `faq.htm` page. Next, select the `whathappens` bookmark from the Bookmark drop-down list. When `whathappens` is displayed in the Bookmark field, the URL field reads `faq.htm#whathappens`. The pound sign in the URL separates the page URL (`faq.htm`) from the specific bookmark name (`whathappens`). Whenever you see a URL that ends with a pound sign followed by text, you are hyperlinking to a bookmark on that page.

13. Choose OK to create the hyperlink. You return to the home page.

14. Choose File, Save (Ctrl+S), or click the Save button on the Standard toolbar to save the page to your Web.

Now it's time to verify that your bookmarks work. Follow these steps:

1. Return to the Frequently Asked Questions page (`faq.htm`) to open it in the page editor.

2. Click the Preview tab at the bottom of the page editor to display the page in Preview mode.

3. From the Table of Contents list at the top of the page, click the What Happens When hyperlink. You advance to the question, as shown in Figure 7.15.

4. Return to Normal View and choose Window, `index.htm` to display the home page.

5. Return to Preview mode, and click the `link to a bookmark on another page` hyperlink. You should advance to the same position on the page that is shown in Figure 7.15.

7

FIGURE 7.15

*When you follow a
hyperlink to a book-
mark, the browser or
preview window
advances to the book-
mark.*

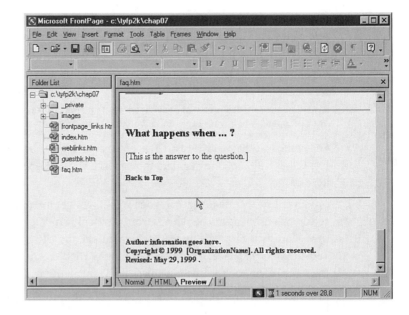

Using Images as Links

You've worked with text hyperlinks so far in this chapter, but you can also use images to create hyperlinks as well. Images are commonly used to create navigation buttons and navigation bars.

Creating image hyperlinks is just as simple as creating text hyperlinks, and the steps are very similar to those you have already learned in this chapter. To create an image hyperlink, you need only click an image and then use the Hyperlink button on the Standard toolbar.

When you create a hyperlink from an image, keep in mind that sometimes people are not using browsers that can display images. These browsers are becoming increasingly rare, but other browsers provide the option of turning off image display. Many people choose not to download images because of the time involved.

The option of turning image display off is not a problem when images are used to enhance the appearance of your pages. When they serve a function such as a hyperlink, however, you must provide an alternative for people who do not want to download all the images. You can provide a text version elsewhere on the page, or you can specify an alternative text representation for the image. You'll use the latter approach in the following task.

There are many ways that you can use images as links, and just as many ways to create navigation systems for your Web. For example, in next week's lessons, you will learn how to use Navigation View in conjunction with FrontPage themes and shared borders to develop navigation systems that automatically link your pages together. You will also learn how to design Web sites that use framesets to display your navigation system.

Navigation View and framesets have advantages and disadvantages. Many people don't like framesets because they divide the browser screen into multiple panes, thereby reducing the amount of space that displays the main content in the Web site. Also, while Navigation View helps you develop navigation bars and banners that are uniform in their appearance, some don't like the uniformity at all and prefer to develop graphics that incorporate varied graphics and more stylish fonts.

As an alternative to framesets and Navigation View, you can develop your own navigation buttons and banners, and use the Include Page component (discussed also in Day 14, "FrontPage Components") to place the navigation bars on one or more pages in your Web. While some of this information will be repeated in Day 14, I'll give you a sneak preview of how to accomplish this now.

Exercise 7.7: Building an Image Navigation Bar

The CD-ROM that accompanies this book includes some images that you will use to create a simple navigation bar. The images can be used to take your readers to all of the pages that you have created so far in this chapter.

To import the images into your Web, and to create a navigation bar, follow these steps:

1. If the Folder List is not displayed beside the page editor, choose View, Folder List to display it.

2. Highlight the images folder and choose File, Import. The Import dialog box appears.

3. Click the Add File button. The Add File to Import List dialog box appears.

4. Use the Look In drop-down list to locate the `tyfp2k\chap07\samples` folder on the CD-ROM that accompanies this book. Highlight `faqs.jpg`, `guestbk.jpg`, `home.jpg`, and `links.jpg`. Then click Open to add the files to your import list.

5. With all four images highlighted in the Import list, choose OK to import the images into your Web.

6. Click the New Page button on the Standard toolbar to create a new blank Web page.

7. Expand the images folder in the Folder List to display the four images.

7

8. Highlight `home.jpg` and drag the filename into your Web page. Release the mouse button to place the image on the first line in your new page.

9. Highlight `guestbk.jpg` and drag the filename into your Web page. Release the mouse button to place the image immediately to the right of the home image.

10. Similarly, place the remaining two images onto your Web page in the following order: `faqs.jpg` and `links.jpg`.

11. Click the Center icon on the Format toolbar to center the four images on your page.

12. Now, you'll add an alternative text representation to the home page. To do this, click the Home image and press Alt+Enter, or right-click and choose Picture Properties from the pop-up window to open the Picture Properties dialog box. It opens to the General tab. In the Text field of the Alternative Representations section, enter **Home**. Choose OK to return to the Web page.

13. Repeat step 12 to add alternative text representations to the remaining three images: `Guest Book` (for `guestbk.jpg`), `FAQs` (for `faqs.jpg`), and `Links` (for `links.jpg`).

14. Now you will create the hyperlinks for each of the images. Again, click the Home image, then select the Hyperlink button on the Standard toolbar. Create a hyperlink to `index.htm`.

15. Click the Guest Book image, and create a hyperlink to `guestbk.htm`.

16. Click the FAQs image, and create a hyperlink to `faq.htm`.

17. Click the Links image, and create a hyperlink to `frontpage_links.htm`.

18. Choose File, Save (Ctrl+S), or click the Save button on the Standard toolbar. Double-click to select the `_private` folder in your Web.

19. Enter **Navigation Bar** for a page title, and **navbar.htm** for the filename. Click Save to save the page. When you're finished, your Web page should look like Figure 7.16.

 Note

If you hide the Folder List, or if you are designing your Web page at higher than 640×480 resolution, you will see all of the navigation buttons appear on the same line in your Web page.

Your new navigation bar displays the alternative text label in the allocated space for each image when your readers have browsers that cannot view images, or have image display turned off. You can place this navigation bar on each of your pages, using the Include

Page component that is furnished with FrontPage. Then in the future, when you need to change your navigation bar, you only need to make the changes to the page you just designed. FrontPage will update the navigation bar on any page where it appears within an Include Page component.

FIGURE 7.16

The completed naviga-
tion bar.

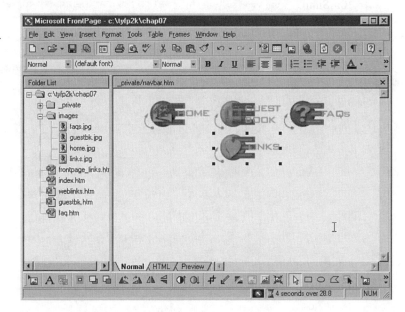

Though you'll learn more about the Include Page component in Day 14, the steps to add them to your pages are simple. Add an Include Page component to each of the four pages in your Web (index.htm, frontpage_links.htm, guestbk.htm, and faq.htm) in the following manner:

- Open one of the pages mentioned in the preceding paragraph.
- Position the insertion point at the top-left corner of the page.
- Choose Insert, Component, Include Page. The Include Page Properties dialog box appears.
- Use the Browse button to open the Current Web dialog box. Double-click the _private folder to select it. Then highlight navbar.htm and choose OK to return to the Include Page Properties dialog box.
- Choose OK to place the Include Page component on your page. You should see the navigation bar appear at the top, as shown in Figure 7.17.
- Click the Save button on the Standard toolbar to save the page to your Web.

7

Tip

> You can also use a quick method to insert all of the Include Page compo-
> nents on your page. After you use the Insert, Component, Include Page com-
> mand to place the component on the first page, copy it into your clipboard
> using Ctrl+C. Then, open each page on which you want the component to
> appear. Position the insertion point at the top-left corner of each page, and
> use Ctrl+V to paste the component at the beginning of each page.

FIGURE 7.17

*The Include Page com-
ponent places the navi-
gation bar on any page
in your Web.*

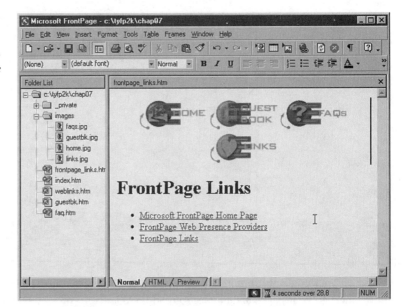

Creating an Imagemap

As an alternative to using several different images to create a navigation bar, you can create one larger image and then designate areas within that image to take a reader to a
page. This type of image is known as an imagemap.

There are advantages and disadvantages to using imagemaps. One advantage to using
them is that your readers have to download only one file instead of several smaller ones.
The browser has to access the remote server only one time to retrieve and download the
image. Imagemaps can also be a lot more creative and visually appealing than their rectangular button counterparts.

On the other hand, the larger image takes longer to download and display completely. In addition, you'll need to add equivalent text links, because imagemaps will not display multiple alternative text representations when image display is turned off.

Still, you can get very creative with imagemaps and a lot of people use them on their Web sites. In the following sections, you'll learn how to configure and use imagemaps on your pages.

Exercise 7.8: Creating Hotspots

You can turn any graphic on your page into a clickable image. Simply select the image, create a hotspot or hotspots on it, and assign a hyperlink to the hotspot.

A hotspot is a rectangular, circular, or polygonal area within an image, and it works the same way as a text or graphic button link. When the reader clicks within the area defined by the hotspot, he or she follows a link to another Web page.

The Picture toolbar includes buttons that let you add hotspots to an image. In this exercise, you'll create another page that could serve as a home page. You'll import a graphic and add some hotspots that link to the pages in your current Web. Follow these steps.

1. Click the New Page button on the Standard toolbar to create a new blank page.
2. Highlight the images folder and choose File, Import. The Import dialog box appears.
3. Click the Add File button. The Add File to Import List dialog box appears.
4. Use the Look In drop-down list to locate the `tyfp2k\chap07\samples` folder on the CD-ROM that accompanies this book. Highlight `puzzle.jpg`, and then click Open to add the file to your import list.
5. With the image highlighted in the Import list, choose OK to import it into your Web.
6. Display the Folder List (View, Folder List), and expand the images folder. Drag `puzzle.jpg` into your blank Web page.
7. Click the Center button on the Format toolbar to center the image on your page.
8. Click to select the image. The Picture toolbar appears at the bottom of the FrontPage interface window.
9. Click the Rectangular Hotspot button on the Picture toolbar. The icon turns into a pencil when you place it over the image. Draw a rectangular hotspot around the green rectangle, beginning at the top-left corner, and releasing the mouse button at the bottom-right corner. The Create Hyperlink dialog box appears.

7

10. Locate `guestbk.htm` in the list of pages in your current Web. Highlight the file-name, then click OK to create your first hotspot hyperlink.

11. Use the resize handles (the small squares) on the rectangular hotspot to adjust the size of the hotspot if necessary.

12. Click the Circular Hotspot button on the Picture toolbar. Draw a circular hotspot around the yellow circle. Begin the hotspot at the center, and drag outward until the circle completely surrounds the circle in the image. Release the mouse to open the Create Hyperlink dialog box.

13. Locate `faq.htm` in the list of pages in your current Web. Highlight the filename, then click OK to create the hotspot hyperlink.

14. Click the circular hotspot in the center, and drag the hotspot to adjust its center point if necessary.

15. Click the Polygonal Hotspot button on the Picture toolbar. Beginning at any point on the red polygon, click with the pencil to set the first point. Move the mouse to the second point you want to set, and click to set the second point. Continue around the polygon in this manner until you arrive back at the point of origin. When you click the first point to close the hotspot, the Create Hyperlink dialog box appears.

16. Locate `frontpage_links.htm` in the list of pages in your current Web. Highlight the filename, then click OK to create the hotspot hyperlink.

17. To adjust any point in the polygonal hotspot, position the cursor over one of the hotspot handles. The cursor turns into a directional arrow and allows you to adjust the position of the hotspot point. To move the entire hotspot, click and drag from the center to reposition it. After all three hotspots are created, your image will look like Figure 7.18.

Tip

You sometimes need to adjust the hotspots on your page so that they do not overlap. However, it might be difficult to see them against the image on which they appear. You can use the Highlight Hotspots button in the Picture toolbar to find hotspots easier. Click the image to activate the Picture tool-bar, then choose the Highlight Hotspots button. The image disappears, and you can adjust the points on your hotspots to prevent overlap.

FIGURE 7.18

*Three hotspots have
been created on the
image to make an
imagemap.*

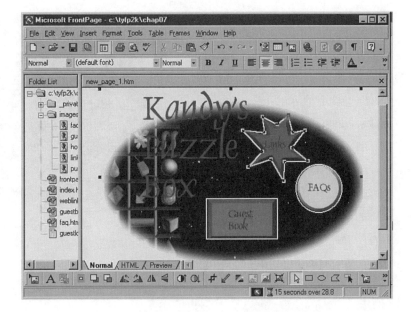

18. Choose File, Save (Ctrl+S) or click the Save button on the Standard toolbar. The Save As dialog box appears.

19. The Save As dialog box might still point to the _private folder, where you saved the navigation bar in the last exercise. Use the Save In box to select the root folder in your Web (the chap07 folder). The other pages that you have created in this chapter should appear in the file list.

20. Change the page title to **Kandy's Puzzle Box**, and enter a filename of **kandys.htm**.

21. Click Save to save the page to your Web.

When you have a Web page that contains only an imagemap, it makes it difficult for non-graphical browsers to enter your Web. Therefore, you might want to add some equivalent text hyperlinks on your page, just in case. In Figure 7.19, you see a brief welcome statement, as well as hyperlinks to the same three pages that have been created on the imagemap. This may seem like excess duplication, but it also ensures that everyone can enter your site.

7

FIGURE 7.19

When you use imagemaps, it is a good idea to include text links that take your visitors to the same pages that are linked from the imagemap.

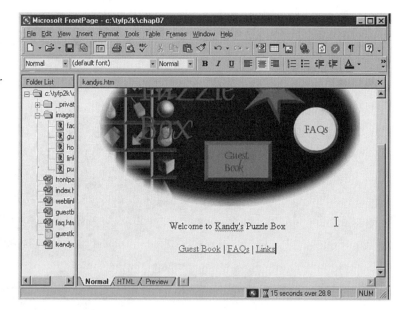

Changing, Unlinking, and Deleting Hyperlinks

It is a fact of life on the Web that sites have a tendency to evolve and change. Ten pages quickly become dozens. They are renamed, relocated, deleted, or divided into other pages.

To change the URL of a text hyperlink or an image hyperlink, do the following:

1. Select the hyperlink that you want to change. For a text hyperlink, place the mouse pointer anywhere within the text that contains the hyperlink or select any part of it. For an image hyperlink, select the image or the hotspot within the image that contains the hyperlink.

2. Click the Hyperlink button in the Standard toolbar. The Edit Hyperlink dialog box, shown in Figure 7.20, appears.

The Edit Hyperlink dialog box contains the same fields and buttons as the Create Hyperlink dialog box, and most should feel very familiar to you at this point. After you make the modifications to your hyperlink, choose OK to exit the dialog box and return to your page.

FIGURE 7.20

Use the Edit Hyperlink dialog box to change existing hyperlinks.

You can also remove a hyperlink from all or part of an existing hyperlink. Follow these steps:

1. Select the text, image, or hotspot from which you want to remove the hyperlink.

2. Click the Hyperlink button in the Standard toolbar to open the Edit Hyperlink dialog box.

3. Delete the path that appears in the URL field so that the URL no longer points to a Web page or file.

4. Choose OK to exit the dialog box. The hyperlink is removed from the selected text.

Summary

In this chapter, you learned how to navigate through your pages and out to other areas of the Internet by using bookmarks and hyperlinks. You learned how to hyperlink pages with text, images, and imagemaps. You are now set to tackle building your Web site from the ground up. In the next lesson, you'll begin to plan the areas that you want to include on your own site. The rest will happen over time.

7

Workshop

Q&A

Q Why is it best to use relative URLs?

A Absolute URLs list the complete path to a page or file. They contain the protocol, server, folder, and filename (for example, `http://www.microsoft.com/frontpage/default.htm` is the absolute URL to the FrontPage home page on Microsoft's Web site). They are best to use when your hyperlinks go to pages that do not reside in your current Web.

Relative URLs contain a partial URL as it relates to the page from which you are creating a hyperlink. And the reason that this is important is that most often you will develop your Web pages on your own computer, and will publish them to the Internet at a later date. If you used absolute URLs to link between the pages on your Web, they would no longer work after being published to the Internet—they'd be looking for the paths on your own computer.

Q Do all browsers support `mailto` hyperlinks?

A No—if a browser does not support a `mailto` hyperlink, the user receives an error message.

Q You haven't mentioned anything about the Target Frame field in the Create Hyperlink or Edit Hyperlink dialog box. What is that all about?

A The Target Frame field applies when you want to link to a page that appears in a frameset. It tells your browser on which frame in the frameset to display the page that you are linking to. For more information about framesets, see Day 12.

Quiz

1. Explain the difference between a hyperlink and a bookmark.
2. What types of hyperlinks can you create in FrontPage?
3. True or false: Absolute URLs are portable.
4. True or false: Bookmark names can contain spaces.
5. What else is important to include on your page when you use images as hyperlinks?

Exercises

1. Create an imagemap for a Web page. When you create your image, remember that there are many who view Web pages at 640×480 resolution, so be sure to preview your Web page at that resolution.

2. Create one or more pages that contain hyperlinks to some of your favorite sites on the World Wide Web. Organize the links in lists that display your links in categories.

Answers to Quiz

1. A hyperlink takes readers to a different page or file on an Internet, intranet, or personal Web server. A bookmark marks a specific location on a Web page, and is an extension of a hyperlink.

2. You can create hyperlinks to pages on the World Wide Web, to pages on a local or network drive, to pages in your current Web, and to email addresses.

3. False. Absolute URLs display a complete path (Web protocol, server, directory, and filename). Relative URLs are portable because they display partial paths.

4. False. Though FrontPage allows you to create bookmark names that contain spaces, they might not work in all browsers. If your bookmarks don't seem to be working correctly in some browsers, double-check your bookmark names for spaces. Better yet, don't use spaces when you assign names to bookmarks.

5. You should include a text equivalent in case some visitors come to your site and cannot or choose not to view images on your pages. By using alternative text representations or adding text hyperlinks on your page, you avoid email saying that people can't navigate through your site.

7

WEEK 2

Enhancing Your Presentation

8

9

10

11

12

13

14

DAY 8

Planning Your Own Web Site

You might think that creating a Web is the first thing to do when you want your own Web site. This is not really true.

A little planning before you take the leap to create a Web may well save a lot of heartache and replanning later. You have already looked at the templates that FrontPage supplies. These templates are great when you have a pre-planned idea that happens to fit with a template, but they're not much help at all when your ideas don't match those of the software writers and designers.

In this chapter you will learn how you can use FrontPage to help you get the most out of your own ideas.

Today you will learn

- How to create a new Web
- How to add, rename, and delete folders
- How to import content into your Web site from your hard drive
- How to import content into your Web site from the World Wide Web

Creating a Web

Creating and planning a Web go hand in hand. FrontPage allows you to create many different types of Webs and customize the layout, or you can start with a single page or even an empty Web and build from there.

One-Page Webs

One of the options that FrontPage offers is a one-page Web, which creates a new Web in the location of your choosing with a single homepage in it.

To create a one-page Web, perform the following steps:

1. Open FrontPage.
2. Select File, New, Web.
3. From the list of options, select One-Page Web.
4. Select a location for the Web, and name it chapter8.
5. Click OK to continue.

FrontPage opens a blank page in Page View for you to work on.

By looking at the Navigation View, you will see that by simply letting FrontPage create a single page for you, the basic structure for your site is already made.

Select View, Navigation and the screen shown in Figure 8.1 appears.

FIGURE 8.1

The Navigation View shows the single home-page created.

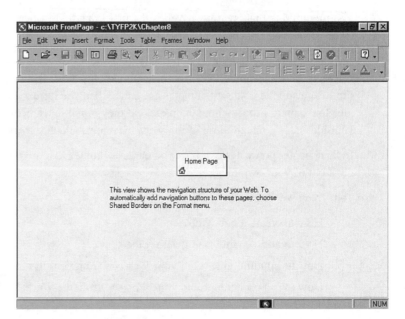

The Navigation View is all ready for you to start adding pages as you create them.

You can add shared borders and themes to a one-page Web in exactly the same way you can with any other type of site.

To add shared borders to a one-page Web, select Format, Shared Borders. The Shared Borders dialog box appears, as shown in Figure 8.2.

FIGURE 8.2

Even with a one-page Web you can set the properties for shared borders. These will affect the pages you create later.

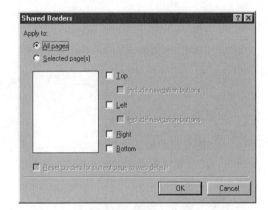

Empty Webs

Another option that FrontPage offers is to create a totally empty Web. This may seem like a strange idea—after all, why would anyone want a Web site with nothing in it?

Although the obvious answer to that question is that no one would, it is sometimes easier to work with a completely blank canvas in order to create exactly what you want.

For example, if you do not want your homepage to be a standard normal page, you can use an empty Web and add only the types of pages you want.

To create an empty Web, perform the following steps:

1. Open FrontPage.
2. Select File, New, Web.
3. From the list of options, select Empty Web.
4. Select a location for the Web, and name it `emptyweb`.
5. Click OK to continue.

FrontPage opens a blank page in Page View for you to work on.

This time, however, if you look at the Navigation View there is nothing there. No pages are added automatically.

You are now free to add any type of page you choose and use it as your homepage.

For example, the following instructions will enable you to have a Narrow Right Aligned Body page as your homepage and to build the navigation structure around it.

Having created your empty Web, ignore the page that FrontPage opened automatically, then do as follows:

1. Select File, New, Page.

2. Choose the Narrow Right Aligned Body option.

3. Click OK. Front Page creates a page that appears as shown in Figure 8.3.

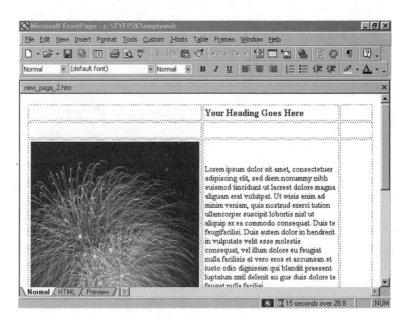

4. Select File, Save.

5. Save the page as index.htm.

6. When prompted to save embedded file, click OK to allow FrontPage to save the embedded image file.

7. Select View, Navigation. The index.htm file you just created is now visible with the little house icon identifying it as the homepage for your Web.

The blank page FrontPage initially created is still open behind your index page, but you can simply ignore this page. It will not affect your Web at all.

Customizing Web Settings

FrontPage offers a large amount of control of the settings for your Web.

The Web Settings option in the Tools menu allows you to set and control the settings that run across your whole Web, such as the Web name, default script language, and the default server message language. It also shows you certain information about your Web, such as the file location, the server currently in use, and the server extensions version where applicable.

To see the default Web settings for a Web, do the following:

1. Open the Web you created called `emptyweb`.

2. From the Tools menu, select Web Settings.

The Web Settings dialog box is displayed, as shown in Figure 8.4.

FIGURE 8.4

The Web Settings dialog box enables you to set up your Web the way you want it.

By default, the dialog box opens to the General tab with the following information displayed:

- *Web Name*—The name you assigned to the Web when you created it.

- *File Location*—The location of the Web on the local machine.

- *FrontPage Server Extensions Version*—The version of the extensions on the local machine.

- *Server Version*—If you are creating a server-based Web, this will show the server you are using.

- *Use Document Check-in and Check-out*—Use this check box if you are using source control (covered on Day 21, "Tracking and Maintaining Your Webs").

Only the top option in this list is customizable from within the Web Settings dialog box. The other details shown are for information purposes only.

You can change the name of the Web simply by typing over what is already there. If you want to change the name of the Web to something more useful, click inside the Web Name box, type the new name, and then click OK to exit the Web Settings dialog box.

The Parameters tab in the Web Settings dialog box is for creating and editing any variables within the Web. Creating variables is covered on Day 14, "FrontPage Components." Unless you have any variables set, this screen is blank.

The Advanced tab has three areas:

- *Set Default Scripting Language*—The three options here are VBScript, JavaScript, and None. This drop-down list enables you to select the scripting language to be used for the scripts that are automatically generated to enforce any data validation settings you apply to form fields. (This will make far more sense once you have learned about forms on Day 18, "Building and Editing Forms.")

- *Show Documents in Hidden Directories*—As you are no doubt aware, FrontPage automatically generates many files when you create a Web site. The pages you create can be seen instantly, but there are many other files you can't normally see. These hidden files usually hold the structure and workings of the Web. They are hidden mainly to ensure that no one accidentally modifies or deletes them. Also, if you create any directories in FrontPage that start with the _ (underscore) character, they too are considered to be hidden directories. Just as there are many reasons why FrontPage puts these folders in hidden directories, there are also reasons why you might want to see them. To show the files in hidden directories, put a check in the Show Files in Hidden Documents check box and then click Apply.

You will be prompted to refresh your Web, as shown in Figure 8.5. Click Yes to continue.

FIGURE 8.5

The Web must be refreshed to show the files in hidden directories.

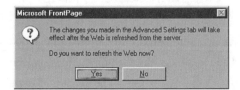

By selecting the Folders View, you will now see any hidden directories in your Web. The changes are most significant when dealing with large Webs or Webs that use themes.

- *Temporary Files*—Whenever you are working within FrontPage, the software auto-matically creates temporary files that are used when you work on pages or embed-ded images. Previous versions of FrontPage made finding these files hard enough, let alone deleting them. FrontPage 2000 has made it as simple as possible by allowing the files to be deleted with the click of a button, making management of these files easy.

Building Your Web Structure

The structure of any Web is vital to its success. Many people make the mistake of think-ing that the structure only relates to how easy a site is to navigate. They don't think about the internal management of files. Keeping a Web neat and tidy on your local machine is just as important as making sure that visitors can find their way around. In the same way that you can manage files in Windows Explorer, FrontPage has the built-in facilities for adding, renaming, and deleting folders and files, making it a straightforward procedure to keep everything in its place. All FrontPage Webs have a folder named images in their structure, giving you a convenient place to store all of your graphics and animations.

In a large Web site, you may well have many pages dedicated to different topics, and keeping them in folders is a simple way of keeping similar files together.

Adding Folders

Adding folders in FrontPage is easy. Follow these steps:

1. Open the chapter8 Web, and then select the View, Folders option.

2. Select File, New, Folder (see Figure 8.6). A new folder immediately appears in the view, with the name in blue ready for you to give it a more meaningful name. You can also right-click in the folders pane and select new folder.

3. Type in **myfolder** and then press Enter.

You now have a folder called myfolder, which you can use for any files you like.

FIGURE 8.6

The New Folder option is located in the File menu.

Renaming Folders

Renaming folders is, again, one of the simplest tasks in FrontPage. To do so, follow these steps:

1. Open the chapter8 Web, and then select the View, Folders option.
2. Single-click on the folder you want to rename—the myfolder you just created, for example.
3. Right-click and select Rename. The folder name turns blue to allow you to edit it.
4. Type the new name for the folder; for this example, type **newname**.

Deleting Folders

Deleting a folder is a simple task, but be very careful before you do because deleting a folder will also delete the contents of it as well.

To delete a folder, follow these steps:

1. Open the chapter8 Web and select the View, Folders option.
2. Single-click on the newname folder.
3. Right-click and then select Delete. The Confirm Delete dialog box, appears as shown in Figure 8.7.
4. Select Yes to delete the folder.

FIGURE 8.7

You are given the chance to change your mind before a folder is deleted.

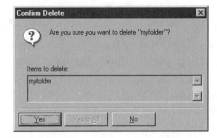

Exercise 8.1: Creating New Folders

Creating new folders is an easy process with FrontPage 2000. To create a new folder, follow these steps:

1. Open the chapter8 Web.
2. Select File, New, Folder. The folder name box appears in blue, ready to be named.
3. Name the folder **workfolder** and then press Enter.

The Folders View now shows the new folder, as shown in Figure 8.8.

FIGURE 8.8

Your new folder is now located in the Folders View.

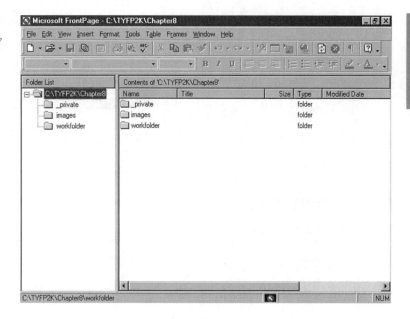

Files can simply be dragged and dropped between folders. FrontPage will update the links between pages as it is moving the files for you.

Adding New or Existing Pages

You can add new pages to your Web either into the main root directory or straight into a folder of your choice.

To add a new page directly into the workfolder you created in the preceding exercise, do the following:

1. Open the `chapter8` Web if it is not already open.

2. Select `workfolder` by single-clicking on it.

3. Click the New Page button on the toolbar. A new page called `index.htm` is created in `workfolder`, as shown in Figure 8.9.

Note

The path to this file is `workfolder/index.htm`. Any file created in a folder takes the path of the folder. This will be represented in the final URL as `http://www.mysite.com/workfolder/index.htm`.

FIGURE 8.9

When you create a new page in a selected folder, it is placed there immediately.

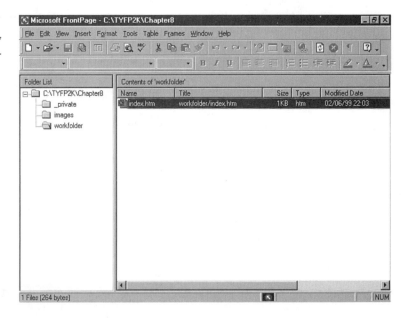

Importing Files or Folders

FrontPage 2000 allows you to import files into your Web from external locations. The most common place to import files from is your own hard drive. You may want to bring in a Word document or an image file to use within the Web, or you may have an existing .htm(l) file that you want to use in the Web.

When you import a file or a folder from your hard drive, a floppy disk, your intranet, or the World Wide Web, Microsoft FrontPage places a copy of the file or folder in your Web, leaving the original intact in its original location. You can create a list of files or folders to import at a later date and even change the URLs of files before importing them.

You can import files or folders directly into a specific folder or subWeb simply by selecting the folder or subWeb first.

Exercise 8.2: Importing Files or Folders

To import a file or folder into your FrontPage Web, perform the following steps:

1. Open the chapter8 Web or whichever Web you want to import the file into.

2. Select File, Import. The Import dialog box appears, as shown in Figure 8.10.

3. Select the files or folders you want to import.

FIGURE 8.10

The Import dialog box allows you to specify where the files are to come from.

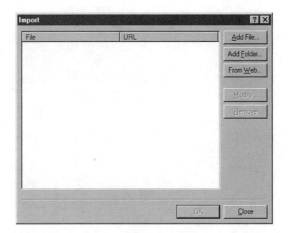

4. To import files, click Add File, and then in the Add File to Import List dialog box that appears, point to the folder where the files you want to import are stored. Select the files, and then click Open.

5. You can change the URL of any file before importing it (either to rename it or to change the file's folder in your Web) by clicking Modify. This opens the Edit URL dialog box.

6. In the File Location Within Your Web box, type the relative URL for the new location of the file. For example, if you type **workfolder/import.htm**, the import.htm page will be saved directly into the workfolder.

7. Click OK.

8. To import a folder, click Add Folder, and then browse to the folder you want to import.

9. Click OK.

10. To import a file or folder from a Web site, click From Web, and the Import Web Wizard appears, as shown in Figure 8.11.

11. Leave the example in the Location box and click Next. The Choose Download Amount dialog box appears, as shown in Figure 8.12.

12. Decide how many levels from the starting page you want to come down—keep in mind that some Web sites are many layers deep.

13. Select a maximum file size to be downloaded.

14. If you only want text and images, put a check mark in the Limit to Text and Image Files check box. Leaving this box blank will cause FrontPage to download all content from the pages.

FIGURE **8.11**

The Import Web Wizard guides you through the process of bringing external files into your Web.

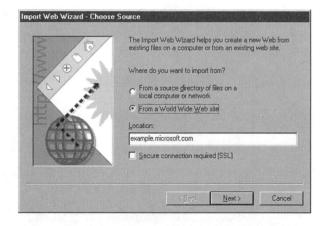

FIGURE **8.12**

You can specify the level of pages to bring in and also a maximum file size.

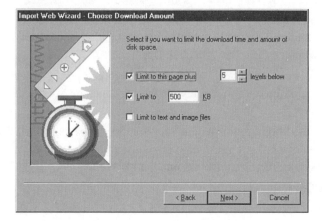

15. Click Next and the wizard displays a congratulations message, as shown in Figure 8.13.

The wizard will now attempt to call in the pages you requested. If the wizard recognizes that the pages were created with FrontPage, it will offer to maintain links, themes, and so on, as shown in Figure 8.14.

The example URL used in the preceding exercise will not result in any pages being downloaded—it is merely for demonstration purposes.

FIGURE 8.13

You have supplied the information; now sit back and let the software do the work.

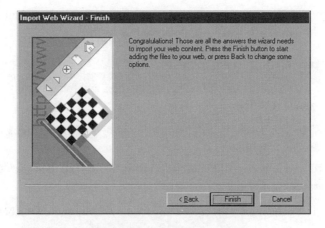

FIGURE 8.14

FrontPage can even recognize which software was used to create the pages you bring in.

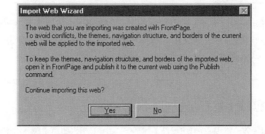

Caution

AUTHOR'S NOTE: Although the software allows you to download complete Web pages and sites from locations all across the World Wide Web, it is neither ethical nor (in many cases) legal to produce someone else's work as your own and SHOULD NOT be done.

Most commercial Web sites have legal notices regarding what you can and cannot do with downloaded material. These notices should always be observed. The following is one example of such a notice:

"All rights, including copyright, in the content of these web pages are owned or controlled for these purposes by the owners of this site.

"In accessing these web pages, you agree that you may only download the content for your own personal non-commercial use.

"You are not permitted to copy, broadcast, download, store (in any medium), transmit, show or play in public, adapt or change in any way the content of these web pages for any other purpose whatsoever without the prior written permission of the site owner."

You can add files from other folders, more folders, or files from other Web sites to the Import list simply by repeating the preceding instructions.

Saving the Import List

You can save your Import list and bring the files and folders into your Web at a later time by doing the following:

1. When you have selected the files and folders to import, click Close. The files are saved on the Import list.

2. To start importing the files, select File, Import and then click OK. The import process will begin.

You can stop the import process at any time by clicking the Stop button.

Note

> If the file you choose to import is a Microsoft Access database file (.mdb extension), you will immediately be prompted to create a database connection.

Importing Other Content

FrontPage 2000 allows you to import files of any type that are supported on your computer.

The list of supported file types could be almost endless, so they will not be listed here.

The most common file types you may import into your Web are image files you intend to use in your pages, .pdf files you intend to create links to, Macromedia Flash Animations, sound files, or video files.

All of these are best imported into the Web before being used. This ensures that the links are always correct, and in the case of an image file, it will prevent the Save Embedded File dialog box from coming up when you have inserted the image onto a page.

The process for importing any file of any type is the same as outlined in the preceding section.

Opening Existing Pages

8

An existing page is any .htm(l) file that has already been created. It doesn't have to be a page of your own making. You can open any .htm(l) page on your computer or at a remote location to either edit it or simply to view it within FrontPage 2000.

If the page is in your current Web, you can double-click the page's icon or filename from any of the views and the page will open in the editing screen.

In the case of imported files, as soon as the import is finished the files are available for editing in the same way as a page you have created yourself.

If the page is in a different Web or on your local filesystem, perform the following steps:

1. Select File, Open. The Open File dialog box appears, as shown in Figure 8.15.

FIGURE 8.15

The Open File dialog box lets you browse to any location to open a page for editing or viewing.

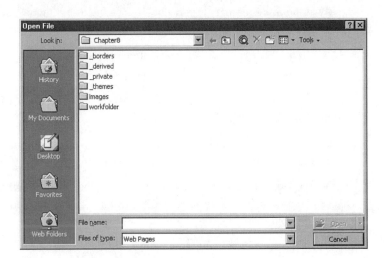

2. Use the icons to browse to the file you want to open—this may be a file on your local machine, a floppy disk, or you can type the full URL to a page on the World Wide Web.

3. If you select a location on the WWW, the file will open for you to edit, but when you save the page, you will be saving it locally—you won't be making changes to an online site.

4. Click Open and the page will open in the Page View for editing.

Browsing Through Your Web

When you have carefully planned your Web site and organized it the way you want, it is nice to see the files you have created and make sure that they are all where you wanted them to be. FrontPage 2000 makes it easy to do just that.

Viewing a Site Summary

FrontPage 2000 has many different reports to display information on many different areas of your Web site. One of these is the Site Summary report. The Site Summary report gives you an overview of your Web, the number and sizes of files and pictures, number and types of hyperlinks, number of incomplete tasks, and so on. The Site Summary report is basically a complete overview of the site at any given time. All of the reports within FrontPage are covered in detail throughout this book, but we will look quickly at the Site Summary report now. To see the Site Summary report, perform the following steps:

1. Open the Web you want to see a summary of.
2. From the View menu, select Reports and then click Site Summary.

The Site Summary report will be displayed, as shown in Figure 8.16. The exact display will obviously depend on the files you have within your Web.

If you want to see files within hidden directories in the Site Summary, you will have to set the Web settings to show them, as covered earlier in this chapter.

Another way to check the files in your Web site is to preview them in a Web browser. This can be done offline in FrontPage 2000 as long as you have a recent Web browser installed on your machine.

With any page open in the editing window, save the page and select File, Preview in Browser or click the Preview in Browser icon. The current page is then displayed. All of your links should be fully functional, giving you the opportunity to test them and see whether the pages look how you want.

FIGURE 8.16

The Site Summary gives an overview of your Web site.

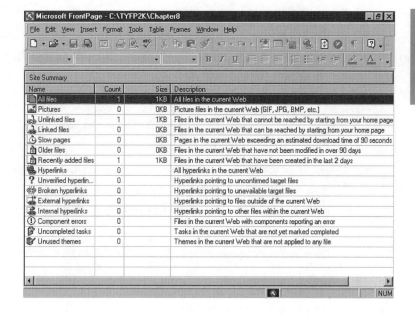

8

Summary

In today's lesson, you learned a bit about planning and managing you own Webs using FrontPage. Tomorrow's lesson covers how to customize the appearance of your Web pages.

Workshop

Q&A

Q If I move a file from one folder to another, what happens to my links?

A FrontPage will update the links as it moves the folders making sure that none break in the process.

Q What happens if I delete a folder that has files I needed after all?

A Before you delete a folder, you will prompted as to whether you are sure you want to delete it. Be very careful—once a folder is deleted, so are its contents.

Q **Can I import a complete Web?**

A Yes, but if it someone else's work DO NOT attempt to pass it off as your own.

Q **If I open a file located in a Web site on the WWW and make changes, will it affect the original Web site?**

A No. As soon as you save the file, it will be saved to your local machine, which won't affect the remote file.

Quiz

1. Is renaming a folder as easy as it is in Windows Explorer?
2. How do you move files from one folder to another?
3. If you import a file, what happens to the original?
4. What file types can you import?
5. Does an existing page have to be in your Web to view or edit it?

Exercises

Now that you have more of an idea about planning your overall Web site, you can try and decide if yours is as well organized as it could be.

1. Look through the files you have and see if you can create some logical folders for keeping files in.
2. See how easily you can import content from other locations. Bring a file from another application into your Web site and link to it directly from FrontPage.
3. Links can be made to any type of file and sometimes it is easier to link to a Word document than it is to convert the information to a Web page.

   If you have a .txt file or a set of documents you want to link to in your Web, import them and just create the links as normal.

   If you have some previously published Web pages, try to import them into your new Web for updating and editing.

Answers to Quiz

1. Yes. Simply select the folder, right-click, and choose Rename.
2. Simply drag them from one location to another.
3. Nothing. The Import command copies the file from its original location, leaving it unchanged.
4. Any file your computer will support can be imported.
5. No. An existing page means any previously created .htm(l) page.

DAY **9**

Changing the Appearance of Your Pages

FrontPage provides multiple ways to assign background images and text colors to your pages. You can create one page with a unique appearance, select others that use the same colors and styles, or create an entire Web that presents pages with consistent appearance. In this chapter, you'll learn all of the various ways that you can change the backgrounds and text colors of your pages.

In today's lesson, you will

- Assign background images, background colors, text colors, and hyperlink colors to a single Web page
- Use the same background properties on multiple pages
- Assign a FrontPage theme to all pages in your Web site
- Add a second theme to selected pages in your Web site
- Customize your FrontPage themes

Dressing Up a Single Page

By default, a standard Web page is rendered in a Web browser with a gray or white background, black text, and three different link colors. Links that have not yet been visited are blue by default; links that have been visited are purple; and active links (those selected but not yet visited) are red.

If it were not for the ability to use different text colors and backgrounds on Web pages, everything on the Internet would look pretty much the same. Different backgrounds and text colors can help your Web pages stand out from the rest, and FrontPage provides several different ways to achieve these results.

Exercise 9.1: Setting Page Properties

The most basic way to assign backgrounds and text colors to a Web page is to set the properties in the Page Properties dialog box. This method uses tags that were introduced in HTML 2.0, making this method a solid choice if you want your Web pages to be compatible with the widest number of browsers.

In this lesson you'll create a Web that does not use a FrontPage theme. This allows you to specify settings by using the Background tab in the Page Properties dialog box. You'll assign background and text properties to a blank Web page. Later, I'll show you an easy way to apply the same settings to other Web pages.

To create the Web and assign background properties to a page, follow these steps:

1. From FrontPage, choose File, New, Web. Create an empty Web named tyfp2k\chap09 on your c: drive.

2. If you do not see the folder list in the left portion of your screen, and a Web page named new_page_1.htm in the right portion of the screen, choose View, Page, and View, Folder List to display them.

3. In order to assign page background and text properties to a Web page, your Web cannot have themes applied to it. To disable themes in the Web, choose Format, Theme. The Theme dialog box appears.

4. Choose to apply the selected theme to All Pages.

5. From the list of themes that appears in the left portion of the Theme dialog box, select (No Theme), and choose OK to exit the Theme dialog box.

Note

When you apply a theme to a Web, you receive a warning that the fonts, colors, bullets, and lines that appear in all pages will be permanently replaced. Choose Yes in the warning box to apply the theme to your Web. You can disable this warning by choosing Tools, Options, and unchecking the Warn Before Permanently Applying Themes check box in the General tab of the Options dialog box.

9

Setting General Page Properties

The General tab of the Page Properties dialog box is shown in Figure 9.1. Applicable to today's lesson are the following properties in this tab:

Location   Displays the path or URL to the Web page.

Title   Displays the title of the Web page. This title should be descriptive of the contents of your Web page.

To continue with today's exercise, display the new_page_1.htm page in the page editor. Then, complete the following:

6. Choose File, Properties. The Page Properties dialog box appears, opened to the General tab (see Figure 9.1).

7. Enter **Web Colors** in the Title field.

FIGURE 9.1

The General tab in the Page Properties dialog box.

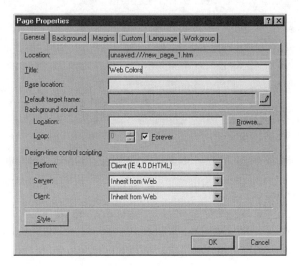

Setting Background Properties

The Background tab in the Page Properties dialog box, shown in Figure 9.2, is where you will enter the remaining settings for your Web page. Here, you assign background images and text and link colors for your Web page. You can also use backgrounds and colors from another page, as you will learn later in this chapter.

FIGURE 9.2

Use the Background tab to assign a background image or color and text colors to Web pages that do not use themes.

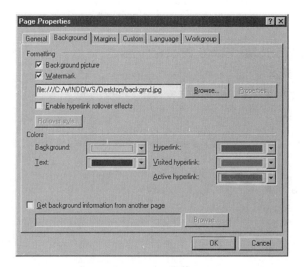

To continue with your current exercise, follow these steps:

8. Click the Background tab, shown in Figure 9.2.

9. To specify a background image for your page, check the Background Picture check box. Click the Browse button. The Select Background Picture dialog box appears.

10. To insert a background picture from the CD-ROM that accompanies this book, click the Select a File on Your Computer button, located in the lower-right portion of the dialog box.

11. Use the Look In box to locate the `tyfp2k\chap09\samples` folder on the CD. Locate `backgrnd.jpg`, and choose OK to return to the Background tab in the Page Properties dialog box.

12. To make the background image a watermark (a stationary background image that does not scroll), check the Watermark check box. Watermarks are an Internet Explorer feature, and may not work in other browsers.

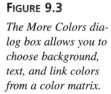

Note

You'll also notice a setting here that allows you to select hyperlink rollover effects. These settings use cascading style sheet properties to change the appearance of the hyperlink when the mouse hovers over the link. Cascading style sheets are discussed further in tomorrow's lesson, "Using Style Sheets."

So far, you have assigned a background image for your Web page. The Colors section of the Page Properties dialog box allows you to select a solid background color, as well as colors for the text and hyperlinks on your pages. When a Web page uses default colors, the word Automatic appears in the Text, Hyperlink, Visited Hyperlink, and Active Hyperlink fields, along with a small square that shows the color each element uses. When you select other colors, the word Automatic is replaced with a solid color square, as shown in Figure 9.2.

Typically, you choose background, text, and link colors that work well with your background image. Even though you are using a patterned background on your Web pages, you also want to select a page background color that is similar in tone to the background image. This way, when a site visitor chooses to turn off images in their browsers, the text and links on your Web pages are still legible.

To select background, text, and link colors, continue with these steps:

13. From the Background drop-down list, choose More Colors to open the More Colors dialog box shown in Figure 9.3. You can select colors from a color matrix using this dialog box.

FIGURE 9.3

The More Colors dialog box allows you to choose background, text, and link colors from a color matrix.

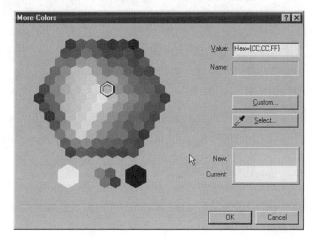

14. Select the color just above and to the right of the center white color in the color matrix (light purple). The Value should read Hex={CC,CC,FF}. Choose OK to return to the Background tab.

15. Similarly, from the Text drop-down menu, choose the last color in the first row of the color matrix. The Value should read Hex={00,00,66}.

16. For the Hyperlink color, choose the last color in the tenth row (the 4th row from the bottom) of the color matrix. The Value should read Hex={99,33,66}.

17. For the Visited Hyperlink color, choose the next to last color in the ninth row (the 5th row from the bottom) of the color matrix. The Value should read Hex={CC,33,99}

18. For the Active Hyperlink color, choose the next to last color in the 2nd row of the color matrix. The Value should read Hex={33,33,FF}.

19. Click OK to exit the Page Properties dialog box. The background image appears on your page.

20. Choose File, Save (Ctrl+S) or click the Save button in the Standard toolbar. The Save As dialog box appears.

21. The title that you entered in step 7 appears in the Page Title field. From the list of folders in your current Web, double-click the _private folder. Then enter **webcolors.htm** in the File Name field.

22. Choose Save to save your page to your Web. The Save Embedded Files dialog box shown in Figure 9.4 appears.

FIGURE 9.4

Use the Save Embedded Files dialog box to save the background image into the image *folder.*

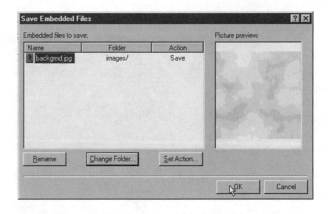

23. Click the Change Folder button. Double-click the images folder to select it. Choose OK to return to the Save Embedded Files dialog box. The Folder column displays images/ as the folder to which your image is saved.

24. Choose OK. Your background image is saved to the images folder, and your style sheet is saved to the private folder.

25. Choose File, Close (Ctrl+F4) to close the Web Colors page.

Exercise 9.2: Using Colors from Another Page

Now that you have created your own FrontPage style sheet, you can easily assign it to another page. You use the Background tab in the Page Properties dialog box to accomplish this task as well. In the following task, you will create a new page based on one of the FrontPage page templates. You will assign the style sheet that you created in the previous task to this Web page.

To assign your style sheet to another page, follow these steps:

1. From FrontPage, choose File, New, Page (Ctrl+N). The New Page dialog box appears.

2. Double-click the One-column Body with Contents and Sidebar page template or highlight the template name and choose OK. The new page appears in FrontPage.

3. Choose Format, Background. The Page Properties dialog box opens to the Background tab shown in Figure 9.5.

FIGURE 9.5

To use background information from one page on another page, check the Get Background Information from Another Page option.

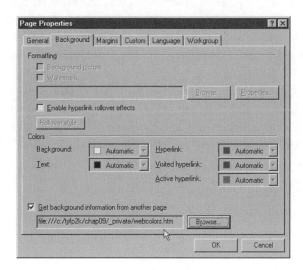

4. Choose the Get Background Information from Another Page option. The choices in the top Formatting section of the Background tab become disabled.

5. Click the Browse button. The Current Web dialog box opens.

6. Double-click the `private` folder to select it, then double-click the `webcolors.htm` page to assign its colors to your new page. You return to the Page Properties dialog box.

7. Click OK. The properties you assigned to your style sheet are assigned to your current page. Optionally, save your practice page to your Web.

You can assign these colors to as many pages in your Web as you like; however, each page has to be done individually by following the preceding exercise with every page. This might seem like a lot of extra work—however, when you later decide to change the look of your Web pages, all you have to do is open the `private/webcolors.htm` page. Change the background image, background color, and text and hyperlink colors, and resave the page to your Web. Automatically, all of the pages that used the background information from that page will be updated.

Adding Themes

In Day 2, "Fast-Track to Webs and Pages," you created a Corporate Presence Web that allowed you the option of selecting a theme as you stepped through the Corporate Presence Web Wizard. You already have some idea of how easy it is to change the entire look of your Web site, including navigation bars and banners. Your pages display a consistent appearance, using the same graphics and fonts throughout the site, or on the pages that you select. Each of the dozens of available themes is professionally designed, and the images and fonts are coordinated to work well together.

Enabling Warnings Before You Apply a Theme

Themes change the way fonts and images appear in your pages. FrontPage 2000 issues a warning before you permanently apply a theme to your Web. When you choose a theme for your Web, you may receive the following warning:

```
Applying a theme to a Web will change the way
fonts, colors, bullets, and lines appear in all pages.
This will permanently replace some of the existing
formatting information. Do you want to apply the theme?
```

Choose Yes to apply your theme or No to cancel the procedure. You can enable or disable this warning through the Options dialog box as follows:

1. From FrontPage, choose Tools, Options. The Options dialog box appears, opened to the General tab shown in Figure 9.6.

2. To disable the warning, uncheck the box that reads Warn Before Permanently Applying Themes. Check the box to enable the warning.

3. Choose OK to exit the Options dialog box and update the setting.

9

FIGURE 9.6

The Options dialog box allows you to enable or disable a warning before you apply themes to your Web.

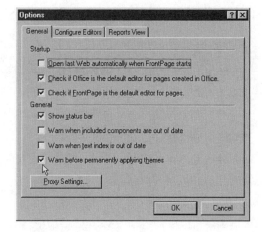

Choosing a Theme

The Themes dialog box is shown in Figure 9.7. You see this dialog box after you choose the Format, Theme command. You can choose to apply a theme to all pages in your Web, or to selected pages. Then, you can select the theme you want to use from the many themes displayed in the left panel of the dialog box. As you highlight one of the names in the Themes list, a preview of the theme appears in the Sample of Themes preview pane at the right.

> **Note**
>
> When you use Themes in your Web pages, you will be unable to change hyperlink colors through the Background tab in the Page Properties dialog box. This tab no longer appears when a page has a theme assigned to it. To change hyperlink colors on a page that uses themes, you will need to modify the theme as discussed later in this chapter.

The Themes dialog box presents the following options:

- *Apply Theme To*—This allows you to choose whether to apply the selected theme to All Pages in your Web, or to Selected Pages.

> **Note**
>
> If you want to apply a theme to selected pages in your Web, choose View, Folders. Select one or more pages from the file list in the right pane in Folders View before you choose the Format, Theme command.

FIGURE 9.7

Use the Themes dialog box to assign a theme to all or some of the pages in your Web.

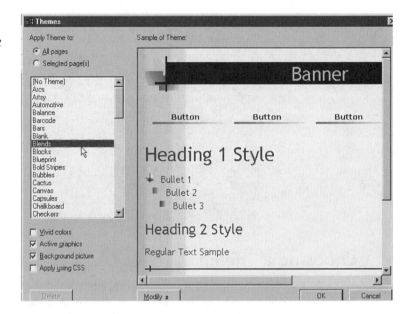

- *Vivid Colors*—Check this option to display brighter text and link colors in your Web pages.

- *Active Graphics*—Check this option to use graphics that change state when a mouse hovers over a navigation button (hover buttons), or when a navigation button is selected. Hover buttons will not work unless viewed in pages that support JavaScript (such as Internet Explorer 3.0 and later, and Netscape Navigator 3.0 and later). When left unchecked, the pages use buttons that do not change state.

- *Background Picture*—Check this option to use a background image on your pages. When left unchecked, the page uses a solid background.

- *Apply Using CSS*—Normally, the information that contains theme settings are stored in hidden folders in your Web. The theme information is specified in several cascading style sheets within these hidden folders. If you check the Apply Using CSS option, FrontPage creates a file named theme1.css in the hidden _themes/*themename* folder of your Web, where *themename* is the name of the theme you selected.

Note To see the hidden folders in your Web, choose Tools, Web Settings to open the Web Settings dialog box. Check the Show Documents in Hidden Directories option in the Advanced tab.

Exercise 9.3: Applying a Theme to a Web

In this exercise, you'll create a Web using the Customer Support Web template. Then you'll apply a Web theme that you choose. Follow these steps:

1. Choose File, New, Web. Select the Customer Support Web template from the Web Sites section. Create the Web in the c:\tyfp2k\custsup folder on your hard drive.

2. After the Web pages appear, choose Format, Theme. The Themes dialog box appears.

3. Select to apply themes to All Pages.

4. From the list of themes, select a theme that is appealing to you, and choose the options you want to apply to your theme. For the example shown in this chapter, I selected the Topo theme, with Vivid Colors, Active Graphics, and Background Picture.

5. Choose OK to apply the theme to all pages in your Web. After FrontPage updates your Web, you will see the theme on all of your Web pages. Figure 9.8 shows the Welcome page (index.htm) as displayed in the page editor.

FIGURE 9.8

A theme is applied to all of the pages in the Customer Support Web.

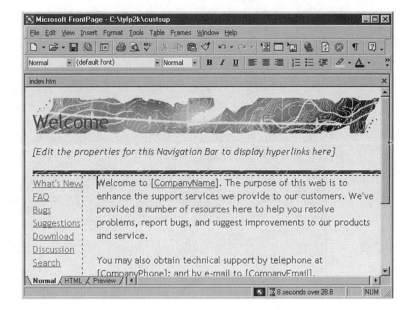

Using Multiple Themes in a Web

The Customer Support Web that you created in the previous exercise contains pages that might stand out more by using another theme. In FrontPage 2000, it's very easy to use more than one theme in a Web. You use Folder View to select one or more pages, and then select a theme for those pages in the Themes dialog box. You'll perform this in the following exercise.

Exercise 9.4: Adding Another Web Theme

Notice that the Customer Support Web contains some pages that are all prefixed with cusu. There are eight such pages, and they relate to the Customer Support Discussion group in this Web. In this exercise, you'll learn how to use more than one theme in a Web. You'll apply a different theme to the pages that are prefixed with cusu.

1. Choose View, Folders. FrontPage displays the list of folders in the left pane, and the list of files contained in the selected folder in the right pane.

2. From the left pane, choose the root folder (labeled C:\tyfp2k\custsup). All pages in that folder appear in the right pane.

3. Shift-click to select all eight files that begin with cusu: cusuaftr.htm, cusuahdr.htm, cusucfrm.htm, cusufoot.htm, cusuhead.htm, cusupost.htm, cususrch.htm, and cusutoc.htm.

4. With these eight pages selected, choose Format, Theme. The Themes dialog box appears again.

5. Select to apply themes to Selected Pages.

6. From the list of themes, select a theme that is appealing to you, and choose the options you want to apply to your theme. Try to select a theme that blends well with the theme you applied with your other pages. This way, people might recognize that they are still on your site, rather than someone else's. For the example shown in this chapter, I selected the Sandstone theme, with Vivid Colors, Active Graphics, and Background Picture.

7. Choose OK to apply the theme to the selected pages in your Web.

8. Choose View, Folder List to hide display of the folder list. This shows your page in full width.

9. Open the Welcome page in the editor (index.htm), and choose the Preview tab in the editor to preview the Web page.

10. Click the Discussion link located in the left navigation bar on the Web page. The Discussion page shown in Figure 9.9 appears. This page uses the first theme that you selected for your Web.

11. Now, click the discussion group link. You should see the Customer Support Discussion page appear in the preview window, as shown in Figure 9.10. This page

uses the theme that you selected as your second choice. Continue navigating through the site to examine which pages use the different themes.

FIGURE 9.9

This page uses the first theme that you selected for your Web.

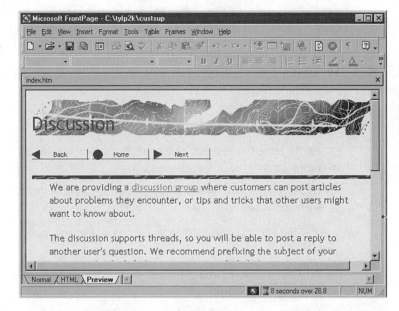

FIGURE 9.10

The Customer Support Discussion page uses the second theme that you selected for your Web.

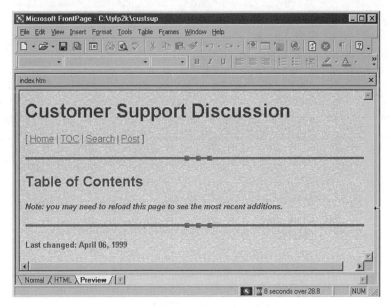

Notes About Themes

When you use themes in your FrontPage Webs, many of the text styles and heading styles that you insert on your pages will automatically use the font faces and colors defined by your Web or page theme. This is true of the following text elements:

- Body text (the font used for Normal paragraphs on your pages)
- Hyperlink text (the color and style of the text used for a hyperlink that the user has not yet followed)
- Visited hyperlink text (the color and style of the text used for a hyperlink that the user has visited)
- Active hyperlink text (the color and style of the text used for a hyperlink that the user is in the process of navigating to)
- Heading 1 through Heading 6 (the color and style of the text used for all heading styles on your pages)

If you use the Paragraph Properties dialog box to format a paragraph, you see the following results:

- When you choose Normal Paragraphs, the selected text will use the body font defined in the theme.
- When you choose Address Paragraphs, the selected text will use an italicized version of the body font defined in the theme.
- When you choose Formatted Paragraphs, the selected text uses a fixed-width font such as Courier.

There are some additional points that should be mentioned, in general, about using the FrontPage Web templates and wizards. The wizards give you an opportunity to choose a graphical theme for your Web before you complete the steps in the wizards. The steps to choose themes in wizards are similar to those that you learned today.

Templates, on the other hand, apply the theme that you last applied to pages in any other Web. If you have not yet applied a theme to any pages, a theme will not be applied to the pages generated by the templates.

Using Bulleted Lists with Themes

When you use bulleted lists in your pages, the List Properties dialog box shown in Figure 9.11 enables you to use the bullet images that are applicable to your current theme or another image that you specify. For more information about bulleted lists, refer to Day 4, "Using Lists to Organize Information."

FIGURE 9.11

You can use the bullet images from your current theme or select another bullet image.

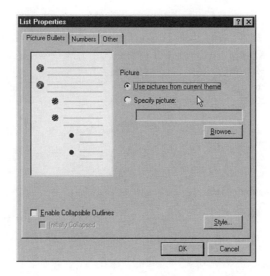

9

Using Horizontal Lines with Themes

When you insert a horizontal line on a Web page that has a theme applied to it, the image used for your Web theme appears. If you double-click on the horizontal line to change its properties, you will notice that the Width, Height, and Color fields in the Horizontal Line Properties dialog box are disabled. However, you will be able to change the alignment of the horizontal line to Left, Center, or Right, as shown in Figure 9.12.

FIGURE 9.12

When themes are applied to your Web pages, you cannot change the width, height, and color of a horizontal line.

Using Page Banners with Themes

When you use the Insert, Page Banner command to insert a page banner on your page, you can select whether your banner appears as an image or as text. This is set in the Page Banner Properties dialog box shown in Figure 9.13. Either selection (Images or

Text) uses the properties associated with the theme applied to your active page. If the current page does not have a theme assigned to it, the page banner inserts the page title as large, bold text. In order for the page banners to appear on your pages, they must be placed in Navigation View, as discussed on Day 9, "Changing the Appearance of Your Pages."

Figure 9.13

When you insert page banners on a page that has a theme, the banner uses the images and fonts associated with the theme. If no theme is applied, the page title appears as large, bold text.

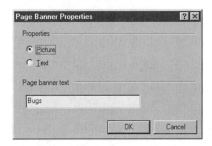

Using Themes with Framesets

Assigning different, but compatible, themes to different frames in framesets may make for an attractive page. You can use one theme for the main pages in your Web, and a different theme for the navigation frames in the frameset. Use the procedure outlined in Exercise 9.4 to apply themes to selected pages.

Using Themes with Background Images

When your page has a theme applied to it, the Format, Background command and its associated properties will not take effect until you remove the theme from the associated page. If you want to change the background image for the entire theme, you will need to modify the theme as discussed in "Modifying Theme Graphics," later in this chapter.

Creating Your Own Themes

The Themes dialog box allows you to make changes to an existing theme. The changes can be subtle, such as selecting a different text or link color. You can also make many changes, such as adding your own background and button graphics. The themes that ship with FrontPage are read-only, and FrontPage will not allow you to save over the top of them. Any time you modify an existing theme, you create a *custom* theme and will be prompted to save it with a different name.

A Modify button appears at the bottom of the Themes dialog box. When you click the Modify button, you are prompted to choose the portion of an existing theme that you want to modify, as shown in Figure 9.14. These choices are Colors, Graphics, and Text.

FIGURE 9.14

You can also modify the colors, graphics, or text in any Web theme.

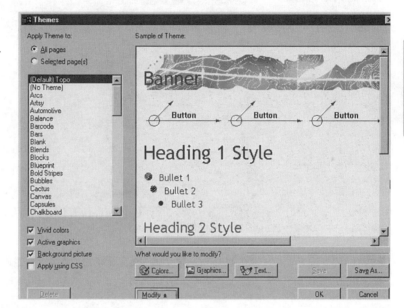

Modifying Theme Colors

When you choose to modify the colors in a theme, the Modify Theme dialog box displays three tabs. The first of these tabs is the Color Schemes tab shown in Figure 9.15. This tab allows you to apply text and link colors from another theme into your current Web theme. From the bottom of the Modify Theme dialog box, you choose whether you want to modify the Normal Colors set, or the Vivid Colors set of your current theme. Scroll through the list until you find another color combination that you like. Double-click to apply the new colors to your current theme. The theme preview displays how your Web pages will look with the new colors.

The Color Wheel tab, shown in Figure 9.16, allows you to adjust the hue and brightness of all colors in the color set. To adjust the hue, click and drag the small circle in the round color matrix until the five squares beneath the color matrix display colors that you like. Then, use the Brightness slider to lighten or darken the colors. Colors get brighter as you move the slider toward the right.

FIGURE 9.15

Use the Color Schemes tab to apply colors from a different theme to your current Web theme.

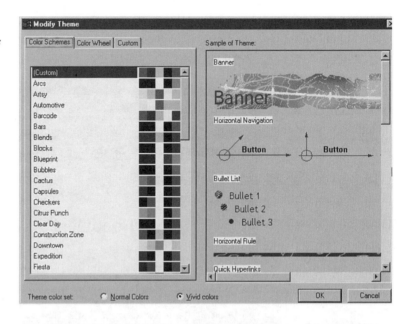

FIGURE 9.16

The Color Wheel tab allows you to adjust the hue and brightness of the colors in your color set.

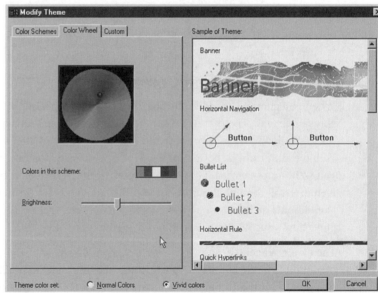

The Custom tab, shown in Figure 9.17, allows you to manually specify the colors that are used in every Web element, from text to table borders. For example, each heading can be a different color, if you want. Select the element that you want to change from the Item drop-down list. Then, choose the color from the Color drop-down list.

FIGURE 9.17

The Custom tab allows you to select custom colors for every element in the theme.

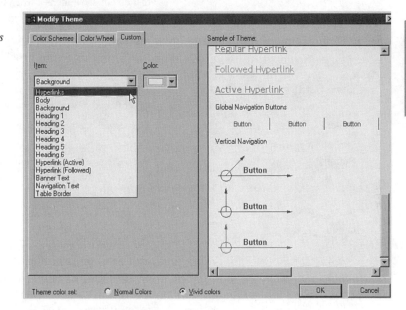

After you select your new colors, choose OK to exit the Modify Theme dialog box.

Modifying Theme Graphics

When you choose to modify theme graphics, you can select different graphics for your Web theme. The background and button graphics can be customized to use graphics that you create yourself. If you want to use images that have transparent areas, apply transparency to the images before you import them into your Web. You might find it easier to select your images if you import all of them into your Web before you modify the theme.

In general, each theme uses the following graphics, with common sizes indicated in Table 9.1:

TABLE 9.1   Graphics Used in Web Themes

Graphic Use	Typical Size	Comments
Background Picture	Varies	Can be either GIF or JPG. Seamless patterns (images that do not show themes when repeated horizontally and vertically) are generally most pleasing.
Banner	600×60	The graphic that displays the title of your Web page. Avoid middle tones, and use light text on dark backgrounds, or dark text on light backgrounds.
Bullet List 1	15×15	The top-level bullet image, which is generally slightly larger than the two lower levels.
Bullet List 2,3	12×12	The second and third level bullet images.
Global Navigation Buttons	95×20	The buttons that are used for top-level pages in your Web. Because they are small, you generally want to keep colors solid rather than using a pattern, so that text is legible.
Horizontal Navigation buttons	140×40	Navigation buttons that are displayed horizontally on your Web page, typically in a top or bottom shared border. If active graphics are used, you'll need to specify three images: one for the button's normal (unselected) state; one for how the button looks when a mouse hovers over it; and one to indicate the current (or selected) page.
Vertical Navigation buttons	140×40	Navigation buttons that are displayed vertically on your Web page, typically in a right or left shared border. See additional comments regarding active graphics for Horizontal Navigation.
Horizontal Rule	450–600×10	The image used for horizontal rules in your Web pages.
Quick Back, Home, Next, Up	100×20	The images used for "quick" navigation buttons that take the reader to same-level pages in your Web. Like Global Navigation Buttons, it is best to use solid colors as text on these buttons is small.

To choose a new theme graphic, select the graphic category from the Item drop-down list in the Picture tab, shown in Figure 9.18. Depending on the selection, one or more additional drop-down lists appear. Use the Browse button beside each drop-down list to select an image from your current Web.

FIGURE 9.18

The Picture tab allows you to customize the images used in your Web theme.

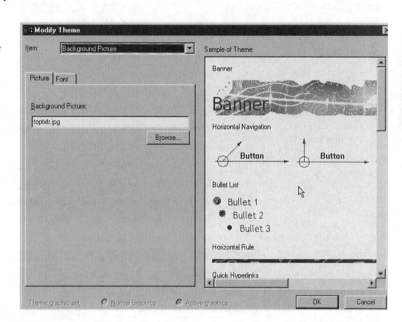

9

To customize the fonts that are used on each navigation button or page banner, click the Font tab shown in Figure 9.19. All fonts that reside on your computer are displayed in the Font list. However, unless the same fonts reside on the receiving end, the text might look different to those who are viewing your page. When you select fonts, also consider readability. Highly decorative fonts can be distracting and hard to read for some people. The Style, Size, Horizontal Alignment, and Vertical Alignment settings allow you to select the font weight, size, and alignment on the navigation buttons.

Modifying Theme Text

When you choose to modify theme text, the dialog box shown in Figure 9.20 appears. The Item list allows you to modify the text used in the body of your Web page, and for the headings.

FIGURE 9.19

The Font tab allows you to customize the fonts that are used on your navigation buttons and banners.

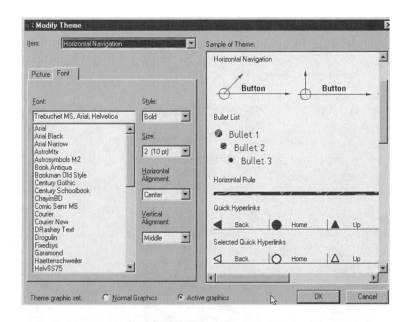

FIGURE 9.20

When you choose to modify theme text, you can change the body and heading fonts on your pages.

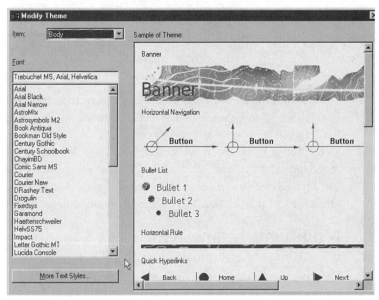

However, you can specify different text properties for just about *any* HTML tag, going well beyond the properties found in standard themes. For this, you need to be familiar with cascading style sheet properties, which are discussed in tomorrow's lesson. When you choose the More Text Styles button at the bottom of the dialog box shown in Figure 9.20, the Style dialog box shown in Figure 9.21 appears. Here, you can specify the appearance of any HTML tag, from basic body text to table data, numbered lists, bulleted lists, and more. Each element on your page can be presented in a consistent manner from page to page.

FIGURE 9.21

The Style dialog box allows you to change the properties of HTML elements that are not found in standard Web themes.

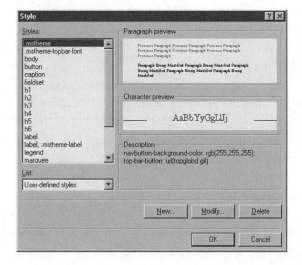

If you're not really handy at creating your own graphics, you can customize the appearance of your pages by using different text and link colors, and different fonts. You can still achieve the "individuality" that you're seeking. Sometimes just a slight change in fonts and color goes a long way to give your site a unique signature!

Summary

You learned today that FrontPage provides many ways to control the appearance of your Web pages. You can assign background, text, and link colors to an individual page, create several pages that share the same background properties, or use themes to apply professionally designed banner graphics, navigation buttons, bullets, horizontal rules, and font faces and colors to your Web pages. FrontPage 2000 also makes it very easy to create and customize your own themes. Today's workshop will help you review what you've learned in this chapter.

Workshop

Q&A

Q Is there a limit to the number of themes that I can use in a Web?

A Not really, no. However, the main reason for using themes is to achieve a relatively consistent appearance throughout the site. One way to achieve consistency while using multiple themes is to use backgrounds, buttons, and text that change in color, but not appearance, from theme to theme. Likewise, if you use themes that share a common color scheme but the graphics vary from theme to theme, this is another way to achieve similarity.

Q I used the Background tab to specify colors for my Web page, and then I applied a theme to all of the pages in my Web. Now the backgrounds that I originally used aren't in the Web Colors page I created. What happened?

A When you assigned the Web theme to all pages in your Web, the theme overwrote the background information that you placed on your Web Colors page. If you want to use both methods in your Web, the next question will help you.

Q You mentioned that the Background tab of the Page Properties dialog box does not appear when themes are used in a Web. Is there a way to use both methods (page backgrounds and themes) in the same Web?

A Yes, there is a way. From Folder View, select all of the pages that you want to assign Background properties to. Choose Format, Theme, and apply (No Theme) to the selected Web pages. The Background tab should appear when you choose the Format, Background or File, Properties command for any of those pages.

Quiz

1. How can you determine when a Web page uses custom background, text, and link colors?
2. What command allows you to use colors from another Web page?
3. What are active graphics?
4. True or false: You can use your own graphics in Web themes.
5. True or false: You can only customize backgrounds, text, headings, and lists in a Web theme.

Exercises

1. Try to apply the lessons you've learned today to your own Web site. Experiment with using more than one theme, if you want.

2. Try your hand at customizing the theme in your own Web site. Sometimes all you need is a variation in text or colors to make a Web site look totally unique.

Answers to Quiz

1. A Web page that uses custom colors displays a value other than Automatic in the Colors section of the Page Properties dialog box. If the Background tab does not appear in the Page Properties dialog box, the page has a theme applied to it.

2. The File, Properties command or Format, Background command allows you to use colors from another Web page. The Background tab of the Page Properties dialog box allows you get background information from another page. This option is disabled when a page uses a Web theme.

3. Active graphics in a Web theme incorporate buttons that respond to selections. A different graphic is used to represent one of three button states: one when a button is not selected, one when a mouse hovers over a button, and one when a page is selected.

4. True. If you are very creative and want to create your own custom buttons, you can easily create a Web theme around them. Select a theme that is close in appearance to what you want to achieve, and go from there.

5. False. When you customize Text theme options, the More Text Styles button allows you to specify text settings for any HTML tag.

9

DAY **10**

Using Style Sheets

Of all the new technologies and standards professional Web developers use on Web sites today, style sheets, also known as Cascading Style Sheets or CSS, are probably the most often used. You may or may not be familiar with them, but you have probably visited a Web site that uses them. For example, Macmillan Computer Publishing makes extensive use of style sheets throughout its Web site. It is most likely that you didn't even notice that style sheets were being used when you visited the Web site. That's because style sheets weren't invented for flashy effects. Rather, Web developers use them to facilitate HTML programming and to cut down on repetitious tags. As we go along, you'll have a chance to cover a large part of CSS, and hopefully, you'll be able to use them comfortably on your Web sites by the end of this lesson. So, without further ado, let's dive into what I think is the most interesting technology available to Web developers at this time.

In today's lesson, you will

- Learn what cascading style sheets are
- Learn to apply styles in FrontPage (inline, embedded, and external)
- Learn some HTML, if you aren't already familiar with it
- Learn to use style sheets to cut down on design time
- Learn to create external style sheets for use on your Web site

What Are Cascading Style Sheets?

A short answer: Style sheets enable you to specify a style for a group of elements (for the rest of this chapter, the term "element" will refer to anything on a Web page), which is automatically used without you having to program it specifically.

A style is formatting that can be applied to an element (remember the definition of an element). For example, you could set the style for a font, which would include, among others: family (or type), size (or point), weight, underline, color, stretch, alignment, and variant. Now, think of the possibilities for a table: border size, border color, background color, and alignment. Repeat this for each row and each cell of the table. As you can see, there are many aspects to style sheets, and it would be impossible to cover everything included in CSS in one chapter. Why, the official CSS reference by the World Wide Web Consortium (also know as the W3C) spans dozens of printed pages! Fortunately, you don't need to know everything that's included in CSS because FrontPage does an excellent job of managing style sheets, and enables you to easily apply styles to elements in your Web pages.

"But what makes style sheets so different?" you may ask. "I am already able to specify most of the font and table styles listed above without using style sheets." Read on, disbeliever…. With the advent of style sheets, you no longer have to specify settings for each element on a page by typing the code. Although this may or may not mean much to you, it can drastically reduce the amount of code on a page, sometimes by as much as 50 percent or more. This has the added bonus of making your file size smaller, which is always welcome on the Web, where bandwidth considerations are high priority. Moreover, it is possible to set styles for all elements in your Web pages, and to reuse these styles throughout your Web site, thus ensuring that your Web site maintains a consistent look and feel. And of course, for those of you who change your desktop theme every day (and who probably do about the same with your Web site), it can take only a couple of minutes to change the styles for your Web, and have the new styles instantly applied to the entire site. Hopefully, you now know why style sheets are so important. Certainly you want to start using them… .

How Styles Are Applied

Style sheets are divided into three areas of application. They can be applied to 1) a single element, for one-time use; 2) a group of elements, for use on one single Web page; and 3) a group of elements, for use on multiple Web pages. The following sections cover each of these types of applications.

Inline Styles

As mentioned in the preceding section, the first, or smallest application of style sheets is one-time use on a single Web page. This is also known as an inline style because the style is defined directly for that one element of the page, and no other element on the page uses it. For example, if you want to set the border size to two pixels for one cell in a large table, and the border for the rest of the table is one pixel wide, you could use an inline style. Most of the time, inline styles are used when you want to do something that you cannot do directly with plain old HTML, such as in the example of the table cell. Another example of this would be setting the spacing between letters in a single word to make it stand out. Think of inline styles as a "quick fix" when you want just the right style for an element in your page.

Embedded Style Sheets

Embedded style sheets are completely different from inline styles in the way they work and in the way they are implemented. An embedded style sheet is used to set styles for groups of elements within the current Web page. For example, if you wanted all of the text in your page to be set to Arial, 10pt., bold, red, and justified (don't try this on the Web, please!), you could simply set the appropriate style rules, or formatting, for the page (using the body tag—don't worry if you don't what it is) in about six lines altogether. Without style sheets, if you had a simple 4×4 table in your Web page, that could take about 30 lines of code or more, and you still wouldn't be able to justify the text. Of course, this is an extreme example, but when you start using style sheets to your advantage, you can simply set the style for the elements on your page, then forget about formatting each little block of text.

External Style Sheets

External style sheets are a lot like embedded style sheets, but their application is different. As the name implies, external style sheets use text files that are not part of the Web page. With external style sheets, the style rules are defined, and then saved to a text file with a CSS extension. They are probably the most useful application of style sheets, since you simply call the style sheet by specifying its path, and the browser takes care of the rest. The implications of this are obvious—one little file can hold the style rules (or formatting) for the entire Web site. When the formatting needs to be changed, only the file is changed, and the changes are immediately reflected throughout the Web site. Easy? Fun? I think so.

The Style Toolbar

Now that you've learned the basics of style sheets, along with the basic vocabulary you'll need to work with them, it's time to see how FrontPage can automate this for you. The first thing you'll want to do is display the Style toolbar by opening FrontPage and then clicking View, Toolbars, Style. The Style toolbar appears in the FrontPage Editor (see Figure 10.1).

FIGURE 10.1

The Style toolbar enables you to easily set styles on elements in your page.

As you can, see the Style toolbar contains only one button. This button opens the Style dialog box, which you can also access using Format, Style (see Figure 10.2). Once you have the Style dialog box open, you may find it a little confusing at first, especially if you're not familiar with HTML tags. The following sections cover the elements in the Style dialog box in more detail.

FIGURE 10.2

The Style dialog box enables you to set style rules on HTML tags and on a selection in your document.

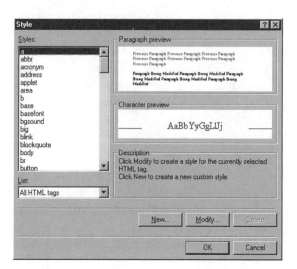

Creating Styles in FrontPage

Creating a style in FrontPage is quite simple. FrontPage divides styles into two major categories—HTML tags and user-defined styles. As you know, styles defined on HTML tags are automatically applied to all of the tags. For user-defined styles, it's a little different. Once you create a style, you'll have to apply it to specific elements on your Web page. We'll go over user-defined styles just after Exercise 10.1, so I won't go into further detail about it now. However, this will help you to get familiar with the Style dialog box shown in Figure 10.2. Notice that the List drop-down box contains two entries: User-Defined Styles and All HTML Tags. For now, the selection that interests us is All HTML Tags.

Modifying Styles for HTML Tags

This section will go over the basic tags you need to understand to work with style sheets. It will give you some basic pointers on which tags are most often used in Web pages with CSS. If you are familiar with HTML tags, you can skip these definitions. Don't worry, you won't find this too hard. Keep in mind that you need to know at least the tags in the following list if you want to successfully use style sheets in your documents.

Tip

> See Appendix A, "HTML 4 Quick Reference," for a complete listing of HTML tags.

- a—This is the anchor tag, used for hyperlinks. Styles applied to this tag will be reflected on all hyperlinks in the Web page.

- body—This is the main tag for any Web page. Styles defined for this tag are applied to the content of the entire page. Note that any style defined on an element will override this tag. For example, if you set style rules for the a and body tags, your hyperlinks will use the style rules set for the a tag rather than those of the body tag when there is a conflict in formatting.

- h1–h6—These are the header tags, which are used when you apply a heading to your text. As you may have guessed, h1 stands for Heading 1, h2 for Heading 2, and so on. If you use headings, you will probably want to set style rules for each of them.

- img—This is the image tag, which is used for every single image in your page. If you want to apply specific formatting to your images, this is the tag you'll want to use.

10

- `input`, `textarea`—The `input` tag is my personal favorite. This tag is used for every form control, with the exception of a multiple line textbox (which, you guessed it, uses the `textarea` tag). You'll most likely want to define the style rules for this tag, especially if you have form controls on your Web page.

- `ol`, `ul`, `li`—These tags are used for lists. The `ol` tag stands for "ordered list," usually a numbered list. The `ul` tag stands for "unordered list," which usually consists of bullets. Finally, the `li` tag stands for "list item." So, if you have a numbered list, it will consist of one `ol` tag, and as many `li` tags as you have items. The same applies for a bulleted list, except that the `ul` tag is used in its place.

- `p`—This is the paragraph tag, which is widely used by FrontPage. For every ¶ you see in the FrontPage Editor, there is a paragraph tag.

- `table`, `tr`, `td`—These three tags are used to create tables. The `table` tag defines the table itself; the `tr` tag defines each table row; and the `td` tag defines table cells.

There, now that wasn't too hard, was it? To modify the display of an HTML tag, all you have to do is select it from the list in the Style dialog box, and then click the Modify button. From there, the Modify Style dialog box will appear (see Figure 10.3). On the bottom-left corner of the dialog box, you'll notice the Format button. This button is used to set the style rules for your HTML tag. When you click this button, a menu pops up that lists your options. You can choose to modify the Font, Paragraph, Border, Numbering, and Position for your selection. Day 3, "Building Basic Web Pages," covered the Font and Paragraph dialog boxes; Day 4, "Using Lists to Organize Information," covered numbering; and positioning will be covered on Day 13, "Working with DHTML and Positioning." We'll go over the Borders and Shading box later in this lesson.

FIGURE 10.3

The Modify Style dialog box enables you to set the style rules (or formatting) for an HTML tag or a user-defined style.

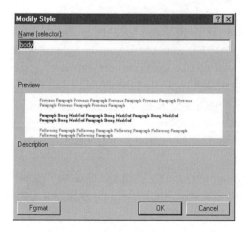

Now that you know about the different applications of styles, the basic HTML tags, and how FrontPage works with style sheets, it's time to start implementing your own styles into your Web pages. The section that follows deals with the basics of styles. If you had trouble with any of the material so far, take your time and read it again. Remember, it's more important to learn than simply to complete the book!

Exercise 10.1: Using Style Sheet Basics

In this exercise, your goal is to create a Web site for a local circus. Since you basically want all of the pages to use the same font, color scheme, and text alignment, you'll define some styles for the home page of your Web site on the body (for the general layout), table, and a (hyperlink) tags. After that, we'll take a look at what style sheets look like in HTML. Follow the steps below, and then see Figure 10.4 for an example of what your page should look like. As always, feel free to explore and add things while following the exercise. After you have completed the exercise, go ahead and play around with the other tags to see what you can accomplish with style sheets.

1. Create a new FrontPage Web, or open an existing one to host the pages your circus Web site will contain, then click File, New, Page, or press Ctrl+N to create a new Web page. Set the title of the page to **The Circus** by right-clicking anywhere in the page and selecting Page Properties from the context menu.

2. Create a new table by choosing Table, Insert, Table. Set the size to two rows, two columns. Set the alignment to Center, the border size to 0, the cell padding to 5, the cell spacing to 0, and the width to 600 pixels, and then click OK. With that in place, select the first row, and merge the two cells inside it using Table, Merge Cells.

3. Now comes the time to define the styles for your page. Open the Style dialog box by clicking the Style button on the Style toolbar, or by choosing Format, Style.

4. Click the body tag once to select it from the list, and then click the Modify button. From there, click the Format button, and then select Font from the drop-down list. Set the font to Verdana, Regular, 10pt. Click OK twice to return to the Style dialog box. You have now set the font family and size for the entire document. Repeat the same procedure for the table tag, then click OK in the Style dialog box to apply your changes. The reason you have to repeat this procedure for the table tag is because some of the style rules applied to the body of the document are not reflected in tables. This is unfortunate, and often annoying, but that's the way it is.

5. Right-click on the top row (which contains the two cells you merged earlier), select Cell Properties, set its horizontal alignment to Center, then click OK. Now, type **Welcome to Dave's Circus** (replace "Dave" with your name), and add two line

breaks after the title, using the Shift+Enter combination. For now, don't add any extra formatting to that text (you may have noticed that it is a little small), since you'll come back on it in Exercise 10,2, where you'll define your own custom style for the title.

6. Now comes the fun part: You'll add a pair of eyes and some teeth to the cell on the right in the second row of the table. You'll find these images on the accompanying CD-ROM under `tyfp2k/chap10/Samples`. They are named `Eyes.gif` and `Teeth.gif`. To do this, first set the horizontal alignment of the cell to Center, and the vertical alignment to Top by right-clicking on it, then choosing Cell Properties. Next, click the Insert Image button from the toolbar in the FrontPage Editor, or choose Insert, Picture, From File. Insert the eyes first, then insert one line break (Shift+Enter), and insert the teeth. (Now take the time to have a laugh, like I did when I was writing this.) After the image of the teeth, insert three line breaks, and type the following text, with a line break between the two sentences:
   `Our circus is devoted to pleasing you, our customer.`
   `Look for our circus at a city near you!`

7. What you want to do now is add some hyperlinks for your viewers to visit. All of the hyperlinks will point to non-existing files, since the purpose is simply to illustrate the use of style sheets with the a tag. First, click the cell on the left in the second row. Set its horizontal alignment to Left, and its vertical alignment to Top, just like you did in the previous step. While you are there, also set the width of the cell to 150 pixels. Now, add the following text, each of the blocks of text separated by one line break (Shift+Enter): `What's New`, `Circus Tour Locations`, `Laughing Out Loud`, `The Giggle Zone`, `Just For Kids`, `Buy Tickets`, `About Us`, and `Circus Actors`. Last but not least (for this step anyway), create hyperlinks pointing to any file or address on the Web (mine all point to `nowhere.htm`) on each of the blocks of text you typed just a second ago.

8. With that done, go back to the Style dialog box (see step 3 for how to access it). You'll notice that you only have two styles listed in the box of styles. That is because the List item is set to User-Defined Styles. Set it back to All HTML Tags, then select the a tag, and click the Modify button. From there, click the Format button, choose Font, and set the font to Trebuchet MS, purple. Click OK all the way out, and watch FrontPage display your style rules for you. Notice that your hyperlinks are displayed at 10pt font size, even though you did not specify this directly. This is because you specified the font size when you set the style rules for the table. Since it wasn't overridden, it remains at 10pt.

9. There, you're all done. Now, to see what style sheets look like in HTML, click the HTML tab at the bottom of the page in the FrontPage Editor. Notice the section

between the `<style>` and `</style>` tags. This is your style sheet (the `<!—` and `—>` tags are to begin and end a comment; a comment tag encloses the style sheet, hiding the code from older browsers). You'll notice that it's quite easy to understand. So, while we're here, we'll add a little bit of code to remove the underline on the hyperlinks in your page, which you unfortunately cannot do with FrontPage. After the last entry in the a section (which should be Font-family: Trebuchet MS), place a semicolon and a space (like this: "; "), and type: **text-decoration: none**; . Now, the a section of your style sheet should look like this (yours will probably be on one line):

```
a {
  color: #800080;
  font-family: Trebuchet MS;
  text-decoration: none;
}
```

Save your page, and click the Preview tab to see what it looks like. See Figure 10.4 for an indication of what your page should look like in the FrontPage Editor.

FIGURE 10.4

An example of what your page should look like after completing Exercise 10.1. Note that style sheets were used in this example to modify the display of the body, table, and a tags.

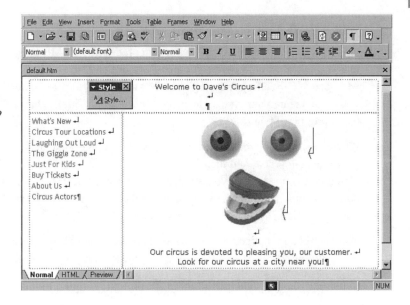

Let's review the exercise you just completed. In it, you should have learned how to implement style rules on HTML tags with FrontPage (we used the body and a tags). You should also have learned that in most cases, style rules are inherited from parent elements. For example, your links (the a, or anchor tags) are displayed at 10pt. font size, even though you never specified the size. That is because the attribute was inherited from the parent element, which is the table tag in this case.

Inheritance can easily be explained if you are familiar with HTML tags—if your tag is enclosed within two other tags, it inherits both the tags' styles. If there is a conflict, the tag "closest" to it (the tag included) has priority. For example, say your page contains an anchor tag (where the font family, size, and color are defined) wrapped inside a div tag (where the alignment and font family are defined), itself wrapped inside the body tag (where the letter spacing and font family are defined). Each tag would be displayed as follows: the a (anchor) tag would use its font family, size, and color, the alignment of the div tag, and the letter spacing of the body tag; the div tag would use its own font family, along with the letter spacing of the body tag; and finally, the body tag would use only its style rules (font family and letter spacing). So you see, things can get a little complicated if you don't sort everything out before you start.

Tip

Inheritance can sometimes be a difficult concept to grasp if you're not a programmer, but it's not that important to know exactly what it is when using CSS—just let your eyes be your guide.

Creating User-Defined Styles

Now that you've seen how styles work on predefined HTML tags, you've surely noticed that style sheets would not be complete without custom styles. For example, if you wanted to create a specific style for your Web site for all titles to be displayed the same way, you could create your own style called "SiteTitle" ("Title" is already taken), then assign the appropriate style rules to it.

It's quite simple to create a custom style in FrontPage. Just click Format, Style to display the Style dialog box, and then click the New button. From there, you'll notice the same dialog box you get when you modify styles for existing HTML elements. All you have to do is type in a name for the style, then set the formatting for your style. Once that is done, just click OK , and you're on your way.

You've probably noticed that we haven't covered each of the formatting dialog boxes yet. So, as promised earlier, the following sections examine these dialog boxes and any differences they have with the standard dialog box. The font, paragraph, and numbering dialog boxes have already been covered in previous chapters, so we won't spend much time on those. The borders dialog box is covered in the "Formatting Borders" section later in this lesson, and the position dialog box will be covered in detail on Day 13, although we'll go over it very briefly here.

Formatting Fonts

When you click the Format button and choose Format Font, a dialog box appears that closely resembles the standard Font dialog box (which is accessed with Format, Font). However, there are a few differences. Most noticeably, there are far fewer effects you can apply to your font than with standard formatting. The reason for this is because most of the standard font formatting effects are either scarcely used or implemented in another way with style sheets. The only other noticeable difference on the Font tab of this dialog box is the list of sizes you can use. The first five entries in the Size box list the scales CSS supports when defining font sizes (see Figure 10.5):

- *Pixels [px]*—Pixels are a measurement used to determine size on a computer screen—for example, if your screen resolution is set to 1024×768, it is 1024 pixels wide by 768 pixels high.
- *Inches [in]*—Hopefully, you know what those are.
- *Millimeters [mm]*—A unit of measurement on the metric scale; you can also use centimeters, with the cm abbreviation.
- *Em square [em]*—The em square is the size of the design grid on which glyphs are laid out. Simply put, use your eyes until you get just the right font size if you really want to use the em square scale.
- *Points [pt]*—Points are the standard unit of measurement used for fonts—for example, in Microsoft Word or Microsoft Excel, when you set the font size to 10, you're actually setting it to 10pt.

FIGURE 10.5

The Font formatting dialog box used with styles enables you to set style rules for your elements. Although it is similar to the standard Font formatting dialog box, there are some important differences.

The entries after the first five are all for points. If you want to use one of the other scales, or use a point size that isn't in the list, simply type the size in along with the scale. For example, if you type "5mm" in the box, you'll see a preview of the font size, and after clicking OK, your font size will be set to five millimeters. The same applies for each of the scales.

The Font dialog box also includes the Character Spacing tab (see Figure 10.6). This tab enables you to set the attributes for the position of the characters on your page. The first element, Spacing, can be set to one of three options: Normal, Expanded, or Condensed. The Normal setting is self-explanatory. The Expanded and Condensed settings increase and decrease, respectively, the spacing between the letters. The By setting enables you to set the number of points by which the characters should be expanded or condensed. The second element of this tab is Position. This simply enables you to raise or lower the text in relation to the characters around it.

FIGURE 10.6

The Character Spacing tab of the Font formatting dialog box enables you to set the spacing and position of your text.

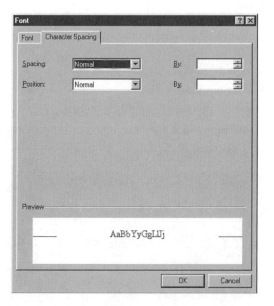

Note

Even though the interface is the same as the standard Font formatting dialog box, only style sheets are used to provide this formatting. When you format your font with the standard dialog box, you are using a mix of HTML (whenever possible) and inline styles (when there are no HTML tags). For all style sheet formatting dialog boxes, the options you see only use style sheets to provide the desired effects.

Formatting Paragraphs

Day 3 already covered basic paragraph formatting, so it won't be covered again here. Suffice it to say that paragraph formatting is implemented almost exactly the same way, whether you use the standard paragraph formatting dialog box or the style sheets paragraph formatting one. You may also have noticed that the dialog boxes are identical. When you use the standard paragraph formatting dialog box, however, most of the options you set use inline styles. This is not the case when you set paragraph formatting options using the Style dialog box because you are specifying the formatting for each element, not for a selection. Keep this in mind when we go over inline styles later in this chapter.

Formatting Borders

Borders are a nice way to jazz up your pages, especially when they contain a lot of data, or if content is scarce. FrontPage enables you to easily create borders and use them. It may be that the only HTML tag you'll use borders on is the `table` tag, but with style sheets, you have a wide variety of options that are not available in standard HTML. For example, in the beginning of this chapter, we discussed some of the benefits of using style sheets with tables. Well, here we are doing just that.

To access the Borders and Shading dialog box, just click the Format button from either the Modify Style or the New Style dialog box. These enable you to set borders on HTML tags (embedded styles). You can also access this dialog box directly from the FrontPage Editor by clicking Format, Borders and Shading. When you access it this way, however, you are using inline styles instead of embedded or external styles.

Note

> You may have noticed references to inline, embedded, and external styles. You don't need to understand them fully yet because they will be covered later in this chapter. When you do come to that portion of the chapter, if you feel uncomfortable with the concepts you can come back to this section for some examples of how FrontPage implements them. Also, you can look over the introduction to style sheets, which described the basic differences between the different implementations of style sheets.

The Borders tab of the Borders and Shading dialog box uses a straightforward interface (see Figure 10.7). You should feel right at home if you've ever used borders and shading in Microsoft Word, from which this dialog box appears to have been borrowed. This dialog box contains four main sections:

- *Setting*—This section enables you to define what the border should look like.
- *Style*—This section gives you the option of setting the border's shape, color, and width. The best way to help you understand what each of the border shapes looks like is for you to click on each one, then examine the Preview section.
- *Preview*—This section, while providing a preview of your borders, enables you to set which sides of the box should have borders.
- *Padding*—This section is used to define the amount of space between the content inside your borders and the edges.

FIGURE 10.7

The Borders and Shading dialog box enables you to set borders and shading on either a selection or an element, such as an HTML tag or a style you have defined.

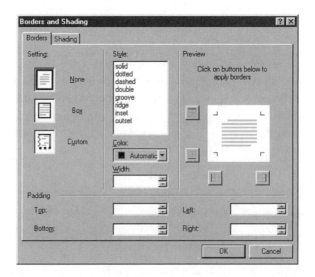

The best way to get comfortable with borders is to experiment with them. A design tip: Try to use borders to divide sections of content within your pages. Be careful, as with any style, not to overdo it. Too many borders on a page will make it look unattractive and dull.

The Shading tab of the Borders and Shading dialog box also has an interface that is easy to follow (see Figure 10.8). The Fill section enables you to set the foreground and background colors for your element. You can also define an image as the background for your element in the Patterns section of the dialog box. From there, you can set the horizontal and vertical position of your background. The Repeat option enables you to set how the background image is repeated. With regular HTML, all background images are tiled and repeated. However, with CSS, you can set it to repeat (just like standard background images), to repeat only on the x-axis (repeat-x), to repeat only on the y-axis (repeat-y), or not to repeat at all (no-repeat). When the background isn't repeated, that's where the horizontal and vertical positions usually come in. As for the Attachment option, Scroll is just like standard HTML, in which the background scrolls with the text, and Fixed is like defining a fixed background—only the text moves, and the background stays in place.

FIGURE 10.8

The Shading tab of the Borders and Shading dialog box enables you to set the foreground color, the background color, and/or a background image for your element.

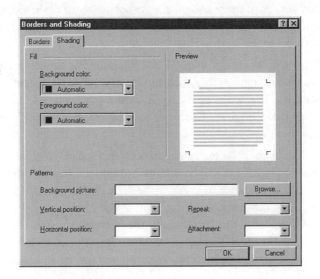

Formatting Numbering

Day 4 covered the Bullets and Numbering dialog box. For that reason, we won't go over this dialog box again. Just keep in mind that when you define your styles in CSS, you can also define how bulleted and numbered lists will appear. This is quite handy because it would be a chore to set a specific format for bulleted and numbered lists on each page of a large Web site.

Formatting Positions

When you choose to format the positioning of an element, you can set it so that it is positioned relatively or absolutely. These concepts are covered on Day 13, so if they sound esoteric for now, that's OK. Relative positioning is positioning in relation to another element, using coordinates. The selected element is always positioned in relation to the closest element from the top and/or left of the page. Absolute positioning refers to positioning an element using coordinates, where (0,0) is the top-left corner of your page.

Exercise 10.2: Getting Fancier with Styles

Finally, the time has come to put into practice what you've learned in this section. In this exercise, you'll work with custom styles. You'll apply these styles to the text on your Web page to make it a little nicer. So, without further ado, follow these steps:

1. If you completed Exercise 10.1, open your Web containing the page, and open that page in the FrontPage Editor. If you didn't complete the exercise, you may want to complete it now, or you may have a hard time following the steps in this exercise.

2. With your page open, click the Style button on the Style toolbar, or click Format, Style. From there, click the New button to create a new style, and set the title (selector) of the style to PageTitle.

3. With the name for the style defined, click the Format button, then select Format Font, and set the font to Jokerman, Bold, 25pt. (type in **25pt**, since it isn't in the list), navy. If you don't have the Jokerman font, you can use any replacement you find suitable. From the Character Spacing tab, set the spacing to Extended, by 3 (type **3** in the By section). Click OK.

4. Click the Format button again, and choose Format Paragraph. Now, set the "spacing after" to 3. This will ensure that your title is separated from the existing content. Click OK twice to return to the Style dialog box. Back at the Style dialog box, notice that there is a new entry in the list of styles called .PageTitle. It has a dot in front of its name to indicate that it is a user-defined style (that is, not an HTML tag). See Figure 10.9 to see what the dialog box should look like now. Notice that in the Description field of this element, you see the style rules you just set.

FIGURE 10.9

The Style dialog box after you have defined some style rules.

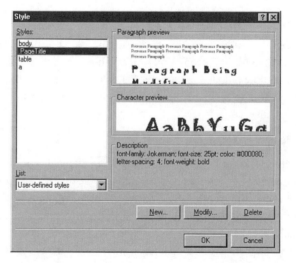

5. Of course, simply defining the style is not enough. You need to apply the style to one or more elements on your page in order to use it. To do that, right-click on the top row of the table that contains your Web page, then choose Cell Properties from the context menu. From there, click the Style button on the bottom-left corner.

In the Class section, set the class to PageTitle. It should be the only entry in the list. You may have noticed that here, the dot before the name of the style is not present. This is because when you use the style, you use its real name—obviously, HTML tags are not available, and as such, there is no need for the dot to indicate a user-defined style. Click OK twice, and your page now has the style applied to the entire cell, so your title is formatted appropriately.

Figure 10.10 shows what your page should look like after completing this exercise.

FIGURE 10.10

What your Web page should look like in the FrontPage Editor after having completed Exercises 10.1 and 10.2.

Modifying Styles

After creating custom styles in FrontPage, you may want to modify and/or delete them if they are no longer needed. This is quite a simple procedure—just use the buttons on the Style dialog box. However, the buttons have different effects, depending on the context. If the user-defined styles are listed, then all of the buttons are activated. We already covered what the New and Modify buttons do, so we won't go over those again. As for the Delete button, if you delete the style rules you defined for an existing HTML tag (such as the body tag), the HTML tag is obviously not deleted. Only the style rules are. On the other hand, if you delete a style you defined, such as the PageTitle style (remember: They are listed with dots in front of their names), the style is deleted, and you must create it again to get it back. This may sound obvious when you are creating your styles, but you may be sorry if you mistakenly delete a style. Remember, though, that you can always undo what you just did by pressing Ctrl+Z, or by choosing Edit, Undo.

Applying Styles in FrontPage

Now that you know the basics of implementing styles with elements, we'll come back to our original discussion of style sheets, in which we examined the three types of style sheets: inline styles, embedded styles, and external styles. You've learned how the first two of these work; you'll learn how FrontPage works with them later in the chapter. The following section discusses external style sheets.

Attaching an External Style Sheet

When working with external style sheets in the FrontPage Editor, you must either type your code or use the Style dialog box. We've already examined what CSS code looks like in a Web page, how to modify HTML elements to apply style rules to them, and how to create your own styles.

If you want to see what external style sheets look like (code-wise), FrontPage comes with some templates already made for you. Remember, external style sheets use a separate file with a CSS extension. You can access these by using File, New, Page and clicking the Style Sheets tab. From there, simply select from the types of style sheets available (see Figure 10.11).

FIGURE 10.11

FrontPage provides some templates to help you with your style sheets. These will appear as plain text pages in the FrontPage Editor.

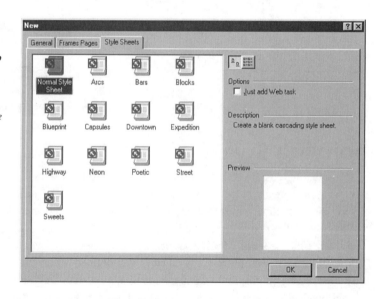

Once you've created your style sheet, and you are ready to attach it to your page, simply click Format, Style Sheet Links from your page. The Link Style Sheet dialog box will appear. From there, you can easily manage the style sheets used in your page. Normally, a page has only one style sheet, but you may want to store your styles in several files, and add only the ones you need in each page. However, this procedure is not recommended because it increases the load on the browser. Note: You may want to refer to the definition of external style sheets if you don't feel comfortable with them yet (see "External Style Sheets," earlier in the chapter).

Exercise 10.3: Adding a Link to an External Style Sheet

In this exercise, you'll take the styles that FrontPage generated for you and place them in a .CSS file (a style sheet). After that, you'll create a link to your style sheet, and the end result should be exactly the same as you had in Exercise 10.2, apart from one major difference. This time, you'll have a single file containing all of your rules, which can be easily modified at a later date if you decide to change the appearance of your page. Although this may seem unimportant, if you have a Web site that spans several hundreds of pages, it's more than an arduous chore to change the format of each page! Just follow these simple steps:

1. Open the Web page (`default.htm`) that you created in Exercise 10.1 and modified in Exercise 10.2. If you did not follow both of these exercises in their entirety, you may have trouble with the steps that follow, so I would recommend you complete them before starting these.

2. With your page open in the FrontPage Editor, switch to HTML View by clicking the HTML tab at the bottom of the editor window. Now, notice the code between the `<style>` and `</style>` tags in your page. This is your style sheet (the lines with `<!` — and `—>` excluded), which should appear in gray. Select the five lines of text, then press Ctrl+C, or use Edit, Copy to copy the text to the clipboard.

3. Click File, New, Page, click the Style Sheets tab, choose Normal Style Sheet, and click OK. In the editor window, press Ctrl+V, or choose Edit Paste to paste your style sheet into the .css file (see the following note).

4. Next, press Ctrl+S, or choose File, Save to save the file, and name it `styles.css`.

5. From there, close the file, and you should revert back to the home page for your Web site, `default.htm`. With that page open, make sure that you are still in HTML View, and delete the embedded style you defined by deleting all of the text between the `<style>` and `</style>` tags (the tags included) at the top of your page. Now, switch back to Normal View, and you should notice that all of the styles have been removed. But do not fear—you will put them back in your page by inserting a link to the style sheet you just created.

6. To do that, click Format, Style Sheet Links, and then click the Add button. Double-click the `styles.css` file you created in step 4, and click OK to apply the link.

10

After a few instants, notice that all of your styles are back. Your page should now look exactly like it did after completing Exercise 10.2, so you can refer to Figure 10.10 to see what it looks like in the FrontPage Editor.

 Note

Although you pasted your code from another page, you could just as easily have reconstructed the entire style sheet by using the Style dialog box. It works the exact same way as it does on a regular Web page, but there is no interface in which to preview your changes.

Removing Links to Style Sheets

Removing a link to a style sheet is even easier than attaching one. Simply choose Format, Style Sheet Links to open the Link Style Sheets dialog box, select the name of the style sheet, and click Remove. Click OK to apply your changes.

Apart from adding and removing links to style sheets, the Link Style Sheets dialog box also enables you to set the order of the style sheets in case of conflicts. However, as mentioned earlier, it is not a good practice to have more than one style sheet.

Using Embedded Styles

Although the title may make it sound complicated, embedded style sheets are a lot simpler than you may assume—you used embedded styles in Exercises 10.1 and 10.2. As explained in the beginning of this chapter, embedded styles are simply style rules that you define, then use on your page. At the code level, they will appear between the `<style>` and `</style>` tags.

The area that wasn't covered, however, is the different ways you can use your custom styles in your pages. In Exercise 10.2, you applied an embedded style you created to a table cell in your page using the Style button on the Cell Properties dialog box. The key to using custom embedded styles is the Style button. You will notice the Style button in just about every context menu (when you select an item in your page and then right-click on it). The only noticeable omissions are with the Paragraph and Font formatting dialog boxes. It's a shame, really, that FrontPage does not provide this button on these dialog boxes. After clicking the Style button from a dialog box, you will notice the dialog box shown earlier in Figure 10.9. From the list of styles, simply select the style you want to use.

Tip If you have defined an external style sheet, and you want to override the formatting for a specific element, simply use an inline style or an embedded style. These always have precedence over external styles. In much the same way, inline styles have precedence over embedded styles.

Applying Inline Styles

In FrontPage, inline styles are applied in much the same way that embedded styles are applied. To create an embedded style, you must again use the Style button on any dialog box it is present on. The difference is that you should not select a class (or style) from the list, but rather, simply use the Format button, and set the formatting for the font, paragraph, border, numbering, and/or position. If a class or ID is already selected, you should delete the entry (just press Delete), otherwise, you will be modifying the embedded style that is selected.

You can also use inline styles in FrontPage when you use features that are not available with standard HTML. If you remember, some dialog boxes use a mix of HTML and CSS to achieve the desired effects. To be more specific, those dialog boxes use HTML and inline styles. If you want to use only inline styles, simply use the Style button, as described in the preceding paragraph, without specifying classes.

Exercise 10.4: Adding Inline Styles

Now that you have learned every aspect of CSS, there is only one aspect you haven't put into practice: inline styles. So, in this exercise, you'll again modify your circus Web page, but this time, you'll apply an inline style to two of your hyperlinks in the left menu to make them stand out from the rest. At the same time, this exercise will help you become more familiar with how to design your pages using style sheets, or when to use each type of style (external, embedded, and inline). Finally, you'll also learn how to apply hyperlink rollover effects. Simply follow the steps below to complete the final phase of your circus Web page:

1. Open your Web in the FrontPage Explorer, and then open the circus Web page in the FrontPage Editor by double-clicking on it from the folders pane. Note: You should complete Exercises 10.1, 10.2, and 10.3 before this one.

2. In the cell on the left containing the hyperlinks pointing to fictitious pages in your Web site, select the first hyperlink, named What's New. Right-click the hyperlink, and choose Hyperlink Properties from the context menu. You can also press Alt+Enter.

3. From there, click the Style button on the far right (one wonders why in this case, the Style button was placed all the way over to the right instead of on the left as in most of the other dialog boxes), click the Format button, and choose the Font Formatting option to open the Font dialog box. By now you should be comfortable with this dialog box, so set the font color to maroon, and the size to 14pt. Click OK all the way out. Notice that on your page, the hyperlink has conserved its font face, which is now defined in your style sheet (Trebuchet MS).

4. Now, select the second hyperlink, named Circus Tour Locations, and repeat steps 2 and 3, setting the font color to green and the type to bold.

5. Finally, you'll enable hyperlink rollover effects. This is done by selecting Format, Background, and placing a check mark in the Enable Hyperlink Rollover Effects box. After that, simply click the Rollover style button, and you can access the font properties. Select fuchsia as the color, and bold as the font weight. Click OK twice.

6. With that done, you may or may not want to check the code of your page. If you are interested, click the HTML tab, and you should notice that on the two hyper-links you modified, there is an extra entry inside the tags, where you see "style=...". This is the direct result of using inline styles. So you see, although your page may look the same on the surface, the ways used to implement inline styles are quite different. With that, check out Figure 10.12 to see what your page should look like in Internet Explorer, version 5.

FIGURE 10.12

What your Web page should look like in Internet Explorer after completing Exercises 10.1 through 10.4. Your circus Web page is now complete.

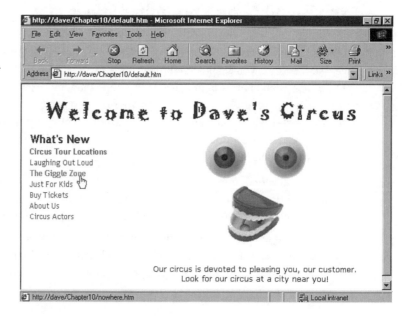

Tip

Unfortunately, FrontPage provides no easy way to set a rollover effect for your hyperlinks when you use an external style sheet. What you can do is simply paste the code from your hyperlink rollover effect into the style sheet. If you click the HTML tab after completing the circus Web page in the preceding exercise, you will notice some code that looks like this: `A:hover {color: #FF00FF; font-weight: bold}`. Simply paste this code on a new line in your CSS file, and voilà, you have a rollover effect on all of your pages.

Using Style Sheets with Your Themes

If you use themes to design your Web sites, you will enjoy this section. Themes already use style sheets to format the content. As such, you can modify the appearance of your themes by changing, among other things, the format of the style sheet used in the theme. Doing so is quite easy. To modify the style sheet used in a theme, simply follow this procedure:

1. With your Web open, click Format, Theme. Select the theme you want to modify from the list of themes.

2. Next, click the Modify button, and click the button marked Text....

3. From there, you'll notice a dialog box that enables you to preview your changes. You have the option of modifying the font for the body and the headings. Obviously, this doesn't offer much in the way of customization, so if you click the More Text Styles button, you'll notice that the standard Style dialog box is back. From there, you should feel comfortable with editing the formatting for the predefined styles, along with the HTML tags.

4. Once your modifications are complete, click the OK button twice to return to the Theme editing dialog box, and click the Save As button to save your theme. Note that you cannot save over a theme that ships with FrontPage. You can, however, save over a theme that you created.

That's about all there is to using style sheets with your themes. Once you are familiar with the Style dialog box, you should be familiar with all of the places that styles sheets are used in FrontPage.

10

Summary

Today's lesson covered the "ins and outs" of style sheets in FrontPage; however, there is a lot we didn't cover. The goal isn't for you to become an expert at style sheets, but rather to gain a basic understanding of the workings of style sheets and how they are used in FrontPage. Hopefully, this lesson has taught you what you'll need to know in the real world about CSS. If you had trouble with any of the concepts presented, perhaps you should reread those sections to ensure that you are comfortable with them. Of course, nothing beats practice, so if you haven't done the exercises on your own, go ahead and do them. If you have, take the time to get creative with style sheets, and soon you'll be using them in almost all of your pages.

Workshop

Q&A

Q Is there a standard for style sheets, or some kind of reference I can use for programming my own style sheets?

A Of course there is, and it's a great one too. The World Wide Web Consortium (also known as the W3C, the organization that sets standards for the Web) created an excellent reference for style sheets and how to use them in your Web pages. This reference is sure to tell you everything you need to know about style sheets. You can find the official reference on the Web at http://www.w3.org/TR/REC-CSS2/.

Q What browsers are style sheets compatible with?

A Currently, the second revision of the style sheets standard, or CSS2, is supported only by Internet Explorer 4 and higher (Netscape Navigator 4.5 partly supports CSS2; however, it is far from being implemented fully or properly). CSS1 is supported by Internet Explorer 3 and higher, and in part by Netscape 4. Microsoft FrontPage uses CSS2.

Q What are the major differences between CSS1 and CSS2?

A CSS1, or the first standard proposed by the W3C for style sheets, comprises of only minimal formatting options that were, for the most part, already available with standard HTML. CSS2, however, contains a lot more formatting options, many of which are not supported with regular HTML. CSS2 also introduces standards for the visually impaired, which enables you to specify how content on your page is read to the user. Unfortunately, this portion of CSS is still widely unused.

Quiz

1. What is the difference between an inline style, an embedded style, and an external style, both in the way they are implemented in FrontPage, and in the way they are used in a Web page?

2. List at least five HTML tags you can set style rules on in the FrontPage Editor (without looking).

3. What is the difference between the standard Font dialog box, accessed with Format, Font, and the one accessed via the Style dialog box? Please be specific.

4. What is the name of the organization that creates and approves standards for the Web?

5. In the FrontPage Editor, how can you create a new style sheet, based upon an existing template?

Exercises

1. If you enjoyed working with style sheets, take the Web page from your exercises and modify it to add more content. Also, add a couple of pages to the Web site, and link the style sheet to each page. This way, you can have a better feel of how CSS spans an entire Web site.

2. If you work with FrontPage themes on your Web sites, try modifying an existing style sheet for a theme, then save the theme, and create a Web site spanning a few pages to explore your theme.

Answers to Quiz

1. An inline style is applied to one element of one page. In FrontPage, inline styles are usually applied with the Style button, found on various dialog boxes. They can also be applied with some standard dialog boxes, when there is no HTML to perform the task. An embedded style is a style that spans one page, but that is applied to an HTML tag or to a user-defined style, thus spanning one or more elements on the page. Embedded styles in FrontPage are created using the Style dialog box. Finally, external styles are defined in a .css file. The file is then linked from one or more pages in a given Web site. In FrontPage, external styles are created by first defining the styles in a CSS file, and then linking the file using the Format, Style Sheet Links option of the FrontPage Editor.

2. Refer to the list in the FrontPage Editor (Style dialog box). The HTML tags we covered at the beginning of this chapter are a, body, h1–h6, img, input, textarea, ol, ul, li, p, table, tr, and td.

3. As with the font, paragraph, and numbering dialog boxes, when accessed via the FrontPage menus, the Font dialog box generates standard HTML and uses inline styles when HTML is not available. On the other hand, when accessed via the Style dialog box, the Font dialog box generates embedded styles in your page.

4. This non-profit organization is known as the World Wide Web Consortium, or the W3C. You can access its Web page at `http://www.w3c.org`.

5. You can create a style sheet in the FrontPage Editor by clicking File, New, Page, and then choosing the Style Sheets tab, and a template, and clicking OK.

DAY **11**

Designing Navigation Systems

How many times have you had an idea for a Web site, but haven't found a good way to help you plan it? You scratch out a few diagrams on a piece of paper to help you plan your pages and how they will link together. Along the way your ideas change, so you erase or scratch out your original ideas and make additions to them. Eventually, you have a stack of papers piled up with pages crossed out, edges torn, and eraser marks all over the place. Your notes are written in five different colors of ink or pencil, and soon they are illegible.

With FrontPage 2000, you don't have to plan your Web pages on placemats or paper anymore. Using the Navigation View in FrontPage, you can plan your site while you create your pages. While doing so, you also create a complete navigation system for your Web. Imagine planning, creating, and linking your Web pages in a few simple steps. As you make changes to your Web, the navigation bars change along with it—automatically! The hardest part of the whole job is figuring out what you're going to put on your site.

In this chapter we will explain

- Navigation Terminology
- Using Navigation View
- Creating Pages in Navigation View
- Using the Navigation Toolbar
- Creating a Printout
- Deleting Pages from Your Navigation Tree
- Using Navigation Bars
- Using Shared Borders
- Setting Navigation Bar Properties
- Modifying a Navigation Bar
- Deleting Navigation Bars

Navigation Terminology

Before you get into designing the navigation system for your Web site, review some of the terminology used in the FrontPage 2000 Explorer. The following list describes terms that are used frequently in Navigation View and navigation bar procedures.

- You can easily design a navigation system for your Web site using Navigation View (shown in Figure 11.1) in FrontPage. By doing so, FrontPage 2000 automatically generates *navigation bars* that provide hyperlinks to other pages in your Web. When you change or move pages, the navigation bars are updated for you automatically.
- *Top-level* pages can be used to designate the main sections in your Web site. Your home page is always a top-level page. However, if you want to include several sections in your Web site, each of which focuses on a specific topic or area of interest, you can create and configure top-level pages for those areas as well. In Figure 11.1, the Home, Main, Interests, and Links pages are all top-level pages.
- A *parent page* is a page that provides navigation links to one or more Web pages that focus on a similar topic or area of interest. In Figure 11.1, the Interests page is a parent page to the Hobbies and Art and Music pages. Similarly, the Hobbies page is a parent page to the Collecting and Reading pages.
- A *child page* is a page that appears after you select a link from a parent page. These pages usually provide more detailed information than the parent page. For

example, the Collecting and Reading pages in Figure 11.1 are "children" of the Hobbies page.

- All child pages that share a common parent page are *peer pages*. They usually share a common focus; for example, the Collecting and Reading pages share the Hobby focus.

- The *active page* is the page that you are currently editing in FrontPage.

- When you use Navigation View to design and plan your navigation system, FrontPage allows you to display navigation bars consistently throughout your Web site. Using *shared borders*, you can repeat content throughout your Web using any combination of top, bottom, left, or right sides of the page. FrontPage uses the content that you add in shared borders on all pages in your Web, or on the pages that you specifically choose.

Figure 11.1 shows the Navigation View in FrontPage.

FIGURE 11.1

The Navigation View.

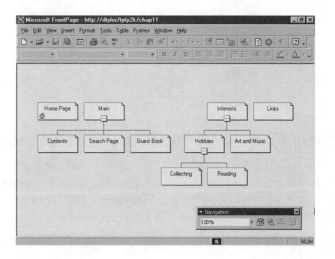

11

> **Note**
>
> Navigation bars and shared borders are an alternative to framesets, which are discussed in Day 12, "Creating and Using Framesets." If your Web site uses frames, you should not use shared borders and navigation bars. Using both on the same pages will make your Web site confusing to navigate.

Using Navigation View

Although you can design your navigation system at any time, you may find it easiest to plan your Web site in Navigation View. You start by creating a FrontPage Web, using the One Page Web template if you are building your Web site from the ground up.

After you create or open a Web, use one of the following procedures to view your Web in Navigation View:

- From FrontPage, choose View, Navigation.
- Click the Navigation icon in the FrontPage Views pane, as shown in Figure 11.2.

FIGURE 11.2

*The Navigation icon in
the FrontPage Views
pane enables you to
see your Web in
Navigation View.*

Creating Pages in Navigation View

In this chapter, you'll create a navigation system and create pages for a personal site. Let's say that you want a main section that holds general pages and other sections that focus on topics that you are interested in. In addition to your home page, you want to create a Web site that contains the following areas:

- The Main area, for general pages such as a guest book, a table of contents, and a search page
- The Interests area, for pages that describe one or more topics in which you are interested
- The Links area, for pages that link to your favorite sites on the World Wide Web

Exercise 11.1: Creating and Naming Top-Level Pages

As mentioned previously, you can begin by creating a One Page Web in FrontPage. This automatically adds your home page to Navigation View and serves as the starting point in your navigation system. To create new top-level pages for the Main, Interests, and Links sections in the Web, follow these steps:

> **Tip**
>
> If you want to undo the changes and additions you made to your navigation system, you can use the Edit, Undo (Ctrl+Z) command, or press the Undo button on the Standard toolbar. The Edit, Redo (Ctrl+Y) command undoes the Undo and reverts back to the changes or additions you originally made.

1. From FrontPage, choose File, New, Web. Create a new disk-based Web using the path c:\tyfp2k\chap11.

2. If you are not already in Navigation View, choose View, Navigation, or click the Navigation icon on the Views pane. Your home page is displayed in Navigation View.

3. Right-click your mouse over an empty area in Navigation View to access the pop-up menu shown in Figure 11.3. Choose New Top Page from the pop-up menu to create a new top-level page. Repeat this procedure two more times to create two more new pages. By default, they are labeled New Page 1, New Page 2, and New Page 3.

FIGURE 11.3

To create a top-level page, right-click over an empty area in Navigation View and choose New Top Page from the pop-up menu.

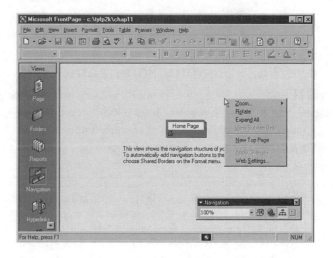

4. To assign the labels that appear in the navigation bars for each page, right-click the New Page 1 icon and choose Rename from the pop-up menu. You can also click the New Page 1 label once to select it and then again to edit the name. The name becomes surrounded by a bounding box and becomes highlighted so you can rename the page. Enter **Main** and press Enter to rename the page.

5. Press Tab to advance to New Page 2, where the label becomes selected for you to relabel the page. Name the second page **Interests**.

6. Press Tab again to advance to New Page 3. Name this page **Links**. Click outside the page to set the name in the last page. Your Navigation View should look like Figure 11.4.

FIGURE 11.4

Four top-level pages created in Navigation View.

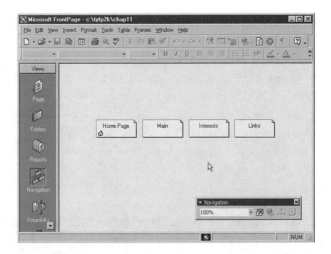

Exercise 11.2: Creating Parent and Child Pages

Now you have four top-level pages in your Web. Any of these four pages can serve as a parent page that will link to pages beneath it. Now you'll use Navigation View to create a couple of pages beneath the top-level page called Interests. If you have interests other than the examples I use in this chapter, feel free to add your own variations.

Note

As you name your pages in Navigation View, try to keep the labels brief—the labels you enter in Navigation View are the labels that appear on your navigation buttons, and can be independent of the title of the page. You can change the title of the page in the Page Properties dialog box, as described later in this chapter.

1. In Navigation View, click the Interests page to make it the active page. The Interests page will now become a *parent page* to other pages beneath it.

2. Click the New Page icon on the Standard toolbar twice. Two new pages appear in Navigation View, each labeled New Page *x*, where *x* is an incremental number. (You can create additional new pages for other interests if you like.) These two new pages are child pages of the Interests page.

3. Label the pages with brief names that describe your own interests, or use the names Hobbies and Art and Music as shown in Figure 11.5.

4. Parent and child pages can continue through multiple levels. For example, you can add different hobby categories beneath the Hobbies page. To do so, select the Hobbies page as the active page. Then click the New Page icon on the Standard toolbar twice to create two child pages beneath the Hobbies page. Name the pages **Collecting** and **Reading**. Your navigation pane will now look similar to Figure 11.5.

FIGURE 11.5

Two additional levels (parent and child pages) are added to the Interests section in the Web.

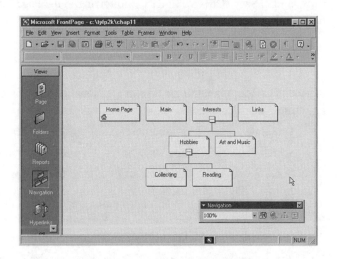

Exercise 11.3: Adding Pages from Your Current Web

You've probably noticed that when you create new pages in FrontPage's Navigation View, you are not given the opportunity to select a template on which to base your new page. All new pages created from Navigation View are based on the Normal page template, which generates a blank page. If you want to use one of the FrontPage templates, you have to create your new pages from Page View. Then, you can add the pages to Navigation View by dragging and dropping pages where you want to place them.

In the following section, you'll create three additional pages (Table of Contents, Search Page, and Guest Book) using some of the FrontPage page templates.

Note   The Table of Contents page contains features that you will learn more about later this week. The Search Page and Guest Book pages contain advanced features that you will learn more about next week.

To create and add template-generated pages to your navigation bar, follow these steps:

1. Choose View, Page, or click the Page icon in the Views pane. The page editor opens.

2. Choose File, New, Page (Ctrl+N). The New dialog box appears.

3. From the list of page templates, double-click Table of Contents. A new Table of Contents page appears in FrontPage.

4. Choose File, Save (Ctrl+S). Enter the following in the Page Title and File Name fields and choose OK to save your page to the home folder in your Web:

Page Title:	`Table of Contents`
File Name:	`contents.htm`

5. Repeat steps 2 through 4 to create two additional pages, using these templates, page titles, and filenames:

Template	**Filename**	**Page Title**
Search Page	`search.htm`	`Search Page`
Guest Book	`gstbook.htm`	`Guest Book`

6. Return to Navigation View (View, Navigation), and display the Folder List (View, Folder List) if it is not already displayed. You will see your new pages listed in the files pane, as shown in Figure 11.6.

7. Click the `contents.htm` page in the Folder List, and drag it into Navigation View. As you drag the page, a ghosted representation of the page follows your mouse cursor. Release the mouse button when the ghosted image of the contents page attaches itself to the Main page in the navigation pane, as shown in Figure 11.7.

Tip   You can also drag and drop pages within Navigation View to rearrange the order in which the pages will appear in your navigation bar. As an example, you might decide later that you want your Main, Interests, and Links pages to become child pages beneath the Home page. Click and drag each page you want to move, and release the mouse button when the ghosted image of the page attaches itself to the new parent in the navigation tree. Any child pages that appear in levels beneath the page you are moving will remain attached to its parent, and will move to the new location as well.

FIGURE 11.6

Return to FrontPage's Navigation View after you create new pages with FrontPage templates. Your new pages appear in the Folder List.

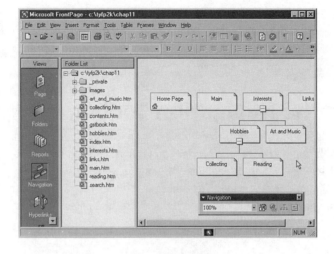

FIGURE 11.7

Release the mouse button when the page you are dragging from the Folder List attaches itself to the page you want to link it to in the navigation pane.

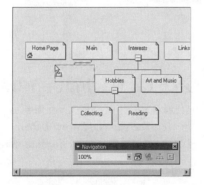

8. Repeat step 7 to attach the remaining two new pages (search.htm and gstbook.htm, in that order) to the Main page in Navigation View. Your Navigation View should now look like the one in Figure 11.8.

FIGURE 11.8

Three template-generated pages are added in the Main section of the Web.

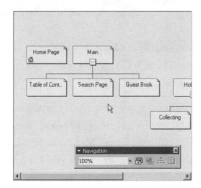

9. Template-generated pages sometimes use page titles that are too wide to display in your navigation buttons. You can shorten the button label by renaming the page in Navigation View. This does not affect the page title or filename. Rename the Table of Contents page `Contents`.

Using the Navigation Toolbar

The Navigation toolbar (see Figure 11.9) appears in the lower-left corner of Navigation View. If you do not see the Navigation toolbar, you can display it if you choose View, Toolbars, Navigation. It contains five buttons, three of which help you display pages in your tree in different ways. The other two buttons help you choose what pages to include in your navigation bars, or to add links to external pages in your navigation bars.

FIGURE 11.9

*The Navigation toolbar
contains commands
that help you view
your navigation tree.*

Viewing Your Hierarchical Navigation Tree

As the number of pages in Navigation View increases, you'll find that you need to scroll through the hierarchical tree to review the pages. However, there are ways that you can focus Navigation View on specific pages, or fit more information in the Navigation View.

Note

> You can expand and collapse branches of the hierarchical trees to focus on other areas, similar to the way that you expand and collapse trees in the Windows Explorer or FrontPage folder lists. Wherever you see a minus sign at the base of a page that is in your navigation tree, you can click to collapse the tree. Conversely, where a plus sign appears, click to expand the tree.

There are three buttons in the Navigation toolbar that enable you to change the way pages are displayed in the navigation panel. You can rotate the tree or zoom out to display all the pages in your navigation system.

- *Zoom*—The Zoom button allows you to view your navigation tree at various zoom levels: 150%, 100%, 75%, 50%, 25%, and Size to Fit. The Size to Fit option displays all pages in your hierarchical tree at the largest resolution possible. Of course, if there are many pages in your Web, the page labels might be illegible.

- *Portrait/Landscape*—This button displays your hierarchical tree in portrait view (the default, which you have seen in figures up to this point), or in landscape view, as shown in Figure 11.10. Rather than appearing at the top of the tree, the top-level pages appear at the left side of the Navigation View. Each sublevel then appears to the right of the preceding level.

FIGURE 11.10

Your navigation tree in landscape view.

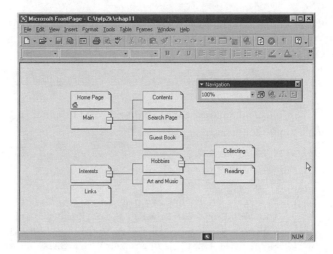

- *View Subtree Only*—You can also focus in on a specific subtree in your Navigation View. For example, if you want to display only the pages in the Main section of the Web you are now creating, click the Main page in Navigation View and then click the View Subtree Only button. FrontPage hides the remaining pages and displays only the Main, Contents, Search Page, and Guest Book pages in Navigation View.

Exercise 11.4: Adding External Pages to Your Navigation Tree

There may be instances when you want to add links to other pages on the World Wide Web in your navigation bars. For example, say you want to add a link to your favorite search engine, or perhaps to your email address or to a newsgroup. The External Link button on the Navigation toolbar allows you to accomplish this. Basically, think of an external link as a page, file, or URL that does not exist in your current Web.

In this exercise, you'll add a navigation link that will send email to your email address when the user clicks it. Follow these steps:

1. Select the Home Page in your Web's Navigation View.

2. Click the External Link button in the Navigation toolbar. The Select Hyperlink dialog box appears, as shown in Figure 11.11.

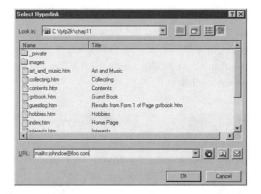

FIGURE 11.11

*When working in
Navigation View, the
Select Hyperlink dia-
log box allows you to
add an external page,
file, or other URL to
your navigation tree.*

3. In the URL field, enter `mailto:` followed by your email address. The entry should look similar to this:

   ```
   mailto:johndoe@foo.com
   ```

Note

To add an external link to a page on the World Wide Web, click the Use Your Web Browser To Select a Page or File button. This small button displays a globe, and appears immediately to the right of the URL field shown in Figure 11.11. FrontPage opens your Web browser and allows you to locate the World Wide Web page that you want to add to your navigation tree. After you find the page, return to FrontPage, where you should see the page URL displayed in the Select Hyperlink dialog box. Choose OK to add the page to your navigation tree.

4. Choose OK to add the mail hyperlink to your navigation tree. You'll see a "page" beneath the Home page. A globe icon appears at the lower-left corner of the mail link, indicating that it is an external link. The email address you entered will be displayed by default on the button. You can rename the button to something more brief, such as Email John or Send Email.

Creating a Printout

You can create a printout of your navigation tree, which is helpful in keeping track of how your pages link to each other. The printouts will be in black and white, and will span multiple pages if your tree requires them. You can preview the printouts before you commit them to paper.

> **Note**
>
> Before you print your Navigation View, be sure to expand or collapse the hierarchical tree to view the pages you want to include in the printout. Choose View, Refresh (F5) while in Navigation View to reset Navigation View so that it displays all pages in your navigation system. Pages that exist in your Web but which have not yet been added to the navigation system will not appear in the printout.

Previewing the Printout

You can use File, Print Preview while in Navigation View to preview what your printout will look like. To preview your printed pages, follow these steps:

1. From Navigation View in FrontPage, choose File, Print Preview. A preview of your navigation tree appears, as shown in Figure 11.12.

FIGURE 11.12

A preview of your navigation tree.

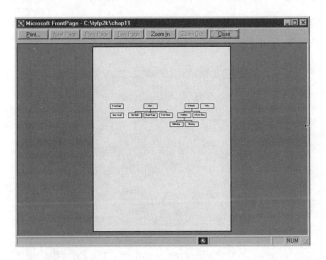

2. To preview the pages in your printout, choose one of the following buttons on the Print Preview toolbar, located at the top of the screen:
   - *Next Page*—Click this button to preview the next page in your printout.
   - *Prev Page*—Click this button to return to the previous page in the printout.
   - *Two Page*—Click this button to preview two pages at the same time after which the button is renamed One Page. To return to a single page display, click the One Page button.
   - *Zoom In*—Click this button to increase the magnification of the page in the preview screen.

- *Zoom Out*—Click this button to decrease the magnification of the page in the preview screen.

3. After you preview your printout, you have two options:

- You can print the pages from the preview window by clicking Print. The Print dialog box appears, where you can configure the number of copies you want to print.
- You can return to FrontPage without printing your pages by clicking Close.

Printing Navigation View

You can print Navigation View from the Print Preview screen, as mentioned in the preceding section. You can also choose File, Print Navigation View (Ctrl+P) or click the Print Navigation View button on the Standard toolbar.

To print your Navigation View, follow these steps:

1. Open the Print dialog box, shown in Figure 11.13, using one of the methods described in the preceding paragraph.

FIGURE 11.13

Use the Print dialog box to select your printer and specify the pages and number of copies you want to print.

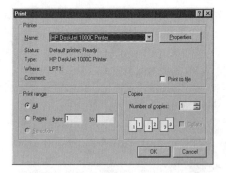

2. Enter or choose the following settings in the Print dialog box:

- In the Printer area, select your printer from the Name drop-down menu. Click the Properties button to select settings that are unique to the printer you selected.
- Check the Print to File check box if you want to print your Navigation View to a file on your hard drive rather than to your printer. The file is saved with a .prn extension.
- In the Print Range area, choose All to print all the pages in Navigation View. Choose Pages to print one or more of a range of pages; enter the starting and ending page numbers in the From and To fields.

- In the Copies area, enter the number of copies that you want to print in the Number of Copies field. Check the Collate check box if you want to collate multiple copies (your printer must support collating).

3. Choose OK to print your pages. You return to FrontPage, and the files are printed.

Deleting Pages from Your Navigation Tree

You can delete pages from your navigation tree from within Navigation View or the Folder List. When you delete pages from the Navigation View, you have the option to either delete the page from your navigation bars or to delete the page from your Web entirely. When you delete a page from the Folder List, it deletes the page from both the navigation bar and the Web.

To delete a page from the navigation pane, follow these steps:

1. From the navigation pane, click the page you want to delete.
2. Press the Del key. The Delete Page dialog box appears (see Figure 11.14).

FIGURE 11.14

Use the Delete Page dialog box to delete a page from your navigation bars or from your FrontPage Web.

3. To delete the page from Navigation View (and therefore from your navigation bars), select the Remove This Page from All Navigation Bars radio button. To delete the page from Navigation View *and* your FrontPage Web, select the Delete This Page from the Web radio button.
4. Choose OK. The page is deleted.

To delete a page from the Folder List, follow these steps:

1. Choose View, Folder List if the folder list is not displayed on your screen.
2. Locate the Web page that you want to delete, and click to select it.
3. Press the Delete key. The Confirm Delete dialog box appears (see Figure 11.15). If the current page links to other pages beneath it, a list of pages appears in the Items to Delete field.
4. Choose Yes to delete the current page or Yes to All to delete the current page and all pages in the Items to Delete field. Choose No to cancel and return to FrontPage.

If you delete a page from your current Web, you cannot undo the action. You need to re-create the page to get it back. Use caution!

FIGURE 11.15

The Confirm Delete dialog box asks whether you are sure that you want to delete pages from your navigation bars.

Using Navigation Bars

So far in this chapter, you've learned how to plan your Web and create pages while you're planning your site. Now it's time to see what you've created as a result of your planning. In the rest of this chapter you'll learn how to display and configure the navigation bars that appear on your pages.

When you double-click one of the pages in Navigation View, FrontPage opens the selected page in the editor. You may not see navigation bars on the page initially. This is because you have to place them there. You can choose to place navigation bars on all pages in your Web automatically. Where special cases are required, you can also place navigation bars on specific pages.

If you always want to locate your navigation bars in the same areas on your Web pages, you can use shared borders, which are covered in the following section.

Using Shared Borders

When you want your pages to look consistent, you generally repeat content from one page to another. In the case of this chapter, for example, you want navigation bars to display in the same areas within all (or most) of your Web pages. You might also want the same logo or copyright and contact information to appear from page to page.

This is where shared borders come in very handy. You can use them to display *any* page elements that repeat from page to page—navigation bars, page footers, banner graphics, and more.

Note

When you create a Web from one of the FrontPage Web templates or wizards, shared borders are automatically created and enabled for you. However, in the case of the Web that you've started today, you'll have to apply them. You can use the Shared Borders dialog box, discussed in the next section, to modify or disable the shared borders, if desired.

Exercise 11.5: Adding Shared Borders to All Pages

In the following task, you'll specify shared borders for all the pages in your small Web. The top shared border will contain a page banner and links to the top-level pages in your Web. The left shared border will display links to child pages (if applicable). The bottom border will display Back and Next buttons and copyright information.

Sounds like a big job, doesn't it? Fortunately, FrontPage makes it relatively easy and painless. To add the borders to your pages, follow these steps:

1. With your Web opened in FrontPage, choose Format, Shared Borders. The Shared Borders dialog box appears (see Figure 11.16).

FIGURE 11.16

You can apply shared borders to the top, left, right, or bottom of each page in your Web.

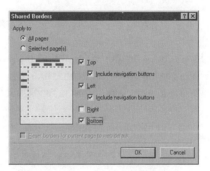

2. In the Apply to section, check All Pages.

3. Check the Top, Left, and Bottom options that appear to the right of the page preview. As you select each option, the page preview updates to give you a preview of where the borders will appear on your pages.

4. To include navigation bars in the top and left shared borders on all pages, check the Include Navigation Buttons options for each of those borders, as shown in Figure 11.16.

5. Choose OK. The shared border settings are applied to all the pages in your Web.

6. From any view in FrontPage, double-click the Home Page to open it in FrontPage. The Home Page opens, and your page is displayed with borders along the edges that you selected. If you have not yet selected a theme, your pages should appear similar to the page shown in Figure 11.17.

FIGURE 11.17

The navigation bar on the Home Page takes you to the main sections in the Web.

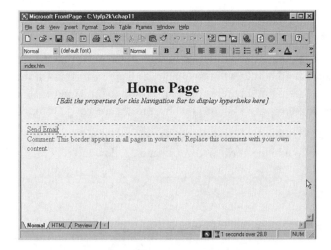

What you see in Figure 11.17 is a page banner at the top of the page, along with a bracketed statement that reads [Edit the properties for this Navigation Bar to display hyperlinks here]. The top navigation bar is there, but you have to configure how you want it to look.

The navigation bar on the side (where it shows Send Email in the figure) is the child link to your email address that you created in Exercise 11.4.

The bottom shared border contains a comment that reminds you that the border appears on all pages in your Web. This is a shared border that you will customize to include a navigation bar and copyright statement.

Note

The steps to apply shared borders to one or more selected pages are similar to those presented in the previous exercise. Instead of applying the shared borders to All Pages, select to apply the border to Selected Page(s) (refer to Figure 11.16).

When a page uses shared borders that are different than the Web default, a check box at the bottom of the Shared Borders dialog box is enabled. The Reset Borders for Current Page to Web default allows you to reset the shared borders back to those you selected for the entire Web.

Setting Navigation Bar Properties

Wherever a navigation bar appears on your pages, you use the Navigation Bar Properties dialog box to configure the buttons that are included in it. This dialog box also allows you to choose between graphical or text navigation buttons.

The Navigation Bar Properties dialog box is shown in Figure 11.18. The first section of the dialog box is the Hyperlinks to Add to Page section, which gives you the following options:

Parent Level	The navigation bar displays buttons that link to the parent page and its peer pages. Example: On your Collecting page, this option displays links to the Hobbies and Art and Music pages.
Same Level	The navigation bar displays buttons that link to the current page and its peer pages. Example: On your Contents page, this option displays links to the Search Page and the Guest Book.
Back and Next	The navigation bar displays buttons that allow the visitor to advance forward or return back to peer pages. Example: On your Search Page, this option displays a Back button (that would go to the Contents page) and a Next button (that would go to the Guest Book).
Child Level	The navigation bar displays buttons that link to the level beneath the current page. Example: On your Main page, this option displays links to Contents, Search Page, and Guest Book.
Top Level	The navigation bar displays buttons that link to the top-level pages in the Web. Example: Main, Interests, and Links pages in your Web.
Child Pages Under Home	The navigation bar displays buttons that link to all child pages of the Home page. In your Web, this option would display a button that links to your Email address.

11

FIGURE **11.18**

Use the Navigation Bar Properties dialog box to configure the content and appearance of your navigation bars.

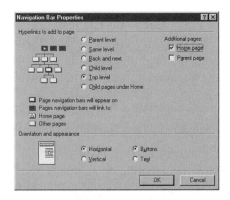

In addition to the preceding options, you can add one or two more options to any of the navigation bars. You can find these in the Additional Pages section at the upper-right corner of the Navigation Bar Properties dialog box:

Home Page   A link to the Home page in your Web will appear in addition to the options you select.

Parent Page   A link to the Parent page will appear in your navigation bar. Links to Parent pages are labeled with the word Up by default.

> **Tip**
>
> By default, FrontPage labels buttons with the word Home (for the Home page), Up (for parent pages), Back (for previous pages), and Next (for next pages). You can change these labels in the Web Settings dialog box. Choose Tools, Web Settings, then click the Navigation tab in the Web Settings dialog box. Enter new labels of your choice in the appropriate fields, or click the Default button to return the labels to their default settings.

In the Orientation and Appearance section of the Navigation Bar Properties dialog box, you find options that configure how the navigation buttons in your navigation bars appear on your pages. You'll probably want to use horizontal orientation for navigation bars that appear at the top and bottom of your pages, and vertical orientation for navigation bars that appear at the left or right of your pages. Choose Buttons to use graphical buttons that are coordinated with your theme. Choose Text to create text navigation bars.

Tip

I find it is generally more presentable to use Text navigation buttons when there are a high number of pages in a navigation bar, because they take up less room. Five or more pages in a horizontal navigation bar will display the buttons on more than one row—text buttons might look better in this case. Experiment to see what you like best. If your Web does not have a theme applied to it, your navigation bars will display as text even if you choose to display them as buttons.

Exercise 11.6: Configuring Navigation Bars

In the following exercise, you'll configure each of the three shared borders that are included on your pages. You'll also apply a theme to the Web, so that your navigation bars use graphical buttons in your navigation bars. I've selected a theme that uses a light background and good contrast for purposes of screen shot clarity—but if you want to select a different theme for your own Web, choose one that you prefer instead.

To complete the exercise, follow these steps:

1. With your Web opened, choose Format, Themes. The Themes dialog box appears.
2. Select the theme that you want to apply to your Web, and configure the theme with the options you like. The only option that you definitely want to choose for this exercise is to apply the theme to all pages in your Web. For this example, I selected the following:

Apply Theme to:	All pages
Theme:	Construction Zone
Options:	Vivid colors
	Active graphics
	Background picture

3. Choose OK. The theme is applied to all pages in your Web.
4. Return to Page View (View, Page) and open your home page in the editor. Now you will see the page with a theme applied to it.
5. In the top border, highlight the text that reads [Edit the properties for this Navigation Bar to display hyperlinks here] and press Alt+Enter, or right-click and select Navigation Bar Properties from the pop-up menu. The Navigation

11

Bar Properties dialog box shown in Figure 11.18 appears. Configure the following options for the top navigation bar:

Hyperlinks to Add to Page:	Top level
Additional Pages:	Home page
Orientation and Appearance:	Horizontal
	Buttons

6. Choose OK to apply the settings to the top navigation bar. Four buttons are displayed as shown in Figure 11.19.

FIGURE 11.19

Your top navigation bar now includes four graphic navigation buttons.

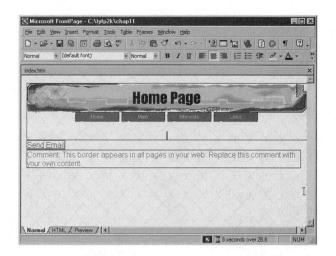

7. For the left navigation bar, you want to display graphic buttons that link to the child pages that appear beneath the current page. When a page does *not* have child pages, FrontPage will not place a navigation border on the left side. Therefore, you might also want to include a button that takes the users back to a parent page for cases such as this. This way your visitors can easily go back to where they were, without having to use the Back button on their browser. To configure the left navigation bar, click the text in the left border that reads Send Email. Press Alt+Enter to open the Navigation Bar Properties dialog box again. Set the following properties:

Hyperlinks to Add to Page:	Child level
Additional Pages:	Parent page
Orientation and Appearance:	Vertical
	Buttons

8. One more shared border to go. Your bottom shared border doesn't contain any navigation bar, but you can add one. To accomplish this, click the Comment in the bottom navigation bar to highlight it. Choose Insert, Navigation Bar to open the Navigation Bar Properties dialog box. Here, you want to add Back and Next buttons that allow the user to navigate to the peer pages of the current page they are viewing (if they exist). We'll also include a link to the home page here, so that the reader doesn't have to scroll all the way back to the top of the page. Set the following properties for the new navigation bar:

Hyperlinks to Add to Page:	Back and next
Additional Pages:	Home page
Orientation and Appearance:	Horizontal
	Buttons

9. Choose OK to apply the settings to the new navigation bar, then press the Center button on the Format toolbar to align the navigation bar to the center of the page.

10. Position the insertion point at the end of the Next navigation button in the navigation bar and press Enter to begin a new line.

11. From the Style drop-down menu in the Format toolbar, choose the Address paragraph style. Enter the following two lines of text, replacing *your name* and *e-mail* with your own name and email address. Your home page should now look like Figure 11.20.

```
Copyright 1999, your name
For questions or comments regarding this page, send email to e-mail.
```

FIGURE 11.20

The comment in the bottom shared border has been replaced with a navigation bar.

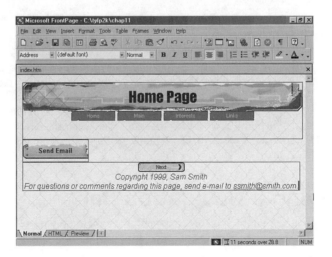

12. Choose File, Save (Ctrl+S), or click the Save button in the Standard toolbar to update the changes to your Web.

You don't get the full effect of the Back and Next buttons on the home page because the home page only contains a link to one peer: a link to your email address in this case. However, when you open the `search.htm` page in the page editor or in a Web browser, you will see three buttons in the bottom navigation bar.

Figure 11.21 shows the bottom of the Main search page as it appears in the FrontPage page editor. Here, the Back button will take you to the Contents page (`contents.htm`). The Home button takes you to the home page (`index.htm`), and the Next button takes you to the Guest Book page (`gstbook.htm`).

FIGURE 11.21

The bottom of the Main search page displays Back, Home, and Next buttons that take the reader to peer pages and to the home page.

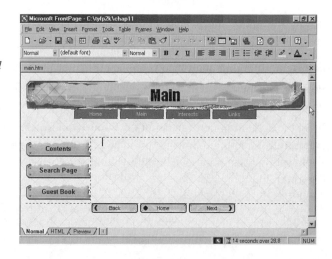

Note

The content that you place in your shared borders is actually stored on separate Web pages that reside in a hidden folder in your Web. To display the pages, choose Tools, Web Settings, and click the Advanced tab in the Web Settings dialog box. Check the Show Documents in Hidden Directories option and press OK. After your Web is refreshed, you will see a folder named _borders, which holds the border pages that you use in your Web.

Modifying a Navigation Bar

After you create your navigation bars and place them on your pages, you can use the commands previously discussed in this chapter to modify your navigation bars in several different ways:

- To change the text labels that appear in the navigation bars, edit the labels in Navigation View, similar to the way you assigned page titles in Exercises 11.1 and 11.2.

- To add or revise links in your navigation bars, add, delete, or move pages in your navigation structure. As you make changes to your navigation system, all your navigation bars update to reflect the changes.

- Use the Navigation Bar Properties dialog box to change the pages that a navigation bar includes. You can also use this dialog box to change from graphic navigation bars to text navigation bars or to change the layout of the navigation bar from horizontal to vertical. To reopen the Navigation Bar Properties dialog box, open the page on which you want to change the navigation bar. Double-click the navigation bar to open the Navigation Bar Properties dialog box. Modify the settings in the dialog box and choose OK to update the changes.

- Remember that when you change a navigation bar that appears in a shared border region on a page, the changes will also apply to any other pages that share the same border settings. If you move a navigation bar from a top shared border to a bottom shared border, for example, the change applies to each page that uses that shared border setting.

- To change the fonts, colors, and graphics that appear on all the pages in your Web, select a new theme from Themes View in FrontPage. To apply changes of this nature to only one page in your Web, select a new theme from FrontPage. To learn more about themes, see Day 9, "Changing the Appearance of Your Pages."

11

Deleting Navigation Bars

It's easy enough to delete a navigation bar, but depending on where you delete it from, you achieve different results.

Here are the steps to delete a navigation bar:

1. Open the page that you want to modify in FrontPage.

2. Select the navigation bar that you want to delete:

   - If the navigation bar appears in a page that does not use shared borders, the navigation bar is deleted from the active page only.

   - If the navigation bar appears on a page that does use shared borders, but appears in the body of the page instead of a shared border region, the navigation bar is removed from the active page only.

   - If the navigation bar appears within a shared border region on a page, the navigation bar is removed from the current page and all other pages that share the same border region.

3. Delete the navigation bar, using one of the following methods:

- Choose Edit, Clear or press the Delete key to remove the navigation bar from your page.
- Choose Edit, Cut (Ctrl+X) to remove the navigation bar from your page and place it into your Windows clipboard. You can paste it into another page using Edit, Paste (Ctrl+V).

Summary

When you use Navigation View in FrontPage, you not only provide links to the key sections and pages in your Web, but you make it easier for your site visitors to find their way around. You learned in this chapter how to create automatic navigation bars that update themselves when you make changes to your Web. You also learned how to use shared borders to place repeated content on all or selected pages in your Web.

Workshop

Q&A

Q Does my Internet service provider have to have the FrontPage Server Extensions installed in order for me to use navigation bars and shared borders?

A When you publish your pages, the navigation bars are saved in standard HTML format. You can publish pages that use this feature to an ISP that does not have the FrontPage Server Extensions installed.

Q Are the navigation bars created by FrontPage 2000 compatible with every browser, or do I have to recommend a specific browser with which to view them?

A If your navigation bars use active graphics, they incorporate hover buttons. Hover buttons are actually small Java applets, so you need to recommend a browser that is capable of displaying Java applets. The most current versions of Netscape Navigator and Internet Explorer are sure to support the latest and greatest features, but it's always best to test your pages in several different browsers to be sure.

Q. Are navigation bars all that I need to create links to all of the pages in my Web?

A. Generally, it's not a good idea to rely solely on the navigation buttons that are automatically generated by FrontPage. The reason for this is that they use Java and graphics to display the links to other pages in your Web. Remember from previous lessons that not all browsers can display these types of features, or that some users choose not to display graphics. It is a good practice to also include a text hyperlink for every navigation button that appears in your Web pages.

Q Can I change the font that is used in my text navigation bars?

A The fonts used with your navigation bars are determined by the theme you use. Cascading style sheet tags are used to determine the fonts and colors of the fonts. For more information about cascading style sheets, see Day 10, "Using Style Sheets."

Q How do I follow a hyperlink in a navigation bar from FrontPage?

A Place the mouse over the navigation button or text in the navigation bar and use the Ctrl+Click shortcut to follow the hyperlink.

Quiz

1. What is the difference between a parent page and a top-level page?
2. What is the difference between a child page and a peer page?
3. True or false: When you create new pages from FrontPage page templates, they are automatically added to your navigation bars.
4. True or false: Your pages always have to use the same shared borders.
5. Can you place other content besides page banners and navigation bars in shared borders?

Exercises

1. If you like the navigation system you designed in this chapter, expand upon it for your own site. Add more pages to your Web and put them where they fit best in your navigation tree. If you prefer designing one of your own, try your skills now while the steps are still fresh in your mind!
2. Try different combinations of settings in the Navigation Bar Properties dialog boxes to see how they look on your pages, and which pages are automatically placed in the navigation bars.

Answers to Quiz

1. A parent page is any page that links to pages in a level directly beneath it. Top-level pages are one or more pages that exist in the highest level of your Web. Your home page is always a top-level page.

2. A child page is a page that has a parent page. Peer pages are two or more child pages that share a common parent.

3. False. Pages generated with FrontPage *Web* templates and wizards are automatically added to navigation bars; but pages generated with *page* templates and wizards have to be added manually in Navigation View.

4. False. Though you might want to use the same shared borders on most of the pages in your Web site, you can also apply and configure shared borders that are specific to a smaller number of pages in your Web.

5. Yes you can. In fact, shared borders don't always have to contain navigation buttons and banners. Company logos and contact information are some items that can easily appear on all of the pages in your Web.

Creating and Using Framesets

No doubt you have browsed the Web and come across some sites that display several pages within multiple panes in a browser window. When you click hyperlinks on one page, the page that it links to appears in another pane. The navigation links remain on the screen as you choose the pages that you want to view. More than likely, the site uses a frameset to display the navigation system.

Think of a frameset as multiple pages in one. The most common way to use framesets is to display hyperlinks and navigation systems that enable users to find information in your Web site without getting too lost. Each region, or frame, in a frameset displays a separate page that is scrollable, just like any other Web page.

FrontPage 2000 enables you to create and edit your framesets in WYSIWYG mode. In addition, you can edit the HTML code associated with your framesets directly.

In today's lesson, you will

- Learn how to create a frameset from a template
- Add and delete frames from a frameset to create your own custom framesets
- Assign properties to framesets and frames
- Learn how to add content to the frames in your framesets
- Create hyperlinks that load pages in your Web to different frames in the frameset

Frames Terminology

In simple terms, a *frameset* is a special kind of page that divides the browser window into multiple sections, called *frames*. When a user navigates to a frameset with a frame-compatible browser, the browser reads the instructions in the frameset page and divides the browser window accordingly.

Figure 12.1 shows what a frameset looks like when you first create it in FrontPage. It is divided into three sections (or frames) that will each display a different Web page.

FIGURE 12.1

A frameset page divides the browser window into multiple sections called frames.

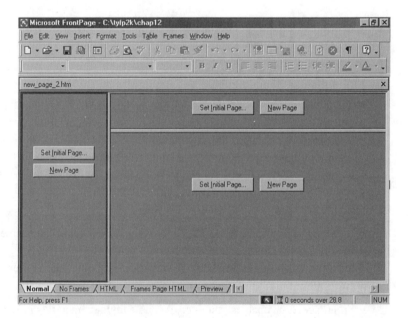

Initially, there is no content displayed in the frameset. Instead, FrontPage displays command buttons that prompt you to create or select the pages that display in each frame of the frameset. As you plan your site, you decide what types of content will be delivered to each of the frames.

In FrontPage terminology, the first pages that display in each frame are called *initial pages*. Initial pages are more commonly known in the HTML world as *source URLs*. To choose the initial page for each frame, click the Set Initial Page button. After you select the initial pages for each frame, FrontPage displays them exactly as they appear in the frameset. For example, Figure 12.2 shows three additional Web pages after they are selected as the initial pages for a frameset that is similar to the one shown in Figure 12.1.

FIGURE 12.2

The pages that first appear in each frame of the frameset are called initial pages, or source URLs.

Now that each frame has a page displayed inside it, the user clicks the links that appear on the pages. If the user clicks a link in the left frame in the frameset shown in Figure 12.2, a new navigation bar appears in the top frame. Likewise, when the user clicks a link in the top navigation bar, a new content page appears in the largest main frame.

In order to direct the pages to the correct frames in the frameset, you'll need to understand what some of the frameset terms mean. The following list briefly describes the terms you will encounter as you develop and design your framesets:

Frameset	A Web page that contains special instructions that divide the browser window into multiple sections, called frames.
Frame	One of the panes, or divisions, in a frameset.

12

Frame name	Each frame in a frameset has a name, much like the houses in a neighborhood can be called "the Smiths's house" or "the Wallaces' house." Frame names aren't URLs (or addresses); they are *descriptions*. Typically, you assign frame names that represent a location in the frameset (left, top, and main, for example).
Target frame	When a user clicks a link on a page in your frameset, the target frame is the name of the frame that the link delivers the page to. Target frames can be assigned to a Web page, or to a hyperlink.
Source URL	Also referred to as the initial page. This is the URL of the page that appears in a frame when browser first loads the frameset.

Yesterday, you built a personal Web site that contained three main areas: a main section, an interests section, and a links section. You used Navigation View to generate navigation buttons for you automatically. The Web site used shared borders and navigation bars to direct visitors to all of the pages in your site.

For the sake of comparison, you'll build a similar Web site in today's lesson, but instead your navigation bars will display in different frames in a frameset. To familiarize yourself with the terminology and procedures, we'll begin with a frameset that uses simple text links for navigation. The final result is shown in Figure 12.3.

Exercise 12.1: Creating a Frameset from a Template

In today's first exercise, you'll begin by creating a two-frame frameset. In exercises that follow, you will learn how to change it into the three-frame frameset that is shown in Figure 12.3.

First, you'll need to create a new Web site and import some content for your frameset. Follow these steps:

1. Choose File, New, Web. Create a new Web and locate it in the tyfp2k/chap12 directory on your C: drive.

2. Highlight the root folder in your new Web, and choose File, Import. The Import dialog box appears.

3. Click the Add File button, and select all of the files in the tyfp2k/chap12/samples folder on your CD-ROM drive. Choose Open to add the files to your import list.

4. Choose OK to import the selected files into your FrontPage Web.

FIGURE 12.3

A three-frame frameset that uses text links for navigation.

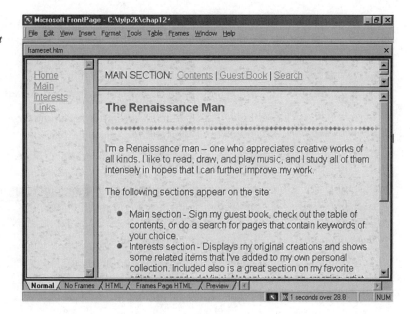

5. To create a new frameset page, choose File, New, Page (Ctrl+N). The New dialog box appears.

6. Select the Frames Pages tab, shown in Figure 12.4.

FIGURE 12.4

The Frames Pages tab in the New dialog box allows you to create a frameset from existing FrontPage templates.

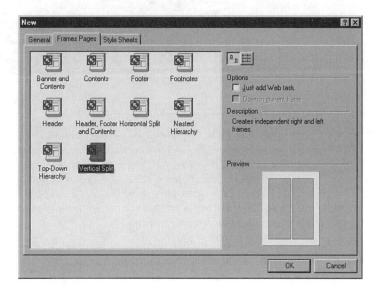

12

7. From the list of available frame templates, highlight the Vertical Split template. A preview and brief description of the frameset appears in the right portion of the New dialog box. The Vertical Split frameset template displays two pages side by side.

8. Choose OK to open the frameset in the page editor. The FrontPage screen displays two frames, as shown in Figure 12.5. Each of the pages contains two buttons:

  - The Set Initial Page button allows you to select the page that initially loads in each frame when the browser first opens the frameset.

  - The New Page button allows you to create a new blank page within a frame.

FIGURE 12.5

Two frames display in FrontPage. Each frame contains two buttons.

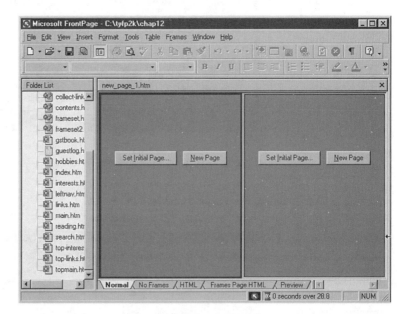

Note

When you select the New Page button in a frameset, a new blank page is created in the selected frame. You can then add content to it as you do any other page. If you want to create a new page using one of the FrontPage templates, do not use the New Page button within the frame. Instead, choose File, New (Ctrl+N). Select your page template from the New dialog box and verify that the Open in Current Frame button in the lower-right corner of the New dialog box is checked. Choose OK to create a new page in the selected frame.

Reviewing Frameset and Frame Properties

FrontPage provides several different frameset templates that should accommodate most of your needs. If you have special needs, you can modify an existing frameset so that it does what *you* want it to do. You can add frames to or delete frames from a frameset, as well as make modifications to the frame names and target frame names.

In order to change a frameset, you have to know what the existing frameset does. To determine this, you look at the properties of the frameset, and the properties of each frame in the frameset.

Frameset Properties

When you have a frameset page opened in the page editor, you can choose the File, Properties command to display the properties for the page. The Page Properties dialog box includes a Frames tab, which is shown in Figure 12.6.

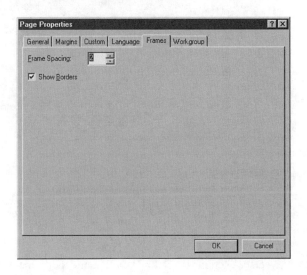

By default, FrontPage creates a frameset that displays borders between each of the frames in the frameset. The spacing between the frames (or, the width of the border) is 2 pixels. The settings in the Frames tab allow you to adjust either or both of these settings.

There are two settings available in the Frames tab:

- *Frame Spacing*—This increases or decreases the amount of spacing between the frames in the frameset. This can be likened to changing the width of the borders between the frames. By default, the width is 2 pixels.

- *Show Borders*—This enables or disables the display of borders between the frames. To create a borderless frameset (a frameset that does not display the "dividers" between the frames in the frameset), uncheck this option. Figure 12.7 shows what your two-frame frameset looks like after the Show Borders option is unchecked. For a completed version of a borderless frameset, refer to Figure 12.2.

FIGURE **12.7**

To create a borderless frameset, uncheck the Show Borders option in the Frames tab.

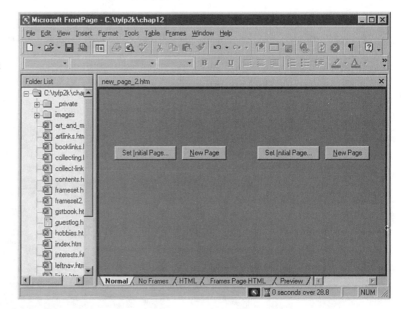

Frame Properties

You can also change the properties of each of the frames in the frameset. The Frame Properties dialog box shown in Figure 12.8 allows you to select several options. To set the properties of a frame, click to make a frame active. A solid blue border surrounds the selected frame. Next, choose Frames, Frame Properties to open the Frame Properties dialog box. Here, you see sections that allow you to name the frame, set its initial page, and choose size, margin, and other options for the currently selected frame. The settings in the top section of the dialog box are as follows:

- *Name*—Allows you to assign a name to the frame in the frameset. Typically, this name represents the physical location of the frame, or a name that describes the content that is to be displayed in each frame. For example, the default frame names for the Vertical Split template that you created in Exercise 12.1 are left (for the left frame) and right (for the right frame). However, if you want to display a navigation bar in the left frame and main Web content in the right frame, you could just as easily call the left frame navigation and the right frame content.

- *Initial Page*—Allows you to select a Web page that initially displays in the frameset when the browser first opens the frameset. Use the Browse button to select a page from your current Web, hard disk, World Wide Web, or to create a new page.

The Frame size setting allows you to specify the width or height of the current frame. Frame widths and heights are defined by one of three units of measurement: Relative, Percent, or Pixels. The differences between them are as follows:

- *Relative*—Defines how the current frame relates to other frames in the frameset. Think of it as a ratio. For example, if you want the left and right frames in your current frameset to be equal in height or width, you assign a Relative value of 1 to each of them (a 1 to 1 ratio). If you want the right frame to be twice as wide as the left frame, assign a Relative value of 1 to the left frame, and 2 to the right frame.

- *Percent*—Specifies a width or height measurement as it relates to the total width or height of the browser window. For example, if you want the left frame to be 35 percent of the total width of the browser window, enter 35 for a measurement and choose Percent from the unit drop-down list.

- *Pixels*—Specifies a width or height measurement in pixels. This is most commonly used when you are displaying graphics in your frame, such as for navigation buttons. The pixel width or height should not be less than the width or height of your images, and you should also take into account the width of scrollbars and page margins that apply to the pages.

The Margins section of the Frame Properties dialog box controls the amount of space from the edge of each frame to the page content that appears in the frame. This setting may not be recognized in some frame-compatible browsers. The settings are

12

- *Width*—Specifies the number of pixels from the left edge of the frame to the content on the page within the frame. By default, the setting is 12 pixels.

- *Height*—Specifies the number of pixels from the top edge of the frame to the content on the page within the frame. By default, the setting is 16 pixels.

Tip To quickly resize one of the frames in FrontPage, click and drag the frame border and release the mouse when the frame is properly sized to hold your page contents.

Finally, the Options setting of the Frame Properties dialog box controls other options that relate to the display of the frame. The settings are

- *Resizable in Browser*—By default, the user is allowed to resize the frame to display the content as he or she chooses. Because people view the Web at varying resolutions, it is generally best to keep this option checked. Unchecking this option prevents the user from resizing frame widths or heights.

- *Show Scrollbars*—By default, scrollbars are shown if needed. When the content of a Web page extends beyond the visible height or width of the frame, scrollbars appear at the right or bottom of the frame. These scrollbars allow the user to scroll to read the portions of the page that are not visible in the frame. Normally, it is wise to display scrollbars if needed. Choose Never to disable the scrollbars, or Always to display scrollbars whether they are necessary or not.

- *Frames Page*—Selecting the Frames Page button in the Frame Properties dialog box displays the Frames tab in the Page Properties dialog box (shown earlier in Figure 12.6).

FIGURE 12.8

The Frame Properties dialog box allows you to specify settings for each frame in the frameset.

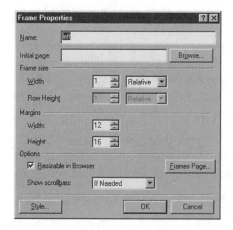

With the basic settings out of the way, you'll now learn how to apply these settings. In the following exercise, you'll convert your two-frame frameset into a three-frame frameset.

Exercise 12.2: Adding Another Frame to the Frameset

While most of the framesets provided with FrontPage are built to accommodate the most common uses, there will be occasions when you will need to make modifications. Additionally, you may start with one type of frameset and decide later that you need to make revisions. This exercise shows you how to add another frame to a frameset.

Right now, your frameset has two frames. The left frame is suitable for navigation bars, and the larger right frame displays the main pages in your Web. In this exercise, you'll divide the right frame into an upper and lower section. The left frame will be 120 pixels wide, and will display a navigation bar that links to the main sections in your Web. The new top frame, 60 pixels in height, will display one of several navigation bars that contain links to the content pages in each section. Finally, the largest main frame will display the pages selected from the top frame. The main frame will consume the remaining space (the full browser window less 120 pixels in width and 60 pixels in height).

> **Note**
>
> I purposely started with a two-frame frameset to show you how to modify an existing frameset. In the future, you might find it easier to start with the frameset template that most closely resembles the final results you want to achieve. After you make the modifications that are discussed in the following steps, your frameset will be very similar to the Nested Hierarchy frameset template that is provided with FrontPage.

To add another frame and change its properties, follow these steps:

1. Click in the right frame in your frameset. A blue border surrounds it.

2. Choose Frame, Split Frame. The Split Frame dialog box shown in Figure 12.9 appears.

FIGURE 12.9

The Split Frame dialog box allows you to split the current frame into two columns or rows.

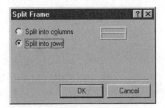

12

3. To split the frame into two rows, choose the Split Into Rows radio button and click OK. Now you have two frames in the right portion of your frameset, making a total of three frames in your frameset.

> **Note**
>
> You also can delete frames from a frameset. If your current frameset has four frames, for example, and you want to change it so that your pages display in three frames, you can use the Delete Frame command in the Frames menu to delete the frame. Click the frame you want to delete, then choose Frame, Delete Frame to remove the frame from your frameset. After you delete a frame, you will need to reassign any default target link or target link settings that pointed to the frame you deleted.

4. To make the left frame 120 pixels wide, select the left frame and choose Frames, Frame Properties. The settings not listed below are to remain at their default settings. Set the following properties for the left frame:

Name   left (default)

Width   120 pixels

5. Choose OK to apply the settings to the left frame.

6. To rename the top-right frame and set it to 60 pixels in height, select the top-right frame and choose Frames, Frame Properties. The settings not mentioned here are to remain at their default settings. Set the following properties for the top-right frame, then choose OK to apply its settings:

Name   top

Column Width   1 Relative (uses the remaining width that is not consumed by the left frame)

Height   60 pixels

7. To rename the bottom-right frame and set it to use the remaining width and height of the browser window, select the bottom-right frame and choose Frames, Frame Properties. The settings not mentioned here are to remain at their default settings. Set the following properties for the bottom-right frame, then choose OK to apply its settings:

Name   main

Column Width   1 Relative (uses the remaining width that is not consumed by the left frame)

Height   1 Relative (uses the remaining height that is not consumed by the top frame)

About Target Frames

Your frameset is designed, and each of the frames has a name. The next step is to identify which pages load into the frameset when the browser first opens the frameset. The frames in your frameset will be used as follows:

- The left frame displays a page that includes hyperlinks to the home page and to the main sections in the Web site (the Main section, the Interests section, and the Links section). When the user clicks on the link that reads Home, the home page displays in the largest main frame. However, when one of the remaining links in the left frame is clicked, the navigation bar in the top frame will change.

- The top frame will display one of three navigation pages that contain links to content pages in the Main, Interests, or Links section in the Web site. When the user clicks on one of the navigation links in the top frame, the content page displays in the main frame.
- The main frame displays the main content in your Web. Clicking links in the main frame will cause the target pages to also display within the main frame.

In order for the pages to be directed to the right frame when the user clicks a link, the browser has to know which frame to direct the pages toward. This is the purpose of *target frame* names, and there are two ways you can assign them:

- When all or most of the hyperlinks on a Web page display target pages in the same frame, you assign a default target frame to the originating page. For example, when the reader selects three of the four links in the left frame, you want a change to occur in the top frame. View the General tab in the Page Properties dialog box for the left frame, and enter the target frame name in the Default Target Frame field. Any link that appears on that Web page will display the linked page in the designated target frame.
- The Home link in your left frame should display in the largest main frame instead of in the smaller top frame (the default target frame you assign to the left page). To achieve this, you assign the target frame name when you create the hyperlink to the home page. By doing so, you override the default target frame assigned to the left page, and the browser directs the page to the frame assigned to the hyperlink.

One additional note about target frames: When a hyperlink does not have a target frame name assigned to it, the link displays the new page in the same frame in which the originating page appears. As a general rule, when links appear on the pages in your main frame, you'll want the new pages to also appear in the main frame.

There is an exception to this rule, however. When you create links to pages stored in other sites on the World Wide Web, you generally do not want to display pages from other sites in your own frameset. One reason for this is that it gives visitors the impression that the external sites are part of your own site, or that you are claiming those pages as your own. In addition, if the external site also uses framesets for navigation, you will display a frameset within a frameset, making both sites extremely difficult to view and navigate.

To avoid displaying external pages in your own frameset, assign the target frame name of _top, discussed later in this chapter in "Other Target Frame Names," to instruct your Web browser to remove the frameset and load the new page in a full browser window.

12

Exercise 12.3: Assigning Target Frames

Let's return to the frameset you have been working on in this chapter to create a page for the left frame in your frameset. This page should contain links that display navigation bars for the Main, Interests, and Links sections of your Web site in the top frame. You'll also include a link that displays the home page in the main frame.

To complete the page for the left frame in your frameset, follow these steps:

1. Click the New Page button in the left frame in your frameset. A new blank page appears in the left frame. The insertion point is ready for you to add content.

 Tip

> If you prefer to edit the content of a framed page in a full browser window, click in the frame you want to edit and choose Frame, Open Page in New Window.

2. Enter the following lines of text, pressing Shift+Enter at the end of each line to insert a normal line break:

   ```
   Home
   Main
   Interests
   Links
   ```

3. Right-click inside the page, and choose Page Properties from the pop-up menu. The Page Properties dialog box appears opened to the General tab.

4. Click the Pencil icon that appears to the right of the Default Target Frame field, which is highlighted in Figure 12.10.

FIGURE 12.10

To assign a default target name to all of the hyperlinks on a Web page, click the Pencil icon at the right of the Default Target Frame field.

Page Properties	? X

General | Margins | Custom | Language | Workgroup |

Location: file:///C./tylp2k/chap12/leftnav.htm
Title: Left Navigation Bar
Base location:
Default target frame: top

Background sound
    Location: Browse...
    Loop: 0   ☑ Forever

Design-time control scripting
    Platform: Client (IE 4.0 DHTML)
    Server: Inherit from Web
    Client: Inherit from Web

    Style...

                              OK   Cancel

5. The Target Frame dialog box shown in Figure 12.11 appears. A preview of your frameset appears in graphic form at the left side of the dialog box. Click the top-right frame in the graphic picture of the frameset. The Target setting field beneath the preview displays top.

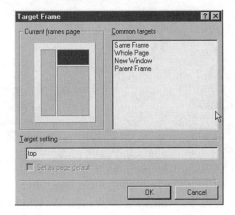

6. Choose OK to return to the Page Properties dialog box, then choose OK again to apply the settings and return to the page editor.

7. Highlight the first line of text in your left navigation bar page (the Home hyperlink), and click the Hyperlink button in the Standard toolbar. The Create Hyperlink dialog box appears.

8. Locate homepg.htm (one of the pages that you imported at the beginning of this chapter). Highlight the page, but don't choose OK yet—remember that you want this page to open in the main frame in the frameset. Right now, you should see Page default (top) displayed in the Target Frame field.

9. Click the Change Target Frame icon (the small pencil) beside the Target Frame field, as shown in Figure 12.12. The Target Frame dialog box reappears.

10. This time, select the bottom-right frame in the graphic representation of your frameset. This assigns the main frame as the target frame for the Home hyperlink.

11. Choose OK to return to the Edit Hyperlink dialog box, then choose OK again to return to the page editor.

12. Highlight the next line on the page in the left frame, which reads Main. Click the Hyperlink button in the Standard toolbar, and create a link to the topmain.htm page in your current Web. Notice that the Target Frame field already displays Page default (top) as the target frame. Choose OK to create the hyperlink.

12

FIGURE 12.12

You assign a target frame to a hyperlink in the Edit Hyperlink dialog box.

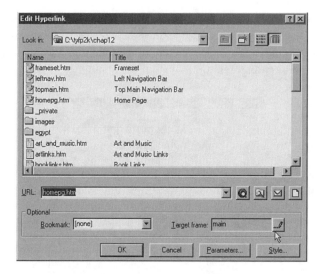

13. Repeat step 12 to create a hyperlink to `top-interests.htm` for the `Interests` hyperlink, and to `top-links.htm` for the `Links` hyperlink.

14. Choose Frames, Save Page. The Save As dialog box appears, displaying a preview of your frameset in the right portion, as shown in Figure 12.13. The preview shows the left frame selected.

FIGURE 12.13

The Save As dialog box displays a preview of your frameset in the right portion

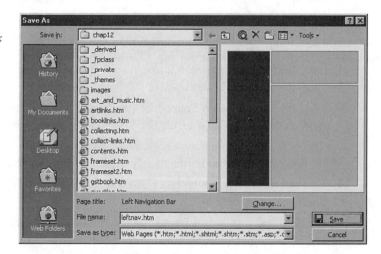

15. Click the Change button to change the title to `Left Navigation Bar` and choose OK to return to the Save As dialog box.

16. Enter `leftnav.htm` in the File Name field.

17. Choose Save. The new page is saved to your Web.

Exercise 12.4: Setting Initial Pages

The left navigation bar that you just created remains onscreen so that the reader can choose which sections in your site he or she wants to view. However, you still need to assign initial pages for the top and main frames in the frameset.

The Main section of your Web site contains pages that will help readers find their way around more easily. Therefore, the Main navigation bar (`topmain.htm`) seems to be a good choice to display in the top frame when the frameset first opens.

 Note | Hyperlinks and target frame names have already been assigned for you on `topmain.htm`, `top-interests.htm`, and `top-links.htm`. They were created using the same steps outlined in Exercise 12.3. Examine these further to learn more about how the pages interact with each other.

The initial page for the main content frame in your frameset should be a page that tells your readers what your site contains. It can be as simple or as complex as you choose, but should contain enough information to get people interested in looking further into your site. Figure 12.14 shows a full-screen example of the Egypt: Land of Mystery page that was shown at the beginning of this chapter. This page is a good example that contains a basic introduction to the Web site. Graphics are also an effective way to draw the reader's attention. The example you'll use in this chapter contains a very brief and general description of what our fictitious site contains.

To assign initial pages for the top and main frames in the frameset, follow these steps:

1. Click the Set Initial Page button in the top frame. The Create Hyperlink dialog box appears.

2. Highlight `topmain.htm` and choose OK to set it as the initial page for the top frame.

3. Click the Set Initial Page button in the main frame. The Create Hyperlink dialog box appears.

4. Highlight `homepg.htm` and choose OK to set it as the initial page for the main frame.

5. Choose File, Save (Ctrl+S) to save your frameset page to your Web.

12

FIGURE 12.14

The initial page for the main frame in your frameset should contain information that tells the reader what your site is about.

Other Target Frame Names

Occasionally, when you work with framesets you encounter situations in which you do not want to load pages in your frameset at all, or you want to direct hyperlinks to the same frame in your frameset. Let's take a couple of common situations that you might encounter when you link to pages on another Web site. One way you can approach this is to display the external pages in a full browser window, removing your frameset from the picture completely. Alternatively, you can display the external pages in another browser window. Two instances of your browser appear simultaneously. One window displays your own frameset, and the other displays the pages on the other site.

Still, there are other times when you want to load a target page in the same frame as the originating page, or you want to direct pages to other frames in a nested frameset (which is described in the following exercise).

The Target Frame dialog box (refer to Figure 12.11) displays a list of special target frame names that fill these needs. The Common Targets list in the right side of the dialog box presents the following choices:

- *Same Frame*—When you choose this option, the Target Setting field displays a target frame of _self. This loads the page to which you are hyperlinking in the same frame that the hyperlink you are following appears in.

- *Whole Page*—When you choose this option, the Target Setting field displays a target frame of _top. This removes the frameset from the current browser window and displays the target page in a full browser window. If any of the hyperlinks in your frames navigate to other sites on the World Wide Web, this is one of two common approaches to display the external pages.

- *New Window*—When you choose this option, the Target Setting field displays a target frame of _blank. This loads the page to which you are hyperlinking in a new browser window and keeps your frameset in the original browser window.

- *Parent Frame*—When you choose this option, the Target Setting field displays a target frame of _parent. This loads the page to which you are hyperlinking in the parent frame if the hyperlink that you are following appears on a child frame.

Exercise 12.5: Dealing with Subcategories

Sometimes, the categories you include on your Web site are too broad to display within a couple of navigation frames because topics can have additional subcategories beneath them. For example, the Interests section in your Web contains two subcategories: Hobbies, and Art and Music. Each of these subcategories can be broken down further. For example, you could have many different hobbies that you want to highlight in separate sections in your Web.

Yesterday, when you used Navigation View to develop a navigation system for a similar Web site, the Hobbies section of the Web branched into two more subcategories: Collecting and Reading. There are two ways that you can add these additional subcategories to your frameset. The following exercise describes both approaches, but in reality you would use one of the two following methods.

Replacing a Frame

The first way you can approach subcategories is to display the subcategories in the same frame as their parent categories. Here, you design another navigation page for the top frame. When the reader clicks the Hobbies link, the top navigation bar is replaced with a navigation bar that displays links to the Collecting and Reading pages. Another link can return the reader back to the previous Hobbies navigation bar.

To create a subcategory page for the Hobbies section, follow these steps:

1. Click the New Page icon on the Standard toolbar to create a new blank page.
2. Enter the following text on the page:

   HOBBIES: Collecting ¦ Reading ¦ Back to Interests
3. Right-click inside the page and choose Page Properties from the pop-up menu. The Page Properties dialog box opens to the General tab.
4. Click the Change Target Frame icon to the right of the Default Target Frame field. The Target Frame dialog box appears.

12

5. You want the links on this navigation bar to display the target pages in the main frame of the frameset. To assign the main frame, enter **main** in the Target Setting field, and choose OK to return to the Page Properties dialog box. Choose OK again to return to the page editor.

6. Highlight the text that reads Collecting. Click the Hyperlink button on the Standard toolbar, and create a hyperlink to the collecting.htm page in your Web.

7. Highlight the text that reads Reading. Click the Hyperlink button on the Standard toolbar, and create a hyperlink to the reading.htm page in your Web.

8. Highlight the text that reads Back to Interests. When the reader selects this link, you want to display the Interests navigation bar in the top frame again. Click the Hyperlink button on the Standard toolbar to open the Create Hyperlink dialog box. Highlight the top-interests.htm page in your Web. The URL of the page displays in the URL field.

9. Click the Change Target Frame icon that displays at the right of the Target Frame field. The Target Frame dialog box appears.

10. From the Common Targets list at the right side of the dialog box, select Same Frame. The Target Setting field displays _self. This instructs the browser to display the linked page in the same frame in which the current navigation bar appears. Choose OK to return to the Create Hyperlink dialog box.

11. Choose OK to return to the page editor.

12. Choose File, Save (Ctrl+S), or click the Save button on the Standard toolbar. Change the page title to Hobbies Navigation Bar, and use a filename of top-hobbies.htm. Click Save to save the new page to your Web.

13. Open or return to the frameset.htm page in your current Web. While pressing the Ctrl key, click the Interests link in the left frame to display top-interests.htm in the top frame of the frameset.

14. Highlight the Hobbies text in the top navigation bar, and click the Hyperlink button in the Standard toolbar. The Create Hyperlink dialog box appears.

15. Locate the top-hobbies.htm page in your Web, and highlight the page to display its URL in the URL field. Then, click the Change Target Frame icon at the right of the Target Frame field.

16. From the Common Targets list, choose Same Frame, and click OK to return to the Create Hyperlink dialog box. Choose OK again to return to the page editor.

17. Choose File, Save (Ctrl+S), or click the Save button on the Standard toolbar to save the updated navigation bar to your Web.

To test how this works, click the Preview tab to display the frameset in Preview mode. If the Interests navigation bar is not displayed in the top frame, click the Interests link in the left frame. Your screen will look similar to Figure 12.15.

FIGURE 12.15

The Interests navigation bar initially displays in the top frame.

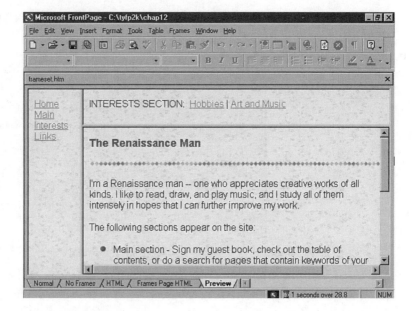

Now, click the Hobbies hyperlink in the top frame. The new navigation bar appears in the top frame, as shown in Figure 12.16. When you click the Collecting and Reading hyperlinks in this navigation bar, the target pages appear in the main frame of the frameset. When you click the Back to Interests hyperlink in the top frame, you return to the navigation bar shown in Figure 12.15.

Using Nested Framesets

Another approach to dealing with subcategories in a Web site is to create a *second* frameset that works within the original frameset. This is called a *nested frameset*.

The original frameset is called the *parent frameset*, and the frameset or framesets that work within it are called *child framesets*. Instead of displaying a targeted page in the main frame of your parent frameset, you display the child frameset within the main (or parent) frame. The child frameset divides the main frame into two or more frames.

The main disadvantage to using this method is that your frameset can get too busy. When too many frames are displayed in a frameset, the viewable area of each frame becomes very small, especially when you view framesets at a lower display resolution. The browser

12

window becomes cluttered with navigation, leaving little room to display the main content in your site. However, if you suggest that your readers view your site at higher resolutions (such as 800×600 or higher), this approach might work well.

FIGURE **12.16**

The Hobbies naviga-tion bar replaces the Interests navigation bar in the top frame.

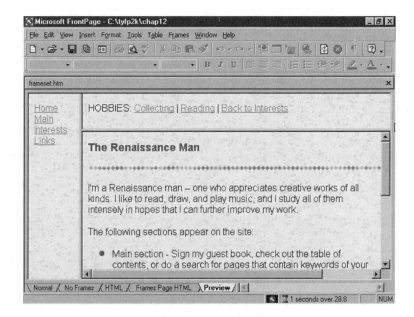

The following exercise demonstrates how you use nested framesets:

1. With the c:\tyfp2k\chap12 Web open, choose File, New, Page (Ctrl+N). The New dialog box appears.

2. Click the Frames Pages tab, and select the Horizontal Split frame from the available frameset options. Choose OK to create the new frameset.

3. Click the Set Initial Page button in the top frame. The Create Hyperlink dialog box appears. Highlight the hobbies.htm page in your current Web, and choose OK. A navigation bar appears in the top frame.

Note

The hobbies.htm Web page is a navigation bar that already has the correct tar-get frame assigned to it. When the reader selects any link in this navigation bar, the pages are loaded in the bottom frame in the new child frameset.

4. Click the Set Initial Page button in the bottom frame. The Create Hyperlink dialog box appears again. Highlight the collecting.htm page in your current Web, and choose OK. A page with the heading of Collecting appears in the bottom frame.

5. Click inside the top frame and choose Frames, Frame Properties. The Frame Properties dialog box appears. Adjust the settings for the top frame as follows, and choose OK to return to the page editor:

Name	top2
Height	60 pixels

6. Choose File, Save (Ctrl+S), or click the Save button on the Standard toolbar. The Save As dialog box appears, displaying the frameset page as the page you are going to save.

7. Change the page title of the new frameset to Hobbies Frameset. Save the frameset with a filename of frameset2.htm. Click the Save button to save the page.

Now that you have designed the second frameset, you need to make the modifications that make it work in the parent frameset. For the following steps, I have created a second example of the Interests navigation bar that appears in the top frame. To proceed, follow these steps:

8. Open the original frameset (frameset.htm) in the page editor.

9. Click inside the Interests link in the left frame, and then click the Hyperlink button on the Standard toolbar. The Edit Hyperlink dialog box appears.

10. In the URL field, change the existing value of top-interests.htm to top-interests2.htm. Choose OK to update the hyperlink information.

11. While pressing the Ctrl key, click the Interests hyperlink in the left frame to display the Interests navigation bar in the top frame.

12. Select the Hobbies link in the top frame, and click the Hyperlink button in the Standard toolbar to open the Edit Hyperlink dialog box. Highlight frameset2.htm as the page to hyperlink to.

13. Click the Change Target Frame button at the right of the Target Frame field. From the Current Frames Page diagram at the left side of the Target Frame dialog box, select the largest frame as the target frame. The Target Setting field displays main.

14. Choose OK to return to the Edit Hyperlink dialog box, and choose OK again to return to the page editor.

15. Choose File, Save to update your main frameset page.

Now, preview your main frameset again by choosing the Preview tab in the page editor. Click the Home link in the left frame to display the initial home page in the main frame. Next, click the Interests link in the left frame to display the Interests navigation bar in the top frame.

Click the Art and Music page in the top frame first. Notice that the main frame displays the Art and Music page in the main frame of the parent frameset, as shown in Figure 12.17.

12

FIGURE 12.17

The Art and Music link displays the target page in the main frame of the parent frameset.

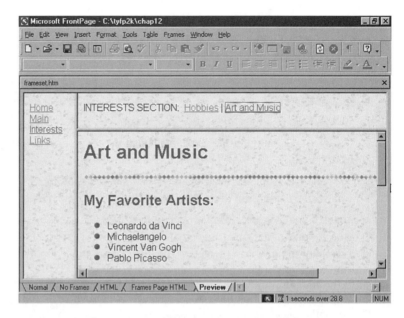

Now, click the Hobbies hyperlink in the top frame. You should see the main page area divide itself into two frames as shown in Figure 12.18. The upper portion displays your Hobbies navigation bar, and the lower portion displays the Collecting page.

FIGURE 12.18

The Hobbies link divides the main frame into two frames, and displays the Hobbies navigation bar beneath the Interests navigation bar.

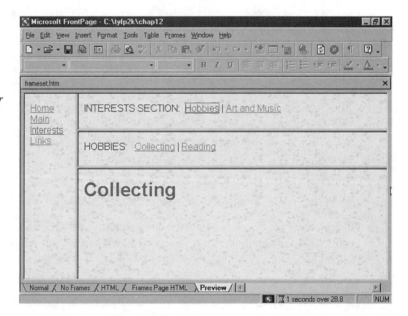

Creating the Alternate Content Page

Frames offer you great flexibility in displaying pages. Don't let your Web site rely totally on that flexibility, however. Many people use browsers that are not compatible with frames. Others use different browsers at different times for various reasons. For example, a user might prefer the way one browser views mail and newsgroups over another, and that choice might not have frame compatibility.

Be considerate to those out there who do not have frame-compatible browsers or who do not use them all the time. Provide alternatives for navigating to the pages that you display within the frames. FrontPage 2000 provides a very easy way to create an alternate content page. If a browser that is not frame-compatible encounters a page with a frameset, the alternate content page displays instead. You can create a Web page that enables the user to navigate to other pages in your site instead of receiving a `This site uses frames but your browser does not support them` message.

In FrontPage 2000, it is very easy to add content to your alternate content page. Instead of using the normal page editing view, you use the No Frames View, shown in Figure 12.19.

FIGURE 12.19

Use the No Frames tab in FrontPage to view and edit the alternate content page.

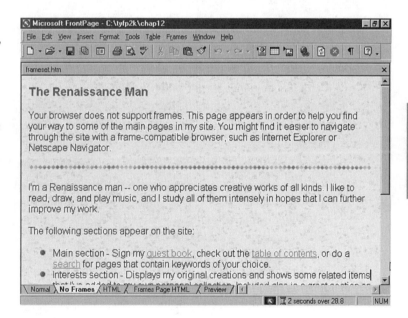

12

If you click the No Frames tab in FrontPage, you can view and edit the alternate content page in WYSIWYG format. By default, the page displays the following text:

`This page uses frames, but your browser doesn't support them.`

It's not a very friendly greeting to present to users who want to see your site, is it? Just imagine how they feel when someone emails them the URL to your site and tells them how great your site is. Then when users navigate to your site without a frame-compatible browser, they receive this message. So much for the interest!

Instead, create a page that links to the other content pages in your site. This way, if someone who does not use a frame-compatible browser navigates to your frameset, they still have a way to read the content you worked so hard at creating.

Summary

In today's lesson, you started with a simple page template and added another frame to it. You learned how to add pages to your framesets and how to create hyperlinks that load pages into specific frames in your frameset. You even learned how to create a page that displays for those who do not use frame-compatible browsers. Now that you know what frames are and what they do, it is time to hit the ground running and develop more framesets of your own.

Workshop

Q&A

Q Can I put anything I want into framesets?

A More or less, yes. You can insert picture presentations, animations, video files, Java applets, forms (such as those used in the discussion groups), and even links to your favorite sites.

Q When I divide pages into frames, how large should I make the graphics?

A The resolutions most commonly used when browsing the Web are 640×480 and 800×600, with the latter being the most common. You can choose the File, Preview in Browser command to display your frameset in any of these resolutions. Use a screen capture program to take a screen shot of the frameset exactly as it appears in your browser at each resolution. That way, you can determine the exact measurements for your graphics. The hard part is deciding whether you want to design your graphics for 640×480 resolution or for 800×600 resolution. It is probably best to design for 640×480 resolution.

Q How many frames can I put in a page?

A As many as you want. Remember, though, that some users display pages at lower resolutions. You do not want to use so many frames that the content of your pages becomes unreadable. If your framesets contain many sections, check them out at

640×480 resolution before you put them on the Web. If you find it difficult to view many frames in that resolution, your visitors will also. Either reduce the number of frames or recommend that your visitors use a higher resolution, such as 800×600 or higher.

Quiz

1. What is the main function of a frameset page?

2. How does a browser know which pages to load into a frameset first?

3. How does the browser know which frame a page should appear in?

4. True or false: It's OK to display other Web sites in my frameset.

5. What happens when a person navigates to your frameset, but does not use a frame-compliant browser?

Exercises

1. Design a frameset that is more suitable to the topics you would like to present in your own Web site. The templates that are furnished with FrontPage serve the needs of the types of framesets you typically encounter on the World Wide Web. Study how the frameset template works before you design your Web content.

2. Try to dress up your frameset more by creating graphic navigation bars instead of using text navigation. Remember, when you size your graphics, to account for any additional width or height that might be needed for scrollbars. Also, it is generally advisable to size your graphics for the least common denominator as far as resolution goes. The lowest resolution is 640×480 for Windows browsers. If you design your graphics for higher resolutions, note somewhere on your page what the recommended video resolution should be for your site.

12

Answers to Quiz

1. A frameset page divides the browser window into multiple sections, called frames.

2. The browser reads the code for the frameset page, and looks for the source URL pages. When you first design your frameset, you can assign the pages by clicking the Set Initial Page button in each frame of the frameset.

3. Target frame names, which can be assigned to an entire page, or to one or more hyperlinks on a page, tell the browser which frame to load a page into.

4. It depends. If you have permission from the author of the other site to display some of his or her content in your own frameset, it's okay. However, if you do get permission, you should also note somewhere in your Web site who the author of that content is, and also make sure that you aren't loading another frameset within your own

frameset. As a general rule, however, you probably want to display pages from other sites in a full browser window, either by removing your frameset or by opening another browser window.

5. Readers must use a frameset-compliant browser to see your framesets. When such a browser is not used, your alternate content page displays in place of the frameset. Use the No Frames tab in the page editor to design a page that will link to the content in your Web.

WEEK 2

DAY 13

Working with DHTML and Positioning

Internet technologies move at such a rapid pace that even the most knowledgeable user can't keep up with everything new. Practically every day, a new technology is devised, even better than the last, and everyone wants to use it. A lot of them expire and aren't heard of again. However, a new technology that has certainly grabbed a lot of attention is DHTML, or *Dynamic HTML*. Ever since its debut, DHTML has been the fashionable technology to use on Web sites, and it still is.

But what is DHTML? Simply put, DHTML is a technology that enables you to create animations and effects programmatically. This saves you from having to use bandwidth-consuming alternatives, such as GIF animations. DHTML turns a plain, run-of-the-mill Web page (or even an entire Web site) into something alive, animated, and dynamic.

So here is where FrontPage steps in. Microsoft FrontPage 2000 enables you to benefit from the eye-candy effects of DHTML while greatly simplifying the process. If you have ever programmed DHTML or used positioning to place elements on a Web page by using a text editor, you know how arduous the process can be! Fortunately, FrontPage automates the insertion of DHTML into a Web page, letting you point and click your way to building a killer Web site.

DHTML and Positioning Terminology

Now that you know what DHTML is, you surely want to start using it, and you probably want to see what you can do. To gain a better understanding of how FrontPage lets you insert DHTML into your Web pages, let's first review some of the basic terminology used in DHTML:

- An *element* is anything on a Web page, including the page itself.
- An *event* is an action, usually fired by a user, to which you can assign a response. Entering a Web site or page, pressing a key, clicking, and even moving are all events.
- A *transition* is an effect that can be applied when changing how an element is displayed within a page or Web site. For example, if you want image_x to be replaced with image_y when you click it (event), the animation played between the time image_x is replaced by image_y is a transition.

Adding Page Transitions

As explained previously, a transition is when the display of an element changes. Page transitions occur when the content displayed in the browser window changes; that is, when moving from one page to another. It is important to understand this concept—otherwise, you may not understand why your pages aren't being displayed like you want them to be.

Choosing an Event

Now that you know what DHTML is, and you know what an event is, you probably want to start adding effects to your pages. Before you dive in, let's look at some of the events available to you in FrontPage that you can set transitions on.

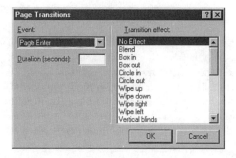

FIGURE 13.1

The Page Transitions window enables you to set page transitions on the current page.

To do that, make sure that the Page icon is selected in the Views pane, then create a new, blank page. Next, choose Format, Page Transition. The Page Transitions dialog box appears, as shown in Figure 13.1. The four main events that you can set transition effects on are covered in the following sections.

Page Enter

As the name implies, this event occurs when you browse to the page—it is fired every time a visitor accesses your page from another page.

Page Exit

The opposite of the Page Enter event, this event is fired every time a visitor leaves your page to go to another (whether it's on your site or not).

Site Enter

In my opinion, the Site Enter event is the most fun to work with. Think of the Site Enter event as an introduction to a play, where the curtain is drawn to show the cast, your Web site. When a visitor enters your Web site, this event is fired. Obviously, the transition cannot occur if your visitor accesses a page that does not contain the transition. If you set a transition to occur on the Site Enter event of your Web site, on a page called my_page.htm, the transition will not occur if your visitor accesses a page named other_page.htm unless you have defined a transition for the same event on this page too. Unlike the Page Enter event, however, if you access my_page.htm again, the event, and thus the transition tied to it, will not occur.

13

Site Exit

Continuing with the analogy of a play, the Site Exit event represents the closing of the curtain. When the visitor leaves your Web site, the Site Exit event occurs.

Note

You may have noticed that when you preview a transition by using the Preview tab in the FrontPage Editor, or when you view your page in your Web browser, the transition doesn't always occur. In the case of a transition occurring on an "enter" event, this usually happens because the contents of the browser window (or the preview mode window) are empty, so there isn't really a change in the display of the element, or the page. In the case of a transition occurring on an "exit" event, try clicking a link to another page, and you'll see the transition play right before your eyes.

Setting Duration

Now that you know all about the four events you can set page transitions on, you'll have to set the duration of the transition. Setting the duration is quite simple. The duration of the transition is in seconds, and can be anywhere from 0 to 30, decimal values included.

Tip

When setting the duration for a transition, you should always use caution—transitions that last too long can frustrate your visitors and make them not want to come back to your Web site. Even a transition whose duration is seven or eight seconds can tend to seem very long. Therefore, it's best to use short values for the duration of the transition—a good duration value for a transition is between two and five seconds. This enables your visitor to have time to view the transition, without it annoying them.

Note that a duration value of zero does not display the transition at all. As for a duration value of one, you may find that the transition is barely displayed. Your best bet is to experiment with different values for the transition duration, and to pick the one you think is best.

Choosing an Effect

And now comes your most important decision—which effect, or transition, should you choose? Although you may find it hard to choose exactly the right effect, always remember one simple rule: If you like it, most of your visitors will too. To help you choose a transition, the following sections go over the different built-in interpage transition effects Dynamic HTML has to offer.

Blend

The Blend transition effect could also be called the fade effect. This effect fades out the content of the current page, while fading in the content of the new page. This is a nice effect, although you may find it to be understated.

Blinds—Vertical/Horizontal

As the name implies, the Blinds transition looks just like venetian blinds opening to reveal the sunlight, your page. This provides a nice effect, although I personally find it a little too square in that the transition doesn't flow as nicely as some of the others.

Box—In/Out

This effect is simply a rectangle that starts from the edges of the browser window and closes in symmetrically on the center of the screen (In). The Out version starts from the center of the browser window and appears to grow to the edges of the window. Both versions of the Box transition effect look good on a Web page.

Checkerboard—Across/Down

The Checkerboard effect divides the screen into tiny squares that wipe across or down. This transition effect closely resembles the Blinds effect, except it is spread out in squares.

Circle—In/Out

The Circle transition is a lot like the Box transition effect, except it is an oval shape instead of a box. A nice, but somewhat plain, transition effect.

Random

Like the name implies, this pseudo-transition effect simply chooses a random effect among those available. You may find that a random transition effect looks good on your Web page—it adds a touch of mystery in that you never know what you're going to get.

Random Bars—Horizontal/Vertical

Random Bars looks like a fuzzy picture on your TV (the Horizontal version anyway). This effect divides the screen into small bars that each move either up or down (Horizontal), or left to right, and vice versa (Vertical). I personally think that this effect doesn't look too good on a Web page.

Random Dissolve

At last, we get to the best of them all, in my opinion. This effect is a granular-like pattern that removes the content of the current page while displaying the content of the new page. Definitely a great choice.

Split—Vertical In/Out, Horizontal In/Out

The Split transition effects always split the page into two sections. The Vertical split could be compared to a curtain—the In version closes in on the center of the screen, like closing curtains, and the Out version starts from the center of the screen and moves out

13

to the edges, like opening curtains. As for the Horizontal split, it could be compared to horizontal doors on a mother spaceship in a science fiction movie, which open (Out) or close (In) for a smaller spaceship.

Strips—Left Down/Up, Right Down/Up

Strips are not similar to the Random Bars effect, as one might expect. Rather, the Strips family of transition effects is more like a diagonal wipe. They start from the left or right, and move diagonally from the upper corner to the opposite bottom corner (Down), and vice versa (Up). My take on these transition effects is that they are mediocre because they don't look very good on a Web page—they are too simple and most of your visitors would probably be unimpressed with them.

Wipe—Up/Down/Right/Left

Perhaps the simplest but most often used of all of the transition effects, is the Wipe. It starts from the side of the screen you choose (Up, Down, Right, or Left) and moves to the opposite side. For example, the Wipe Up transition effect starts from the bottom and literally wipes the contents from the previous page away, displaying the contents of the new page as it moves up.

Exercise 13.1: Adding a Page Transition

At last comes the time when you get to follow a walk-through to set up a transition effect. In this exercise, you'll create two Web pages. The first will be a welcome screen with a message telling your visitors to sit back and get ready to enjoy the Web version of your play, entitled "The Quest for a Better Web Page with DHTML." This page will contain a link to the second page. The second page will contain a transition effect on the Page Enter event. The transition effect for the Page Enter event will be a Vertical Out Split (you can choose another transition if you prefer).

Wait until you see how painless FrontPage makes this process. Just follow these easy steps, and you'll have an introduction to your play, along with a page (which will be blank for now) with the play's contents.

1. Create or open an existing FrontPage Web to host the two pages your Web site will contain, and then click File, New, Page, or press Ctrl+N to create a new page.

2. Choose File, Save, or press Ctrl+S to save the page you just created. Name the page intro.htm, and set the title of the page to DHTML Play Introduction by right-clicking anywhere on the page and choosing Page Properties, or by clicking Format, Background, and clicking the General tab.

3. Repeat steps 1 and 2 to create another page, which you will save under the name of DHTML_play.htm. Set the title of the page to The Quest for a Better Web Page with DHTML.

4. Now, go back to `intro.htm` by double-clicking on the file in the Folder List pane, then press the Center button on the toolbar or click Format, Paragraph to set the alignment to Center, and, at the cursor position, type **Welcome to the play The Quest for a Better Web Page with DHTML**.

5. Between the words "play" and "The Quest," press Shift+Enter twice to insert two line breaks, then select the title of the play, and set the size to 5pt using the toolbar, or by clicking Format, Font. Also, press Ctrl+B, or press the Bold button on the toolbar to make the text stand out with boldface type.

6. Next, press Enter twice after the title of the play, and type **Click here to start viewing the play**. Select the text you just typed, and make it into a hyperlink pointing to `DHTML_play.htm`. To do that, press the Hyperlink button on the toolbar, or press Ctrl+K. In the subsequent dialog box, double-click `DHMTL_play.htm`.

7. Save your changes to the page. Your page should now resemble the page displayed in Figure 13.2.

FIGURE 13.2

Your page, intro.htm, should be similar to the page displayed here in the FrontPage Editor.

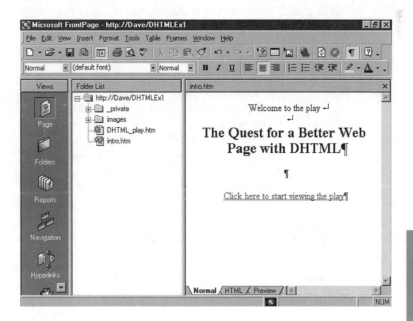

8. Next, double-click `DHTML_play.htm` in the Folder List pane to start editing that page. To make the transition more obvious from one page to the other, start by changing the background color to Navy, and the text color to white. To do that, choose Format Background, set the Background and Text colors, and then click OK.

9. Moving right along, type **Content goes here...** at the top of the page.

13

10. Now comes the time to set the page transition. To set the transition, click Format, Page Transition to display the Page Transitions dialog box, and select the default event, Page Enter. Next, type in a duration of 5, in order to make the transition last five seconds (just long enough to display it, but not long enough to annoy anyone).

11. Last, choose the Split Vertical Out transition effect, and click OK to apply the transition to the page.

12. All that's left now is to save your changes, and to preview the pages. To do that, double-click intro.htm in the Folder List pane and click the Preview in Browser button from the toolbar, or use File, Preview in Browser to display the page. Once the page is displayed in your browser, click the link you created marked Click here to start viewing the play to see the transition effect play right before your eyes. Make sure that you preview your page in Microsoft Internet Explorer 4 or higher, or you won't see the transition effect.

If you found this exercise a little difficult, don't despair. Simply follow the steps again to add a page transition, and you'll see—in no time, you'll be using page transitions left and right on your pages.

> **Tip**
>
> It is wise to consider how many transitions you use in your pages, so that you don't overuse them. You may find it better not to use transition effects, for example, on every single page in your Web site, since this may confuse or annoy your visitors. A good rule of thumb to follow is never more than one page transition per section in your Web site.
>
> If you feel that you are at a lack for animation effects, there are lots more exciting features of DHTML we haven't covered yet, which you'll surely enjoy using in your pages.

Removing Page Transitions

Now that we've covered the basics of how to insert a page transition, you may want to know how to remove one, in case you add too many.

The good news is that removing a page transition couldn't be any easier. To remove a page transition, simply follow these steps:

1. With your page open in the FrontPage Editor, click Format, Page Transition to show the Page Transitions dialog box.

2. Select the event you want to remove the page transition effect from, select the option No Effect from the Transition Effect window, and then click OK.

As you can see, removing a page transition effect is just as easy as adding one.

The DHTML Effects Toolbar

At last, this section covers what is, in my opinion, the best part of DHTML in FrontPage: the DHTML Effects toolbar. With this powerful little toolbar, you can click up a DHTML storm of great design.

First, you might want to display the DHTML Effects toolbar, if it's not already visible. To do that, open FrontPage, then click View, Toolbars, DHTML Effects. You should see the toolbar appear, with all of the options disabled, as shown in Figure 13.3.

If you are working at a lower resolution, you may find that the toolbar takes up a lot of screen space. You can easily resize the toolbar so that it's displayed in two, even three, sections. To do that, just place your pointer to the left or right of the toolbar until it changes to a two-way arrow, and simply drag it inward until it folds on itself. You can also drag the toolbar and dock it at any place you find convenient if you have a little more screen real estate.

FIGURE 13.3

The DHTML Effects toolbar enables you to animate your Web pages with ease.

Note

If the DHTML Effects toolbar does not appear, or if you cannot edit page elements, you may have set your browser compatibility to an older version.

To change page options, click Tools, Page Options, then place a checkmark in the Dynamic HTML box. Also, place a checkmark in the CSS 1.0 and CSS 2.0 boxes while you're at it. Another way to do this is to set compatibility to Microsoft Internet Explorer and Netscape Navigator, and to set version compatibility to 4.0 browsers and higher.

Also note that many animations you can set on your pages in FrontPage won't work with older browsers, and many are restricted to Microsoft's Internet Explorer, versions 4.0 and higher.

13

As mentioned earlier, all of the options on the DHTML Effects toolbar are disabled. To activate the toolbar, simply insert an element (remember, an element can be just about anything on your page, although it's usually text or an image), select the element, and you will see the On section of the toolbar activated.

Here is a quick review of the sections of the toolbar, so that you can feel more at ease with it.

The first section, On, enables you to set the event you want your effect to be played on.

The second section of the toolbar, Apply, is for selecting the effect you want to apply to your element, and selecting its settings.

The second to last item from the left, Remove Effect, is a button that you can click to remove an effect from your page.

Finally, the last item on the toolbar, the Highlight Dynamic HTML Effects button, does exactly as its name implies. I suggest that you leave this feature on. You'll surely find it useful when tinkering with the settings for each DHTML effect you set.

Now that you know what the elements of the toolbar are, you'll surely want to know more about what each of the events, effects, and settings do. They are covered in the following sections.

Animating Text and Images

Although you can animate just about anything on a page, we'll stick to animating text and images in this section, since you probably won't have to set a Dynamic HTML effect on anything else. Also, text and images are the most visual examples of Dynamic HTML in action. A note though: Just as with page transitions, be careful not to overdo it. Some DHTML on a Web page looks good, but if you don't use it properly, it can easily make your site unattractive.

Choosing an Event

Well, I've probably kept you on the edge of your seat, wanting to add a Dynamic HTML effect on an element in your page. This is exactly what you'll do now, starting with learning which events you can set an effect on. The key to Dynamic HTML isn't really in setting the effect (although it plays a major role) but rather, it's in setting the event you want the transition to occur on.

Click

This event occurs when you click on an element. Although this event is useful, you may not find it so great when adding DHTML effects, since most of the time when users click on an element in a page, it's a hyperlink that leads them to another portion of the site.

Double-Click

The Double-Click event occurs when you double-click an element. Again, my observation from the Click event may apply, and even more so, since it is rare that users double-click on a Web page. Moreover, some novice mouse users have a hard time with double-clicking, which may prevent your animation from ever being displayed.

Mouse Over

This is most definitely the preferred event for text and image animation on the Web. Since you usually move your mouse around a page before clicking on a link, you are usually certain that your DHTML will be executed. If you are using a fourth- or fifth-generation (or higher) browser, you'll notice that Microsoft uses this event extensively on its Web site, usually for text elements. This makes an otherwise boring page filled with text come alive, especially when you use it on a hyperlink.

Page Load

This event occurs when your page is loaded. It is similar to a page transition, but you don't have to be coming from another page (as in the Page Enter and Site Enter events) in order for it to execute. This event is probably the most often used in animating images with DHTML. I personally prefer this event because it is displayed immediately, and it doesn't wait for any specific user intervention (unlike the preceding three events).

Choosing an Effect

Now that you know which events are available, you probably also want to know which effects you can set. DHTML provides several effects to choose from, and you'll probably want to try all of them out on your own. For each effect covered, I'll specify on which events you can set it, and for which type of element (text or image) it is available. I'll also go over what each effect does.

Fly Out

This effect yields the same result when applied to text and to images. It is available on the Click and Double-Click events only. In both the case of text and images, it makes the element move from its initial position to the position you specify in the settings section. The positions are quite self-explanatory—they are To Left, To Top, To Bottom-Left, To Bottom-Right, To Top-Right, To Top-Left, To Top-Right by word, and To Bottom-Right by word. A note on the "by word" effects: They simply move each word to the desired position one by one. Although these effects are available in the FrontPage Editor when an image is selected, they are obviously no different than the others.

13

Formatting

Only applicable to text elements, this effect is available on the Click, Double-Click, and Mouse Over events. Combined with the Mouse Over event, this effect is probably the most used on text-based Web pages today. I think that this effect is the best of all of the available effects because it can easily single out a portion of text when the mouse passes over it. The term Formatting includes many things, even though its name may make it sound simple. In FrontPage, you have two options in the Settings section of the DHTML Effects toolbar when you select this effect: Choose Font and Choose Border.

If you select Choose Font, you can set just about anything, just as you would for regular text. From choosing a new font and size, to setting the character spacing, you have a plethora of options. If you select Choose Border, you can set box and shading options.

Don't let the Settings section of the toolbar fool you for this effect, however. You can set both the font and border settings for the same event, and it will work fine.

Drop In by Word

This effect, applicable to both text and images, is quite nice on Web pages. It can only be set on the Page Load event because the words drop in one by one to their intended position, which is impossible if they are already in place(as they are with the other three events). Unfortunately, there are no settings for this element, so you cannot set the speed of the drop. My take on this effect is that you might want to restrict it to short sentences. Otherwise, the user has to wait until a long paragraph of text is dropped into place, and this can be quite annoying.

Elastic

The Elastic effect can be set on text and images, but only on the Page Load event, for the same reasons mentioned in the preceding section. When I first saw this effect play, I found it quite cute. If you choose the From Right setting, the text zips in from the right, passes its position, then bounces into place. If you choose the From Bottom setting, the text quickly flies by its intended position from the bottom of the screen, then bounces into place—a nice little effect your visitors will probably find amusing.

Fly In

The Fly In effect is almost the exact opposite of the Fly Out effect. This effect can be set on text and on images alike, and just like the previous two effects, it can only be set on the Page Load event for the same reasons. Refer to the Fly Out effect for the available settings for this effect. You might find it nice to use in conjunction with or in place of the Drop In by Word effect on your Web pages.

Hop

This effect also can only be set on the Page Load event, and it can be set on either text or images. This effect is quite hard to describe, so you might want to try it out yourself to see what it does. Personally, I found that this effect took a little too long to execute. A note on the effect when applied to text: Each word seems to spiral into position, like the Drop In by Word effect.

Spiral

This effect applies to text and images alike, and can only be set on the Page Load event. The element quickly comes in from the right, spiraling around its position, and almost immediately takes its intended place. I found this effect to be quite annoying.

Wave

Again, this effect applies to text and images, and is a Page Load effect. This effect looks exactly like the Hop effect, just that it takes a little longer to complete, and the element appears to bounce around a little bit. I was not impressed at all by this event, and as such, I would not recommend it for frequent usage on a Web page.

Wipe

This effect can be used with text and images, but unfortunately, it can only be set on the Page Load event. There are three settings for this effect: Left to Right, Top to Bottom, and From Middle. The only one of these three settings that isn't obvious is the From Middle setting—it wipes from the middle of the page, vertically divided. A suggestion: When I applied this effect to text with the Left to Right setting, I found it looked like a typewriter banging letters one by one—a surprising little twist. You'll probably find that this effect is quite appealing and fun to use on your pages.

Zoom

Like the previous effects, it can be applied to text and to images, on the Page Load event only. However, even though it can be applied to images, this effect doesn't do anything special. The image simply drops into place. There are two settings for the effect: In and Out. The Out effect starts with a large element, and progressively resizes it to its intended position. The In setting does just the opposite. This may have been a nice effect to use on your Web pages, but since it doesn't work properly with images, I found it a little bit annoying with plain text.

Swap Picture

This effect applies only to images, and can be set on the Click and Mouse Over events only. This event is used quite often on Web pages of popular Web sites. A note, though: Unfortunately, the size of your existing images has to be the same as that of the image

13

from which you intend to swap, or the swapped image will be stretched and skewed to fit into the dimensions of the previous image. If image_x is 50 pixels wide and 100 pixels high, image_y should be 50 pixels wide and 100 pixels high also, or it will be stretched (or shrunk) to fit into a 50-pixel wide and 100-pixel high frame. The good news about this effect is that it is reversible. If you set the image to swap on the Click event and a visitor clicks the image, the image changes, but if they click on it again, it will change back. The same applies to the Mouse Over event.

Choosing Settings

The basics of choosing settings were covered in the previous section, "Choosing an Event," but it is important to note that when you do not choose a setting for your effect, FrontPage does not apply the effect to your element. For example: If I were to set a Swap Picture effect on the Mouse Over event of my image, but I didn't set the picture to swap with, it would be as if I had not applied any effect at all. You may find this obvious now, as you are reading this, but I personally have been caught quite a number of times by this situation. Just a note of caution before you go yelling for help to a knowledgeable friend!

Exercise 13.2: Animating Your Page

Now comes the time to start putting into practice what you've learned so far. During this exercise, you'll work on the DHTML play you created in Exercise 13.1, so if you haven't done it yet, you might want to go back and take the time to do it before you start on Exercise 13.2.

You'll modify your first page to add an animation to make the welcome text bounce using the Elastic effect. On your welcome page, you'll also add a text effect to make the hyperlink to the page containing your play appear bigger and in bold type when the mouse passes over it. As for the page with the actual play, you'll add two images to represent your actors, and make them fly out to the top right of the screen when they are clicked. Does all that sound like fun? Well, it is! As with the previous exercise, feel free to let your imagination run wild—nothing prevents you from adding some extra effects here and there! To get it working, follow these steps:

1. Open the Web that includes your play in the FrontPage Explorer. Also, open the introduction file, `intro.htm`, by double-clicking on it in the Folder List pane so that you can start adding effects to it.

2. Make sure that the Dynamic HTML toolbar is visible on your page. To do that, click View, Toolbars, DHTML Effects. Now, select the text `Welcome to the play The Quest for a Better Web Page with DHTML`, which should contain two line

breaks between the words "play" and "The Quest." From there, in the On drop-down box on the DHTML Effects toolbar, select the Page Load event, choose the Elastic effect in the Apply section, and choose From Bottom in the settings section. In the FrontPage Editor, a light blue box should appear around your selection to indicate that you have added a DHTML effect.

3. Now that you have set the animation you want to play on the Page Load event, you'll want to set an effect to make the hyperlink on the page appear bigger and in bold face when the mouse passes over it. To do that, select the hyperlink on the page (marked Click here to start viewing the play), then, from the DHTML toolbar, choose Mouse Over as the event, Formatting as the effect (it's the only one available in the Apply section), and click Choose Font in the Settings section. You should see the Font dialog box appear. Set the font style to bold, and the font size to 14pt. Again, notice the visual feedback indicating that you have successfully added the effect. See Figure 13.4 for an indication of what your page should look like in the FrontPage Editor.

FIGURE 13.4

An indication of what your page should look like after following steps 1 through 3.

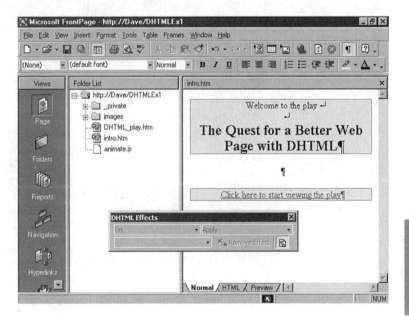

4. Save your page, and open the page containing your play, named DHTML_play.htm. If you finished Exercise 1, you'll want to set the background color back to light yellow instead of blue (so that the images are more visible), and the text color back to the default black. Also, remove the sentence you added, so that the page is blank (be careful not to remove the page transition though).

5. From there, insert the two images for the actors, the first separated from the second by five spaces. You will find the images on your CD-ROM under tyfp2k/chap13/ Samples. They should be named DirtyGuy.gif and SkinnyGuy.gif. You should also center the content of the page by pressing the Center button on the toolbar.

6. With your images in place, click on the first image, and using the DHTML toolbar, create a Fly Out to Top-Right animation on the Click event. If you have trouble doing this, refer to step 3 for more help on how to set each section of the animation effect. Once you have added the effect, you may have noticed that FrontPage places a blue rectangle around the entire area containing the images. This is because, for images, DHTML effects are set in groups on a "per-group" basis. This is not the case with text animations. You may also want to add a Back to introduction hyperlink so you can easily browse between the pages. Now, save your page, and see Figure 13.5 to see what your page should look like.

FIGURE 13.5

This is how your page should look after following steps 1 through 6.

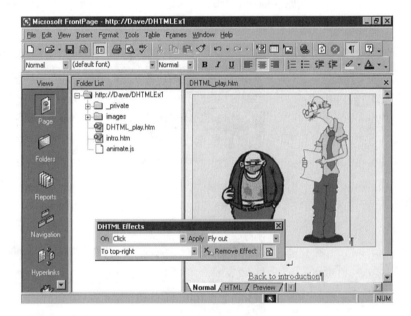

7. And now comes the fun part. To preview your page, double-click the intro.htm page, and click the Preview in Browser button on the toolbar. Check out each of the animations you added by executing the appropriate events (in the case of the hyperlink on the first page, pass your mouse pointer over it, and in the case of the images on the second page, click on them to see what happens). Again, make sure

that you are viewing your pages in Microsoft Internet Explorer 4 or higher. Note that you can always see your animations again by clicking the Refresh button in your Web browser.

The Positioning Toolbar

Now that you've seen how you can easily add animations to your Web pages with Dynamic HTML, it's time to start learning what makes DHTML so great. This section is a little more complicated than the others, but don't despair! FrontPage makes it so easy to position text and images in your pages, you'll soon find that it's child's play.

You will, however, need a little vocabulary lesson on positioning terms before you learn how positioning is used in FrontPage. Here are the terms you should be familiar with for this section, along with short descriptions:

- *Positioning* is the placement of elements at specific places on a Web page, using coordinates.

- *Absolute positioning* is the placement of an element at specific coordinates within a Web page, regardless of the other elements on the page. An example of this is an image being placed at coordinates (100, 100). Note that in computer terms, positioning an element at (100, 100) means 100 pixels left and 100 pixels down from the top left corner of the screen, or this case, the browser window, unlike in mathematics, where the origin is the center of the screen.

- *Relative positioning* isdescribes the positioning in relation to another element, using coordinates. For example, image_y can be placed five pixels to the left and two pixels down from image_x.

- *Wrapping* is the placement of other elements on the page around a given element.

- *CSS 2.0* is the acronym used for Cascading Style Sheets, version 2.0. CSS 2.0 and positioning are sometimes used interchangeably, but CSS 2.0 refers to the functional specification, while positioning refers to what you can do with CSS.

- *Z-order*, *z-plane*, and *z-index* are synonyms meaning the position of an item on the z-axis (spatial position). Since Web pages aren't 3-dimensional, this can seem bizarre. But in fact, it isn't. If two images are overlapping, which one should be displayed on top of the other? Typically, this was determined by the placement of an image in the source code of a Web page. However, with DHTML, most elements have a z-index attribute that enables their placement to be based on a value—the higher the z-index value, the higher it is in the stack. This is also referred to as *layering*.

13

The time has finally come to examine the Positioning toolbar. To display it, click View, Toolbars, Positioning. See Figure 13.6 to see what the Positioning toolbar looks like when activated. Remember that just like the Dynamic HTML Effects toolbar, all the sections of the toolbar are disabled until you select an element to apply the settings to.

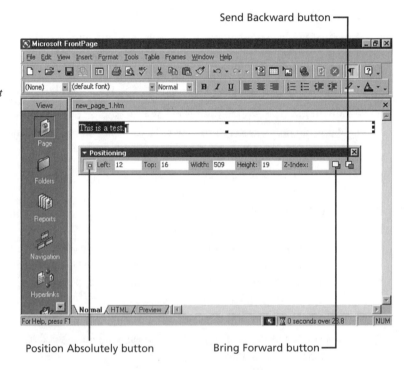

FIGURE 13.6

The Positioning toolbar enables you to place elements like text and images at specific coordinates on your Web page.

Send Backward button

Position Absolutely button   Bring Forward button

Starting from the left, the Positioning toolbar contains eight buttons or sections. The Position Absolutely button enables you to position an element at absolute coordinates on your page. Remember the definition of absolute positioning? If you select an element on your page, then click this button, you will see all of the other buttons on the toolbar light up, indicating that they are enabled.

Each section is quite straightforward: The Left text box is used to specify the x coordinates of the element, and the Top text box is used to set the y coordinates of the element (all from position (0,0), the top-left corner of the browser window). In fact, if you go ahead and select some text or an image, and then click the Position Absolutely button on the toolbar, you'll see the default coordinates appear (refer to Figure 13.6). Notice that the text is at (12,16) by default.

The Width and Height sections enable you to set the width and height of an element. In the case of text, you can set the dimensions of the box around it. In the case of an image, you can set its dimensions, and the FrontPage Editor will immediately resize it accordingly.

Note

In the case of an image, you can set the width and height using the Positioning toolbar, even if it isn't positioned absolutely. This is not the case with text, since it's the box around the text that is resized, not the text itself.

FIGURE 13.7

Coordinates are set from the top-left edge of the Web page. The width and height of the text are positioned absolutely and images can also be set using the Positioning toolbar. Note, too, that a visual cue in the form of an anchor indicates that an image has been positioned absolutely.

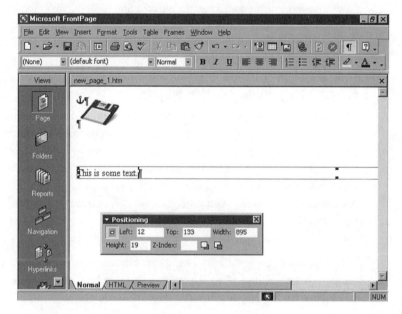

Last but not least come the Z-Index text box and the Bring Forward and Send Backward buttons. Since they are related to each other, they will be examined together. If you remember the definition of z-indexing, you will remember that it's how DHTML enables you to set the position of an element in 3-D. It can be a complicated concept to grasp, but FrontPage makes it relatively easy to use. By clicking the Bring Forward and Send Backward buttons, FrontPage sets the z-index of an element for you. If you try it out yourself, you'll see that pressing these buttons increments (Bring Forward) or decrements

13

(Send Backward) the z-index value. To help you grasp the concept of layering (or z-indexing) in your pages, just think of a stack of objects, for example, CDs. If you have a stack of 10 CDs, and CD #5 has a z-index of zero (the default for all elements), then CD #4 will have a z-index of -1, CD #3 a z-index of -2, while CD #6 will have a z-index of 1, and so on. Any element on your page, including the page itself, could be compared to CD #5, in that all elements start out with a z-index of zero. Elements are always placed in relation to the page. A higher z-index value brings an element forward, while a lower one sends it to the back of the stack.

Positioning Text and Images

Now that you know how to use the Positioning toolbar, we'll look into some other elements. The first of two that we'll look at before diving into another exercise is how to choose the wrapping style. From there, we'll continue on to choosing the correct positioning style (absolute or relative).

Choosing Wrapping Style

The wrapping style of an element allows you to position it either to the left or to the right of the page, with content flowing around it. Even though this effect can be mimicked for an image with the alignment property of an element, we will cover it anyway, since it is part of FrontPage, and since it is integrated into it. However, you should use the alignment properties of elements instead of using positioning, whenever possible, to maintain maximum compatibility with older browsers. Alignment was introduced into positioning because when you have several elements relatively or absolutely positioned on a page, the alignment schema used in older browsers cannot be used.

All of the wrapping style positioning capabilities are neatly tucked away into the Position dialog box (see Figure 13.8). To open this dialog box, choose Format, Position. The following are the three different wrapping styles you can set:

- *None*—This is the default for all elements. It is used to remove positioning previously applied to an element.
- *Left*—This enables you to align elements to the left side of the page. Content around the positioned element flows around the element, as the graphic indicates.
- *Right*—Elements positioned to the right side of the page have content flowing around them at the top, left, and bottom.

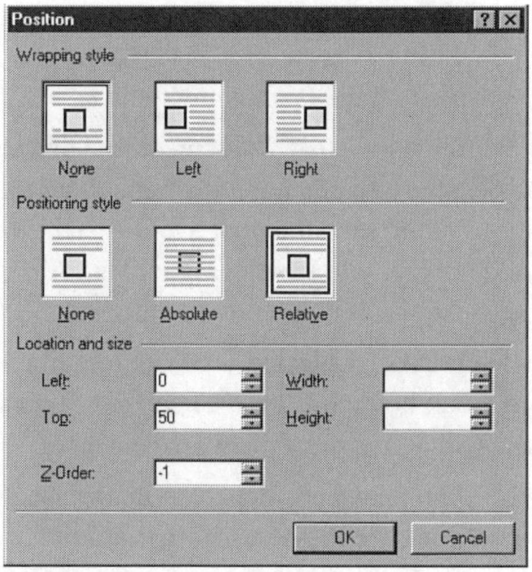

FIGURE **13.8**

The Position dialog box enables you to set complex positioning schemas.

Choosing Positioning Style

Positioning… a word that can mean so much. Since you already know what relative and absolute positioning are, you are probably wondering which you should use in your Web pages. A short and concise answer: Try not to use absolute positioning unless you have to. You should try to avoid absolute positioning in part because only fourth-generation and higher Web browsers will read it, so users with older browsers won't see any difference. Also, you shouldn't use absolute positioning and DHTML together because the results of this mix will be unpredictable at best. Therefore, your best bet is to stick with relative positioning, whenever possible. In order for you to understand the differences and the similarities between each, the next two exercises will cover positioning.

Exercise 13.3: Using Absolute Positions

In this exercise, you'll add some text and an image to your play, and position the image absolutely on the page. Both the text and image will be added on the introduction page, intro.htm, which you should have if you followed Exercises 13.1 and 13.2.

To position an image absolutely on the page, follow these steps:

1. Open the Web containing your DHTML play in the FrontPage Explorer, and double-click the intro.htm page to open it in the FrontPage Editor.

2. Place your cursor after the two DHTML animation effects, and add one line break with the Shift+Enter combination.

13

3. At the cursor position, insert the image named Planet_lines.gif, which can be found on your CD-ROM in the tyfp2k/chap13/Samples directory. Then, click the Position Absolutely button on the Positioning toolbar.

4. After clicking the button, notice that your cursor remains at the same place it was, but that you cannot see the paragraph marker behind the image, even though it's there. To solve this problem, send the image to the back of the stack by clicking the Send Backward button on the Positioning toolbar. Also, set the Left property for the image to 100, and the Top property to 200.

5. Insert three more line breaks by placing your cursor at the last line break, and set your font format to Arial, bold, 8pt. Type Copyright Technology Theatre. All rights reserved., with a line break between sentences.

6. That's all there is to it! You have positioned an image absolutely on your page. To see what it looks like, click the Preview in Browser button. Make sure you are using a compatible browser, such as Microsoft Internet Explorer 4.0 or higher. Once the page is displayed in your browser, you might find that it doesn't look so great, especially if you are working on a really large monitor, like I am—the graphic will be all the way over to the left, with no text even close to it. However, you will see what absolute positioning is all about when you resize your browser window to a smaller size. Try it out; everything on the page moves except that image you positioned absolutely. See Figure 13.9 for an example of what your page should look like in the FrontPage Editor.

FIGURE 13.9

A view of what your page should look like in the FrontPage Editor after Exercise 13.3. Notice that the image of the planet is selected, and that it is absolutely positioned.

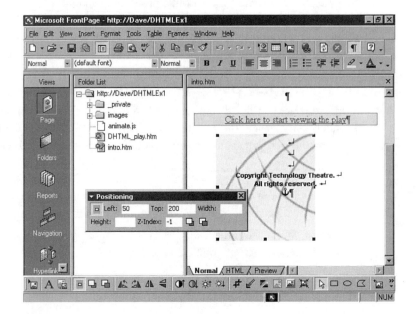

Exercise 13.4: Using Relative Positions

In this exercise, you'll change the image you positioned absolutely in Exercise 13.3, so that it is relatively positioned instead, with the copyright information displayed in top of it.

To position an image relatively on the page, follow these steps:

1. Remove the absolute positioning on your image in the FrontPage Editor by clicking the image to select it, and then clicking the Position Absolutely button on the Positioning toolbar to toggle the positioning state of the image.

2. Remove the line breaks before the copyright text, and drag the image so that it takes its place before the copyright text. After the image is in its new position, you'll notice that the text is stuck to it. You should separate it with a line break (Shift+Enter).

3. Set relative positioning on the element by clicking Format, Position to open the Position dialog box (refer to Figure 13.8). Select Relative in the Positioning Style area and click OK. Note that you can continue using the Position dialog box instead of the toolbar, but it's easier to use the toolbar because it allows you to continue working on your page without clicking OK all the time. Set the Left value to 0, and the Top value to 50. Remember that with relative positioning, elements are placed using the position of the element above them. Therefore, positioning your image relatively at (0,50) will place it 50 pixels under the hyperlink to enter the play, regardless of the user's configuration.

4. In order for the copyright text to be displayed, you will have to set the z-index of your image. To do that, simply select the image and click the Send Backward button on the Positioning toolbar.

5. Finally, save your page, and preview it in your browser. Notice that the copyright text appears on top of the image. See what happens if you set the z-index to 0, and you should gain a better understanding of how relative positioning works, if you haven't fully grasped the concept yet. See Figure 13.10 for an indication of what your page should look like in the FrontPage Editor.

13

FIGURE 13.10

An example of what your page should look like after Exercise 13.4. Notice that the Positioning toolbar indicates the relative coordinates of the image.

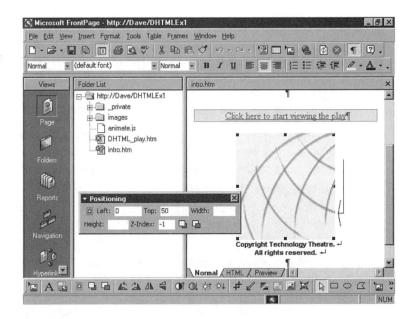

Layering Text and Images

Since you now know how to work with the z-index, we'll approach layering from a different angle, just to make sure that you have fully grasped the concept. If you recall the example I gave about a stack of CDs, it will be useful in this section. Basically, when you work with FrontPage, all you have to do is use the handy buttons on the Positioning toolbar, and you'll be all set.

Changing Z-Order

Let's review how you can change the z-index, or z-order, of a block of text or an image.

When you want your element absolutely positioned, in the FrontPage Editor, just select the element, and use the Send Backward and Bring Forward buttons.

However, FrontPage has the annoying tendency of assuming that you always want your element absolutely positioned as soon as you set the z-index using the Positioning toolbar. Fortunately, it's easy enough to fix by using the Position dialog box (refer to Figure 13.8). For relative positioning, simply set the image to be relatively positioned, then set the appropriate properties. (This makes you wonder why a Position Relatively button wasn't added to the Positioning toolbar.) Fortunately, there is a workaround you can use for this seemingly obvious omission. Just click the arrow pointing down to the left of the title of the Positioning toolbar window, select Add or Remove Buttons, and click

Customize. From there, click the Commands tab, if it isn't already selected, then click the Format in the Categories section, and drag the Position word from the Commands window onto your toolbar. This will enable you to have one-click access from the Positioning toolbar to the Position dialog box. I found this particularly handy when working with positioning, since you often have to position elements relatively, not absolutely.

Exercise 13.5: Layering Images

In this, the last exercise for the chapter, you'll work with layering and relative positioning, so that you can see how both of these concepts integrate to help you build a better Web site.

Specifically, you'll start by adding an image to the page containing your play, `DHTML_play.htm`. Once that is done, you'll place a new image, that of a stick of dynamite, in the forefront with your two original images behind it.

To layer images, follow these steps:

1. Open your Web in the FrontPage Explorer, and double-click `DHTML_play.htm` to open the file containing your play.

2. Next, add the image named `Dynamite.gif`, found on your CD-ROM under `tyfp2k/chap13/Samples`, immediately after the DHTML Effect you set in Exercise 13.2 (or before the link back to the introduction page, if you added one).

3. With the image selected, open the Position dialog box, click Relative to relatively position the image, and set the image's z-index to -1 by typing `-1` in the Z-Order field. At the same time, set the Top property to -125, so that the stick of dynamite moves up 75 pixels.

> **Note**
>
> A pixel is the unit of measurement used on a screen in computers. Magnified 16 times, a pixel is about 3/16 of an inch.

13

4. Now, save the page, and click the Preview in Browser button from the toolbar in the FrontPage Editor to see what your page looks like. Notice that the stick of dynamite appears behind the two images of the actors, even though it doesn't in the FrontPage Editor. Also, take note that if you click on one of the two actors, they fly away, but the stick of dynamite doesn't move. This is because the image is not part of the dynamic HTML effect you added earlier. If you wanted it to move with the other two images, all you would have to do is place it inside the light blue rectangle in the FrontPage Editor.

This concludes the exercise on layering. You should be more familiar with the concept, now that you have seen it in action. Remember that the reason the stick of dynamite appears behind the other two images is because you set the z-index value to -1. Had you set it to zero or to a positive value, it would have appeared on top of the other two images because when there is no z-index set, images appear in the order they appear in the source code (or in this case, the order you see them on your page).

 Note   Although text layering wasn't covered extensively, the same principles apply to text as for images. See the "Workshop" section at the end of the chapter for an exercise on using positioning with text and setting the z-index of text and images.

Summary

In this chapter you have learned about page transitions, DHTML effects, and positioning. Page transitions help you to provide an introduction to your Web page or Web site (Enter) or to provide a grandiose exit (Exit). DHTML animations enable you to quickly add animations to your Web pages—animations that look great and load quickly, which is essential on the Web. Finally, positioning, a concept you may have found difficult to grasp, was examined to reveal how absolute and relative positioning works, and how you can work with the z-index value to better your Web.

Workshop

Q&A

Q With which Web browsers is the technology we examined compatible?

A Currently, only Microsoft's Internet Explorer, version 4 and higher, supports the topics we examined. Netscape Navigator 4 and 4.5 provide shaky support for positioning at best. However, the next version of Netscape Navigator promises to be fully compliant with the specifications for the technology we examined. If you plan to use the technology we examined in your Web pages, your best bet would be to restrict the content to users of Microsoft's Internet Explorer, versions 4 and higher.

Q Where can I get more information on programming my own Dynamic HTML and using positioning myself?

A A great start is Microsoft's Internet Client SDK. It contains a wealth of information on using the technology we covered in Internet Explorer. You'll find all of this at `http://msdn.microsoft.com`. You will probably also want to pay a visit to the World Wide Web Consortium's Web site, the entity that defines standards for the Web, at `http://www.w3c.org`.

Quiz

1. What are the events on which you can set a page transition. (Hint: There are four.)

2. What is an event?

3. How do you set a DHTML effect on your page in the FrontPage Editor?

4. If an element is absolutely positioned on your Web page at coordinates (0,500), in which corner of the screen will it be (choose between top-left, top-right, bottom-left, and bottom-right)?

5. What visual cues does FrontPage provide when you set a DHTML effect? When you absolutely position an element?

Exercises

1. If you liked using page transitions, create a three-page Web site, and place the transition effect of your choice on at least two of the four events available, with at least one transition effect per page.

2. A fun exercise: Find two images that blend nicely, or that display a cause-effect relationship, such as a stick of dynamite exploding, and set a Swap Picture DHTML effect on the Mouse Over event of the first image.

3. If you feel you need to work with positioning a little more, insert two images on a Web page, then place text positioned relatively on top of one or both of the images.

Answers to Quiz

1. The four events you can set a page transition on are Page Enter, Site Enter, Page Exit and Site Exit.

2. As we covered in the beginning of this chapter, an event is an action, usually fired by a user, to which you can assign a response. Entering a Web site or page, pressing a key, clicking, and even moving are all events.

13

3. You can set DHTML effects on elements in your page by using the DHTML Effects toolbar. All you have to do is set the event, the effect, and the settings.

4. An element absolutely positioned at coordinates (0,500) will appear in the bottom-left corner of your page. Remember that the origin is the top-left corner of the screen.

5. When you set a DHTML effect, FrontPage places a light blue rectangle around the element containing the effect, if you left this option turned on. When you absolutely position an element, FrontPage displays a little picture of an anchor on your page to indicate the element's state.

DAY 14

FrontPage Components

What Is a FrontPage Component?

The word *component* is used to describe many things in FrontPage, but in a nutshell, components are additions to basic HTML that quickly and simply add functionality and style to your Web site. You can see from the list in Figure 14.1 that the term covers many different things.

In today's lesson, you will

- Learn how to insert a hover button on your Web page
- Learn how to insert and configure a hit counter
- Include pages within pages
- Substitute information on your pages
- Create and display variables
- Insert a Table of Contents
- Learn how to use navigation bars

FIGURE **14.1**

FIGURE **14.1**

The Component flyout menu allows you to add enhancements to your Web site quickly and easily.

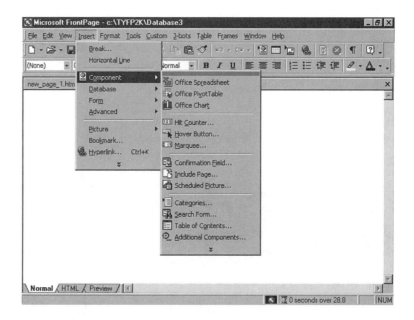

Using and Reusing Information

FrontPage allows you to reuse information already contained within your pages without having to re-create it over and over again. You can do this by using include pages, variables, the navigation bars, and the built-in Table of Contents to automate many procedures. Even one set of hover buttons can be used across the whole site using cut-and-paste without having to keep remaking the same buttons with the same link information.

Hover Buttons

Hover buttons are one of the easiest ways to add animation to your Web pages without having to learn any scripting languages. Like any button, hover buttons contain hyperlinks to pages or files. The big difference between normal buttons and hover buttons is that when a visitor clicks on or points to a hover button it can glow, display a picture, or play a sound effect.

Exercise 14.1: Inserting a Hover Button on Your Page

To insert a hover button on your page, follow these steps:

1. In Page View, position the cursor where you want to create a hover button.

2. On the Insert menu, point to Component, and then click Hover Button. The Hover Button Properties dialog box appears (see Figure 14.2).

FIGURE 14.2

The Hover Button Properties dialog box lets you decide how you want your buttons to look.

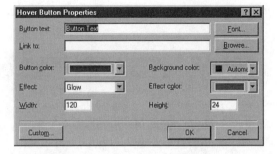

3. In the Button Text box, type the text label for the hover button. If you want to use a custom picture that already contains a text label, you can leave this blank. Remember that if you type a long label, you will have to adjust the width of the hover button to accommodate the long label.

4. In the Link To box, type the URL of the page or file you want to display when the hover button is clicked. Or, click Browse to locate the page or file.

5. Select a color for your button in the Button Color box. If you click Custom and select a picture to use for the hover button, modifying the button color has no effect.

6. In the Effect box, choose the visual effect that will be displayed when a site visitor moves the mouse pointer over the button.

7. Select the size of your button in the Width box. This is set in pixels. Remember that if you click Custom and select a picture to use for the hover button, the width you type here should match the width of the picture.

8. Type the height of the button, in pixels, in the Height box. Remember that if you click Custom and select a picture to use for the hover button, the height you type here should match the height of the picture.

9. Select the background color for your button in the Background Color box. Although you cannot select it to be transparent, you can select the same color as your page background.

10. Choose a color from the Effect Color box for the effect you selected in step 6. Whatever you choose here will appear over the button color.

11. Click the Font button to open the Font Properties dialog box, and select the font, size, style, and color of the text on your button.

12. Click OK to return to Page View.

You will learn about the custom button in the following section.

14

Once you have made your selections, you will see your button on the page. It should
look something like Figure 14.3.

FIGURE 14.3

*You won't see the
effects of your hover
button until you pre-
view the page.*

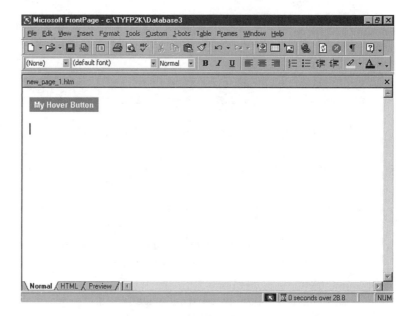

Setting a Picture for a Hover Effect on Your Hover Button

You can set a picture for a hover effect on a hover button. When a visitor points to the
hover button, the picture is displayed. Follow these steps:

1. In Page View, right-click the hover button you have just created and then select
   Hover Button Properties on the shortcut menu.

2. Click the Custom button.

3. In the On Hover box, type the URL to the picture you want to use for the hover
   effect, and then click OK. Alternatively, you can click Browse to locate the picture.

4. In the Width and Height boxes, type the width and height of the picture in pixels,
   and then click OK. It is very important that the size of the hover button matches the
   size of the picture you use for the hover effect.

Setting the Properties for a Hover Button

You can modify the text label, default hyperlink, effects, colors, and size of a hover button at any time without having to delete the button and start again.

In Page View, right-click the hover button you want to modify, and then click Hover Button Properties on the shortcut menu. You will then be able to modify any or all of the properties for the button.

Adding Sound Effects to Your Hover Button

Do the following to add a sound effect to a hover button that you have already created. When a site visitor comes to your page and clicks or points to the hover button, the sound effect is played.

1. In Page View, right-click the hover button you want to modify, and then click Hover Button Properties on the shortcut menu.

2. Click Custom.

3. In the Play Sound area, select the action and the sound effect.

To play the sound effect when a site visitor clicks the hover button, type the URL of the sound effect in the On Click box. Or, click Browse to locate the sound effect.

 Note

Because hover buttons are actually Java applets, you can use only .au format sound files for sound effects; you cannot use .midi or .wav files. Furthermore, the .au files must be in 8-bit, 8000 Hz, mono, u-law format.

To preview the hover button as it will appear when a site visitor browses to the page on the World Wide Web, click the Preview tab, or click Preview in Browser on the File menu.

Hit Counters

A hit counter is quite simply what it says it is. It counts the number of "hits" your Web site gets. It displays the total on the page so that anyone coming to the site can see how many others have been there.

FrontPage offers various styles of hit counters for you to display on the page, or you can apply your own number graphics by creating a custom picture in GIF format. The picture must be a single image with the numbers 0 to 9, evenly spaced.

A hit counter will work only for pages within your own Web, and must be hosted on a server with the FrontPage extensions installed.

14

Exercise 14.2: Adding a Hit Counter to Your Pages

To add a hit counter to your pages, follow these steps:

1. In Page View, position the insertion point where you want to place the hit counter.

2. On the Insert menu, point to Component, and then click Hit Counter. The Hit Counter Properties dialog box as shown in Figure 14.4 appears.

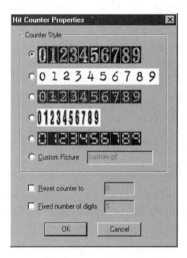

3. Under Counter Style, select the style of hit counter you want to use from the options FrontPage gives you, or click Custom Picture if you want to use your own pre-prepared graphic. If you select the custom option, you will need to add the relative path to the .gif file you have created—for example, `images/counter.gif`.

4. You can choose to have the hit counter start at any number you want. It never looks impressive for a visitor to go to a site and find that he is visitor number 0002. As long as you remember the number you set, you will always know the "actual" number of visitors. To set the counter to a specific number, select the Reset Counter To box, and then type the number at which you want the counter to start. You can also reset the counter to any number after it is on the site.

5. To display a fixed number of digits in the hit counter, select the Fixed Number of Digits box, and then type the number. For example, to display 005 rather than 5, select this option and type 3. When you have made your selections, click OK to continue.

[HitCounter] is displayed on the page as a placeholder for the hit counter. Your selected image or style will be displayed when you publish the page or preview it in a browser, as shown in Figure 14.5.

FIGURE **14.5**

FIGURE **14.5**

The hit counter is only displayed when the page is previewed in a browser.

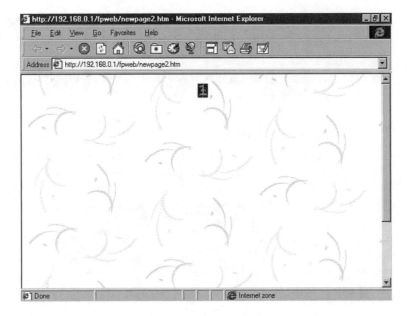

Resetting a Hit Counter to Zero (or Another Number)

After you add a hit counter to a page, you can reset the counter to zero. You might wonder why you would want to do this. A good example would be that after you test your Web online for errors, you may want to cancel the hits that have been created by your own visits. To do this, follow these steps:

1. In Page View, double-click the [HitCounter] placeholder. The Hit Counter Properties dialog box that you have already seen appears.

2. Select the Reset Counter To box, and then type **0** in the box. As already mentioned, you can select any number of your choice in this box.

Including Pages Within Pages

With FrontPage 2000 it is easy to include the contents of one HTML page within another. This makes it easy to have repeated content displayed in more than one place at a time without having to keep changing all of the affected pages. For example, if you have a copyright notice or legal information appearing on multiple pages within your site, it would make sense to be able to update all of the pages at the same time. The Include Page component makes this a simple task. Note however, that you can only include pages that are in your own Web and not any external data using this method.

14

You will need to have two HTML pages for this: one for the included information to appear in, and one that is the included page. To include a page within a page, do the following:

1. Make a page that simply says 'this is included information' and save it into your open Web as include.htm.
2. Then, in an open page decide where you want the contents of the included page to appear, and position the insertion point there.
3. On the Insert menu, select Component and then click Include Page. The Include Page Properties dialog box appears, as shown in Figure 14.6.

FIGURE 14.6

The Include Page Properties dialog box allows you to type in the URL or use the Browse option to find the file you want.

4. In the Page to Include box, type the relative URL to include.htm, or click Browse to find the file.
5. Click OK to continue.

You will see instantly that the text 'this is included information' appears on the selected page as shown in Figure 14.7. Now imagine the included information is needed on many pages within your site. All you have to do is include the page in each required location and it will be updated everywhere at once. Much easier than changing the same information over and over again.

Substituting Information—The Substitution Component

You have already seen how easy it to change information in many pages using the include component, and you also know that by using shared borders you can have the same information shared across multiple pages or even a whole Web. Unfortunately, that isn't always enough for all occasions.

FIGURE 14.7

As soon as you click OK, the information from the included page appears.

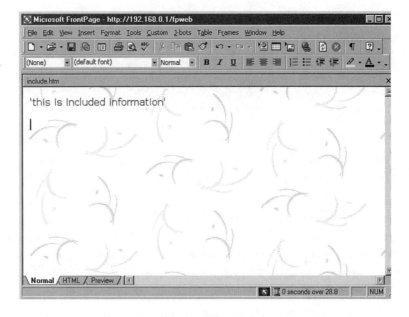

For this reason, FrontPage offers you the chance to use the Substitution component to get around this problem.

Imagine that you have a long list of products available on your site, and each product has a name and a stock code. The name of the product may remain the same, but the stock code needs to change. It could be tedious to have to change this everywhere it appears; however, using variables makes this as simple as possible. The first thing you need to do is define the variables for your content.

Defining a Variable

If the stock code changes, you simply change the value of the variable you defined, and then the new stock code is automatically displayed in your Web.

To define a variable, do the following:

1. On the Tools menu, click Web Settings to open the Web Settings dialog box, and then click the Parameters tab.

2. Click Add. The Add Name and Value dialog box appears as shown in Figure 14.8.

14

FIGURE **14.8**

*Use the Add Name and
Value dialog box to
define your variables.*

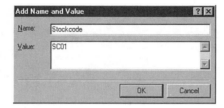

3. In the Name box, type a name for the variable, such as **Stockcode**.

4. In the Value box, type a value for the variable, such as **SC01**.

5. Click OK to close the dialog box.

Displaying a Variable on a Page

After you have created a variable, you can display the value of it on a Web page. A variable can be either a system variable (such as the author's name, the name of the person who last modified the page, the description of the page, and so on), or as in this case, a variable you have defined.

To display a variable on a page, follow these steps:

1. In Page View, position the insertion point where you want to display your variable.

2. On the Insert menu, point to Component, and then click Substitution. The Substitution Properties dialog box appears, as shown in Figure 14.9.

FIGURE **14.9**

*The Substitution
Properties dialog box
allows you to select
which variable you are
going to add to your
page.*

3. In the Substitute With box, make your selection from the drop-down list. As soon as you make your selection, the value of your variable will be displayed on the page at the insertion point, as shown in Figure 14.10.

FIGURE **14.10**

*As soon as you select
your variable, it
appears on your page.*

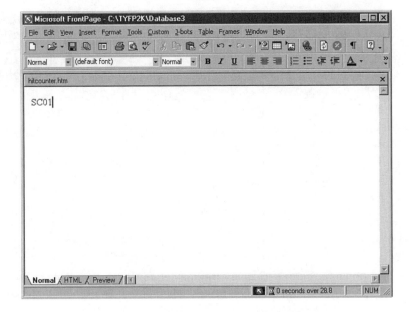

FIGURE **14.10**

*As soon as you select
your variable, it
appears on your page.*

Exercise 14.3: Using the Substitution Component

Now that you know the basics of creating a variable, this exercise will demonstrate how
to use them a little more.

Assume that you want to have an author credit on your page, or a dated copyright notice.
In this exercise you will create a variable and then change it to see how it affects the
pages. Follow these steps:

1. Create a variable using the steps outlined in the "Defining a Variable" section.
   Name it **copyright** and give it the value **1999**.

2. On any Web page on which you want to display copyright information, click the
   insertion point where you want the variable to appear.

3. Type **This site is the copyright of** '***yourname***' (replace 'yourname' with
   your name) and then leave a space to add the date. This is the line of text the variable will complete. The page should look something like Figure 14.11.

4. Select Insert Component, and then select Substitution.

5. Choose the copyright variable in the drop-down list that appears. The number 1999
   should now appear immediately after '*yourname*', as shown in Figure 14.12.

14

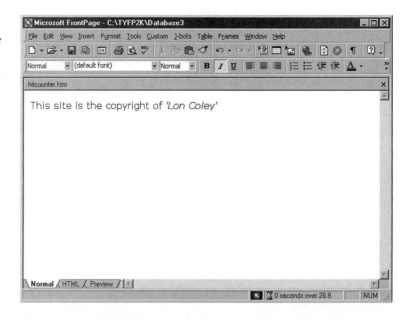

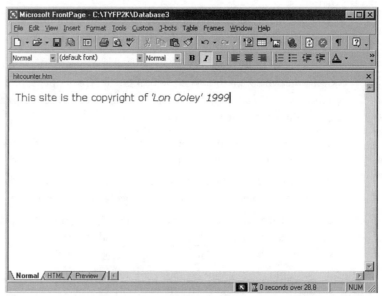

6. Select Tools, Web Settings, Parameters. Select the copyright variable and then choose Modify. Change the value to **2000**.

7. Save the page and then select View Refresh. Your page should change immediately to reflect the modification to the variable.

Once you have changed the variable in the Web Settings dialog box, the changes will be reflected immediately across the whole Web. This applies to all the variables you may use within your Web. It is by far the simplest way of making sure that your important information is kept up-to-date in all locations.

Using the Table of Contents

Navigation and ease of travelling through a Web site are both of paramount importance. Both navigation and the creation of a table of contents can be automated within FrontPage 2000. The software allows you to create a self-generating table of contents based simply on the navigation structure of your Web, and pages with hyperlinks that are not included in the navigation structure. Anyone visiting the site can see at a glance the full contents of the site, making it easy to find out any areas of the site they may have missed or not even realized were there.

The table of contents can be contained within a page of your Web, or it can be a separate page. It is normal practice that a large site will have a dedicated table of contents, whereas a small site may well have this located within a page of normal content.

Adding a Table of Contents to Your Site

To add a table of contents to your site, follow these steps:

1. In Page View, position the insertion point where you want to create a table of contents.

2. On the Insert menu, point to Component, and then click Table of Contents. The Table of Contents Properties dialog box appears, as shown in Figure 14.13.

FIGURE 14.13

The Table of Contents Properties dialog box allows you to select the starting point for your listing.

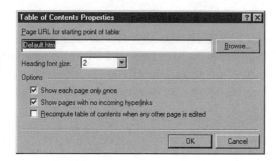

14

3. In the Page URL for Starting Point of Table box, type the relative URL of the page to use as the starting point for the table of contents, or click Browse to locate the page. The starting point determines which pages are leftmost in the table of contents. Normally, the starting point will be your homepage, but it can be any page you select.

4. In the Heading Font Size drop-down list box, select the paragraph style for the heading (the top-level entry, or starting page) of the table of contents. To exclude the starting page from the table of contents, select None.

There are three check boxes at the bottom of the dialog box. These are as follows:

- *Show Each Page Only Once*—Each page in your Web will be displayed only once within the table of contents. It is very common for some pages in a Web to be linked to multiple times (for example, the homepage), which can make your table of contents look confusing to a visitor.

- *Show Pages with No Incoming Hyperlinks*—This option displays pages in the table of contents that have no links to them. Be careful before selecting this option— normally, a page with no hyperlinks is out-of-date or is unlinked for some other reason.

- *Recompute Table of Contents When Any Other Page Is Edited*—Every time you edit a page in your Web, FrontPage will check that the table of contents is still accurate and update it accordingly. However, this process can take a long time and can significantly increase the time it takes to save pages. A better alternative would be to simply open and save the page containing the table of contents. This will cause the page to recalculate the links and update itself.

You can also organize the table of contents using categories, which will be covered in the following section.

Categorizing a File

Once your Web grows to a reasonable size, management is of paramount importance. We will be looking at site maintenance in greater detail as the book goes on, but for now we will cover categorizing your pages. Using categories to group pages, pictures, and so on can make managing your site easier and in many cases more effective.

To add pages to a category, follow these steps:

1. On the View menu, point to Reports, and then click Categories.

2. Select a file in your Web that you want to categorize by clicking on it once.

3. Right-click on the selected file and select Properties.

4. Click the Workgroup tab. A properties dialog box with the Workgroup tab displayed appears as shown in Figure 14.14.

FIGURE 14.14

The Workgroup tab displays a list of categories for you to choose from.

5. In the Available Categories box, select the check boxes of the categories for this file. If a page or file fits into more than one category, you can select multiple categories.

Tip

It is easy to categorize many files at the same time. From within the Categories report (select View, Reports, Categories), select all of the files you want to categorize, then right-click to display the shortcut menu, and then select Properties. Click the Workgroup tab, and then in the Items Belong to These Categories box, select the categories for the selected files.

Exercise 14.4: Creating Custom Categories for Your Pages

FrontPage supplies a choice of categories that in most cases will suffice for most people. If, however, the categories supplied don't seem to meet your needs you can create your own categories and then add your pages to them. Follow these steps:

1. In the Categories report, select a file that you need to create a category for.

2. Right-click on the file.

3. Select Properties, and then select Workgroup.

14

4. Click the Categories button. The Master Category List dialog box appears, as shown in Figure 14.15.

FIGURE 14.15

The Master Categories List dialog box allows you to add categories more appropriate to your own Web.

5. Type a name for the new category, such as **My Category**, then click Add to add it to the list. Click OK to return to the Master Category List. My Category is now available in the Available Categories list, as shown in Figure 14.16.

FIGURE 14.16

As soon as you click OK your new category is added to the list.

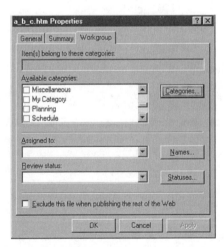

Scheduling Information to Be Included

Now that you know how to include information from one page in another, we will look at ways that FrontPage enables you to choose not only what is displayed on your pages, but also when it is displayed.

The Include Picture and Include Scheduled Information components both allow you to specify when certain information will be displayed on a page.

Scheduling a Page or Picture to Appear

FrontPage allows you to set information to be displayed during a specific timeframe. This is useful in many ways. You may want to publish a press release on a given day, but have it prepared in advance, or you may have some special offers on a site that will become invalid after a given date.

The obvious question at this point is what happens to the page when there is nothing scheduled to appear. It's a very good question, and FrontPage makes sure that this is not a problem. You can specify a normal file or default picture to be displayed outside the allotted time. When there are no special items scheduled to appear on your Web page, this image will display so you can avoid having a blank space on the page.

It is worth noting that the time for the scheduled event is picked up from the Web server's time clock, which may be different from your own. If the actual hour the advertisement should appear is important, make sure that you set the times correctly for the server that will be hosting your pages.

Exercise 14.5: Using the Scheduled Include Components

To use the Scheduled Include components, follow these steps:

1. In Page View, position the insertion point where you want to display another page or picture.

2. On the Insert menu, point to Component.

3. Select Scheduled Include Page or Scheduled Picture. The Scheduled Picture Properties dialog box opens, as shown in Figure 14.17.

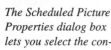

FIGURE 14.17

The Scheduled Picture Properties dialog box lets you select the content for a given timeframe.

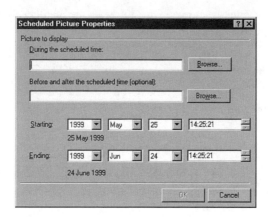

14

4. In the During the Scheduled Time box, type the relative URL of the page or picture to include, or click Browse to find the file you want to use.

5. In the Starting section, specify the year, month, day, and time at which you want to start displaying the page or picture.

6. In the Ending section, specify the year, month, day, and time at which you want to stop displaying the page or picture.

7. To specify the page content for all other times, browse to the normal picture or file that will be used on the pages whenever there is not a scheduled include.

8. When you have selected all of the options, click OK to continue.

If your scheduled times are current, the file or picture you specified will be shown; if not, the page will not be changed until the date you specified.

Now all kinds of information is available to the people coming to visit the site, but there are still more components that have not yet been mentioned.

One of the most commonly used components is the Marquee component, which is discussed in the following section.

Adding a Marquee to Your Page

A marquee is a page element that is set to display a horizontally scrolling text message. Used carefully, the marquee can be effective in displaying information that you want to be sure your visitors see. It must be noted, however, that the marquee feature is not supported in Netscape at all. There are some JavaScript options, but you would have to search the Internet for those.

To insert a marquee, do the following:

1. In Page View, click where you want to create the marquee, or select the text that you want to display in the marquee.

2. On the Insert menu, point to Component, and then click Marquee. The Marquee Properties dialog box appears as shown in Figure 14.18.

3. In the Text box, type the line of text you want the marquee to display. If you are using text that you selected from your pages, this is automatically contained in the text box.

4. Specify the direction you want the text to move in the Direction box.

5. In the Speed box, specify the speed at which the text will scroll and the length of any delay you choose to set. The delay specifies in milliseconds the length of time before the marquee begins to move.

6. Specify how the text will move in the Behavior box.

7. In the Alignment box, set the properties for how the marquee will align with any adjacent text.

8. Set a size in Width and Height boxes for the area your marquee is to take up on the page.

9. In the Repeat area, determine whether the marquee will be displayed continuously in the browser while the visitor is there, or if you don't want this, specify the number of times for the marquee to appear.

10. Use the Background Color option to set a colored area behind the scrolling text. This is best used to make your text stand out from the rest of the page.

FIGURE 14.18

The Marquee Properties dialog box covers all of the things you need to set.

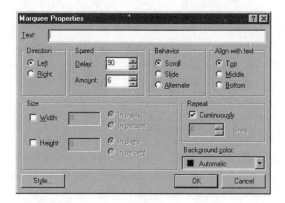

Format the Font in a Marquee

Once you have the text and size of the marquee set, you may want to enhance your marquee by formatting the font used in the marquee. To format the font in a marquee, do the following:

- In Page View, right-click the marquee you want to format, and then click Font Properties on the shortcut menu.

- To set the font how you want it, simply modify the settings in the Font dialog box, as shown in Figure 14.19.

- To expand or condense the spacing between characters, or to raise or lower the text, modify the settings on the Character Spacing tab.

- To change any of the settings for a marquee, double click on the marquee in Page View to open the dialog box already shown.

14

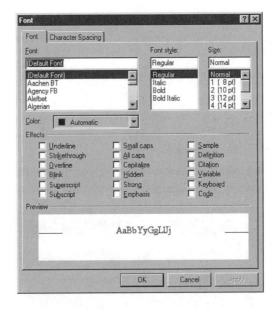

FIGURE 14.19

Changing the font properties for the mar-quee is only a click away.

You have now seen almost all of the automated components that FrontPage uses to make your site look better and be more user-friendly.

I have deliberately left the most important component, the navigation component, until the end because nothing is worse for a visitor than a site that is badly organized or diffi-cult to navigate. The following section looks at navigation bars.

Navigation Bars

FrontPage uses its own Navigation View to help generate links for you when using themes and shared borders, but you don't have to use the navigation bars within a shared border. You can add them anywhere on any page.

Adding a Navigation Bar to a Page

A navigation bar is a set of text or button hyperlinks that a site visitor uses to get to the pages in your Web site. A typical navigation bar might have buttons to the site's home page and to each of the main top-level pages. When you add a navigation bar to a page, FrontPage generates the navigation hyperlinks based on your Web structure as displayed in the Navigation View.

To add a navigation bar to a page, click to place the insertion point where you want the navigation bar to appear, then select Insert Navigation Bar. The Navigation Bar Properties dialog box appears (see Figure 14.20) and you can set the following options:

- Vertical or horizontal layout for the navigation bar—for example, use a horizontal navigation bar across the top of a page, and use a vertical navigation bar down the side of the page.

- The type of hyperlinks to display—buttons or text. Buttons can be used only in conjunction with a theme because it is the theme that supplies the button graphic.

- Which hyperlinks to display on the navigation bar. For example, you can choose from the following:

  Parent Level (pages above the current page)

  Same Level (pages on the same level as the current page)

  Back and Next (hyperlinks for browsing a sequence of same-level pages)

  Child Level (pages under the current page)

  Top Level (top level of your Web)

  Child Pages Under Home (child pages of the homepage)

  Links to the Web's homepage and/or a page's parent page

FIGURE 14.20

The Navigation Bar Properties dialog box allows you to select the level of the links to appear.

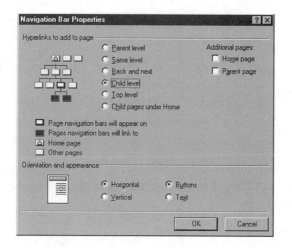

The quickest way to set up a navigation system for your Web is to look at the option of using shared borders containing a navigation bar. This is achieved by adding a navigation bar within a shared border. It is then carried across all the pages that have the shared border set. Setting a navigation bar within a shared border has the same properties just discussed.

14

Other Components

You have now learned many of the components offered within FrontPage. Those not covered in today's lesson will be discussed in other chapters throughout the book. All of the Office components, for example, are covered on Day 15, "Integrating with Office 2000."

Summary

Now that you have looked at all of the ways FrontPage can help you to use and reuse information, spend the workshop time looking at your Web and finding ways of making life easier.

Create some variables relevant to your site and see how easy it is to update them.

Create a table of contents page for your site and format it to show all of the pages in your Web. See how easy it will be for visitors to know where they have and haven't been.

Categorize your pages and then use the categories as a basis for a contents listing on your site.

Although setting up some of these can take a little time, it is well worth it in the long run.

The more information you can reuse and automate, the simpler it will be to maintain and update your site without fear of creating errors.

Workshop

Q&A

Q If I have a picture to include for a few days do I have to have a blank space before and after it?

A No—just make sure you set a picture or file for the dates not in the "include" period.

Q Why can't I see my marquee in Netscape?

A You will see the text, but it is static. The marquee tag is not supported in Netscape browsers.

Q Will everyone be able to see my hover buttons?

A Because hover buttons are Java applets, anyone who has Java turned off will not see them.

Q Can I use the hit counter without FrontPage extensions?

A No—it is one of the components that need the extensions to function.

Quiz

1. What format must sound files be in to work on hover buttons?

2. Can shared borders show different navigation levels?

3. Will pages within folders starting with an underscore appear in your Table of Contents?

4. Can you format the text and background in a marquee?

5. Can you update a page just by modifying a variable?

Exercises

1. Create a blank page in your Web and see how many of the components you learned about today you can use in a single page.

2. Create a marquee to introduce a hit counter on your page.

There are many ways to use the components covered in today's lesson. Learn how to use them to the best effect, and you can save yourself time and effort when you create your next Web.

Answers to Quiz

1. They must be in .au format because the hover buttons are Java applets.

2. Any navigation bar in a shared border will have the same properties in all the pages it appears in, but you can have more than one navigation bar in the same shared border.

3. No. They are hidden.

4. Yes. You can select any font and background color you like.

5. Yes. As soon as you modify the value for a variable, the changes will be reflected in the Web.

14

WEEK 3

Advanced Features and Publishing

15

16

17

18

19

20

21

Integrating with Office 2000

Many of you have used Microsoft Office before and many have used previous versions of FrontPage. Now Microsoft has taken the massive leap to make FrontPage an integral part of the Office family of products.

When Microsoft Office was first released as a piece of software in the marketplace, the Internet was far from the publicly accessible utility it is today. Even the more recent versions of Microsoft Office that had some Web functionality were not made or marketed with Web integration in mind.

FrontPage 2000 has been designed with the same principles of integration that the whole of the Office family has had all along. This has now been extended to FrontPage, making it a true member of the Office family.

If you have used previous versions of Microsoft Office, such as Office 97, you may remember how frustrating it was to create Web pages from your Excel spreadsheet or PowerPoint presentation. Even translating Word documents, which are similar to Web pages, ended up with less than stunning results.

When Office 97 was released, the Web was only a few years old. At that time it was almost impossible to predict what the Web was becoming or what features users would want. Everyone knew the Web was going to have a huge impact on the world, but nobody really knew what to do with it. Both the Web and Microsoft Office have come a long way since then. These days, most companies understand how important a role the Web can play in creating distributed systems where employees can share documents with each other and the world. Making Office 2000 Web-enabled was a major design goal.

Microsoft Word, Excel, and PowerPoint can now create Web pages without losing functionality. PowerPoint 97 users had to suffer seeing their carefully crafted presentations reduced to a slideshow of pictures when exported to HTML. PowerPoint 2000 enables you to save your PowerPoint presentation to a Web page without losing functionality.

Telling you that it is easy to do certainly doesn't mean that there is nothing to cover in this chapter.

Today you will learn

- The basics of converting Word documents and documents from other, non-Microsoft word processors such as Corel WordPerfect into Web pages
- How to use the new Office Web Components that were created to allow some document sharing between Office 2000 users
- How to use FrontPage with Access 2000

Editing Web Pages Created with Office 2000

Word, Excel, and PowerPoint use a new technology called XML (eXtensible Markup Language) to maintain much of their original formatting. XML is a close cousin to HTML but is far more robust because it allows you to create and format tag definitions. XML was created to help describe not only how something should look, but also what it is. It enables you to define your own formatting styles for headings or paragraphs in Word and have that same formatting available in your Web page.

XML does have its limitations, mainly because it is still in its infancy. The newest versions of both Microsoft Internet Explorer and Netscape Communicator incorporate the ability to view pages that use XML, but older versions do not.

Working with Word and Text Files

Microsoft Word is one of the most common file formats you may need to convert into a Web page. Although the information you see here is focused on Microsoft Word, much of it can be applied to other word processors such as Corel WordPerfect.

Opening and Inserting Text Files

There's nothing simpler to work with than a plain ASCII text file. Text files also pose the least amount of questions and problems when trying to import a document into a Web page. There is a file called web1.txt on the accompanying CD-ROM. For this chapter you will need to create a new empty Web called chapter15.

Open a blank page in the chapter15 Web.

To open and insert the web1.txt file, perform the following steps:

1. Locate the web1.txt file on your CD with Windows Explorer and double-click on the file to launch the file in Notepad.
2. In Notepad, highlight the text to insert into FrontPage or use Edit, Select All to highlight the entire document.
3. Copy the highlighted text using Ctrl+C or the Edit, Copy command.
4. In FrontPage, position the cursor where you want the text placed.
5. Paste the text using Ctrl+P or the Edit, Paste command.
6. Close Notepad.

The text you selected from Notepad appears where you selected in the Web page. Your page should now look like Figure 15.1.

After you insert the text file, you may need to adjust the formatting because some text files have hidden line breaks at the end of each line.

FIGURE 15.1

Inserting a .txt file into your Web page is easy, but it may need formatting after you insert it.

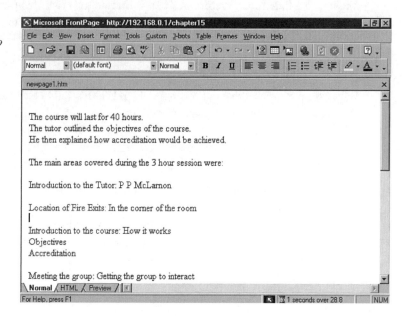

Working with RTF Files

Rich Text Format (RTF) is an industry standard for exchanging formatted text. An RTF file is much like a Word file, allowing you to specify different fonts, font sizes, and a host of other things common to most word processors. If you haven't heard of RTF before, you're not alone.

RTF can help you because it is an industry standard. That means that many companies create products that offer the capability to export their files into an RTF format. You've probably been given a file that couldn't be opened in your word processor because the person who gave you the file didn't have the same version or brand as you. RTF enables people to exchange information without having to go to the trouble of finding special plug-ins or conversion programs.

When FrontPage converts a document such as Microsoft Word, it first converts it into RTF. You may be wondering why doesn't it just convert the Word document into HTML, which is perfectly understandable. FrontPage uses RTF to level the playing field so to speak. Instead of having to create separate ways to convert a Word document or a WordPerfect document into HTML, it makes sense to use the capabilities for Word or WordPerfect to convert to RTF. That RTF file can then be converted into HTML without much hassle.

RTF does have some drawbacks, however. For example, if you want to convert a Word document that has pictures and text precisely positioned on your page, you may find that some of your formatting will be lost in the transition. Although files converted to RTF might take a little time to reformat when converted to HTML, you will probably save much more time than if you try to find a way to save the original to HTML or convert it into another file format.

Inserting Files into Pages

Have you ever wished that converting a file to HTML could be as easy as drag-and-drop? Well your wish is here. FrontPage allows you to drag a file from Windows Explorer or your desktop right into FrontPage. FrontPage will automatically figure out what type of file you have and use the appropriate converter. There's no catch involved—just drag, then drop. Just make sure you have a page open to drop your document into.

When you drag a file into a Web page, FrontPage will detect the type of file you are attempting to paste into the page. Some files might not be recognizable by FrontPage and will return an error. When you drag a Microsoft Word document into a Web page, FrontPage will check to see which version of Word the document was saved in. Then, FrontPage will do whatever is needed to convert it to RTF. Once FrontPage has converted

15

the document to RTF, it can easily convert the RTF document into HTML and paste it into the page. You may experience a delay depending on how large the Word file is because larger files require more time and memory to convert into RTF and HTML.

Note

> The best way to insert a Word document is by dragging the file from Windows Explorer into the Web page. Often, dragging and dropping a file from FrontPage's Folder View will simply result in a link to the file being placed in the page and not the document itself.

Exercise 15.1: Using Word Documents in Your Web

On the accompanying CD, along with the file web1.txt you will find web1.rtf and web1.doc. This is the same file saved in different formats.

Locate the web1.doc file on the CD, and then in Windows Explorer click the Copy button. On the page you have in FrontPage, place the cursor where you want to paste the Word document.

You will see that the fonts and sizes set in the original document have all been retained.

This file has been used deliberately to highlight one small issue when importing Word documents—the formatting from Word has been retained exactly (see Figure 15.2). On this occasion, it's not a good thing!

FIGURE 15.2

Inserting a .doc file into your Web page brings all of the formatting from Word with it.

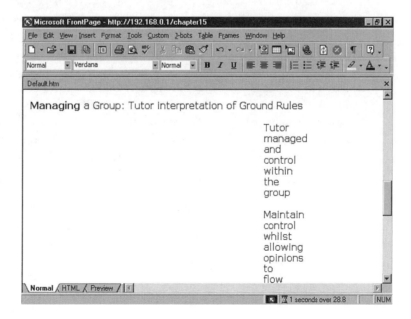

When the Word document was created, the initial formatting was achieved by serious overuse of the Tab key. When the file is brought into FrontPage, this is displayed in the HTML by the `<blockquote>` tag. You need to be aware that you should make correct use of the Tab key in Word to ensure correct formatting of your Web pages.

To amend the file in FrontPage, you will need to use the Decrease Indent button on the areas that appear too far to the right of the page. The Tab key in Word is read into FrontPage as an indent. When you use the Tab key in FrontPage it inserts the code for the spacebar. There are no tabs in HTML which is why the code reads as a number of spaces.

Working with the Office Web Components

Microsoft Excel has become one of the most common spreadsheet programs around today. Spreadsheets are a great way to visualize information because they lay everything out in an organized fashion. Many people inside a company may use a single spreadsheet. A spreadsheet for the current budget may require the input of accountants, managers, engineers, marketing, and sales. With this need for shared data, Microsoft has created the Office Web Components.

Inserting Office Spreadsheets

Prior to FrontPage 2000 and Office 2000, spreadsheets were non-interactive Web pages. You can still save an Excel spreadsheet as a Web page with no interactivity, and for static information this is fine. Excel 2000 also now has an option to save as a Web page with interactivity. However, Excel spreadsheets can now be inserted into a Web page for editing. This enables items like a budget report to be adjusted online instead of having to pass the same document to a number of people. You can even designate a location to download the Office Spreadsheet component from. The only requirement is that users must be using Internet Explorer as their browser because the Office Spreadsheet component is an ActiveX control and will not work under Netscape Navigator. We have included a file called web1.xls on the CD to give you some sample data to use for the spreadsheet parts of this chapter.

To insert an Office Spreadsheet component, perform the following steps:

1. Place your cursor in the position you want the spreadsheet to appear.
2. From the FrontPage menu, choose Insert, Component, Office Spreadsheet. The Office Spreadsheet component will be inserted into the page, as shown in Figure 15.3.

FIGURE 15.3

The Office Spreadsheet looks and acts exactly like an Excel spreadsheet.

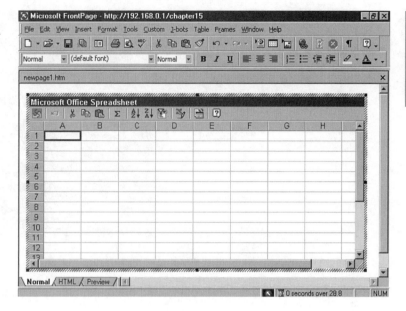

3. Because the Office Spreadsheet component is an ActiveX control, you will be able to set its appearance by right-clicking on it and selecting ActiveX Control Properties. The ActiveX control properties are discussed in detail in Chapter 17, "Adding Advanced Web Technologies."

4. Once you have inserted the Office Spreadsheet control, you can essentially perform any task that you would in a normal Excel spreadsheet. To access the properties for the control, click the Properties Toolbox button in the Office Spreadsheet Control toolbar to open the Spreadsheet Properties Toolbox, as shown in Figure 15.4. The options for formatting the control are identical to Excel and too numerous to discuss in this one chapter.

After you have inserted a spreadsheet, you can begin working with the spreadsheet as if you were in Excel. The Office Spreadsheet control is the best place to design your spreadsheets because it is limited to one sheet. You can use pre-existing Excel spreadsheets by copying and pasting the cells from your Excel spreadsheet into the Office Spreadsheet component.

FIGURE 15.4

The Spreadsheet Properties Toolbox formatting options are identical to Excel.

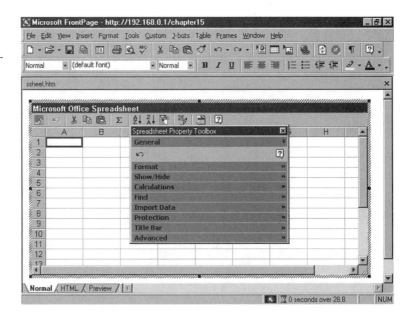

PivotTables

PivotTables and Office Charts are new items, and although actually designed as part of the Microsoft SQL Server 7 data-warehousing product, they can be used for data such as an Excel spreadsheet or Access database. Databases used by a data warehouse are a little different than the databases used by Access or an Excel spreadsheet because they are three-dimensional in nature. An Excel spreadsheet is a series of columns and rows and is two-dimensional, whereas a data warehouse uses a cube with rows and columns, much like stacking spreadsheets on top of each other infinitely. PivotTables and Pivot Charts are designed to help visually analyze this information. To insert a PivotTable into a Web page, perform the following steps:

1. Place your cursor in the position you want the PivotTable to appear.

2. From the FrontPage menu choose Insert, Component, PivotTable. The PivotTable will be inserted into the page, as shown in Figure 15.5.

3. To set up the PivotTable, click the Property Toolbox button (second active button from the right side of the toolbar). The PivotTable Property Toolbox dialog opens, as shown in Figure 15.6.

FIGURE 15.5

The PivotTable can be used to group together items such as monthly and quarterly sales.

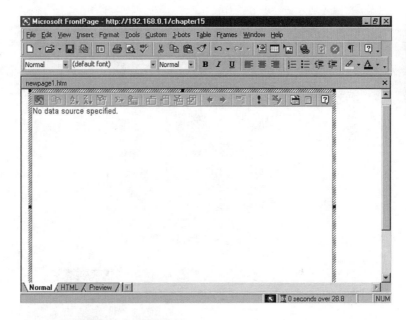

FIGURE 15.6

The PivotTable has a number of options for connecting to a data source as well as for locking rows so they cannot be edited.

4. Once you have inserted the PivotTable you will need to find a data source for it. This can be an Excel spreadsheet, an Access database, a SQL Server, or any number of other data sources. To choose or create a connection to a data source, select the Data Source tab on the PivotTable Property Toolbox. The Data Source tab will expand as shown in Figure 15.7.

5. Choose Connection and click on the Connection Editor button. The Data Link Properties dialog appears, as shown in Figure 15.8.

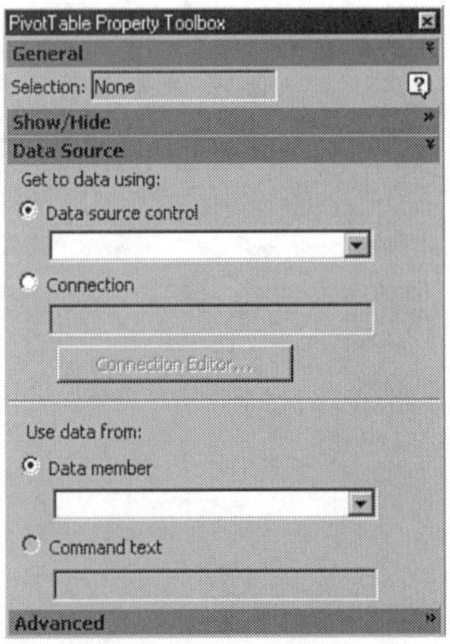

FIGURE 15.7

The Data Source sheet selects the data source for your PivotTable.

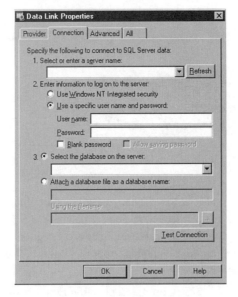

FIGURE 15.8

The Data Link Properties dialog determines what type of data source you are connecting to, as well choosing the file or server that contains the data source.

6. By default, the Data Link Properties are set up to connect to a SQL Server database because the PivotTable is really a data-warehousing tool. You can change this by selecting a different driver from the list available on the Provider tab. To use Access or Excel as a data source, select the driver marked "Microsoft OLE DB Provider for ODBC Drivers," and then select the Connection tab to choose an existing ODBC connection.

7. If you do not have an existing connection, you will need to create one. To do this, go into Control Panel and click on ODBC Data Sources. You will need to add a new data source that points to the correct .xls or .mdb file.

> **Note**
>
> You will need to make sure that your ISP/WPP supports this function—they will need to set up a matching data source on their server for you as well.

8. After you choose a connection and close the Data Link Properties dialog, you will be returned to the PivotTable Property Toolbox. You will then need to select where the information comes from by using the Data Member drop-down menu. If the connection is to an Access database, you will be selecting from a list of tables in the database.

9. Once you select the connection and data member, the PivotTable will alter itself to prepare for customization. Your screen will look like Figure 15.9.

FIGURE 15.9

The pivot table is now ready to be customized.

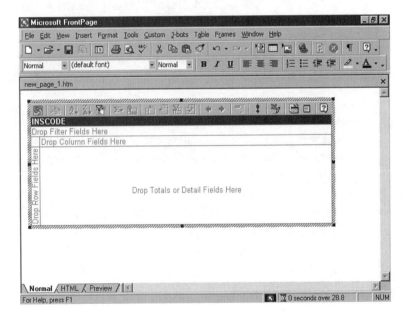

10. In order to drag and drop fields into the PivotTable, you need to make the Field List visible. Choose the Show/Hide tab in the PivotTable Property Toolbox, as shown in Figure 15.10.

FIGURE 15.10

You need to make the Field List visible before you can customize your PivotTable.

11. Choose the Field List button to display the Field List. The Field List contains all the fields from the data source to be placed in the PivotTable.

12. From the Field List you can drag and drop fields into the PivotTable.

You can begin placing fields into the PivotTable right away, but make sure you save your page beforehand. It's always good to have a page you can revert to quickly to avoid unnecessary annoyances, especially since placing fields in the PivotTable is tricky and you may get frustrated for a while before the fields appear as you intend.

Inserting Charts

Charts are a great way to display information. The Chart component makes use of data that already exists in the page, such as an Office spreadsheet or a PivotTable. The chart cannot be set to use just any data source, only one that has been used in the page.

To add a chart to a Web page, follow these steps:

1. Place your cursor in the position you want the chart to appear.

2. From the FrontPage menu choose Insert, Component, Office Chart. The Office Chart Wizard dialog will appear, as shown in Figure 15.11. The Chart Wizard dialog box will guide you through the required steps. The dialog box is clearly labeled as it takes you through the three steps required to insert the chart.

FIGURE 15.11

The Chart component has over 40 different types of charts for you to display your data.

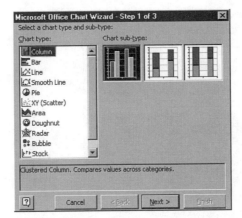

3. From Step 1, you can choose which type and sub-type of chart you want to use, such as bar, line, and pie charts. Once you have chosen the type and sub-type of chart, click the Next button to proceed to Step 2 of the Chart Wizard (see Figure 15.12).

FIGURE 15.12

If you have more than one data source on the page you can select the one whose data you want to use.

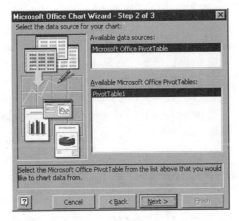

4. From Step 2, you can choose which data source you want to use. If you have multiple data sources on a page, such as several Office spreadsheets, you will be able to choose the type of source, such as Office Spreadsheet, and the data source, such as Spreadsheet1. Once you have chosen the source for your data, click the Next button to proceed to Step 3 of the wizard (see Figure 15.13).

FIGURE **15.13**

*You must now choose
which fields to display
in your chart.*

5. Step 3 will look slightly different for each type of chart and each type of data source. If the data source was an Excel spreadsheet and the Chart type was a Pie chart, then you will see two sections to Step 3—the Series and the Category (x) Axis.

6. The top portion, Series, contains information that goes into the chart itself. If you are using an Excel spreadsheet as the data source, enter the name of the chart in the Name field, and the range of cells to use for the data, such as B1:B11.

7. The bottom portion, the Category (x) Axis Labels, is used to generate the legend for the chart. Use this field to enter the fields where the legend can be generated from, such as A1:A11. I have selected this example of fields to use because most people tend to use column A for things such as titles, and column B for things such as Sales. The fields to enter here would normally be dependant upon the way you have your spreadsheet laid out.

The chart is a powerful tool to view your data with, but does require a bit of knowledge about the different chart types. Better chart documentation can be found in Microsoft Excel where the Chart component was originally used.

Exercise 15.2: Using the Office Spreadsheet and Chart

This exercise will use the Office Spreadsheet and then use a Chart component to display a graphic view of the spreadsheet data. For this example you will create a spreadsheet that contains a list of people and their purchases.

1. Create a new Web page to place the spreadsheet and chart into.

2. From the FrontPage menu, choose Insert, Component, Office Spreadsheet.

3. Beginning with Row 1 in Column A, enter the following. Each line represents one row so the first entry is Row 1 Column A, the second entry is Row 2 Column A, and so on.

Client

Mrs J Buckley

Mr V A Patel

Ms R Truman

Mrs D Patel

Mr W White

Mr J Salem

Mrs P Smith

Mr R Roberts

Miss E Tugby

Mrs J Whiteley

Mr P Dale

Mrs L Lai Won

Your spreadsheet should now look like Figure 15.14.

FIGURE 15.14

The spreadsheet with a list of clients.

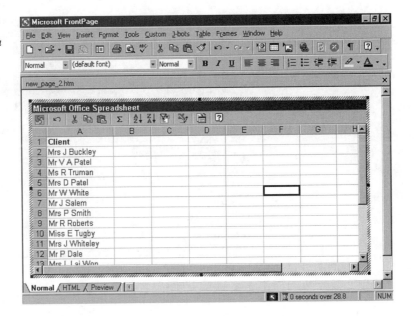

4. Beginning with Row 1 in Column B, enter the following. Each line represents one row so the first entry is Row 1 Column B, the second entry is Row 2 Column B and so on.

Premium

70

90

70

100

120

80

70

90

70

120

90

80

Your spreadsheet should now look like Figure 15.15.

FIGURE 15.15

The spreadsheet now shows clients with their premiums.

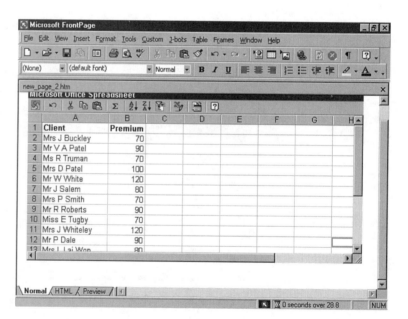

5. Now that the data is in the spreadsheet, you can add a chart. Place your cursor on the page somewhere below your spreadsheet. From the FrontPage menu, choose Insert, Component, Office Chart to display Step 1 of the Office Chart Wizard.

6. Choose the Pie type chart and the first Pie Subset. Press the next button to proceed to Step 2 of the Office Chart Wizard.

7. Step 2 of the wizard selects the data source for the chart. Since there is only one data source it will already be selected and you can click the Next button to proceed to Step 3.

8. Step 3 of the wizard sets up the chart with the data from the Office Spreadsheet. This will probably be completely blank. If the Series combo box is empty, select the Add button to add your first series of data.

9. In the Name box, enter **Premiums**.

10. In the Values box, enter **B1:B13**. This will use the values from column B to populate our Pie.

11. In the Category (x) Axis Labels field enter **A1:A13**. This will use the corresponding values from column A in the legend for the Chart. Your Step 3 of the wizard should look like Figure 15.16.

FIGURE 15.16

The chart is now ready to add to the page.

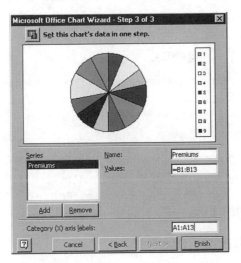

12. Click the Finish button to exit the wizard and update the Chart. Your finished page should look like Figure 15.17.

To see how powerful these two features are, try editing the values in the spreadsheet and see how they reflect in the chart. You might also want to adjust the settings for the spreadsheet, which can be edited from within a Web page.

FIGURE 15.17

The chart is now complete.

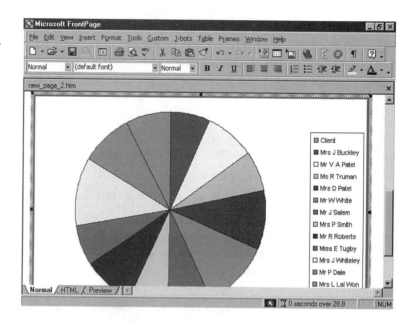

Working with Access

Access is a database utility. Access enables users to create database tables that hold information, as well as the forms used to put information into the database. If you haven't worked with databases before you don't need to worry—you won't be seeing a lot of theory or technical explanations.

If your Web site will be hosted on a Web server running Internet Information Server 3.0 or greater, then you can use FrontPage to create Web pages that use the information in an Access database. FrontPage can limit the number of records returned and even break your results into multiple pages.

Adding Database Results

Keeping Web page content current can be a hassle, especially when you have lots of data. In cases like these you may want to use a database to store your information. We have supplied a sample database on the CD called Wine List1.mdb, which you can use for this part of the chapter.

To add database results to a Web page, perform the following steps:

1. Open a Web page and position your cursor where you would like to put the database results.

2. From the FrontPage menu choose Insert, Database, Results. The Database Results Wizard opens, as shown in Figure 15.18.

FIGURE 15.18

Before you can begin choosing fields for your results, you must choose or create a data source.

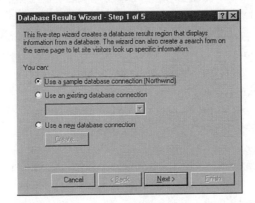

Step 1 of the Database Results Wizard has three options—Use a Sample Access Database, Use an Existing Database Connection, and Use a New Database Connection.

3. Select Use a New Database Connection and click Create. The Web Settings dialog will open with the database page selected.

4. Click the Add button to add a connection to your sample database. This will open the New Database Connection dialog, as shown in Figure 15.19.

FIGURE 15.19

If you haven't already created a database connection, you can do that easily with the New Database Connection dialog.

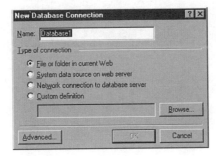

5. The New Database Connection dialog has the following options:

Name—This field allows you to name your new database connection or enter the name of a database connection that might exist on your computer but has not been used by FrontPage.

File or Folder in Current Web—This option allows you to select a database file that exists in your current FrontPage Web.

System Data Source on Web Server—This option allows you to select a pre-existing database connection that exists on the server. This connection could be to any sort of database, such as an Access 2000 database, a Microsoft SQL Server database, or any other database that supports ODBC.

Network Connection to a Database—This option allows you to create a connection to a database that exists somewhere else on the network. Database servers are often on separate servers from the Web server.

Custom Definition—This option allows you to choose a .dsn file that holds the information about a custom data source definition.

Advanced button—Clicking the Advanced button opens the Advanced Connection Properties dialog box (see Figure 15.20). This dialog allows you to set advanced connection properties such as a username and password to use to access the database, the connection timeout, and other custom parameters.

To use the sample database, you will first need to import it into your Web. Click the Browse button to browse to the database file we have supplied. By default the browse will search for Access .mdb files, but you can select other types of data sources.

FIGURE 15.20

With the Advanced Connection Properties dialog you can set parameters that enable you to customize your database connection for the specific capabilities of your database, whether it's Microsoft Access or an Oracle database server.

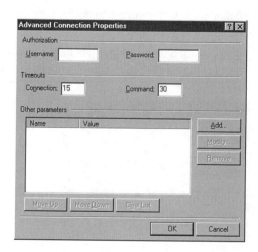

6. Click OK to close the New Database Connection dialog and create the connection.

7. Select the new database connection and click OK. You will notice that the Database Results Wizard now has the Use an Existing Database Connection option selected and it is already set to your new database connection.

8 Select Next to continue to Step 2 of the wizard, as shown in Figure 15.21.

FIGURE 15.21

You can either select your results from a table in the database, or use custom SQL queries that you write.

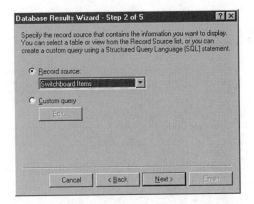

Note

Sometimes when adding a new connection, you may receive an error when you reach Step 2 of the Database Results Wizard. This error means that FrontPage isn't able to open this new connection properly in order to get a list of tables in the database. The best way to resolve this is to simply save your work, close all applications, and reboot. FrontPage should be able to open the database connection after the system has rebooted. I would like to be able to tell you why this happens, but it's seems to simply be a slight glitch which occurs periodically.

9. Step 2 of the Database Results Wizard has the following options:

   Record Source—This drop-down list contains a list of tables available inside the database. Use this to choose the exact table where the results will come from.

   Custom Query—Selecting this option allows you to enter your own query information written in SQL. Selecting the custom query option and choosing the Edit button will open the Custom Query dialog box, as shown in Figure 15.22.

   The Custom Query dialog enables you to write your own SQL statements to develop complex queries to the database, to insert fields from a form, or to paste the contents of the clipboard. Pasting the clipboard contents allows you to use a tool such as Access 2000 to develop your queries graphically, then copy the SQL code created by the query and paste it into the SQL Statement field.

10. Click the Next button. Step 3 of the Database Results Wizard appears, as shown in Figure 15.23.

FIGURE 15.22

You can write your own SQL queries to obtain information from your database or, if you don't know SQL, you can copy SQL from an Access Query and paste it into SQL Statement field.

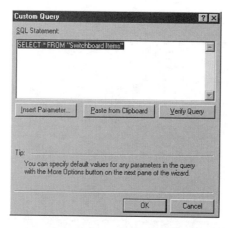

FIGURE 15.23

You can select which fields you want to be listed in the database results.

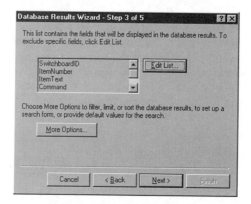

11. Step 3 of the Database Results Wizard contains the two following buttons:

Edit List—Selecting the Edit List button opens the Displayed Fields dialog (see Figure 15.24). With the Displayed Fields dialog you choose which fields are displayed by moving them into the Displayed Fields list. You can also control their order by moving the fields higher in the list to appear closer to the first column, or lower in the list to appear near the last column. Fields that you don't want displayed will be listed in the Available Fields list.

More Options—Selecting the More Options button opens the More Options dialog box (see Figure 15.25). The More Options dialog box enables you to limit the number of records returned in your results, which improves the download time of a page, or to set some text if there are no records available. It also has two more buttons, the Criteria button used to set certain criteria such as Date greater than June 10, 1999, and the Ordering button used to choose which fields you want to sort by

15

and whether they should sort ascending (least to greatest) or descending (greatest to least). If you change your mind then you can always use the Defaults button to restore your settings to the FrontPage defaults.

Click OK when you have completed your options and to return to Step 3 of the Database Results Wizard.

FIGURE 15.24

You can add, remove or change the order in which fields appear.

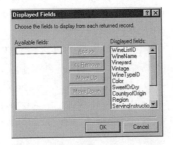

FIGURE 15.25

The More Options dialog box helps you set the way the visitor will see the results.

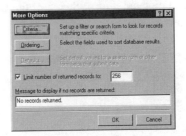

12. When finished, click the Next button. Step 4 of the Database Results Wizard appears, as shown in Figure 15.26.

FIGURE 15.26

There are a number of formatting options for your results to give them a professional feel.

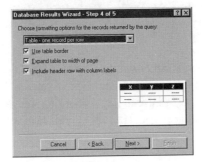

13. Step 4 is for choosing the format you want to display your results in. You have three options, a table with one record per row, a list with one field per item, and a drop-down list with one record per item.

Table – One Record per Row—The most common option for database results displays the results in a row and column format where each row is a distinct record and each column is a field in the database. You can choose to have a table border, expand the table to fill the width of the page, and to include a header row with column names.

List – One Field per Item—The List displays a record with one field per line. This format displays information similarly to a form. You can choose to add field names before each result, to use a separating line between each record in the database, and how you want the fields to appear, such as a paragraph or a bulleted list.

Drop-Down List – One Record per Item—A Drop-Down list will create a drop-down list box filled with the results of a database. You can choose a value to display in the list, and a hidden value that is actually used by a form handler. This is useful to display the name of a company and then pass their corporate ID number to a form handler.

14. Click Next when you have completed Step 4. Step 5 of the Database Results Wizard Is displayed, as shown in Figure 15.27.

FIGURE 15.27

The last step lets you choose to display all the records together, or to separate them into multiple pages for easier reading.

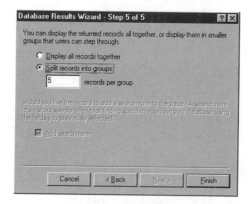

15. Step 5 is the final step and enables you to choose to display all the records on one page, or to break the results into multiple pages. If you are displaying a large number of results, it may be best to use multiple pages to increase download time. Use the Records Per Group field to decide how many records will appear per page.

16. Click the Finish button to close the wizard and begin generating the database results component.

17. You will be prompted at this point to rename the page with an .asp extension. This is the file extension required for this page to function correctly.

Adding Column Values

After you create your database results, you may realize that you really needed another field or two to be displayed. Instead of going back and repeating the whole Database Results wizard process again, you can simply add a column to your existing Database Results component.

To add a column from your database to an existing Database Results component, perform the following steps:

1. Position your cursor in the location you want to add your database column to. If you are adding it to a table, you will probably need to add a separate table cell for it because the Add Column component won't do that for you.

2. From the FrontPage menu, choose Insert, Database, Column Value. The Database Column Value dialog appears (see Figure 15.28).

FIGURE 15.28

Adding database columns is simple because it uses information you have already provided with the database results.

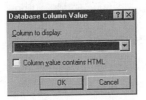

3. The Database Column Value uses the information you have already provided for the Database Results to make things simple. The Database Column Value dialog has two fields:

    Column to Display—This drop-down list contains all the fields that you can display. Select one from the list to add that column to your Database Results. Be careful—the list contains all the fields, not just the ones you haven't used yet.

    Column Value Contains HTML—Use this option to ensure that any HTML code contained in your database field is preserved properly. Not checking this option may mean that any HTML code you have in the field will end up being displayed in the browser.

4. Click OK once you have chosen your options to close the Database Column Value dialog and apply your changes.

Configuring Queries

There are two ways to create custom queries, by writing your own or using a database tool such as Access 2000. Databases are queried using a language known as SQL

(Structured Query Language). SQL can be a little tricky to learn and requires a knowledge of database theory and design. You can avoid this by creating a query in Access and viewing the SQL generated by the query.

As you saw previously, FrontPage tries to make it easy to copy and paste SQL queries from a database such as Access 2000 by adding a Paste from Clipboard button. This lets you copy the SQL query code from an Access query to the clipboard and then paste the contents of the clipboard into the custom query box.

If you aren't using Access as your database, chances are you can still create queries and view the underlying SQL code generated by them. To find out if this is possible, consult your database's documentation.

Exercise 15.3: Interfacing with Databases

The accompanying CD contains a sample database for you to use in this exercise. Although it is a basic database, it should give you an idea of how databases can interface with Web sites. Any set of data that is liable to frequent change is perfect for using with FrontPage because it saves you having to keep exporting static pages.

Open a new page in your FrontPage Web and immediately save it as `default.asp`. To do this, click on the Save button and then use the drop-down list to select the Active Server Pages option.

1. From the FrontPage menu, choose Insert, Database, Results to begin the Database Results Wizard.

2. Select Use a New Database Connection and click the Create button. This opens the Web Settings dialog to the Database page.

3. Click the Add button to open the New Database Connection dialog. In the Name field enter `Wine List`. Click the Browse button and select the `WineList1.mdb` file in your Web.

4. Click OK to close the dialog.

5. Click OK to close the Web Settings dialog and return to the Database Results Wizard.

6. Select the Sales connection from the list and click the Next button to proceed to Step 2 of the wizard.

7. From the Record Source list, select the Wine List table and click Next to proceed to Step 3 of the wizard.

8. Click the Edit List button to open the Displayed Fields list. Edit the Displayed Fields so that the Available Fields box contains Wine Name, Vintage, Color, and SweetOrDry, as shown in Figure 15.29. Click the Next button to proceed to Step 4 of the wizard.

FIGURE 15.29

The Available Fields will display Wine Name, Vintage, Color, and SweetOrDry fields in that order.

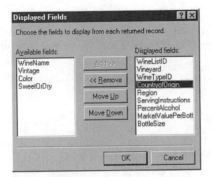

9. Step 4 of the Wizard gives you the formatting options list. Choose the Table—One Row per Record option. Uncheck the Use table border, Expand table to width of page, and Include header row with column labels. Click the Next button to proceed to Step 5 of the Database Results Wizard.

10. Select the Display All Rows Together option so that all of the wines are listed. Click the Finish button to close the wizard and generate the Database Results area. The Database Results will appear in the page as shown in Figure 15.30.

FIGURE 15.30

The Database Results won't show the actual database values until viewed through a browser, but they can be formatted as if they were normal text.

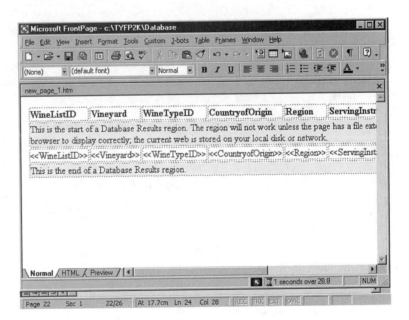

Click the Preview in Browser button to view the page and the database results.

Note   The database results will appear if viewed through the browser, but only if your Web is running through a Web server that supports Active Server Pages.

Using Office Macros

Have you ever found yourself performing the same series of tasks over and over in an application? This behavior is not only tedious, but boring as well. Macros are scripts that you can write that will perform these tasks simply by invoking the macro. If, for example, one of your projects uses a number of Webs you could create a macro that would open all of these Webs for you without having to open each individually.

Macros are created using a special version of Visual Basic called Visual Basic for Applications (VBA). VBA is an extension of the Visual Basic language specifically for use inside of applications. Because it is based on Visual Basic you will be able to find a wealth of material on programming with it. The best place to start learning is at Microsoft's Visual Basic Web site at http://msdn.microsoft.com/vbasic/.

FrontPage and the other Office 2000 applications expose certain functions for use with Macros. This is called an Object Model because it describes an object and what it contains. Each application in Office 2000, such as FrontPage and Word, is an object. The Object Model describes the different functions you can call for each object or the properties that can be set. The Object Model itself is a bit beyond the scope of this chapter and book, but here is a peek at how it works.

In this example, you will create a simple macro that opens two Web sites. You will need to have two Webs created already in order to use this macro, but you should still see how it works even if you don't have them ready.

To add a macro to FrontPage, perform the following steps:

1. From the FrontPage menu choose Tools, Macro, Macros. The Macro dialog box opens (see Figure 15.31).

2. The Macro dialog has the following fields:

   Macro Name—Use this field to enter the name of a new macro.

   Run—This button will run a macro that you have selected.

   Cancel—Closes the Macro dialog.

   Step Into—This allows you to run the macro, but one line at a time. This is very useful when trying to figure out where a problem occurs.

15

Edit—Opens the macro in the VB editor in order to be edited.

Create—Will create the starting framework for a macro after you have entered a name for your macro in the Macro Name field.

Delete—Deletes a macro that you have selected.

Macros In—Enables you to list macros that are only in FrontPage, or in other applications that you may have open such as Word 2000.

3. In the Macro Name field, type `OpenWeb`.

4. Click the Create button to create the OpenWeb macro and open the new macro in the Visual Basic editor, as shown in Figure 15.32.

FIGURE 15.31

With macros you can script some of your most common tasks in FrontPage to save you time.

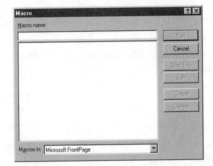

FIGURE 15.32

This version of the Visual Basic editor is a little different than the full version of Visual Basic, but still has many of the features that make it an easy product to use and learn.

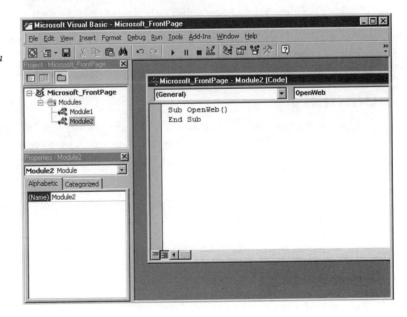

5. A macro is a special type of function called a subroutine. All macros will begin with `Sub macroname()` and end with `End Sub`. The code between these is the actual macro. In the OpenWeb macro, add the following code between the `Sub OpenWeb()` and the `End Sub`:

```
Dim objFirstWeb As Web

Set objFirstWeb = Webs.Add("pathtoweb", "username", "password")
MsgBox ("Web Opened")

objFirstWeb.Close
MsgBox ("Web Closed")

Application.Quit
```

Replace `pathtoweb` with the URL or file path to the Web (such as `http://localhost/myweb` or `c:\my webs\myweb\`). You can leave the username and password empty or delete them altogether. If you are trying to open a Web on an NT or UNIX server, you may need to enter your username and password.

6. Press F5 or select Run, Run Sub/User Form to run the macro. The macro will open FrontPage and the Web you specify in the pathtoweb. The macro will then display a dialog saying the Web is opened. After clicking the OK button, FrontPage will close the Web and display another dialog saying the Web is closed. After clicking the OK button, FrontPage will quit.

7. To exit the Visual Basic editor, select Alt+Q or File, Quit.

While this may not be the most glamorous or exciting example, it is simple and should begin to give you some ideas of what you could do with macros.

Summary

This chapter has covered the basics of using some of the new Office component features in FrontPage 2000. Use the workshop time to learn a little more about how they can enhance your Web pages. Don't forget that some of them will only work in Internet Explorer.

Use the sample spreadsheet and database files to create pages that use their functionality. Try formatting the output to suit your needs.

Create a page to display some database results, then try changing the order the results are displayed in. Just because things are in a certain order in the database doesn't mean that they have to be the same in your Web pages.

Try to learn a little more about Access. Look at the SQL View in some of your queries to see how they are made up.

15

Make a basic PowerPoint presentation complete with transition effects and see how they look when used in a Web. They can make great Web pages and enhance a corporate feel to your site.

Workshop

Q&A

Q **Can I use a database in my Web if I am not using Internet Information Server 3.0 or greater?**

A No. The technology that FrontPage uses to access databases is available to IIS versions 3 and above only. This technology, called Active Server Pages, is built into IIS 3.0 and greater and allows complex scripts to be written in the same page as HTML. While Active Server Pages are being ported to other operating systems and Web servers by third-party vendors, FrontPage is not designed to work with them.

Q **Why can't I see the Office Spreadsheet, PivotTable, or Chart on the Insert, Component menu?**

A In order to use these components your compatibility settings under page options must be set to Internet Explorer only. In most cases when these items don't appear it is because the page options are either set to Netscape Navigator, or to browsers without ActiveX support. Since these items are ActiveX controls they will not be listed when compatibility has been set to Netscape Navigator.

Quiz

1. Can you actually perform spreadsheet commands using the spreadsheet component?

2. Can you actually perform database functions using the database component?

3. Will you need to reformat a text file if you cut and paste it into your FrontPage Web?

4. What does .asp stand for?

5. What is SQL?

Exercises

1. Add some new records to the sample spreadsheet and database files we have supplied.

2. Using the database used earlier in the chapter, add some new records and see how quickly these are displayed in your results.

3. Add components from these to your Web pages. As an alternative, see if you can create a new database or spreadsheet that is relevant to your own project.

4. See if you can create an appropriate PowerPoint presentation and implement it as part of your Web site. This is easy to do in FrontPage 2000.

Answers to Quiz

1. Yes. The spreadsheet component allows you to manipulate the data and input fields and so on.

2. No. It is designed to show results from a database, not for database creation.

3. Most likely yes. The .txt file extension is the simplest form of text file and does not support fonts, sizes, and so on.

4. Active Server Pages. The file type required to display the results from a database.

5. Structured Query Language. The language used in database queries.

DAY 16

Adding Your Own HTML Code

Why You May Need More Than Just FrontPage 2000

Even though FrontPage 2000 is the most up-to-date Web design, development, and management tool available, there may still come a time when it's just not enough.

Web Design is never finished; even the most experienced professional will tell you that there is no such thing as a finished Web site. As technology develops and more techniques become widely available, software becomes out of date.

FrontPage makes almost every Web design task simple and straightforward, and for many people reading this book, it is all you will ever need. For others, however, it is simple a case of "The more you learn—the more you want to do."

For this reason, FrontPage 2000 makes it easier than ever to work directly with the HTML code, whether you want to add some code you may have found on the Internet or edit the code actually generated by FrontPage—it has never been easier.

Like all software, each version of FrontPage has developed and added new features. The first version of FrontPage allowed you to see the code and do nothing with it; FrontPage 97 and 98 allowed you to edit the code—but was just as likely to change it back for you. FrontPage 2000 no longer tries to change code you add, in fact it offers the tools to make working in HTML View a simple process.

This chapter will cover

- Working in HTML View
- Using the HTML Component
- Revealing HTML Tags in the FrontPage Editor

Working in HTML View

To start with, you will create a page in the normal way, and then look at the HTML and how FrontPage can help you to use it as an editing tool:

1. Open FrontPage and create a new empty Web called `chapter16`.
2. Then using an empty page, type the following text, using the Enter key at the end of each line:

   ```
   I have indented this sentence from the rest.

   We can add to the page using the HTML view.

   The tags for the page are color coded

   This sentence is right aligned

   This one is left aligned and bold

   And this one is in the middle and underlined

   I have used the font Verdana as well as different colors and sizes
   to do this page
   ```

3. Format the text you typed so that it looks like Figure 16.1.

FIGURE **16.1**

*The text you typed
with formatting
applied.*

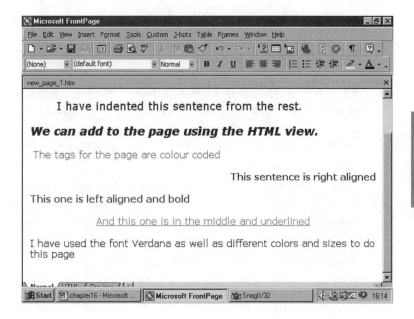

4. Save the page as code.htm.

5. Click on the HTML tab to see the code for the page. It should look like Figure 16.2.

FIGURE **16.2**

*The HTML view of the
text you typed.*

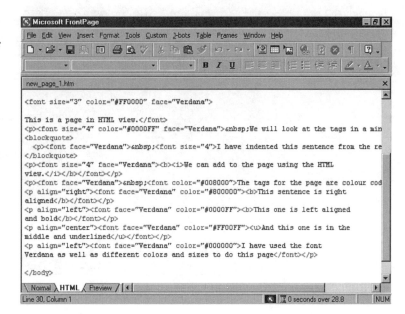

As you see, the only colors that appear at this stage are black for the text we typed and the default blue to indicate the tags. FrontPage 2000, however, gives us many options to change and customize this view.

Working Within the HTML View

Working with raw HTML can become a little confusing, especially if you have a large page and are trying to differentiate between the code and your actual content. To help differentiate between text and HTML, FrontPage 2000 uses color coding in the HTML View.

Color-coding allows you to better separate HTML tags from the text of your Web page. The HTML View uses different colors to identify HTML tags, attribute names, attribute values, comments, scripts, and normal text. FrontPage98 used color coding in HTML View to display different tags; FrontPage 2000 now builds upon that, actually allowing you to customize the colors to suit your taste and choice.

To customize the color-coding feature of the HTML View, perform the following steps:

1. From the FrontPage Menu, choose Tools, Page Options. This opens the Page Options dialog box shown in Figure 16.3.
2. Select the Color Coding tab to display the Color Coding page shown in Figure 16.4.

FIGURE 16.3

The Page Options dialog box.

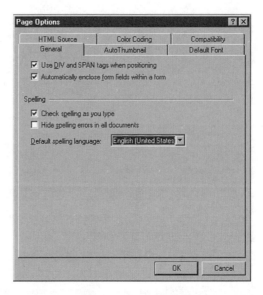

FIGURE **16.4**

The Color Coding tab.

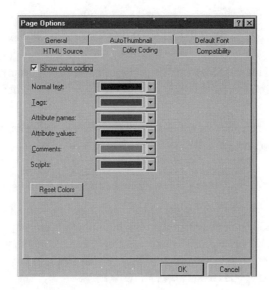

The Color Coding tab offers choices to make the HTML View easier to read. The Color Coding page has the following options:

- *Show Color Coding*—Enabled by default, this check box enables you to toggle on or off the color coding for the HTML View.

- *Normal Text*—This color chooser enables you to choose the color to designate the normal text that will appear in your Web page. The color of the text in the HTML View will not affect the color of your text in Normal View. The default color for this is black.

- *Tags*—This color chooser enables you to choose the color of the HTML tag itself. The default color for this is blue.

- *Attribute Names*—Some tags have attributes that can be set, such as the width attribute of the image tag. This color chooser enables you to choose the color for any HTML attribute names. The default color for this is blue.

- *Attribute Values*—An attribute such as an image's width, needs a value such as 50. This color chooser enables you to choose the color for any HTML attribute value. The default color for this is black.

- *Comments*—HTML has a special comments tag so you can put your own comments into a page to help identify what the code does. An example of a comment is `<!--This is a comment -->`. This color chooser enables you to choose the color for any comments. Since FrontPage stores some of the FrontPage component information as comments, they will also appear this color. The default color for this is gray.
- *Scripts*—This color chooser enables you to choose the color of any script code, such as JavaScript or VBScript, contained in your page. The default color for this is maroon.
- *Reset Colors*—This button allows you to reset all the colors to the default settings.

Try changing the colors from the default and see if you prefer a combination other than the default offered. Remember that the reset button will take everything back to this default if you find your selections don't work or become confusing.

Editing Your Page in HTML View

The HTML View of FrontPage 2000 looks and works just like a text editor. You have the facilities to copy, paste, and move blocks of text around. Simply select part of the page you want to work with, and then right-click to see the normal list of text options.

While in HTML View, right-clicking on the actual HTML allows you to easily bring up the Tag Properties dialog box, as shown in Figure 16.5.

FIGURE 16.5

You can open the Tag Properties dialog box by right-clicking on a tag while in HTML View.

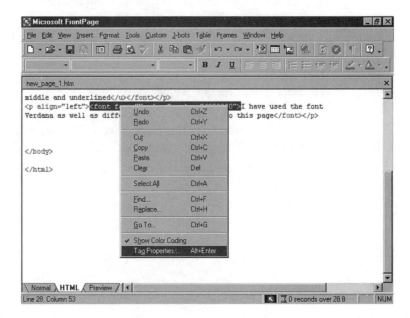

Another feature new to FrontPage 2000 is the ability to add a FrontPage Component or even a table while working in the HTML View. In previous versions you could edit the code once it was generated, but not actually use the Insert, Table option. Adding a table while in HTML View will insert the table code right away if you want.

Anyone who has experience with previous versions of FrontPage will remember how difficult it was to edit FrontPage-generated HTML. Often, after adjusting a tag here or putting a space there, FrontPage would go ahead and reformat things its own way regardless of what you may have wanted. With FrontPage 2000, Microsoft has gone to a lot of effort and a long way toward making sure that this does not happen anymore. The HTML View in FrontPage is now a comprehensive editing tool in its own right, rather than an often frustrating way to see how FrontPage had changed your code.

Using the HTML Component

Previously, the HTML component was the only way to stop FrontPage attempting to "tidy-up" your code. Even though FrontPage 2000 doesn't try to reformat your code, it is still a nice option to be able to add raw HTML even when working in Normal View.

The HTML component creates a special grouping of tags to identify your inserted code. This code is platform independent because it is stored as a comment, which means Web servers and browsers will ignore it.

To insert HTML using the HTML component, perform the following steps:

1. Open the page you want to add the HTML to, or create a blank page.

2. Position the cursor where you want the HTML to be inserted.

3. Select Insert, Advanced, HTML from the FrontPage menu to display the HTML Markup dialog box, as shown in Figure 16.6.

FIGURE 16.6

The HTML Markup dialog box enables you to insert any HTML into a page without worrying how FrontPage will format it.

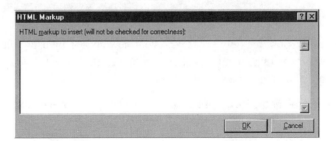

4. Enter the following:

```
<p><font face="Tahoma" size="3" color="#0000FF"><b> This bright, bold
blue text is in the Tahoma font and is being added using the insert
HTML option and will not be immediately displayed in the normal
view</b></font>
```

5. When finished, click OK to close the HTML Markup dialog box.

Having clicked OK, don't panic. You won't be able to see the effect your insertion has just had in the Normal View. Click on the Preview tab and you will see that your page has changed. It now appears as in Figure 16.7, complete with new blue text at the bottom.

FIGURE 16.7

The HTML you added appears in the window when you click on the Preview button.

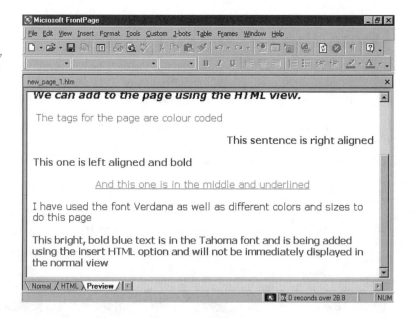

In Normal View, the only way to see your new code is by using the new Reveal Tags (View, Reveal Tags) feature as shown in Figure 16.8. The HTML you inserted shows as a blue question mark in a yellow rectangle.

We will look at the Reveal Tags option in more detail in the next section.

Revealing HTML Tags

Revealing HTML tags is a brand new feature in FrontPage 2000. Although some other Web design packages have had this feature for a while, it is new to FrontPage, and acts as a middle point between working in Normal View and editing the raw code.

As shown in Figure 16.8, FrontPage will display HTML tags inside of a special tag icon. Clicking on a tag, as shown in Figure 16.9, will highlight the tag and its contents, making it easier to see what that tag is affecting. Holding the mouse over a selected tag will give you more information.

FIGURE 16.8

The Reveal Tags option is another new feature in FrontPage 2000.

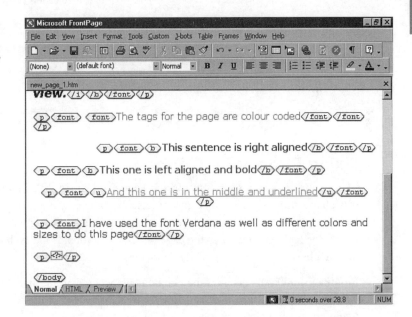

| Note | FrontPage only displays tags after the opening body tag. It does not display any tags that are located in the header portion of the page. These include the <title> tag and any meta tags you may add to your pages. |

Revealing tags will not affect the HTML contained in the page or the layout of the page itself. Revealing tags is simply a way to gain an understanding of what FrontPage is doing behind the scenes while eliminating the need to switch views all the time.

FIGURE 16.9

FIGURE **16.9**

Select a tag with Reveal Tags turned on to see what it is affecting.

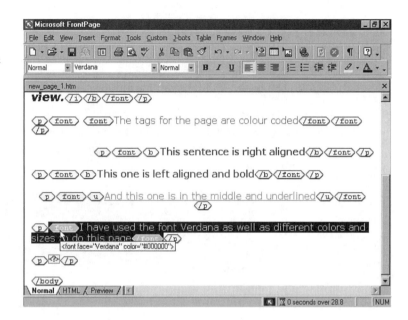

Fixing Errors with Go To

Many users of previous versions of FrontPage complained that finding errors on a page was almost impossible. Script errors are usually shown by number. FrontPage 98 had no facility to show these, making debugging a problem script a nightmare. Previous users of FrontPage had to count down the page one line at a time. If the Web page had several hundred lines, this became quickly annoying.

FrontPage 2000 now displays the line numbers when working in HTML View. Try highlighting one line of text, and then look to the very bottom of the screen—you will see a line number and column number displayed.

FrontPage 2000 has another new feature that allows you to jump directly to any line on the page. This enables you to find the problem line quickly without having to waste time scrolling down the page.

To jump to any line in the page, perform the following steps:

1. Open the page you have been working on in this chapter.
2. Click on the HTML tag.
3. Right-click anywhere on the page and select Go To. The Go To Line dialog box opens, as shown in Figure 16.10.
4. In the Enter Line Number field, enter the number of the line you want to go to.
5. Click OK to close the dialog box and move to that line in the document.

FIGURE 16.10

The new Go To Line feature allows you to immediately jump to any line in a page.

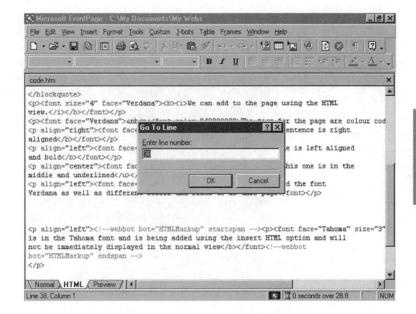

16

Formatting HTML Source

As already mentioned, previous versions of FrontPage were famous (or more to the point, infamous) for formatting HTML in the way it wanted to. FrontPage 2000 has not only stopped this, but allows you to format the HTML the way *you* want to.

Those with little or no knowledge of HTML will have no interest in how the code behind their pages looks. However, for many others it is a vital part of the Web creation process. You may want your pages to look a certain way so you can read the HTML easier, or, if you are part of a company or Web development team, you may have strict regulations to work within. With more integration possible between Web applications, you may find that something you are using needs things in a certain way. FrontPage 2000 gives you this level of control over almost every tag available in HTML 4.0.

To set the options for formatting the HTML source, perform the following steps:

1. Use the page you have been working with in this chapter.
2. From the FrontPage menu, choose Tools, Page Options. Select the HTML Source tab of the Page Options dialog box, as shown in Figure 16.11.

FIGURE 16.11

FrontPage offers you full control over how your HTML is written and laid out in your Web pages.

3. The General section of the HTML Source page has the following options for saving files:

   Preserve Existing HTML—When FrontPage opens a file it will keep the existing HTML format. When FrontPage saves a file, it will save any new HTML in the format you specify, thus preserving the original formatting of the HTML when the page was opened.

   Reformat Using Rules Below—Choosing this radio button will allow FrontPage to immediately reformat the HTML of any page that you open to the formatting options you set.

   Base on Current Page—FrontPage can scan a Web page and attempt to determine how it is formatted. This button will scan the page and try to set the default HTML Source formatting to match the formatting of the current page.

4. The Formatting section of the HTML Source page has the following options:

   Tag Names Are Lowercase—Checking this option will force FrontPage to write all HTML tags in lowercase (such as <p> instead of <P>). This is a readability option as some people prefer to see tags in a particular case so they can easily be identified.

Attribute Names Are Lowercase—Checking this option will force FrontPage to write the attribute names of HTML tags in lowercase (such as `<p align>` instead of `<p ALIGN>`). Again, this is a readability option. Some people choose to use lowercase HTML tags and uppercase attributes for quick identification, but choose the setting most comfortable for you to read.

Allow Line Breaks Within Tags—Some tags can become very long once you add all the attributes and can scroll off the side of the page. Allowing line breaks can help you see better by keeping the tag from going off the side of the page. If you use custom programs that read your Web pages for one reason or another, they might have difficulty with tags that run onto multiple lines.

Indent—With this option you can choose the number of Spaces, or Tabs, to indent at the beginning of each line. This helps keep the HTML code from butting up against the edge of the document and often makes for easier reading. The default is two spaces.

Right Margin—This allows you to choose the number of characters in each line. FrontPage will make sure that nothing goes beyond this point, unless it has to (such as when HTML tags are set to be on one line). The default is right margin 80 characters.

Tags—This list contains almost every tag in HTML 4.0. Some tags may not be present that were in earlier versions because they were never really used (such as the `<person>` tag) or have been removed from the latest version of the HTML standard. By selecting a tag, you can choose from a series of formatting options. Some options will not be available for every tag however.

Line Breaks—The Line Breaks section has several settings that allow you to control the line spacing around a tag. You may want certain tags to be spaced for easy reading. The line breaks section allows you to add lines before and after a beginning tag, and before and after an ending tag. Some tags, such as a table tag, have both a beginning `<table>` and an ending `</table>` tag. Tags that don't have an ending tag, such as an image (`<img>`), will have their before and after ending tag fields disabled. Look at a Web page's HTML and try to figure out which parts you have the most trouble finding. Tables are good to place space around because you can put tables within tables, which can be hard to find in the HTML, and tables can be a very important part of a Web page so you will want to spot them easily.

16

Omit Start Tag—There are some tags that don't require a beginning tag to be specified. The <head> tag is a good example. The head tag itself is only a container for other tags such as the <title> and <meta> tags. Most browsers will be able to assume where it should be even if the tag isn't present. Only tags that have an optional start tag will be able to use this option. Use this option only if you understand HTML because it could have consequences to the way browsers view your document.

Omit Endtag—Some tags, such as the paragraph (<p>) tag, don't require an ending tag. Most browsers will be able to determine where an ending tag should be and don't require a closing tag. The <p> tag is probably the most famous of these because very few authors used the ending tag, and even fewer knew that it actually existed because they were taught by examples that had no ending tag. You may find it easier to use ending tags, especially when starting out reading HTML so you definitely know where things begin and end. Other users might find extra tags like the </p> tag annoying and a waste of space.

Indent Contents—This allows you to force a tag to indent a little way into the page for readability. The following code shows tags that are difficult to read because they aren't indented:

```
<table>
<tr>
<td> This is the first table cell.</td>
<td> This is the second table cell.</td>
</tr>
</table>
```

Compare the previous code to this new code that shows how indenting can make your HTML easier to read and identify elements.

```
<table>
 <tr>
  <td> This is the first table cell.</td>
  <td> This is the second table cell.</td>
 </tr>
</table>
```

Reset—This button returns the source formatting to the installed default settings.

5. After you have chosen your formatting options, click OK to close the Page Options dialog box and apply the new settings.

After you make changes to the HTML source formatting, look at the effect the formatting has had. If you are happy with it, that's fine, but if not, remember you can return to the default settings at any time by clicking the Reset button. If you are planing on formatting individual tags, then it is best to do so one at a time. This makes it easier to see the effect your changes are having.

Floating Frames: An Example of Coding

16

Although FrontPage was designed recently and is aimed to support almost every type of technology, one gap in this support is the use of floating frames. Floating frames are an oddity in Web design, and although not fully supported in all browsers, they are a perfect example for using hand coding.

What Are Floating Frames?

Floating frames were introduced by Microsoft in Internet Explorer 3 and were recently made part of the newest HTML standard, HTML 4. Floating frames are very different from normal frames because they don't use a frameset like the frames discussed in Chapter 12, "Creating and Using Framesets."

These floating frames, perhaps better known as inline frames, are like putting little windows inside your Web pages.

You might wonder what use these special frames might be good for. If you visit MSNBC at `<http://www.msnbc.com>` then you have probably already seen one and didn't know it. MSNBC uses floating frames often in their online articles to give extra background or related information about an article. Because you can control the height and width of a floating frame, you can pack a lot of information into it without taking up a large part of your page.

Unfortunately, even though the `<iframe>` tag has been added to the latest HTML standard, it is still only supported in Internet Explorer. You will need to have a back-up plan for anyone viewing your site in Netscape or any of the older browsers.

Exercise 16.1: Adding a Floating Frame to Your Web Page

Before you begin, you may want to look over the following attributes for the floating frame's `<iframe>` tag. Any value listed as *n* refers to any number.

TABLE 16.1 Floating Frame Attributes

Attribute Name	Value	Description
Align	Left or Right	Aligns the inline frame to the left or the right.
Border	*n*	Sets a border around the inline frame exactly like that of a table.
Frameborder	Yes or No	Displays a border like that of a normal frame.
Height	*n*	The height of the inline frame in pixels.
Marginheight	*n*	The amount of space, in pixels, that separates the inline frame from content above and below it.
Marginwidth	*n*	The amount of space, in pixels, that separates the inline frame from content to the left and right of it.
Name	Text	Defines the target name for any hyperlinks.
Scrolling	Auto | Yes | No	Tells the inline frame to scroll when necessary, to always have scrollbars, or to never have scrollbars.
Src	Url	The URL to the source of the inline frame.
Width	*n*	The width of the inline frame in pixels.

You will be starting with a new page for this exercise. Save and close the code.htm page you have been working with so far and then follow these steps:

1. Open FrontPage and create a new blank page.

2. From the FrontPage menu choose Table, Insert Table to display the Insert Table dialog box.

3. Set the number of rows to 1 and columns to 2.

4. Make the table 100% wide.

5. Click OK to create the table.

6. Position your cursor in the right-hand table cell and type the following:

   `This text is not inside the inline frame`
   Your page should look something like Figure 16.12.

7. Position your cursor in the left-hand table cell.

8. Switch to the HTML View. The code should look something like Figure 16.13.

FIGURE 16.12

Basic text typed in the right-hand cell.

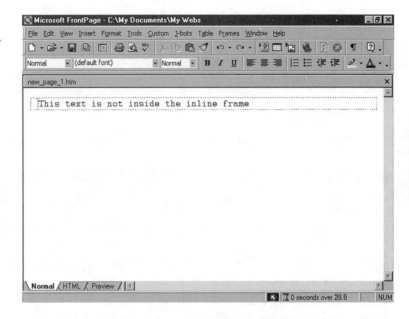

16

FIGURE 16.13

FrontPage keeps the cursor in the same place when you switch to HTML View.

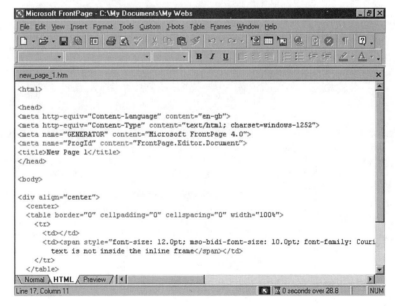

9. Type the following.

```
<iframe width="200" height="200" scrolling="auto">
If you are seeing this then your browser doesn't support inline frames.
</iframe>
```

This will create an inline frame 200 pixels high by 200 pixels wide with automatic scrolling.

10. Switch to Normal View. Your page should look something like Figure 16.14.

FIGURE 16.14

Although we have been working in HTML View, Normal View shows us what we have created to date.

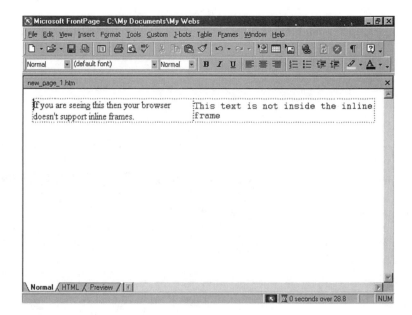

11. Save your page with the name `inline_frame.htm`.

12. Click the Preview in Browser button. If you are using Internet Explorer 4 (or higher) you will see a screen similar to Figure 16.15.

   If you are using any other browser, your display will resemble Figure 16.16. Notice that the text you added is visible—telling visitors that they are missing something on this page.

13. Keep this saved page because you will be working with it again in a few minutes.

FIGURE 16.15

The page you are working on when viewed in a browser that supports inline frames.

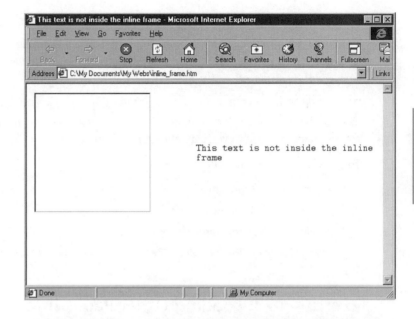

FIGURE 16.16

The same page in a browser that offers no support for the `<iframe>` tag.

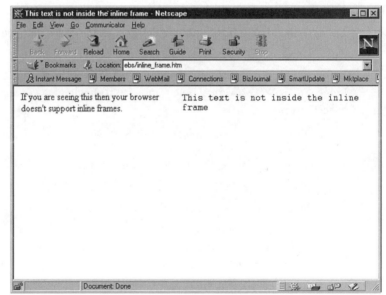

Exercise 16.2: Naming Your Floating Frame

The name you give your floating frame is very important. Naming inline frames is very similar to naming frames. The name you give a frame is used to target where any links in a page will be displayed.

With inline frames, the idea is usually that links in your page will open a specified document within the inline frame. Targeting an inline frame works identically to targeting a normal frame, but before you can target a frame you need to name it.

To name an inline frame, follow these steps:

1. Open `inline_frame.htm`.
2. Switch to HTML View and locate the `<iframe>` tag.
3. Replace the line containing the initial `<iframe>` tag with the following:

   `<iframe width="200" height="200" scrolling="auto" name="myinlineframe">`

4. Save the page.

Exercise 16.3: Loading Other Pages into Your Floating Frame

The contents of your floating frame depends on the pages that you load into them. If you don't specify a source page, you will see a plain window as you did in Figure 16.15.

Before you begin this exercise you will need to create a page to load into your inline frame. You will use a very simple frame, but it should give you a good idea of how the concept works.

Create a new page in your `chapter16` Web. Type the following single line of text.

`This is being displayed in my inline frame.`
Save this page as `inside_frame.htm`. You are now ready for this exercise.

1. Open `inline_frame.htm` and switch to the HTML View.
2. Locate the `<iframe>` tag and replace it with the following.

   `<iframe width="200" height="200" scrolling="auto"`
   `name="myinlineframe""src="inside_frame.htm">`

   The `src` attribute is the source where the page to be displayed within the inline frame comes from. If you named this page differently or want to use another page, simply change the `src` attribute value.

3. Preview the page in Internet Explorer 4 (or higher) and your page should look something like Figure 16.17.

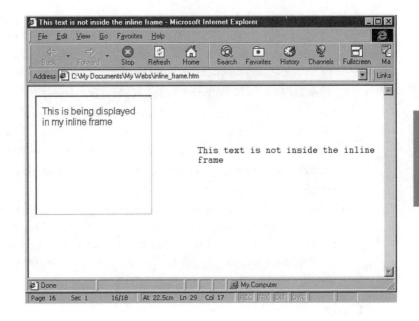

FIGURE 16.17

The text you typed in inside_frame.htm appears inside the framed area of your page.

16

Summary

Now that you are more confident about how the HTML View can be used, try experimenting with it to understand the raw code behind the pages you make.

Start with an existing page you have created and read it in HTML View. Once you are pretty sure that you understand things, you can move on to create a page using just the HTML View. See how do without the benefit of seeing the page immediately. Once you have a page, however basic, use the Reveal Tags option to see your tags in action. Remember that clicking on a tag will show everything it affects.

Use the iframe.htm page you created to see how inline frames can be used effectively. Changing the text you typed in inside_frame.htm will immediately be changed in the browser. Try inserting images into inline frames.

Workshop

Q&A

Q Do I have to know any HTML to take advantage of the HTML View?

A No you don't, but a knowledge of HTML can't hurt. There are just some things that a WYSIWYG editor can't always handle properly, or that arc best done by hand-coding to ensure proper results. FrontPage also has limitations, not because of its design, but because of HTML itself. Understanding a bit about the HTML behind everything can help you understand the limitations and save you from hours of toiling to get something to work that isn't yet possible with the Web.

Q How do I know if my hand-coded HTML is correct?

A Switching from HTML View to Normal View will give you an immediate idea of whether what you are doing is correct. If the page looks how you expect, then carry on. If not, then look again at the code and see if you can spot your mistake.

Q Are the quotes used in HTML tag attributes such as `align="right"` necessary?

A Most current browsers will accept `align="right"` as well as `align=right`. Using quotes around attribute values is the proper way to do things. New technologies are coming, such as XML, that could have problems working with HTML attributes that do not use quotes. In XML, for example, all tag attribute values *must* be surrounded in quotes.

Quiz

1. How do you get rid of reveal tags?
2. How do you get rid of tag colors you may set and not like?
3. Can you see the effects of code added with the HTML component in Normal View?
4. Can you use inline frames with all browsers?

Exercises

Besides the exercises already covered in this chapter you might try the following:

1. Use the HTML component and HTML View to add some text to your Web page and make it bold using `<b>` before the text and `</b>` after.
2. Use the HTML component and HTML View to add an image to your Web page.
3. Use the HTML component and HTML View to add a simple table to your Web page.

When trying each of these, start with the HTML component first to give you an idea of how to position things. Then try using the HTML View. The HTML View will be harder at first because you have to learn to identify parts of your page by the HTML. Look up some HTML tags that you might want to try such as different types of lists and try adding them. Becoming familiar with the HTML View and how to work with HTML can set you apart from other users and help you identify and solve problems when they do occur.

Answers to Quiz

1. Simply go to the View menu and uncheck the Reveal Tags option.

2. The Page Options screen has the HTML source button; click the Reset button to return to the default settings.

3. No. This will not display in Normal View.

4. Definitely not. Currently only IE4 (or higher) supports the use of inline frames.

16

DAY 17

Adding Advanced Web Technologies

Adding Advanced Technologies to Your Web Site

Even with all the capabilities of HTML, DHTML, JavaScript, and the numerous other technologies you've already seen throughout this book, sometimes it just isn't enough. What if you could create a program that could run in a Web page to extend its capabilities? Imagine the possibilities—you could do virtually anything. Luckily for us, this capability does exist in three advanced technologies discussed in this chapter.

As you'll see, each of these technologies is a little different, but each offers certain capabilities to build exciting new features into your Web pages.

This chapter covers

- Plug-ins and what they are
- Using Java applets

- Adding ActiveX to your pages
- Adding scripts to your pages
- Using Design Time Controls

Plug-Ins and What They Are

Browsers can be extended by the use of a technology called plug-ins. I imagine that all of us at one time or another have gone to a site and been told we needed "something else" to see the contents of the page. Common plug-ins include those for Flash Animations and Real Media Players.

In this instance the term plug-in refers to the files required for viewing the page correctly.

Netscape, for example, has hundreds of plug-ins available for download, and they each do a specific task or show a specific program.

Importing a Plug-In into Your Web

Although you can import the plug-in file directly into your Web (usually a library file with the .dll suffix), most companies prefer that you refer your users to their download page to obtain the plug-in. In the case of a Flash Animation, Macromedia actually supplies a button that can act as a link to the download page. Other options include a simple text link saying "download plug-in here." Unlike some advanced technologies, Flash Animations need to be made by the user and are not freely downloadable from the Internet.

Exercise 17.1: Inserting a Plug-In into Your Page

In design terms, the phrase plug-in is slightly misleading. Rather than the viewer application, you are actually referring to the file that needs the plug-in. Inserting a plug-in works indirectly; you insert the file that needs the plug-in and the browser tries to do the rest. For this exercise you will be using the `flower.swf` file on the CD-ROM that accompanies this book. This animation was created for this book by Jan Hart at `www.ariadne-webdesign.co.uk`.

Create a new Web called `chapter17` to use with the exercises in this chapter.

To insert a plug-in into your Web page, perform the following steps:

1. Open FrontPage.
2. Import the `flower.swf` file from the CD-ROM into your `images` directory.
3. Open the page into which you want to insert the plug-in.

4. Give this page a black background.

5. Move your cursor to the position you want your plug-in to appear.

6. From the FrontPage menu, choose Insert, Advanced, Plug-in. The Plug-in Properties dialog box opens, as shown in Figure 17.1.

Figure 17.1

In FrontPage, the insert plug-in option actually means that you plug-in the file.

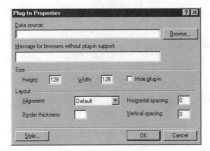

7. The Plug-in Properties dialog box has the following options:

Data Source—This field allows you to browse for the file that you want the plug-in to display, not the plug-in itself—in this case the path and filename to `flower.swf`.

Message for Browsers Without Plug-in Support—Use this field to display a message for browsers that don't support plug-ins. For this exercise, type **To view this page you need the plug-in for Flash.**

Height—This is the height of the plug-in in pixels. Make this 240 pixels.

Width—This is the width of the plug-in in pixels. Make this 340 pixels.

Hide Plug-In—Checking this will hide the plug-in symbol in the FrontPage editor. This is useful if you are using sound files because you won't need to worry about the placement or size of the plug-in on the page. Don't check this option for this exercise.

Alignment—This sets the alignment for the plug-in to determine how other items such as text flow around it. Set this option to Default.

Border Thickness—Determines how thick, in pixels, the border around the plug-in is. Leave this option blank.

Horizontal Spacing—Use this field to create a buffer between your plug-in and any content to the left or right of it. Like height and width, this is also in pixels. Leave this set to 0.

Vertical Spacing—Use this field to create a buffer between your plug-in and any content above or below it. Like height and width, this is also in pixels. Leave this set to 0.

17

8. Once you have chosen your options for the plug-in, your completed dialog box should look like Figure 17.2. Click OK to close the Plug-in Properties dialog box and apply your changes.

The completed Plug-in Properties dialog box.

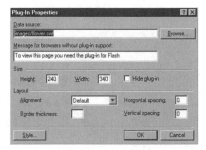

Back in Normal View, the plug-in displays onscreen as an icon (see Figure 17.3). The placement of the icon represents the alignment you selected above, and the handles indicate the area of the animation on the page.

FIGURE 17.3

The plug-in icon and handles represent the amount of space needed for the animation.

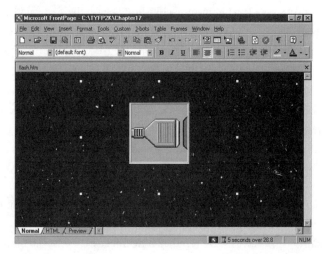

To view the actual animation, you will need to either click on the Preview tab in FrontPage, or save the page as `flash.htm` and use the Preview in Browser option. You access Preview in Browser option is by selecting File, Preview in Browser. Your page should look like Figure 17.4.

Note This assumes you actually have the Macromedia Flash viewer installed.

FIGURE 17.4

The Flash Animation as displayed in your browser window.

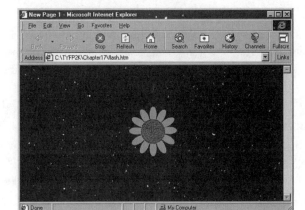

Although you have inserted this animation as a plug-in, Macromedia recommends that you use Aftershock, which is shipped with the Flash program. The software also includes instructions for editing and adding to the raw HTML, to avoid looping and so on.

Using Java Applets

Java applets are used usually to give your pages a little something different. They can be image effects, navigation systems, or simply moving images.

Java applets are very different from JavaScript (which will be covered later in this chapter). An applet is a predesigned piece of code that plugs-in to your page to give the desired effect.

Not all browsers support the use of Java applets, and not all users like the download time added to a page when using them.

Java applets can come in all shapes and sizes. If you have used FrontPage's Hover Button then you have already seen an applet in action. Applets are commonly used to provide scrolling text similar to a marquee, a clock on a Web page, or even a rotating banner ad.

Importing a Java Class File

Java applets are compiled into files that have a .class extension. You can think of the .class file as a program that can only be run from your browser. To use an applet, this file must be available from the user's browser. The .class file doesn't have to be in your Web site; it can be on someone else's, but it is best to rely on files that are only in your Web.

To import a Java .class file, use the File, Import feature to locate and import the .class file into your Web. You may want to create a special directory ahead of time for your .class file. Most users will use a directory called Java to keep all their class files.

Exercise 17.2: Inserting and Configuring a Java Applet

Unfortunately, Java applets can't just be dropped into a Web page. There are a number of features that need to be configured in order for the applet to work properly. Each applet is configured differently because each applet has different needs. You can tell an applet to do things by passing it information in the form of a parameter.

Java applets can be downloaded from many different places on the Internet. The one you will use is called fireworks and was created by and downloaded from Fabio Ciucci at www.anfyjava.com. The files you need for this are located in a folder called fireworks on the accompanying CD-ROM.

To insert an applet into a Web page and configure it, perform the following steps:

1. Open the chapter17 Web if it is not already open.
2. Create a new folder called Java.
3. Locate the fireworks folder on the CD, and import all of the files into the Java directory you just created.
4. Open a new page in the Java folder to insert a Java applet into.
5. Position your cursor in the location you want to display the applet.
6. From the FrontPage menu, choose Insert, Advanced, Java Applet. The Java Applet Properties dialog box opens, as shown in Figure 17.5.
7. The Java Applet Properties dialog box has the following fields:

   Applet Source—This is the name of the Java .class file. You only need to specify the classname file and not the full URL, in this case, firewks.class.

   Applet Base URL—This is the URL to the .class file not including the filename. If your .class file was in a different directory to the page, the base URL would be http://www.mysite.com/Java/ . Because your page is in the same directory, you can leave this blank.

Message for Browsers Without Java Support—Use this field to display a message for any browsers without Java support that view the page. Insert the following text: **You are missing a great Java applet here!!!!**

Applet Parameters—Web pages pass information to an applet through parameters. Each parameter has a name and a value. Each applet has its own parameter names that it will accept, so you will need to read the applet documentation carefully to understand how it works. You can add parameters with the Add button, modify them with the Modify button, or remove them with the Remove button. The firewks.txt file in the fireworks folder has full details of the parameters required for this applet.

Horizontal Spacing—This is the number of pixels that separate the applet from other content to the left or right of it. Leave this set to 0.

Vertical Spacing—This is the number of pixels that separate the applet from other content above or beneath it. Leave this set to 0.

Alignment—This is the alignment of the applet and works identically to the picture alignment Set this to Default.

Height—This is the height of the applet in pixels. Leave this set to 400 for this exercise.

Width—This is the width of the applet in pixels. Set this to 500 for this exercise.

The completed dialog box should look like Figure 17.6.

17

FIGURE 17.5

The Java Applet Properties dialog box looks simple because Java applets get all their information through parameters.

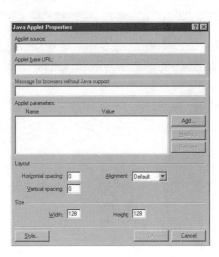

FIGURE 17.6

The completed Java Applets Properties dialog box shows information about size and location, as well as the required parameters.

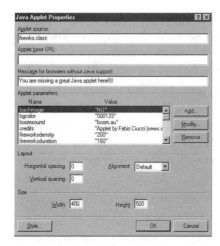

8. Once you have chosen your settings for the applet, click OK to close the Java Applet Properties dialog box.

9. Save this page as `applet.htm`.

Back in Normal View, the plug-in displays onscreen as an icon (see Figure 17.7). The placement of the icon represents the alignment you selected, and the handles indicate the area of the applet on the page.

FIGURE 17.7

The plug-in icon and handles represent the space needed for the applet.

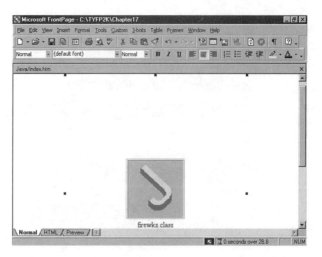

To view the applet in action, you will need to either click on the Preview tab in FrontPage, or save the page as `flash.htm` and use the Preview in Browser option. Your page should look like Figure 17.8.

Note

This assumes you have support for Java applets enabled on your browser.

FIGURE 17.8

The Java applet as displayed in your browser window.

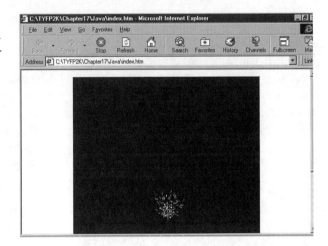

17

You may want to preview your page and verify that the applet behaves properly. Some applets can cause browsers to stall or even crash.

Online Resources for Java Applets

Java has been exploding into both the Web development and programming circles for several years. This explosion has sparked hundreds of Web sites with thousands of applets available for free or to purchase. With all this information, where do you begin? Here are two sites that offer information on Java Applets:

- Sun Microsystems, the creator and backing force behind Java, is always a good place to start. While some of this information may be way too technical, it offers links to other sites that are developing Java applets or have good resources available for Java. You can access Sun's Java Pages at either http://java.sun.com or http://www.javasoft.com.

- If you're looking for Java applets to use in your pages, you can search for them at developer.com's Java Directory. This directory contains thousands of applets grouped into specific categories such as Special Effects and Animation. This site is located at http://www.developer.com.

Adding ActiveX to Your Pages

There is some confusion as to what ActiveX is. Many people compare ActiveX to Java, which is an apples to oranges comparison. Whereas Java is a programming language, ActiveX is a way of programming. ActiveX enables programs to talk to each other. If you're confused at first, don't worry. ActiveX can confuse even veteran programmers.

Programs that are written using the ActiveX standard are usually meant to be used by other programs. Because they are usually used by other programs they are called *ActiveX controls*. You've probably seen an ActiveX control already and didn't even realize it. Most of the boxes, buttons, and lists that you use in programs such as Microsoft Office are ActiveX controls. The reason for this is simple: reuse. You can use the same ActiveX control over and over again in lots of different Web pages and applications. Internet Explorer itself is an ActiveX control that allows developers to put custom Web browsers into their own applications.

Using ActiveX in a Web page comes with a price, however—currently ActiveX controls can only be used by Internet Explorer. In fact, the restrictions of using an ActiveX control in many ways far outweigh the benefits. They are only supported within a Windows environment, are only viewable (except in a few cases) when using current versions of Internet Explorer, and in some cases are seen as a security risk. The best place for using ActiveX controls is within an intranet environment when the Web designer/developer has complete control of the environment in which the control is being used.

Inserting an ActiveX Control

Inserting ActiveX controls is a little different than inserting plug-ins. You can insert the ActiveX control and configure most of the parameters automatically directly from information stored in the control. More experienced users can also configure a control to run from a remote location.

To insert an ActiveX control, follow these steps:

1. Open the page you want to insert an ActiveX control into.

2. Position your cursor in the location you want to display your ActiveX control.

3. From the FrontPage menu, choose Insert, Advanced, ActiveX. The Insert ActiveX Control dialog box opens, as shown in Figure 17.9. Your page options must be set to Internet Explorer Only or Custom with ActiveX enabled.

4. Select an ActiveX control to insert from the list, or choose the Customize button to display a complete list of ActiveX controls (see Figure 17.10).

FIGURE 17.9

The list of ActiveX controls may not contain all the controls available, but only the ones set to be displayed.

FIGURE 17.10

You can customize the list of ActiveX controls by checking all the controls you want to display.

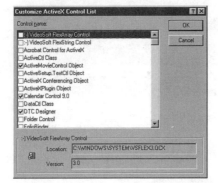

5. Once you have inserted the ActiveX control, right-click on it and select Properties.

6. Each ActiveX control will typically have its own property page in addition to two common property pages—the Object page and the Parameters page.

7. The Object page has the following options, as shown in Figure 17.11.

Name—A name for your ActiveX Control Object. This can be anything as long as it is one word without spaces and is unique for that page.

Alignment—Sets the alignment for the control and works identically to the picture alignment.

Border Thickness—The thickness in pixels of the border to be displayed around the ActiveX control.

Horizontal Spacing—The number of pixels that separate the applet from other content to the left or right of it.

Vertical Spacing—The number of pixels that separate the applet from other content above or beneath it.

Height—This is the height of the applet in pixels.

Width—This is the width of the applet in pixels.

Alternative Representation—This enables you to display a custom message in HTML to be displayed on a browser that does not have ActiveX capabilities.

Code Source—This is the location of the ActiveX control file on a network reachable by users of your Web.

FIGURE 17.11

Most of the options will no doubt seem routine by now, but the few that are new are very important.

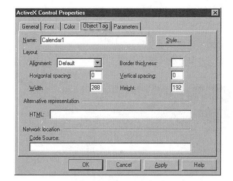

8. The Parameters page allows you to add, modify, and remove parameters to pass to the ActiveX control. Like a Java applet, each ActiveX control uses its own set of parameters and values. Read any documentation you have on an ActiveX control before changing any settings.

9. Once you have chosen your settings, click OK to close the ActiveX Controls Properties dialog box and apply your changes.

Online Resources for ActiveX Controls

Because ActiveX controls can be used by Web browsers and applications alike, they are becoming popular tools for programmers and Web designers. Unfortunately, most of the Web sites available are geared more toward a programmer than a Web developer. Even if you aren't a programmer, there are some pretty cool sites for you to visit.

- *The Microsoft ActiveX site*—If you are a programmer or you're just interested in finding out the details on ActiveX, then visit http://www.microsoft.com/com/activex.asp. This site is rather technical so don't worry if you don't understand anything for a while. ActiveX can take a good bit of time to actually understand how it all works.

- *Microsoft Agent*—Microsoft Agent may be one of the coolest ActiveX controls around. An Agent is a character such as a genie, a robot, or the Office 2000 Assistants. Agents are animated, they can talk, and they can even be voice activated by you. Microsoft Agent is free and can be incorporated into a Web page or program. Just be ready to learn a little bit on how to script it. You can find more about Microsoft Agent at http://msdn.microsoft.com/msagent.

- *ActiveX.com*—This site, sponsored by CNET, is one of the best places to find ActiveX controls to fit your needs. This site lists ActiveX controls by categories, such as Browser Enhancements. To help you find just the right control you can even run a search through their listings to find a control to download and try. You can find the ActiveX.com site at `http://www.activex.com`.

Exercise 17.3: Adding ActiveX Controls to a Web Page

This exercise is almost identical to Exercise 17.1 except you will be using an ActiveX control instead of a plug-in. You may need to install the Flash ActiveX control player before working this example. A copy of the Flash ActiveX control is included on the CD-ROM that accompanies this book. You will also need the `flower.swf` file from the `chapter17` Web on the CD.

1. Open a page to insert the ActiveX control into or create a new page.

2. Click the Center formatting button to move your cursor to the middle of the page. Press the Return key a couple times to bring your cursor more toward the exact middle of the page.

3. From the FrontPage menu, choose Insert, Advanced, ActiveX Control.

4. Choose the ShockWave Flash Object from the list, if available. If it is not available, choose the Customize button to display the full list of ActiveX controls and check the ShockWave Flash Object. You will then be able to select it from the list.

5. Click OK to close the dialog box and apply your changes.

6. Your page should appear blank except for a small area that is now selected. Right-click over this area and choose ActiveX Control Properties. The ActiveX Control Properties dialog box should appear with the Flash Properties tab selected, as shown in Figure 17.12.

FIGURE 17.12

Each ActiveX control has its own unique property page in addition to the normal ActiveX control property pages.

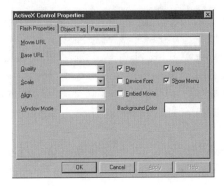

17

7. In the Flash Properties page, enter **images\flower.swf** in the Movie URL field.

8. From the Quality field select AutoHigh to ensure the highest quality playback.

9. Uncheck the looping option so the animation only plays once.

10. Click the Object Tag tab to display the Object page.

11. Set the Height to 240 pixels.

12. Set the Width to 320 pixels.

13. Click OK to close the ActiveX Controls Properties dialog box.

14. Unlike the plug-in and the applet, an ActiveX control will display in normal mode. Your page should now look like Figure 17.13.

15. Save your page as **activex.htm** and use the Preview in Browser option to view your ActiveX control. Your final page should look something like Figure 17.13.

FIGURE 17.13

Your new page should now display your ActiveX Shockwave movie.

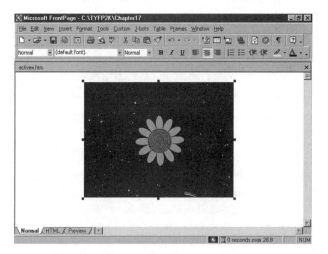

Adding Scripts to Your Pages

Before JavaScript came along, Web pages just sat there. You couldn't move your mouse over a hyperlink and see a message in the status bar and you couldn't do anything interactive that didn't require a plug-in. The Web scripting revolution changed that when JavaScript and VBScript entered the into the browser. Once they appeared a whole new world full of action opened up for the Web.

A scripting language is very similar to a normal programming language except for one major detail—before you can use a normal programming language you have to "compile" it.

Compiling means taking the code that was written and converting it into machine language. Once a program is compiled, it's ready to go. FrontPage, for example, was compiled right before it was placed on CD to be sent to manufacturing. Scripting languages don't have to be compiled; they are run as necessary. When you move your mouse over an image, a script may be referred to that will change the image while the mouse is over it.

There are two choices when it comes to scripting languages, JavaScript and VBScript.

JavaScript, originally named LiveScript, was developed by Netscape to add scripting features to the Navigator browser. Netscape renamed LiveScript to JavaScript after Sun released the Java programming language. Despite the similarity in name, they are two very different languages. JavaScript works well in both Navigator and Internet Explorer, but you might run into minor differences.

VBScript is based on the popular Visual Basic programming language. It is easy to learn and use, and is a powerful scripting language. Some development tools, such as Visual C++, even let you script common tasks with VBScript. Currently, VBScript is limited to Internet Explorer, although plug-ins to allow VBScript to be used for Navigator are available for purchase.

17

 Note

Although as stated here JavaScript is the more widely compatible language, it is always worth checking that *any* script you run will work in the browser you choose. VBScript is only supported in Internet Explorer, but there are still issues surrounding both JavaScript and JScript as well.

Setting the Default Scripting Language

FrontPage 2000 can be configured to write either JavaScript or VBScript. JavaScript is recommended because it works in the widest variety of browsers; VBScript is currently limited to Internet Explorer only.

To set the default scripting language for your Web, perform the following steps:

1. Open the chapter17 Web you want to set the default scripting language for.

2. From the FrontPage menu, choose Tools, Web Settings. This opens the Web Settings dialog box.

3. Select the Advanced tab to display the Advanced settings page, as shown in Figure 17.14.

FIGURE 17.14

FrontPage allows you to choose the default scripting language for your Web.

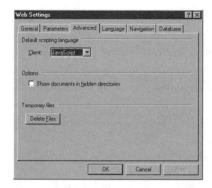

4. The Default Scripting Language section has a drop-down list called Client. This list sets the default browser scripting language to JavaScript, VBScript, or none.

5. When you have chosen the default scripting language, click OK to close the dialog box and save your changes.

Using JavaScript

JavaScript can be used in a Web for everything from animation to applications. JavaScript is now widely supported and can be viewed in almost every browser.

Note

In Tools, Page Options, the Compatibility tab allows you to select the targeted browser for your Web. If you target your Web for compatibility with Microsoft Web TV in the Browsers drop down list, JavaScript will be disabled by default.

To enable or disable JavaScript, follow these steps:

1. Select Tools, Page Options and then click on the Compatibility tab.

2. To enable or JavaScript, select the JavaScript check box; to disable JavaScript, clear this check box.

Using VBScript

Microsoft VBScript can be used in your Web for everything from forms to database queries. However, some Web browsers still don't support VBScript, so pages containing VBScript may not display or may produce errors when visited by people using those browsers.

As previously mentioned, FrontPage 2000 allows you to create your Web for compatibility with specific browsers and technologies.

You can have VBScript enabled or disabled, but even if you have VBScript enabled, targeting your Web for browsers without support for it will lead to the commands for inserting or using VBScript being grayed out.

To enable or disable VBScript, follow these steps:

1. Select Tools, Page Options and then click on the Compatibility tab.
2. To enable or disable VBScript, select or clear the VBScript check box.

The Microsoft Script Editor

The Microsoft Script editor can be used for writing either JavaScript or VBScript in your Web pages. To locate the Microsoft Script editor, select Tools, Macros, Microsoft Script Editor.

Note

If you target your Web for compatibility with Netscape Navigator Only, Both Internet Explorer and Navigator, or Microsoft Web TV in the Browsers box, VBScript is automatically disabled by default. Although you can override this setting, it will most likely lead to errors on your pages.

The Visual Basic Editor

You can use the Visual Basic Editor from within FrontPage 2000 to create macros, applications, controls, and forms for your Web. This obviously requires a prior knowledge of scripting, but means that you can create Webs and change their structure within a programming environment. For example, you could use the Visual Basic Editor to create a new folder and then convert that folder to a Web. To get to the Visual Basic Editor, select Tools, Macros and then click Visual Basic Editor.

You can also use the Microsoft Script editor to write VBScript the same way you use it to write JavaScript.

Using Design Time Controls

This section covers Design Time Controls because FrontPage 2000 has the facility to insert them into a Web page. Unfortunately, as a new feature in FrontPage 2000, the software does not ship with any examples. Therefore, until such time as you have located and downloaded at least one DTC, the Insert, Advanced, Design Time Control option will be grayed out.

17

The information that follows is for general purposes, assuming that in time Design Time Controls will be freely downloadable for you to add to your pages.

A Design Time Control (DTC) is a special kind of control because your users will never know it is there. Design Time Controls are like ActiveX controls because they run when the Web page they are in is called. When the Web page is requested, the DTC is the first thing to run. Its output is then placed into the page itself.

Design Time Controls are meant to extend FrontPage from third-party companies. A typical job for a DTC would be to generate a chart for real-time results of a user poll or a picture based on text that is entered into a form.

DTCs are relatively new so there aren't a lot of them available yet, but there will be in the near future. DTCs were originally introduced with FrontPage's cousin, Visual Interdev 1.0. Because they were introduced with Visual Interdev many companies will focus on their capability to extend Visual Interdev over FrontPage. If you find a DTC that you like but it was designed for Visual Interdev, you may want to ask whether it also supports FrontPage 2000.

Adding and Configuring Design Time Controls

Design Time Controls are very similar to ActiveX controls. As a matter of fact, the Object Tag and Parameters pages for an ActiveX control are identical to those used by DTCs. Like ActiveX controls, each DTC will have it's own unique property page.

To insert a Design Time Control into your page, perform the following steps:

1. Open a page to insert the Design Time Control into or create a new page.
2. Click the Center formatting button to move your cursor to the middle of the page. Press the Return key a couple times to bring your cursor more toward the exact middle of the page.
3. From the FrontPage menu, choose Insert, Advanced, Design Time Control.

Most controls have their own special image that will be displayed in the page so you can identify one DTC from another.

Showing Design Time Controls

As already mentioned, Design Time Controls when inserted display their own image to indicate which DTC you are using. This image can take up a lot of space, so FrontPage 2000 offers the facility to remove the image and simply display one line of text containing the name of the DTC. This clears the area to enable you to finish the design of your page as normal. To show or hide the DTC image, Select Insert, Advanced, Show Design Time Controls.

Summary

Locating and using Plug-Ins and applets for your site can be a fun way to enhance your learning.

Remember that every ActiveX control or Applet will ship with it's own parameters, which you will have to configure to make it work.

Searching the Internet is far and away the best source of add-ins for your Webs. Try to locate some new ones rather than just seeing something on someone else's site and trying to use it.

Think carefully about whether adding these things into your site will be an improvement for visitors or whether they will simply be bells and whistles that perform no function.

If you have a company or business site, make sure that the features will be visible to your visitors. Using fancy features is definitely a bad idea if no one (or hardly anyone) will see them.

Think carefully about the additional download time that may be required for people to view your pages.

If you use applets, animations, and so on and they play a part in the navigation of your site, make sure that people will be able to get to your pages if they don't have the required support.

Workshop

Q&A

Q Why don't I see any Design Time Controls in FrontPage?

A FrontPage doesn't come with any special DTCs. You might see some depending on whether any other products are also loaded onto your computer, such as Microsoft Visual Interdev or Microsoft Site Server Tools. Most DTCs are developed by third-party software vendors as additions to Microsoft development products like Visual Interdev and FrontPage.

Q Will my VBScript work in all browsers?

A No. There are still quite a few browsers that don't offer support for VBScript. If you have selected compatibility options, don't try to override them.

Q Can I download Flash Movies/Animations?

A There may be a few sources on the Internet where this can be done, but on the whole, Flash Animations are not freely available.

Q Why can't I just add an applet to my page?

A Applets all come with their own instructions; you must read these carefully and make sure that you upload the .class files to the correct directory.

Quiz

1. How do you give instructions to an applet?
2. Of the three advanced features that can be inserted into a Web page (ActiveX, Java, or plug-in) which one works in all browsers?
3. Where were Design Time Controls first introduced?
4. Will JavaScript be supported in all browsers?
5. How do you make an ActiveX control you downloaded visible in the ActiveX control list?

Exercises

1. Practice inserting plug-ins and Java applets. Make sure that you read the instructions carefully when using Java applets. Any mistake in the parameter instructions can lead to the applet not working at all.
2. Try changing the size and alignment settings for the plug-ins, and see what effect it may have. Making something bigger can result in distortion, whereas making it smaller can make it too small to bother with.
3. Locating Design Time Controls compatible with FrontPage 2000 may be difficult for a while, but see if you can, and then configure one for use on your pages. Remember that the parameter and object tags will appear very similar to those you have already practiced with.

Answers to Quiz

1. Applets receive instructions through parameters consisting of a name, such as color, and a value, such as blue.
2. Java is the best feature to use because it is supported in all but the oldest versions of Microsoft Internet Explorer and Netscape Navigator.
3. Design Time Controls were first introduced in Visual Interdev 1.0, and are brand new to FrontPage 2000.
4. Almost. Nearly every browser offers support for JavaScript (but not Web TV, currently).
5. To see a newly downloaded ActiveX control, use the Customize button to add it to the selectable list.

DAY **18**

Building and Editing Forms

Forms are used all over the Internet. They are the simplest and quickest means of gathering information from your site visitors, and unlike email you can control the type and format of the information visitors send you. From simply asking for someone's email address to a complete life history, a form can gather the information you require in a matter of minutes.

In today's lesson, you will learn

- How to create a form using the Form Page Wizard
- How to add form fields
- How to create validation rules for form fields
- How to create a confirmation page
- How to rename form fields
- How to edit form fields

What Is a Form?

A form is a collection of fields that you use for gathering information from visitors to your Web site. Visitors fill out a form by typing text, clicking radio buttons and check boxes, and selecting options from drop-down lists. After filling out the form, site visitors submit the data they entered. The steps in creating a form include

- Deciding what kind of information to collect, and then starting a form
- Adding fields to the form
- Setting data entry rules for your form fields
- Setting up how you want to handle the information you collect from the form
- Setting up a confirmation page

The first step is to decide what kind of form you want to create, and what kind of information you want to gather with it. Forms have a variety of uses, such as:

- Gathering contact information about your visitors
- Collecting order or billing information
- Getting feedback about the quality and content of your site

After you decide what kind of form you want to create, you can either start with a blank form and add to it, or you can use a template or wizard to create the form for you. FrontPage makes creating forms easy using supplied templates, which can be customized for your own needs.

In the following exercise, you will create a form to collect information about people visiting your Web site—who they are, where they are, what they think about the site, as well as the date and time of their visit.

 Note

> Forms created using the FrontPage templates need to be published to a Web server with the FrontPage extensions installed to function correctly.

Exercise 18.1: Creating a Form Using the Form Page Wizard

To create a form using the Form Page Wizard, follow these steps:

1. Create a new empty FrontPage Web called Chapter18.
2. Choose File, New, Page and select the Form Page Wizard. The Form Page Wizard appears, as shown in Figure 18.1.

FIGURE 18.1

The Form Page Wizard guides you through the steps to create a form.

3. To start entering information for your form fields, click the Next button to bring up the screen shown in Figure 18.2.

FIGURE 18.2

Step 2 of the Form Page Wizard allows you to add new questions to your form or modify existing ones.

18

4. Here you can add questions for your visitors to answer when they visit your Web site (you can also edit questions on an existing form). Click the Add button shown in Figure 18.2 to see the selection of categories for the form fields, as shown in Figure 18.3.

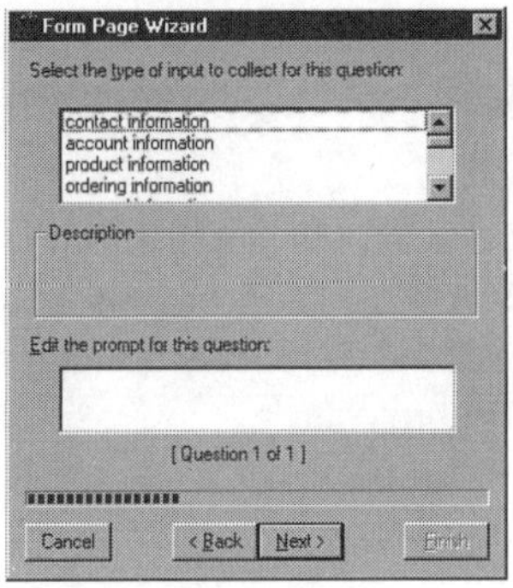

FIGURE 18.3

FrontPage offers a choice of categories for your form questions.

The available categories are

- *Contact Information*—Generates fields for information such as the user's name and phone number.

- *Account Information*—Generates fields for a user's username and password. This is often used in conjunction with the user Registration form, which we'll discuss on Day 19, "Handling Forms with FrontPage Components."

- *Product Information*—The fields generated ask the user for product name, model, serial number, and other useful product information.

- *Ordering Information*—Prompts the user for the products they want to purchase as well as billing and shipping information.

- *Personal Information*—Similar to the Contact Information, but prompts the user for more personal information such as age, height, and gender.

- *One of Several Options*—Generates a drop-down list, radio buttons, or a list of several options from which the user is to choose only one.

- *Any of Several Options*—Produces a list of choices from which the user can select multiple options.

- *Boolean*—Generates a check box or radio buttons for yes/no or true/false questions.

- *Date*—Generates a formatted text box for a date field in mm/dd/yy, dd/mm/yy, or free format.

- *Time*—Generates a formatted text box for a time field in hh:mm:ss in am/pm, military time, or a free format.

- *Range*—Generates a ranged response from 1 to 5, bad to good, and disagree strongly to agree strongly. Can be formatted to use radio buttons or a drop-down list.

- *Number*—Generates a text box that will only accept numeric input.

- *String*—Generates a text box that can accept any alphanumeric values and can have a limited length.

- *Paragraph*—Generates a text area that allows for any information the visitor wishes to write.

5. Select the Contact Information option in the top half of the box, and in the bottom half edit the default text to read `Let us know how we can get in touch with you`, and then click Next. You will see the screen in Figure 18.4, where you can select which information you want to collect.

FIGURE 18.4

Having chosen to receive contact information, you can now be more specific in the information visitors need to supply.

Leave the default selections for this exercise and then click Next to continue.

Note

It is worth mentioning that many people are still wary of giving personal information over the Internet unless it is really necessary, so avoid asking for home addresses and phone numbers where possible.

Figure 18.5 shows that your question now appears as number 1 in the list.

FIGURE 18.5

Your question immediately appears as number 1 in the list.

18

6. Click the Add button to return to the category listing, and use the scrollbar to select the Date option.

7. In the lower half of the screen, change the question to `Please let me know today's date:`. Click the Next button to bring up the screen shown in Figure 18.6.

FIGURE 18.6

There are three possi-ble date formats to choose from when asking visitors to fill in a date field.

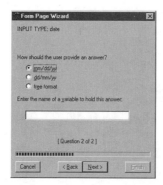

Here you can select the format for your visitors to enter the date. Remember that people in different parts of the world write the date in different ways. Commonly in the U.S. it will mm/dd/yy, whereas in the UK it will be dd/mm/yy. The free for-mat option allows visitors to type the date however they want.

8. Select the mm/dd/yy option. In the lower part of the screen, you are prompted to give a name for the variable to hold this information. Type the word **date** and then click Next to continue.

9. There are now two questions listed for your form. Click on Add to return to the category listing and then select the Time option.

10. Change the question in the lower part of the screen to read **Please let me know the time in your part of the world:** and click Next to see the screen shown in Figure 18.7.

FIGURE 18.7

You can choose from one of three time for-mats for your visitors to use.

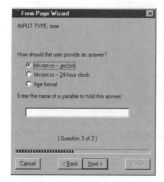

This is where you select the format for visitors to enter the time. Again, there are three choices. You can choose from a standard 12-hour am/pm option, a 24-hour clock option, or you can allow visitors to type the date in their own way.

11. Select the hh:mm:ss option and in the lower half of the screen type the word **time** as the name for the variable. Click Next to continue. You will now see three questions listed. Click Add to see the category listing and select one of several options. Change the question to read **Where in the world are you?** and click Next to see the screen in Figure 18.8.

FIGURE 18.8

Insert a list of choices for your visitor to pick from and the type of list they will see.

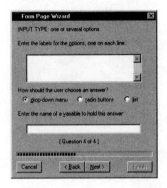

12. This screen presents you with the opportunity to name the choices the visitor will have, as well as how they will make their selection from the choices offered. In the top half of the screen, type the following choices (one on each line):

    USA

    Canada

    Europe

    Africa

    India

    Asia

    Australia

13. In the next section, choose how the visitor will make their selection from your list. The three possibilities are a drop-down menu, radio buttons, or from a list. Select the drop-down Menu option. In the lower part of the screen, type **where** as the name for the variable. Click Next to continue.

    You will now have four questions showing in your list. These appear in the same order as in Figure 18.9. You have now all of the questions for your form.

18

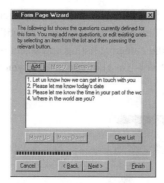

FIGURE 18.9

All four of the questions you have added appear in the list in the order you created them.

14. Click Next to continue. The screen, as shown in Figure 18.10, allows you to select the formatting for your completed form page.

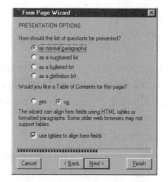

FIGURE 18.10

FrontPage allows you to choose from four presentation options for your form.

The options on this screen allow you to decide the layout of the questions on your page. The options for layout are self-explanatory and use formatting terms already covered in this book. If you create a form to collect specific answers to a list of questions, it is a good idea to present the questions as a numbered list. This makes it easier for the visitor to follow.

15. The questions we are asking are quite general and are therefore best formatted as normal paragraphs. To do this, select the Normal Paragraphs option.

16. The Table of Contents option, if selected, generates a TOC at the top of the form page. This is a useful feature when dealing with large forms, but is not necessary for a small form like the one you are creating. Leave this option set to No (which is the default).

The last option on this screen determines the HTML layout of the finished page. By default the form will be formatted using tables. You can, however, select to use formatted paragraphs instead. If you suspect your Web site will have a high proportion of visitors using older browser versions that don't offer support for tables, then it is best to deselect the tables option.

17. You will use tables for your form, so leave the Align Using Tables option selected and click Next to continue. You will then see the screen shown in Figure 18.11.

FIGURE **18.11**

Choose how you want the results of your form to be saved.

This is where you will choose how the results of your form are saved. The first option saves the results to a Web page of your choice, the second option is to have the results saved to a text file, or you can use a custom cgi script. The best option for you will depend on the type of service your ISP has given you. Many ISPs will tell you what form types you can and cannot use, so it is best to check with them. Tomorrow's lesson covers form handlers in detail.

18. For this exercise you will be saving the results to a text file. Select the Save Results to a Text File option. Front Page will name this text file `formrslt.txt` by default, and there is no need to change this.

19. Click Next to continue and you will see that FrontPage now has enough information to generate your Form Page.

Figure 18.12 confirms this fact, and asks you to click Finish to see your form page. Click Finish and FrontPage generates the form for you.

Your finished form page should look like Figure 18.13.

18

FIGURE 18.12

You have now supplied all of the information needed by FrontPage to create your form.

FIGURE 18.13

The finished form.

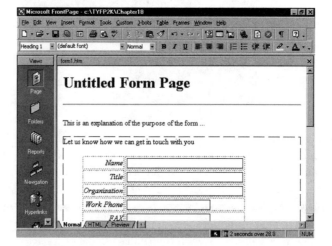

Congratulations! You have now made your own form page.

Save this page as form1.htm and give it the title **My First Form Page**.

Now that you have your form page, you can start to customize it, and look in more detail at how some of the components in it work.

The following sections discuss form fields and how you can use them to customize your form.

Types of Form Fields

There are quite a few different types of form fields. Some of them you may never use, whereas some will appear in every form you make. Each type of form field has a slightly different look and purpose.

What Is a Form Field?

Form fields are the individual fields on a form that are used to gather information.

Anywhere a visitor can type information, make a selection, or choose an answer is a form field. Your form uses the following types of form fields:

- *Text Boxes*—For the visitor to type his or her name and so on
- *Drop-down Menu*—For the visitor to select his or her location.
- *Buttons*—For the visitor to submit the form when complete or to reset the form if he or she makes a mistake.

Each type of field operates a little differently, so choose the fields for your forms depending on the way you want site visitors to enter information.

There are six very common types of form fields, which are discussed in the following sections.

One-Line Text Box

Use one-line text boxes to collect a small amount of text, such as a name, email address, or a phone number. Figure 18.14 shows the Name, Title, Organization, and other fields, which are just some of the one-line text boxes used to create your form.

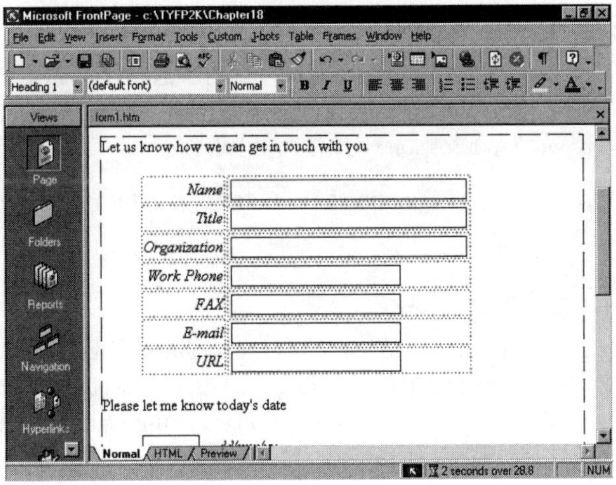

18

FIGURE 18.14

A selection of one-line text boxes from your form.

Radio Button

Use radio buttons when you want the site visitor to select only one option from a group. Although you didn't use radio buttons in your form, you have probably seen them many times. Radio buttons usually come in sets and offer the visitor a set of choices to select from. Figure 18.15 shows a set of radio buttons allowing a selection of a, b, or c.

FIGURE 18.15

A set of radio buttons labeled a, b and c.

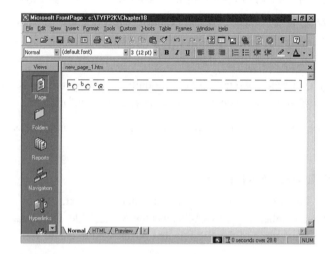

Drop-Down Menu

Use a drop-down menu to offer the site visitor a list of choices. This field is similar to using a group of radio buttons, but it takes less space on your form. You can configure a drop-down menu to allow one or multiple selections.

Figure 18.16 shows the drop-down menu from your form inviting visitors to tell you their location.

Scrolling Text Box

Use scrolling text boxes to collect one or more lines of text, such as a visitor's comments about your Web site. This field scrolls as required to accommodate varying amounts of text. Figure 18.17 shows a scrolling text box inviting visitors to leave their comments.

FIGURE 18.16

The Location drop-down menu from your form.

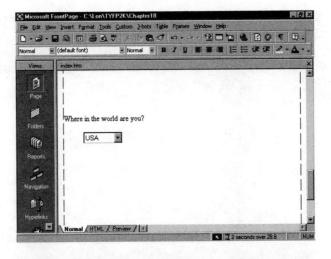

FIGURE 18.16

The Location drop-down menu from your form.

FIGURE 18.17

A scrolling text box allows visitors to leave their own comments.

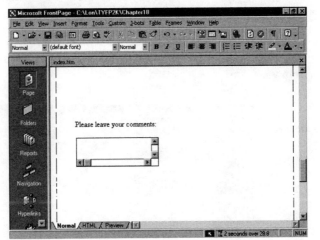

FIGURE 18.17

A scrolling text box allows visitors to leave their own comments.

18

Check Box

Use check boxes for optional items. These are often used on sites offering to send updates to a visitor as shown in Figure 18.18. The site visitor can select or clear the check box. Visitors can also select multiple items or no items at all.

FIGURE 18.18

FIGURE 18.18

A check box can be used to let people choose whether or not they want to be informed of site updates.

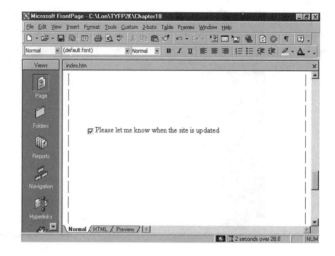

Push Button

Use push buttons to let site visitors submit the form after filling it out, clear fields by resetting the form, or run your custom scripts. Figure 18.19 shows the submit and reset buttons from your form.

FIGURE 18.19

Your form has submit and reset buttons to either send the information or clear the form in case of input errors.

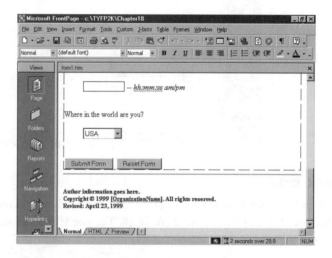

That's all of the common types of form fields. Now you can customize the way your form page looks and see what is going on behind the scenes. Your form looks simple enough onscreen, but it is actually quite a complex utility.

The page as created by the wizard is very boring to look at. As the only page in a new Web it probably has no theme, and has plain black text on a white background. Editing these properties of a form page is the same as editing any other page.

You can add a theme to the page in the normal way using the Format, Theme command. I have selected the tidepool theme for my sample form page, (the tidepool theme is one of the additional themes that can be installed from the CD-ROM that accompanies this book) but you can select any theme of your choice.

You can edit the text on the page the same way as any other type of page.

Change the Phrase Untitled Normal Page to read `Who are you? What's the time?`

The page is looking friendlier already. A bit of color and a welcoming title has made a huge difference.

The next line on the form page should be edited to give an introduction to the purpose of the form. Change this to read `It's always nice to know who is visiting and what time they called in. Please fill in the details below and then click on submit`.

Your Form Page should now look something like Figure 18.20, depending on the theme you have selected.

18

FIGURE 18.20

A little color and friendly text makes a huge difference to even a simple form.

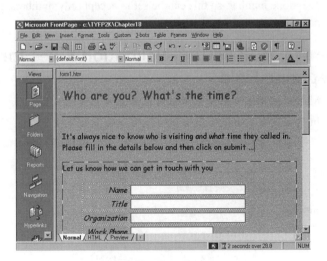

Validating Form Fields

The next step in creating a usable form is to set rules for entering data into your form fields. These data entry rules, also called *validation rules*, ensure that a site visitor fills out the form correctly. For example, you could set up an order form for your products, but unless the customer's name, address, and payment information are correctly entered, you would be unable to complete and process the order.

Text Box Validation

You can specify the type of data to allow and set other criteria for one-line and scrolling text boxes. For example, to collect a credit card number, set up a one-line text box to accept only numbers and hyphens, and disallow all other characters. You can also require a fixed number of characters so that a site visitor does not omit a number by mistake.

To set data entry rules for a text box, you can specify the following:

- The type of data to allow (text, integers, or numbers) and the format
- Whether an entry in the field is required
- The minimum and maximum length for the entry
- Conditions for the data—for example, on your form you request the visitor's work telephone number, so this can be set to accept only numbers, spaces, hyphens, and parentheses

Exercise 18.2: Setting Validation Rules for the Work Telephone Field

1. Make sure the form you created is open.
2. In Page View, double-click the text box called Work Phone. The Text Box Properties dialog box shown in Figure 18.21 appears.

FIGURE 18.21

The Text Box Properties dialog box.

3. Click Validate to see the Text Box Validation dialog box shown in Figure 18.22.

FIGURE 18.22

The Text Box Validation dialog box.

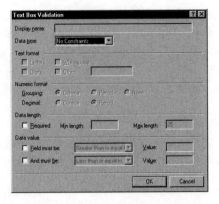

4. In the Data Type list, click the type of data to allow in the field, for example, Number.

5. If you limit the data to Text, select the types of characters to allow in the field—Letters, Digits, White space (spaces, tabs, carriage returns, and line feeds), or Other (different characters such as commas and hyphens). If you select Other, type the characters in the box.

6. If you limit the data to Integer or Number, specify the character to allow for grouping. You can disallow any punctuation, allow periods to group numbers as in 123.456.789, or allow commas to group numbers as in 123,456,789.

7. If you limit the data to Number, specify the character to use for decimal points. You cannot use the same character for both Grouping and Decimal.

8. To require that a site visitor type an entry in the Data Length text box field, select Required.

9. To specify the minimum number of characters to allow in the text box, type a value in the Min Length box. Phone numbers usually have at least six numbers, so this could be used as a minimum.

10. To specify the maximum number of characters to allow in the text box, type a value in the Max Length box. Remember that phone numbers can contain many numbers including international, national, and area codes as well as the basic number, so don't be too restrictive. I would suggest leaving this blank.

11. To specify a value constraint, such as requiring the value in the field to be greater than 10, select Field Must Be, and then click the condition from the corresponding list. In the Value box, type the value for the constraint. To specify a second constraint, select And Must Be, then specify a condition and value. This is not appropriate for a phone number field so it can be ignored here.

18

12. In the Display Name box, type **WorkPhone** to identify the text box for the visitor. This name is displayed to the visitor in a message if they submit the form and do not meet the requirements you have set for the text box. For example, the site visitor would see "Please enter a value for the *WorkPhone* field."

13. Click OK twice to get back to the normal FrontPage screen.

Radio Button Validation

You can require a selection to be made from a group of radio buttons. For example, a form could have two radio buttons, Yes and No. If a site visitor tries to submit the form without making a selection, a message is displayed.

Follow these steps:

1. In Page View, double-click a radio button in the group for which you want to set a rule.

2. Click Validate.

3. To require the site visitor to select one of the radio buttons, select Data Required.

4. In the Display Name box, type a name to identify the radio button group for the site visitor. This name is displayed to the visitor in a message if the visitor submits the form without selecting a radio button from that group. This helps the visitor identify which field(s) they need to go back to and complete.

Drop-Down Menu Validation

You can require a visitor to make a choice from a drop-down menu, set the minimum and maximum number of choices to allow, and disallow the first choice from being selected (for example, disallow the first item from being selected if it is an instruction, such as "Select an item").

The following are options you have for setting data entry rules for a drop-down menu:

- You can set validation rules for the way you want site visitors to enter data in a drop-down menu.

- You can make sure that site visitors make a selection. If a selection is not made and a site visitor tries to submit the form, a message is displayed.

- If the drop-down menu allows multiple selections, you can specify a minimum and maximum number of selections to allow.

Exercise 18.3: Editing and Adding a Validation Rule to the Drop-Down Menu in Your Form

First you will add a top option that says **select the nearest area**:

1. In Page View, double-click the Drop-down Menu form field asking for the visitors to tell you their location. The Drop-Down Menu Properties dialog box appears, as shown in Figure 18.23. The top (USA) option is set to be selected by default.

FIGURE 18.23

The Drop-Down Menu Properties dialog box.

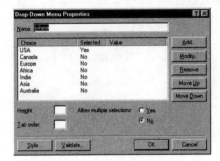

2. Click Add.

3. In the Add Choice dialog box, type **select the nearest area** and leave the initial value set to not selected.

4. Click OK to return to the main properties dialog box.

5. The new choice now appears at the bottom of the list. To move it to the top of the list, click on it to select it, and then click the Move Up button until it appears at the top of the list, as shown in Figure 18.24.

FIGURE 18.24

The addition you have just made now appears at the top of the list.

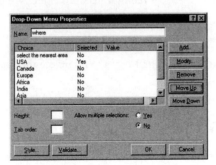

Now change the initial state of the USA option to not selected. To do this:

6. Open the properties box for the drop-down menu if it is not still open.

18

7. Click on the USA option to select it.

8. Click Modify to see the Modify Choice dialog box shown in Figure 18.25.

FIGURE 18.25

You can change the properties of any of your options in the Modify Choice dialog box.

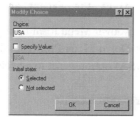

9. Click Not Selected and then click OK to return to the properties dialog box.

Now add a validation rule to disallow the first selection:

1. Click Validate to open Drop-Down Menu Validation box.

2. Select Data Required to ensure that the site visitor makes a selection from this drop-down list.

3. To restrict a site visitor from selecting the first choice in the drop-down menu, select Disallow First Item.

4. In the Display Name box, type `location`. This name is displayed in a message if the visitor submits the form and does not meet the requirements you have set for the drop-down menu. For example, the site visitor would see "Please enter a value for the *Location* field".

5. Click OK twice to return to the normal page view.

6. You will be prompted to enter an integer in the Height field. Enter the number 1. This field controls how many of the options are visible without clicking the drop-down arrow.

7. Save the page to save all the changes you have made.

When tested, your form will now prompt users to complete the fields for which you have added validation rules.

Advanced Form Features

Now that you have seen a basic form and how to edit some of the components in it, we can now move on to some of the more advanced features of forms and how they can enhance the way your forms work and look.

Renaming Form Fields

Every form field has a unique name to distinguish itself from every other field in the form. FrontPage will automatically assign names to the form fields, such as T1 for the first text box in the form or D1 for the first drop-down menu in the form. Additional text boxes will be labeled T2, T3, T4, and so on. The same applies for all other form fields. While it's nice that FrontPage does this for you, it leaves a little bit to be desired when it comes to reading the data entered by the user, so you may want to change the names to something more helpful.

To change the name of a form field:

1. Open the Form Field dialog box by double-clicking on the field whose name you want to change. It doesn't matter which type of form field you are clicking on (with the exception of pictures, which we will look at in a minute); the double-click will open the properties box for it.

2. Type the new name for the form field in the Name text box, making sure that the name doesn't conflict with any other form fields.

Buttons

There are three types of standard buttons, a "normal" button, a "submit" button, and a "reset" button. The submit button is used to send the information that has been entered in the form to the form handler on the Web server. The reset button will simply return all the form fields to their default values, erasing any user input without sending it to the Web server.

The normal button is different from the submit and reset buttons in that it doesn't automatically do anything.

Normal buttons are used mainly when developers are using client-side scripting with JavaScript or VBScript. A good example of scripting a normal button is a mortgage calculator. Since the formulae used to calculate a mortgage payment are well known, they can easily be scripted into a Web page. In this case, the normal button would be used to call the script function that calculates the user's mortgage payment.

Form Handlers

A form handler is vital to any form that is created for use on the Internet. Simply put, it is a script or executable file that sits on the Web server and processes the form information passed from the browser. The FrontPage Server Extensions already have a built-in form handler that doesn't require any additional setup. If your Web site will be hosted on

18

a server that does not support the FrontPage Server Extensions, you will need to look at some other types of form handlers. Different types of Form Handlers are covered fully on Day 19.

Picture Form Fields

The picture form field allows you to use a picture of your choice to submit a form instead of the default grey button. A nice example of this could be to use an image of a magnifying glass to submit a search on a page.

To insert a picture into your form, perform the following steps:

1. Open the form you created in Exercise 18.1.
2. Place your cursor where you want the picture to be.
3. From the FrontPage menu choose Insert, Form, Picture. The Picture dialog box shown in Figure 18.26 appears.

FIGURE 18.26

The Picture dialog box.

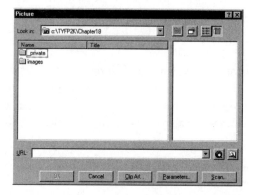

Inserting a picture as a form field is exactly the same as inserting an image into a page.

4. Move to the location of the image to insert and select the image. Click the OK button to insert the picture.
5. Right-click on the inserted picture and choose Form Field Properties. The Picture Properties dialog box shown in Figure 18.27 appears.

Note   Do not double-click on the image to get the properties—this will open your default image editor if you have one installed, or an error message if you don't.

18

Figure 18.27

The Picture Properties dialog box.

6. All the picture property tabs are identical to those found on the image property tabs with one exception, the Form Field tab. Use the Name field to assign a name to the picture. You could name it anything from "Submit" to "Send Comments."

   If you name the button "Submit," it can then be used in place of the default grey button created by the wizard.

7. Click OK to close the Picture Properties dialog box.

Hidden Fields

To include information in the form results that you do not want site visitors to see, you can add hidden fields to your form.

Each hidden field has a name and a value. When the form is submitted, the names and values of the hidden fields are included in the form results, along with the names and values from the visible form fields.

For example, if you have several different forms that use the same custom form handler, you could use a hidden field to identify each form by using a unique name or number.

Note

The default confirmation page displays hidden fields and their values. If you do not want the site visitor to see this information, create a custom confirmation page as described in the following section.

To add a hidden field called to your form, follow these steps:

1. In Page View, right-click the form, and then click Form Properties on the shortcut menu.

2. Click Advanced.

3. Click Add. This will open the Name/Value Pair dialog box shown in Figure 18.28.

FIGURE **18.28**

*The Name/Value pair
dialog box opens as
soon as you click Add.*

4. In the Name box, type **Form1**.

5. In the Value box, type the value to associate with the field. (The value can be any text.) Type **WebFormOne**.

6. Click OK three times to return to the normal page view.

7. Save the page with the latest changes.

Confirmation Pages

A confirmation page is a Web page that the visitor sees in the Web browser after successfully completing and submitting your form. FrontPage creates a default confirmation page, which doing the job, but it lacks style and personality. It is better to create your own confirmation page, and there are two ways of doing this:

1. Select File, New, Page, Confirmation Form to create the FrontPage default confirmation page.

2. Create a custom confirmation page.

With a confirmation page, you can display the contents of form fields. The site visitor can confirm that the information was entered correctly and, if necessary, can return to the form and fill it out again. You can also personalize the confirmation page; for example, if you request the site visitor's name in your form, you can display it on the confirmation page.

Make a written note of the form fields you want to confirm before starting this. You cannot swap between screens during the following process.

To create a custom confirmation page, follow these steps:

1. In Page View, click the New Page button.

2. On the page, type the text you want to display after a site visitor has submitted the form.

Then, to display information back to the visitor from a form field:

3. Place the cursor where you want to display the visitor's name.

4. On the Insert menu, point to Component, and then click Confirmation Field.

5. In the Name of Form Field to Confirm box, type the exact name of the field from which to display information (**Contact_FullName**), and then click OK.

   The name of the field is displayed in brackets on the form, as shown in Figure 18.29. When the confirmation form is displayed to the site visitor, this field will display the site visitor's entry instead.

6. Repeat these steps for each field you want to display.

7. Click Save.

8. Type the URL and the page title, and then click Save.

FIGURE 18.29

The form field name is displayed in brackets in the editor screen.

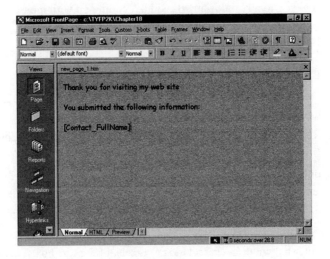

Finally, to assign the confirmation page to your form:

1. Open the page containing your form by double-clicking the file in the Folder List.

2. Right-click the form, and then click Form Properties on the shortcut menu.

3. Click Options, and then click the Confirmation Page tab.

4. In the URL of Confirmation Page box, type the name and location of the confirmation page you just created, or click Browse to locate it.

18

Exercise 18.4: Reinforcing the Learning

This exercise is designed to reinforce the commands you have already looked at and to clarify any points that need further explanation. These points will be covered again on Day 19 when we look at form handlers and the different types of form wizards. The following explains in depth about the most common form fields and how to use them. Use the workshop time to add them to a blank page and see how to use them without the benefit of FrontPage doing all of the work for you. In the Chapter18 Web, select File, New, Page or click on the New Page icon.

You will be presented with a blank Web page (or one with the theme from the current Web, if applied.)

Don't worry that this isn't a form page. If any form field is inserted on an area of a page that isn't in a form, FrontPage will automatically create a form complete with submit and reset buttons and put the new form field inside. While experimenting, you may want to insert a blank form by choosing Insert, Form, Form from the FrontPage menu. This will allow you to add fields at will without ending up with multiple forms cluttering up your page.

To add a one-line text box, follow these steps:

1. Place your cursor where you want the text box to be.

2. From the FrontPage menu, choose Insert, Form, One-Line Text Box. This will insert a one-line text box where your cursor is.

3. Right-click the one-line text box and select Form Field Properties to open the Text Box Properties dialog box.

4. In the Name field, enter a name for this field that will describe the information you are gathering.

5. In the Initial Value field, enter any text that you would like to appear in the box before the user starts typing.

6. Enter the width in characters, not pixels, of the text box. This does not set a maximum length for what the user can type in the text box, only how wide the box is. If you set your width to 40, any extra characters will simply cause the text box to scroll sideways. The default value is 20 characters wide.

7. If this text box will be accepting a user's password, select the Yes radio button in the Password field to cause anything the user types into the box to appear as an asterisk (*). By default, the Password field is set to No.

8. When you are done editing, click OK to close the Text Box dialog box.

When naming a form field, don't use spaces in the field names because they can cause errors. Web designers usually will give a form field a descriptive name that combines two or more words, such as TheTime. The use of capital letters helps make reading the name easier.

Editing Scrolling Text Boxes

A scrolling text box is very similar to a one-line text box, except that it can be several rows high. To insert a scrolling text box, perform the following steps:

1. Place your cursor where you want the scrolling text box to be.

2. From the FrontPage menu, choose Insert, Form, Scrolling Text Box. This will insert a scrolling text box where your cursor is.

3. Right-click on the text box and choose Form Field Properties. The Text Box Properties dialog box used for scrolling text boxes appears.

4. In the Name field, enter a name for this field that describes the information you are gathering.

5. In the Initial Value field, enter any text that you would like to appear in the box before the user starts typing. For example, "Please complete our form".

6. Enter the width in characters, not pixels, of the text box. This does not set a maximum length for what the user can type in the text box, only how wide the box is. Depending on the browser, your user's comments may wrap to the next line, or begin scrolling sideways when they enter more characters than specified in your width. The default value is 20 characters wide.

7. Use the Number of Lines field to control how many rows high your scrolling text box will be. The more user input you are expecting, the higher your box should be to give visitors the largest working space possible. By default, the number of lines is set to the minimum height of two.

8. When you are done editing, click OK.

Editing Check Boxes

Check boxes are useful when you have a very simple yes/no or true/false question. Check boxes are often used when many selections can be made, such as "Check all television shows you watch" or "Check your favorite items for sale here."

To insert a check box, perform the following steps:

1. Place your cursor where you want the check box to be.

2. From the FrontPage menu, choose Insert, Form, Check Box. This will insert a check box where your cursor is.

3. Right-click on the check box and choose Form Field Properties. The Check Box Properties dialog box appears.

4. In the Name field, enter something that helps describe the question you are asking. Since check box answers are a simple yes or no, it is very important to create a meaningful name.

5. In the Value field, enter text that will appear as the answer in the results. For the favorite items for sale example, you would probably just use a value of "True" or "Yes" for each check box.

6. Use the Initial State field to decide whether the box is checked by default. Many Web sites will have some check boxes already checked that often say "I would like more information," or "I do not want to be put on your mailing lists."

7. Once you have finished editing the check box, click OK to close the Check Box Properties dialog box.

Editing Radio Buttons

Radio buttons are used when a question requires the user to select only one answer from two or more available. To insert a radio button, perform the following steps:

1. Place your cursor where you want the radio button to be.

2. From the FrontPage menu, choose Insert, Form, Radio Button.

3. Right-click on the radio button and choose Form Field Properties. This opens the Radio Button Properties dialog box.

4. Use the Group Name field to control which group of radio buttons this button will be a part of.

5. In the Value field, define what information the form saves if this button is checked.

6. The Initial State will make this radio button Selected or Not Selected when the user first views the page. Make sure that there is only one button in the group that is selected, otherwise errors could occur in your form (FrontPage will not warn you when this occurs).

7. Once you have finished editing the radio button, click OK to close the Radio Button Properties dialog box.

Once you have added your first radio button in a group, it might be easiest to simply copy and paste it however many times you will need it; then you only have to edit the value of each radio button.

Editing Drop-Down Menus

We used a drop-down menu in form1.htm and looked at some of the ways to customize it. The following steps will enable you to add a drop-down menu and edit the properties to suit your needs:

1. Place your cursor where you want the drop-down menu to be.
2. From the FrontPage menu choose Insert, Form, Drop-Down Menu. This will insert a drop-down menu where your cursor is.
3. Right-click on the drop-down menu and choose Form Field Properties. The Drop-Down Menu Properties dialog box appears.
4. Use the Name field to enter a descriptive name for the menu.

To add your first choice to the drop-down menu, perform the following steps:

1. Click the Add button. The Add Choice dialog box appears.
2. Use the Choice field to enter a phrase or sentence that describes the choice.
3. Check the Specify Value check box to enable you to enter a value for the menu item that is different from the Choice field.
4. The Initial State field sets the menu item as Selected or Not Selected. Only one menu item can be selected in a drop-down menu.
5. Click OK to close the Add Choice dialog box and return to the Drop-Down Menu Properties dialog box.
6. Repeat steps 1 through 5 to add additional questions.
7. Once you have finished editing the drop-down menu, click OK to close the dialog box.

Contrary to what most people think of a drop-down menu box, you can set the Height field so it appears as a scrollable list instead of a drop-down menu. Any height value greater than 1 will create a scrolling list. The Height and the Allow Multiple Selections will cause the list to appear differently.

A drop-down menu can be set to allow multiple selections by selecting the Yes or No radio buttons. For a normal drop-down menu of Height 1, the Allow Multiple Selections field should be set to No because it is difficult to choose multiple items in a short box. Likewise, the Height should be set to greater than 2 (usually around 5) if Allow Multiple Selections is set to Yes.

18

To move a menu item up or down the list, perform the following steps:

1. If the Drop-Down Menu Properties dialog box is not already open, right-click on the drop-down menu and select Form Field Properties.
2. Click on the menu item you want to move in order to select it.
3. Click the Move Up button to move the menu item further up the list or click on the Move Down button to move the menu item further down the list.
4. When finished, click OK to close the Drop-Down Menu Properties dialog box.

To modify a menu item, perform the following steps:

1. If the Drop-Down Menu Properties dialog box is not already open, right-click on the drop-down menu and select Form Field Properties.
2. Click on the menu item you want to modify in order to select it.
3. Click the Modify button. The Modify Choice dialog box appears. The Modify Choice dialog box is identical to the Add Choice dialog box.
4. When finished, click OK to close the Drop-Down Menu Properties dialog box.

To remove a menu item from the list, perform the following steps:

1. If the Drop-Down Menu Properties dialog box is not already open, right-click on the drop-down menu and select Form Field Properties.
2. Click on the menu item you want to remove in order to select it.
3. Click the Remove button and the menu item will be removed from the list.
4. When finished, click OK to close the Drop-Down Menu Properties dialog box.

Summary

On Day 19, you will learn about form fields in more detail, but more specifically, you will learn about form handlers, what they do, and how they work. A detailed explanation of the FrontPage extensions will be included not just in reference to forms, but also all of the components that FrontPage generates automatically.

Workshop

Q&A

Q Will my form work without FrontPage extensions?

A No. Because FrontPage uses its own form handler, you can only use FrontPage generated forms on a FrontPage-enabled server unless you are using a custom form handler.

Q **I want my form results emailed to me—can I have them saved to a text file as well?**

A Yes, simply leave the .txt filename in the dialog box after configuring the form to send results by email, and you will get an email and an entry in the .txt file.

Q **I want to add a hidden field to my form. Will this show in the confirmation page?**

A Yes, unless you create a custom confirmation page. The default confirmation page will show the results of all fields.

Quiz

1. How do you change and edit the properties of a form field?

2. What are the most common types of form fields?

3. What happens if you add a form field into a normal page?

4. Can you select more than one radio button at a time?

Exercises

1. Look at the different form-related wizards and see if any of them will fit your needs. Add a feedback form to your site to let visitors tell you what they think. Remember that you can format a forms page in the same way as a normal HTML page with themes, backgrounds, and so on.

2. Experiment with adding form fields to a blank page. See how the different fields look and act within your pages. Notice what happens when you add a form field into a non-forms page.

3. Create a form from scratch to add into your Web. Rather than use a wizard, just insert the form fields that you want to use.

Answers to Quiz

1. Either double-click the form field to launch the Form Field Properties dialog box, or right-click and select Form Field Properties from the menu.

2. Radio buttons, text boxes, scrolling text boxes, check boxes, drop-down menus, and submit/reset buttons are the most common types of form fields.

3. Adding a form field into a normal page causes FrontPage to add a form into the page. This is indicated by the presence of dashed lines around the form.

4. No. Radio buttons allow only a single selection.

18

DAY 19

Handling Forms with FrontPage Components

In the last lesson, you made a form for visitors to tell you where they are in the world and what the current time is. That's the easy bit. You make the form, a visitor fills it in, and you get the results. Simple, really.

Well, not that simple unfortunately. Every form on the Internet needs something else to make it work, and that something is a *form handler*. A form handler is a program or script that sits on a Web server and quite literally "handles" the information for the Web server.

Whenever a form is submitted, the Web server sends it to a form handler to be processed. Form handlers are different from normal programs and scripts because they use the Common Gateway Interface (CGI) to get and return information. A normal program uses a mouse or keyboard to send information to the computer and a monitor or printer to send some information back to the user. A Web server uses CGI to format your form results so they can be passed to a form handler. When the form handler receives this information, it can do anything with the information, such as save it to a file, perform some calculations on it, and even return it to a Web page with some special information based on what was entered in the form.

Today you will learn

- How to use FrontPage form handlers
- How to use and configure the Save Results component
- How to use the Registration component
- How to use and configure the Discussion component
- How to save form results
- How to create and configure confirmation pages
- How to create and configure validation pages
- How to test forms

Using FrontPage Form Handlers

FrontPage comes with its own set of form handlers built in to the FrontPage server extensions, which are pieces of script that automate many procedures and make it possible for even novice users to create forms, use databases, and have a search facility on their Web sites.

We'll cover the server extensions as well as their uses and drawbacks at the end of this chapter. For now we'll look at them only in reference to forms.

 Note

> It's vital that you understand that for a FrontPage form to work, your finished Web site must reside on a server that fully supports the FrontPage extensions. Even if you have a Web server on your local machine and can test forms and other FrontPage components on your hard drive, unless your ISP (or WPP—Web Presence Provider) offers support for FrontPage, your forms will *not* work.

FrontPage server extensions are available free of charge to ISPs and WPPs. Microsoft keeps a worldwide list of companies offering support for FrontPage extensions on its FrontPage Web site (`http://www.microsoft.com/frontpage`). If you're not certain whether you have this support from your ISP, either check the list or call your ISP directly before attempting to use the FrontPage form handler.

FrontPage comes with several of the most common types of form handlers used on the Web. Each form handler has its own special purpose. The different types include the Save Results Form component, the Registration component, the Search component, and the Discussion Web. As long as you have FrontPage support for your Web site, you won't have to do anything else to make your forms work. The following sections look at the different types of form handlers in detail.

The Save Results Component

The Save Results component is the workhorse of all form handlers. It's the most widely used form handler of all. It lets you capture the information your users enter into your forms and saves this information to text files, HTML files, or a database. It can even email the results to you. If you just want to ask some questions of your users, this is the form component for you. This is the type of form handler associated with the form created on Day 18, "Building and Editing Forms." The visitor fills in the form, and the results are then "saved" and sent back to you.

The Registration Component

The Registration component (also known as the *User Registration Page*) lets you get a rough idea of who is using your site by asking users to create usernames for themselves before entering your Web. It even keeps track of the users throughout their visits, which is great when you're using discussion forms. For example, you might want to make sure that people who post to a discussion are who they say they are.

The Discussion Component

The Discussion component allows you to create what is known as a *threaded discussion* to a new or existing Web. A threaded discussion means that users can post comments and questions, and other users can reply. The replies are listed under the original post, thus creating a thread. The Discussion Component Wizard allows you to decide how the pages it generates should look, whether you want a table of contents, and whether you want the discussion to be searchable.

19

Where You Can Store Form Results

A form can save your results to a file or a database, or it can send them directly to an email address. Wherever the Web server stores your form results, it must be someplace that the Web server can always reach. This limits the locations to which you can save a file or database. It must be the Web server itself or a computer permanently attached to the Web server through a network. You should never tell a form to save results to your hard drive, for example.

Storing Results on Your Web Site

Storing your form results as part of your Web site makes the results easily accessible to you. To view the results of a form that saves to your Web, you have to open the Web that exists on the server, not your local copy.

FrontPage will usually try to save your form results to a directory named _private. The underscore in front of the word *private* means that this is a "hidden" directory. Hidden directories aren't listed with normal directories, which keeps them relatively hidden. Hidden is very different from *restricted*—the files are still accessible by everyone, but they need to know the *exact* name of the directory and file. Because FrontPage uses _private by default, and many thousands of people use FrontPage, you would be well advised to create a new hidden directory to prevent people from snooping around for your form results. FrontPage uses default filenames as well, making it quite simple for other FrontPage users to guess where your results are kept. To view hidden files, you need to check the Show Documents in Hidden Directories check box found on the Advanced tab of the Web Settings dialog box.

Storing Text and HTML Results

All the data in the world won't do you any good if you can't read it easily. As the following list shows, the Save Results component gives you a number of options when it comes to saving the information from your form. Some of these options are designed with the user in mind, making it easier to read the results when they come in and some are designed to be read by a database such as Microsoft Access 2000.

- Formatted text within HTML
- Formatted text
- Text database using a comma as a separator
- Text database using a tab as a separator
- Text database using a space as a separator

Saving the form results as a text database can help you if you're going to import your results into a Microsoft Excel spreadsheet or an Access database. Before you choose which text database format to use, check to see which type of delimiter your application can handle. Some applications may only be able to import text databases that use a comma as a separator, whereas others might use a tab. Finding this out beforehand can save you a lot of trouble later on.

Exercise 19.1: Deciding Where and How to Save Your Form Results

To specify where and how to save your form results, perform the following steps:

1. Open the page form1.htm you created on Day 18 and right-click to see the Form Properties dialog box, as shown in Figure 19.1.

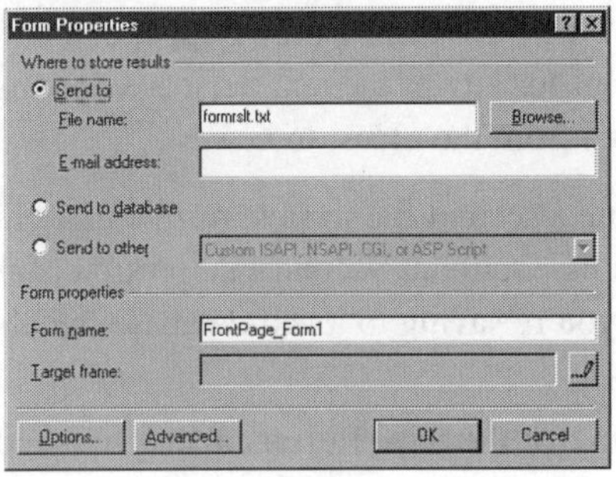

FIGURE 19.1

The Form Properties dialog box is the place to set up the form handler.

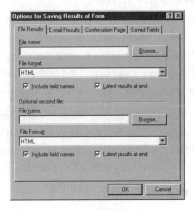

2. Click the Options button to open the Options for Saving Results of Form dialog box, as shown in Figure 19.2.

FIGURE 19.2

There are a variety of options for the Save Results component.

19

3. Select the File Results tab if it's not already selected.

4. In the upper section of the File Results page, you can set the following options:

   - *File Name*—This field contains the path to the form results file. By default, FrontPage creates a file called formrslt.txt located in the _private directory of your Web. You can choose another file by clicking the Browse button or typing in a filename of your own choosing, in which case FrontPage will create the file for you.

- *File Format*—From this list, you can choose the file format for your form results file. The option Text Database Using Comma as a Separator is selected by default. The full list of file formats is listed in Table 19.1.
- *Include Field Names*—Toggling this field on allows the form handler to save the field names alongside the results. This can help you quickly identify information such as name, email address, and comments.
- *Latest Results at End*—Determines whether the form results are inserted into the beginning of the form results file or appended onto the end of it. This box will be grayed out for any of the text database options because databases prefer to import data from the oldest to newest.

5. You may want to create a second file to save results in a different format. If so, change the settings in the Optional Second File portion of the Save Results dialog box. This is useful if you're saving to a text database but also want a second file that's more readable.

6. Click the OK button to exit the Save Results dialog box and return to the Form Properties dialog box.

7. Click OK to exit the Form Properties dialog box.

Sending Results Through Email

In addition to sending the results of your form to a file, you can also configure a form to send the results to you through email. This feature is great when you need to be notified immediately when someone fills out a form. This is especially useful for customer service and support forms as well as product inquiries and orders. Configuring email has two parts—configuring the form and configuring the server extensions.

Before you get too exited with the idea of sending form results through email, first find out whether your ISP or WPP supports this feature. Depending on how its service is set up, you might not find all the features you want; therefore, you should ask questions first before wasting time and energy on something that will never work.

Choosing to Save Results to Email

Setting a form handler to email a copy of a form's results can save you the time of having to check the form results file every so often to see if anyone has posted to it. We'll use Form1.htm again for this example, but the same rules apply regardless of the form.

Exercise 19.2: Sending a Copy of the Form by Email

To send a copy of your form by email, perform the following steps:

1. Right-click anywhere within the form box and select Form Properties from the list to open the Form Properties dialog box, shown previously in Figure 19.1.

2. In the E-Mail Address field, enter the email address to which you want to send a copy of the form results.

3. You can click the OK button to close the Form Properties dialog box or click the Options button to open the Options for Saving Results of Form dialog box, shown previously in Figure 19.2.

4. Select the E-Mail Results tab, as shown in Figure 19.3.

FIGURE 19.3

When you email your form results, you can specify the email address to send them to. The other options allow you to select a reply address and subject line.

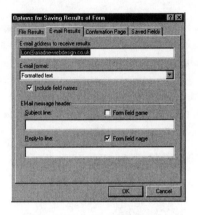

5. In the E-mail Address to Receive Form Results field, enter the email address that you want to receive a copy of the form results.

6. The E-mail Format drop-down list allows you to format the email you receive with the same options as a form results file.

7. Select Include Field Names to send the field names along with the field results.

8. The Subject Line field allows you to enter your own message to use as the subject for the email sent by the form. By default, the email subject will be "Form Results." This is helpful when you want to identify the emails from your form quickly and easily. You can also use the results from a form field by checking the Form Field Name check box and entering the form field name whose data you want send in the Subject Line field.

9. The Reply-to Line field can be used to specify the From line of an email. If your form requests a user's email address, you can specify the From line to be the user's email address by entering in the field name from your form that prompts the user for his or her email address. In the case of the form1.htm example, the field name would be "Contact_Email".

10. Click OK to close the Options for Saving Results of Form dialog box.

11. Click OK to close the Form Properties dialog box.

19

> **Note**
>
> If you're creating this Web on a machine that doesn't have a server or doesn't support FrontPage extensions, you'll be informed at this point that the email function is not configured. If you know your ISP will support the feature when the Web is published, this can safely be ignored.

Configuring Your Mail Server

In order to send a copy of your form results by email, the FrontPage server extensions must be configured with some basic information. Configuring the server extensions for email must be done on the Web server hosting the site. If you're publishing your site to a Web hosted by your ISP, your ISP will need to set this feature up for you. The following instructions will configure a local machine to handle email but have no bearing on the ISP's setup. If you're not running a local Web server or only intend to use the email facility via an ISP, you can ignore the following steps.

To configure the FrontPage server extensions on a Windows NT machine, perform the following steps:

1. Open the FrontPage Server Extensions Administrator utility.
2. Right-click the name of the Web server or virtual server and select Properties. Click the Settings button. The Email Settings dialog box will open, as shown in Figure 19.4.

FIGURE 19.4

The Web server's properties page allows you to set up your local machine to handle email, but you must still get your ISP to configure the remote server for online email results.

3. The Email Settings dialog box has the following options:
   - *Web Server's Mail Address*—The email address that will appear in the From line of the email.
   - *Contact Address*—The email address of the contact person for the Web site. This is used by the server extensions to display a contact email address when certain FrontPage components fail.

- *SMTP Mail Address*—The name of the SMTP server the email messages will be routed through. Ask your ISP or host what the address of the SMTP server is. Usually this is in the form of `mail.someserver.com`.

- *Mail Encoding*—Sets the encoding scheme for emails. The default value is 8-bit encoding, but you can change this if you need to support different email clients. The default encoding should be fine for almost every email client.

- *Character Set*—The character set that the email will be sent in. Each character set listed in the drop-down menu corresponds to a different language.

4. When you've completed setting your email options, click OK to return to the properties page.

5. Click OK to close the properties page and then exit the FrontPage Server Extensions Administrator.

Sending Results to a Database

FrontPage 2000 makes it easier than ever to save your form results directly to a database. Database design is an entire topic in itself, and there are many books already on the subject. FrontPage can actually create the database for you, which is what the following instructions are for, although they can easily be used to connect to an existing database. If you let FrontPage create your database, you'll see that your folders view has added an database file with an `.mdb` extension.

Note

You'll again need to contact your ISP before using this option. Not all ISPs (or WPPs) offer support for databases as a standard service. It may be offered as an additional (paid) service, or it might not be offered at all. All pages that utilize the database option will need to be renamed with an `.asp` extension (FrontPage will prompt you to do this at the appropriate time).

19

Exercise 19.3: Sending the Form Results to a Database

To save the results of your form to a database, perform the following steps:

1. If it's not already open, open `form1.htm`.

2. Position your cursor anywhere in the form area and then right-click and select Form Properties. This will open the Form Properties dialog box.

3. In the Where to Store Results section, select the Send to Database option.

4. Click the Options button. The Options for Saving Results to Database dialog box will open, as shown in Figure 19.5.

FIGURE 19.5

Aside from the Connection section, configuring your form to save to a database is almost identical to saving to a text file.

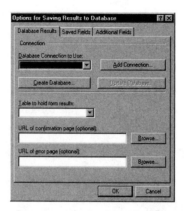

5. The top half of the page is for choosing database connections.

- *Database Connection to Use*—This drop-down menu lists all the database connections already available. If you haven't created a database connection, use the Add Connection feature.

- *Add Connection*—This button launches the Database Web Settings page. This page allows you to create new database connections to file databases, system databases, network databases, or custom connections.

- *Create Database*—This button creates an Access database. The database will contain a column for each of the fields in your form.

- *Update Database*—If you modify your database and add new fields, the Update Database button can be used to make sure the new fields are also added to your database.

6. Click the Create Database button to create an Access database. This process may take a few minutes depending on the size of your form.

7. The Table to Hold Results In drop-down menu lists all the tables available in the database. Newly created databases will have only one table named Results.

Databases store their information in *tables*. A table consists of columns and rows, much like an Excel spreadsheet. Each column is a separate form field, and each row is a specific record. When you save your results to a database, one row is created, and the values from your form fields are stored in their appropriate columns.

You can easily set a confirmation page or error page for your form in FrontPage 2000. Follow these steps:

1. You can specify a confirmation page for your form by entering the path to the page in the URL of Confirmation Page field, or you can use the Browse button to locate the confirmation page you want to use.

2. You can specify an error page for your form by entering the path to the page in the URL of Error Page field, or you can use the Browse button to locate the error page you want to use.

3. Once you've set the properties on the Database Connection page, click the tab labeled Saved Fields to determine which form fields to save.

4. The Saved Fields page, shown in Figure 19.6, allows you to determine which fields are saved to your database. By default, all the fields in your form are selected. You can remove fields from the list by selecting the field and clicking the Remove button.

FIGURE 19.6

The Saved Fields page allows you to choose which fields you want to save. By default, all fields are selected.

5. If there are any form fields that don't appear in your current list (for example, if you remove a field and then later realize that you actually wanted to save it), choose the Add button to display the Add Field dialog box, shown in Figure 19.7. This dialog box lets you pick which form field to save and the name of the field in the database to save it to.

FIGURE 19.7

The Add Field dialog box allows you to pick a field to add as well as which database field to store it in.

6. In addition to adding and removing fields from the list of fields to be saved, you can specify which database field the form fields are saved to. When FrontPage makes an Access database, it names the fields in the database exactly the same as those in your form. You may have to modify each of the form's fields so that they're saved to the proper database field.

19

Again, this is a good reason why you shouldn't use spaces in form field names. Although Access supports spaces in field names, the ASP code that's created when you use a database in FrontPage might struggle with them.

7. When you've selected all the form fields to save to the database, choose the Additional Fields tab. The Additional Fields page is displayed (see Figure 19.8).

FIGURE 19.8

As well as saving the fields from your form, FrontPage allows you to save additional information from the visitor's Web server.

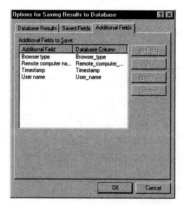

8. The Additional Fields page looks very similar to the Saved Fields page, except the fields listed come from the Web server. The most useful field, in most cases, is the Browser Type option. This enables you to keep an eye on the type of software your visitors are using when they come to your site. This information can be a huge help in designing and maintaining a site that's accessible to all your visitors.

9. When you select the Database option and click OK to exit back to the form, you're prompted to rename the page to the ASP format. This indicates that the page uses Active Server Pages technology, which is explained in more detail later.

Sending Results to a Custom Script

Don't let the term *custom script* mislead you—often there's very little that's custom about the script. The term *custom script* is loosely used to describe any form handler that's provided for a particular task, such as saving a form's results or creating a threaded discussion. When FrontPage refers to a custom script, it means any script that isn't part of the FrontPage server extensions.

All custom scripts use special methods to talk to the Web server. You already learned about CGI, but there are other popular custom script programming techniques such as

ISAPI, NSAPI, and ASP. These are briefly explained in this section, but they're all subjects for study in their own right. To create your own scripts using these technologies, you'll need programming skills.

ISAPI stands for the *Internet Standard Application Programming Interface*. ISAPI was developed by Microsoft as a way to write applications for use with its Web servers, but ISAPI has been adopted by other Web server manufacturers as well. ISAPI applications are usually created in a language such as C or C++ and cannot be modified unless you have access to the source code and a compiler.

NSAPI stands for *Netscape Server Application Programming Interface*. NSAPI was developed by Netscape as a way to write applications for its Web servers. Like ISAPI, NSAPI has also been adopted by other Web server manufacturers and is usually programmed in C or C++.

Active Server Pages (ASP) was developed by Microsoft for use on version 3.0 and higher Web servers. ASP allows you to mix scripting code and HTML on the same page, making it much easier and faster to develop custom scripts. ASP is usually programmed in VBScript or JScript, but it can be extended to use other scripting languages such as PerlScript. ASP is also the extension used for pages that involve database connectivity.

If you need to use a custom script, you should definitely talk to your ISP or hosting service. Most ISPs have a very strict policy regarding form handlers. Many ISPs have their own form handlers, which are the only ones acceptable to them. These are usually provided free of charge and come with some technical support about setting them up on your site.

If your ISP or hosting service allows you to use a custom form handler, you'll still need some technical knowledge. You can't simply download a handler and assume it will work in your setting: You'll need to know the specifics of the ISP's Web server. You'll definitely want to know what their operating system is, because a form handler written in the C programming language and compiled on Windows NT won't run on UNIX. There are many other "clashes" like this, so find out as much as you can before attempting to use a custom form handler.

These days, even the free ISPs offer some support for forms, so unless you want to engage in quite a learning curve, you'd be well advised to see what they offer first.

If you still want to attempt this yourself, the first step should be to ask your ISP or hosting server about supporting Perl. Perl is one of the most common scripting languages, and scripts written in Perl can be run on any Web server that has a Perl interpreter installed. Most UNIX servers have Perl interpreters built in to them, but Windows NT will need one installed. Therefore, you should always ask your ISP whether it supports

19

this language, and, if not, whether it's prepared to offer support. As well as being able to run on many different platforms, Perl has literally thousands of free scripts available on the Web.

Here are some of the most popular CGI and Perl sources:

- Matt's script archive at www.worldwidemart.com/scripts/
- The CGI Resource Index at http://www.cgi-resources.com/
- The Yahoo! CGI index at http://dir.yahoo.com/Computers_and_Internet/ Internet/World_Wide_Web/CGI___Common_Gateway_Interface/

It's entirely possible that you'll have to try a few scripts before you get one that meets your needs. Also, many of them need to be modified to fit your requirements, field names, and so on. The sites that offer free scripts usually have instructions accompanying them, but you'll need to be prepared for quite a bit of work as well as trial and error.

To configure a FrontPage form to use a custom form handler, open form1.htm and then follow these steps:

1. Right-click anywhere inside the form box and select the form properties to bring up the Form Properties dialog box.

2. Click the Send to Other radio button and select CGI, ISAPI, NSAPI, or ASP Script from the drop-down list.

3. Click the Options button to open the Options for Custom Form Handler dialog box, as shown in Figure 19.9.

FIGURE 19.9

A form made with FrontPage can also be set up to use a custom script or form handler.

4. In the Action field, enter the absolute URL of the form page. An absolute URL is the entire URL from the server name all the way to the form handler. If your form handler is named myform.cgi located in the cgi-bin directory of your Web and your server is named www.myserver.com, your absolute URL might look like this:

   http://www.myserver.com/cgi-bin/myform.cgi

5. Choose the POST or GET method from the Method field, depending on which your form supports. With POST, the results are sent directly to the form, whereas with

GET, the results are passed to the form by adding them onto the end of the URL, like so:

```
http://www.myserver.com/cgi-bin/myform.cgi?field1=somevalue
```

6. Use the Encoding Type option only if your form requires a special encoding scheme. By default, FrontPage uses the standard application/x-www-form-urlencoded scheme.

7. Click OK to close the Custom Form Handler dialog box.

8. Click OK to close the Form Properties dialog box.

After you set up your form to use a custom form handler, you may want to try it a few times to make sure it works. If you're testing it locally and it works fine, don't just publish it to your hosting server and forget about it; instead, give it a few tries to make sure it works.

Configuring Confirmation Page Options

A *confirmation page* is a special page used to let users know that the form they just put their information into actually did something. A confirmation page can also return the results of a field or fields from a form page.

Using Confirmation Pages

We looked at confirmation options a little bit in Chapter 18. Now it's time to look at them in more detail. A confirmation page is a great page to use for displaying a message such as "Thank you for your comments" or "Your request will be dealt with in the near future." The confirmation page is just like any other page, but before you can have your form link to a confirmation page, you need to make one first.

Exercise 19.4: Using a Confirmation Page

To begin, open form1.htm. To configure your form to use a confirmation page, perform the following steps:

1. Right-click anywhere on your form and select Form Properties to open the Form Properties dialog box.

2. Click the Options button to open the Options for Saving Results of Form dialog box.

3. If you're saving the results to a file, select the Confirmation Page tab, as shown in Figure 19.10. In the URL of Confirmation Page field, enter the path to the confirmation page created on Day 18 or use the Browse button to locate this file.

19

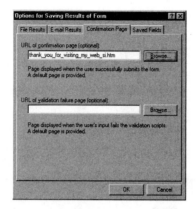

FIGURE 19.10

*Browse to the confir-
mation page you
created in Chapter 18.*

4. If you're saving your results to a database, click the Option button to open the
   Options for Saving Results to Database dialog box. In the URL of Confirmation
   Page field, enter the path to the file or use the Browse button to locate the file.

5. Once you've selected the confirmation page location, click the OK button to close
   the dialog box.

Adding Confirmation Fields to a Page

If you want to let a user know what he or she entered into the form, you can add *confirmation fields* to the confirmation page. These fields simply return the results that were
sent by the user when the form was submitted. You can use this to personalize the confirmation page by printing the user's name, or you can use it to list all the information submitted for the user to verify or print out.

To add a confirmation field to your confirmation page, perform the following steps:

1. Open your confirmation page and place your cursor where you want the confirmation field to be.

2. From the FrontPage menu bar, choose Insert,Component, Confirmation Field. This
   will open the Confirmation Field Properties dialog box.

3. Enter the name of the form field you want to appear on your confirmation page.
   Click OK when finished.

Using Validation Failure Pages

FrontPage will normally use a client-side script to validate form results, but it can be set
up to report errors to a different page, much like a confirmation page is used to report

success. There's nothing fancy with a validation page—it simply lets you tell your viewers that they encountered an error. If you want, you can also use confirmation fields in a validation page; however, the validation page has no way of knowing which field caused an error. To use a validation page for a form, you must turn off the client-side scripting option for your Web.

To configure your form to use a validation error page, perform the following steps:

1. Open the Web that has the form you want to use a validation failure page for.

2. From the FrontPage menu bar, choose Tools, Web Settings.

3. Click the Advanced tab to display the Advanced options page.

4. From the Client field of the Default Scripting Language section, choose <None> to use no scripting language.

5. Click OK when you have finished.

Once you've turned off the default scripting language for your Web, you can set the form to use your validation error page. Follow these steps:

1. Open the form page that you want to set to use a validation failure page.

2. Right-click anywhere inside the form and select Form from the context menu.

3. If you're saving results to a file, select the Confirmation tab (refer to Figure 19.10). In the URL of Validation Failure Page field, enter the path to the file or use the Browse button to locate the file.

4. If you're saving your results to a database, click the Option button to open the Options for Saving Results to Database dialog box. In the URL of Error Page field, enter the path to the file or use the Browse button to locate the file.

5. Click OK to close the Form Properties dialog box.

The validation failure page doesn't tell you what went wrong with the information a user enters into your form, but it will let the user know that something went wrong. A validation failure page is especially useful if you have users whose browsers are incapable of supporting JavaScript or VBScript.

Choosing the Data to Save

Sometimes you might want to store the results of every field or specify the order in which the fields are saved in your results files. You'll also need to determine how to save the date and time as well as any other extra information the Web server can provide.

19

Form Fields to Save

You might not want to save all the information from your form, such as button values. Yes, believe it or not, a button is actually a form field, and the value of a submit button can be saved along with the rest of your form. You may also want to specify the order in which your fields are saved.

Exercise 19.5: Deciding Which Fields to Save

To specify which form fields you want to save, perform the following steps:

1. Open form1.htm.

2. Right-click anywhere inside the form and select Form Properties from the list. This will open the Form Properties dialog box (refer to Figure 19.1).

3. Click the Options button to display the Options for Saving Results of Form (refer to Figure 19.2).

4. Click the Saved Fields tab to display the Saved Fields page, as shown in Figure 19.11. By default, all the fields in your form are saved.

FIGURE 19.11

In addition to saving fields from your own form, you can also save some extras that the Web server provides.

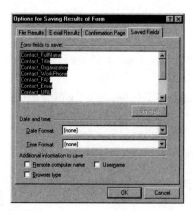

5. The Form Fields to Save text box lists all the form fields in your form. You can specify which form fields you want saved by removing any unwanted fields from this list. You must be careful to list only one form field per line.

6. You can move a form field up or down in the list by deleting it and then retyping it in the new location.

7. If you've removed a form field and decide you want to add it again, you can type its name in the Form Fields to Save text box. Order is important, so if you want the field to appear at the top of the list, enter it at the top of the list.

8. If you've removed fields from the Form Fields to Save text box, the Save All button will be enabled. Choosing this button will replace any fields you typed or order changes you made in the Form Fields to Save text box with the complete list of form fields available in their original order.

9. When you've selected the fields you want to save and have placed them in their proper order, click the OK button to close the Options for Saving Results of Form dialog box.

10. Click OK to close the Form Properties dialog box and save your changes.

Date and Time Format

Many people have a preference for how a date should appear and can easily misread a date that's not in the expected format. For example, is 12/3/99 December 3, 1999 or is it March 12, 1999? There's no way for you to tell unless you specify how you want your dates and times saved. FrontPage saves both the date and the time with the form results, so it's important that you can easily identify when the results were saved. If this is a customer service form, you'll want to be able to respond as quickly as possible, so the date and time are very important.

To choose a date and time format, perform the following steps:

1. Open the form1.htm page created in Chapter 18.

2. Right-click anywhere inside the form and select Form Properties from the list. This will open the Form Properties dialog box (refer to Figure 19.1).

3. Click the Options button to display the Options for Saving Results of Form (refer to Figure 19.2).

4. Click the Saved Fields tab to display the Saved Fields page (refer to Figure 19.11).

5. The Date and Time section of the page has the following fields:

   • The Date Format drop-down list contains a variety of different date formats you can choose from. When a user saves the results of your form, FrontPage will record the date along with the user's results. Setting the date format gives you control over how FrontPage will save the date.

   • The Time Format drop-down list contains a variety of common time formats you can choose from. Like the date format, FrontPage will use this format when saving the time a form's results are saved.

6. When you've selected the date and time formats, click the OK button to close the Options for Saving Results of Form dialog box.

7. Click OK to close the Form Properties dialog box and save your changes.

19

Additional Information to Save

In addition to form fields and the date and time, many Web servers can provide some additional information. Some of this information won't be useful to a normal Internet Web site but may be useful for an intranet Web site (a special type of Web site used inside a company for company data such as Human Resources information).

To save additional information with your form, perform the following steps:

1. Open form1.htm.

2. Right-click anywhere inside the form and select Form Properties from the list. This opens the Form Properties dialog (refer to Figure 19.1).

3. Click the Options button to display the Options for Saving Results of Form (refer to Figure 19.2).

4. Click the Saved Fields tab to display the Saved Fields page (refer to Figure 19.11).

5. The Additional Information to Save section of the page has the following options you can choose:

   - *Remote Computer Name*—This field lets you save the name of the remote computer. On the Internet, this might have little or no value for you because you'll probably only get an IP address.

   - *Username*—The username is usually the account name the user is logged in as or the user's IP address. Sometimes this field will be blank. It's probably best used on an intranet site to help determine which user has filled out the form.

   - *Browser Type*—This field enables the form to record which type and version of Web browser was used to fill out the form. If you've ever wondered which browsers your site is most commonly viewed with, this is a great way to find out, and it can help you figure out which browsers to design your site for.

6. When you've selected the additional information you want to save with your form, click the OK button to close the Options for Saving Results of Form dialog box.

7. Click OK to close the Form Properties dialog box and save your changes.

Testing Forms on Your Computer

To test any form you create with FrontPage, you'll need a Web server. This is not a limitation of FrontPage or the FrontPage form handlers. All form handlers require input from a Web server and cannot operate without one. Luckily, Microsoft provides free Web servers for use on all Windows 95/98 machines as well as NT Workstation and Server machines.

About the Microsoft Personal Web Server

The Microsoft Personal Web Server (PWS) is a close cousin to the industrial-strength Internet Information Server for Windows NT Server. You can download a current version of PWS for your system from the Microsoft Web site. If you have Windows 98, PWS is located on your CD-ROM.

Configuring a Form to Use a Custom Script

Configuring a form to use a custom script is a fairly straightforward operation. The key item to remember is that FrontPage itself doesn't interact with the script—that's the job of the Web server. This means if you've set up your form properly, chances are any problems you have are related to the custom script itself or the Web server.

To configure a form to use a custom script, use the following steps:

1. Import the custom script into the FrontPage Web that will make use of the script. It's almost a Web tradition to place custom scripts in a directory called cgi-bin or cgi. Some ISPs or hosting providers require you to use a particular directory name, and they will be able to tell you what it is if that's the case.

2. Open the page that contains the form you want to configure to use the custom form handler.

3. Right-click anywhere on the form and select Form Properties. This displays the Form Properties dialog box (refer to Figure 19.1).

4. From the Set to Other drop-down menu, select ISAPI, NSAPI, CGI, or ASP.

5. Click the Options button. This displays the Options for Custom Form Handler dialog box, shown in Figure 19.12.

19

FIGURE 19.12

Although primarily designed to work with FrontPage extensions, a form can be configured to work with a custom script.

6. In the Action field, enter the absolute URL to the form handler.

Using Discussion Groups and Discussion Webs

Discussion groups enable users of your Web site to post comments and questions. Other users can also reply to these comments and questions, thus creating what is known as a *discussion thread*, where you have a series of posts and replies. Discussion groups are excellent forums for product support because users who have questions can receive answers from other knowledgeable users or the company staff.

The Discussion Web Wizard

Discussion groups are created with the Discussion Web Wizard. This wizard allows you to create a new Web or to add the discussion Web to your existing Web. You may want to create a new Web for your discussion Web to make publishing and management easier, because discussion Webs can create a large number of files.

Exercise 19.6: Creating a Discussion Web

To create a discussion group with the Discussion Web Wizard, perform the following steps:

1. From the FrontPage menu, select File, New, Web to display the New dialog box.

2. Choose Discussion Web Wizard.

3. Use the Specify the Location of the New Web field to specify the Web server you want to create the discussion Web on as well as the name of the discussion Web. If you want to add the discussion group to an already existing Web that's currently open in FrontPage, check the Add to Current Web check box.

4. Click the OK button. The Discussion Web Wizard will appear, as shown in Figure 19.13, with a page explaining the how the wizard works. Click Next to move on to the next page.

FIGURE 19.13

The Discussion Web Wizard talks you through setting up a discussion Web.

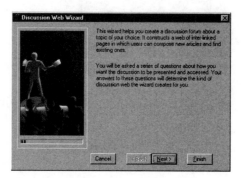

5. The second page of the wizard, shown in Figure 19.14, has several options you can choose for your Web (we'll select all these options for this example):

- *Submission Form*—You can see that this is a required part of the form. Without it, visitors would not be able to post their comments.

- *Table of Contents*—This is a highly recommended option because it creates the list of posts made to the group, thus making the posts easier to follow.

- *Search Form*—The search form is a special type of Search Form Component that's set to search only the discussion group and not any other part of your Web site. If you expect that your discussion Web will have a large amount of traffic, it's a good idea to offer visitors a chance to look for messages using a search form rather than having to scroll through all the postings.

- *Threaded Replies*—This gives the discussion Web a newsgroup-type look. Replies are shown connected to their initial posting and display slightly indented to make it obvious that they are replies. This makes it easy for visitors to follow a specific topic.

- *Confirmation Page*—A confirmation page informs the user that his or her post has been submitted.

FIGURE 19.14

You need to decide which settings your discussion Web will have.

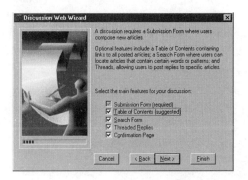

6. Once you've chosen your options for the discussion group, click the Next button. The third page of the wizard will be displayed (see Figure 19.15).

7. The third page of the Discussion Web Wizard is used to determine the name for your discussion site and has the following options:

19

FIGURE **19.15**

FIGURE **19.15**

Before you get too far, you need to choose a name for your new discussion group as well as a place to put it.

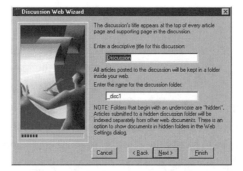

- *Enter a Descriptive Title for This Discussion*—This will be the name FrontPage inserts into your discussion pages as a title for the group. Choose a title that isn't just meaningful to you but also to your visitors. (We'll name ours "Learning FrontPage 2000.")

- *Enter the Name of the Discussion Folder*—Discussion groups use hidden folders named _disc by default. There's no need to change this from the default, although as is the case with the _private folder, anyone who is proficient with FrontPage will know that this is the name of the hidden folder. Each _disc folder is created with a different number at the end, starting with the first discussion group you create (_disc1). Each discussion group needs to have its own folder, both for searching purposes and to prevent errors when the posts are written to the server.

8. When you've chosen a name for the discussion group and its folder, click the Next button. The fourth page of the wizard will be shown (see Figure 19.16).

FIGURE **19.16**

You can select from three options to specify which fields your visitors need to fill out.

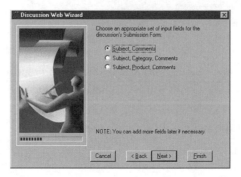

9. The fourth page of the wizard offers you three different choices for fields users can enter information into:

- *Subject, Comments*—Allows users to enter a subject for their posts and provides a scrolling text box for users to enter their comments. (This is the option we'll select.)

- *Subject, Category, Comments*—Allows users to enter a subject for their posts and a category that they name. It also provides a scrolling text box for users to enter their comments.

- *Subject, Product, Comments*—Allows users to enter a subject for their posts as well as a product name or number. It also provides a scrolling text box for users to enter their comments. (This is a useful option for a commercial site offering customer support for products.)

10. Select the "Subject, Comments" option and click Next to continue. The resulting page is shown in Figure 19.17.

FIGURE 19.17

Using a Web server that supports the User Registration Component allows you to limit the access to your discussion group.

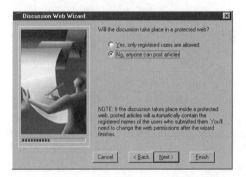

11. The fifth page gives you the option to limit access to the discussion group using the Registration component (covered later in the chapter). Alternatively, you can allow anyone to post messages. Because we have not discussed user registration yet, select the No, Anyone Can Post Articles option and then click Next to see the resulting screen, shown in Figure 19.18.

19

FIGURE 19.18

FrontPage gives you two options for the order your messages are displayed.

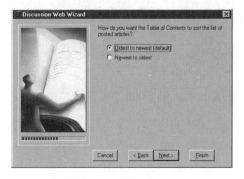

12. Select the Newest to Oldest option here, because most people prefer to see recent postings first. The default is actually to see older messages first, but for users who are coming to your site frequently to use the discussion Web, it can soon become frustrating to scroll through a growing list to find the newest articles. Click Next to continue setting up your discussion Web.

13. In the initial setting, you selected the Table of Contents option. With this selected, FrontPage can generate a table of contents to use as the front page for the discussion Web, as shown in Figure 19.19. This is a nice idea because visitors can instantly get an idea of what's there. Select Yes and then click Next.

FIGURE 19.19

Use your discussion group's table of contents as the main page of the Web.

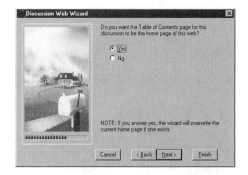

14. Because we chose to add a search form in our discussion Web, the Discussion Web Wizard page shown in Figure 19.20 is displayed. The options here are all explained by their titles—each will show exactly what it says it will. They allow you to choose how the results of a search will be displayed to the user. Select the "Subject, Size, Date" option—this will give a visitor enough information.

FIGURE 19.20

You have four possible choices for how a visitor will receive the results of a search in your discussion Web.

15. The next screen, shown in Figure 19.21, gives you the option to apply a theme to your discussion Web. Clicking Choose Web Theme will open the normal Choose Theme dialog box. For this example, you can add a custom theme to the discussion

Web. You can select any theme to match your site, or you can choose not have one at all. Once you've applied a theme or chosen not to apply a theme, click Next to continue.

FIGURE **19.21**

You can add a theme to match the rest of your site by clicking the Choose Web Theme button.

16. In Figure 19.22, you can select a frameset for your discussion group. The best option to select here is the Dual Interface option; this will allow visitors who use older browsers with no support for frames to still use your discussion group. Simply clicking the other radio buttons here will give you a preview of the layout for each option. Select the Dual Interface option and then click Next.

FIGURE **19.22**

Select from a choice of three frame-based layouts or choose a "no frames" option.

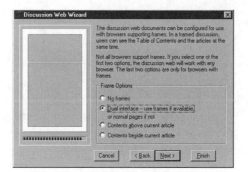

17. The screen shown in Figure 19.23 is displayed next. You have now supplied all the information FrontPage needs to create your discussion group. Click the Finish button to allow FrontPage to create your discussion Web.

18. If you now look at the folders view in FrontPage, you should see the files listed, as shown Figure 19.24. This is the list of files created by FrontPage using the example we just worked through.

FIGURE 19.23

FrontPage now has enough information to create your discussion Web.

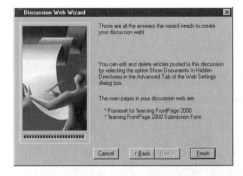

FIGURE 19.24

FrontPage creates a set of files for your discussion Web.

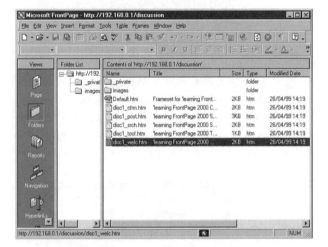

19. When viewed in your Web browser, the page displays as shown in Figure 19.25, with the Contents section at the top of the page and the main details, instructions, and links for posting an article below it. You can edit the text in this frame the same way as editing any other text in FrontPage.

Configuring the Discussion Group

Once the discussion Web has been created, you should look at the pages and make any changes you feel are appropriate, such as adding graphics or banners throughout your site. Editing the design of the page is exactly the same as editing any other pages you've created.

FIGURE 19.25

When previewed in a browser, your discussion Web shows the frame layout and options for posting articles.

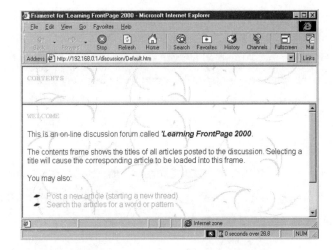

Using the Registration Component

The User Registration component can be used to force a visitor of your Web site to first enter a name, password, and email address.

This component is not in any way offering security to your site, because visitors can type in any information they want, and you have no way of checking it for accuracy or honesty.

What the Registration component actually does is help you keep track of who is coming to the site. In the case of a discussion Web, it ensures that visitors posting messages are actually who they say they are. Once a name and password have been registered by a visitor, no one else is able to use it.

Creating Registration Pages

The most common way of using this component, as already mentioned, is in conjunction with a discussion Web. The registration page must be placed in your root Web to which the discussion Web is a subWeb—for example, with the following domain:

```
http://www.mysite.com/discusson/
```

The registration page would be placed in the main mysite.com Web, not in the discussion subWeb.

This page has to be outside the subWeb, which will require registration, simply because putting it within the same subWeb would create a "Catch-22" situation. No registration form, no access to the subWeb; no access to the subWeb, no chance to fill in the form, and so on.

19

The easiest way to create a registration form is by using the User Registration Page template. Follow these steps:

1. Open the root Web to which you're going to add a "registration required" subWeb.

2. On the File menu, point to New and then click Page.

3. On the General tab, click User Registration and then click OK.

FrontPage automatically creates a user registration form. This form is shown in Figure 19.26.

FIGURE 19.26

The registration page, when generated, is filled with comments and instructions about how it works.

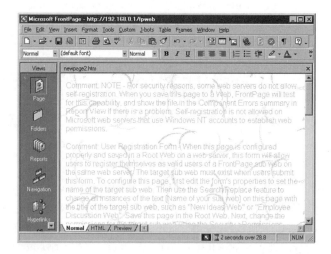

4. Right-click the form and then click Form Properties on the shortcut menu. The Form Properties dialog box displays. Notice that this time the Send to Other box is already checked and says Registration Form Handler.

5. Click Options and then click the Registration tab, as shown in Figure 19.27.

FIGURE 19.27

The Options for Registration Form Handler dialog box. In the Web name box, type the name of the protected Web site.

The Registration component includes the following fields:

- *Web Name*—You must choose a valid subWeb as a destination—for example, the discussion Web you created.

- *Username Fields*—This is automatically populated from the form.

- *Password Field*—This is automatically populated from the form.

- *Password Confirmation Field*—This is automatically populated from the form. This is the field that makes visitors type their passwords twice to ensure they haven't made a typing error the first time.

- *Require Secure Password*—This check box is selected by default, and it forces the visitor to enter a "secure" password. This is defined as being at least six character long and cannot match the username, even partially.

- *URL of Registration Failure Page*—Use this field to designate a page to be displayed if the user's registration fails.

6. Click the File Results tab. The file in which the usernames of site visitors are saved is displayed in the File Name box. By default, this file is located in the _private folder of the root Web.

7. Click OK and then click OK again.

8. Customize the fields on the form as needed. For example, change the phrase [OtherWeb] to the name of your protected Web site (for example, "discussion"). You can then customize the instructions on the form and change the text labels on the fields.

The Registration Form can be set to use custom form field names if you choose to create your own registration page.

When you've chosen your options, click OK to close the dialog box.

In addition to the configuring Registration Component, you'll also need to limit the target Web so that only registered users have access.

To limit the access to the target subWeb, perform the following steps:

1. Open the subWeb you want to have your users register for.

2. From the FrontPage menu bar, choose Tools, Permissions, Security.

3. On the Settings tab, choose Use Unique Permissions for This Web.

4. On the Users tab, choose Only Registered Users Have Browse Access.

19

Using the Registration Component on Your Server

The Registration Component works with all the Web servers supported by the FrontPage server extensions, except for Microsoft's Internet Information Server and the Personal Web Server.

Internet Information Server

You may be wondering why Microsoft would release a product that wouldn't work on its own servers. There are several good reasons for this. Microsoft Web servers implement security in a slightly different fashion than some other Web servers. Both IIS and the PWS rely on the security inherent in the operating system's file format.

Security is not an easy topic to cover, and even the basics would take more than a few chapters. In a nutshell, Windows NT is designed with strict security guidelines that the Registration Component violates in that it allows anyone to register as a user to gain access to Web pages and files that you want private. Also, the Registration Component doesn't offer security, and the information is simply entered by the visitor and is not checked at all.

The FrontPage Server Extensions and Components

I've made numerous mentions of the FrontPage server extensions without ever really explaining them.

Table 19.1 will hopefully give you an understanding of what they are and how they work. The following discussion should help to explain some of the features and which of them need the extensions.

FrontPage components are built-in FrontPage objects that are evaluated and executed when an author saves a page or, in some cases, when a user browses the page. FrontPage components generate HTML, or, in some cases, client-side or server-side script code.

Runtime components expand dynamically when the page containing the component is fetched by a browser, or for form handler components, when a form is submitted. This is similar to a CGI script running on the server. Authoring-time components expand only when the page is saved, not when the page is fetched by a browser.

Components identified as *runtime* require extensions on the server. Components identified as *author time* do not require extensions but may require additional files to be uploaded.

TABLE 19.1   Some of the FrontPage Components and Whether They Need the FrontPage Extensions

Component	Type	Purpose
Banner Ad Manager	Authoring time	Allows images to be automatically displayed and rotated in sequence. Users can click the images to follow a hyperlink.
Comment	Authoring time	Text that authors can view in the FrontPage Editor but that will not be displayed by a Web browser, similar to "hidden text" in a word processor. Comment text appears purple in the FrontPage Editor and retains the character size and other attributes of the current paragraph style. Comments are particularly useful for instructions embedded in templates.
Confirmation Field	Runtime	Includes the values of fields in a form on the confirmation page.
Default Form Handler (also called *Save Results Component*)	Runtime	Appends the contents of a form to a file on the server in any of eight formats (suitable for importing into databases, feeding into a mail merge with Microsoft Word, viewing in a text editor, viewing in a Web browser, and so on). This form handler can also be configured to email the form's contents.
Discussion	Runtime	Creates a threaded discussion group.
Hit Counter	Runtime	Monitors and displays the number of visits a page has received.
Hover Button	Authoring time	A button on a Web page that contains an animation that's activated when the mouse moves over the button or is clicked on the button.
Include Page	Authoring time	Replaced with the contents of a page in the FrontPage Web. If the included page changes, it is reincluded. Note that the Include Page component is not the same as a server-side include. Server-side includes dynamically include pages when the page is fetched. The Include Page component only updates the included data when the page is saved.
Marquee	Authoring time	Creates a horizontal scrolling text window.

19

continues

TABLE 19.1 CONTINUED

Component	Type	Purpose
Page Banner	Authoring time	Creates a banner across the page with the page's title. Text or images are used, based on the FrontPage theme selected for the Web.
Registration	Runtime	Allows end users to add themselves to the list of users permitted to browse a protected Web by registering a username and password.
Scheduled Image	Authoring time	Similar to the Scheduled Include FrontPage component, except that only an image is included.
Scheduled Include	Authoring time	Similar to the Include Page component, but the inclusion is only effective during a specified time period, before and after which the inclusion is automatically disabled (or, optionally, a different page is included).
Search	Runtime	Performs a full-text search over all pages in a Web or over all messages in a discussion group.
Substitution	Authoring time	Performs macro substitutions, allowing the values of data items (such as a company's address) to be centralized for easy updating.
Table of Contents	Authoring time	Displays a complete outline of all pages in a Web and optionally updates that outline whenever any page is added, deleted, or renamed within the Web.
Timestamp	Authoring time	Indicates when a page was last edited by an author or (optionally) when it was last automatically updated, in various date and time formats.

FrontPage 2000 makes it possible to avoid using features that require the server extensions simply by turning them off.

To Enable or Disable the FrontPage Server Extensions

If you know that the server that will be hosting your Web does not offer support for the FrontPage extensions, it may be better to turn them off. When you disable the FrontPage extensions for a Web, the runtime components are grayed out and you're unable to use them. To disable the FrontPage extensions, do the following:

1. Select Tools, Page Options and then select the Compatibility tab.

2. To prepare your Web for a server that offers no support for the FrontPage server extensions, deselect the Enabled with Microsoft FrontPage Server Extensions check box.

3. If you clear this check box, the following commands will be unavailable:

- Hit Counter
- Confirmation Field
- Include Page
- Scheduled Include Page
- Categories
- Search Form
- Additional Components

The FrontPage Server Extensions and Publishing Your Web

You don't have to have the FrontPage extensions on the Web server to have a successful Web site. As long as you remember the components and features that require the extensions, your Web site should always work on the server you use.

How the Server Extensions Affect Publishing

FrontPage only has full functionality when combined with a Web server that offers support for the FrontPage extensions. As you've already seen, there are numerous features that will not work without these extensions. Here are the benefits of having your Web hosted on a server that offers FrontPage extensions:

- Your Web will have full FrontPage functionality when it's published. Without the server extensions, the features listed previously will not work.

- FrontPage can maintain both your files and hyperlinks. Every time you publish the Web, FrontPage compares the files on your local computer to the files on the Web server. For example, if you move or delete a file in your local Web, FrontPage will update and correct any hyperlinks to it.

- After you've published the Web, you'll be able to open and edit it directly on the ISP's Web server. You'll also be able to publish it back to your local machine.

- FrontPage can publish your Web using HTTP (Hypertext Transfer Protocol) instead of the standard FTP.

Managing the Files on the Web Server

Even in these days when some ISPs offer "unlimited Web space," this is still not the norm. Just like any other computer program, file management is vital to the long-term success of your project. Deleting orphaned and old files can be the only way to keep the size of your Web down.

19

When you've published your complete Web once, FrontPage can synchronize the files on your local Web with the published files on the Web server. Each subsequent time you use the publish feature, FrontPage will compare the files locally to those on the hard drive and offer to do the following:

- When you've deleted files from your Web locally, FrontPage will prompt you about deleting the same files on the Web server.

- FrontPage can also match other actions on the Web server, such as moving and renaming files.

Create Your Own Search Page

You can create your own search page through the New Page dialog box and modify it to fit your site, or you can create a Web page and then select the Insert, Component, Search Form command.

A search form is a very important part of any Web site, and it requires careful attention to detail. Anyone can simply insert a component to act as a search facility, but it takes careful consideration to add a successful search component to your site. Visitors will need to know how to use the search facility you're offering. Almost everyone has used the major search engines and will know that they each work in a slightly different way. Make sure you give instructions to your site visitors about the language they can use, how to look for more than one word at a time, and so on. The Search Page template gives hints and tips about this that are worth reading even if you don't want to use the template for your site. A search engine with bad instructions or no instructions is a waste of everyone's time.

Summary

In terms of information covered and learning involved, today's lesson has already covered a lot. Day 18 also covered information about creating forms, so rather than making another general form, you can now try to create one of the most commonly used form types on the Internet—the search form.

The search form is unique in that it reads information in your Web site and helps a visitor find something specific.

Workshop

Q&A

Q Why doesn't my confirmation page ask the users to confirm that the information they entered is correct?

A The confirmation page is only designed to confirm that the contents of the form have been received, not that they're correct.

Q Why can't I change the order in which fields are saved in a database as I can when saving to a text file?

A Unlike a text file, the order of fields in a database isn't important. Once a text file is created, the order of fields cannot easily be changed. With a database, however, reports and queries can be created to display fields in any order at all. Therefore, the way the data is received has no importance.

Quiz

1. What's the most common use for a registration page?

2. If you disable the FrontPage extensions, can you still use the discussion Web?

3. When someone registers with your discussion Web, does FrontPage check the information?

4. Do all forms need a handler?

5. Can you use the Registration Component with IIS?

Exercises

1. Experiment with different settings and layouts for the discussion Web. Find a format that best suits your needs.

2. Turn off the FrontPage extensions and see how it affects your site. It's best to find this out before publishing your site.

Answers to Quiz

1. To register people with a discussion Web.

2. No, the discussion Web requires the FrontPage extensions to function correctly.

3. No, the information is simply stored for reference. Users can use any names they want.

4. Yes, all forms require a handler of some description.

5. No, it violates the inherent security settings.

19

DAY 20

Testing and Publishing Your Web

Okay, your Web is finished and you're ready to send it online. Is it easy? Well, it would be if you could guarantee that you've made no mistakes in your work.

Luckily, FrontPage comes with various built-in reports and views that can make it easy for you to check what you've done before you send your site live on the Internet.

Today you will learn

- How to view hyperlinks at a glance
- How to recalculate hyperlinks in your Web
- How to verify that hyperlinks are correct
- How to fix component errors
- How to fix content errors
- How to get your Web online
- How to publicize your Web

Hyperlinks

Everyone who has used the Internet, and certainly those who have made Web pages (however basic), will know what a hyperlink is. The hyperlinks in the pages we've made throughout this book are the main navigation structure for the Information Superhighway. Being able to let people get to long, complicated URLs just by clicking a mouse is what helps to make the Internet as popular as it is today.

Viewing Hyperlinks

If you've ever wondered how the Web got its name, you only have to look at the Hyperlinks View in FrontPage to understand. Because a single Web page can point to hundreds of other Web pages, and each of those hundreds of others can point to hundreds of other Web pages, you can become overloaded just trying to think about this tangled "Web" of files. The Hyperlinks View helps by showing how one page relates to other pages. This view let's you see what a page's links point to, as well as what other pages in your Web might point to it.

 Note   The figures shown in this chapter are from pages made specially to demonstrate the screens.

As shown in Figure 20.1, the Hyperlink View is divided into two panes—one to show your files and folder, and another to show the links between files. If you don't see the files and folder, you can view them by selecting View, Folder List. In order to view the links from and to a page, you must first choose a starting page by selecting any page in your Web from the left pane. To select a file, simply click the filename, and it will be displayed in the Hyperlink View on the right.

Pages that link to the page you've selected will appear on the left of the page. You need to remember that the Hyperlinks View can't show pages that link to your page that aren't in your Web. Links from the page you selected are displayed on the right of your page. The Hyperlinks View will show links that refer to images, emails, and Web pages that aren't in your Web.

All hyperlinks, whether they're to Web pages, images, or emails, will have an arrow extending to them from the page you've selected to start with. If a page that's linked to has an box with a plus sign in it, you can click the plus sign to view the links that extend from that page, as shown in Figure 20.2. To prevent your view from getting too cluttered, you can only expand one link from one page at a time in each direction (pages that point to the page you're viewing and pages that the page you're viewing link to).

FIGURE 20.1

The Hyperlink View can help you visualize how your Web pages work together, but it can get a little confusing if you have a large number of linked pages.

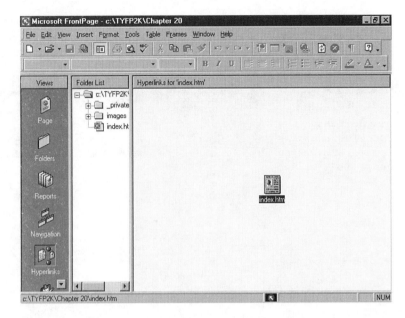

FIGURE 20.2

Clicking the plus sign allows you to see the links to and from a page.

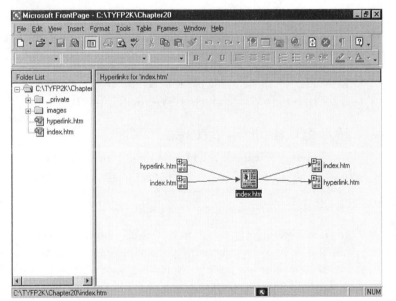

Hyperlinks Inside Pages

A hyperlink inside a page either points back to the page or points to a bookmark within the page. When there's a hyperlink inside a page, the Hyperlink View will display a link to another copy of that page. This can be useful for immediately spotting pages with bookmarks in them. Figure 20.3 shows that the page index.htm has a bookmark in it; you'll notice that it points to itself again, and again, and again.

FIGURE 20.3

Pages with bookmarks can clutter up your view as they link back to themselves, all the way to infinity and beyond.

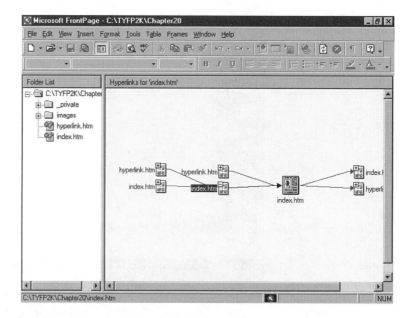

To enable hyperlinks inside pages to be displayed, right-click anywhere on the right pane of the Hyperlink View and select Hyperlinks Inside Page.

Hyperlinks to Pictures

When most people think of a hyperlink to an image, they think of a link that takes them to an image. *Hyperlinks to pictures* refers to any image that's included in your page. Hyperlinks to images will appear and behave the same way other links do, except you'll see an image icon instead of a Web page icon.

To allow hyperlinks to images to be viewed, right-click anywhere on the right pane of the Hyperlinks View and select Hyperlink to Pictures. As you can see in Figure 20.4, the hyperlink to an image displays as a picture icon with the path and filename attached.

Repeated Hyperlinks

In some pages, you'll repeat the same link several times. By default, the Hyperlinks View will ignore multiple hyperlinks to the same page, but you can have the Hyperlinks View display them. Repeated hyperlinks can be pages, images, or emails, as shown in Figure 20.5.

FIGURE **20.4**

An image file displays as an icon with the filename in the Hyperlinks View.

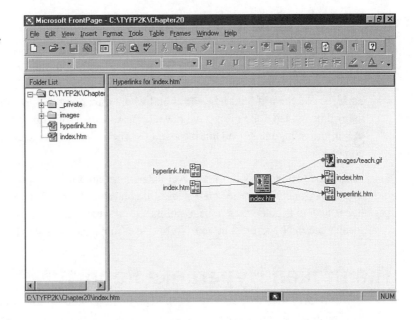

To display repeated hyperlinks, right-click on the right pane of the Hyperlinks View and select Repeated Hyperlinks.

FIGURE **20.5**

Turning off repeated hyperlinks avoids confusion when you have one page that repeats the same link a number of times, but turning it on can help you see if one of them might be wrong.

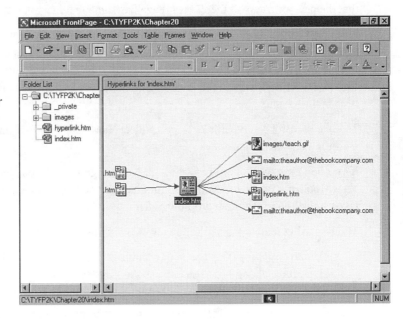

20

Recalculating Hyperlinks

Recalculating links sounds neat, but what exactly does it do? This is one of those crucial features that's often forgotten about but is very important to the health of your Web site. FrontPage keeps track of certain things about your Web site, such as the keywords in each file and the different hyperlinks and where they point to. Updating this information takes time, which none of us have nowadays. As a trade-off, FrontPage doesn't update this information unless you tell it to—that's where the Recalculate Hyperlinks option comes in.

Recalculate Hyperlinks lets the server extensions build new lists of keywords and links. The Hyperlinks View relies on the information created when FrontPage recalculates hyperlinks to decide where a page points to and what pages might point to a page. To recalculate the hyperlinks in your Web, select Tools, Recalculate Hyperlinks.

The Broken Hyperlinks Report

If you've ever tried to manually check hyperlinks, you know how time consuming it can be. This often becomes a trade-off; you could spend time making your site better and adding more content, or you could spend your time verifying that links to other Web sites still work. Nothing will annoy a visitor to your site more than clicking a link only to find that the page or site isn't there. FrontPage has some features that can help you here.

FrontPage can generate a number of reports that can help keep you informed of different aspects of your Web site. Reports are covered in Chapter 21, "Tracking and Maintaining Your Webs," but there are two reports that need to be discussed in this chapter: the Broken Hyperlinks Report and the Component Errors Report, which you'll see a little later in this chapter.

To open the Broken Hyperlinks Report, select View, Reports, Broken Hyperlinks from the FrontPage menu bar.

If you don't see the Reporting toolbar shown in Figure 20.6, you can open it by selecting View, Toolbars, Reporting from the FrontPage menu. You can then select the Broken Hyperlinks Report from the drop-down list.

The Reporting toolbar has the following two buttons:

- *Edit Hyperlinks*—This opens the details of whatever link is selected in the Edit Hyperlinks dialog box. You can use the Edit Hyperlinks dialog box to correct the URL and replace it in any or all of the pages with the broken hyperlink.
- *Verify Hyperlinks*—This begins the process of querying each hyperlink in the report to verify whether it's broken or correct. Because only one link is searched at

a time, this may take several minutes, especially if you have a lot of links to external Web sites.

FIGURE 20.6

The Broken Hyperlinks Report can be accessed from the new Reporting toolbar.

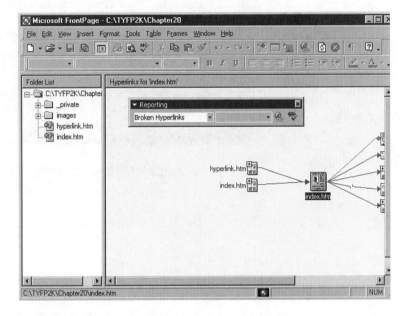

Click the Verify Hyperlinks button to see if you have any broken hyperlinks.

If FrontPage finds any broken links within your Web, a screen similar to the one shown in Figure 20.7 will appear (we'll look at how to fix this link shortly).

Hyperlink Status

FrontPage keeps tracks of the hyperlinks in your Web as well as their status. This means that if FrontPage has identified a broken link, it will remember until you fix it. The Broken Hyperlinks Report has three status codes:

- *Unknown*—Denoted by a question mark in the Status field. This means that FrontPage hasn't checked to see whether this link is valid yet.

- *OK*—Identified by a check mark symbol in the Status field. This means that FrontPage has checked this link and found it to be good.

- *Broken*—Identified by a broken chain link symbol in the Status field. This means that FrontPage has checked the link and received an error instead of a page.

Most of the time when you start this report, you'll see a number of hyperlinks with the Unknown status, as shown in Figure 20.8. Links that point to other Web sites (known as *external hyperlinks*) will always have an Unknown status every time you start FrontPage.

20

Now, FrontPage doesn't forget which external links are good and which are bad, but if an external link is marked as OK, it will be removed from the report. The big trouble with this is that a page or site that's good today may be removed forever tomorrow, so you can never know when an external link will be gone for good.

FIGURE 20.7

The Broken Hyperlinks Report shows the information you need to fix any broken links.

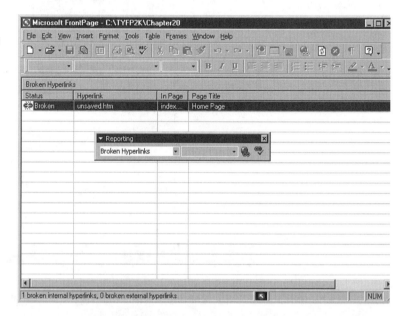

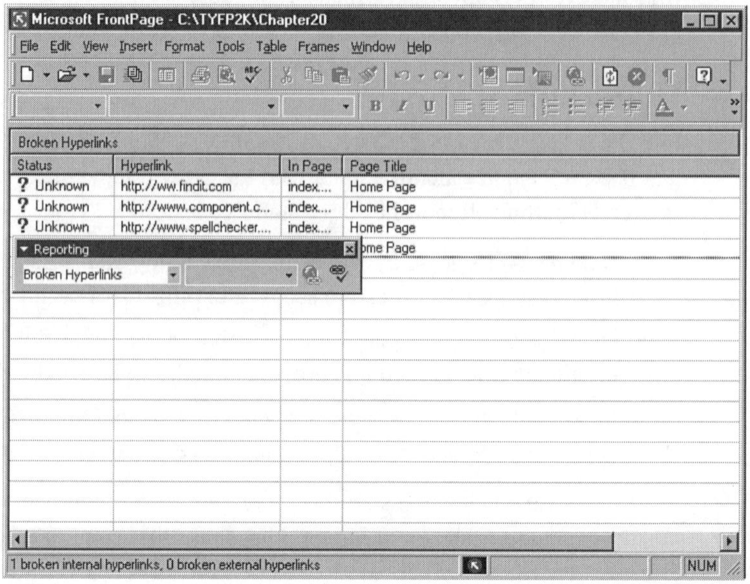

FIGURE 20.8

Links that FrontPage hasn't checked before or can't verify without connecting to the Internet appear as "unknown" links.

Verifying Hyperlinks

You can verify the hyperlinks in the Broken Hyperlinks Report by clicking the Verify Hyperlinks button. If you have a large Broken Hyperlinks Report or a lot of links to other Web sites, you might want to grab something to drink, go for a walk, or have some supper. FrontPage is very quick at verifying your local hyperlinks, but it has to call up each hyperlink that's not part of your Web and wait for a response.

If you don't want to wait, there is something you can do. When you click the Verify Hyperlinks button on the Reporting toolbar, FrontPage will display the Verify Hyperlinks dialog box, shown in Figure 20.9. This nifty dialog box will let you search all the pages or only the ones you select. You can select a range of pages by left-clicking with your mouse on the first file and then holding the Shift key while you click on the last file. You can also select individual pages by holding the Ctrl key while you left-click the filename.

FIGURE 20.9

If verifying hyperlinks is taking too long, you can stop it and restart it again later, as long as you don't close the Web.

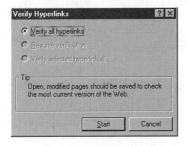

If the verification is going for a long time, you can use the Esc key to stop the report. If you decide you want to pick up where you left off, click the Verify Hyperlinks button again and select Resume Verification. You can only resume the verification process if you don't close the Web. If you close the Web, FrontPage will start at the beginning again.

Fixing Internal Hyperlinks

Fixing broken links that point to pages in your own Web site should be a top priority. Users browsing your site can forgive you if a link to another Web site breaks, but they'll have little patience when it comes to links to your own pages.

Exercise 20.1: Fixing Internal Hyperlinks

To fix an internal hyperlink, perform the following steps:

1. Click the broken internal hyperlink you want to repair from the Broken Hyperlinks Report.

2. Click the Edit Hyperlink button in the Reporting toolbar or double-click the broken hyperlink. The Edit Hyperlink dialog box, shown in Figure 20.10, opens.

20

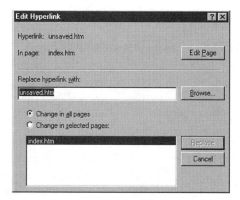

FIGURE 20.10

The Edit Hyperlink feature allows you to fix bad links in one or many pages, as required.

3. If you already know the full path to the correct file, enter it into the Replace Hyperlink With field or use the Browse button to browse to the file you want to replace the bad link with.

4. The Edit Hyperlink dialog box also let's you choose which pages to replace this hyperlink in. Here are your options:

   - *Change in All Pages*—This option will automatically correct this link in all the pages that the bad link appears in.

   - *Change in Selected Pages*—This option allows you to select the pages you want this hyperlink to be corrected in from the list below the radio buttons.

5. Click the Replace button when finished to begin replacing the links.

Once FrontPage has finished replacing the link in all the pages you specified, the Broken Hyperlinks Report will refresh itself. After the refresh, the fixed link should no longer be visible in the report.

Fixing Hyperlinks to the World Wide Web

Fixing hyperlinks to the World Wide Web works almost the same as fixing internal hyperlinks. To find the correct external hyperlink, FrontPage will use your Web browser so you can browse to the correct destination page or site.

To fix an external hyperlink, perform the following steps:

1. Click the broken external hyperlink you want to repair from the Broken Hyperlinks Report.

2. Click the Edit Hyperlink button in the Reporting toolbar or double-click the broken hyperlink. The Edit Hyperlink dialog box will open.

3. Click the Browse button to open the Select Hyperlink dialog box, as shown in Figure 20.11. Click the icon of the world with a spyglass on it (directly to the right of the URL field) to open your Web browser.

FIGURE 20.11

This is the same Select Hyperlink dialog box shown previously on Day 7, "Adding Links and Bookmarks."

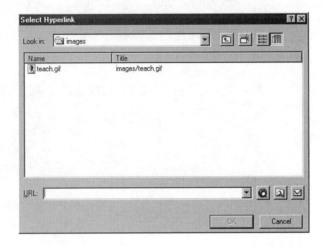

4. With your Web browser, browse to the Web site or page you want to replace the bad link with. Return to FrontPage when you've found the correct page or Web site. The URL field will now contain the corrected URL.

5. Select the page or pages you want to be fixed and then click the Replace button.

6. When FrontPage is finished correcting the hyperlinks, it will return you to the Broken Hyperlinks Report.

Fixing Component Errors

Component errors can pop up almost anywhere, and when they do, it's incredibly annoying. Running the Recalculate Hyperlinks command will often cure many of these errors, especially those caused by pointing to the wrong location for the server extensions. Some of them are caused by other problems, such as deleting the page a table of contents uses as its starting page.

There are several ways to find information about a component error but only one way to find the actual error. To find a component error you must use the Component Errors Report. This report will give you a list of all pages in your Web that have a broken component. To see this report, select View, Reports, Component Errors.

20

From the component report shown in Figure 20.12, or any other view that lists files, you can get more information about a page by right-clicking the page and selecting Page Properties. If the Web page has an error, a new sheet is added to the Page Properties dialog box called Component Errors. The Component Errors sheet will list any component errors in the page as well as the reason why there are errors. The errors aren't lengthy and don't tell you directly how to fix the problems, but knowing what the problems are is usually enough, as demonstrated in the next two examples.

FIGURE 20.12

The Component Errors Report is a handy tool to find out which components aren't working.

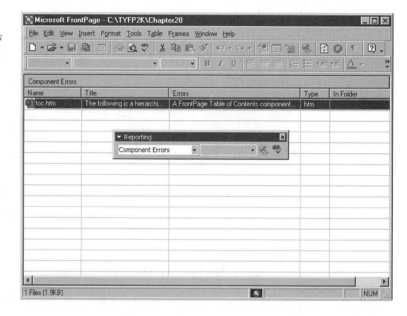

Figure 20.12 shows a Component Error Report indicating that there's a problem with toc.htm.

Right-clicking the Errors column and selecting Properties will show more information (see Figure 20.13).

If you find errors, always use Recalculate Hyperlinks before you go about trying to fix them. If you're lucky, this will fix some of your component errors. It's also a good idea to use Recalculate Hyperlinks after you fix a component error to make sure it doesn't come back.

If you keep getting errors in your published site and not on your local site, try connecting to your published site directly and then use Recalculate Hyperlinks. Sometimes there are differences in the files that your local server extensions use and the server extensions your hosting Web server uses. Usually, this happens when publishing from Windows to UNIX, but it can happen with other operating systems as well.

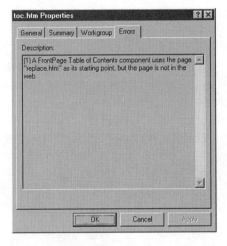

FIGURE 20.13

More information about the error being reported can be obtained by selecting the Properties option.

Fixing Content Errors

Aside from the technical errors that can occur with a FrontPage server component or a broken hyperlink, you can also make content errors. Content errors are, in fact, far more likely, because we are all human and therefore prone to making mistakes at times. A content error might be a simple misspelling of a word in one page or a hundred pages. It could also refer to something that, in fact, is not an error of your making, but one born out of changes to the factual content of your site. Imagine a company Web site listing the names of all its employees—when a staff change occurs, the Web site is immediately wrong. FrontPage 2000 not only enables you to check your spelling and find and replace words in a single page, it also enables you to perform these actions across an entire Web.

Performing an Across-the-Web Spell-Check

Good spelling is vital in a Web site—whether it's a simple home page or a multinational company's Web site. People browsing to your Web site are less likely to take you or your site seriously if you have spelling mistakes in your pages. This will also reflect on the services or products your site might sell. Imagine what potential customers think when they see a site that has spelling mistakes in it: What kind of problems might the products have?

Back on Day 3, "Building Basic Web Pages," you read about how to perform spell-checking a page at a time. You're now ready to take that a step further and check a range of pages or even an entire Web.

20

Exercise 20.2: Performing a Spell-Check

To spell-check across pages or an entire Web, perform the following steps:

1. Open the Web you want to spell-check and select the Folders View.

2. From the FrontPage menu bar, select Tools, Spelling or press the F7 key. The Spelling dialog box will appear, as shown in Figure 20.14.

FIGURE 20.14

You can quickly check the spelling in one or all of your pages.

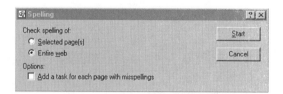

3. The Spelling dialog box has the following options:

   • *Check Spelling Of*—This can be set for an entire Web or selected pages. If you choose the Selected Page(s) option, you can select any pages that appear in the Folder View.

   • *Add a Task for Each Page with Misspellings*—This option, if checked, will add a task to the Web's task list for each page that has misspellings in it.

4. When you've set your options for the spell-check, click the Start button.

5. As the spell-check searches the pages, it will display them along with their status (Edited or Not Edited), the number of misspelled words, and the misspelled words. Double-click any of the pages to correct the misspelled words. This will open the page for editing and launch the normal spell-checking utility.

6. After you've corrected the spelling in a page, you'll be prompted to save and close the page and either continue to the next page or cancel. You can choose not to save and close the page if you need to edit it further. To continue with the next document in the list, click the Next Document button (or Cancel if you want to stop the spell-checking).

7. When you've finished checking the last page in the list, you'll be asked to save and close the edited page. You can choose not to save and close this page, as described in step 6. To finish spell-checking, click the OK button (or the Cancel button to cancel).

Performing an Across-the-Web Find

On Day 3 you used the Find command to find some text in a page that you had open for editing. Now that you've moved beyond working with single pages, you're ready to use Find across multiple pages or an entire Web.

The Find dialog box shown in Figure 20.15 looks almost identical to the Find dialog box you were shown in Chapter 3, with two exceptions. You can select multiple pages or an entire Web to search, and you can also search in the HTML code itself. If you need to refresh your memory on the other options in the Find dialog box, refer to the "Finding and Replacing Text" section of Chapter 3.

In previous versions of FrontPage, many users complained that they were unable to perform a find-and-replace operation in the HTML code. This has been addressed fully in FrontPage 2000.

FIGURE 20.15

Finding text in your Web site has never been easier, and you can even look in the HTML code, too.

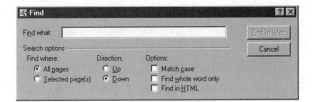

Exercise 20.3: Finding Text Within Your Pages or Web

To find text in a number of pages or across a Web, perform the following steps:

1. From the FrontPage menu bar, select Edit, Find or press Ctrl+F. The Find dialog box shown in Figure 20.15 will open.

2. The Find Where section has several choices, depending on which view you're in.

   - *Current Page*—This choice is only available if you're editing a page. It will limit itself to the page you're editing.

   - *All Pages*—This choice is available in any view. Select this radio button if you want to perform a Find operation on every page in your Web.

   - *Selected page(s)*—This choice is available in any view except Page View. You can use this to limit the Find operation to the pages you select. You can select pages from the folders listed in the Folders list. If you don't have the Folder list enabled, you can enable it by selecting View, Folder List.

   If you're in any view other than the Page View, you'll also have the next option.

   - *Find in HTML*—If checked, the Find operation will also search the HTML code for the text you enter. This is useful for changing someone's email as it appears in a browser as well as the HTML code used to make the actual hyperlink to the email address.

3. Once you've entered the text you want to find as well as the range of pages, click the Find In Web button to begin the Find operation.

20

4. As Find locates pages that have the text you're looking for, it will list them along with the count of how many times the text occurs in the pages.

5. Double-clicking a page will open that page for editing and allow you to use Find just as you did in Chapter 3. There's one addition, however. When Find has moved into a Web page, a new button will appear called Back to Web. Clicking this button returns you to the Find results for the entire Web or the range of pages you searched.

Performing an Across-the-Web Replace

Like the find and spell-check operations, replacing text across a Web works almost identically to replacing text in a page. An across-the-Web Replace works the exact same way as an across-the-Web Find, except for the addition of the Replace box, shown in Figure 20.16.

From the FrontPage menu bar, select Edit, Replace. The Replace dialog box shown in Figure 20.16 will be displayed.

FIGURE 20.16

Replacing across the Web makes it easy to change email addresses in every page without having to find the text page by page.

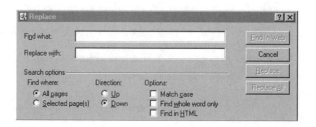

Once all the pages with the word or phrase you want to change have been found, you must use the Replace feature to go into each page, one by one, to replace the text.

Getting Your Web Online

So, you built a Web, tested it, and are now ready to get it online. But how do you get it online? FrontPage allows you to publish your Web to Web servers with or without the FrontPage server extensions installed. However, there's a difference between publishing to a server with the FrontPage server extensions and publishing to one without the FrontPage server extensions.

Publishing to a FrontPage Server

FrontPage uses the Hypertext Transfer Protocol (HTTP) to publish your Web to a Web server. Because the FrontPage server extensions use HTTP, FrontPage can talk directly with the Web server, which is very different than publishing to a non-FrontPage server, which we'll talk about in the next section.

Here are just a few of the benefits of being able to publish to a server with the FrontPage server extensions:

- You can restrict access to your Web.
- You can assign other users the ability to edit your Web.
- You can work in groups.
- You can create task lists.
- Your publishing is more secure using HTTP than it is using FTP.
- You can connect directly to the server to edit pages.
- You're able to use FrontPage components that rely on the FrontPage server extensions.

To publish your disk-based or server-based Web to a Web server with the FrontPage server extensions, perform the following steps:

1. Open the disk-based or server-based Web that you want to publish.

2. From the FrontPage menu bar, choose File, Publish Web. The Publish Web dialog box will open, as shown in Figure 20.17.

FIGURE 20.17

Publishing to a FrontPage Web is easy with the Publish Web command.

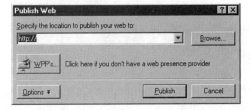

3. The Publish Web dialog box has the following fields:
    - *Specify the Location to Publish Your Web To*—Enter the full URL to which you're publishing (that is, the URL people will use to find your site). If you're publishing to a root Web, you'll only need to enter the domain name after http://. If you're publishing a subWeb, enter the domain name plus the name of the subWeb you're publishing to—for example, http://www.mysite.com/mysubWeb/.
    - *WPPs*—Choosing this button will open your browser to a Web page with information on Web Presence Providers who offer Web-hosting services using the FrontPage server extensions.

20

Select the Options button to see the following:

- *Publish Changed Pages Only*—This option checks the list of local files and the times they were last modified and compares them to files that are already on the server. FrontPage will then publish any newer files as well as any files that weren't already on the server. FrontPage will always prompt you before it overwrites a file just in case there was a mistake.
- *Publish All Pages, Overwriting Any on the Server*—This option will publish the entire Web and overwrite any files that are already on the server. Depending on the size of your Web, this option can take a long time.
- *Include SubWebs*—Checking this field will also publish any subWebs associated with the Web you're publishing.
- *Secure Connection Required (SSL)*—This field uses a secure form of HTTP called HTTPS to publish pages to the Web server. Before using this setting, contact your host to see if it supports HTTPS, which is more expensive to implement and requires a special setup.

4. Once you've chosen the destination for your Web and the options you want, click the Publish button to begin the publishing process.
5. When publishing is complete, you'll be notified with a dialog box. FrontPage will create a hyperlink to your newly published site.
6. Click this hyperlink to see the results of all your hard work.

Publishing to a Non-FrontPage Server

You might find yourself publishing to a Web server that doesn't have the FrontPage server extensions installed, or maybe the server extensions aren't available for that specific server. When you publish your Web, FrontPage will first determine whether the server you're publishing to supports the FrontPage server extensions. If the server doesn't, FrontPage will use what's known as the File Transfer Protocol (FTP) to transmit your Web pages. Unlike HTTP and the rest of the Web, FTP has been around for a long time, almost since the earliest days of the Internet.

Each ISP, company, or Web-hosting service will set up its FTP publishing differently, so you should contact it first to understand its procedures. Some ways in which it might set up its servers will cause a delay between when you publish the content to your FTP site and when it appears on the Web server. Regardless, you should find out what the process is so you don't waste valuable time tracking down what you think is a bug but turns out to be normal operating procedure for the ISP.

Publishing to a non-FrontPage server will work almost the same as publishing to a FrontPage server, except you'll use FTP to publish. When you publish your Web, you'll need to use `ftp://` in place of `http://` and then list the full URL to the directory that you'll be publishing to, such as `ftp://ftp.mysite.com/users/me`. The Secure Connection Required option will not work with a non-FrontPage server because it uses HTTPS to publish, which is only supported by the FrontPage server extensions. When attempting to publish a Web that contains FrontPage components that rely on the FrontPage server extensions to a site without FrontPage support, you'll receive a warning telling you that these components will not work and which components they are.

Publicizing Your Web

You've now published your Web site and are ready for the Web masses to descend upon it. The only problem is how to let the world know it exists. The two most popular ways to publicize your Web site are through search engines and banner ads.

A search engine such as Lycos (`http://www.lycos.com`) works very much like the FrontPage Search Component. A search engine won't just go out and find your Web site; you have to tell each search engine you would like it to visit your site and add your pages to its database. Once you ask a search engine to visit your site, it will look at the first page in your site and then follow as many links in your site as it can find. This process of moving from page to page is often known as *spidering*, and the programs many search engines use to look at your site are called *spiders* or *robots*. This is the Web after all, so we're bound to find some spiders in it somewhere.

As a search engine visits each page in your site, it makes a record of all the keywords in a page as well as the URL for the page. This process of making a record of the keywords and URLs is often called *indexing*. Each search engine is designed a little differently, and they tend to have minds of their own, but many search engines have provided us a way to control which keywords our pages will be found under.

HTML provides a special type of tag called the meta tag, which comes from the term *metadata*. Metadata is really data about data (or in this case, information about the contents of a Web page). There are lots of different variations of meta tags, but the two we're going to look at in terms of getting our site publicized are *keyword* and *description*.

Adding Keywords and a Description to a Web Page

The keyword meta tag allows you to specify which keywords you want your page to appear under. The keywords are simply a list of words separated by commas. The goal of every Web designer is to get his or her pages into the first 10 results of a search. If your page is in the top 100, your chances of being noticed are slim.

20

A description meta tag is just a description of your page or your site. Not everyone uses descriptions, but you might want to use one at least on your home page. Because the description is really only useful on a search engine, use it only when you need to and be as brief as possible. Don't describe the history of your company in great detail or a complete list of products, but do describe who your company is and what it does.

Exercise 20.4: Adding Keywords and a Description to a Web Page

To add keywords and a description to a Web page, perform the following steps:

1. In FrontPage, open the Page Properties dialog box by right-clicking anywhere on your Web page and selecting Page Properties or from the FrontPage menu bar, select File, Properties.

2. Click the Custom tab on the Page Properties dialog box to display the page shown in Figure 20.18.

3. The user variables already displayed are quite obvious from their descriptions; they tell you the software used, the theme applied (if any), and the type of document you're dealing with.

FIGURE 20.18

The Custom tab lists both user-defined variables and special ones used only by browsers and the Web server.

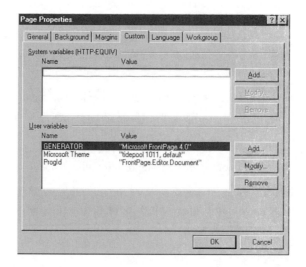

4. In the bottom half, labeled User Variables, click the Add button to display the User Meta Variable dialog box, shown in Figure 20.19. The User Meta Variable dialog box has two fields:

   • *Name*—This is the name of the meta variable—in this case, *keywords*.

- *Value*—This is the real content of the meta tag. Here's where you would type the keywords for your page.

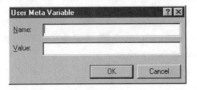

5. In the Name field, type **Keywords**. In the Value field, type a list of keywords, separating each word by a comma and a space. A list of keywords for a site relating to this book might include the following keywords: FrontPage, Microsoft, Software, Books, Sams, and Teach Yourself.

6. When you're done adding keywords, click the OK button to return to the Page Properties dialog box. You'll see that the Keywords variable has been added to the list, as shown in Figure 20.20.

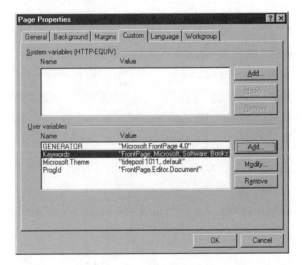

7. To add a description to your page, click the Add button to display the User Meta Variable dialog box again.

8. In the Name field, type **Description**. In the Value field, type a brief description of your page or your site. For a site that provides backup support for this book, for example, the description might be "Web site offering backup support for the *Sams Teach Yourself FrontPage 2000 in 21 Days* book."

20

9. When you've finished adding your description, click OK to close the User Meta Variable dialog box. The description is now included in the list.

10. Click OK to close the Page Properties dialog box and add the description to your page.

11. This process needs to be repeated, step by step, for every page you want to add keywords or a description to.

You'll notice when you return to Page View that you cannot see any sign of the description or keywords you added. This is correct; they're held in the code of the page and not displayed in normal view. Click the HTML tab and you'll see at the top of the page where the keywords and description appear. Figure 20.21 shows the description and keywords used in the examples.

FIGURE 20.21

The keywords and description are visible only when you switch to HTML View.

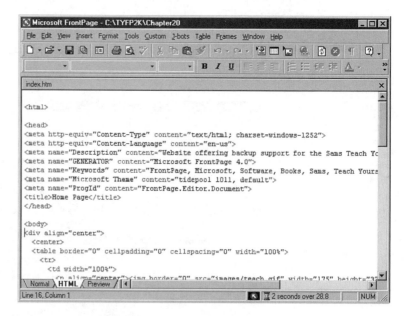

It's a good idea to start using keywords right away. Adding keywords early on, before your Web gets too many pages, will save you plenty of time and effort. Descriptions are a little different, and you may only want to use a description for one or two pages, but placing one in your main page is always a good idea, even when you have a very small site.

Using the Banner Ad Manager

Another way to promote sites is through banner ads. A *banner ad* is simply a graphic on a page that links to another site. This banner is usually a certain size (468 pixels wide by

60 pixels high is the industry norm) and is fairly small to ensure a quick download. You might want to trade banners with friends so they can put your banner on their sites or you can put their banners on your site. This approach is mutually beneficial because it can increase your traffic as well as your friends' traffic. If your site becomes very popular, you may even want to sell banner ad space for certain pages.

You can use the Banner Ad Manager to define how many seconds a banner ad is on a page, what the order of the pictures is, and what they link to. The Banner Ad Manager does have a limitation in that it can only link to one page, even though it lists a number of pictures. You can get around this by having the Banner Ad Manager link to a "sponsors" page, where you list your sponsors.

To add a banner ad to your page, perform the following steps:

1. On the page where you want to place the banner ad, move the cursor to the location where the banner ad is to appear.

2. From the FrontPage menu bar, select Insert, Component, Banner Ad Manager. The Banner Ad Manager Properties dialog box will open, as shown in Figure 20.22.

FIGURE 20.22

Use the Banner Ad Manager to schedule a series of banner ads for your page.

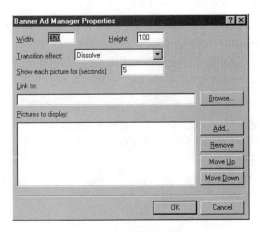

3. The Banner Ad Manager Properties dialog box has the following fields:

    • *Width*—This is the width, in pixels, of the image. The normal industry banner ad is 468 pixels wide. If an image is wider than this, the extra will simply be cut off.

    • *Height*—This is the height in pixels of the image. The normal industry banner ad is 60 pixels high. If an image is taller than this, the extra will simply be cut off.

20

- *Transition Effect*—This is the effect that will take place when moving from one image to another. The transition effects include None, Blinds Horizontal, Blinds Vertical, Dissolve, Box In, and Box Out.
- *Show Each Picture for (seconds)*—This is where you set the time in seconds that each picture will be displayed in the banner ad.
- *Link To*—This field allows you to specify the page or URL to link to when someone clicks the banner ad. You can only have one link per Banner Ad Component, so you may want to plan things carefully.
- *Pictures to Display*—The list of pictures, in order from first to last, that the Banner Ad Manager will display in the page.

4. In the Width field, enter the width, in pixels, of the *widest* banner image you're going to insert, or you can use the industry standard of 468.

5. In the Height field, enter the height, in pixels, of the *tallest* banner image you're going to insert, or you can use the industry standard of 60.

6. In the Transition Effect field, select the desired transition between images (or None if you don't want a transition effect).

7. In the Link To field, enter the URL to the page you want the banner ad to link to, or you can use the Browse button to locate the page.

8. To add a picture to the Banner Add Manager, click the Add button and select the picture you want to appear in the banner ad.

9. Repeat step 8 for as many pictures as you want to appear.

10. You can move pictures higher in the list by selecting the picture and clicking the Move Up button, or you can move pictures lower in the list by selecting the picture and clicking the Move Down button.

11. You can remove pictures from the list by selecting the picture and clicking the Remove button.

12. When you've added all the pictures to your list and have them in the proper order, click the OK button to close the Banner Ad Manager Properties dialog box.

When using banner ads, try to keep the file size of the ads small so your viewers don't have to wait while the banner downloads. Also, don't cycle through a lot of banner ads on one page, because they can become a distraction and an annoyance to viewers. You can add a banner ad to as many pages as you like and have them all link to one single sponsor's page.

Summary

Make sure you have no errors in your pages before you publish them.

If you don't already have an ISP (or WPP), use the facility within the File, Publish menu option to locate one that offers the services you require.

Speak to some friends who have Web sites and see if they would be interested in having a mutual link-sharing scheme. Then, all you need to do is get banner-sized images from your friends and can create your own Banner Ad Manager.

For practice doing this, try to create a few different banners that you would like to use as advertisements for your site and see which look the best.

Do an Internet search for sites that offer advice on getting found on search engines. Also, get yourself a list of search engines that you would like to be seen on. Although most people use the "known" ones—Yahoo!, Excite, and AltaVista—there are, in fact, many thousands of search engines all over the world.

Workshop

Q&A

Q **I've submitted my site to a search engine but it doesn't show up. Why not?**

A Search engines receive tens of thousands of request every day to add or update sites. Often, your site will get added to a queue (first come, first serve). Some search engines will only spider sites on certain days of the week or month. Even if your site is spidered immediately, it might not be added to the database for a few days. You might even have to wait several days or even weeks before your site shows up in the search engines.

Q **I've lost the local copy of my Web site after I published it. What can I do?**

A If the server on which you published your Web has the FrontPage server extensions, then this is easy. Most FrontPage users think of publishing in only one direction, from your computer to a server. What most users don't realize is that you can go the other way, too. FrontPage doesn't care; it just needs two Web servers to work with. You can publish your Web site back to your computer by opening the Web you published to the server just as you would when you open your local Web. It's best to use the exact same URL to open your Web that you used to publish it (such as `http://www.mysite.com/myWeb/`). Once you open the Web, you can publish it back to your local computer by using your local computer's name

20

(`http://mycomputer/myWeb/`). If your server doesn't support the FrontPage server extensions, you can use an FTP client such as WS_FTP to copy the files from the server back to your computer, where you can then import them into a new Web.

Q My WPP doesn't have the server extensions, can I still use the File, Publish command?

A Yes, but FrontPage will actually default to its own built-in FTP protocol, so none of the components needing the extensions will work.

Q Can I make my banner ad as big as I want?

A You can make the file any size, but if it's bigger than the industry standard file size, you'll find that the excess is always cut off.

Quiz

1. How many sites can a banner ad link to?

2. Can you find and replace text within HTML code?

3. How do you see hyperlinks to and from a page?

4. Can you resume a Verify Hyperlinks Report?

5. If you delete your table of contents' starting page, which report will show the error?

Exercises

1. This exercise is more about preparing your site for publishing and publishing your site than it is about adding items. The best exercises you can do are to simply practice finding words in your site. Find works the same way as Spell-check and Replace, but it won't change any of your text, so it's the least error-prone way of getting practice with these tools.

2. If you're going to publish your site to a server with the FrontPage server extensions, you can test the publishing feature locally by simply publishing to a different Web on your local computer. When you're done testing the publishing locally, you can simply delete the duplicate Web.

3. Try developing a set of keywords for your site. Think of every useful word you can. You may want to get a thesaurus out to look up similar words, because not everyone thinks like you do. If you use the keyword *automobile*, people searching for the word *vehicle* might not find your site.

Answers to Quiz

1. Only one page can be linked to, regardless of the number of banners.

2. Yes, this is a new feature in FrontPage 2000.

3. In the Hyperlinks View, click a plus on a page to expand it.

4. Only if you haven't closed FrontPage since you started it.

5. The Component Error Report will show the problem.

20

DAY 21

Tracking and Maintaining Your Webs

Okay, the site is built, the content is fine, and it's live on the Internet. Now it's time to put your feet up and relax.

If only it were that simple!

Building and publishing your Web site is really only the beginning: After you build it, you have to keep it going by adding new content and features. Today, we'll discuss task lists to help you keep track of what you need to do, reports to help analyze your Web site, and general maintenance of your Web and the FrontPage server extensions.

In today's lesson, you will learn

- How to use task lists
- How to use the reports offered by FrontPage
- How to configure you Web settings
- How to check pages in and out of your Web
- How to maintain your Web

Task Lists

You can use a task list to organize all the things you need to do for your Web site, such as creating graphics, adding pages, and making big changes. A task list will allow you to prioritize tasks and give detailed information and instructions about each task. If you're working with a group, tasks can also be assigned to individuals in your group. To see the Task View, select View, Tasks.

Showing Your Task History

FrontPage keeps track of all the tasks that have been entered into the task list, including current and completed tasks. With the Task View, you can see both current and completed tasks. Normally the Task View will only display the current tasks, as shown in Figure 21.1. Because FrontPage keeps track of all the tasks, even the completed ones, you can view them by showing the Task History (see Figure 21.2).

FIGURE 21.1

The Task View lets you keep track of all the tasks for your Web that you have yet to complete.

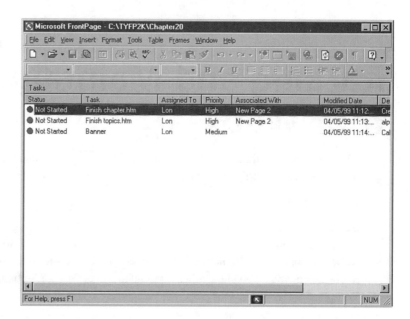

To show the entire Task History, perform the following steps:

1. Switch to the Task View of your Web.

2. Right-click a blank area of the Task View and select either Show Task History or Edit, Task, Show History.

FIGURE 21.2

The Task History will show you all the tasks for your Web, both completed and uncompleted.

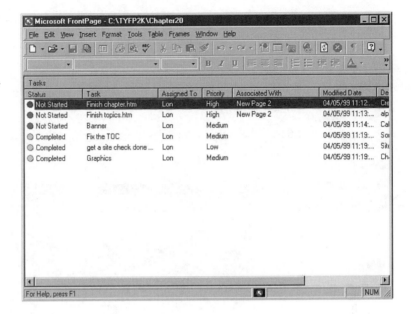

Adding Tasks

You have two ways to add a task to your task list: by adding a task in the Task View or by adding a task while editing a Web page. The two methods are almost identical, except that when you create a task while editing a Web page, the task becomes associated with that particular Web page.

Exercise 21.1: Adding Tasks

To add a task, perform the following steps:

1. Right-click a blank area of the Task View and select New Task or select Edit, Task, Add Task from the FrontPage menu bar. The New Task dialog box appears, as shown in Figure 21.3.

2. Enter or choose the following options:

   - *Task Name*—Enter a descriptive name for your task. The name should convey as much meaning as possible at a glance—for example, "Graphics for home page."

   - *Priority*—Choose a priority for this task: Low, Medium, or High. FrontPage will default to Medium.

21

- *Assigned To*—Choose the appropriate user to assign this task to. If you're not working in a group, FrontPage will list only your current account. You can type in a name that isn't in the drop-down menu.

- *Description*—Enter text that describes what you need done or the steps you need to perform to complete the task—for example, "Improve text quality on home page logo."

3. In addition to these fields, the New Task dialog box also displays the following noneditable fields:

FIGURE 21.3

Adding a new task is easy—you can assign it to someone, set a priority, and give it a name.

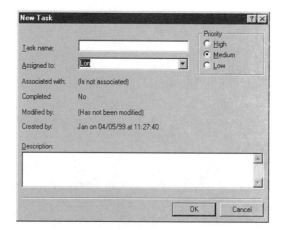

- *Associated With*—If you added the task while editing a Web page, the task will become automatically associated with it and the path to the file will be displayed.

- *Completed*—Shows whether the task has been completed. Upon creation, this will automatically be No. When complete, the task disappears from the default Task View, and the status becomes green with the word *Completed* showing when you view the Task History.

- *Modified By*—Displays the user account that last modified the task information as well as the date and time of modification.

- *Created By*—Displays the user account that created the task as well as the date and time of creation.

4. Click OK when finished to close the New Task dialog box.

Tasks may seem trivial at first glance, but once your site gets larger, they may prove useful for planning and making changes. When there is more than one person working on a site, a task list is a great way to keep track of changes and updates other people might want you to make.

Deleting or Marking Tasks Completed

Sometimes after you create a task, you might decide you don't want to do it. The best option in that case is to delete it. Deleted tasks won't appear in the Task History.

To delete a task from your Web's task list, perform the following steps:

1. Switch to the Task View for your Web.
2. Select the task you want to delete by clicking it.
3. Delete the task by pressing the Delete key or by right-clicking the task and choosing Delete. A confirmation box will appear to verify whether you really want to delete the task. Choose Yes to delete the task.

 Note

> You can also delete tasks that are marked as completed when you're viewing the Task History.

When you've completed a task, you can mark it as completed. Marking a task as completed will remove it from the current list of tasks and place it into your Task History. If this task isn't important, you may want to delete it so you don't clutter up your history.

To mark a task as completed, perform the following steps:

1. Switch to the Task View for your Web.
2. Select the task you want to mark as completed by clicking it.
3. Right-click the task and select Mark As Completed or select Edit, Task, Mark As Completed from the FrontPage menu bar.

Reports

As you've already seen in this book, FrontPage 2000 has many new features from previous versions. One of the most significant features is the new reports FrontPage can now produce for you. We covered a couple of these on Day 20, "Testing and Publishing Your Web," and we'll now look at the rest of them.

The new reporting features make it simple for you to find out if any of your Web pages are slow to load without having to open the pages. You can also see a list of the files that have been changed lately, how many broken links you have, and even which pages are checked out by someone else editing your Web site.

21

The new reporting feature is very powerful and can produce a detailed report for just about every aspect for your site. It's the easiest way to see how your site is going to perform even before it's published.

To use any of the reports with team functions, such as assignments, you'll need to open the Web the team works from. Do not your local copy (unless your team is working with your local copy). If you don't open the same version your team uses, you might not have the most current information about assignments or files that are checked out.

To switch to the Reports View in FrontPage 2000, select View, Reports. If the Reporting toolbar shown in Figure 21.4 doesn't display automatically, select View, Toolbars, Reporting.

FIGURE 21.4

The Reporting toolbar makes switching between reports easy.

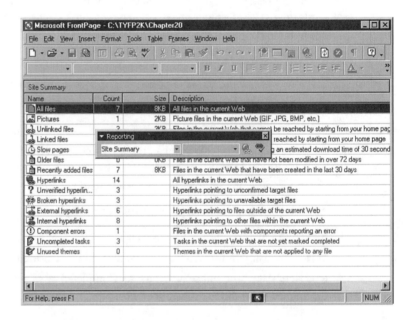

The Reporting toolbar has the following four sections (from left to right):

- *Report*—The Report drop-down menu lists all the different reports you can create with FrontPage.

- *Report Setting*—The Report Setting drop-down menu will change its values depending on which report is selected. For reports such as the Older Files report, this menu will be a list of days so you can identify how old a document has to be before being listed. In other reports, such as the Slow Pages report, this menu will be listed in seconds so you can identify how slow a slow page is.

- *Edit Hyperlinks*—If you're viewing a report that lists hyperlinks, such as the Broken Hyperlinks report, this button will open the Edit Hyperlink dialog box for whatever link you've selected.

- *Verify Hyperlinks*—If you're viewing a report that lists hyperlinks, such as the Broken Hyperlinks report, this button will allow you to verify any links in the report, including links to other Web sites.

Site Summary

As you can see in Figure 21.5, the Site Summary report provides an overview of your site, including summary information from most of the reports. Double-click any entry in this view to get more information.

FIGURE 21.5

The Site Summary report gives you an overview of all the individual reports for your Web.

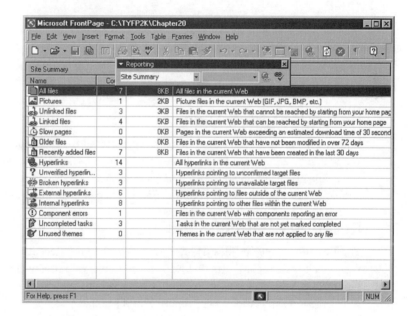

All Files

The All Files report will provide you with a list of all the files in your Web site. As you can see in Figure 21.6, the All Files report will show more than just the filename, size, and when it was last modified. The All Files report also lists the title of the page (untitled pages will simply display the full path to the file), the type of file, which user modified the file last, and any comments that may be included with the file. To change the way this report looks, simply click in any of the title bars. Doing this, you can view the files by name, size, and so on.

21

FIGURE 21.6

The All Files report lists every file in your Web and allows you to organize them by name, size, or title.

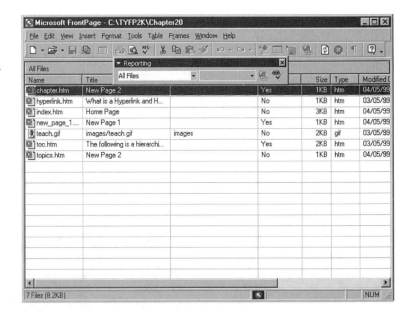

Recently Added Files

With the Recently Added Files report, you can see all the files that were added to your site within a certain time frame, as shown in Figure 21.7. The Report Settings menu gives you a range of days from zero days (today), all the way through 365 days. By double-clicking any of the files in the report, you can open that file for editing.

Recently Changed Files

The Recently Changed Files report is very similar to the Recently Added Files report, except that it shows any files that were added to the Web or any changes made. Compare Figure 21.8, which shows the Recently Changed Files report, with Figure 21.7, which shows the Recently Added Files report. You'll see that some of the files will be the same because any new file is considered a changed file. Like the Recently Added Files report, you can use the Report Settings drop-down menu to specify how many days you want the list to go back.

FIGURE 21.7

With the Recently Added Files report, you can find out which files have been added lately. This becomes really useful if you have a lot of pages to keep track of or you work in a team.

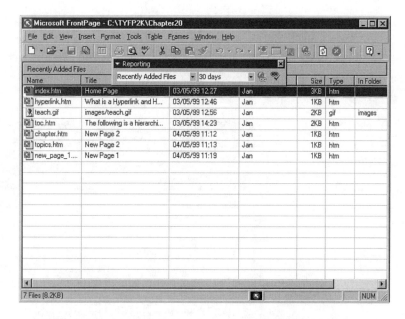

FIGURE 21.8

You can always find the last file that was worked on with the Recently Changed Files report.

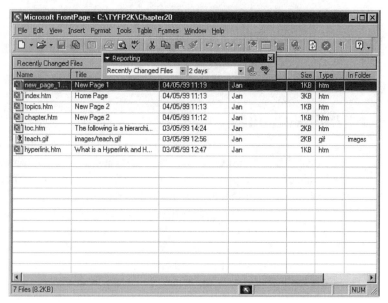

Older Files

The Older Files report is useful for finding files that you haven't changed in some time. Unlike the Recently Added Files or Recently Changed Files reports, the Older Files report lists all files that are older than a certain amount of days. Using the Report

21

Settings drop-down menu, you can specify the minimum age for a file, such as any files that are older than 30, 60, or even 90 days. The Report option goes as high as 365 days. Figure 21.9 shows an older files report for a large site that's not changed very often. For large Web sites, this comes in very handy when you need to find pages that have been around for some time that might need updating.

FIGURE 21.9

With the Older Files report, you can find files that have been on your site for a long time.

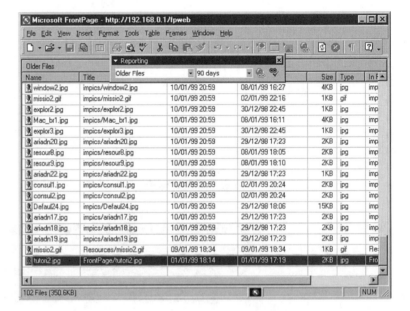

Unlinked Files

As a Web site grows, the Unlinked Files report, shown in Figure 21.10, becomes more important. It's not hard to create a Web page and then forget to make a link to it. Using the Unlinked Files report shows you all the files in your Web that don't have pages in your Web that link to them. You might also remove a link to a file and then forget to delete the file itself. These extra files can take up valuable server space, show up unwanted in the search bot, or even slow down the time it takes to publish your site. Figure 21.10 is taken from a large site with many unlinked files. It's worth mentioning at this point that there may be times you create pages that deliberately have no links or that you remove the links from. Caution must be used when deleting files you might want at a later date.

FIGURE 21.10

The Unlinked Files report will help you find any orphaned files in your site.

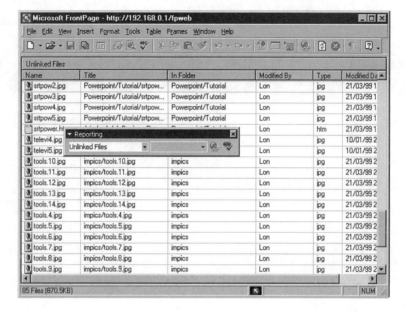

Slow Pages

The patience level of most Web surfers today is around 14 to 16 seconds. If your pages don't load fast enough, most visitors will become bored, then irritated, and then leave your site. As you can see from the Slow Pages report shown in Figure 21.11, this page will take over 100 seconds to download. This report can be very helpful in determining which pages need to be trimmed down or broken into smaller pages. If you have pages that are exceptionally large and you can't break them into smaller pages, make sure any links to these pages mention that they're large and will take some time to download. Warning users ahead of time will often keep them from getting irritated because they already know a page is slow and have made a choice to view it. Although the report in Figure 21.11 is set to 90 seconds to show an extreme example, you would normally use the drop-down list to select a range of time in seconds that a page must be slower than, such as slower than 20 seconds.

21

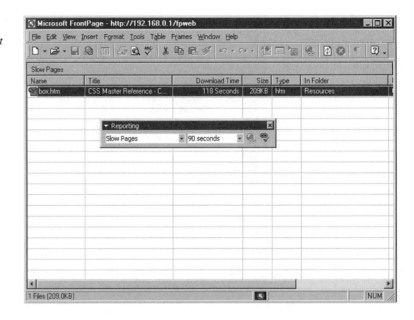

FIGURE 21.11

The Slow Pages report lets you identify files that might need to be edited or split to reduce the download time.

Broken Hyperlinks

Whenever a file is deleted, or even just moved or renamed, there's a chance that somewhere in your Web there's a link pointing to this file. This means that when a file is deleted, all the links to it will now show as broken. Sometimes when a file is moved or renamed, there can still be a link pointing to the old location or name. The Broken Hyperlinks report, shown in Figure 21.12, lets you see all the files that have a broken hyperlink in them. This list will show any broken internal hyperlinks and a question mark for any unknown external hyperlinks. By clicking the Verify Hyperlinks button on the Reports toolbar, you cause FrontPage to verify the existence of links to files outside your Web site. Double-clicking any of the files listed in the report will open the Edit Hyperlink dialog box. You can find more information on the Broken Hyperlinks report on Day 20.

Component Errors

Bugs can creep up in your Web site from time to time. Sometimes these bugs affect a FrontPage component, and FrontPage will need to report the error. If there's an error, such as the starting page for the table of contents was deleted, you can find it listed in the Component Errors report, shown in Figure 21.13. It's good to check for component errors whenever you delete pages from your Web or make major changes in the layout or structure of your site. The best time to run this report is right before you publish changes to your site so you can catch them before you put them on the Web for the world to see. (The Component Errors report is covered in detail on Day 20.)

FIGURE 21.12

The Broken Hyperlinks report will let you see any broken links before your users do.

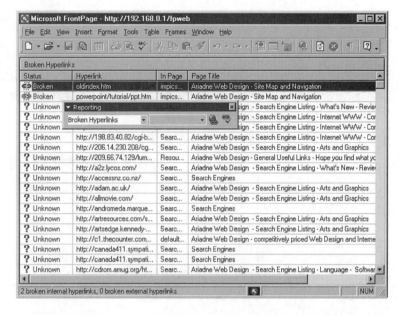

FIGURE 21.13

Use the Component Errors report to find out whether there are any problems with your FrontPage components.

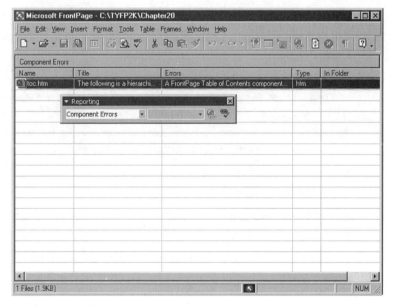

Review Status

If your Web has been set to use the Review Status feature, you can use the Review Status report shown in Figure 21.14 to list all the files in your Web as well as their review status, who they're assigned to, their review date, and who they were reviewed by.

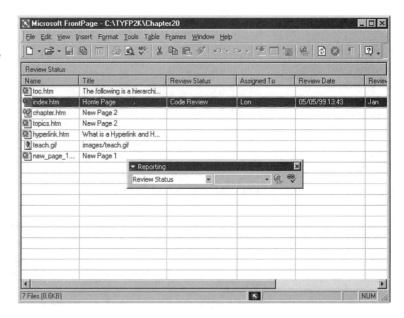

FIGURE 21.14

With the Review Status report you can see who has been assigned to review a page and what the review function is.

List Files by Review Status

To use the Review Status feature fully, you'll first need to have set the review status for a page.

You can set the review status for a file indicating what type of review the file needs, such as a code review for an Active Server Page, or where the file stands in the processes before publishing. If you've set the review status for the files in your Web, you can use the Review Status report to sort the files in your Web by review status. You can also look at the dates the files were last reviewed and who reviewed them.

To sort the report alphabetically by review status, review date, or reviewer, click the appropriate column heading.

To modify the review status for a file, click the cell in the Review Status column, click the cell again, and then type or select a review status.

To assign a file to a person or workgroup, click the cell in the Assigned To column, click the cell again, and then type or select a person or workgroup.

You can set the review status for multiple files at one time, or you can assign multiple files at one time. In the Review Status report, select the files you want to set or assign a review status for, right-click to display the shortcut menu, and then click Properties. Click the Workgroup tab and then in the Review Status or Assigned To box, select the review status, person, or workgroup for the selected files.

Assigned To

If you work in a group, the Assigned To report can help you keep track of any pages assigned to you as well as to others in your group. As you can see in Figure 21.15, the Assigned To report is very useful for viewing the progress of your teammates. This report shows all the pages in your site and who they have been assigned to.

FIGURE 21.15

The Assigned To report allows you to quickly see which pages have been assigned to the members in your team.

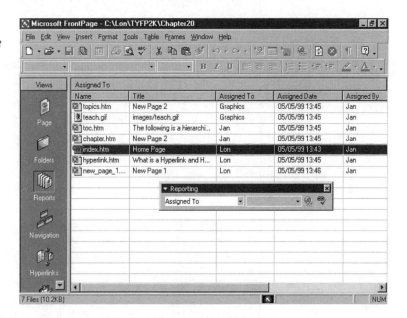

Categories

If you remember "Categorizing Your Content" back on Day 14, "FrontPage Components," you know you can assign a category to a Web page. The Categories report, shown in Figure 21.16, displays all the files that match the category you select in the Report Settings drop-down menu. If you select the (all categories) option, the Categories report will list all the pages in your Web, just like the All Files report.

Publish Status

While you're working on your Web, you may decide that some pages just aren't ready yet and flag them not to be published.

To flag a file not to be published, from inside an open page, right-click and select Page Properties, Workgroup. The check box for Not to Publish is empty by default.

The Publish Status report, shown in Figure 21.17, will list all the files in your Web as well as their publish status.

21

FIGURE 21.16

The Categories report lets you view all the pages in all categories or an individual category.

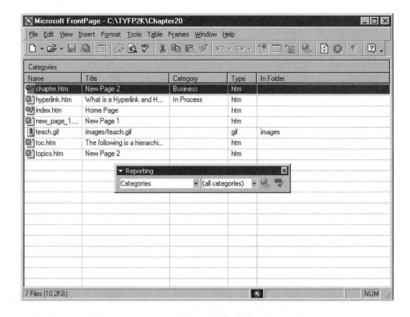

FIGURE 21.17

The Publish Status report allows you to see which files in your site are set not to publish.

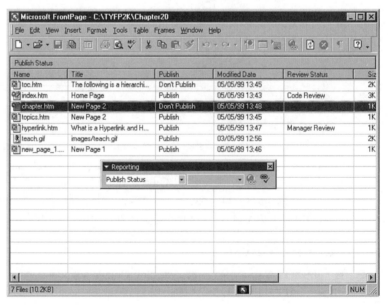

Checkout Status

List Files by Checkout Status allows you to see which files are currently checked out of your Web.

If your Web uses source control to manage files by checking them in and out from a server, you can use the Checkout Status report to see at a glance who has checked out which files.

The Checkout Status report lists all the files in your Web. The Checked Out By column shows who has the file checked out, the Version column shows the most recent version of the file that was checked out, and the Locked Date column shows the date the file was checked out (and therefore *locked*).

To check out a file that isn't locked, right-click the file and then click Check Out on the shortcut menu.

To open and edit it a file, right-click the file and then click Open on the shortcut menu.

To check in a file that you've checked out, right-click the file and then click Check In on the shortcut menu.

The Checkout Status report lists the normal file attributes you expect, such as name, size, and type. In addition to these, the report also shows the name of the user who has checked out the file, the version number of the file, and the date and time that the file was locked for exclusive use. FrontPage will usually list the files that are checked out first. You can identify files that are checked out by a red check mark before the filename. Files that aren't checked out have a green circle in front of them. You may have to scan through the list of files to find the ones that are checked out because there's no way to sort the results based on checkout status. This report will only appear if you have version control enabled for a Web.

Checking Pages In and Out of Your Web

Checking pages in and out of your Web can be done from almost any view or report in FrontPage. There are two easy methods for checking in and out files, and both can be performed from almost any view or report, such as the Folders View or the Unlinked Files report.

Double-click the file you want to check out (of course, assuming that it already hasn't been checked out). This will open a dialog box asking you to verify that you want to check the file out. You can also right-click the file and select Check Out to check out the file.

If you accidentally check out the wrong file, you can right-click the file you accidentally checked out and select Undo Check Out.

To check files back in, right-click the file and select Check In.

21

Web Maintenance

Every Web site needs maintenance now and again, whether it's to remove an old subWeb, add an administrator, or to just recalculate your Web. If you aren't a system administrator in charge of your own server, you might not have to do all of these tasks, but some of them you'll probably want to know about—even if you only work on a test Web server on your PC.

Administering Your Webs

Up until now, we haven't talked much about the FrontPage server extensions other than how to publish using them and what components need the server extensions. Well, now it's time to see what the server extensions can do for you by themselves. The next few items we'll look at all require you to open the Server Extensions Administrator program, so you might want to open it up now and look around so you'll be more comfortable with the next few examples.

Deleting Webs

Users of previous versions of FrontPage will remember that you could delete Webs directly in the FrontPage Explorer. FrontPage 2000 has moved many of the tasks such as deleting Webs into the FrontPage Server Extensions Administrator (which is good, because it's much harder to accidentally delete Webs now).

To delete a FrontPage Web, perform the following steps:

1. In the FrontPage Server Administrator, click the subWeb you want to delete.
2. Right-click the subWeb and choose Task, Delete Web. You'll then be reminded that this action is permanent. If you really want to delete the Web, click OK; otherwise, click Cancel.

Enabling and Disabling Authoring

The FrontPage server extensions will also let you disable authoring for a Web. In a nutshell, this allows you to turn off (or on) the ability for someone with FrontPage to publish or modify a particular Web. Now, you may wonder why you would want to do such a thing (and frankly, you'll probably never need to, but we're going to cover it just in case). Who knows, you might go on vacation and want to make sure nobody changes your Webs.

Exercise 21.2: Enabling and Disabling Authoring

To enable and disable authoring on a FrontPage Web, perform the following steps:

1. Right-click the root Web and select Properties. The Properties dialog box will open, as shown in Figure 21.18.

FIGURE 21.18

You can choose to disable authoring for an entire Web site through the Server Extensions Administrator.

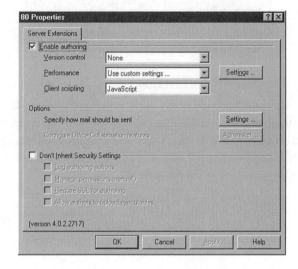

2. Uncheck Enable Authoring to prevent FrontPage users from publishing or modifying Webs. Check Enable Authoring to allow FrontPage users to publish or modify Webs.

Adding Administrators

Administrators are users who can do anything to a Web, including deleting and adding subWebs, so you'll want to be careful who you give Administrator access to your Webs. The first way is through the Tools, Security menu in FrontPage 2000, which we'll discuss later in this chapter in "Adding Security." Here we look at adding an administrator to a FrontPage Web using the Server Extensions Administrator.

To add an administrator to a Web, perform the following steps:

1. If the Web server is PWS or IIS 4 or later, right-click the Web you want to add an administrator to and select New, Server Extensions Administrator.

   Alternatively, select New, Administrator if the Web server is not IIS 4 or later. The New Administrator dialog box will open, as shown in Figure 21.19.

2. If the Web server is IIS 4 or later, enter the name of a valid Windows user account.

   Alternatively, enter a new user name in the Username field and a password in both the Password and Confirm Password fields.

For a better description of how security works on a Web, see the "Adding Security" section, later in this chapter.

21

FIGURE 21.19

You can add administrators to your Web without opening the Web in FrontPage.

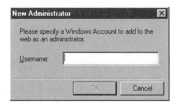

Checking the Server Extensions

Over a period of time, little errors can occur in the settings for your Web site. Luckily, the server extensions have a feature that will go through and check Webs to make sure they're functioning properly. Even if nothing is obviously wrong, it's good to use the Check Server Extensions feature as a preventative measure. You never know when a little error is about to spring into a bigger error.

To check the server extensions, perform the following steps:

1. Right-click the Web (subWeb or root Web) that you want to check and select Task, Check Server Extensions. This will open the Check Web dialog box, as shown in Figure 21.20.

FIGURE 21.20

The Check Server Extensions feature will scan your Web(s) for errors, report any that are found, and attempt to correct them.

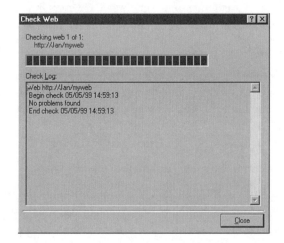

2. If you're running Windows NT on an NTFS partition, you'll be asked whether you want to tighten security. Click Yes if you want FrontPage to tighten security.

   The Check Web dialog box will log any errors and display them.

Recalculating Your Web

Whenever you make major changes to your site, such as adding or changing a number of Web pages, it's a good idea to *recalculate* your Web. Recalculating a Web tells the Web server to make sure any references to the FrontPage components are pointing to their proper location on the server. If you put a hit counter in one of your pages, recalculating will make sure that it actually points to the location of the hit counter executable.

If you're using the Search Component, it's important to recalculate your Web often. Indexing your Web pages—going through and tracking all the keywords—takes time. Because indexing every time you save a page would create an unbearable delay, FrontPage instead uses the Recalculate Web function to index all your pages in a Web at one time. If you don't recalculate your Webs often, you may find that your Search Component returns links to deleted pages and that new pages don't appear.

To recalculate a Web, right-click the Web (subWeb or root Web) you want to recalculate and select Task, Recalculate Web.

Converting Directories and Webs

The FrontPage 2000 server extensions now allow you to convert an existing Web to a directory as well as to convert directories to Webs. Converting directories to Webs is especially useful if you want to break a large Web into smaller subWeb pieces or if you want to hand over part of a site to someone else to maintain.

Converting directories to Webs is almost identical to creating Webs with the FrontPage server extensions. As a matter of fact, the act of converting a directory to a Web calls up the same wizard as creating a new Web.

To launch the wizard to convert a directory into a Web, right-click the directory you want to convert. The New SubWeb Wizard will open with the directory information already filled in for this Web.

FrontPage 2000 also lets you perform the opposite and make a Web a directory. This can be useful when you need to combine a subWeb back into its parent Web. When the conversion is complete, the directory will then appear as part of the parent Web in FrontPage.

To convert a subWeb into a directory, perform the following steps:

1. Right-click the Web you want to convert into a directory and select Task, Convert Server Extensions Web to Directory (see Figure 21.21). This will open the Convert Web to Folder dialog box. Before you convert a subWeb into a directory, read the warning carefully so you don't regret this action later.

21

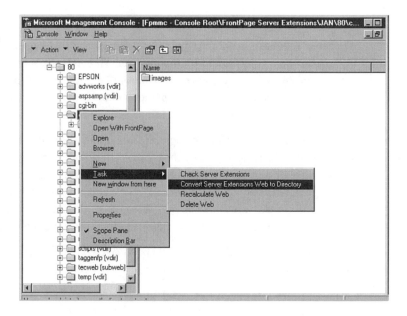

2. Read the dialog box carefully, because items such as navigation and task lists will be lost. If you want to begin the conversion, click Yes; otherwise, click No.

Configuring Web Settings

Now that we've covered most of the administrative functions of both FrontPage and the FrontPage server extensions, there are a few more optional settings that we need to discuss.

Changing Your Web's Name and Title

For one reason or another, you may get tired of the name you chose for one of your Webs, or you may decide it just isn't descriptive enough. Well, if you can change the names of Web pages, why not the name of your Web site?

Exercise 21.3: Changing the Name of Your Web

To change the name of your Web, perform the following steps:

1. In FrontPage, open the Web you want to change the name of.

2. In the FrontPage menu bar, select Tools, Web Settings. This will open the Web Settings dialog box.

3. On the General tab, enter the new name for your Web in the Web Name field.

4. Click OK when you've finished changing the name.

Displaying Documents in Hidden Directories

You may have created directories that begin with an underscore (such as _hidden) so that the files in them won't appear when someone lists the files in your Web. Well, this leaves the you with a problem: You can't see these directories and the files that are in them, either. FrontPage 2000 has a setting that will allow you to see these hidden directories without making them visible to everyone else.

To display documents in hidden directories, perform the following steps:

1. From the FrontPage menu, select Tools, Web Settings. This will open the Web Settings dialog box.
2. Click the Advanced tab to display the Advanced Web Settings page.
3. Check the box labeled Show Documents in Hidden Folders.
4. Click OK to close the Web Settings dialog box.

Setting the Default Web and HTML Encoding Languages

Not everyone speaks English, and many of us may need to design a Web page in another language, such as Spanish or even Japanese. With the new capabilities in FrontPage and Office 2000 to use multiple languages on one computer, these new features will become important as more users try their hand at writing in other languages.

When the FrontPage server extensions report errors, you'll definitely want be able to read and understand them. The server extensions can be told not only which language to report errors in but also which language components such as the Search Component should use in Web pages that return results.

To change the language used for server extension messages, perform the following steps:

1. In FrontPage, open the Web you want to set the language for.
2. From the FrontPage menu bar, select Tools, Web Settings to open the Web Settings dialog box.
3. Click the Language tab to open the Language Web Settings page.
4. From the Server Message Language drop-down menu, select the language you want FrontPage to use for the FrontPage components and error reports.
5. Click OK when finished to close the Web Settings dialog box.

If the server extensions can be told to use a different language, why not FrontPage itself? FrontPage can use a number of languages to author Web pages in, but you need to make sure there's a special HTML tag to tell browsers which language your pages are encoded

21

in so they can read your pages. The following instructions will set the default language for every page and can always be changed in individual Web pages from the General tab of the Page Options dialog box.

Exercise 21.4: Setting the HTML Encoding Language

To set the HTML encoding language for your Web, perform the following steps:

1. In FrontPage, open the Web you want to set the language for.
2. From the FrontPage menu bar, select Tools, Web Settings to open the Web Settings dialog box.
3. Click the Language tab to open the Language Web Settings page.
4. From the Default Page Encoding section, select the language setting you want all your pages in the Web to use.
5. Click OK when finished to close the Web Settings dialog box.

Setting Default Navigation Button Labels

You may find that the default button labels of Home, Up, Back, and Next just don't have enough spice for your Web site. Have no fear: You can be as creative as you want and change these anytime (although it's always good to change these when starting a Web to limit the number of problems you may have).

To change the default navigation button labels, perform the following steps:

1. In FrontPage, open the Web site whose default navigation labels you want to change.
2. From the FrontPage menu bar, select Tools, Web Settings to open the Web Settings dialog box.
3. Click the Navigation tab to open the Navigation Web Settings page.
4. Enter or choose the following options:
   - *Home*—The name of the root page of your Web site. This will always be the top page in your Navigation View.
   - *Parent Page*—Refers to the page that's directly above a page in the Navigation View.
   - *Previous Page*—Used when you have a number of grouped pages to link to the previous page in the group.
   - *Next Page*—Used when you have a number of grouped pages to link to the next page in the group.
5. Click OK when finished to close the Web Settings dialog box.

Adding Security

Put simply, *security* is the process of restricting access of files and directories to certain files. There are various ways to keep track of who gets access to which files, but all security measures save user names and passwords together in a form of database. On Windows NT, user accounts are kept in a specialized database called the Security Accounts Manager (SAM), but other operating systems and even some Web servers will have their own specialized user database.

FrontPage implements security on a Web-to-Web basis and cannot set security on individual files. The way FrontPage performs security will differ depending on the Web server, because FrontPage uses the security that's built into the Web server. With the exception of IIS, the Web servers that support the FrontPage server extensions will allow you to create new users to add to your Web as well as to limit the Web access to specific users. IIS does not allow you to create users because it makes use of Windows NT's native security features, which prohibit how users are created. IIS will still allow you to limit who can access your Web, but the user must have a registered Windows NT account. Users of the Personal Web Server on Windows 95/98 will not be able to use security locally, because FAT and FAT32 have no file security whatsoever. Even Personal Web Server works much the same as IIS does, but only the Windows NT Workstation version of PWS supports permissions, because it has the capability of using the secure NTFS file format. If you're using Windows NT, perform the following steps:

1. Open the Web you want to restrict access to.

2. From the FrontPage menu bar, choose Tools, Security, Permissions. This will open the Permissions dialog box for the Web.

3. If this is a subWeb, you'll see a page to inherit permissions from the parent or to use unique permissions. If you want to use permissions that are different than the parent Web, choose the Use Unique Permissions for This Web radio button. By default, FrontPage will use the same permissions as the parent Web.

4. The Users tab allows you to add or remove users from your Web as well as to restrict access to only registered users. If you want to have only registered users view your Web, choose Only Registered Users Have Browse Access.

5. You can use the Add button to add or remove users from the list as well as to determine their access levels. FrontPage provides three choices:

    - *Browse*—Browse access means this user can only view pages in your Web but not alter them.

    - *Author*—Author access allows a FrontPage user to create, change, and delete Web pages and directories in the Web but does not allow the user to create new Webs.

21

- *Administrate*—Administrate access has all the capabilities of Author access, except it allows the user to create new Webs.

6. Once you've finished, click the OK button to close the dialog box and apply your changes.

Summary

Regardless of whether you've published your Web, it's worth taking some time to check on it.

Work through the reports covered in this chapter and make sure you don't have any errors or files that will cause a huge download time.

If you find any long pages that are not really changeable or cannot be cut down, you should add a link somewhere telling the visitors that they will be in for a bit of a wait.

Use the other reports to check on the overall functionality of the site. If you've published your site but still find that the Tasks View is showing incomplete tasks, check which tasks they are. It may be that you've completed the tasks but not cleared them from the list.

Get into the habit of adding tasks to the list when you create new pages. As your site grows, maintenance becomes more and more important.

If your site has been published, make sure you've checked it online as well. Even the most careful planning and checking of a local Web is worth nothing if things go wrong once it's uploaded. Check all your pages, links, forms, and any other components you've added.

Workshop

Q&A

Q Why can't I create new administrators with IIS?

A IIS relies on the security features of Windows NT Server for authenticating users. When IIS asks for your user name and password, it's actually pulling this information from the NT Server's SAM. If IIS allowed accounts to be created, it would have to add them to the SAM. This would violate the security of the server as well as any computers in the server's domain. Windows NT's security meets certain standards established by the Department of Defense to prevent this sort of security violation. This close affiliation with Windows NT's security makes IIS very safe and secure, but it also means that to add a user, you need to talk to an administrator for the Web server and have him or her add the account.

Q How do I delete a FrontPage Web?

A This feature has now been moved to the Server Extensions Administrator. Select the subWeb you want to delete, and select Task, Delete Web.

Q Should I recalculate my Web?

A It's important to recalculate your Web regularly, especially after adding or changing pages. Recalculating ensures that all the links to components point to the right locations.

Q Can I change the title of my FrontPage Web?

A Yes. From the Tools menu, select Web Settings. In the Web Name tab, type whatever you want to call the Web.

Q I don't want the navigation buttons on my page to read "parent page." How do I change this?

A Selecting Tools, Web Settings, Navigation allows you to change the labels for any of the navigation buttons.

Quiz

1. What does the Site Summary report do?

2. What's the patience level of most site visitors?

3. How do you know which pages will not be published?

4. When is a Web site complete?

Exercises

1. Look at the Unlinked Files report in FrontPage. See what each of the files are before deleting them. Deleting a file from a FrontPage Web is an irreversible action. Therefore, you might want to create a new folder in the Web called "Old Files" and move the pages showing as unlinked to this folder.

2. If you started with a Web called "myWeb" or now have lots of Webs created by following the examples in this book, now would be a good time to delete them.

   Remember that disk-based Webs can be deleted using the Delete command in Windows Explorer, but server-based Webs need to be deleted using the Server Extensions Administrator.

Now that we're at the end of Day 21, it's time to clean up your computer and make sure you have a working Web site (that is, it does what you want and looks the way you intended).

21

If not, go back through the lessons and either work through them again or revise any points you're unsure of.

Answers to Quiz

1. The Site Summary report provides the overview of your site.

2. On average, a visitor will only wait 14 to 16 seconds for a page to load.

3. The Publish Status report lists all your pages and shows you simply which pages are not going to be published.

4. Never! A Web site can always be updated, increased, or modified.

APPENDIXES

A

B

C

APPENDIX **A**

HTML 4 Quick Reference

This appendix provides a quick reference to the elements and attributes of the HTML 4.0 language, as specified by the World Wide Web Consortium. It is based on the information provided in the *HTML 4.0 Specification*, revised April 24, 1998. The latest version of this document can be found at `http://www.w3.org/TR/REC-html40/`.

To make the information readily accessible, this appendix organizes HTML elements by their function in the following order:

- Structure:

  `BDO, BODY,` Comments, `DIV, !DOCTYPE, H1...H6, HEAD, HR, HTML, META, SPAN, TITLE`

- Text Phrases and Paragraphs:

  `ACRONYM, ADDRESS, BLOCKQUOTE, BR, CITE, CODE, DEL, DFN, EM, INS, KBD, P, PRE, Q, SAMP, STRONG, SUB, SUP, VAR`

- Text Formatting Elements:

  `B, BASEFONT, BIG, FONT, I, S, SMALL, STRIKE, TT, U`

- Lists:

  `DD, DL, DT, LI, MENU, OL, UL`

- Links:

  A, BASE, LINK

- Tables:

  CAPTION, COL, COLGROUP, TABLE, TBODY, TD, TFOOT, TH, THEAD, TR

- Frames:

  FRAME, FRAMESET, IFRAME, NOFRAMES

- Embedded content:

  APPLET, AREA, IMG, MAP, OBJECT, PARAM

- Style:

  STYLE

- Forms:

  BUTTON, FIELDSET, FORM, INPUT, ISINDEX, LABEL, LEGEND, OPTION, SELECT, TEXTAREA

- Scripts:

  SCRIPT, NOSCRIPT

Within each section the elements are listed alphabetically and the following information is presented:

- Usage—A general description of the element.
- Start/End Tag—Indicates whether these tags are required, optional, or illegal.
- Attributes—Lists the attributes of the element with a short description of their effect.
- Deprecated—Lists deprecated attributes—attributes that are still supported in HTML 4.0 and in most browsers, but that are in the process of being phased out in favor of newer techniques, such as style sheets.
- Empty—Indicates whether the element can be empty.
- Notes—Relates any special considerations when using the element and indicates whether the element is new, deprecated, or obsolete.

Common Attributes and Events

The HTML 4.0 specification includes several attributes that apply to a significant number of elements. These are referred to as %coreattrbs, %i18n, and %events throughout this appendix and are explained below.

%coreattrs

Four attributes are abbreviated as %coreattrs in the following sections. They are

- id="..."   A global identifier

- `class="..."`   A list of classes separated by spaces
- `style="..."`   Style information
- `title="..."`   Provides more information for a specific element, as opposed to the TITLE element, which entitles the entire Web page

%i18n

Two attributes for internationalization (i18n) are abbreviated as `%i18n`:

- `lang="..."`   The language identifier
- `dir="..."`   The text direction (`ltr`, `rtl`)

%events

The following intrinsic events are abbreviated `%events`:

- `onclick="..."`   A pointing device (such as a mouse) was single-clicked.
- `ondblclick="..."`   A pointing device (such as a mouse) was double-clicked.
- `onmousedown="..."`   A mouse button was clicked and held down.
- `onmouseup="..."`   A mouse button that was clicked and held down was released.
- `onmouseover="..."`   A mouse moved the cursor over an object.
- `onmousemove="..."`   The mouse was moved.
- `onmouseout="..."`   A mouse moved the cursor off an object.
- `onkeypress="..."`   A key was pressed and released.
- `onkeydown="..."`   A key was pressed and held down.
- `onkeyup="..."`   A key that was pressed has been released.

Structure

HTML relies upon several elements to provide structure to a document (as opposed to structuring the text within) as well as provide information that is used by the browser or search engines.

<BDO>...</BDO>

Usage	The bidirectional algorithm element is used to selectively turn off the default text direction.
Start/End Tag	Required/Required.
Attributes	`lang="..."` The language of the document.
	`dir="..."` The text direction (`ltr`, `rtl`).
Empty	No.
Notes	The `dir` attribute is mandatory.

<BODY>...</BODY>

Usage	Contains the content of the document.
Start/End Tag	Optional/Optional.
Attributes	%coreattrs, %i18n, %events
	onload="..." Intrinsic event triggered when the document loads.
	onunload="..." Intrinsic event triggered when document unloads.
Deprecated	The following presentational attributes are deprecated in favor of setting these values with style sheets.
	background="..." URL for the background image.
	bgcolor="..." Sets background color.
	text="..." Text color.
	link="..." Link color.
	vlink="..." Visited link color.
	alink="..." Active link color.
Empty	No.
Notes	There can be only one BODY, and it must follow the HEAD. The BODY element can be replaced by a FRAMESET element.

Comments <!-- ... -->

Usage	Used to insert notes or scripts that are not displayed by the browser.
Start/End Tag	Required/Required.
Attributes	None.
Empty	Yes.
Notes	Comments are not restricted to one line and can be any length. The end tag is not required to be on the same line as the start tag.

<DIV>...</DIV>

Usage	The division element is used to add structure to a block of text.
Start/End Tag	Required/Required.
Attributes	%coreattrs, %i18n, %events.

A

| Deprecated | The `align` attribute is deprecated in favor of controlling alignment through style sheets.

`align="..."` Controls alignment (`left`, `center`, `right`, `justify`). |
| Empty | No. |
| Notes | Cannot be used within a P element. |

`<!DOCTYPE...>`

| Usage | Version information appears on the first line of an HTML document and is a Standard Generalized Markup Language (SGML) declaration rather than an element. |

`<H1>...</H1>` through `<H6>...</H6>`

Usage	The six headings (H1 is the uppermost, or most important) are used in the BODY to structure information in a hierarchical fashion.
Start/End Tag	Required/Required.
Attributes	`%coreattrs`, `%i18n`, `%events`.
Deprecated	The ALIGN attribute is deprecated in favor of controlling alignment through style sheets.

`align="..."` Controls alignment (`left`, `center`, `right`, `justify`). |
| Empty | No. |
| Notes | Visual browsers will display the size of the headings in relation to their importance, with H1 being the largest and H6 the smallest. |

`<HEAD>...</HEAD`

| Usage | This is the document header and contains other elements that provide information to users and search engines. |
| Start/End Tag | Optional/Optional. |
| Attributes | `%i18n`.

`profile="..."` URL specifying the location of META data. |
| Empty | No. |
| Notes | There can be only one HEAD per document. It must follow the opening HTML tag and precede the BODY. |

\<HR\>

Usage	Horizontal rules are used to separate sections of a Web page.
Start/End Tag	Required/Illegal.
Attributes	%coreattrs, %events.
Deprecated	align="..." Controls alignment (left, center, right, justify).
	noshade="..." Displays the rule as a solid color.
	size="..." The size of the rule.
	width="..." The width of the rule.
Empty	Yes.

\<HTML\>...\</HTML\>

Usage	The HTML element contains the entire document.
Start/End Tag	Optional/Optional.
Attributes	%i18n.
Deprecated	version="..." URL of the document type definition specifying the HTML version used to create the document.
Empty	No.
Notes	The version information is duplicated in the \<!DOCTYPE...\> declaration and is therefore not essential.

\<META\>

Usage	Provides information about the document.
Start/End Tag	Required/Illegal.
Attributes	%i18n.
	http-equiv="..." HTTP response header name.
	name="..." Name of the meta information.
	content="..." Content of the meta information.
	scheme="..." Assigns a scheme to interpret the meta data.
Empty	Yes.

A

<SPAN>...</SPAN>

Usage	Organizes the document by defining a span of text.
Start/End Tag	Required/Required.
Attributes	%coreattrs, %i18n, %events.
Empty	No.

<TITLE>...</TITLE>

Usage	This is the name you give your Web page. The TITLE element is located in the HEAD element and is displayed in the browser window title bar.
Start/End Tag	Required/Required.
Attributes	%i18n.
Empty	No.
Notes	Only one title allowed per document.

Text Phrases and Paragraphs

Text phrases (or blocks) can be structured to suit a specific purpose, such as creating a paragraph. This should not be confused with modifying the formatting of the text.

<ACRONYM>...</ACRONYM>

Usage	Used to define acronyms.
Start/End Tag	Required/Required.
Attributes	%coreattrs, %i18n, %events.
Empty	No.

<ADDRESS>...</ADDRESS>

Usage	Provides a special format for author or contact information.
Start/End Tag	Required/Required.
Attributes	%coreattrs, %i18n, %events.
Empty	No.
Notes	The BR element is commonly used inside the ADDRESS element to break the lines of an address.

\<BLOCKQUOTE\>...\</BLOCKQUOTE\>

Usage	Used to display long quotations.
Start/End Tag	Required/Required.
Attributes	%coreattrs, %i18n, %events.
	cite="..." The URL of the quoted text.
Empty	No.

\<BR\>

Usage	Forces a line break.
Start/End Tag	Required/Illegal.
Attributes	%coreattrs, %i18n, %events.
Deprecated	clear="..." Sets the location where next line begins after a floating object (none, left, right, all).
Empty	Yes.

\<CITE\>...\</CITE\>

Usage	Cites a reference.
Start/End Tag	Required/Required.
Attributes	%coreattrs, %i18n, %events.
Empty	No.

\<CODE\>...\</CODE\>

Usage	Identifies a code fragment for display.
Start/End Tag	Required/Required.
Attributes	%coreattrs, %i18n, %events.
Empty	No.

\<DEL\>...\</DEL\>

Usage	Shows text as having been deleted from the document since the last change.
Start/End Tag	Required/Required.

Attributes	%coreattrs, %i18n, %events.
	cite="..." The URL of the source document.
	datetime="..." Indicates the date and time of the change.
Empty	No.
Notes	New element in HTML 4.0.

`<DFN>...</DFN>`

Usage	Defines an enclosed term.
Start/End Tag	Required/Required.
Attributes	%coreattrs, %i18n, %events.
Empty	No.

`<EM>...</EM>`

Usage	Emphasized text.
Start/End Tag	Required/Required.
Attributes	%coreattrs, %i18n, %events.
Empty	No.

`<INS>...</INS>`

Usage	Shows text as having been inserted in the document since the last change.
Start/End Tag	Required/Required.
Attributes	%coreattrs, %i18n, %events.
	cite="..." The URL of the source document.
	datetime="..." Indicates the date and time of the change.
Empty	No.
Notes	New element in HTML 4.0.

`<KBD>...</KBD>`

Usage	Indicates text a user would type.
Start/End Tag	Required/Required.
Attributes	%coreattrs, %i18n, %events.
Empty	No.

<P>...</P>

Usage	Defines a paragraph.
Start/End Tag	Required/Optional.
Attributes	%coreattrs, %i18n, %events.
Deprecated	align="..." Controls alignment (left, center, right, justify).
Empty	No.

<PRE>...</PRE>

Usage	Displays preformatted text.
Start/End Tag	Required/Required.
Attributes	%coreattrs, %i18n, %events.
Deprecated	width="..." The width of the formatted text.
Empty	No.

<Q>...</Q>

Usage	Used to display short quotations that do not require paragraph breaks.
Start/End Tag	Required/Required.
Attributes	%coreattrs, %i18n, %events.
	cite="..." The URL of the quoted text.
Empty	No.
Notes	New element in HTML 4.0.

<SAMP>...</SAMP>

Usage	Identifies sample output.
Start/End Tag	Required/Required.
Attributes	%coreattrs, %i18n, %events.
Empty	No.

\<STRONG\>...\</STRONG\>

Usage	Stronger emphasis.
Start/End Tag	Required/Required.
Attributes	%coreattrs, %i18n, %events.
Empty	No.

\<SUB\>...\</SUB\>

Usage	Creates subscript.
Start/End Tag	Required/Required.
Attributes	%coreattrs, %i18n, %events.
Empty	No.

\<SUP\>...\</SUP\>

Usage	Creates superscript.
Start/End Tag	Required/Required.
Attributes	%coreattrs, %i18n, %events.
Empty	No.

\<VAR\>...\</VAR\>

Usage	A variable.
Start/End Tag	Required/Required.
Attributes	%coreattrs, %i18n, %events.
Empty	No.

Text Formatting Elements

Text characteristics such as the size, weight, and style can be modified by using these elements, but the HTML 4.0 specification encourages you to use style sheets instead.

\<B\>...\</B\>

Usage	Bold text.
Start/End Tag	Required/Required.
Attributes	%coreattrs, %i18n, %events.
Empty	No.

\<BASEFONT\>

Usage	Sets the base font size.
Start/End Tag	Required/Illegal.
Deprecated	size="..." The font size (1 through 7 or relative).
	color="..." The font color.
	face="..." The font type.
Empty	Yes.
Notes	Deprecated in favor of style sheets.

\<BIG\>...\</BIG\>

Usage	Large text.
Start/End Tag	Required/Required.
Attributes	%coreattrs, %i18n, %events.
Empty	No.

\<FONT\>...\</FONT\>

Usage	Changes the font size and color.
Start/End Tag	Required/Required.
Deprecated	size="..." The font size (1 through 7 or relative).
	color="..." The font color.
	face="..." The font type.
Empty	No.
Notes	Deprecated in favor of style sheets.

\<I\>...\</I\>

Usage	Italicized text.
Start/End Tag	Required/Required.
Attributes	%coreattrs, %i18n, %events.
Empty	No.

\<S\>...\</S\>

Usage	Strikethrough text.
Start/End Tag	Required/Required.
Attributes	%coreattrs, %i18n, %events.
Empty	No.
Notes	Deprecated in favor of style sheets.

\<SMALL\>...\</SMALL\>

Usage	Small text.
Start/End Tag	Required/Required.
Attributes	%coreattrs, %i18n, %events.
Empty	No.

\<STRIKE\>...\</STRIKE\>

Usage	Strikethrough text.
Start/End Tag	Required/Required.
Attributes	%coreattrs, %i18n, %events.
Empty	No.
Notes	Deprecated in favor of style sheets.

\<TT\>...\</TT\>

Usage	Teletype (or monospaced) text.
Start/End Tag	Required/Required.
Attributes	%coreattrs, %i18n, %events.
Empty	No.

\<U\>...\</U\>

Usage	Underlined text.
Start/End Tag	Required/Required.
Attributes	%coreattrs, %i18n, %events.
Empty	No.
Notes	Deprecated in favor of style sheets.

Lists

You can organize text into a more structured outline by creating lists. Lists can be nested.

<DD>...</DD>

Usage	The definition description used in a DL (definition list) element.
Start/End Tag	Required/Optional.
Attributes	%coreattrs, %i18n, %events.
Empty	No.
Notes	Can contain block-level content, such as the <P> element.

<DIR>...</DIR>

Usage	Creates a multi-column directory list.
Start/End Tag	Required/Required.
Attributes	%coreattrs, %i18n, %events.
Deprecated	compact Compacts the displayed list.
Empty	No.
Notes	Must contain at least one list item. This element is deprecated in favor of the UL (unordered list) element.

<DL>...</DL>

Usage	Creates a definition list.
Start/End Tag	Required/Required.
Attributes	%coreattrs, %i18n, %events.
Deprecated	compact Compacts the displayed list.
Empty	No.
Notes	Must contain at least one <DT> or <DD> element in any order.

<DT>...</DT>

Usage	The definition term (or label) used within a DL (definition list) element.
Start/End Tag	Required/Optional.

Attributes	%coreattrs, %i18n, %events.
Empty	No.
Notes	Must contain text (which can be modified by text markup elements).

<LI>...</LI>

Usage	Defines a list item within a list.
Start/End Tag	Required/Optional.
Attributes	%coreattrs, %i18n, %events.
Deprecated	type="..." Changes the numbering style (1, a, A, i, I), in ordered lists, or bullet style (disc, square, circle) in unordered lists.
	value="..." Sets the numbering to the given integer beginning with the current list item.
Empty	No.

<MENU>...</MENU>

Usage	Creates a single-column menu list.
Start/End Tag	Required/Required.
Attributes	%coreattrs, %i18n, %events.
Deprecated	compact Compacts the displayed list.
Empty	No.
Notes	Must contain at least one list itcm. This element is deprecated in favor of the UL (unordered list) element.

<OL>...</OL>

Usage	Creates an ordered list.
Start/End Tag	Required/Required.
Attributes	%coreattrs, %i18n, %events.
Deprecated	compact Compacts the displayed list.
	start="..." Sets the starting number to the chosen integer.
	type="..." Sets the numbering style (1, a, A, i, I).
Empty	No.
Notes	Must contain at least one list item.

\<UL\>...\</UL\>

Usage	Creates an unordered list.
Start/End Tag	Required/Required.
Attributes	%coreattrs, %i18n, %events.
Deprecated	compact Compacts the displayed list.
	type="..." Sets the bullet style (disc, square, circle).
Empty	No.
Notes	Must contain at least one list item.

Links

Hyperlinking is fundamental to HTML. These elements enable you to link to other documents.

\<A\>...\</A\>

Usage	Used to define links and anchors.
Start/End Tag	Required/Required.
Attributes	%coreattrs, %i18n, %events.
	charset="..." Character encoding of the resource.
	name="..." Defines an anchor.
	href="..." The URL of the linked resource.
	target="..." Determines where the resource will be displayed (user-defined name, _blank, _parent, _self, _top).
	rel="..." Forward link types.
	rev="..." Reverse link types.
	accesskey="..." Assigns a hotkey to this element.
	shape="..." Enables you to define client-side imagemaps using defined shapes (default, rect, circle, poly).
	coords="..." Sets the size of the shape using pixel or percentage lengths.
	tabindex="..." Sets the tabbing order between elements with a defined tabindex.
Empty	No.

A

<BASE>

Usage	All other URLs in the document are resolved against this location.
Start/End Tag	Required/Illegal.
Attributes	`href="..."` The URL of the linked resource.
	`target="..."` Determines where the resource will be displayed (user-defined name, _blank, _parent, _self, _top).
Empty	Yes.
Notes	Located in the document HEAD.

<LINK>

Usage	Defines the relationship between a link and a resource.
Start/End Tag	Required/Illegal.
Attributes	`%coreattrs, %i18n, %events.`
	`href="..."` The URL of the resource.
	`rel="..."` The forward link types.
	`rev="..."` The reverse link types.
	`type="..."` The Internet content type.
	`media="..."` Defines the destination medium (screen, print, projection, braille, speech, all).
	`target="..."` Determines where the resource will be displayed (user-defined name, _blank, _parent, _self, _top).
Empty	Yes.
Notes	Located in the document HEAD.

Tables

Tables are meant to display data in a tabular format. Tables are widely used for page layout purposes, but with the advent of style sheets this is being discouraged by the HTML 4.0 specification.

<CAPTION>...</CAPTION>

Usage	Displays a table caption.
Start/End Tag	Required/Required.
Attributes	`%coreattrs, %i18n, %events.`

Deprecated	align="..." Controls alignment (left, center, right, justify).
Empty	No.
Notes	Optional.

`<COL>`

Usage	Groups columns within column groups in order to share attribute values.
Start/End Tag	Required/Illegal.
Attributes	%coreattrs, %i18n, %events.
	span="..." The number of columns the group contains.
	width="..." The column width as a percentage, pixel value, or minimum value.
	align="..." Horizontally aligns the contents of cells (left, center, right, justify, char).
	char="..." Sets a character on which the column aligns.
	charoff="..." Offset to the first alignment character on a line.
	valign="..." Vertically aligns the contents of a cell (top, middle, bottom, baseline).
Empty	Yes.

`<COLGROUP>...</COLGROUP>`

Usage	Defines a column group.
Start/End Tag	Required/Optional.
Attributes	%coreattrs, %i18n, %events.
	span="..." The number of columns in a group.
	width="..." The width of the columns.
	align="..." Horizontally aligns the contents of cells (left, center, right, justify, char).
	char="..." Sets a character on which the column aligns.
	charoff="..." Offset to the first alignment character on a line.
	valign="..." Vertically aligns the contents of a cell (top, middle, bottom, baseline).
Empty	No.

A

<TABLE>...</TABLE>

Usage	Creates a table.
Start/End Tag	Required/Required.
Attributes	`%coreattrs`, `%i18n`, `%events`.

`width="..."`   Table width.

`cols="..."`   The number of columns.

`border="..."`   The width in pixels of a border around the table.

`frame="..."`   Sets the visible sides of a table (`void`, `above`, `below`, `hsides`, `lhs`, `rhs`, `vsides`, `box`, `border`).

`rules="..."`   Sets the visible rules within a table (`none`, `groups`, `rows`, `cols`, `all`).

`cellspacing="..."`   Spacing between cells.

`cellpadding="..."`   Spacing in cells.

Deprecated	`align="..."` Controls alignment (`left`, `center`, `right`, `justify`).
	`bgcolor="..."` Sets the background color.
Empty	No.

<TBODY>...</TBODY>

Usage	Defines the table body.
Start/End Tag	Optional/Optional.
Attributes	`%coreattrs`, `%i18n`, `%events`.

`align="..."`   Horizontally aligns the contents of cells (`left`, `center`, `right`, `justify`, `char`).

`char="..."`   Sets a character on which the column aligns.

`charoff="..."`   Offset to the first alignment character on a line.

`valign="..."`   Vertically aligns the contents of cells (`top`, `middle`, `bottom`, `baseline`).

Empty	No.

<TD>...</TD>

Usage	Defines a cell's contents.
Start/End Tag	Required/Optional.
Attributes	%coreattrs, %i18n, %events.

axis="..." Abbreviated name.

axes="..." axis names listing row and column headers pertaining to the cell.

rowspan="..." The number of rows spanned by a cell.

colspan="..." The number of columns spanned by a cell.

align="..." Horizontally aligns the contents of cells (left, center, right, justify, char).

char="..." Sets a character on which the column aligns.

charoff="..." Offset to the first alignment character on a line.

valign="..." Vertically aligns the contents of cells (top, middle, bottom, baseline).

Deprecated	nowrap="..." Turns off text wrapping in a cell.

bgcolor="..." Sets the background color.

height="..." Sets the height of the cell.

width="..." Sets the width of the cell.

Empty	No.

<TFOOT>...</TFOOT>

Usage	Defines the table footer.
Start/End Tag	Required/Optional.
Attributes	%coreattrs, %i18n, %events.

align="..." Horizontally aligns the contents of cells (left, center, right, justify, char).

char="..." Sets a character on which the column aligns.

charoff="..." Offset to the first alignment character on a line.

valign="..." Vertically aligns the contents of cells (top, middle, bottom, baseline).

Empty	No.

<TH>...</TH>

Usage	Defines the cell contents of the table header.
Start/End Tag	Required/Optional.
Attributes	%coreattrs, %i18n, %events.

axis="..." Abbreviated name.

axes="..." axis names listing row and column headers pertaining to the cell.

rowspan="..." The number of rows spanned by a cell.

colspan="..." The number of columns spanned by a cell.

align="..." Horizontally aligns the contents of cells (left, center, right, justify, char).

char="..." Sets a character on which the column aligns.

charoff="..." Offset to the first alignment character on a line.

valign="..." Vertically aligns the contents of cells (top, middle, bottom, baseline).

Deprecated	nowrap="..." Turns off text wrapping in a cell.

bgcolor="..." Sets the background color.

height="..." Sets the height of the cell.

width="..." Sets the width of the cell.

Empty	No.

<THEAD>...</THEAD>

Usage	Defines the table header.
Start/End Tag	Required/Optional.
Attributes	%coreattrs, %i18n, %events.

align="..." Horizontally aligns the contents of cells (left, center, right, justify, char).

char="..." Sets a character on which the column aligns.

charoff="..." Offset to the first alignment character on a line.

valign="..." Vertically aligns the contents of cells (top, middle, bottom, baseline).

Empty	No.

A

<TR>...</TR>

Usage	Defines a row of table cells.
Start/End Tag	Required/Optional.
Attributes	`%coreattrs`, `%i18n`, `%events`.
	`align="..."` Horizontally aligns the contents of cells (`left`, `center`, `right`, `justify`, `char`).
	`char="..."` Sets a character on which the column aligns.
	`charoff="..."` Offset to the first alignment character on a line.
	`valign="..."` Vertically aligns the contents of cells (`top`, `middle`, `bottom`, `baseline`).
Deprecated	`bgcolor="..."` Sets the background color.
Empty	No.

Frames

Frames create new "panels" in the Web browser window that are used to display content from different source documents.

<FRAME>

Usage	Defines a `FRAME`.
Start/End Tag	Required/Illegal.
Attributes	`name="..."` The name of a frame.
	`src="..."` The source to be displayed in a frame.
	`frameborder="..."` Toggles the border between frames (`0`, `1`).
	`marginwidth="..."` Sets the space between the frame border and content.
	`marginheight="..."` Sets the space between the frame border and content.
	`noresize` Disables sizing.
	`scrolling="..."` Determines scrollbar presence (`auto`, `yes`, `no`).
Empty	Yes.

\<FRAMESET>...\</FRAMESET>

Usage	Defines the layout of FRAMES within a window.
Start/End Tag	Required/Required.
Attributes	rows="..." The number of rows.
	cols="..." The number of columns.
	onload="..." The intrinsic event triggered when the document loads.
	onunload="..." The intrinsic event triggered when the document unloads.
Empty	No.
Notes	FRAMESETs can be nested.

\<IFRAME>...\</IFRAME>

Usage	Creates an inline frame.
Start/End Tag	Required/Required.
Attributes	name="..." The name of the frame.
	src="..." The source to be displayed in a frame.
	frameborder="..." Toggles the border between frames (0, 1).
	marginwidth="..." Sets the space between the frame border and content.
	marginheight="..." Sets the space between the frame border and content.
	scrolling="..." Determines scrollbar presence (auto, yes, no).
	height="..." Height.
	width="..." Width.
Deprecated	align="..." Controls alignment (left, center, right, justify).
Empty	No.

A

<NOFRAMES>...</NOFRAMES>

Usage	Alternative content when frames are not supported.
Start/End Tag	Required/Required.
Attributes	None.
Empty	No.

Embedded Content

Also called inclusions, embedded content applies to Java applets, imagemaps, and other multimedia or programmatic content that is placed in a Web page to provide additional functionality.

<APPLET>...</APPLET>

Usage	Includes a Java applet.
Start/End Tag	Required/Required.
Deprecated	align="..." Controls alignment (left, center, right, justify).
	alt="..." Displays text while loading.
	archive="..." Identifies the resources to be preloaded.
	code="..." The applet class file.
	codebase="..." The URL base for the applet.
	height="..." The width of the displayed applet.
	hspace="..." The horizontal space separating the image from other content.
	name="..." The name of the applet.
	object="..." The serialized applet file.
	vspace="..." The vertical space separating the image from other content.
	width="..." The height of the displayed applet.
Empty	No.
Notes	APPLET is deprecated in favor of the OBJECT element.

<AREA>

Usage	The AREA element is used to define links and anchors.
Start/End Tag	Required/Illegal.
Attributes	shape="..." Enables you to define client-side imagemaps using defined shapes (default, rect, circle, poly).
	coords="..." Sets the size of the shape using pixel or percentage lengths.
	href="..." The URL of the linked resource.
	target="..." Determines where the resource will be displayed (user-defined name, _blank, _parent, _self, _top).
	nohref="..." Indicates that the region has no action.
	alt="..." Displays alternative text.
	tabindex="..." Sets the tabbing order between elements with a defined tabindex.
Empty	Yes.

<IMG>

Usage	Includes an image in the document.
Start/End Tag	Required/Illegal.
Attributes	%coreattrs, %i18n, %events.
	src="..." The URL of the image.
	alt="..." Alternative text to display.
	height="..." The height of the image.
	width="..." The width of the image.
	usemap="..." The URL to a client-side imagemap.
	ismap Identifies a server-side imagemap.

A

Deprecated	`align="..."` Controls alignment (`left`, `center`, `right`, `justify`).
	`border="..."` Border width.
	`hspace="..."` The horizontal space separating the image from other content.
	`vspace="..."` The vertical space separating the image from other content.
Empty	Yes.

<MAP>...</MAP>

Usage	When used with the AREA element, creates a client-side imagemap.
Start/End Tag	Required/Required.
Attributes	`%coreattrs`.
	`name="..."` The name of the imagemap to be created.
Empty	No.

<OBJECT>...</OBJECT>

Usage	Includes an object.
Start/End Tag	Required/Required.
Attributes	`%coreattrs, %i18n, %events`.
	`declare` A flag that declares but doesn't create an object.
	`classid="..."` The URL of the object's location.
	`codebase="..."` The URL for resolving URLs specified by other attributes.
	`data="..."` The URL to the object's data.
	`type="..."` The Internet content type for data.
	`codetype="..."` The Internet content type for the code.
	`standby="..."` Show message while loading.
	`height="..."` The height of the object.
	`width="..."` The width of the object.
	`usemap="..."` The URL to an imagemap.
	`shapes=` Enables you to define areas to search for hyperlinks if the object is an image.

A

name="..."   The URL to submit as part of a form.

tabindex="..."   Sets the tabbing order between elements with a defined tabindex.

Deprecated	align="..." Controls alignment (left, center, right, justify).	
	border="..." Displays the border around an object.	
	hspace="..." The space between the sides of the object and other page content.	
	vspace="..." The space between the top and bottom of the object and other page content.	
Empty	No.	

<PARAM>

Usage	Initializes an object.
Start/End Tag	Required/Illegal.
Attributes	name="..." Defines the parameter name.
	value="..." The value of the object parameter.
	valuetype="..." Defines the value type (data, ref, object).
	type="..." The Internet media type.
Empty	Yes.

Style

Style sheets (both inline and external) are incorporated into an HTML document through the use of the STYLE element.

<STYLE>...</STYLE>

Usage	Creates an internal style sheet.
Start/End Tag	Required/Required.
Attributes	%i18n.
	type="..." The Internet content type.
	media="..." Defines the destination medium (screen, print, projection, braille, speech, all).
	title="..." The title of the style.

Empty	No.
Notes	Located in the HEAD element.

Forms

Forms create an interface for the user to select options and submit data back to the Web server.

`<BUTTON>...</BUTTON>`

Usage	Creates a button.
Start/End Tag	Required/Required.
Attributes	%coreattrs, %i18n, %events.
	name="..." The button name.
	value="..." The value of the button.
	type="..." The button type (button, submit, reset).
	disabled="..." Sets the button state to disabled.
	tabindex="..." Sets the tabbing order between elements with a defined tabindex.
	onfocus="..." The event that occurs when the element receives focus.
	onblur="..." The event that occurs when the element loses focus.
Empty	No.

`<FIELDSET>...</FIELDSET>`

Usage	Groups related controls.
Start/End Tag	Required/Required.
Attributes	%coreattrs, %i18n, %events.
Empty	No.

`<FORM>...</FORM>`

Usage	Creates a form that holds controls for user input.
Start/End Tag	Required/Required.

Attributes   `%coreattrs`, `%i18n`, `%events`.

`action="..."`   The URL for the server action.

`enctype="..."`   Specifies the MIME (Internet media type).

`onsubmit="..."`   The intrinsic event that occurs when the form is submitted.

`onreset="..."`   The intrinsic event that occurs when the form is reset.

`target="..."`   Determines where the resource will be displayed (user-defined name, `_blank`, `_parent`, `_self`, `_top`).

`accept-charset="..."`   The list of character encodings.

`method="..."`   The HTTP method (`post` or `get`).

Empty   No.

`<INPUT>`

Usage   Defines controls used in forms.

Start/End Tag   Required/Illegal.

Attributes   `%coreattrs`, `%i18n`, `%events`.

`type="..."`   The type of input control (`text`, `password`, `checkbox`, `radio`, `submit`, `reset`, `file`, `hidden`, `image`, `button`).

`name="..."`   The name of the control (required except for `submit` and `reset`).

`value="..."`   The initial value of the control (required for radio and check boxes).

`checked="..."`   Sets the radio buttons to a checked state.

`disabled="..."`   Disables the control.

`readonly="..."`   For text password types.

`size="..."`   The width of the control in pixels except for text and password controls, which are specified in number of characters.

`maxlength="..."`   The maximum number of characters that can be entered.

`src="..."`   The URL to an image control type.

alt="..." An alternative text description.

usemap="..." The URL to a client-side imagemap.

tabindex="..." Sets the tabbing order between elements with a defined tabindex.

onfocus="..." The event that occurs when the element receives focus.

onblur="..." The event that occurs when the element loses focus.

onselect="..." Intrinsic event that occurs when the control is selected.

onchange="..." Intrinsic event that occurs when the control is changed.

accept="..." File types allowed for upload.

Deprecated	align="..." Controls alignment (left, center, right, justify).
Empty	Yes.

<ISINDEX>

Usage	Prompts the user for input.
Start/End Tag	Required/Illegal.
Attributes	%coreattrs, %i18n.
Deprecated	prompt="..." Provides a prompt string for the input field.
Empty	Yes.

<LABEL>...</LABEL>

Usage	Labels a control.
Start/End Tag	Required/Required.
Attributes	%coreattrs, %i18n, %events.

for="..." Associates a label with an identified control.

disabled="..." Disables a control.

accesskey="..." Assigns a hotkey to this element.

onfocus="..." The event that occurs when the element receives focus.

onblur="..." The event that occurs when the element loses focus.

Empty   No.

`<LEGEND>...</LEGEND>`

Usage	Assigns a caption to a FIELDSET.
Start/End Tag	Required/Required.
Attributes	%coreattrs, %i18n, %events.
	accesskey="..." Assigns a hotkey to this element.
Deprecated	align="..." Controls alignment (left, center, right, justify).
Empty	No.

`<OPTION>...</OPTION>`

Usage	Specifies choices in a SELECT element.
Start/End Tag	Required/Optional.
Attributes	%coreattrs, %i18n, %events.
	selected="..." Specifies whether the option is selected.
	disabled="..." Disables control.
	value="..." The value submitted if a control is submitted.
Empty	No.

`<SELECT>...</SELECT>`

Usage	Creates choices for the user to select.
Start/End Tag	Required/Required.
Attributes	%coreattrs, %i18n, %events.
	name="..." The name of the element.
	size="..." The width in number of rows.
	multiple Allows multiple selections.
	disabled="..." Disables the control.
	tabindex="..." Sets the tabbing order between elements with a defined tabindex.
	onfocus="..." The event that occurs when the element receives focus.

onblur="..." The event that occurs when the element loses focus.

onselect="..." Intrinsic event that occurs when the control is selected.

onchange="..." Intrinsic event that occurs when the control is changed.

Empty   No.

\<TEXTAREA\>...\</TEXTAREA\>

Usage   Creates an area for user input with multiple lines.

Start/End Tag   Required/Required.

Attributes   %coreattrs, %i18n, %events.

name="..." The name of the control.

rows="..." The width in number of rows.

cols="..." The height in number of columns.

disabled="..." Disables the control.

readonly="..." Sets the displayed text to read-only status.

tabindex="..." Sets the tabbing order between elements with a defined tabindex.

onfocus="..." The event that occurs when the element receives focus.

onblur="..." The event that occurs when the element loses focus.

onselect="..." Intrinsic event that occurs when the control is selected.

onchange="..." Intrinsic event that occurs when the control is changed.

Empty   No.

Notes   Text to be displayed is placed within the start and end tags.

Scripts

Scripting language is made available to process data and perform other dynamic events through the SCRIPT element.

<SCRIPT>...</SCRIPT>

Usage	The SCRIPT element contains client-side scripts that are executed by the browser.
Start/End Tag	Required/Required.
Attributes	type="..." Script language Internet content type.
	src="..." The URL for the external script.
Deprecated	language="..." The scripting language, deprecated in favor of the type attribute.
Empty	No.
Notes	You can set the default scripting language in the META element.

<NOSCRIPT>...</NOSCRIPT>

Usage	The NOSCRIPT element provides alternative content for browsers unable to execute a script.
Start/End Tag	Required/Required.
Attributes	None.
Empty	No.

Character Entities

Table A.1 contains the possible numeric and character entities for the ISO-Latin-1 (ISO8859-1) character set. Where possible, the character is shown.

Note Not all browsers can display all characters, and some browsers might even display characters different from those that appear in the table. Newer browsers seem to have a better track record for handling character entities, but be sure to test your HTML files extensively with multiple browsers if you intend to use these entities.

TABLE A.1   ISO-LATIN-1 CHARACTER SET

Character	Numeric Entity	Character Entity (if any)	Description
	`&#00;`–`&#08;`		Unused
	`&#09;`		Horizontal tab
	`&#10;`		Line feed
	`&#11;`–`&#31;`		Unused
	`&#32;`		Space
!	`&#33;`		Exclamation mark
"	`&#34;`	`&quot;`	Quotation mark
#	`&#35;`		Number sign
$	`&#36;`		Dollar sign
%	`&#37;`		Percent sign
&	`&#38;`	`&amp;`	Ampersand
'	`&#39;`		Apostrophe
(	`&#40;`		Left parenthesis
)	`&#41;`		Right parenthesis
*	`&#42;`		Asterisk
+	`&#43;`		Plus sign
,	`&#44;`		Comma
-	`&#45;`		Hyphen
.	`&#46;`		Period (fullstop)
/	`&#47;`		Solidus (slash)
0–9	`&#48;`–`&#57;`		Digits 0–9
:	`&#58;`		Colon
;	`&#59;`		Semicolon
<	`&#60;`	`&lt;`	Less than
=	`&#61;`		Equal sign
>	`&#62;`	`&gt;`	Greater than
?	`&#63;`		Question mark
@	`&#64;`		Commercial "at"
A–Z	`&#65;`–`&#90;`		Letters A–Z
[	`&#91;`		Left square bracket

A

Character	Numeric Entity	Character Entity (if any)	Description
\	&#92;		Reverse solidus (backslash)
]	&#93;		Right square bracket
^	&#94;		Caret
—	&#95;		Horizontal bar
`	&#96;		Grave accent
a–z	a–z		Letters a–z
{	&#123;		Left curly brace
|	|		Vertical bar
}	&#125;		Right curly brace
~	&#126;		Tilde
	&#127;–Ÿ		Unused
			non-breaking space
¡	&#161;	&iexcl;	Inverted exclamation
¢	&#162;	&cent;	Cent sign
£	&#163;	&pound;	Pound sterling
	&#164;	&curren;	General currency sign
¥	&#165;	&yen;	Yen sign
¦	&#166;	¦ or brkbar;	Broken vertical bar
§	&#167;	&sect;	Section sign
¨	&#168;	&uml;	Umlaut (dieresis)
©	&#169;	&copy;	Copyright
ª	&#170;	&ordf;	Feminine ordinal
‹	&#171;	&laquo;	Left angle quote, guillemet left
¬	&#172;	&not;	Not sign
-	&#173;	&shy;	Soft hyphen
®	&#174;	&reg;	Registered trademark
¯	&#175;	&hibar;	Macron accent
°	&#176;	&deg;	Degree sign
±	&#177;	&plusmn;	Plus or minus
^{2}	&#178;	&sup2;	Superscript two
^{3}	&#179;	&sup3;	Superscript three

continues

TABLE A.1 CONTINUED

Character	Numeric Entity	Character Entity (if any)	Description
´	&#180;	&acute;	Acute accent
µ	&#181;	&micro;	Micro sign
¶	&#182;	&para;	Paragraph sign
·	&#183;	&middot;	Middle dot
¸	&#184;	&cedil;	Cedilla
¹	&#185;	&sup1;	Superscript one
º	&#186;	&ordm;	Masculine ordinal
›	&#187;	&raquo;	Right angle quote, quillemet right
¼	&#188;	&frac14;	Fraction one-fourth
½	&#189;	&frac12;	Fraction one-half
¾	&#190;	&frac34;	Fraction three-fourths
¿	&#191;	&iquest	Inverted question mark
À	&#192;	&Agrave;	Capital A, grave accent
Á	&#193;	&Aacute;	Capital A, acute accent
Â	&#194;	&Acirc;	Capital A, circumflex accent
Ã	&#195;	&Atilde;	Capital A, tilde
Ä	&#196;	&Auml;	Capital A, dieresis or umlaut mark
Å	&#197;	&Aring;	Capital A, ring
Æ	&#198;	&AElig;	Capital AE diphthong (ligature)
Ç	&#199;	&Ccedil;	Capital C, cedilla
È	&#200;	&Egrave;	Capital E, grave accent
É	&#201;	&Eacute;	Capital E, acute accent
Ê	&#202;	&Ecirc;	Capital E, circumflex accent
Ë	&#203;	&Euml;	Capital E, dieresis or umlaut mark
Ì	&#204;	&Igrave;	Capital I, grave accent
Í	&#205;	&Iacute;	Capital I, acute accent
Î	&#206;	&Icirc;	Capital I, circumflex accent
Ï	&#207;	&Iuml;	Capital I, dieresis or umlaut mark
Ð	&#208;	&ETH;	Capital Eth, Icelandic
Ñ	&#209;	&Ntilde;	Capital N, tilde
Ò	&#210;	&Ograve;	Capital O, grave accent

Character	Numeric Entity	Character Entity (if any)	Description
Ó	&#211;	&Oacute;	Capital O, acute accent
Ô	&#212;	&Ocirc;	Capital O, circumflex accent
Õ	&#213;	&Otilde;	Capital O, tilde
Ö	&#214;	&Ouml;	Capital O, dieresis or umlaut mark
×	&#215;	&times;	Multiply sign
Ø	&#216;	&Oslash;	Capital O, slash
Ù	&#217;	&Ugrave;	Capital U, grave accent
Ú	&#218;	&Uacute;	Capital U, acute accent
Û	&#219;	&Ucirc;	Capital U, circumflex accent
Ü	&#220;	&Uuml;	Capital U, dieresis or umlaut mark
Ý	&#221;	&Yacute;	Capital Y, acute accent
Þ	&#222;	&THORN;	Capital THORN, Icelandic
ß	&#223;	&szlig;	Small sharp s, German (sz ligature)
à	&#224;	&agrave;	Small a, grave accent
á	&#225;	&aacute;	Small a, acute accent
â	&#226;	&acirc;	Small a, circumflex accent
ã	&#227;	&atilde;	Small a, tilde
ä	&#228;	&aauml;	Small a, dieresisor umlaut mark
å	&#229;	&aring;	Small a, ring
æ	&#230;	&aelig;	Small ae diphthong (ligature)
ç	&#231;	&ccedil;	Small c, cedilla
è	&#232;	&egrave;	Small e, grave accent
é	&#233;	&eacute;	Small e, acute accent
ê	&#234;	&ecirc;	Small e, circumflex accent
ë	&#235;	&euml;	Small e, dieresis or umlaut mark
ì	&#236;	&igrave;	Small i, grave accent
í	&#237;	&iacute;	Small i, acute accent
î	&#238;	&icirc;	Small i, circumflex accent
ï	&#239;	&iuml;	Small i, dieresis or umlaut mark
ð	&#240;	&eth;	Small eth, Icelandic
ñ	&#241;	&ntilde;	Small n, tilde
ò	&#242;	&ograve;	Small o, grave accent

A

continues

TABLE A.1   CONTINUED

Character	Numeric Entity	Character Entity (if any)	Description
ó	&#243;	&oacute;	Small o, acute accent
ô	&#244;	&ocirc;	Small o, circumflex accent
õ	&#245;	&otilde;	Small o, tilde
ö	&#246;	&ouml;	Small o, dieresis or umlaut mark
÷	&#247;	&divide;	Division sign
ø	&#248;	&oslash;	Small o, slash
ù	&#249;	&ugrave;	Small u, grave accent
ú	&#250;	&uacute;	Small u, acute accent
û	&#251;	&ucirc;	Small u, circumflex accent
ü	&#252;	&uuml;	Small u, dieresis or umlaut mark
´y	&#253;	&yacute;	Small y, acute accent
þ	&#254;	&thorn;	Small thorn, Icelandic
ÿ	&#255;	&yuml;	Small y, dieresis or umlaut mark

APPENDIX B

Cascading Style Sheet Quick Reference

Cascading Style Sheets (or CSS for short) allow for advanced placement and rendering of text and graphics on your pages. Text, images, and multimedia can be applied to your Web pages with great precision. This appendix provides a quick reference to CSS1, as well as those properties and values that are included in the CSS2 recommendation dated May 12, 1998.

> **Note**   This appendix is based on the information provided in the Cascading Style Sheets, Level 2 W3C recommendation dated May 12, 1998, which can be found at http://www.w3.org/TR/REC-CSS2/.

To make the information readily accessible, this appendix organizes CSS properties in the following order:

- Block-level properties
- Background and color properties

- Box model properties
- Font properties
- List properties
- Text properties
- Visual effects properties
- Aural style sheet properties
- Generated content/automatic numbering properties
- Paged media properties
- User interface properties
- Cascading Style Sheet units

How to Use This Appendix

Each property contains information presented in the following order:

- Usage—A description of the property
- CSS1 values—Legal CSS1 values and syntax
- CSS2 values—Legal CSS2 values and syntax
- Initial—The initial value
- Applies to—Elements to which the property applies
- Inherited—Whether the property is inherited
- Notes—Additional information

Deciphering CSS values is an exercise that requires patience and a strict adherence to the rules of logic. As you refer to the values for each property listed in this appendix, you should use the following scheme to understand them.

Values of different types are differentiated as follows:

- **Keyword values**—Keywords are identifiers, such as `red`, `auto`, `normal`, and `inherit`. They do not have quotation marks.
- **Basic data types**—These values, such as `<number>` and `<length>`, are contained within angled brackets to indicate the data type of the actual value used in a style statement. It is important to note that this refers to the data type and is not the actual value. The basic data types are described at the end of this appendix.
- **Shorthand reference**—Values that are enclosed in angled brackets and single quotation marks, such as `<'background-color'>` within the `background` property,

indicate a shorthand method for setting the desired value. The values identified in `background-color` are available for use in the `background` property. For example, if you choose to set the background color for the document body you can choose to do so by using either BODY { background: red } or BODY { background-color: red }.

- **Pre-defined data types**—Values within angled brackets without quotes, such as `<border-width>` within the `'border-top-width'` property, are similar to the basic data types but contain predefined values. For example, the available values for `<border-width>` are thin, thick, medium, and `<length>`.

When there is more than one value available, they are arranged according to the following rules:

- **Adjacent words**—Several adjacent words indicate all values must be used but can be in any order.
- **Values separated by bars "¦"**—The bar separates two or more alternatives, only one of which can occur.
- **Values separated by double-bars "¦¦"**—The double bar separates two or more options, of which one or more must occur in any order.
- **Brackets "[]"**—Brackets group the values into statements that are evaluated much like a mathematical expression.

When evaluating the values listed in this appendix, the order of precedence is that adjacent values take priority over those separated by double bars and then single bars.

In addition to this, special modifiers may follow each value or group of values. These are the following:

- ***** **(asterisk)**—The preceding type, word, or group occurs zero or more times
- **+** **(plus)**—The preceding type, word, or group occurs one or more times
- **?** **(question mark)**—The preceding type, word, or group is optional
- **(curly braces) "{}"**—Surrounding a pair of numbers, such as {1,2}, indicates the preceding type, word, or group occurs at least 1 and at most 2 times

Block-Level Properties

Block-level elements are those that are formatted visually as blocks. For example, a paragraph or a list is a block.

bottom, left, right, top

Usage	Specifies how far a box's bottom, left, right, or top content edge is offset from the respective bottom, left, right, or top of the box's containing block.
CSS2 Values	`<length>`	`<percentage>`	`auto`	`inherit`
Initial	`auto`
Applies to	All elements.
Inherited	No.
Notes	Percentage refers to height of containing block.

direction

Usage	Specifies the direction of inline box flow, embedded text direction, column layout, and content overflow.
CSS1 Values	`ltr`	`rtl`
CSS2 Values	`inherit`
Initial	`ltr`
Applies to	All elements.
Inherited	Yes.
Notes	See `unicode-bidi` for further properties that relate to embedded text direction.

display

Usage	Specifies how the contents of a block are to be generated.
CSS1 Values	`inline`	`block`	`list-item`
CSS2 Values	`run-in`	`compact`	`marker`	`table`	`inline-table`	`table-row-group`	`table-column-group`	`table-header-group`	`table-footer-group`	`table-row`	`table-cell`	`table-caption`	`none`	`inherit`
Initial	`inline`
Applies to	All elements.
Inherited	No.

float

Usage	Specifies whether a box should float to the left, right, or not at all.
CSS1 Values	none	left	right
CSS2 Values	inherit
Initial	none
Applies to	Elements that are not positioned absolutely.
Inherited	No.

B

position

Usage	Determines which CSS2 positioning algorithms are used to calculate the coordinates of a box.
CSS2 Values	static	<relative>	<absolute>	fixed	inherit
Initial	static
Applies to	All elements except generated content.
Inherited	No.

unicode-bidi

Usage	Opens a new level of embedding with respect to the bidirectional algorithm when elements with reversed writing direction are embedded more than one level deep.
CSS2 Values	normal	embed	bidi-override	inherit
Initial	normal
Applies to	All elements.
Inherited	No.

z-index

Usage	Specifies the stack level of the box, and whether the box establishes a local stacking context.
CSS2 Values	auto	<integer>	inherit
Initial	auto

| Applies to | Elements that generate absolutely and relatively positioned boxes. |
| Inherited | No. |

Background and Color Properties

Where HTML allows you to specify background and color properties for text, link, and background on a global basis in the document head, CSS includes similar properties that allow you to customize colors for individual elements. The following properties are those that affect foreground and background colors of page elements.

background

Usage	Shorthand property for setting the individual background properties at the same place in the style sheet.
CSS1 Values	[<'background-color'> ‖ <'background-image'> ‖ <'background-repeat'> ‖ <'background-attachment'> ‖ <'background-position'>]
CSS2 Values	inherit
Initial	Not defined.
Applies to	All elements.
Inherited	No.

background-attachment

Usage	If a background image is specified, this property specifies whether it is fixed in the viewport or scrolls along with the document.
CSS1 Values	scroll | fixed
CSS2 Values	inherit
Initial	scroll
Applies to	All elements.
Inherited	No.

background-color

| Usage | Sets the background color of an element. |
| CSS1 Values | <color> \| transparent |

CSS2 Values	inherit
Initial	transparent
Applies to	All elements.
Inherited	No.

background-image

Usage	Sets the background image of an element.
CSS1 Values	<uri> | none
CSS2 Values	inherit
Initial	none
Applies to	All elements.
Inherited	No.
Notes	Authors should also specify a background color that will be used when the image is unavailable.

background-position

Usage	Specifies the initial position of the background image, if one is specified.
CSS1 Values	[[<percentage> | <length>](1,2) | [top | center | bottom] || [left | center | right]]
CSS2 Values	inherit
Initial	0% 0%
Applies to	Block-level and replaced elements.
Inherited	No.

background-repeat

Usage	Specifies whether an image is repeated (tiled) and how, if a background image is specified.
CSS1 Values	repeat-x | repeat-y | repeat | no-repeat
CSS2 Values	inherit

B

Initial	repeat
Applies to	All elements.
Inherited	No.

color

Usage	Describes the foreground color of an element's text content.
CSS1 Values	`<color>`
CSS2 Values	`inherit`
Initial	Depends on browser.
Applies to	All elements.
Inherited	Yes.

Box Model Properties

Each page element in the document tree is contained within a rectangular box and laid out according to a visual formatting model. The following elements affect an element's box.

border

Usage	A shorthand property for setting the same width, color, and style on all four borders of an element.
CSS1 Values	`['border-width' ‖ 'border-style'	<color>]`
CSS2 Values	`inherit`
Initial	Not defined for shorthand properties.
Applies to	All elements.
Inherited	No.
Notes	This property accepts only one value. To set different values for each side of the border, use the `border-width`, `border-style`, or `border-color` properties.

border-bottom, border-left, border-right, border-top

Usage	Shorthand properties for setting the width, style, and color of an element's bottom, left, right, or top border (respectively).
CSS1 Values	['border-bottom-width' ‖ 'border-style' ‖ <color>]
	['border-left-width' ‖ 'border-style' ‖ <color>]
	['border-right-width' ‖ 'border-style' ‖ <color>]
	['border-top-width' ‖ 'border-style' ‖ <color>]
CSS2 Values	inherit
Initial	Not defined.
Applies to	All elements.
Inherited	No.

border-color

Usage	Sets the color of the four borders.
CSS1 Values	<color> (1,4) ‖ transparent
CSS2 Values	inherit
Initial	The value of the <color> property.
Applies to	All elements.
Inherited	No.
Notes	This property accepts up to four values, as follows:
	One value: Sets all four border colors
	Two values: First value for top and bottom; second value for right and left
	Three values: First value for top; second value for right and left; third value for bottom
	Four values: Top, right, bottom, and left respectively

B

border-bottom-color, border-left-color, border-right-color, border-top-color

Usage	Specifies the colors of a box's border.
CSS1 Values	`<color>`
CSS2 Values	`inherit`
Initial	The value of the `<color>` property.
Applies to	All elements.
Inherited	No.

border-style

Usage	Sets the style of the four borders.
CSS1 Values	`none	dotted	dashed	solid	double	groove	ridge	inset	outset`
CSS2 Values	`inherit`
Initial	`none`
Applies to	All elements.
Inherited	No.
Notes	This property can have from one to four values (see notes under `border-color` for explanation). If no value is specified, the color of the element itself will take its place.

border-bottom-style, border-left-style, border-right-style, border-top-style

Usage	Sets the style of a specific border (bottom, left, right, or top).
Values	Same as `border-style`.
Initial	`none`
Applies to	All elements.
Inherited	No.

border-width

Usage	A shorthand property for setting border-width-top, border-width-right, border-width-bottom, and border-width-left at the same place in the style sheet.
CSS1 Values	[thin | medium | thick] | <length>
CSS2 Values	inherit
Initial	Not defined.
Applies to	All elements.
Inherited	No.
Notes	This property accepts up to four values (see notes under border-color for explanation).

border-bottom-width, border-left-width, border-right-width, border-top-width

Usage	Sets the width of an element's bottom, left, right, or top border (respectively).
CSS1 Values	[thin | medium | thick] | <length>
CSS2 Values	inherit
Initial	medium
Applies to	All elements.
Inherited	No.

clear

Usage	Indicates which sides of an element's box or boxes may not be adjacent to an earlier floating box.
CSS1 Values	none | left | right | both
CSS2 Values	inherit
Initial	none
Applies to	Block-level elements.
Inherited	No.

B

height, width

Usage	Specifies the content height or width of a box.
CSS1 Values	`<length>` | `auto`
CSS2 Values	`<percentage>` | `inherit`
Initial	`auto`
Applies to	All elements but non-replaced inline elements and table columns; also does not apply to column groups (for `height`) or row groups (for `width`).
Inherited	No.

margin

Usage	Shorthand property for setting `margin-top`, `margin-right`, `margin-bottom` and `margin-left` at the same place in the style sheet.
CSS1 Values	`<length>` | `<percentage>` | `auto`
CSS2 Values	`inherit`
Initial	Not defined (shorthand property).
Applies to	All elements.
Inherited	No.

margin-bottom, margin-left, margin-right, margin-top

Usage	Sets the bottom, left, right, and top margins of a box (respectively).
CSS1 Values	`<length>` | `<percentage>` | `auto`
CSS2 Values	`inherit`
Initial	0
Applies to	All elements.
Inherited	No.

max-height, max-width

Usage	Constrains the height and width of a block to a maximum value.
CSS2 Values	`<length>`	`<percentage>`	`inherit`
Initial	100%
Applies to	All elements.
Inherited	No.
Notes	Percentages refer to the height of the containing block.

min-height, min-width

Usage	Constrains the height and width of a block to a minimum value.
CSS2 Values	`<length>`	`<percentage>`	`inherit`
Initial	0
Applies to	All elements.
Inherited	No.
Notes	Percentages refer to the height of the containing block.

padding

Usage	Shorthand property that sets `padding-top`, `padding-right`, `padding-bottom`, and `padding-left` at the same place in the style sheet.
CSS1 Values	`<length>`	`<percentage>`
CSS2 Values	`inherit`
Initial	Not defined.
Applies to	All elements.
Inherited	No.

B

padding-top, padding-right, padding-bottom, padding-left

Usage	Specifies the width of the padding area of a box's top, right, bottom, and left sides.
CSS1 Values	`<length>`	`<percentage>`
CSS2 Values	`inherit`
Initial	0
Applies to	All elements.
Inherited	No.
Notes	Values cannot be negative. Percentage values refer to the width of the containing block.

Font Properties

Far more powerful than the font tags and attributes found in HTML 4.0, Cascading Style Sheets allow you to affect many additional elements of a font. CSS1 font properties assume that the font is resident on the client's system and specify alternative fonts through other properties. The properties proposed in CSS2 go beyond that, allowing authors to actually describe the fonts they want to use, and increases the capability for browsers to select fonts when the font the author specified is not available.

font

Usage	A shorthand property for setting `font-style`, `font-variant`, `font-weight`, `font-size`, `line-height`, and `font-family` at the same place in the style sheet.
CSS1 Values	`[['font-style' || 'font-variant' || 'font-weight']? 'font-size' [/'line-height']? font-family`
CSS2 Values	`caption	icon	menu	message-box	small-caption	status-bar	inherit`
Initial	See individual properties.
Applies to	All elements.

Inherited	Yes.
Notes	Percentages allowed on `font-size` and `line-height`. For backward compatibility, set `font-stretch` and `font-size-adjust` by using their respective individual properties.

font-family

Usage	Specifies a list of font family names and generic family names.
CSS1 Values	`[[<family-name>` | `<generic-family>` `[,]* [<family-name>` | `<generic-family>]`,
CSS2 Values	`inherit`
Initial	Depends on browser.
Applies to	All elements.
Inherited	Yes.
Notes	`<family-name>` displays a font family of choice (Arial, Helvetica, or Bookman, for example). `<generic-family>` assigns one of five generic family names: `serif`, `sans-serif`, `cursive`, `fantasy`, or `monospace`.

font-size

Usage	Describes the size of the font when set solid.
CSS1 Values	`<absolute-size>` | `<relative-size>` | `<length>` | `<percentage>`
CSS2 Values	`inherit`
Initial	`medium`
Applies to	All elements.
Inherited	The computed value is inherited.
Notes	Percentages can be used relative to parent element's font size.

font-size-adjust

Usage	Allows authors to specify a z-value for an element that preserves the x-height of the first choice substitute font.
CSS2 Values	`<number>` | `none` | `inherit`

Initial	none
Applies to	All elements.
Inherited	Yes.
Notes	Percentages can be used relative to parent element's font size.

font-stretch

Usage	Specifies between normal, condensed, and extended faces within a font family.
CSS2 Values	normal	wider	narrower	ultra-condensed	extra-condensed	condensed	semi-condensed	semi-expanded	expanded	extra-expanded	ultra-expanded	inherit
Initial	normal
Applies to	All elements.
Inherited	Yes.

font-style

Usage	Requests normal (roman or upright), italic, and oblique faces within a font family.
CSS1 Values	normal	italic	oblique
CSS2 Values	inherit
Initial	normal
Applies to	All elements.
Inherited	Yes.

font-variant

Usage	Specifies a font that is not labeled as a small-caps font (normal) or one that is labeled as a small-caps font (small-caps).
CSS1 Values	normal	small-caps
CSS2 Values	inherit
Initial	normal

Applies to	All elements.
Inherited	Yes.

font-weight

Usage	Specifies the weight of the font.
CSS1 Values	normal	bold	bolder	lighter	100	200	300	400	500	600	700	800	900
CSS2 Values	inherit
Initial	normal
Applies to	All elements.
Inherited	Yes.
Notes	Values 100 through 900 form an ordered sequence. Each number indicates a weight that is at least as dark as its predecessor. Normal is equal to a weight of 400, while bold is equal to a weight of 700.

List Properties

When an element is assigned a display value of list-item, the element's content is contained in a box, and an optional marker box can be specified. The marker defines the image, glyph, or number that is used to identify the list item. The following properties affect list items and markers.

list-style

Usage	Shorthand notation for setting list-style-type, list-style-image, and list-style-position at the same place in the style sheet.
CSS1 Values	['list-style-type' || 'list-style-position' || 'list-style-image']
CSS2 Values	inherit
Initial	Not defined.
Applies to	Elements with display property set to list-item.
Inherited	Yes.

list-style-image

Usage	Sets the image that will be used as the list item marker.
CSS1 Values	`<uri>` | `none`
CSS2 Values	`inherit`
Initial	`none`
Applies to	Elements with `display` property set to `list-item`.
Inherited	Yes.

list-style-position

Usage	Specifies the position of the marker box with respect to the line item content box.
CSS1 Values	`inside` | `outside`
CSS2 Values	`inherit`
Initial	`outside`
Applies to	Elements with `display` property set to `list-item`.
Inherited	Yes.

list-style-type

Usage	Specifies the appearance of the list item marker when `list-style-image` is set to `none`.
CSS1 Values	`disc` | `circle` | `square` | `decimal` | `lower-roman` | `upper-roman` | `lower-alpha` | `upper-alpha` | `none`
CSS2 Values	`leading-zero` | `western-decimal` | `lower-greek` | `lower-latin` | `upper-latin` | `hebrew` | `armenian` | `georgian` | `cjk-ideographic` | `hiragana` | `katakana` | `hiragana-iroha` | `katakana-iroha` | `inherit`
Initial	`disc`
Applies to	Elements with `display` property set to `list-item`.
Inherited	Yes.

Text Properties

The following properties affect the visual presentation of characters, spaces, words, and paragraphs.

letter-spacing

Usage	Specifies the spacing behavior between text characters.
CSS1 Values	`normal	<length>`
CSS2 Values	`inherit`
Initial	`normal`
Applies to	All elements.
Inherited	Yes.

line-height

Usage	Specifies the minimal height of each inline box.
CSS1 Values	`normal	number	<length>	<percentage>`
CSS2 Values	`inherit`
Initial	`normal`
Applies to	All elements.
Inherited	Yes.

text-align

Usage	Describes how a block of text is aligned.
CSS1 Values	`left	right	center	justify`
CSS2 Values	`<string>	inherit`
Initial	Depends on browser and writing direction.
Applies to	Block-level elements.
Inherited	Yes.

B

text-decoration

Usage	Describes decorations that are added to the text of an element.
CSS1 Values	none | underline | overline | line-through | blink
CSS2 Values	inherit
Initial	none
Applies to	All elements.
Inherited	No.

text-indent

Usage	Specifies the indentation of the first line of text in a block.
CSS1 Values	\<length> | \<percentage>
CSS2 Values	inherit
Initial	0
Applies to	Block-level elements.
Inherited	Yes.

text-shadow

Usage	Accepts a comma-separated list of shadow effects to be applied to the text of an element.
CSS2 Values	none | \<color> | \<length> | inherit
Initial	none
Applies to	All elements.
Inherited	No.
Notes	Text shadows may also be used with :first-letter and :first-line pseudo-elements.

text-transform

Usage	Controls the capitalization of an element's text.
CSS1 Values	capitalize | uppercase | lowercase | none

CSS2 Values	`inherit`
Initial	`none`
Applies to	All elements.
Inherited	Yes.

vertical-align

Usage	Affects the vertical positioning of the boxes generated by an inline-level element.
Values	`baseline` | `sub` | `super` | `top` | `texttop` | `middle` | `bottom` | `text-bottom` | `sub` | `<percentage>`
CSS2 Values	`inherit`
Initial	`baseline`
Applies to	Inline-level and table-cell elements.
Inherited	No.

white-space

Usage	Specifies how whitespace inside the element is handled.
CSS1 Values	`normal` | `pre` | `nowrap`
CSS2 Values	`inherit`
Initial	`normal`
Applies to	Block-level elements.
Inherited	Yes.

word-spacing

Usage	Specifies the spacing behavior between words.
Values	`normal` | `<length>`
CSS2 Values	`inherit`
Initial	`normal`
Applies to	All elements.
Inherited	Yes.

B

Visual Effects Properties

The following properties affect visual rendering of an element.

`clip`

Usage	Defines what portion of an element's rendered content is visible.
CSS2 Values	`<shape>` | `auto` | `inherit`
Initial	`auto`
Applies to	Block-level and replaced elements.
Inherited	No.

`overflow`

Usage	Specifies whether the contents of a block-level element are clipped when they overflow the element's box.
CSS2 Values	`visible` | `hidden` | `scroll` | `auto` | `inherit`
Initial	`visible`
Applies to	Block-level and replaced elements.
Inherited	No.

`visibility`

Usage	Specifies whether the boxes generated by an element are rendered.
CSS2 Values	`visible` | `hidden` | `collapse` | `inherit`
Initial	`inherit`
Applies to	All elements.
Inherited	No.

Aural Style Sheet Properties

Aural style sheets, a proposed media type for CSS2, are primarily used for the blind and visually impaired communities. Page contents are read to the user. The aural style sheet "canvas" uses dimensional space to render sounds in specified sequences as page elements are displayed and selected.

azimuth

Usage	Allows you to position a sound. Designed for spatial audio, which requires binaural headphones or 5-speaker home theater systems.
CSS2 Values	`<angle>` | [[`left-side` | `far-left` | `left` | `center-left` | `center` | `center-right` | `right` | `far-right` | `right-side`] || `behind`]| `leftwards` | `rightwards` | `inherit`
Initial	center
Applies to	All elements.
Inherited	Yes.

B

cue

Usage	Shorthand property for `cue-before` and `cue-after`. Plays a sound before or after an element is rendered.
CSS2 Values	`cue-before` | `cue-after` | `inherit`
Initial	Not defined (shorthand property).
Applies to	All elements.
Inherited	No.

cue-after, cue-before

Usage	Plays a sound after (`cue-after`) or before (`cue-before`) an element is rendered.
CSS2 Values	`<uri>` | `none` | `inherit`
Initial	none
Applies to	All elements.
Inherited	No.

elevation

Usage	Allows you to position the angle of a sound. For use with spatial audio (binaural headphones or 5-speaker home theater setups required).
CSS2 Values	`<angle>` | `below` | `level` | `above` | `higher` | `lower` | `inherit`

Initial	`level`
Applies to	All elements.
Inherited	Yes.

pause

Usage	A shorthand property for setting `pause-before` and `pause-after` in the same location in the style sheet.
CSS2 Values	`<time>` | `<percentage>` | `inherit`
Initial	Depends on browser.
Applies to	All elements.
Inherited	No.

pause-after, pause-before

Usage	Specifies a pause to be observed before or after speaking an element's content.
CSS2 Values	`<time>` | `<percentage>` | `inherit`
Initial	Depends on browser.
Applies to	All elements.
Inherited	No.

pitch

Usage	Specifies the average pitch (frequency) of the speaking voice.
CSS2 Values	`<frequency>` | `x-low` | `low` | `medium` | `high` | `x-high` | `inherit`
Initial	`medium`
Applies to	All elements.
Inherited	Yes.
Notes	Average pitch for standard male voice is around 120hZ; for female voice it is around 210hZ.

pitch-range

Usage	Specifies variation in average pitch. Used to vary inflection and add animation to the voice.
CSS2 Values	`<number>`	`inherit`
Initial	50
Applies to	All elements.
Inherited	Yes.

play-during

Usage	Specifies a sound to be played as a background while an element's content is spoken.
CSS2 Values	`<uri>`	`mix?`	`repeat?`	`auto`	`none`	`inherit`
Initial	`auto`
Applies to	All elements.
Inherited	No.

richness

Usage	Specifies the richness, or brightness, of the speaking voice.
CSS2 Values	`<number>`	`inherit`
Initial	50
Applies to	All elements.
Inherited	Yes.

speak

Usage	Specifies whether text will be rendered aurally, and in what manner
CSS2 Values	`normal`	`none`	`spell-out`	`inherit`
Initial	`normal`
Applies to	All elements.
Inherited	Yes.

B

speak-header

Usage	Specifies whether table headers are spoken before every cell, or only before a cell when it is associated with a different header than a previous cell.
CSS2 Values	`once` | `always` | `inherit`
Initial	`once`
Applies to	Elements that have header information.
Inherited	Yes.

speak-numeral

Usage	Speaks numbers as individual digits (100 is spoken as "one zero zero", or as a continuous full number (100 is spoken as "one hundred").
CSS2 Values	`digits` | `continuous` | `inherit`
Initial	`continuous`
Applies to	All elements.
Inherited	Yes.

speak-punctuation

Usage	Speaks punctuation literally (period, comma, and so on) or naturally as various pauses.
CSS2 Values	`code` | `none` | `inherit`
Initial	`none`
Applies to	All elements.
Inherited	Yes.

speech-rate

Usage	Specifies the speaking rate of the voice.
CSS2 Values	`<number>` | `x-slow` | `slow` | `medium` | `fast` | `x-fast` | `faster` | `slower` | `inherit`
Initial	`medium`

Applies to	All elements.
Inherited	Yes.

stress

Usage	Specifies the height of "local peaks" in the intonation of a voice. Controls the amount of inflection within stress markers.
CSS2 Values	`<number>`	`inherit`
Initial	50
Applies to	All elements.
Inherited	Yes.
Notes	A companion to the `pitch-range` property.

voice-family

Usage	Specifies a comma-separated list of voice family names.
CSS2 Values	`<specific-voice>`	`<generic-voice>`	`inherit`
Initial	Depends on browser.
Applies to	All elements.
Inherited	Yes.

volume

Usage	Specifies the median volume of a waveform. Ranges from 0 (minimum audible volume level) to 100 (maximum comfortable level).
CSS2 Values	`<number>`	`<percentage>`	`silent`	`x-soft`	`soft`	`medium`	`loud`	`x-loud`	`inherit`
Initial	`medium`
Applies to	All elements.
Inherited	Yes.
Notes	Silent renders no sound at all. x-soft = 0, soft = 25, medium = 50, loud = 75, and x-loud = 100.

B

Generated Content / Automatic Numbering Properties

CSS2 introduces properties and values that allow authors to render content automatically (for example, numbered lists can be generated automatically). Authors specify style and location of generated content with `:before` and `:after` pseudo-elements that indicate the page elements before and after which content is generated automatically.

content

Usage	Used with `:before` and `:after` pseudo-elements to generate content in a document.
CSS2 Values	`<string>` | `<uri>` | `<counter>` | `attr(X)` | `open-quote` | `close-quote` | `no-open-quote` | `no-close-quote` | `inherit`
Initial	empty string
Applies to	`:before` and `:after` pseudo-elements.
Inherited	All.

counter-increment

Usage	Accepts one or more names of counters (identifiers), each one optionally followed by an integer. The integer indicates the amount of increment for every occurrence of the element.
CSS2 Values	`<identifier>` | `<integer>` | `none` | `inherit`
Initial	`none`
Applies to	All elements.
Inherited	No.

counter-reset

Usage	Contains a list of one or more names of counters. The integer gives the value that the counter is set to on each occurrence of the element.
CSS2 Values	`<identifier>` | `<integer>` | `none` | `inherit`
Initial	`none`
Applies to	All elements.
Inherited	No.

marker-offset

Usage	Specifies the distance between the nearest border edges of a marker box and its associated principal box.
CSS2 Values	`<length>` | `auto` | `inherit`
Initial	`auto`
Applies to	Elements with `display` property set to `marker`.
Inherited	No.

quotes

Usage	Specifies quotation marks for embedded quotations.
CSS2 Values	`<string>` | `<string>+` | `none` | `inherit`
Initial	Depends on browser.
Applies to	All elements.
Inherited	Yes.

Paged Media Properties

Normally, a Web page is displayed as a continuous page. CSS2 introduces the concept of paged media, which is designed to split a document into one or more discrete pages for display on paper, transparencies, computer screens, and so on. Page size, margins, page breaks, widows, and orphans can all be set with the following properties and values.

marks

Usage	Specifies whether cross marks, crop marks, or both should be rendered just outside the page box. Used in high-quality printing.
CSS2 Values	`crop` | `cross` | `none` | `inherit`
Initial	`none`
Applies to	Page context.
Inherited	N/A.

orphans

Usage	Specifies the minimum number of lines of a paragraph that must be left at the bottom of a page.
CSS2 Values	`<integer>` | `inherit`
Initial	2
Applies to	Block-level elements.
Inherited	Yes.

page

Usage	Used to specify a particular type of page where an element should be displayed.
CSS2 Values	`<identifier>` `:left` | `:right` | `auto`
Initial	`auto`
Applies to	Block-level elements.
Inherited	Yes.
Notes	By adding `:left` or `:right`, the element can be forced to fall on a left or right page.

page-break-after, page-break-before

Usage	Specifies page breaks before the following element or after the preceding element.
CSS2 Values	`auto` | `always` | `avoid` | `left` | `right` | `inherit`
Initial	`auto`
Applies to	Block-level elements.
Inherited	No.

page-break-inside

Usage	Forces a page break inside the parent element.
CSS2 Values	`avoid` | `auto` | `inherit`
Initial	`auto`

Applies to	Block-level elements.
Inherited	Yes.

size

Usage	Specifies the size and orientation of a page box.
CSS2 Values	`<length>`	`auto`	`portrait`	`landscape`	`inherit`
Initial	`auto`
Applies to	Page context.
Inherited	N/A.

widows

Usage	Specifies the minimum number of lines of a paragraph that must be left at the top of a page.
CSS2 Values	`<integer>`	`inherit`
Initial	2
Applies to	Block-level elements.
Inherited	Yes.

Table Properties

The CSS table model is based on the HTML 4.0 table model, which consists of tables, captions, rows, row groups, columns, column groups, and cells. In CSS2, tables can be rendered visually and aurally. Authors can specify how headers and data will be spoken through attributes defined previously under "Aural Page Properties."

border-collapse

Usage	Selects a table's border model.
CSS2 Values	`collapse`	`separate`	`inherit`
Initial	`collapse`
Applies to	Table and inline table elements.
Inherited	Yes.

border-spacing

Usage	In separated borders model, specifies the distance that separates the adjacent cell borders.
CSS2 Values	`<length>` | `<length>` `?` | `inherit`
Initial	0
Applies to	Table and inline table elements.
Inherited	Yes.

caption-side

Usage	Specifies the position of the caption box with respect to the table box.
CSS2 Values	`top` | `bottom` | `left` | `right` | `inherit`
Initial	`top`
Applies to	Table caption elements.
Inherited	Yes.

column-span, row-span

Usage	Specifies the number of columns or rows (respectively) spanned by a cell.
CSS2 Values	`<integer>` | `inherit`
Initial	1
Applies to	Table-cell, table-column, and table-column-group elements (`column-span`); table-cell elements (`row-span`).
Inherited	No.

empty-cells

Usage	In separated tables model, specifies how borders around cells that have no visible content are rendered.
CSS2 Values	`borders` | `no-borders` | `inherit`
Initial	`borders`

Applies to	Table cell elements.
Inherited	Yes.

table-layout

Usage	Controls the algorithm used to lay out the table cells.
CSS2 Values	auto	fixed	inherit
Initial	auto
Applies to	Table and inline table elements.
Inherited	No.
Notes	Fixed table layout depends on the width of the table and its columns. Auto table layout depends on the contents of the cells.

User Interface Properties

User interface properties allow customization of cursor appearance, color preferences, font preferences, and dynamic outlines.

cursor

Usage	Specifies the type of cursor which displays for a pointing device.
CSS2 Values	<uri>	auto	crosshair	default	pointer	move	e-resize	ne-resize	nw-resize	n-resize	se-resize	sw-resize	s-resize	w-resize	text	wait	help	inherit
Initial	auto
Applies to	All elements.
Inherited	Yes.

outline

Usage	Shorthand property for setting outline-color, outline-style, and outline-width.
CSS2 Values	outline-color	outline-style	outline-width	inherit
Initial	See individual properties.

Applies to	All elements.
Inherited	No.
Notes	Similar to `border` property, creates an outline around visual objects such as buttons, active form fields, imagemaps, and so on. Using `outline` property instead of `border` property does not cause reflow when displaying or suppressing the outline. Outlines can also be non-rectangular.

outline-color

Usage	Specifies the color of the outline.
CSS2 Values	`<color>` | `invert` | `inherit`
Initial	`invert`
Applies to	All elements.
Inherited	No.

outline-style

Usage	Specifies the style of the outline.
CSS2 Values	same as `<border-style>` | `inherit`
Initial	`none`
Applies to	All elements.
Inherited	No.

outline-width

Usage	Specifies the width of the outline.
CSS2 Values	same as `<border-width>` | `inherit`
Initial	`medium`
Applies to	All elements.
Inherited	No.

Cascading Style Sheet Units

Several Cascading Style Sheet attributes use standard units to define measurements, styles, colors, and other identifiers. Throughout this appendix, unit measurements have been enclosed within brackets (< >). The following section lists the values associated with each unit type.

B

`<absolute-size>`

Absolute sizes refer to font sizes computed and kept by the user's browser. The following values are from smallest to largest:

```
xx-small
x-small
small
medium
large
x-large
xx-large
```

`<angle>`

Angle values are used with aural style sheets. Their format is an optional sign character (+ or -) immediately followed by a number. The following are angle units:

deg	degrees
grad	grads
rad	radians

`<border-style>`

These properties specify the type of line that surrounds a box's border. The `border-style` value type can take one of the following:

none	Forces border width to zero
dotted	A series of dots
dashed	A series of short line segments
solid	A single line segment
double	Two solid lines, with the sum of the two lines and the space between them equaling the value of `border-width`

groove	Renders a border that looks as though it is carved into the canvas
ridge	Renders a border that looks as though it is coming out of the canvas
inset	Renders a border that looks like the entire box is embedded into the canvas
outset	Renders a border that looks like the entire box is coming out of the canvas

`<border-width>`

The `border-width` property sets the width of the border area. It can take one of the following values:

thin	A thin border
medium	A medium border
thick	A thick border
`<length>`	An explicit value (cannot be negative)

`<color>`

Colors can be defined by keyword (as defined in HTML 4.0) or by a numerical RGB specification. The accepted formats are:

Keyword:	aqua | black | blue | fuchsia | gray | green | lime | maroon | navy | olive | purple | red | silver | teal | white | yellow
#rgb	example for Blue: { color: #00f }
#rrggbb	example for Blue: { color: #0000ff }
rgb (integer range)	example for Blue: { color: rgb(0,0,255) }
rgb (float range)	example for Blue: { color: rgb(0%, 0%, 100%) }

`<family-name>`

Fonts can be specified by the name of a font family of choice. Examples of this are `Arial`, `Times New Roman`, `Helvetica`, `Baskerville`, and so on. Font family names that contain whitespace (tabs, line feeds, carriage returns, form feeds, and so on) should be quoted.

<frequency>

Frequency identifiers are used with aural style sheets. The format is a number immediately followed by one of the following identifiers:

Hz   Hertz

kHz   kilo Hertz

<generic-family>

Authors are encouraged to use generic font family names as a last alternative, in case a user does not have a specified font on his or her system. Generic font family names are keywords, and must not be enclosed in quotes. The following are examples of each:

serif	Times New Roman, MS Georgia, Garamond
sans-serif	Arial, Helvetica, Futura, Gill Sans
cursive	Zapf-Chancery, Caflisch Script
fantasy	Critter, Cottonwood
monospace	Courier, MS Courier New, Prestige

<generic-voice>

Generic voices are the aural equivalent of generic font family names. The following are possible generic voice values:

male

female

child

<integer>

An integer consists of one or more digits ("0" through "9"). It may be preceded by a "-" or a "+" to indicate the sign. Also see <number>.

<length>

Lengths are specified by an optional sign character ("+" or "-") immediately followed by a number with or without a decimal point, immediately followed by one of the following unit identifiers:

Relative values:

em   The font size of the relevant font

B

| ex | The x-height of the relevant font |
| px | Pixels, relative to the viewing device |

Absolute values:

pt	Points (1/72nd of an inch)
in	Inches
cm	Centimeters
mm	Millimeters
pc	Picas (12 points, or 1/6 of an inch)

<number>

A number can consist of an integer, or it can be zero or more digits, followed by a dot (.), followed by one or more digits. Numbers may be preceded by a "-" or a "+" to indicate the sign. Also see <integer>.

<percentage>

Percentage values are always relative to another value, such as a length. The format is an optional sign character ("+" or "-"), immediately followed by a number, immediately followed by "%".

<relative-size>

Relative sizes are interpreted relative to the font size of the parent element. The following are possible values:

```
larger
smaller
```

<shape>

In CSS2, the only valid shape value is rect(<top> <right> <bottom> <left>), where the latter four descriptors specify offsets from the respective sides of the box.

<specific-voice>

Specific voice values are the aural style sheet equivalent of font-family. Values are specific names of a voice (for example: teacher, comedian, preacher, and so on).

`<time>`

Time units are used with aural style sheets. Their format is a number immediately followed by one of the following identifiers:

ms   milliseconds

s   seconds

`<uri>`

URI (or Uniform Resource Indicators) values are used to designate addresses of page elements such as images. The format of a URI is `url(`, followed by optional whitespace, followed by an optional single quote or double quotation mark, followed by the URI itself, followed by an optional single or double quote, followed by optional whitespace, followed by `)`. To clarify, here is an example:

```
BODY { background: url("http://www.foo.com/images/background.gif") }
```

B

APPENDIX C

Installing FrontPage 2000

In this lesson, you learn how to install FrontPage 2000 on your PC.

Installing FrontPage 2000 on Your PC

Installing FrontPage on your PC is relatively easy and should take you only a few minutes. FrontPage requires that you are at least running Windows 95/98. You can also install FrontPage on a PC running Windows NT. While FrontPage is mostly compatible with Microsoft Internet Explorer version 3.0 and later, some features do require IE 4.0 or later. If you are running Netscape, you should be using at least version 4.0 or later.

If you have already installed Microsoft Office 2000 you might already have FrontPage installed. If you purchased the standalone version of FrontPage 2000, or if FrontPage was not installed during the installation of Office 2000, then you need to install it. Here's what you need to do to install FrontPage 2000:

1. Insert your FrontPage CD-ROM in your CD-ROM drive.

2. If you do not have the Autorun CD feature turned on, from the Start menu, select Run and type **X:\SETUP**, where X:\ is the drive letter of your CD-ROM drive. In a few seconds, you will see the setup opening screen (see Figure C.1).

FIGURE C.1

The FrontPage setup opening screen.

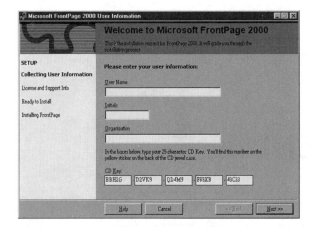

3. Enter the requested information in the opening screen (see Figure C.2) and select Next>> to continue.

FIGURE C.2

Entering your personal information into FrontPage setup.

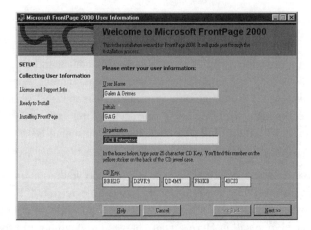

4. The next screen is the license agreement (see Figure C.3). Read the agreement and select I accept the Terms in the License Agreement and then select Next>> to continue with the installation.

FIGURE C.3

You must accept the license agreement to install FrontPage.

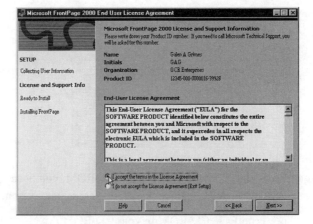

5. At the next screen, select the Install Now icon (at the top of the screen) to begin installing FrontPage 2000 into C:\Program Files\Microsoft Office\, or D:\Program Files\Microsoft Office if your programs are installed on your D drive (see Figure C.4).

FIGURE C.4

You can decide during setup where you want FrontPage installed on your PC.

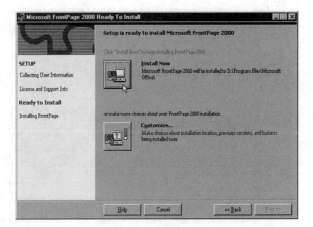

If you want to install FrontPage into a different folder, select the Customize icon and then enter the name of the folder where you want to install FrontPage. Depending on the speed of your PC, the installation should take approximately 10–20 minutes.

6. When the installation is complete, FrontPage will indicate that and prompt you to select OK to continue. You will then be prompted to restart your PC to complete FrontPage's configuration (see Figure C.5). Go ahead and select Yes to restart (reboot) your PC.

FIGURE C.5

After installing FrontPage, you need to restart your PC before you can run the program.

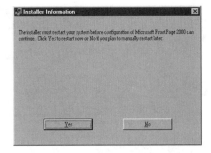

If you install FrontPage from the Office 2000 CD-ROM, you need to perform a custom installation and select FrontPage to be installed. Here is what you need to do:

1. Insert your FrontPage CD-ROM in your CD-ROM drive.
2. If you do not have the Autorun CD feature turned on then from the Start menu, select Run and type **X:\SETUP**, where X:\ is the drive letter of your CD-ROM drive. In a few seconds, you will see the Maintenance Mode opening screen (see Figure C.6).

FIGURE C.6

Office 2000 Maintenance Mode opening screen.

3. Select Add or Remove Features.
4. Highlight Microsoft FrontPage for Windows (see Figure C.7).

FIGURE C.7

Selecting.

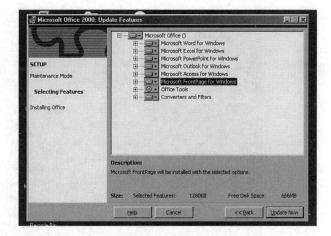

5. Select the Update Now button to begin installing FrontPage. The installation procedure begins and in a few minutes the maintenance mode program will indicate that FrontPage was installed.

Running FrontPage for the First Time

After the installation is completed and your computer has been restarted, you should start FrontPage to make sure the installation went okay, and so you can start becoming familiar with the program.

To start FrontPage for the first time, do the following:

1. Select Programs from the Start menu.

2. Select the Microsoft FrontPage icon to start the program (see Figure C.8). The program begins in a few seconds.

Tip

You can save yourself a little time and effort in starting FrontPage by creating a shortcut on your desktop or your Quick Launch toolbar if you are using Windows 98 and IE4.

3. In a few seconds, you will see the opening screen and then the FrontPage main interface (see Figure C.9).

FIGURE C.8

The Microsoft FrontPage icon you use to start FrontPage.

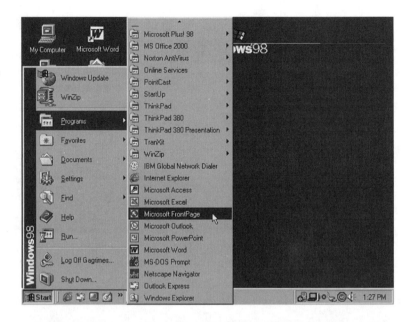

FIGURE C.9

The main FrontPage 2000 user interface.

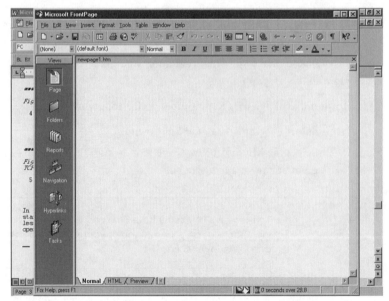

4. The first time you start FrontPage, it will take a few minutes to acquire your PC's hostname and TCP/IP address. You may also be prompted as to whether you want to set FrontPage as your default HTML editor. This is information it will need later when you use FrontPage to publish your Web to the Internet (see Figure C.10).

FIGURE C.10

FrontPage attempts to acquire your PC's hostname and TCP/IP address the first time you start the program.

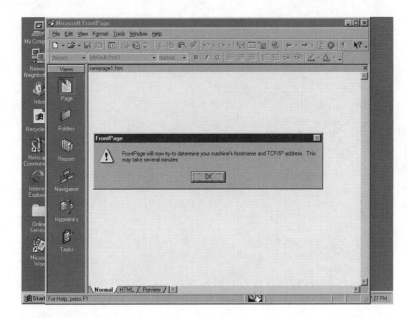

5. Take a few minutes to look over the user interface to start getting familiar with it. Don't worry about developing a detailed familiarity with the interface now. That will come in the next lesson.

In this lesson, you learned how to install FrontPage on your PC and had some time to become familiar with the main user interface. In the next lesson, you start developing a more detailed familiarity with the operation of the FrontPage editor.

INDEX

X-Y-Z

SAMS
Teach Yourself
in 21 Days

Sams Teach Yourself in 21 Days teaches you all the skills you need to master the basics and then moves on to the more advanced features and concepts. This series is designed for the way you learn. Go chapter by chapter through the step-by-step lessons or just choose those lessons that interest you the most.

Sams Teach Yourself Web Publishing with HTML 4 in 21 Days
Laura Lemay and Denise Tyler
ISBN: 0-672-31345-6
US $29.99/CAN $42.95

Other Sams Teach Yourself in 21 Days Titles

Java 2
Laura Lemay and Rogers Cadenhead
ISBN: 0-672-31638-2
US $29.99/CAN $44.95

XML
Simon North and Paul Hermans
ISBN: 1-57521-396-6
US $29.99/CAN $44.95

Photoshop 5
T. Michael Clark
ISBN: 0-672-31300-6
US $39.99/CAN $56.95

Access 2000
Paul Cassel
ISBN: 0-672-31292-1
US $29.99/CAN $44.95

Active Server Pages 2
Sanjaya Hettihewa
ISBN: 0-672-31333-2
US $34.99/CAN $50.95

Visual InterDev 6
Michael Van Hoozer
ISBN: 0-672-31251-4
US $34.99/CAN $50.95

Internet Programming with Visual Basic
Peter Aitken
ISBN: 0-672-31459-2
US $29.99/CAN $44.95

Visual J++ 6
Rick Leinecker
ISBN: 0-672-31351-0
US $29.99/CAN $44.95

Sams Teach Yourself Perl in 21 Days
Laura Lemay
ISBN: 0-672-31305-7
US $29.99/CAN $44.95

Sams Teach Yourself Microsoft Office 2000 in 21 Days
Laurie Ulrich
ISBN: 0-672-31448-7
US $29.99/CAN $44.95

www.samspublishing.com

All prices are subject to change.

Visit the
Sams Teach Yourself
Microsoft FrontPage 2000
in 21 Days
Web site at:

http://www.fp2k.com/

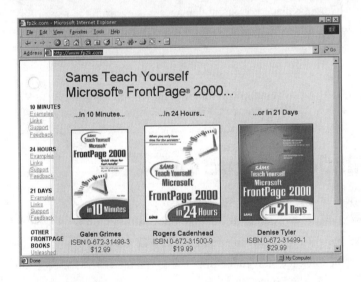

Here you'll find:

- **Example files:** Some of the examples—complete with graphics and media files—will be available online.

- **Updated links to the sites mentioned in the book:** If a site has moved elsewhere, we'll update it here.

- **Answers to reader questions:** Questions that aren't already covered in the book's Q&A sections can be found here.

- **Corrections and clarifications:** When errors are brought to our attention, they'll be described on the site along with the corrected text and any other material that's relevant.

CD-ROM Licensing Agreement

By opening this package, you are agreeing to be bound by the following agreement:

- You may not copy or redistribute the entire CD-ROM as a whole. Copying and redistribution of individual software programs on the CD-ROM is governed by terms set by individual copyright holders.

- The installer and code from the author(s) are copyrighted by the publisher and the author(s). Individual programs and other items on the CD-ROM are copyrighted or are under GNU license by their various authors or other copyright holders.

- This software is sold as-is without warranty of any kind, either expressed or implied, including but not limited to the implied warranties of merchantability and fitness for a particular purpose. Neither the publisher nor its dealers or distributors assume any liability for any alleged or actual damages arising from the use of this program. (Some states do not allow for the exclusion of implied warranties, so the exclusion may not apply to you.)

Note

This CD-ROM uses long and mixed-case filenames requiring the use of a protected-mode CD-ROM driver.

Installation Instructions

- Insert the CD into the CD-ROM drive.
- From the Windows desktop, double-click the My Computer icon.
- Double-click the icon representing your CD-ROM drive.
- Double-click the icon called Start.exe to run the CD-ROM program.

Note

If you have Windows installed on your computer, and you have the AutoPlay feature enabled, the Start.exe program will begin automatically when you insert the *Sams Teach Yourself Microsoft FrontPage 2000 in 21 Days* CD into your CD-ROM drive.